The Language of Hunter-Gatherers

C000102270

Hunter-gatherers are often portrayed as 'others' standing outside the main trajectory of human social evolution. But even after eleven millennia of agriculture and two centuries of widespread industrialization, hunter-gatherer societies continue to exist. This volume, using the lens of language, offers us a window into the inner workings of twenty-first-century hunter-gatherer societies – how they survive and how they interface with societies that produce more. It challenges long-held assumptions about the limits on social dynamism in hunter-gatherer societies to show that their languages are no different either typologically or sociolinguistically from other languages. With its worldwide coverage, this volume serves as a report on the state of hunter-gatherer societies at the beginning of the twenty-first century, and readers in all geographical areas will find arguments of relevance here.

TOM GÜLDEMANN is Professor for African Linguistics and Sociolinguistics at Humboldt University, Berlin. He specializes in African linguistics, with a particular focus on languages subsumed under 'Khoisan' in the Kalahari Basin area of southern Africa as well as on Bantu and wider Niger-Congo.

PATRICK MCCONVELL has worked on Australian Indigenous languages, especially in the Northern Territory and Western Australia. He has published extensively on the social history of hunter-gatherer languages in general, and language shift, code-switching and mixing of languages.

RICHARD A. RHODES is Associate Professor of Linguistics at University of California, Berkeley and an internationally recognized expert in Algonquian studies. His recent work has focused on descriptive syntax and nineteenth-century Ojibwe/Ottawa documents.

The Language of Hunter-Gatherers

Edited by

Tom Güldemann

Humboldt University, Berlin, and Max Planck Institute for the Science of Human History, Jena

Patrick McConvell

Australian National University, Canberra

Richard A. Rhodes

University of California, Berkeley

CAMBRIDGE
UNIVERSITY PRESS

CAMBRIDGE
UNIVERSITY PRESS

Shaftesbury Road, Cambridge CB2 8EA, United Kingdom

One Liberty Plaza, 20th Floor, New York, NY 10006, USA

477 Williamstown Road, Port Melbourne, VIC 3207, Australia

314–321, 3rd Floor, Plot 3, Splendor Forum, Jasola District Centre, New Delhi – 110025, India

103 Penang Road, #05–06/07, Visioncrest Commercial, Singapore 238467

Cambridge University Press is part of Cambridge University Press & Assessment, a department of the University of Cambridge.

We share the University's mission to contribute to society through the pursuit of education, learning and research at the highest international levels of excellence.

www.cambridge.org
Information on this title: www.cambridge.org/9781009299558

DOI: 10.1017/9781139026208

First published 2020
First paperback edition 2022

A catalogue record for this publication is available from the British Library

ISBN   978-1-107-00368-2   Hardback
ISBN   978-1-009-29955-8   Paperback

Cambridge University Press & Assessment has no responsibility for the persistence or accuracy of URLs for external or third-party internet websites referred to in this publication and does not guarantee that any content on such websites is, or will remain, accurate or appropriate.

Dedicated to the memory of Jane Hill and Jørgen Rischel, whose chapters in this volume and their overall academic oeuvre make outsized contributions to the field this volume addresses

Jane Hill and Jørgen Rischel

Contents

Figures

x

Maps

Tables

Contributors

GREGORY D. S. ANDERSON Living Tongues Institute for Endangered Languages, Salem, OR, USA

BALTHASAR BICKEL University of Zürich, Switzerland

JULIETTE BLEVINS City University of New York, USA

JOSÉ BRAUNSTEIN Academia Nacional de Ciencias de Buenos Aires, Argentina

CECIL H. BROWN Harvard University, Cambridge, MA, USA

NICLAS BURENHULT Lund University, Sweden

MARK DONOHUE Living Tongues Institute for Endangered Languages, Salem, OR, USA

PATIENCE EPPS University of Texas, Austin, USA

TOM GÜLDEMANN Humboldt University, Berlin and Max Planck Institute for the Science of Human History, Jena

ELLEN DRÖFN GUNNARSDÓTTIR Johns Hopkins University, Baltimore, USA

K. DAVID HARRISON Swarthmore College, PA, USA

MARK HARVEY University of Newcastle, Australia

JANE H. HILL University of Arizona, Tucson, USA

PATRICK MCCONVELL Australian National University, Canberra

JOHANNA NICHOLS University of California, Berkeley, USA

LAWRENCE A. REID University of Hawaii, Manoa, USA

WILLEM J. DE REUSE University of North Texas, Denton, USA

RICHARD A. RHODES University of California, Berkeley, USA

JØRGEN RISCHEL University of Trier, Germany

MALCOLM ROSS Australian National University, Canberra

GRAZIANO SAVÀ Università degli Studi di Napoli "L'Orientale" Naples, Italy.

ANTONIA SORIENTE Università degli Studi di Napoli "L'Orientale" Naples, Italy.

MARK STONEKING Max Planck Institute for Evolutionary Anthropology, Leipzig, Germany

PETER SUTTON SOAS University of London, UK

MAURO TOSCO University of Turin, Italy

EDWARD J. VAJDA Western Washington University, Bellingham, USA

ALEJANDRA VIDAL Universidad Nacional de Formosa, Argentina

Preface

This book has had a long, maybe overlong history. It originated in papers that contributors to this volume presented at an international workshop, "Historical linguistics and hunter-gatherer populations in global perspective," at the Max Planck Institute for Evolutionary Anthropology Leipzig in the summer of 2006. The workshop was organized by the first editor and his colleague Alena Witzlack-Makarevich (see https://www.eva.mpg.de/fileadmin/content_files/lin guistics/pdf/HunterGatherer_webpage_2006.pdf), generously sponsored by the Institute's Department of Linguistics. We would like to thank the then director, Bernard Comrie, for his crucial support as well as Claudia Schmid for her skillful conference coordination.

Following the workshop, the idea arose among the editors of this volume to make the content of the workshop public through a selection of the papers presented. That, however, left some key gaps, so to achieve better areal and thematic coverage of the topic, additional contributions were solicited.

As is obvious from the date of the workshop, this book has been a long time coming. We would therefore like to express our particular gratitude to the contributors who stayed the course for all these years. The topic is such that the volume and its individual contributions have lasting relevance to a field deeply concerned about marginalized languages.

In the final phases of the production of this book, we received tremendous administrative help from Edwin Rhodes for which we herewith express our deepest gratitude. We acknowledge the financial and institutional support granted us by the Humboldt University Berlin, the University of California, Berkeley, and the Australian National University in connection with the production of the volume itself.

It is our hope that this book will inspire further in-depth study of the languages and linguistic history of forager populations the world over.

The editors

Part I

Introduction

1   Hunter-Gatherer Anthropology and Language

Tom Güldemann, Patrick McConvell, and Richard A. Rhodes

1.1   Introduction

Foragers are often portrayed as "others" standing outside the main trajectory of human social evolution, which began with the Neolithic Revolution. In some forms of this narrative, foragers are static, left behind in the tide of history by their dynamic cousins, the farmers.

In anthropology and archaeology, the pillars holding up this view are being undermined as studies revealing dynamism and cultural change among foragers claim more attention. In particular, key tenets of the conventional narrative, such as the "wave of advance" of farmers that marginalizes and eventually eliminates foragers, are being reconsidered (Bellwood and Renfrew 2002). In regions such as Southeast Asia the conventional wisdom that there is a huge economic, social, and demographic gulf between farmers and foragers is being questioned (Fix 1994; Gibson and Sillander 2011). It has come to light that there were forager societies that did not fit the stereotype of small, isolated bands. They were, in fact, organized into large-scale, complex polities (Arnold 1996). Add to this the fact that the literature in this debate has paid far too little attention to the Western Hemisphere. At the time of contact, North and South America were home to large numbers of forager groups, many in long-term relationships with neighboring agriculturalists. Even more telling, agriculture continued to expand in North America up to the time of first contact (Galinat 1985: 277), leaving a picture, not of a dynamic unidirectional spread of agriculture, but of a much more subtle system of groups moving into agriculture with a lingering significant role for foraging, especially hunting and fishing. As the Western Hemisphere transitions are much more recent, the mechanisms are much less speculative. The dynamic balance between forager groups, agricultural groups, and groups in transition is clear. Conversation around the mechanisms of transition at work in the remote past of the

We acknowledge the Linguistics Department of the Max-Planck Institute for Evolutionary Anthropology, Leipzig, for hosting the conference that gave birth to this book, and other assistance to editors and contributors.

Neolithic could benefit greatly from a serious look at North America, where the more recent time frame allows us to see that there was both the adoption of agriculture by some and its abandonment by others. The fact that the process was not complete in North America at the time of contact allows us to see the balance of power between groups with very different calorie acquisition regimes. In particular, we see that the change was gradual over the course of centuries. Such a gradual shift cannot be obvious at the remove of seven to ten millennia.

The basic overview of North American subsistence at contact has long been known and is uncontroversial (Driver and Massey 1957; Driver 1969). Moreover, there was a well-established precontact transcontinental trade network that brought materials from the coasts to the interior and vice versa (Driver 1969). The most prominent of those networks, the Hopewell Interaction Sphere (Seeman 1979), has been thoroughly studied and continues to be a topic of interest (Sarich 2010). What is significant for us is that these trade networks linked native polities with different subsistence regimes. Even though the onslaught of overwhelming numbers of Europeans has radically changed the dynamic, there are still places in the Western Hemisphere where such balances continue to exist (see Epps, Chapter 22).

Studies of language and language change can contribute to this change of perspective on foragers, as the chapters in this volume show. Forager languages are not different in kind from farmer languages (Bickel and Nichols, Chapter 3), and the kinds of changes they undergo are likewise parallel. Foragers expand and migrate into new or abandoned areas, taking their languages with them (Rhodes, Chapter 20), forming the treelike structures well known in comparative historical linguistics. This makes analysis and reconstruction of forager languages using standard methods possible, a fact well known among linguists since Bloomfield's (1925) seminal paper on the reconstruction of Algonquian. It is not useful to dichotomize farmer and forager languages. Categorizing farmer languages as being based primarily on such migration and phylogeny and forager languages as being based primarily on stasis and diffusion of linguistic elements is dubious at best (e.g., Nettle 1999; for a critique see McConvell 2001). In fact, both types of processes are found in both types of economy. Among foragers themselves there is a range of different levels of contribution of phylogeny and diffusion (Bowern et al. 2011).

Understanding the patterns of prehistoric change through linguistic prehistory, including that of foragers, can illuminate the overall prehistory of continents and regions. This can be combined with and complement the evidence of archaeology, genetics, and other disciplines. The focusing of efforts on farmer language expansion in recent times (Bellwood and Renfrew 2002) and the popularization of this view (Diamond and Bellwood 2003) led to neglect or even denial of forager language expansion. But a sober evaluation of readily available evidence makes it truly impossible to deny that forager languages also spread. This evidence is abundant in the history and linguistic prehistory on all continents. The received position may be recasting the framework to include forager language spreads (Bellwood 2014), but this book shows that forager dynamism is more widespread and complex than the received view accepts.

While the end of the last ice age may have been the backdrop to the invention of agriculture and animal husbandry in some places, it also had very marked effects on the hunter-gatherer populations who did not make this transition during the period from 13,000 to 7,000 years ago. As the glaciers retreated and the world climate grew warmer, hunter-gatherers were able to move into a wider variety of foraging environments, utilize a wider variety of species and occupy regions that would have been effectively uninhabitable in the Pleistocene (Richerson et al. 2001; Kennett and Winterhalder 2006: 3).

These population movements in the early Holocene went hand in hand with the expansion of languages. In some cases this was the "initial colonization" of some areas or at least the reoccupation of regions sparsely populated until that time. In fact, owing to the aforementioned circumstances, there is every reason to expect spreads of forager languages in the early-to-mid Holocene. In North America it is clear that those spreads continued into recent millennia, for example, the eastward movement of Algonquians out of the Columbia Plateau into the Great Lakes region, on into eastern Canada, and down the East Coast of what is now the United States (Denny 1992; Goddard 1994). Eastern Algonquians and Southern Great Lakes Algonquians took up agriculture late, mostly after those expansions (Fowler and Hall 1978: 560; Snow 1978: 58). Algonquian forager expansion has continued northwestward into the historical period (see Rhodes, Chapter 20).

But the most dramatic forager spread in North America in the historical period was the spread of the Dakhota across the Missouri at the end of the eighteenth and beginning of the nineteenth centuries. At first contact they were primarily buffalo hunters (Radisson 1961: 14, 142). With the arrival of the horse, they sought to expand west of the Missouri, where there were entrenched agriculturalists: the Arikawa, Pawnee, and Mandan. It was only in the wake of a series of smallpox epidemics, seriously weakening the Arikawa and decimating the Mandan, that the Dakhota succeeded (DeMallie 2001: 731).

Hunter-gatherers have undergone major transitions or revolutions of their own. These involved turning toward a broad spectrum of food resources, including those that are not highly ranked but are nevertheless dependable despite having high handling costs (Bird and O'Connell 2006; see §1.4 for more discussion). Developing a broad spectrum of resources was almost as revolutionary as the rise of agriculture during the Neolithic. And broadening the resource base is often linked to the idea of intensification. The broad spectrum may have been based predominantly on adopting various techniques of food processing, but the motivation may well have been to provide sustenance for large ritual and social gatherings (Lourandos 1997). As Bettinger (1994) argues, the arrival of migrants may force local indigenous groups into marginal territory where intensification becomes a necessity, in spite of the fact that both groups may be foragers.

It is important to recognize that different groups of foragers emerge with different subsistence strategies, different social organizations, and different cultural complexes. This fact is particularly apparent when taking a broad view across the indigenous peoples of North America (Driver and Massey 1957). These groups of foragers spread languages and developed new linguistic patterns, even in contact with farmers. Issues of this type are crucial in Epps (Chapter 22).

This introduction first addresses the question of who should be considered foragers in §1.2. Following in §1.3 we consider the effect the concept of the Neolithic Revolution has had on forager studies. Then §1.4 discusses timelines for forager development, independent of farming. The topic of §1.5 is forager language spread, an oft-ignored aspect of forager prehistory. We then move away from prehistory to look at the features that have been attributed to forager societies and their potential relations with language in §1.6. This includes how foragers' life patterns are different from those of food producers, how analysts have divided foragers themselves into types based on their different ways of organizing aspects of society, and the importance of language in the concept of a "dialect tribe," often used in research on foragers. §1.7 returns to questions of change first raised in relation to transitions and language spreads, this time focused on social dynamics, again challenging the "static" stereotype of the forager. Most foragers have lived in close contact with food producers for many hundreds or thousands of years, and the kinds of interactions found between the two groups are explored in §1.8. Many such interactions involve the social and geographical marginalization of foragers, which is discussed in §1.9. §1.10 addresses the effects of language contact between food producers and foragers that fall short of language shift. Then §1.11 highlights unusual cases in which people have "reverted" from food production to foraging. Finally, the introduction closes with a brief conclusion.

1.2   Who Are Foragers?

The term "hunter-gatherer" is generally being replaced by "forager" in the literature. While both terms are used interchangeably in this book, we prefer to use the term "forager" in theoretical contexts. This is in part because it is shorter and simpler, but more substantively because the term *forage* goes beyond hunting and gathering to include fishing, a primary food source for a significant number of nonagricultural groups, notably in North America (Driver 1969), and does not exclude foragers who also derive part of their livelihood from trading. Finally, the term "foraging" "diminishes an improper emphasis on the singularity of hunting," while highlighting "the diversity always present" (Griffin 1981: 34).

How do we define foragers? Binford (2002: 116) characterizes them as "[groups who] do not organize themselves to control food production through strategic modifications in the organization of the ecosystems that they exploit." This definition is negative vis-à-vis farmers and herders, who do engage in such "strategic manipulations," but it is also likely to be somewhat inaccurate. There is significant evidence that some North American hunting cultures manage game populations (Feit 2004: 122). This could be legitimately considered a strategic manipulation of resources. The paleoethnobotanical literature crucially addresses how the use of plant material develops into full-fledged domestication (see Minnis 2003, 2004). But other sources also take a line to Binford's, defining foraging as a mode of gaining a livelihood that is distinct from food production. A useful approach can be to define food production as exerting control over the reproductive cycle of one's caloric resources.

It has been stressed by a number of writers that some foragers do intervene to some extent in the reproduction of wild food resources, for instance, by scattering seeds or replanting tubers. This could be viewed as a matter of degree. In order to approach the matter statistically, the Ethnographic Atlas (White 1986, 1990) uses calculations based on the amount of nutrition that comes from hunting, wild food gathering, fishing, farming, and animal domestication. For further discussion of such issues, see §1.3.

Apart from attending purely to the question of how food is obtained, other aspects of foragers have been highlighted in the literature. These include in particular aspects of their exchange practices and ideology, such as food sharing and egalitarianism (Barnard 2002). Barnard suggests that universal kinship – the practice of assigning kinship terms to all members of the community and associated groups – is a feature of hunter-gatherers. It is not clear whether these features are exclusively associated with foragers or more widespread including small-scale farmer and herder groups also. For further discussion see §1.6.

Other characteristics are often seen to be closely associated with foragers. One is high mobility of residence ("nomadism"). But the correlation, nomadism with foragers and sedentism with farmers and pastoralists, is weak (for some discussion and references see Ember [1978] and Ember and Ember [2010]). The fishers of the American northwest coast, for instance, are only partially and seasonally mobile (Suttles 1990: 4). Conversely, some cultivators and herders are highly mobile. The size of the community among hunter-gatherers is often reckoned to be small, but again many farmer groups are also small. If these demographic characteristics were more robust it may be possible to compare them with features of language, such as degree of language contact phenomena, which may correlate with numbers of contacts with other groups.

As stressed previously, foragers are diverse along several dimensions, due to social changes they have undergone internally or due to their relationships with other groups, be they farmers or pastoralists. In the latter case there are contrasts between foraging people who have lived in a world composed largely of foragers until the last couple of centuries, those who have been in long-term equilibrium with agriculturalist neighbors, and those who have been long encapsulated as minorities in a world of farmers, pastoralists, and large polities. These differences can have significant effects including effects on language, such as forager groups shifting to speak the farmer or pastoralist languages (McConvell 2001). Between the ends of the spectrum lie intermediate cases, a number of which are illustrated in this book, where the languages are in a mutual steady state of contact without spread. The range of activities engaged in by different forager or borderline forager groups also exhibits considerable diversity, including hunting, gathering, fishing, and occasionally systematic trading. Another dimension of diversity is coastal – seafaring vs. terrestrial orientation.

The "borderline" cases include:

(a) Reliance on marine and other aquatic resources that "correlates positively with permanence of settlement, group size, levels of hierarchy, degree of stratification, restrictions on access to resources and form of domestic organization" (Pálsson 1988: 202). Such sedentary foragers are a far cry from the nomadic bands said to typify foragers.

(b) Nomadic agriculturalists, such as slash-and-burn farmers in the Amazon, New Guinea, and other places. As well as having a propensity for movement in some cases, they also often rely quite heavily on hunting and gathering for their diet, so that it becomes difficult to allocate them unambiguously to the farmer or forager category. It has been suggested that in the Amazon, self-identification as primarily farmers or foragers is at least as important as a balance of subsistence activities. Epps and Stenzel (2013: 19–21) describe the dichotomy between River People and Forest People in the Upper Rio Negro, which divides them roughly between farmers and foragers (primarily hunters) respectively. Other writers cited in this source have emphasized complementary exchange between these groups that is similar to the symbiosis found between farmers and foragers elsewhere, e.g., in Central Africa.

However, despite their distinct identities as farmers and foragers, in their subsistence practice the Amazonian groups all tend to mix modes to an extent.

This raises questions about the linguistic correlates that have been proposed by Brown (Chapter 4) comparing foragers and farmers/horticulturalists with regard to differences in their taxonomic structures for plants, and how they fare when applied to such borderline cases. Epps (2013) in an Amazonian regional study writes, "The Vaupés languages shed new light on the relationship between subsistence pattern and ethnobiological nomenclature: comparative evidence supports the basic generalization that hunter-gatherer systems have fewer binomial terms (specific/varietal levels); but language contact may level differences in flora-fauna terminology, primarily via calquing of binomials – even while subsistence differences are maintained."

Some speech communities who were made up of foragers have changed more definitively to become farmers or herders. But in some cases the change has gone in the reverse direction. These changes are sometimes accompanied by language shift, but not always. If there is a shift it is to a language associated with the new subsistence strategy. However, when there is no language shift or when the stable outcome is bilingualism, the original heritage language inevitably undergoes a transformation, at least in the vocabulary related to subsistence activity, through borrowing or coining of new terms. Attempted reconstruction of such changes in historical linguistics has been used in detailing and dating phases of transition to new forms of subsistence (cf. Ehret 2011).

Of course, over the last few hundred years, many forager groups have come to rely less on hunted and foraged food, since they have generally been incorporated into wider economies. In this book, we allocate groups to the forager category, taking as a reference point ethnographic descriptions at first colonial/scientific contact. And, since ours is a linguistic study, historically attested foraging groups are not considered if there is a complete lack of linguistic data. Güldemann and Hammerström (unpublished manuscript) deal in more detail with the languages considered under the rubric of "forager languages" regarding their classification and geographical and demographic characteristics.

1.3   Social Evolution and the Neolithic Revolution

The dominant paradigm in the scientific study of prehistory in the twentieth century was the Neolithic Revolution – the revolution being the move away from foraging to farming and herding. It is the centerpiece of most schemes of social evolution.

The paradigm shift to the notion of a Neolithic Revolution brought along a presumption that many other features of society necessarily change with the change to agriculture. The anthropology of the 1960s saw such things as concepts of property flowing from the Neolithic change in production.

The easy dichotomization of calorie acquisition into foraging on the one hand and farming and herding on the other which the metaphor of "revolution" suggested turned out to be unrealistic in a way similar to how the other social evolutionist schemes of the nineteenth century were received. Ideas of property, for instance, did not arrive with the Neolithic Revolution, although this view is widely held (Trigger 1998). Evidence from language helps to erode some of these questionable ideas (Kelly 1995: 163). One might expect that expressions of possession and property were very different in forager and farmer societies if an entirely new set of concepts was ushered in by the Neolithic Revolution. In fact, there is no such huge difference between the way forager languages deal with these ideas and the way that others do. If differences exist they are generally more subtle than one might expect.

The notion of the Neolithic Revolution as a watershed in social evolution can be useful because it throws forager societies into relief and enables us to focus on their special characteristics. However, in practice, it often leads to a singular focus on the rapid and precipitous changes and a corresponding neglect of the less dramatic changes throughout the long period of forager prehistory, worthy of investigation in their own right. That is, the Neolithic is seen as the motor of dynamism par excellence that has led to the mistaken corresponding assumption that there is little major change or dynamism among forager/hunter-gatherer societies.

This assumption has affected widely accepted views of linguistic prehistory as well. Dixon proposed the "punctuated equilibrium" view that most of prehistory is dominated by an equilibrium state in which massive diffusion is the prime mechanism of change, wiping out evidence of families formed by bursts of divergence called "punctuations." His hypothesis relegates the role of the comparative method in investigating divergence to relatively recent "punctuations." Nettle (1999) took Dixon's model and married it to the "Neolithic Revolution" model, attributing the long equilibria primarily to foragers and the "punctuations" to the expansion of farmer and herder languages (see McConvell 2001 for a critique). In recent years, however, the pendulum seems to have swung back, and both "punctuated equilibrium" and the attribution of cultural stasis and immobilism to foragers are now less in vogue (Bellwood 2013).

The portrayal of the agricultural revolution as the key transition in a unidirectional and unilineal evolutionary scheme has been challenged, e.g., by Layton et al. (1991), who see possibilities of "evolution" in the opposite direction from agriculture or herding to foraging, and emphasize the prevalence of mixed agriculture-foraging economies known as low-level food production. Certainly this "devolution" from food production to foraging has occurred, possibly even on a large scale (see Chapter 21 by Hill on the Great Basin United States and Chapter 6 by Güldemann on southern Africa). The common use of the term "devolution" in relation to this phenomenon underlines the dominance of the belief in unidirectional evolution embedded in the discourse about these matters.

1.4   Timelines for Foragers and Forager Languages

While debate still rages over the factors leading to the invention of food production, most authors allow that its timing, at the end of the Pleistocene and beginning of the Holocene eras, was no accident. After millennia in the grip of the most recent ice age, the world became a wetter and warmer place. Plants and animals became more abundant. More diverse species were found in a much greater variety of places. This huge transformation led to the invention of agriculture and animal husbandry in Eurasia in the period 13,000 to 7,000 years ago, but it also had very marked effects on forager populations themselves.

First, foragers were able to occupy regions which would have been uninhabitable, or virtually so, in the Pleistocene, so they moved into a wider variety of foraging environments and utilized a wider variety of species (Richerson et al. 2001; Kenett and Winterhalder 2006: 3). In some cases, this would for all intents and purposes be the "initial colonization" of some areas or the full colonization of formerly sparsely populated areas. Those involved in these migrations would probably have been some of the groups who were on the edge of such "fallow" areas and by virtue of having spent some time foraging in those areas would have been preadapted to them. The most likely to expand in a "wave of advance" across these regions would have been those who had developed technologies, and forms of social organizations to cope with the new challenges. It must be remembered that the early Holocene had a fluctuating and volatile climate throughout the world, and in particular the marginal environments being reoccupied were highly unpredictable in climate and therefore resource availability. Sea level rise in the early Holocene would have caused movement inland and probably conflict. Rather than all the groups on these new frontiers expanding simultaneously and equally successfully, certain groups are likely to have had specific proclivities and advantages that propelled them over large areas to form widespread subgroups and families.

There is a second historical development that would have affected a world exclusively populated by foragers. In an attempt to better explain the adoption of agriculture, Flannery (1969) proposed the notion of a "broad spectrum revolution" before the onset of the Neolithic. His proposal was based on robust archaeological indications that pre-Neolithic foragers in a number of areas changed their type of foraging. The major result was a reliance on a new subsistence base that came from a wider food spectrum more equilibrated between high- and low-value resources. Such a shift in strategy not only allowed a forager group to make more effective use of an area it had already settled, but also facilitated their expansion into regions with fewer high-value resources. Groups with such strategies would have outcompeted groups with a more "conservative" foraging mode. In other words, the expansion of forager groups at the expense of others in the early Holocene is highly likely to have occurred. Again, such population expansions would have gone hand in hand with the expansion of languages.

These observations cast doubt at one possible reading of the farming/language dispersal hypothesis and similar approaches to prehistory. Although scholars such as Renfrew, Bellwood, and others may not necessarily deny the possibility of widespread language spread on the part of foragers, they still bracket forager language shift, calling into question the agency of forager societies – a point that chapters in this volume directly contradict (Hill, Chapter 21; McConvell, Chapter 16; and Rhodes, Chapter 20).

[forager] language shift was surely always localized under Neolithic social conditions. Bellwood (2011: 375)

Their huge emphasis on farmers being the bearers of widespread new language families invites the conclusion that the geographical scale of forager language spreads and possible resulting phylogenetic diversification are viewed as qualitatively different from those of food producers. According to Renfrew the abstraction from individual historical cases and the generalization of an apparent correlation to population types is at the very heart of the hypothesis:

The approach [viz. the farming/language dispersals hypothesis] has the undoubted merit, whatever the final outcome of the discussion and debates currently underway, of lifting the discussion out of and beyond the specifics of each individual case of a particular language family, and looking rather at the more general processes involved in the formation of language families, and at the correlates between the linguistic and the social or historical processes involved. (Renfrew 2003: 3)

Before embarking on the farming/language dispersals hypothesis Renfrew worked with what he called the "demography/subsistence model" in which he assumed that:

a new group of persons (speaking a different language) will not find it easy to become established within the territory in question unless it has available to it something which will allow it to compete successfully, in terms of subsistence procurement, with the existing population. (Renfrew 1989b: 118)

It is worth noting that this view does not, in fact, follow from any specific subsistence type. It is totally compatible with the foregoing observations that foragers with different strategies could compete with one another for territory and the more successful spread their languages in a way similar to that Renfrew envisaged for farmers. It has even been proposed that purely material/economic differentials are not the only factors. Expanding populations may well have advantageous characteristics in ideology and/or social organization. Denny (1992, p.c.), for example, suggests that Cree culture (including language) supplanted Boreal Forest culture on the strength of Algonquian ritualism.

This kind of more nuanced approach is also necessary to account for the historical dynamics between food producers to explain so-called "secondary dispersals." See, for example, Comrie's (2002) discussion of the Indo-European language family, which follows Diebold (1992) in linking Indo-European spreads to early speakers utilizing either agriculture or pastoralism, each with its own dynamics.

This approach solves a potential dilemma within the farming/language dispersals model. Several large families, which emerged in tandem with farming dispersals, cannot be associated with farming in their early historical stages (e.g., no reconstructed lexicon for food production). Archaeological evidence seems to back up the linguistics in some cases. Some large families are clearly associated with foraging in their earliest stages of spread, for instance, Finno-Ugric (according to Nichols and Rhodes [2018]) proto-Finnic speakers were foragers with a sideline in trading furs). Thus the first expansion phase seems to have occurred in a time when the speakers of early varieties of a language were foragers who out-competed other forager populations long before taking up food production. Linguistic reconstruction, including tracking of loanwords, can, in the best cases, detect strata with innovations in vocabulary reflecting stages within a forager economy as well as transition to farming and/or herding.

By combining linguistics with archaeology and other prehistoric disciplines it is possible to assign fairly reliable dates to such strata and stages, and thus construct timelines. Because dates from linguistics alone are not always arrived at in a fully reliable way,[1] some practitioners of different disciplines are wary of this method, fearing that it can lead to circularity.

Some people outside linguistics (and some inside) have looked with skepticism at the estimates arrived at of many widespread language families as being 10,000 to 5,000 years old – i.e., dating from the early-to-mid Holocene. Where these dates have been associated with food production, the dating has generally gained favor, but in the case of forager language families the dates have been seen as an odd coincidence and probably some artifact of the linguists' methods and assumptions (Gruhn 1997). But in fact, following the logic just outlined, there is every reason to believe that there were spreads of forager languages in the early-to-mid Holocene.

The widely known limitation on the ability of lexicostatistics to detect family groupings has often been brought into this discussion. There are certainly problems with lexicostatistics. It is undeniable that evidence of linguistic relatedness is lost fairly consistently over time and that trying to establish a genetic relationship with time depths of over 10,000 years – i.e., roughly the Pleistocene – one finds that the evidence becomes vanishingly scant. Most linguists use lexicostatistics only as one type of evidence in arriving at classification and usually rely more heavily on evidence of shared innovations in subgroups as favored by the comparative method. A language 'family' established by this method may be 10,000 years old or more, but it could well be a subgroup of a larger older family that cannot be solidly established. Much energy is currently being devoted to trying to establish the validity of such macro-families whose proto-languages, given their Pleistocene vintage, would have been spoken by foragers. While these endeavors are of interest, it is also important to look at how and why forager languages expanded in the early Holocene because this is more accessible to us.

1.5   Forager Language Spreads

Forager language expansions are not confined to the early Holocene. They also occurred later, in the period 5,000–1,000 years ago. In Australia they are correlated with later rounds of reoccupations of sparsely populated regions (deserts, mountains, islands) (Veth 2006; Hiscock 2008) and are correlated with both climate change and the development of toolkits and techniques adapted to these environments. The El Niño Southern Oscillation (ENSO) is the dominant weather pattern in the Pacific region. The oscillation was muted in the early Holocene, but became more marked in the mid-Holocene around 5,000 years ago. Turney and Hobbs (2006) argue that a new intensity of activity on the landscape in many areas of Queensland corresponds exactly with the onset of the modern ENSO pattern at 5000 BP. These events could also be correlated with language spreads (for instance, in this case the early expansion of Pama-Nyungan). Subsequent spreads in the period 2000–1000 BP (Western desert spread, spread of Maric languages in Queensland) may have other environmental contexts. Recent studies are producing evidence of a spurt in population growth among Australian foragers in the late Holocene (Williams et al. 2015).

It should be noted that foragers are also involved in two kinds of language spread, as are other populations. One is *skirting* movement into areas that are unoccupied or sparsely occupied at the time, and the other is *encroaching* movement, where there was already a resident population and the mechanism of spread is language shift to the newcomers' language.[2] These processes are attested in historical times and can be inferred for prehistoric language spreads of foragers, using evidence such as the influence of substratal languages (the languages of the preexisting populations before language shift). This kind of process is often classed as a kind of borrowing or diffusion, but is importantly different as a social process, and has its characteristic linguistic effects (McConvell 2009).

So far we have focused on the spread of languages into empty or sparsely populated zones that in the skirting-encroaching model (McConvell 1996, 2001; Evans and McConvell 1998) are referred to as skirting phases. However, many of the language spreads in the Holocene would have been encroaching, i.e., involved people moving into territory already occupied by other language groups. Encroaching frequently entails language shift, either the newcomers shifting to the language of the resident population, or the indigenous group shifting to that of the newly arriving migrants. The latter scenario requires a more nuanced modeling of the sociolinguistics, absent under the "normal" conditions of a colonial master class or an influential lingua franca. Investigating this is one of the key tasks of linguistic prehistory of foragers. It requires careful comparison with ethnographic cases of multilingualism and language shift. Chapters in this volume (Chapter 16 by McConvell and Chapter 21 by Hill) debate the value of the skirting-encroaching hypothesis for Australia and North America specifically.

The spreads of languages suggested by these models and studies are very different from the picture of "punctuated equilibrium" proposed by Dixon. In that view language spreads and divergence of families took place soon after the initial colonization of continents and then little happened aside from diffusion of elements between languages. Dixon himself (2002: 33; 659–668) actually contradicts that general model when he allows that "minor punctuations" may have taken place later and cites environmental changes as a cause.

Foragers, as mentioned previously, have themselves undergone major transitions or "revolutions" involving a turn to a "broad spectrum" of food resources to include those that are not highly ranked because they have high handling costs but have the advantage of being dependable (Bird and O'Connell 2006). Such adjustments in calorie acquisition regimes can be almost as revolutionary as a shift to agriculture, and, like agriculture, are often discussed in the literature as "intensification." In Australia these are based predominantly on various techniques of food processing. A major transition of this kind for the arid zones was the expansion of seed grinding that occurred in the mid Holocene. Linguistic reconstruction can shed great light on this process and its timing (McConvell and Smith 2003). It is, however, unclear whether this change involved major movements of people, because technological know-how is diffusible and in fact seems to have been diffused, to judge from the linguistic evidence. In such cases language spread may not be implicated, only the spread of vocabulary along with ideas, artifacts, and skills. However, if groups that had new techniques accessed resources among and around groups that did not, they would win a battle of "competitive exclusion" (Bettinger and Bauhoff 1982) with the residents with a narrower diet, and then language spread could occur primarily by population replacement.

North America is home to two notably wide spreads of languages led by foragers. The Algonquians, whose common language date is generally agreed to be ca. 3500 BP, spread as foragers into the upper Midwest and ultimately into Quebec/Laborador starting in 1400 BP (Denny 1991, 1992). The Athabaskans, whose homeland has long been recognized as being in the interior of Alaska and the adjacent Canadian territory, spawned spreads down the Pacific coast in the vicinity of the present California-Oregon border, and to what is now the American Southwest. These Apacheans spreading into agriculturalist territory are reported to have been buffalo hunters at the time of earliest contact by the Spanish (Winship 1904: 65, 112, 194).

1.6   Features of Forager Life and Their Relation to Language

We will outline some of the proposals regarding the differences between forager society and culture and those of food producers and go on to point out problems with many of the assumptions behind those proposals – some of which have already been mentioned (see §1.1). Because imagining what the linguistic consequences of some of these questionable assumptions might be could lead to a tortuous hypothetical discussion, we will simply mention a few of the more concrete proposals in this section and show how linguistic evidence might cast light on them.

For instance, it had been a common assumption that ideas of property would be absent in foragers (Trigger 1998). This is not empirically the case (Myers 1988) and hypotheses that there would be linguistic absences of property related words and expressions, are not supported (Keen 2010, chapter 3). Similar arguments can be made on the basis of the existence of ownership terms in Proto-Algonquian (Aubin, 1975), ca. 3500 BP, predating the adoption of agriculture in the family by at least two millennia.

However, there do seem to be some effects on the structure of terminologies, such as those of flora, which are statistically significant when foragers and farmers are broadly surveyed. These differences relate to the different ways in which farmers deal with plants in cultivation and the foragers' orientation toward wild plants (Brown, Chapter 4). For instance, there seems to be pro-liferation in varietal terminology among cultivars. This can sometimes be matched by foragers' plant terminology, however. Other generalizations are less robust (Brown, Chapter 4; Bowern et al. 2014).

Kelly (1995: 14–15; Isaac 1990) sets out a "generalized foraging model" strongly influenced by Lee and de Vore (1968) and their notion of "nomadic style" with the following features:

1. Egalitarianism. Mobility constrains accumulation of property and inequality.
2. Low population density. Population intentionally kept below carrying capacity; people come together in large aggregations seasonally for social purposes.
3. Lack of territoriality. Caused by resource variability, requiring movement from region to region; defended territories maladaptive.
4. Minimum of food storage. Due to nomadism and plentiful resources.
5. Flux in band composition. Maintaining social ties requires movement and visiting; disputes solved by group fission.

There are counterexamples to these characteristics among various groups of foragers. Assuming that they do have some validity in forager groups, what are the potential effects in language?

Where there is Egalitarianism (feature 1), social classes are absent and the kind of sociolinguistic variation found in class-based societies will also be absent. Further, there may be an implication that there will be no dominance of one language group over others, at least among forager groups. This might be extended to include lack of lingua francas among foragers not in contact with nonforager groups. This is not necessarily a question of political dominance, although lingua francas are usually the language of a group that is widespread and powerful as compared with the groups that use it as a second language. While there is no evidence for lingua francas in precolonial Australia, for instance, Rhodes (1982, 2012) provides evidence for lingua francas in the American Great Lakes area. Inequalities and hierarchies do exist in the category of societies named "complex hunter-gatherers" so it would be useful to investigate whether language dominance exists or has existed in other situations like that reported by Rhodes.

The assumption that there are no sociolinguistic differences becomes an issue when we come to discuss the mechanisms of language spread among foragers. One of the common explanations for widespread languages that accounts for many cases of language shift today and in the past is that the spreading language has been a lingua franca that is eventually adopted as a first language by groups previously using it as a second language. If this explanation does not fit the facts of forager language ecology in earlier times, then we must look elsewhere.

We should point out that multilingualism is widely reported among forager groups. Being multilingual fits well with the notions of seasonal social aggregations (feature 2), moving from region to region (feature 3), and maintaining social ties by visiting (feature 5). Multilingualism is valuable for ease of communication with bands in other areas. It also implies that groups and individuals travel not only within their own language territory but outside it, a situation widely recorded for traditional times. The fact that marriages take place between people speaking different languages means that children generally learn both their father's and mother's language. If postmarital residence includes periods with both the wife's and husband's families, then bilingualism including the spouse's tongue will be common.

Fission of groups mentioned in (5) could lead to language shift. If one or both groups moved into the orbit of a different language group, it could result in the intrusive group adopting the language of the new location or converting the new neighbors to the breakaway group's language. This possible scenario of language spread is discussed further in the text that follows.

Lack of "territoriality" is a controversial point. In Australia, in southern Africa, and throughout North America forager groups have strong attachments to particular areas of country. These attachments often have a religious and mythological charter to validate them (Barnard 2002: 14). In Australia the attachment also usually involves a direct tie between the land and the language spoken on it. That tie is also validated by a charter (Rumsey 1993). Furthermore, there is a great deal of vocabulary and expressions affirming the affiliation of persons and groups to land. However, as stressed in point (3), this does not often prevent groups from moving into other groups' "countries" for foraging purposes. In Australia the use of violence to deter trespassers is relatively rare.[3]

More generally there is variation in the extent to which people of similar culture and language have territorial barriers and actively defend territory. High "territoriality" in this sense has been correlated with high resource levels and high predictability of them, which makes defense a worthwhile proposition. This model has been put forward for Great Basin foraging societies where societies in the northeast with dense reliable resources are most "territorial" (Thomas 1981; Kelly 1995: 190–192).

If boundaries do exist, and are generally correlated with languages, but are more or less permeable in different zones, then one might expect different relationships between languages. Multilingualism may be more highly developed in the zones where access to other "countries" is relatively free, and perhaps borrowing of both words and grammatical patterns may be greater.

While various authors have sought to explain the dichotomy between foragers and food producers (Lee 1988; Barnard 2002), others are more concerned with describing and explaining differences between foragers. One of the most influential schemes has been that of Woodburn (1980) which distinguishes between immediate-return and delayed-return societies.

This is often interpreted as equivalent to the distinction between egalitarian (immediate-return) and non-egalitarian (delayed-return) but the relationship is not so simple.

Australian Aborigines, for instance, are normally seen as highly egalitarian. Kelly (1995) classed them as delayed-return because of their marriage practices that incorporate delayed return of a spouse at some future time after an initial marriage between groups (Kelly 1995: 31).

In fact, there is a gradation of egalitarianism among Australian Aborigines. In some areas there is a tendency for some men to become leaders or "bosses," using the currency of religious prestige and polygynous marriage rather than material accumulation. In a sense, varieties of a delayed return marriage system go hand in hand with this kind of development. It can be argued that having a large number of wives (and children) provides an older man with the labor that can make his group a leader in foraging and able to host religious gatherings. These "bosses" are usually reputedly "good hunters" (which may relate to the "show-off" aspects of hunting prowess, Bliege-Bird et al. 2001) but being a good hunter can also be the product of a good team of sons, sons-in-law, and brothers-in-law as hunters. "Bosses" are rich in people rather material goods. The high incidence of polygyny and leadership varies quite markedly within Australia. There is some level of correlation between high-resource regions and the polygyny-leadership complex; it is not absolute and the two cultural traits must be regarded as partially independent sociocultural variables (Keen 1982, 2004, 2006).

It is possible that the extent of nodal leadership has an impact on the distribution of languages. In areas where men can achieve nodal leadership status the language spoken by such men could achieve a kind of dominance through his and his brothers' children speaking it, and indirectly by others learning it to interact with them and because it is prestigious. While not a lingua franca in the generally accepted sense, such a language could acquire the kind of status that would set the scene for others to shift to it.

Another way of subcategorizing foragers is whether they are sedentary or nomadic. The archetype has been the nomad, but most groups fall somewhere in a cline between some sedentary periods and some (or a great deal of) nomadism that is generally constrained to their own territory or familiar neighboring areas. In many parts of Australia and the Kalahari Basin, for example, constraints often revolve around availability and predictability of water sources ("tethered foraging": Kelly 1995: 127).

Relatively sedentary groups, or those that engage in very constrained rounds of foraging within the language-group country, may exhibit a tendency to be less bilingual/multilingual and not to borrow words or structures from neighboring languages. In the Top End of the Northern Territory of Australia (Harvey, Chapter 15) this appears to be the case and this contrasts with the situation elsewhere in Australia. Similarly, the "territoriality" dimension discussed earlier, which may often go along with relative sedentism, could be the basis for emphasizing linguistic differences.

Forager studies have been dominated by ecological and demographic models, and language has rarely been in focus. And yet one of the key concepts of influential models has taken language to be a defining characteristic – the "dialect tribe." This concept was developed especially in Australia by Tindale and Birdsell and used as the basis of modeling of forager populations that divided into such units approximating to the "magic number" 500 (Birdsell 1953, 1973; Hunn 1994).

There is an assumption in much of the discussion of "dialect tribes" that is seriously at variance with the facts in many places, viz. that the group of people who speaks one language or dialect are also endogamous exclusively, or almost exclusively in marrying within the group and thus being a "breeding population" (Kelly 1995: 209). This model was also supported by Dixon (1976), for Australia. But ethnographic data show high levels of intermarriage between language groups in most regions of Australia.

Multilingualism in the sense of use of a number of neighboring languages by individuals was very common among Australian Aborigines in traditional times, and persists until the present in some areas. This often correlates with marriage between different language groups so that mother and father, and other members of the close family, were from different language groups. In some larger groups covering a wider territory such as the Warlpiri the levels of multilingualism were lower except in areas adjacent to other language territories (Mary Laughren pers. commun.).

Earlier descriptions of foragers tended to ascribe patrilineal descent and patrilocal postmarital residence to them[4] but what has emerged from later surveys has revealed a much more mixed picture. Some groups in Australia that stress patrilineal descent most strongly also have an ideology of the father's language (the clan language) being the first and most important for any individual, even though the mother's language is usually learned too. Patrilocal residence, where it is consistently practiced, also tends to reinforce this kind of picture but in practice periods of residence among affines are quite common for men, leading to husbands learning their wife's language and the children being more proficient in the mother's language. It is possible that certain marriage and postmarital residence patterns, in conjunction with other factors, could lead to language shift and language spread.

Similarly, with types of marriage an earlier generalization that foragers generally practice cross-cousin marriage has not been fully borne out although the proportion of foragers with one or other variety of cross-cousin marriage is quite high (59% of groups surveyed by Lee and De Vore permitted it: 1968:

338). Both old and recent revived theories of the prehistory of kinship and marriage are proposing that cross-cousin marriage is the primeval form (Allen 2004), so if this were correct one might expect foragers to tend in this direction. There are problems with this hypothesis however (see McConvell 2018, which deals with this and the ascription of section systems to early societies).

The impact of cousin marriage on language really depends on the type of system. If repeated bilateral "sister exchange" arrangements exist for several generations between groups that speak different languages one might expect the development of a long-term societal bilingualism between these groups and possibly some degree of convergence.

1.7   Social Dynamics of Forager Societies

Many of the models of forager society and economy have treated them as static. If they have dealt with change it has mainly been either cyclical change within a basic equilibrium, or radical change brought about by colonization in the last few hundred years. When radical changes are portrayed solely as the product of colonial impacts, it leaves the impression that the era before contact was one without change.

This emphasis may be related to the generally static ahistorical analyses produced by functionalist social anthropology, coupled with an unquestioned assumption that there was a lack of change among forager groups (sometimes itself exaggerated in the literature).

For example, "mobility" has been seen as something that occurs as a result of resource fluctuation or population pressures, but in which people of one group move around within a relatively restricted territory foraging, rather than moving into new areas or expanding territories. Even studies of "settlement" are largely confined, in human ecology models, to seasonal relocation of base camps within a territory rather than radical change in location. It should, however, be noted that the modeling of initial settlement or colonization of new zones has been the focus of some work in archaeology, see Moore (2001), Kelly (2003), and Bird and O'Connell (2006), the latter two dealing with ethnographic and archaeological examples among foragers.

A substantial amount of modeling of the linguistic prehistory of North American language families has been done by linguists and anthropologists using the classical comparative method, allied to hypotheses of migration. In a number of these models, the issue of whether the proto-language was spoken by foragers comes up. Athabaskan, as mentioned earlier, is one which was shown to have moved from the Canadian north to areas on the Pacific coast and ultimately, the Apachean branch moved into the southwestern United States: in his classic study, Sapir (1936) includes changes of meaning of roots, some of which also provide evidence of change to farming in some of the southern languages, although the earliest contact suggests that only some bands practiced marginal agriculture (cf. Brugge 1983: 490–491).

Another of the well-examined case studies in prehistory where language spread has featured prominently in the argument is that of the Great Basin (Bettinger and Baumhoff 1982; Bettinger 1991; Madsen and Rhode 1994; Kaestle and Smith 2001; Bird and O'Connell 2006). Unlike "initial colonization" cases here there was already a resident population that was at least partially displaced by the newcomers but also partially absorbed as the residents adopted the newcomer's language, yielding a biogenetic picture of a large influx of new genes that are related to those of people to the southwest. This is encroaching in terms of the McConvell hypothesis but is reanalyzed by Hill (Chapter 21). One hypothesis about the interaction of the newcomers and the residents is that it was one of "competitive exclusion" enabled by the fact that the newcomers exploited a wider range of resources than the residents. The outcome is a mixture of displacement and absorption of the resident groups according to Bird and O'Connell, the latter presumably to be equated to language shift on the part of the residents. It is not clear just where and when each process occurred.

In fact, though, some of the ecological-demographic models do allow for a "safety valve" that adds dynamics to this static picture. In Winterhalder's (1986) scheme (see also Kelly 1995: 169–170), "migration" is one option, alongside nonlocal exchange. In situations in which there is high variation (unpredictability) of daily returns and the group all experience abundance and scarcity at the same time, then sharing is not a practical option. The "migration" here is not necessarily long term. These models have not generally focused on long-term major changes, as noted by Winterhalder and Kennett (2006).[5]

Kelly (1995: 198–200) modifies Winterhalder's model to address variation in and among groups rather than individuals, and where major resources fail for all people in all neighboring groups, long-distance migration is an option that can be taken up. An instance of this is cited from among the Nuataqmit Eskimos, who moved 600 km when the supply of caribou virtually disappeared (Burch 1971). Catastrophic resource fluctuations like this might account for long-distance movements known to have taken place among Eskimos and other forager groups (cf. Fortescue 1997, and Ives 1990 on Athabaskan migration),[6] and to have been responsible for current widespread and noncontiguous distributions of linguistic subgroups.

In some regions such climatic variation and unpredictability may be extreme enough to cause regular relocations owing to catastrophic decline in resources in one region, followed by reoccupation of the abandoned region later when resources are replenished. This may be a motor of relatively rapid spread of languages in such regions (for instance deserts: see Veth, Smith, and Hiscock 2005).

This kind of thinking allows us to connect with the modeling of spreads most associated with the work of population geneticists. The most well known is the "demic diffusion" or "wave of advance" model – "demic diffusion" being used to suggest that movement of people drove the advance of agriculture. This stands in contrast to the anti-migrationist view, quite entrenched in archaeology of the time, which saw such innovations as diffusion of cultural elements only (cf. McConvell 2010). The "wave of advance" model has focused exclusively on the spread of agriculture, and with it the spread of farmers' languages. It builds on the commonly accepted idea that food production boosts the population to the extent that food producers have to move on to other areas to find enough cultivable land and pasture (land already populated by foragers in most cases). However, an increase in foraging activity and efficiency can also cause population expansion and, as population rises, pressures for groups to hive off from the current territory, as we have seen earlier. So "wave of advance" models may be applicable in at least some situations to foragers.

The generality of this idea may have had less impact in forager studies not only because it was applied only to food producers, but also because of the overemphasis on homeostatic models of population increase among foragers. It is simply assumed that population of forager groups level off when (or often long before) carrying capacity is reached (Kelly 1995: 228). Emphasis is often placed on natural and deliberate population controls, or moving into social change models, on the possibility of the formation of hierarchies to deal with this "scalar stress." The other option allowed in some models, but less discussed, is siphoning off population through fission and migration (Kelly 1995: 305), which could lead to changes in language distribution.[7]

The fate of languages in the "wave-of-advance" process has not always been entirely clear. Not only is there migration of some food producers into forager regions bringing their language with them, but there is language shift on the part of (former) foragers to the language of the food-producing newcomers as part of the model. This would explain the dilution of the genetic profiles of the original food producers as they move further and further away from their original homelands.

It is not the case that foragers always shift to food producer's languages when they adopt food production, nor is it the case that they always maintain their ancestral language when they eschew food production (McConvell 2001).[8] Many studies recently (e.g., in Kennett and Winterhalder 2006) seem to show that the forager economy survives for some time alongside the food producers until it finally dwindles and becomes marginalized. The Philippine Negritos (Reid, Chapter 10), the Pnan of Borneo (Soriente, Chapter 11), and the Central African Pygmies (Bahuchet 2012) have all shifted to the food producers' languages while at the same time they maintained foraging in the context of conventionalized exchange of goods and services with the food producers. This may have occurred in some of these other slow transitions as well.[9]

1.8   Interaction between Foragers and Food Producers

The conscious (or unconscious) position that views foraging peoples as isolated and static has long been entrenched in anthropology. This "isolation" view has often led to a tendency to assume that modern foragers reflect, in a more or less direct way, how humans lived before the Neolithic. However, a number of case studies have shown quite convincingly that many forager groups have changed considerably, especially in areas where food production has been present for some time. Such an "integration" or "interdependence" approach has gained wide acceptance (cf. Headland and Reid [1989] and the following comments by other authors).

What interdependence means for our concerns is that the longer food producer groups have been in an area with forager societies, the more fruitful and necessary it is to study the languages of the forager societies because of the insight their languages provide to the mutual interaction with nonforaging groups. Since the relevance of the amount of interaction differs considerably from area to area based on foragers needs, it is useful to distinguish between different types of foragers in terms of their relation to food-producing subsistence regimes and the peoples following them. Adding this typology of foragers to those already discussed in § 1.5.[10] Bellwood (2005b: 28–39), for example, has attempted to provide such a classification of foragers, proposing three groups.

> Group 1: The "niche" hunter-gatherers of Africa and Asia
> Group 2: The "unenclosed" hunter-gatherers of Australia, the Andamans, and the Americas
> Group 3: Hunter-gatherers who descend from former agriculturalists

Since Bellwood's (2005b) focus is on early agricultural peoples and their history, foragers only play a background role and no significant attention is paid to their languages. Since we are primarily concerned with foragers, and particularly the historical dynamics of their languages, it is necessary for us to make a more fine-grained classification. In focusing on the linguistic identity of forager groups we find that we need to largely reject Bellwood's basic classification in the foregoing. We argue that what different types there are reflect a historical trend toward ever stronger integration into a food-producing world. A serious look at the language situation yields a rather neat five-way classification of foragers.

> Group A. Largely independent foragers with a linguistic affiliation distinct from food-producers

Group B. "Encapsulated" foragers with a linguistic affiliation distinct from food producers

Group C. "Encapsulated" foragers with a linguistic affiliation to food producers

Group D. "Encapsulated" foragers with a food producer language but a distinct dialect

Group E. More fully incorporated and acculturated foragers with caste-like status

Bellwood's classifications and ours show little overlap, apart from his Group 2 corresponding to our Group A (both representing the largely independent foragers dealt with in §1.4.). In particular, our classification does not recognize the distinction between Bellwood's Groups 1 and 3, or what Ellen (1994) refers to as "primary food collectors" and "secondary food collectors." That is, groups with a continuous foraging tradition, some of them having undergone language shift to a food producer language, on the one hand, and as opposed to, on the other hand, former food-producing groups who shifted their subsistence type to foraging (a process called variously in the literature "devolution" or "reversion"). But we know that there are some "primary food collectors" who have shifted their language to a food-producer language, e.g., Pygmies (Bahuchet 2012).

We believe our classification is more insightful because language shift, or lack thereof, is more telling of the relationships between foragers and food producers than the accidents of geography and history that give rise to Bellwood's groups. In particular, either of Bellwood's Groups 1 and 3 can speak a language straightforwardly descended from that of their remote ancestors, or can show varying degrees of linguistic assimilation with neighboring food producers.

The classification in question is also related to the problem that, in a number of cases, the historical evaluation of foragers in terms of these distinct scenarios is actually a hotly debated issue, which will be discussed later in more detail. As the distinction, as such, is obviously very important, not the least from a linguistic perspective, we will dedicate some discussion to the attested phenomenon of subsistence shift from food production to foraging.

1.9   Geographical and Linguistic Marginalization of Foragers

There is no simple and direct correlation between the presence of forager languages and different geographical conditions across the globe. Instead, the best explanation for the modern geographical pattern seems to be of a historical nature. The current geographical distribution of forager languages is best explained in negative terms. That is, it corresponds to the best possible survival of foraging modes and the viability for independent foraging societies relative to competing groups with other subsistence types. The situation is particularly complex in North America, where prior to the arrival of Europeans there was a complex network of trade interlocking foragers and agriculturalists (Baugh and Ericson 1994). The mere existence of such a robust system implies significant agency on the part of the foragers, some of whom occupied niches as the traders. The Ottawa, for example, first contacted by the French in 1615, were the preeminent traders and middlemen of the early contact period (cf. Feest and Feest 1978: 772–774).[11]

Map 1.1 shows the occurrence of forager languages in contrast to the geographical areas of early precolonial food production (using our current global forager language list from the Appendix; see Güldemann and Hammarström [unpublished manuscript] for a final inventory). It can be argued that these distributions are to a large extent complementary. The still discernible "compact" or at least forager-rich areas can be characterized as the geographical periphery of food-producing areas. They roughly delineate the limits of the Neolithic Revolution, whose earliest centers started out from temperate areas around or relatively close to the Equator, before the onset of the industrial revolution. Because the secondary impact of Neolithic expansions, urbanization and metallurgical development, was relatively low or entirely absent from Australia and large parts of North and South America, these areas are still the richest in forager groups and also display large families composed exclusively of forager languages. Southern Africa and Siberia, where foragers also maintained a more salient presence, seem to represent the food-producing periphery in a more attenuated form. These areas are largely unsuitable for traditional forms of farming, so foragers interacted mainly with pastoralist groups.[12] Güldemann and Hammarström (unpublished manuscript) present a more detailed discussion of this general finding.

The concept of forager territories as "food-producing peripheries" can also be applied on a micro-geographical level, namely in the zones where foragers share the same larger area with food-producing groups. One obvious geographical dichotomy exists between foragers in arid and semi-arid areas vs. food producers in better watered zones. This is, for example, attested in southern Africa for the San as opposed to Khoekhoe pastoralists and Bantu agro-pastoralists (cf. Güldemann, Chapter 6).

Another pattern, recurrent on several continents, is that foragers inhabit(ed) the more forested parts of a region while food producers predominantly used more open country. This can be observed in Siberia with Taiga foragers (cf. Vajda, Chapter 17) as opposed to Tundra reindeer herders. This is evident even within close-knit ethnolinuistic groups, for example, among the Yukaghir, Enets, and Nenets. In North America, the penetration of subsistence agriculture into the Woodlands was quite late, ca. 1000 BP (Scarry 2003) as compared

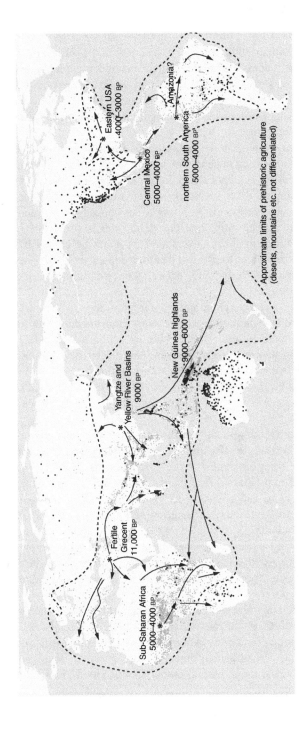

Map 1.1 Forager languages and early food production across the globe. Larger black dots indicate forager languages while smaller grey dots indicate food-producer languages.

The following labels appear on the map:

Eastern USA 4000–3000 BP

Amazonia?

Central Mexico 5000–4000 BP

northern South America 5000–4000 BP

Approximate limits of prehistoric agriculture (deserts, mountains etc. not differentiated)

New Guinea highlands ~9000–6000 BP

Yangtze and Yellow River Basins 9000 BP

Fertile Crescent 11,000 BP

Sub-Saharan Africa 5000–4000 BP

to the Southwest (ca. 3000 BP; Ford 1981), the Midwest, and the South (ca. 3000–2350 BP, Gremillian 2003: 33) (see esp. Smith and Cowan 2003: 117). In East Africa, too, Okiek foragers were encountered predominantly along the forested mountain slopes along the Rift Valley while their pastoralist and agro-pastoralist neighbors preferred the savannah areas. Finally, many of the scheduled tribes in India, among which foraging traits are salient, are also found frequently in forested zones.

The two last examples show that the tendency of forest regions to be "reserved" for foragers can go hand in hand with an altitudinal differentiation, in that mountains are potentially a longer refuge for foragers. We are, however, not aware of good examples of a landscape-related dichotomy between foragers and food producers exclusively in terms of an opposition between highland and lowland areas. The altitudinal correlation might simply be a function of the primary factor of forest coverage. This might be caused by two factors: first, highlands without forests can be utilized intensively by food producers, in particular by pastoralists; and second, deforestation progresses far more rapidly at low altitudes.

The tropical rain forests as larger geographical configurations recurrently attest for yet another territorial pattern: food producers often generally settle along river courses and possibly other major communication routes, while foragers settle in and subsist on the forest interiors. This holds, for example, in Equatorial Africa between farmers and Pygmies (Bahuchet 2012), in Borneo between Forest Dayak and Penan foragers (Soriente, Chapter 11), and in the Amazon between Tucanoan groups and Hup foragers (Epps, Chapter 22).[13]

All these different microgeographical patterns seem to represent variants of a universal theme: like the global pattern they do not say much about inherent properties of the foraging mode and the social units associated with it, but rather something about external factors, viz. – how well foragers can compete with nonforagers in that environment. Foragers hold out longest in ecological zones that are less suitable for agriculture and thus peripheral for the various food-producing subsistence modes. The marginalization and obliteration of foraging societies even in these areas today is largely associated with later European colonization possessing technology that allows for relatively stable food production even under less favorable ecological conditions.

The Neolithic Revolution and the subsequent expansion of food producers have split up forager populations in many areas into demographically and geographically smaller groups. The most extreme reflex of this process is the elevated incidence of isolate or unclassified languages and very small linguistic lineages spoken by foragers deep within predominantly food-producing territory. This pattern obtains irrespective of the overall ecological conditions.

To mention a few examples, this holds for Kujarge, Ongota, Hadza, and Sandawe in dry areas in northern and eastern Africa; for Kusunda and Nihali in mountainous regions of northern South Asia; and for Nadahup and Cacua-Nukak around the Vaupés area of the Amazon rain forest in northern South America.

In the past the global marginalization of foraging subsistence types was at times conceived of in terms of these groups being physically "pushed out" of food producer ranges, implying their migration into other areas that had fewer resources and thus were less competed for. It is, however, an empirical question whether this scenario applies for a certain region and was at all important. There is reason to doubt that story. In some areas this forager emigration hypothesis has been shown to be a myth without much historical substance, for example, the San in South Africa (Szalay 1995). It is not uncommon in North America for agriculture to spread from one group to another rather than the agricultural group dispossessing a forager group, e.g., Apacheans and most Eastern Algonquian groups. This again points to the fact that for many North American groups the adoption of agriculture was gradual prior to contact with Europeans.

There are also indications from a more general perspective that cast doubt on the very likelihood of the forager emigration hypothesis. First, the territoriality of many forager groups and their strong ideological attachment to their home areas (cf. the concept of "topophilia," Yuan 1990) suggest that they would tend to stay and try to adapt to whatever changing conditions rather than migrate away. Second, it is questionable whether the possibility of migration was an available option in the first place. Given that foragers had adapted to marginal areas already during the "broad spectrum revolution," most such ranges were already occupied when the territorial pressure by food producers ensued with the Neolithic Revolution so that immigration attempts would have met with considerable resistance by foragers already in place. Under this perspective it needs in fact to be investigated whether there are any well attested historical cases of significant forager emigration at all due to marginalization by food producers and, if there are, what their specific circumstances were.

In purely linguistic terms, the marginalization of foragers is reflected today by a far higher degree of language endangerment, when compared to languages spoken by food-producers – not necessarily in absolute terms, but rather relative terms. For example, looking at Whalen and Simons' (2012) global data about endangered lineages, on a global scale the proportion of endangered forager languages is high. Our lists of forager languages and lineages paint a similar picture. A great portion of our list is extinct or moribund languages; most of the other cases are latently endangered. The number of relatively secure languages is a tiny minority of the overall population.

1.10   Language Contact between Foragers and Food Producers

Undoubtedly, food-producing groups are responsible for the most dramatic changes affecting the profile of foraging populations in the recent human past. This is equally true from a linguistic perspective. The widespread and long-standing sociolinguistic prestige of many food-producer languages implies that they exert a strong, contact-mediated influence on neighboring forager languages, even when the forager languages are maintained. For example, the lexical domain might be expected to change by incorporating vocabulary referring to new technologies and social practices. This in turn can even bring about considerable systemic changes, as in biological taxonomy, kinship terminology, etc. Lexical borrowing can, however, go far beyond this canonical type. This has happened in some languages without obvious relatives to such an extent that they are difficult to classify. See the discussion on Ongota by Savá and Tosco (Chapter 5) and consider similar cases in Africa such as Shabo (Schnoebelen 2009) and Kujarge (Doornbos and Bender 1983; Lovestrand 2013).

The above type of "canonical" language contact situation should be distinguished from the linguistic impact of food producers on foragers immediately before language shift takes place. Here, the extent and type of interference is presumably related more to the effects of increasing communicative dominance of the prestige language(s) and eventually the accompanying attrition of the original language. A case in point seems to be the current situation of Gyeli-Kola spoken by pygmy foragers in southwestern Cameroon according to the information by Grimm (2015). Gyeli-Kola presumably originated in a language shift by the pygmies toward a language of an early layer of Bantu colonization, represented today by the pygmies' closest linguistic relatives speaking Kwasio. But subsequently there emerged a separate pygmy language. In the modern period of increased sociolinguistic pressure, however, Gyeli-Kola has diversified into various dialects according to different regionally dominant contact languages. The splitting up of Gyeli-Kola into a Kwasio dialect, a Bulu dialect, a Basaa dialect etc. arguably reflects the first phase in the possible process of full linguistic acculturation. At the other end of such a developmental scale is the Tuu language, Nǁng in the southern Kalahari of South Africa. It was effectively dormant for several decades, especially during the Apartheid era, being replaced by a local variety of Afrikaans. After being reactivated, it was used again by remnant speakers. Through intensive efforts towards language documentation it is now spoken with a notable Afrikaans interference in lexicon, phonology, and morphosyntax.

In contrast to the aforementioned patterns, forager languages can also show strong linguistic resilience under certain conditions, which are still to be investigated fully. Consider the following recurrent pattern: a forager language belongs genealogically to a family with a clear population history involving food production as the result of shift, but it is a separate language rather than a mere dialect, which is the expected first result of a simple language shift. This implies that the foragers must have had a sufficiently long and partly independent linguistic history in order to maintain or develop its considerable degree of distinctiveness. Such a situation applies, for example, to various groups among the Pygmies in Central Africa (Bahuchet 2012; Grimm 2015), the Okiek or (N)dorobo foragers in eastern Africa (Rottland and Voßen 1977), and the Negritos in the Philippines (Reid 2009; Chapter 10). As Reid has shown for the last case, this partial post-shift isolation by foragers sometimes can even produce a historical-comparative picture whereby their languages retain conservative linguistic traits that have been lost in the closest relatives spoken by the ultimate food-producing language donors. Forager languages can thus even be of importance for the historical assessment of food-producer groups and their languages.

Contact-induced linguistic transfer between food producers and foragers is recurrently modeled as a kind of one-way street from the former to the latter, apparently starting out from the modern sociolinguistic differential existing between the two types of groups. However, it is far from clear whether such a relation is universal and even less so whether it has been relevant throughout their history of interaction. It is instead conceivable that food producers, when entering forager areas for the first time where they did not have an established demographic advantage, were partly dependent on the local foragers for environmental knowledge. That fosters various patterns of population contact that lead to a considerable amount of feature transfer into the food producing population profile. From a linguistic perspective, this is modeled as a substrate. Such a scenario is proposed by Güldemann (Chapter 6) for the interaction between San forager groups and different layers of herding and agricultural colonizers in southern Africa on the basis of structural features. It is so extensive that the status of a lineage as an immigrant linguistic group may not at all be obvious. This substrate effect even promises to recover some interesting relics of the linguistic forager heritage in areas whose language profile has been completely shifted to that of colonizing food producers. Such research has been especially attractive with respect to lexical traits, some examples of which are Letouzey (1976) and Bahuchet (1992, 1993) on the so-called *Baakaa pygmies in the western part of the African rain forest, Reid (1994) on the Philippine Negritos, and Blench and Walsh (2010) on the Mikea in Madagascar. This type of research, however, is still in its infancy. It requires as complete a picture as possible for all forager and nonforager languages involved historically and this is not the case for most areas. It is thus a promising line of research to extend the search for forager substrates in the future to nonlexical domains and even food-producing languages. For example, the suggestive lexical similarities between Great Andamanese and Austro-Asiatic proposed by Blevins (Chapter 9) may go back to conventional horizontal transfer on the Southeast Asian mainland before the ancestor of Great Andamanese immigrated to its modern island territory. Of course, the lexical similarities could also be explained by Great Andamanese belonging to a geographically more widely distributed lineage occupying parts of the adjacent mainland, which left a strong substrate effect in colonizing Austroasiatic-speaking populations. How sparse sound evidence for substantial forager substrates in modern languages of food producers may still be, it is premature at this stage to exclude the possibility that certain groups, especially those reflecting early Neolithic expansions, still retain features of original forager populations.

1.11   From Food Production to Foraging

One of the key points that comes out of a closer examination of the history, both archaeological and linguistic, of foragers is that there are instances of "reversion" whereby food producers become foragers because of adaptation to a new environment, climate change, economic stress, social stress, and/or economical niche specialization. One can identify four possible cases of devolution/reversion according to linguistic outcome, but only three are attested:

(a) Separate identity but no distinct language variety: unattested so far
(b) Dialectal variety of a food producer language, e.g., Chatham Island Moriori of Maori, Mikea of Bara Malagasy
(c) Separate language, e.g., Mlabri (Rischel, Chapter 7); Tasaday (Reid 1992, 1996, 1997)
(d) Distinct lineage, e.g., Numic in Uto-Aztecan (Hill, Chapter 21), parts of Kalahari Khoe in Khoe-Kwadi (Güldemann, Chapter 6)

These cases are of particular interest in the general debate, because the shift from food production to foraging has been elevated to a kind of "mainstream" pattern from a more theoretical perspective. In postmodern discourse over approaches to anthropology starting in the late 1960s, it became popular to deny that modern foragers in different areas of the globe could be historically continuous. Cases in point are South India (cf. the concept of "professional primitives" by Fox 1969), the Amazon region (as per the complete devolution theory by Lévi-Strauss 1968 and Lathrap 1968), Borneo (see Blust 1972; Hoffman 1986; and Bellwood 1999 for the assumed devolution on the part of the Pnan), New Guinea (see the response by Specht 2003 to Roscoe 2002), and Central Africa (cf. Blench 1999 on pygmies).

Note that all the aforementioned cases pertain to densely forested tropical regions. They are related to more theoretical works dealing with individual areas where another challenge to the assumption of forager continuity is posed by Headland (1987), Bailey et al. (1989), and their ilk. These works have questioned generally whether forager subsistence in tropical forest environments, entirely independent of resources directly or indirectly enabled by neighboring horticulture, is at all possible. The authors argue that the virtual absence of modern, fully independent rain forest foragers in the ethnographic and archaeological records suggest that existing foragers in this habitat are a "secondary" adaptation depending on the vicinity of horticulture. There is ample linguistic and nonlinguistic evidence to cast serious doubts on this kind of approach. See Güldemann and Hammarström (unpublished manuscript) for a more detailed discussion from a linguistic perspective.

1.12   Conclusions

We have argued in this introduction for a view of foragers that recognizes that they have significant agency when interacting with food producers. It is conceivable they may be in a steady state as foragers, whether in contact with food producers or not. While history has shown that food producers ultimately absorb, convert, or marginalize most forager societies, there are still, 11,000 years on, places where groups maintain a foraging lifestyle in contact with food producers. A close look at those situations provides evidence to suggest that the interaction is in no way appropriately characterized as that of food producers linguistically (and by extension culturally) "steamrolling" foragers societies (Diamond 1997). Most tellingly, North America at the time of contact had a wide-ranging trade network interlocking food producers and foragers, including societies with very mixed calorie acquisition regimes.

In places where foragers have found niches, the Arctic and Subarctic; the Australian and South African deserts; and the deep jungle in Africa, South America, and South Asia, they have long histories of cultural survival, even if that survival is now, in the age of broad technological reach, at risk. How these forager groups interact with food producers now can be instructive of how interactions of the past played out. One must, of course, beware of potential anachronisms – twentieth-/twenty-first-century postindustrial food producers are not Neolithic food producers. Nor are twentieth-/twenty-first-century foragers, many with quite modern tools acquired from food producers, the same as their remote post-Ice Age cultural forebears. Nonetheless, there is an abundance of evidence to contribute to the discussion of how agriculture spread in the Neolithic, but it remains largely unreferenced in the current debate.

Furthermore, this volume directly addresses a large, and largely untapped, source of evidence regarding the relations between foragers and food producers, namely language. The conventional wisdom on the relevance of language looks only at the macro level. All the languages and language families that are now the most widespread and have the largest numbers of speakers belong to food producers. Such a view, however, completely overlooks the masses of evidence to be gleaned from the details of language. Linguists have long known that language contact leaves traces and that the nature of those traces follow from the nature of those contacts. That is to say, there is a second archeological record in the languages themselves. This volume brings the first round of detailed linguistic evidence to bear on the question.

Chapter 3 by Bickel and Nichols shows that there is no evidence that foragers' languages are in any essential way different from food producers' languages. What differences there may be arise in the vocabulary, since the vocabulary of a language reflects what the speakers most talk about. Brown (Chapter 4) shows that botanical terms differ between foragers and food producers. In his chapter he points out that binomial botanical terminology appears to have arisen with the domestication of plants.

Chapter 2 by Gunnarsdóttir and Stoneking sheds light on the genetics of hunter-gather groups. By comparison with food-producing groups, hunter-gather groups in general have low genetic diversity. They suggest that the lower genetic diversity displayed by some hunter-gatherer groups indicates that the lineages are ancient, and by implication that their foraging lifestyle may be a direct continuation of ancient foraging. But this is true only of some groups.

The remainder of the volume consists of case studies. We begin in Africa.

Savà and Tosco (Chapter 5) discuss the Ongota, a very small, and highly endangered Ethiopian group speaking a language isolate typologically quite distinct from neighboring languages. Based on an historical analysis, they suggest the distant ancestral group of the Ongota reverted to hunting and gathering, but show that the Ongota have long maintained a distinct ethnic identity.

Güldemann's chapter (Chapter 6) addresses a puzzle in Khoisan studies. Khoisan is a general label for the three major, but unrelated language families in southern Africa with phonemic clicks. The groups speaking Khoe-Kwadi languages display more cultural heterogeneity than those of the other two families, who are uniformly foragers but whose languages are more distant. His conclusion goes against the received wisdom in that the ancestors of the Khoe-Kwadi groups are proposed to have come into the region not as foragers but rather as pastoralists and were the first food producers, preceding the arrival of the Bantu.

Having finished with Africa we continue with papers on South and Southeast Asia.

Rischel's contribution (Chapter 7) starts with an overview of hunter-gatherer groups throughout South and Southeast Asia. Some, perhaps many, of these groups were once part of the larger food-producing community and, for a variety of reasons, left to forage. He then turns to a case study of the Mlabri, a Mon-Khmer speaking group of hunter-gathers whose territory straddles the northernmost section of Thai-Lao border. Their language is closely related to Tin and Lua'. The genetic and linguistic evidence regarding the Mlabri seem to suggest different histories. But Rischel puts forth a convincing analysis that the Mlabri are a case of cultural reversion relatively recent in origin.

Reid (Chapter 10) presents an overview of the Negrito groups of the Philippines, examining their prehistoric relationship with the encroaching Austronesian food producers and, arguing from linguistic evidence, how they interacted with their food-producing neighbors.

Soriente (Chapter 11) discusses Penan Benalui, a hunter-gather group from the interior of Borneo. Her work clarifies the linguistic relationships between the sedentary, food-producing Kenyah groups and the Penan Benalui against the background of a broader regional view of hunter-gatherers.

Blevins (Chapter 9) untangles the knotty problem of the Andamanese languages of the aloof Negrito Andamanese hunter-gatherers, who formerly spoke as many as fourteen languages. She shows that there is a basic north-south divide between Great Andamanese to the north and Ongan languages to the south. She addresses the controversy about whether the differences are ancient – Andamanese being Austroasiatic, and Ongan being Austronesian – or whether the two populations were an ancient population speaking a single language and Ongan comes to look like Austronesian through contact effects.

Burenhult's contribution (Chapter 8) addresses the Semang foragers of the Malay peninsula, who speak Aslian languages, which constitute a distinct branch of Austroasiatic. He concludes from a combination of genetic and linguistic evidence that the phenotypically distinct Semang are remnants of ancient hunter-gathers who may have been in a complex relationship with neighboring food producers, but who nonetheless represent a continuity stretching back to the Holocene.

The next section of the book addresses Australia and New Guinea.

Ross' contribution (Chapter 12) surveys Eastern Oceania and grapples with the essential problem of New Guinea, the fact that it is so resource rich that individual groups can live independently of other neighboring groups. Hence, New Guinea is home to the most genetic diversity of languages and language families in the world. Furthermore, the richness of resources also allows for sedentary foraging next to some cultivars developed more than 9,000 years ago.

Donahue's contribution (Chapter 13) reinforces the findings of Nichols and Bickel (Chapter 3), in that he finds differences in the languages of hunter-gatherers, even when those languages are related to food-producer languages, but there is no consistency in how they are different. Possibly the most interesting aspect of Donahue's paper is his showing that, in New Guinea, the distinction between hunter-gatherer and food producer is less than fully clear.

McConvell's contribution (Chapter 16) grapples with the conundrum that Australia was a continent of hunter-gatherers, effectively isolated from the rest of the world until the eighteenth-century arrival of the Europeans. This creates the temptation for the researcher to view Australia as a kind of laboratory for the study of hunter-gatherer culture in pre-Neolithic times. But that view ignores three major facts. First, Australian hunter-gatherer cultures are quite diverse and have interacted prolifically for millenia. Second, Australian ecology is dramatically different from much of the rest of the world. Third, nearly two centuries of interactions with colonizing Europeans, before anthropological interest arose, have dramatically distorted the aboriginal cultures. The implications of these facts for reconstructing crucial vocabulary in Pama-Nyungan are explored.

Harvey's contribution (Chapter 15) deals with the important concept in Australia of land-language relations. He examines the evidence for shifts in such relationships in the non-Pama-Nyungan area and the implications of these shifts as evidence for population shifts.

Sutton's contribution (Chapter 14) explores two questions relevant to Australian languages. Some Australian groups are historically very small, ca. 200. What sociological conditions of this hunter-gatherer society allowed languages to persist at such extremely low numbers? And on the other hand, there were very big (for Australia) languages. Were these super-languages differently underpinned socially, or were they merely cases of recent expansion? This discussion touches on issues relevant to Dixon's model of punctuated equilibrium.

The fifth section of the book addresses languages found in northeastern Eurasia.

Anderson and Harrison contribute a chapter (Chapter 18) on two languages found on the south Siberia taiga, Tofa and Todzhu. Both groups are on the forager-food producer borderline. They are hunter-gatherers with reindeer herds. Both speak Turkic languages as a result of a language shift. The chapter addresses the evidence for language shift with cultural retention, including substrate effects and linguistically encoded knowledge systems.

Vajda's contribution (Chapter 17) addresses issues around the aboriginal hunter-gatherer groups of the middle Yenisei region of central Siberia. These groups speak related languages that are typologically very different from the suffixing, agglutinative languages of other Siberian language families whose speakers are pastoralists. A scattering of Yeniseic substrate elements appear across a vast area of Inner Eurasia, but Yeniseic typological traits were not borrowed. Instead the grammatical structures of Yeniseic languages were profoundly affected by the surrounding languages, while their vocabulary was almost untouched.

The sixth section of the book addresses languages found in North America.

Hill's contribution (Chapter 21) addresses a long-held hypothesis that two branches of northern Uto-Aztecan, Takic and Numic, differ in the amount of substrate influence they show. She shows that Takic does not, in fact, show more than Numic, and she raises questions about commonly held views of what happens linguistically when shifting environmental conditions cause groups to contract. She is looking at groups that have a particularly rich archeological record.

Rhodes' contribution (Chapter 20) addresses the question of whether hunter-gatherer groups can display agency in language spread. Looking at historically attested data for the last 500 years, he shows that all types of language spreads, migratory and nonmigratory, have taken place in the Great Lakes region of North America. He shows that the spreads were driven by hunter-gatherers. These facts call into question assumptions made by archeologists about the agency of foragers vis-à-vis food producers.

Chapter 19 by de Reuse grapples with the question of primitivism and the Sapir-Whorf hypothesis. It has long been conventional wisdom that Eskimoan languages have many words for "snow." de Reuse shows that, once one factors out the extraordinarily complex morphology typical of all Eskimoan languages, Yupik has exact two stems distinguishing snow on the ground from falling snow. At the same time, Eskimoan languages have a technical vocabulary for talking about any weather, sea, and ice conditions that affect Eskimo life, particularly regarding hunting and gathering activities, and that includes "snow."

The seventh and final section of the book addresses issues in the languages of South America.

Epps' contribution (Chapter 22) addresses a situation that is found around the world where hunter-gatherers and neighboring food producers are in a so-called symbiotic relationship. The hunter-gatherers supply forest products and sometimes labor; the food-producers provide carbohydrates. Epps points out that the relationship is very asymmetric in favor of the food producers, but nonetheless there are places where the asymmetrical relationship is stable enough to last for generations. Often the asymmetry leads to language shift to the food producer's language, but sometimes the hunter-gatherers maintain a stable bilingualism. This chapter provides a case study of the relationship between the northwest Amazonian hunter-gatherer groups speaking Nadahup (Makú) languages and food producers speaking Tukanoan languages.

Vidal and Braunstein (Chapter 23) present a description of the hunter-gatherer peoples of the Gran Chaco region of central lowland South America. They examine the various Chaco languages, which are all seriously underdocumented, from an historical perspective and provide evidence for contact among all the hunter-gatherer groups in that area, through a brief comparative examination. Addressing one of the oldest enigmas of the Chaco, they consider the pressures under which groups forced in the Chaco by colonization disappeared, assimilated, or reformed and hence disappeared from or suddenly emerged in the historical record. Their explanation proposes ethnogenic dynamics based on currently known processes of cultural change and mixture. In this dynamic, the hunter-gatherer culture acts as a lowest common denominator enabling assimilation of even formerly agrarian groups.

The march of history is clear. Food producers can, and in general do, out-produce foragers. This generally puts food producers in positions of relative economic power with respect to foragers. But where the story gets interesting is in the niches, where food production is marginal – often for reasons of climate – or where foraging brings other advantages. Beyond that, most of us are so citified that we forget that until the rise of agribusiness, hunting played an important role in farming across much of the globe, if for no other reason than vermin control, and the calories are a byproduct.

In their respective niches, foragers have much to teach us about the balance of power, cultural coherence, and economics on the margins. These lessons have been poorly learned when it comes to theorizing about the transition to agriculture from the Neolithic on.

It is hoped that this volume with contributions spanning the globe will help bring the light of facts about forager languages to bear on some of the most fundamental questions regarding how the human race got to be where it is.

NOTES

1. The method of dating from linguistics alone, glottochronology, is problematic.
2. These two types were formerly called "upstream" and "downstream" respectively (McConvell 2010) but McConvell (2013) has now adopted the new terminology because the geographical metaphor caused confusion.
3. The need for explicit permission from those most closely associated with the country and the threat of violence to keep "strangers" out seems to vary among different groups, even in relatively close proximity for instance in Australia. There could be an ecological determinant here – the more defended boundaries seem to occur in more resource-rich zones, where the need for people to forage outside their normal territory is less. Consequently, people crossing boundaries in this way are suspected of having ulterior motives of a different kind, such as revenge raids, carrying off

women, and the like, and dealt with accordingly. A problematic case is that where a region of low resources abuts on to a region of higher resources. The group in the low-resource area may see it as legitimate practice to forage in the high-resource area in times of need, but those in the high-resource area may be less amenable to this practice, as it has not been part of their tradition to such an extent.

4. Murdock (1949: 204) stated, however, that bilocal residence particularly suited the foragers' lifestyle. This generalization is challenged by Ember (1978).

5. It should be noted that this is beginning to be addressed in recent work.

6. This may particularly be the case for groups heavily reliant on migrating herds or flocks of game where the usual paths of the animals are disrupted by some natural phenomenon.

7. Kelly (1995; 254–256) also makes an argument that sedentism can lead to an increase in the rate of population growth.

8. The other possibility of food producers adopting the language of foragers does not seem to be attested. This may be a premature generalization.

9. Many publications stress the unusual nature of the foraging life in tropical rain forests and warn against drawing general analogies from it, however.

10. Compare this typology of foragers with those already discussed definitional traits given in §1.5.

11. The situation is even more complicated. Groups such as the Ottawa, who are not unusual in proto-historical North America, practiced a mixed subsistence regime, supplementing their hunting and trade with some agriculture (Feest and Feest 1978: 774).

12. It is an interesting question in its own right to determine whether, and if so why, herding as a major subsistence component is more "tolerant" to cohabitation with relatively independent foragers.

13. It should not be concluded, of course, that landscape-related ethnic "dichoto-mies" are tied to differences in subsistence. Aikhenvald (2008), for example, reports an opposition between "river-dwellers" and "jungle-dwellers" along the Sepik River who cannot be distinguished obviously in terms of foraging vs. food production and speak languages which might also be remotely related to each other within a proposed wider Sepik family (Foley 2008). Further research is needed, however, because both the subsistence assignment to groups and the genealogical classification of languages are quite problematic in New Guinea.

References

Aikhenvald, Alexandra. (2008). *The Manambu language of East Sepik, Papua New Guinea*. Cambridge: Cambridge University Press.

Allen, Nick J. (2004). Tetradic theory: An approach to kinship. In R. Parkin and L. Stone (eds.), *Kinship and family: An anthropological reader*. Oxford: Blackwell, 231–235.

Arnold, Jeanne. (1996). The archaeology of complex hunter-gatherers. *Journal of Archeological Method and Theory* 3(2): 77–126.

Aubin, George F. (1975). *A Proto-Algonquian dictionary*. National Museum of Man, Mercury Series. Canadian Ethnology Service Paper no. 29. Ottawa: National Museums of Canada.

Bahuchet, Serge. (1992). Histoire d'une civilisation forestière 1: dans la forêt d'Afrique centrale; les pygmées aka et baka. *Bibliothèque de la SELAF 322. Ethnoscience 8.* Leuven: Peeters.

Bahuchet, Serge. (1993). Histoire d'une civilisation forestière 2: la rencontre des agriculteurs – les pygmées parmi les peuples d'Afrique centrale. *Bibliothèque de la SELAF 344. Ethnoscience 9.* Leuven: Peeters.

Bahuchet, Serge. (2012). Changing language, remaining Pygmy. *Human Biology* 84(1): 11–43. Retrieved from: www.bioone.org/doi/full/10.3378/027.084.0101

Bailey, Robert, M. Jenike, L. Head, et al. (1989). Hunting and gathering in tropical rain forest: Is it possible? *American Anthropologist* 91: 55–92.

Barnard, Alan. (2002). The foraging mode of thought. In Henry Stewart, Alan Barnard, and Keiichi Omura (eds.), *Self- and other images of hunter-gatherers.* Senri Ethnological Studies 60. Osaka: National Museum of Ethnology, 5–24.

Baugh, Timothy G., and Jonathon E. Ericson (eds.). (1994). *Prehistoric exchange systems in North America.* New York: Plenum Press.

Bellwood, Peter. (1999). Archaeology of Southeast Asian hunters and gatherers. In Richard B. Lee, and Richard Daly (eds.), *The Cambridge encyclopaedia of hunters and gatherers.* Cambridge: Cambridge University Press, 284–288.

Bellwood, Peter. (2005a). Examining the farming/language dispersal hypothesis in the East Asian context. In Laurent Sagart, Roger Blench, and Alicia Sanchez-Mazas (eds.), *The peopling of East Asia: Putting together archaeology, linguistics and genetics.* Abingdon: RoutledgeCurzon,17–30.

Bellwood, Peter. (2005b). *First farmers: The origins of agricultural societies.* Oxford: Blackwell.

Bellwood, Peter. (2011). Holocene population history in the Pacific Region as a model for worldwide food producer dispersals. *Current Anthropology* 52–54: S363–S378.

Bellwood, Peter. (2013). *First migrants: Ancient migration in global perspective.* Chichester: Wiley/Blackwell.

Bellwood P. (ed.). (2014). *The global prehistory of human migration.* Hoboken, NJ: Wiley-Blackwell, 327–332.

Bellwood Peter, and Colin Renfrew (eds.). (2002). *Examining the farming/language dispersal hypothesis.* Cambridge: MacDonald Institute for Archaeological Research, University of Cambridge.

Bettinger, Robert. (1991). Doing Great Basin archaeology recently: Coping with variability. *Journal of Archaeological Research* 1: 43–66.

Bettinger, Robert L. (1994). How, when, and why Numic spread. In David B. Madsen and David Rhode (eds.), *Across the west: Human population movement and the expansion of the Numa.* Salt Lake City: University of Utah Press, 44–55.

Bettinger, Robert, and Martin Baumhoff. (1982). The Numic spread: Great Plains cultures in competition. *American Antiquity* 47: 485–505.

Binford, Lewis. (2002). *In pursuit of the past: Decoding the archaeological record.* Berkeley: University of California Press.

Bird, Douglas, and James O'Connell. (2006). Behavioral ecology and archaeology. *Journal of Archaeological Research* 14: 143–188.

Birdsell, Joseph Benjamin. (1953). Some environmental and cultural factors influencing the structuring of Australian aboriginal populations. *American Naturalist* 87: 171–207.

Blench, Roger. (1999). Are the African Pygmies an ethnographic fiction? In H. Biesbrouck, S. Elders, and G. Rossel (eds.), *Central African hunter-gatherers in a multidisciplinary perspective: Challenging elusiveness.* Leiden: Research School for Asian, African, and Amerindian Studies (CNWS), Leiden University, 41–60.

Blench, Roger, and Martin T. Walsh. (2010). The vocabularies of Vazimba and Beosi: Do they represent the languages of the pre-Austronesian populations of Madagascar? Retrieved from: www.rogerblench.info/Language/Isolates/Vazimba %20vocabulary.pdf

Bliege-Bird, Rebecca, Eric Smith, and Douglas Bird. (2001). The hunting handicap: Costly signalling in human foraging strategies. *Behavioral Ecology and Sociobiology* 50: 9–19.

Bloomfield, Leonard. (1925). On the sound system of central Algonquian. *Language* 1 (4): 130–156.

Blust, Robert A. (1974). The Proto-North Sarawak vowel deletion hypothesis. PhD thesis, University of Hawaiʻi.

Bowern, Claire, P. Epps, R. Gray, J. Hill, P. McConvell, and J. Zentz. (2011). Does lateral transmission obscure inheritance in hunter-gatherer languages? *PLoS ONE* 6(9): e25195.

Bowern, Claire, H. Haynie, C. Sheard, et al. (2014). Loan and inheritance patterns in hunter-gatherer ethnobiological systems. *Journal of Ethnobiology* 34(2): 195–227.

Brugge, David M. (1983). Navajo prehistory and history to 1850. In Alfonso Ortiz (vol. ed.), *Handbook of North American Indians, Vol. 10: Southwest.* Washington, DC: Smithsonian Institution Press, 489–501.

Burch, Ernest. (1971). The caribou/wild reindeer as a human resource. *American Antiquity* 37(3): 339–361.

Comrie, Bernard. (2002). Farming dispersal in Europe and the spread of the Indo-European language family. In P. Bellwood and C. Renfrew (eds.), *Examining the Farming language dispersal hypothesis.* Cambridge: McDonald Institute for Archaeological Research, 409–419.

DeMallie, Raymond J. (vol. ed.). (2001). *Handbook of North American Indians*, Vol. 13: *Plains.* Washington, DC: Smithsonian Institution Press.

Denny, J. Peter. (1991). The Algonquian migration from plateau to midwest: Linguistics and archaeology. In W. Cowan (ed.), *Papers of the 22nd Algonquian conference.* Ottawa: Carleton University, 103–124.

Denny, J. Peter. (1992). The entry of the Algonquian language into the Boreal Forest. Paper read to the Canadian Archaeological Association, London, Ontario, May 1992.

Diamond, Jared M. (1997). Linguistics: The language steamrollers. *Nature* 389: 544–546.

Diamond, Jared, and Peter Bellwood (2003). Farmers and their languages: The first expansions. *Science* 300(5619): 597–603.

Diebold, Richard. (1992). The traditional view of the Indo-European paleo-economy: Contradictory evidence from anthropology and linguistics. In E. Polome and W. Winter (eds.), *Reconstructing languages and cultures.* Berlin: de Gruyter Mouton. 317–368.

Dixon, R. M. W. (1976).Tribes, languages and other boundaries in northeast Queensland. In Nicholas Peterson (ed.), *Tribes and boundaries in Australia.* Canberra: AIAS, 204–238.

Dixon, R. M. W. (2002). *Australian languages: Their nature and development.* Cambridge: Cambridge University Press.

Doornbos, Paul, and M. Lionel Bender. (1983). Languages of Wadai-Darfur. In M. Lionel Bender (ed.), *Nilo-Saharan language studies.* Committee on Northeast African Studies Monographs 13. East Lansing: African Studies Center, Michigan State University, 42–79.

Driver, Harold E. (1969). *Indians of North America* (2nd edn). Chicago: University of Chicago Press.

Driver, Harold E., and William C. Massey. (1957). Comparative studies of North American Indians. *Transactions of the American Philosophical Society, New Series* 47(Pt. 2).

Ehret, Christopher. (2011). *History and the testimony of language.* Berkeley: University of California Press.

Ellen, Roy. (1994). Modes of subsistence: Hunting and gathering to agriculture and pastoralism. In Tim Ingold (ed.), *Companion encyclopedia of anthropology: Humanity, culture and social life.* London: Routledge, 197–225.

Ember, Carol. (1978). Myths about hunter-gatherers. *Ethnology* 17: 439–444.

Ember, Carol, and Melvin Ember. (2010). *Cultural anthropology.* Upper Saddle River, NJ: Prentice-Hall.

Epps, Patience. (2013). Inheritance, calquing or independent innovation? Reconstructing morphological complexity in Amazonian numerals. *Journal of Language Contact* 6(2): 323–357.

Epps, Patience, and Kristine Stenzel. (2013). Introduction. In Patience Epps and Kristine Stenzel (eds.), *Upper Rio Negro: Cultural and linguistic interaction in northwestern Amazonia.* Rio de Janeiro: Museu Nacional; Museu do Índio/Funai, 13–50.

Evans, N., and P. McConvell. (1998). The enigma of Pama-Nyungan expansion in Australia. In Roger Blench and Matthew Spriggs (eds.), *Archaeology and language,* Vol. 2. London: Routledge, 174–191.

Feest, Christian F., and Johanna E. Feest. (1978). Ottawa. In Bruce G. Trigger (ed.), *Handbook of North American Indians,* Vol. 15. Washington, DC: Smithsonian Institution Press, 772–786.

Feit, Harvey A. (2004). Hunting and the quest for power: The James Bay Cree and Whitemen in the 20th century. In R. Bruce Morrison and C. Roderick Wilson (eds.), *Native peoples: The Canadian experience* (3rd edn). Toronto: McCelland & Stewart, 101–128.

Fix, Alan. (1994). *Migration and colonization in human micro-evolution.* Cambridge: Cambridge University Press.

Flannery, Kent. (1969). Origins and ecological effects of early domestication in Iran and the Near East. In P. Ucko and G. Dimbleby (eds.), *The domestication and exploitation of plants and animals.* Chicago: Aldine, 73–100.

Foley, William. (2008). *The Papuan languages of New Guinea.* Cambridge: Cambridge University Press.

Ford, Richard I. (1981). Gardening and farming before A.D. 1000: Patterns of prehistoric cultivation north of Mexico. *Journal of Ethnobiology* 1(1): 6–27.

Fortescue, Michael. (1997). Dialect distribution and intergroup interaction in Greenlandic Eskimo. In P. McConvell and N. Evans (eds.), *Archaeology and*

Linguistics: Aboriginal Australia in global perspective. Melbourne: Oxford University Press, 111–122.

Fowler, Melvin L., and Robert L. Hall. (1978). Late prehistory of the Illinois area. In Bruce G. Trigger (vol. ed.), *Handbook of North American Indians*, Vol. 15: *Northeast*. Washington, DC: Smithsonian Institution, 560–568.

Fox, Richard G. (1969). "Professional primitives": Hunters and gatherers of nuclear South Asia. *Man in India* 49(2): 139–160.

Galinat, William. (1985). Domestication and diffusion of maize. In R. Ford (ed.), *Prehistoric food production in North America*. Anthropological Papers, Museum of Anthropology, University of Michigan, No. 75. Ann Arbor: University of Michigan Press, 245–278.

Gibbon, Guy E., and Ames, Kenneth M. (1998). *Archaeology of prehistoric Native America: An encyclopedia*. New York: Routledge.

Gibson, Thomas, and Kenneth Sillender. (2011). *Anarchic solidarity: Autonomy, equality and fellowship in South-east Asia*. Yale South-east Asian Studies Monographs. New Haven, CT: Yale University Press.

Goddard, R. H. Ives. (1994). The west-to-east cline in Algonquian dialectology. In William Cowan (ed.), *Actes du 25e congrès des Algonquinistes*. Ottawa: Carleton University, 187–211.

Gremillion, Kristen. (2003). Eastern Woodlands overview. In Paul E. Minnis (ed.), *People and plants in ancient eastern North America*. Washington, DC: Smithsonian Institution Press, 17–49.

Griffin, P. Bion. (1981). Hunting, farming and sedentism in a rain-forest foraging society. In S. Kent (ed.), *Farmers as Hunters: The implications of sedetism*. Cambridge: Cambridge University Press, 61–75.

Grimm, Nadine. (2015). A grammar of Gyeli. PhD thesis, Institute for Asian and African Studies, Humboldt University Berlin.

Gruhn, Ruth. (1997). Language classification and models of the peopling of the Americas. In P. McConvell and N. Evans (eds.), *Archaeology and Linguistics: Aboriginal Australia in global perspective*. Melbourne: Oxford University Press.

Headland, Thomas. (1986). Why foragers do not become farmers: A historical study of a changing ecosystem and its effect on a Negrito hunter-gatherer group in the Philippines. Unpublished PhD dissertation, University of Hawaii.

Headland, Thomas. (1987). The wild yam question: How well could independent hunter-gatherers live in a tropical rain forest ecosystem? *Human Ecology* 15: 463–491.

Headland, Thomas N., and Lawrence Reid. (1989). Hunter-gatherers and their neighbors from prehistory to the present. *Current Anthropology* 30(1): 43–51.

Hill, Jane H. (1996). *Languages on the land: Toward an anthropological dialectology*. David Skomp Distinguished Lectures in Anthropology. Bloomington: Department of Anthropology, Indiana University.

Hill, Jane H. (2001). Proto-Uto-Aztecan. *American Anthropologist New Series* 103(4): 913–934.

Hill, Jane H. (2008). Northern Uto-Aztecan and Kiowa-Tanoan: Evidence of contact between the Proto-languages? *IJAL* 74: 155–188.

Hiscock, Peter. (2008). *Archaeology of ancient Australia*. London: Routledge.

Hoffman, Carl L. (1986). *The Punan: Hunters and gatherers of Borneo*. Studies in Cultural Anthropology, 12. Ann Arbor: University Microfilms International Research Press.

Hunn, Eugene. (1994). Place-names, population density and the magic number 500. *Current Anthropology* 35(1): 81–85.

Isaac, Barry. (1990). Economy, ecology and analogy: The !Kung San and the generalised foraging model. In K. Tankersley and B. Isaac (eds.), *Early Paleoindian economies of Eastern North America.* Greenwich, CT: JAI Press, 323–335.

Ives, John. (1990). *A theory of northern Athabaskan prehistory.* Boulder, CO: Westview Press.

Kaestle, F., and D. Smith. (2001). Ancient mitochondrial DNA evidence for prehistoric movement: The Numic expansion. *American Journal of Physical Anthropology* 115: 1–12.

Keen, Ian. (1982). How some Murngin men marry ten wives. *Man New Series* 17(4): 620–642.

Keen, Ian. (2004). *Aboriginal economy and society.* Melbourne: Cambridge University Press.

Keen, Ian. (2006). Constraints on the development of enduring inequality in late Holocene Australia. *Current Anthropology* 17(1): 7–38.

Keen, I. (ed.) (2010). *Indigenous participation in Australian economies.* New South Wales: ANU Press.

Kelly, R. I. (1995). *The foraging spectrum: Diversity in hunter-gatherer lifeways.* Washington, DC: Smithsonian Institution Press.

Kelly, Robert. (2003). Colonization of new land by hunter-gatherers. In H. Rockman and J. Steele (eds.), *The colonization of unfamiliar landscapes: The archaeology of adaptation.* London: Routledge, 44–57.

Kennett, Douglas J., and Bruce Winterhalder (eds.). (2006). *Behavioral ecology and the transition to agriculture.* Berkeley: University of California Press.

Lathrap, Donald. (1968). The 'hunting' economies of the tropical forest zone of South America: An attempt at historical perspective. In Richard Lee and Irven Devore, eds. *Man the hunter.* Chicago: Aldine, 23–29.

Layton, R., R. Foley, E. Williams, et al. (1991). The transition between hunting and gathering and the specialized husbandry of resources: A socio-biological approach. *Current Anthropology* 32(3): 255–274.

Lee, Richard, and Irene deVore (eds.). (1968). *Man the hunter.* Chicago: Aldine.

Letouzey, René. (1976). Contribution de la botanique au problème d'une éventuelle langue pygmée. *Bibliothèque de la SELAF 57/8.* Paris: SELAF.

Levi-Strauss, Claude. (1968). The concept of 'primitiveness'. In Richard Lee and Irven Devore (eds.), *Man the hunter.* Chicago: Aldine, 349–352.

Lourandos, Harry. (1997). *Continent of hunter-gatherers: New perspectives on Australian prehistory.* Cambridge: Cambridge University Press.

Lovestrand, Joey. (2013). East Chadic B: Classification and description progress report. *Journal of West African Languages* 40(1): 105–130.

Madsen, David B., and Rhode, David. (1994). *Across the west: Human population movement and the expansion of the Numa.* Salt Lake City: University of Utah Press.

McConvell, Patrick. (1996). Backtracking to Babel: The chronology of Pama-Nyungan expansion in Australia. *Archaeology in Oceania* 31: 125–144.

McConvell, Patrick. (2001). Language shift and language spread among hunter-gatherers. In C. Panter-Brick, P. Rowley-Conwy, and R. Layron (eds.), *Hunter-gatherers:*

Social and biological perspectives. Cambridge: Cambridge University Press, 143–169.

McConvell, Patrick. (2009). Loanwords in Gurindji, a Pama-Nyungan language of Australia. Chapter and database in M. Haspelmath and U. Tadmor (eds.), *Loanwords in the world's languages: A comparative handbook*. Berlin: Mouton de Gruyter, 790–822.

McConvell, Patrick. (2010). The archaeolinguistics of migration. In J. Lucassen, L. Lucassen, and P. Manning (eds.), *Migration history in world history: Multidisciplinary approaches*. Leiden: Brill, 151–190.

McConvell, Patrick. (2013). Comment on Denham's 'Beyond Fictions of Closure'. *Mathematical Anthropology and Cultural Theory*. 5(3).

McConvell, Patrick. (2018). The birds and the bees: The origins of sections in Queensland. In P. McConvell, P. Kelly, and S. Lacrampe (eds.), *Skin, kin and clan: the dynamics of social categories in indigenous Australia*. Canberra: ANU Press, 219–270.

McConvell, Patrick, and Mike Smith. (2003). Millers and mullers: The archaeolinguistic stratigraphy of seed-grinding in Central Australia. In H. Andersse (ed.), *Language contact in prehistory: Studies in stratigraphy*. Amsterdam: Benjamins, 177–200.

Minnis, Paul E. (ed.). (2003). *People and plants in ancient eastern North America*. Washington, DC: Smithsonian Institution Press.

Minnis, Paul E. (ed.). (2004). *People and plants in ancient western North America*. Washington, DC: Smithsonian Institution Press.

Moore, John. (2001). Evaluating five models of human colonization. *American Anthropologist* 163(2): 395–408.

Murdock, George. (1949). *Social structure*. New York: Macmillan.

Myers, Fred. (1988). *Pintupi country, Pintupi self: Sentiment and politics among Western Desert Aborigines*. Washington, DC: Smithsonian Institution Press.

Nettle, Daniel. (1999). *Linguistic diversity*. Oxford: Oxford University Press.

Nichols, Johanna, and Richard A. Rhodes. (2018). Vectors of language spread at the central steppe periphery: Finno-Ugric as a catalyst language. In R. Iversen and G. Kroonen (eds.), *Digging for Words: Archaeolinguistic case studies from the XV Nordic TAG Conference held at University of Copenhagen, April 16–18, 2015*. Oxford: British Archaeological Reports, 58–68.

Ortiz, Alfonso (vol. ed.) (1983). *Handbook of North American Indians*, Vol. 10: *Southwest*. Washington, DC: Smithsonian Institution Press.

Pálsson, Gísli. (1988). Hunters and gatherers of the sea. In Tim Ingold, David Riches, and James Woodburn (eds.), *Hunters and gatherers 1: History, evolution and social change*. New York: Berg, 189–204.

Radisson, Pierre Esprit. (1961). *The explorations of Pierre Esprit Radisson, from the original manuscript in the Bodleian Library and the British Museum*, edited by Arthur T. Adams, modernized by Loren Kallsen. Minneapolis, MN: Ross and Haines.

Reid, Lawrence A. (1992). The Tasaday language: A key to Tasaday prehistory. In Thomas N. Headland (ed.), *The Tasaday controversy: An assessment of the evidence*. Washington, DC: American Anthropological Association, 180–193.

Reid, Lawrence A. (1994). Possible non-Austronesian lexical elements in Philippine Negrito languages. *Oceanic Linguistics* 33(1): 37–72.

Reid, Lawrence A. (1996). The Tasaday tapes. In *Pan-Asiatic linguistics: Proceedings of the 4th international symposium on languages and linguistics*, January 8–10, 1996, Vol. 5. Salaya, Thailand: Institute of Language and Culture for Rural Development, Mahidol University, 1743–1766.

Reid, Lawrence A. (1997). Linguistic archaeology: Tracking down the Tasaday language. In Roger Blench and Matthew Spriggs (eds.), *Theoretical and methodological orientations: Archaeology and language 1*. One World Archaeology 27. London: Routledge, 184–208.

Reid, Lawrence A. (2009). Hunter-gatherer and farmer symbiosis from a linguist's point of view. In Kazunobu Ikeya, Hidefumi Ogawa, and Peter Mitchell (eds.), *Interactions between hunter-gatherers and farmers: From prehistory to present*. Senri Ethnological Studies 73. Osaka: National Museum of Ethnology, 263–269.

Renfrew, A. Colin. (1989a). Models of change in language and archaeology. *Transactions of the Philological Society* 87(2): 103–155.

Renfrew, A. Colin. (1989b). *Archaeology and language: The puzzle of Indo-European origins*. London: Penguin.

Renfrew, A. Colin. (2003). *Figuring it out: What are we? Where do we come from?* London: Thames & Hudson.

Rhodes, Richard A. (1982). Algonquian trade languages. In Wm. Cowan (ed.), *Papers of the thirteenth Algonquian conference*. Ottawa: Carleton University, 1–10.

Rhodes, Richard A. (2012). Algonquian trade languages revisited. In K. Hele and J. R. Valentine (eds.), *Papers of the fortieth Algonquian conference*. Albany: SUNY Press, 358–369.

Richerson, Peter, Robert Boyd, and Robert Bettinger. (2001). Was agriculture impossible during the Pleistocene but mandatory during the Holocene? *American Antiquity* 66(3): 387–411.

Rottland, Franz, and Rainer Voßen. (1977). Grundlagen für eine Klärung des Dorobo-Problems. In Wilhelm J. G. Möhlig, Franz Rottland, and Bernd Heine (eds.), *Zur Sprachgeschichte und Ethnohistorie in Afrika: Neue Beiträge afrikanistischer Forschungen*. Berlin: Dietrich Reimer, 213–238.

Rumsey, A. (1993). Language and territoriality in Aboriginal Australia. In M. Walsh and C. Yallop (eds.), *Language and culture in Aboriginal Australia*. Canberra: Aboriginal Studies Press,191–206.

Sapir, Edward. (1949/1936). Internal linguistic evidence suggestive of the northern origin of the Navaho. In D. Mandelbaum (ed.), *Selected writings in language, culture and personality*, 213–224. Berkeley: University of California Press. *American Anthropologist* 38(2): 224–235 [1936].

Sarich, Steven. (2010). Deconstructing the Hopewell Interaction Sphere. *Nebraska Anthropologist*. Paper 59.

Scarry, C. Margaret. (2003). Patterns of wild plant utilization in the prehistoric eastern woodlands. In Paul E. Minnis (ed.), *People and plants in ancient eastern North America*. Washington, DC: Smithsonian Institution Press, 50–104.

Schnoebelen, Tyler. (2009). (Un)classifying Shabo: Phylogenetic methods and results. In Peter K. Austin, Oliver Bond, Monik Charette, et al. (eds.), *Proceedings of conference on language documentation and linguistic theory 2*. London: School of Oriental and African Studies, 275–284.

Seeman, Mark F. (1979). *Hopewell Interaction Sphere: The evidence for interregional trade and structural complexity.* Indianapolis, IN: Indian Historical Society.

Smith, Bruce D., and C. Wesley Cowan. (2003). Domesticated crop plants and the evolution of food production economies in eastern North America. In Paul E. Minnis (ed.), *People and plants in ancient eastern North America.* Washington, DC: Smithsonian Institution Press, 105–125.

Snow, Dean. (1978). Late prehistory of the East Coast. In Bruce G. Trigger (vol. ed.), *Handbook of North American Indians,* Vol. 15: *Northeast.* Washington, DC: Smithsonian Institution, 58–69.

Specht, Jim. (2003). On New Guinea hunters and gatherers. *Current Anthropology* 44(2): 269–271.

Struever, Stuart, and Gail L. Houart. (1990). Analysis of the Hopewell Interaction Sphere. In Wayne Suttles (vol. ed.), *Handbook of North American Indians,* Vol. 7: *Northwest Coast.* Washington, DC: Smithsonian Institution, 1990.

Suttles, Wayne. (1990). *Handbook of the North American Indians,* Vol. 7: *North-west Coast.* Washington, DC: Smithsonian Institution Press.

Szalay, Miklós. (1995). *The San and the colonization of the Cape: 1770–1879; conflict, incorporation, acculturation.* Quellen zur Khoisan-Forschung 11. Köln: Rüdiger Köppe.

Thomas, D. H. (1981). Complexity among Great Basin Shoshones, the world's least affluent hunter-gatherers? In S. Koyoma and D. H. Thomas (eds.), *Affluent foragers: Pacific coast, east and west.* Osaka: National Museum of Ethnology, 19–52.

Trigger, Bruce G. (vol. ed.). (1978). *Handbook of North American Indians,* Vol. 15: *Northeast.* Washington, DC: Smithsonian Institution Press.

Trigger, Bruce G. (1998). *Sociocultural evolution: Calculation and contingency.* Malden, MA: Blackwell.

Turney, Christian, and Douglas Hobbs. (2006). ENSO influence on Holocene Aboriginal populations in Queensland, Australia. *Journal of Archaeological Science* 33(12): 1744–1748.

Veth, Peter. (2006). Social dynamism in the archaeology of the Western Desert. In B. David, B. Barker, and I. McNiven (eds.), *The social archaeology of Australian indigenous societies.* Canberra: Aboriginal Studies Press, 242–253.

Veth, P., M. Smith, and P. Hiscock (eds.). (2005). *Desert peoples: Archaeological Perspectives.* Oxford: Blackwell.

Whalen, Doug, and Gary F. Simons (2012). Endangered language families. *Language* 88: 151–173.

White, Douglas (ed.) (1986). Introduction. Ethnographic atlas. *World Cultures.* 6(3). (based on G. Murdock et al.).

White, Douglas. (1990). Ethnographic atlas map tabulations. Retrieved from: http://ec lectic.ss.uci.edu/~drwhite/worldcul/wldvol63.htm (with Michael Fischer).

Williams, Alan N., Sean Ulm, Chris S. M. Turney, David Rohde, and Gentry White (2015). Holocene demographic changes and the emergence of complex societies in prehistoric Australia. *PLoS* June 17, 2015. Retrieved from: http://dx.doi.org/10.1 371/journal.pone.0128661

Winship, George Parker (ed. and trans.). (1904). *The journey of Coronado, 1540–1542, from the City of Mexico to the Grand Canon of the Colorado and the Buffalo Plains of Texas.* New York: A. S. Barnes & Company,

Winterhalder, Bruce. (1986). Diet choice, risk and food sharing in a stochastic environment. *Journal of Anthropological Archaeology* 5(4): 369–392.

Woodburn, James. (1980). Hunters and gatherers today and reconstruction of the past. In E. Gellner (ed.), *Soviet and Western anthropology*. London: Duckworth.

Woodburn, James. (1990). Hunters and gatherers today and reconstruction of the past. In E. Gellner (ed.), *Soviet and Western Anthropology*. London: Duckworth.

Yuan, Yi-F. (1990). *Topophilia: A study of environmental perceptions, attitudes, and values*. New York: Columbia University Press.

2 Genetic Landscape of Present-Day Hunter-Gatherer Groups

Ellen Dröfn Gunnarsdóttir and Mark Stoneking

2.1 Introduction

Hunter-gatherer groups have been comprehensively studied from a multidisci-plinary perspective over the last few decades, particularly in an anthropological and linguistic context. More recently, molecular geneticists have contributed to the field, focusing on the genetic landscape of hunter-gatherer groups from evolutionary and historical standpoints, especially in comparison to agricultural groups. Hunter-gatherer groups have often been used as models of ancient lifestyles of modern humans, especially in classical anthropology. There is a similar tendency among evolutionary geneticists to automatically assume that contemporary hunter-gatherer groups can be used as a model to better understand our evolutionary past. However, there is no simple way to define a hunting and gathering mode of subsistence; even though the term "hunting and gathering" implies a specific mode of subsistence, many groups practice both partial hunting and gathering and partial agriculture.

In cultural anthropology, many different terms are used to describe the various levels of hunting and gathering, but in genetic studies there is a tendency to simplify the term, with groups often defined as either hunter-gatherer or food-producing groups, not taking into account the various levels (see, e.g., Chapter 5 by Savá and Tosco, this volume). It is also known that some groups that had practiced hunting and gathering in the past have changed to farming, and vice versa. Known cases where hunter-gatherer groups have changed recently from hunting and gathering to farming are, for example, the Khoisan people in southern Africa and Navajo and some Apache populations in the southwestern United States (Diamond and Bellwood 2003). Agricultural groups that changed to a hunting and gathering mode of subsistence when they had reached areas unsuitable for farming include Polynesian hunter-gatherer groups on the Chatham Islands and New Zealand, a Uto-Aztecan hunter-gatherer group in the Great Basin of North America derived from farmers from Mexico, and Punan hunter-gatherer groups in Borneo derived from Austronesian farmers (Diamond and

Table 2.1 *Number of languages spoken by regionally defined hunter-gatherer groups*

Region	Languages	Language families
South America	160	65
North America	250	52
Northeast Eurasia	33	8
Australia	271	28
New Guinea	330	86
Tropical Asia	147	18
Africa	87	23

Information taken from Tom Güldemann, Chapter 6, this volume.

Bellwood 2003). Furthermore, Oota et al. (2005) showed that a hunter-gatherer group from Thailand, the Mlabri, appears to have originated from an agricultural group and later changed to hunting and gathering. The group had no mitochondrial DNA (mtDNA) diversity and very low Y-chromosome diversity. However, interdisciplinary studies indicate that the group recently originated from an agricultural group. Therefore, caution is advised when interpreting genetic data and it is important not to jump to conclusions based on genetic data alone. Interdisciplinary perspectives should always be considered when inferring our evolutionary past to get a more holistic picture. Undoubtedly, modern hunter-gatherer groups differ from their Pleistocene ancestors and are not relics of those populations.

Hunting and gathering is still practiced globally. Although it is difficult to predict how many hunter-gatherer groups there are in the world today, the number of languages spoken regionally by hunter-gatherer groups (Table 2.1) gives some idea of their worldwide distribution. Population densities of hunter-gatherer groups are habitually smaller than those of agricultural groups, tending to be around ten to seventy-five individuals, with seasonal variance (Kelly 1995).

Around the fifteenth to sixteenth centuries, when European colonization began in Africa, the Americas, and Asia, approximately a third of the world's peoples were hunter-gatherers, but since then hunter-gatherer groups have declined drastically (Biesele et al. 2000). Moreover, during the spread of agriculture some 6,000 to 12,000 years ago (depending on geographical location), many hunter-gatherer groups were undoubtedly assimilated, while those groups that still maintained a hunting and gathering mode of subsistence migrated to areas unsuitable for agriculture, often because of pressure from the incoming agricultural group. Modern-day hunter-gatherer groups are still under pressure from agricultural groups, and as a consequence many of them have adopted agricultural practices. As a result, hunter-gatherer groups are declining rapidly, emphasizing the importance and urgency of multidisciplinary research on their genes, languages, and culture.

2.2   Genetic Markers and Analysis

2.2.1   mtDNA, Y Chromosomes, and Autosomal Markers

Several markers are used to examine evolutionary history and genetic variation. To date, the uniparentally inherited mtDNA and the nonrecombining part of DNA of the Y chromosome (NRY) have been the most informative genetic markers for examining population ancestry and history, but autosomal DNA markers are increasingly being used for studies of human population genetic structure and variation. In early studies, classical markers based on the products of genes, such as serum proteins and blood groups, were commonly used in molecular anthropology, but with advances in DNA technologies such markers are no longer utilized in studies on human evolution.

To understand the properties of these markers and how they are used, we will give a short introduction to the most commonly used genetic markers; more information can be found in an introduction to molecular anthropology written specifically for linguists (Pakendorf 2007). MtDNA is a double-stranded circular DNA molecule that is not located in the nucleus with the chromosomal DNA, but in cytoplasmic organelles of eukaryotic cells called mitochondria, which are responsible for producing energy for the cell. MtDNA is relatively small, containing only 16,569 nucleotides in humans (in contrast to the 3.3 billion nucleotides of autosomal DNA that comprise the human genome), and its entire sequence was determined in 1981 (Anderson et al. 1981). MtDNA has a high copy number per cell, making it easy to extract. It is inherited exclusively through the maternal line and only daughters can pass it on to the next generation. MtDNA does not undergo recombination like autosomal DNA (i.e., non-sex-determining chromosomes – there are 22 pairs of such chromosomes in the nucleus of the cell, along with a pair of sex-determining chromosomes); that is, it does not undergo the process by which segments of the members of each pair of chromosomes in a parent are exchanged during the production of eggs or sperm. MtDNA also has a high mutation rate compared to nuclear DNA. All of these qualities of mtDNA make it a very suitable genetic marker in population and evolutionary genetics studies, and it has been used extensively since the late 1980s (Pakendorf and Stoneking 2005; Güldemann and Stoneking 2008).

Because mtDNA is maternally inherited, it can be used to trace the maternal history of a population. The so-called hypervariable region of mtDNA, which consists of about 400 nucleotides, has been widely used in population genetics studies to infer genetic variation between and within populations (Stoneking et al. 1991; Helgason et al. 2000; Salas et al. 2000, 2002; Pereira et al. 2001), mainly because it has a high mutation rate and a convenient size for analysis. More recently, it has become increasingly common to sequence the entire mtDNA genome (Horai et al. 1995; Ingman et al. 2000; Tanaka et al. 2004; Barnabas et al. 2006; Gonder et al. 2006; Pierson et al. 2006; Abu-Amero et al. 2007). By analyzing the entire mtDNA genome, the maximum amount of information possible is extracted, and phylogenetic relationships are better resolved.

The Y chromosome is the male counterpart of mtDNA. It is also uniparentally inherited and passed from fathers to sons. It is much larger than mtDNA, containing about 60 million nucleotides, 95% of which do not recombine (hence called the nonrecombining part of the Y chromosome [NRY]) (Jobling and Tyler-Smith 2003). Because the Y chromosome is male specific, it has been used to trace the paternal history of populations (Jobling and Tylersmith 1995; Hammer et al. 2001; Underhill et al. 2001a, 2001b; Cruciani et al. 2002; Hurles et al. 2002; Cruciani et al. 2007). Typically, NRY variation is analyzed by typing informative single-nucleotide polymorphisms (SNPs), which involve a mutation at a single nucleotide, and/or the analysis of microsatellite markers, which are short DNA segments that show variation in the number of tandemly repeated core sequence and hence are also called short tandem repeats (STRs). The aforementioned qualities of mtDNA and the Y chromosome make these markers a convenient tool in molecular anthropology. At present, information from both mtDNA and the Y chromosome are used in population history studies because together they provide insights into both the paternal and the maternal history of populations (Knight et al. 2003; Cordaux et al. 2004; Hudjashov et al. 2007; Nasidze et al. 2007; Pakendorf et al. 2007; Tishkoff et al. 2007).

Autosomal markers have also been used to study genetic variation in molecular anthropology. Autosomal markers, which include STRs, SNPs, and copy number variations (CNVs), can be informative for the level of admixture and genetic structure (Rosenberg and Nordborg 2006; Friedlaender et al. 2008; Kayser et al. 2008; Li et al. 2008). Because mtDNA and the Y chromosome are only two loci, using autosomal markers adds multiple loci and gives a fuller picture of the genetic variation and history of human populations.

2.2.2   *Haplogroups and Haplotypes*

At this point, it is important to introduce a few concepts that are used when genetic data are analyzed and interpreted. When dealing with *haploid* data, i.e., from genomes that have no homologous pairs (and hence no recombination), such as those from the mitochondrial genome, sequences can be assigned to

Table 2.2 *Haplogroups and haplotypes*

a) mtDNA sequences			
Position	**1**	**2**	**Haplogroup**
Sequence 1	ATATGGCTAGAGGCTA		A
Sequence 2	ATATGGCTAGAGGCTG		A
Sequence 3	ATTTGGCTAGAGGCTA		B
Sequence 4	ATTTGGCTAGAGGCTT		B
b) Y-chromosome SNPs and STRs			
Position	**1**	**2**	
Haplotype 1	G	(ATA)x12	C
Haplotype 2	G	(ATA)x10	C
Haplotype 3	C	(ATA)x11	D
Haplotype 4	C	(ATA)x13	D
	SNP	**Y-STR**	

(a) Position 1 variation indicates haplogroup membership whereas position 2 variation reflects variation among sequences that belong to the same haplogroup. (b) Position 1 indicates haplogroup membership and position 2 (number of Y-STR repeats, where x12 refers to an allele with 12 copies of the ATA repeat, x10 refers to an allele with 10 copies of the ATA repeat, etc.) reflects haplotype variation.

haplogroups. Haplogroups are groups of sequences that share some of the same polymorphic sites and are therefore all derived from a common ancestor; see Table 2.2a. Major haplogroups share the same basal polymorphic sites that coalesce far back in time, i.e., near the root of the phylogenetic tree. Major mtDNA haplogroups include haplogroups L, M, and N. Haplogroup L is the oldest and most diverse mtDNA haplogroup, and it is the most common haplogroup in Africa. Haplogroups M and N are found largely outside of Africa and are the basal lineages of all other haplogroups outside of Africa.

Like mtDNA, the Y chromosome is also haploid, and as such, haplogroups can be defined. Y-chromosome haplogroups are defined by differences in the nonrecombining part of the chromosome, where a single phylogeny can be constructed. Major Y-chromosome haplogroups are A and B, which are found in sub-Saharan Africa; haplogroup A is the most diverse and oldest Y-chromosome haplogroup.

The term *haplotype* refers to a set of sequences (in the case of mtDNA) or STR genotypes (in the case of the Y chromosome) that further discriminate chromosomes within the same haplogroup. As such a set of chromosomes may belong to the same haplogroup (Table 2.2a) and yet the chromosomes may be unique haplotypes. Because of recombination and the diploid state of autosomal DNA, the term haplogroup is generally not used to describe autosomal DNA variation.

2.3   Genetic Diversity in Hunter-Gatherer Groups

2.3.1   *Reduced Diversity in Hunter-Gatherer Groups Relative to Agriculturalists*

Molecular anthropological studies on the origins and genetic variation of hunter-gatherer groups have shown that they generally exhibit very low genetic diversity (Vigilant et al. 1991; Watson et al. 1996; Weiss and von Haeseler 1998; Excoffier and Schneider 1999; Chen et al. 2000; Oota et al. 2001; Endicott et al. 2003; Thangaraj et al. 2003; Schmitt et al. 2004; Oota et al. 2005), particularly when compared to neighboring agricultural groups (Thangaraj et al. 2003; Destro-Bisol et al. 2004; Quintana-Murci et al. 2008). For example, low mtDNA diversity has been observed among the Aché Natives of Paraguay (Schmitt et al. 2004), Andaman Islanders (Endicott et al. 2003; Thangaraj et al. 2003), and pygmy hunter-gatherer groups in western Africa (Vigilant et al. 1991; Watson et al. 1996; Chen et al. 2000; Quintana-Murci et al. 2008) compared to neighboring agricultural groups; see Figure 2.1. In some of these studies, Y-chromosome and autosomal variation was also analyzed,

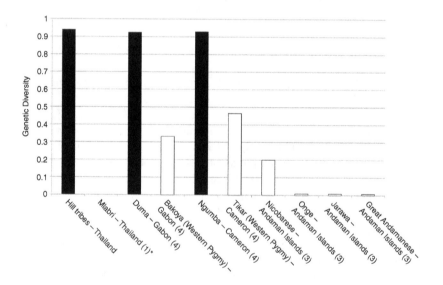

Figure 2.1 Genetic diversity of hunter-gatherer and agricultural groups. Hill Tribes – 0.94, Mlabri – 0, Duma – 0.925, Bakoya – 0.333, Ngumba – 0.93, Tikar – 0.464, Nicobarese – 0.2, Onge – 0.008, Jarawa – 0.008, Great Andamanese – 0.007. *The Mlabri have no genetic diversity. (1) Oota et al. (2005); (2) Schmitt et al. (2004); (3) Thangaraj et al. (2003); (4) Quintana-Murci et al. (2008).

revealing the same pattern, namely lower genetic variation for hunter-gatherer than for agricultural groups.

In Figure 2.1, agricultural groups are depicted with black bars and hunter-gatherer groups with white bars. Genetic diversity is measured as gene diversity on a scale from 0 to 1, with 0 indicating the lowest diversity and 1 the highest. Data from neighboring agricultural groups from the Andaman Islands and Paraguay were not available for comparison.

Some studies have also shown deep divergence of mtDNA lineages of hunter-gatherer groups, for example, the !Kung in Botswana (Vigilant et al. 1991). A study by Knight et al. (2003) showed that the Ju|'hoansi and Hadzabe in southern Africa have mtDNA haplotypes that diverge at the root of the human mitochondrial phylogenetic tree. The study found these two groups also had unique Y-chromosomal haplotypes and were genetically very distant from each other. It has, however, been argued that this seemingly deep divergence could rather reflect genetic drift and subsequent lineage lost (Tishkoff et al. 2007; Güldemann and Stoneking 2008). Deep genetic divergence can be heavily influenced by ancient population splits, isolation, and genetic drift resulting from small population sizes. Old unique haplogroups can indicate an ancient population split followed by isolation, whereas recent bottlenecks alter frequencies of haplogroups that are not very old. Hence, to the extent that there are old unique haplogroups in hunter-gatherer groups, there may be support for ancient population splits, but distinguishing between the two is not straightforward.

2.3.2   *Forces Influencing Genetic Diversity*

Before discussing what kind of forces are most likely to have influenced the low genetic diversity and deep divergence among hunter-gatherer groups, it is necessary to introduce some basic terms used in population genetics. *Genetic drift* refers to the random fluctuation of allele[1] frequencies from generation to generation due to chance. The rate of genetic drift strongly depends on population size: the smaller the population size, the greater the change in allele frequencies between generations, and the faster alleles can reach fixation or be lost. When referring to population size, it is not the census population size that matters, but rather the *effective population size* (N_e), which is essentially the number of breeding individuals in a population that contribute to the next generation. Effective population size can be used to estimate the effect of genetic drift in populations. Because genetic drift strongly influences genetic variation in small populations, it has the greatest effects when a population has undergone a *bottleneck* or a *founding event*. A bottleneck event refers to a severe reduction in population size whereas a founding event refers to a small population that has split from a bigger population and migrated to a new area.

How, then, might demographic events such as genetic drift and bottlenecks influence the genetic diversity of hunter-gatherer groups? The rise and spread of agriculture is the most recent event that has potentially greatly influenced the genetic diversity of hunter-gatherer groups. It is believed that when agricultural expansions began some 6,000 to 10,000 years ago, hunter-gatherer groups migrated to marginal areas when agricultural groups expanded and settled in areas suitable for agriculture. As a consequence, hunter-gatherer groups started living in areas not suitable for agriculture and sometimes less suitable for hunting and foraging, resulting in a reduction in effective population size (Thangaraj et al. 2003). Therefore, hunter-gatherer groups went through bottlenecks as a result of the cultural and demographic expansion of the Neolithic technology and peoples.

It has been proposed that hunter-gatherer groups had small effective population sizes even before the expansion of agriculture (Knight et al. 2003; Destro-Bisol et al. 2004). In support of the argument for preagricultural bottlenecks, Knight et al. (2003) claimed the deep genetic divergence that they observed between the San and Hadzabe indicated that the groups had already been isolated by the time of the Bantu expansion, when Bantu-speaking farmers started spreading around southern Africa around 1,500 years ago.[2] In another study, Quintana-Murci et al. (2008) concluded from the composition of the hunter-gatherer and agriculturalist mtDNA gene pool of Central Africa[3] that the ancestors of groups leading to hunter-gatherers on one hand and farmers on the other split not later than 70,000 years ago and remained isolated from each other until around 40,000 years ago, when gene flow started to occur between them. They also concluded that the gene flow between hunter-gatherer groups and farmers persisted until a few thousand years ago, at which time the mtDNA gene pool of the agricultural groups was enriched by the expansion and intergroups migration of other surrounding groups, explaining why their mtDNA gene pool is more diverse than that of the hunter-gatherer groups. The rise of agriculture is then not the only force that created differences in the genetic diversity between agricultural and hunter-gatherer groups; these can also be attributed to other demographic forces (e.g., population expansion and increased migration rates) that might have happened long before.

Yet, evidence for agricultural expansions to have reduced genetic diversity in hunter-gatherer groups remains. In a study by Excoffier and Schneider (1999) mtDNA diversity in sixty-two worldwide populations was analyzed for evidence of a population expansion. Their results indicate that only hunter-gatherer groups and most Amerindian groups in the study showed no evidence of a Pleistocene expansion. Moreover, genetic distances between populations revealed that populations exhibiting no evidence of an expansion were also most distant from other populations. According to the study, the lack of a

Pleistocene expansion signature in hunter-gatherer groups is best explained by population bottlenecks in these groups in response to the Neolithic transition, and expansions of other groups at that time. Accordingly, during the Pleistocene all human groups experienced a population expansion and the oldest one took place in Africa, as evidenced by the increased genetic diversity found there compared to other continents. Quintana-Murci et al. (2008) also demonstrated signatures of population expansions in agricultural groups in sub-Saharan Africa, but not for hunter-gatherer groups, again contrasting the different demographic histories for the agricultural and hunter-gatherer groups. As such, it is reasonable to assume that as a general response to agricultural expansions, hunter-gatherer groups experienced severe population bottlenecks effects. As a result, hunter-gatherer groups had a reduction in their effective population size (N_e) and a strengthening of the effect of genetic drift. This is arguably the major factor influencing the increased genetic distances and decreased genetic diversity of these groups, although evolutionary events that preceded the rise of agriculture may still have had an important effect on genetic variation in hunter-gatherer groups.

2.3.3   Interactions between Hunter-Gatherer Groups and Agricultural Groups

The influence of agricultural expansions on hunter-gatherer groups has been most extensively studied in Africa in relation to the Bantu expansion; these studies have demonstrated a huge impact of the Bantu expansion on the genetic diversity of African hunter-gatherer groups (Poloni et al. 1997; Excoffier and Schneider 1999; Hammer et al. 2001; Cruciani et al. 2002; Salas et al. 2002; Knight et al. 2003; Destro-Bisol et al. 2004). These studies demonstrate that during the Bantu expansion, hunter-gatherer groups became more marginalized. The marginalization of hunter-gatherer groups influenced their contact with other groups, resulting in limited gene flow between them. There was limited gene flow not only between agriculturalists and hunter-gatherer groups, but also between different hunter-gatherer groups in Africa.

Despite limited gene flow between hunter-gatherer groups and agricultural groups, studies of both mtDNA and Y-chromosome diversity indicate that there has undeniably been some admixture between them, and that it has been sex biased. There are differences in levels of mtDNA and Y chromosome diversity in these groups that are associated with cultural affiliation. In general, differences between groups are bigger for the Y chromosome than for mtDNA (Seielstad et al. 1998; Oota et al. 2001), and it has been suggested that this might reflect a higher female migration rate because of patrilocality (Seielstad et al. 1998; Destro-Bisol et al. 2004). Patrilocal residence is a social construction whereby women move to their husband's residence after marriage, while matrilocality is the reverse. Because most human populations practice patrilocality rather than matrilocality, migration rates are higher for females than for males, which would tend to decrease differences between groups for mtDNA and increase them for the Y chromosome. Support for this hypothesis comes from a study of mtDNA and Y-chromosome variation in matrilocal groups, where the opposite pattern (larger differences for mtDNA than for the Y chromosome) was observed (Oota et al. 2001).

Differences in the effective population size among males and females may also cause differences in genetic diversity between the Y chromosome and mtDNA. For example, polygyny can lead to a more structured Y-chromosome than mtDNA pattern because the effective population size for males in this case is smaller than for females (Seielstad et al. 1998). Polygyny would result in greater differences between groups and reduced levels of variation within groups for the Y chromosome. Polygyny, possibly along with warfare, has been invoked as an explanation for the drastically reduced Y-chromosome variation, but normal levels of mtDNA variation, observed in some groups from West New Guinea (Kayser et al. 2003).

Polygyny is generally higher among agricultural groups and they are more commonly patrilocal, whereas hunter-gatherer groups can be matrilocal. Cultural anthropologists have also demonstrated that marriages between women from hunter-gatherer groups and men from agricultural groups is commonly accepted, but the reverse case of women from agricultural groups marrying men from hunter-gatherer groups is seldom observed. This has been referred to as hypergyny, where women marry men of slightly higher status, and it has been noted among the Hadza, Efe, and Okiek hunter-gatherer groups in Africa (Spielmann and Eder 1994).

In a study by Wood et al. (2005) a difference in female and male migration rates among agricultural and hunter-gatherer groups from forty populations of Africa was observed. In general, the Y-chromosome diversity was less correlated with geography than was mtDNA diversity. According to the study this difference could be explained by Bantu males dispersing over longer distances or in greater numbers than Bantu females. They claim that it is likely that Bantu farmers admixed with hunter-gatherer groups, usually Bantu men marrying the women from hunter-gatherer groups. In such cases the children would habitually become farmers in their father's village. Their study supports the hypothesis that Bantu farmers had a great influence on genetic variation in sub-Saharan Africa and that Bantu farmers replaced hunter-gatherer groups to some extent, with asymmetric gene flow between them. A study by Quintana-Murci et al. (2008) supports the hypothesis that there has been asymmetric maternal gene flow between hunter-gatherer groups and agricultural groups in the hunter-gatherer to farmer direction.

It is evident from these studies that the Bantu expansion influenced the genetic diversity of hunter-gatherer groups in Africa, but more because of marginalization than admixture. Initially, when hunter-gatherer groups and farmers met, there was no barrier of gene flow between them. However, sociocultural inequalities were later created between them that had a negative effect on the gene flow across the groups (Quintana-Murci et al. 2008). The kind of cultural influences that were discussed in the foregoing can greatly influence genetic variation, especially in the case of hunter-gatherer groups because their small population size makes them vulnerable to such influences. To summarize, it is evident that there has been a sex-biased gene flow between hunter-gatherer groups and agricultural groups in sub-Saharan Africa and that it has influenced the genetic landscape of present-day hunter-gatherer groups, at least in Africa.

2.3.4   Evidence of Shared Ancestry between Local Hunter-Gatherer Groups?

It could be assumed that different hunter-gatherer groups within the same geographic region, show a close genetic affinity especially when compared to non-hunter-gatherer groups as they often share common phenotypic features (like the short stature among pygmy hunter-gatherer groups in Africa) and cultural traits. When dealing with such questions in molecular anthropology, the traditional approach is to analyze haplotype diversity and haplogroup frequencies, to make inferences about shared ancestry and migration patterns. In this way it has been demonstrated that some hunter-gatherer groups carry paternal and maternal lineages that belong to the deepest clades known among modern humans (Behar et al. 2008). Such observations can indicate that hunter-gatherer groups share a deep common ancestry.

Some haplogroups are chiefly found in hunter-gatherer groups in Africa and are rare in other groups. The mtDNA haplogroups L0d and L0k are found at high frequencies in the Khoisan and are almost absent in other populations (Vigilant et al. 1991). Pygmy groups in Africa mainly have the mtDNA haplogroup L1c (Destro-Bisol et al. 2004), and the sub-haplogroup L1c1a is the only surviving clade in pygmy hunter-gatherer groups of Central Africa, whereas agricultural groups show a higher level of haplogroup diversity (Quintana-Murci et al. 2008). L1c is also found in agricultural groups, and the ancestral group carrying L1c lineages gave rise to current day agricultural – and hunter-gatherer groups more than 70,000 years ago (Quintana-Murci et al. 2008). The reduced haplogroup diversity found in hunter-gatherer groups in Africa might possibly be explained by the asymmetric gene flow between hunter-gatherer groups and farmers; hunter-gatherer women moved to farmer groups, thereby possibly reducing the genetic diversity of hunter-gatherer groups. But for the movement of hunter-gatherer women into agricultural groups to influence genetic diversity it would have to have been extensive. Furthermore, it would then be expected that genetic diversity was lower for the mtDNA than for the Y chromosome, but that is not the case. Therefore, the main genetic impact of agricultural groups on hunter-gatherer groups was through assimilation and marginalization, i.e., bottlenecks in those that survived, thereby reducing genetic diversity.

Even though some studies have illustrated elevated genetic differentiation between hunter-gatherer groups and agricultural groups, in Central Africa these groups do share the most common mtDNA haplogroups (Quintana-Murci et al. 2008). Because of the high sharing of L1c1a lineages there must have been maternal gene flow between these groups after they split. Almost all L1c1a lineages are more diverse among hunter-gatherer groups and almost all of them are found in Bantu farmer groups in Central Africa, giving support to the hypothesis that there was gene flow in the hunter-gatherer to farmers direction in that region (Quintana-Murci et al. 2008).

As to whether or not there is a shared common ancestry of different hunter-gatherer groups, there are at the moment insufficient genetic data to give a clear answer to this question. Not many studies have been done on genetic distances and ancestry between hunter-gatherer groups outside of Africa, but several studies on the genetic landscape of hunter-gatherer groups in Africa have revealed that even within the same continent, genetic distances between different hunter-gatherer groups can vary significantly. This has been observed among pygmy groups in western and eastern Africa, indicating a lack of recent maternal common ancestry for those groups (Quintana-Murci et al. 2008). However, a study by Tishkoff et al. (2004), showed that the Mbuti (in Eastern Africa) and Biaka (in Western Africa) Pygmy hunter-gatherer groups are closely related and both these groups were more related to West African populations than East African populations. Furthermore, a shared ancestry among Khoesan speakers (Hadza, Sandawe, San, and !Xun/Khoe) and Pygmies (Mbuti in Central Africa, Baka, and Bakola in Cameroon) is supported by analysis of autosomal STRs in a recent study on the genetic structure of Africans (Tishkoff et al. 2009). In contrast, a lack of shared ancestry among tribal populations in India was observed through large genetic distances among populations along with reduced mtDNA diversity, indicating population isolation, reduced effective population sizes from bottleneck effects, and enhanced genetic drift (Cordaux et al. 2003).

To resolve this kind of inconsistency it is important to analyze more markers and increase sample sizes to truly understand the genetic link between these groups. Also, other methods of analysis are needed. Rather than focusing only on shared haplotypes and calculating divergence estimates based on haplogroups, model-based approaches using extensive simulations promise to be much more informative for addressing these questions, especially because they allow the investigation of which demographic scenarios are best supported by the data. For example, Tishkoff et al. (2007) used a model-based approach and showed that their data could not distinguish among three scenarios for relationships among east African and southern African hunter-gatherer groups.

What seems to be palpable is that hunter-gatherer groups do show greater genetic distances from agricultural groups and have a deep divergence. As mentioned before, a significant reduction of genetic diversity was observed among the Khoisan in Africa, and their mtDNA lineages diverge very early from other types of mtDNA lineages (Vigilant et al. 1991). Their mtDNA gene pool contains mainly L0d and L0k haplogroups which are almost absent in other populations.

Similar patterns have been detected with Y-chromosomal studies. The Y-chromosome haplogroup distribution in Africa demonstrates major differences in the genetic landscape between hunter-gatherer groups and agricultural groups. Haplogroup B2b is found at high frequency in hunter-gatherer groups in Africa (Knight et al. 2003; Wood et al. 2005) whereas it is almost absent in agricultural groups (Güldemann and Stoneking 2008). On the other hand, the Y-chromosome haplogroup E3a is commonly associated with the Bantu expansion and is found at high frequency in Bantu populations (Underhill et al. 2001b). In summary, numerous studies have shown that many haplogroups found in hunter-gatherer groups are absent in agricultural populations, or present at very low frequencies. This indicates a different evolutionary history for hunter-gatherers and agricultural groups and supports the hypothesis that hunter-gatherer groups have undergone isolation and population reduction since the Neolithic transition, if not earlier. As hunter-gatherer groups have lineages that are not found in agricultural groups, it is safe to assume that the genetic variation observed among them is not only caused by reduction of genetic diversity, but also because of population bottlenecks and genetic drift. The fact that hunter-gatherer groups have lineages that are only found among them must indicate a deep ancestry for those groups and considerable isolation from other groups. Even though there has been some maternal gene flow in the hunter-gatherer to Bantu direction in Africa, some unique mtDNA haplotypes are found in hunter-gatherer groups and not in agricultural groups, showing the preservation of their unique demographic history and ancestry.

2.4   Future Directions

Recently there have been major improvements in obtaining genetic data. Next-generation sequencing technologies allow high-throughput sequencing at a greatly reduced cost, making the resequencing of whole genomes a possibility in the near future. Even now, not only do these technologies make it feasible to re-sequence the entire mtDNA genome (as opposed to just the hypervariable region), but the resequencing of selected genomic regions (both Y-chromosome and autosomal) is also possible. Moreover, existing technologies allow up to one million polymorphic sites to be genotyped simultaneously. These new technologies are contributing greatly to population genetic analyses by providing genetic data on an unprecedented scale.

Producing large amounts of genetic data with these new technologies further allows the application of new and innovative analytical techniques. New model-based analyses incorporate extensive simulations to make inferences about demographic history, providing more accurate estimates of population history. These kinds of analysis will improve our understanding and interpretation of the extensive data that can now be produced with high-throughput sequencing and genotyping technologies. Instead of analyzing only small parts of two loci (the Y chromosome and mtDNA), whole mtDNA genomes, larger parts of the Y chromosome and multiple loci can be incorporated into molecular anthropology. New technologies and methods for analyzing the genetic data will undoubtedly provide more and deeper insights into the demographic history and the evolutionary history of hunter-gatherer groups, and we can expect a lot more studies on this topic in the near future. But new technologies are not sufficient to give answers to all the remaining questions, what is also needed to get a better understanding of the genetic diversity of hunter-gatherer groups, is to get more samples from further hunter-gatherer groups, especially outside Africa because most studies on the genetics of hunter-gatherer groups have focused on Africa.

Note Added in Proof

This chapter was written in 2006 and last updated in 2009, and hence does not reflect developments since then.

Acknowledgments

We thank the Max Planck Society for funding; Tom Güldeman for the invitation to write this review and for valuable discussion; and Brigitte Pakendorf, David Hughes, Irina Pugach, and Frederick Delfin for useful comments and discussions on the manuscript.

NOTES

1. An allele is one form out of many alternative forms of DNA sequence at a specific location in the genome.
2. But see Güldemann and Stoneking (2008) for an alternative interpretation

3. Agricultural groups in the study: Akele, Ateke, Benga, Duma, Eshira, Evlya, Ewondo, Fang, Galoa, Kota, Makina, Mitsogo, Ndumu, Ngumba, Nzebi, Obamba, Orungu, Punu, and Shake. HG groups were Mbuti, Babongo, Baka (in center and southwest Cameroon and northeast Gabon), Bakola, Bakoya, Biaka, and Tikar.

References

Abu-Amero, K. K., A. M. Gonzalez, J. M. Larruga, T. M. Bosley, and V. M. Cabrera. (2007). Eurasian and African mitochondrial DNA influences in the Saudi Arabian population. *BMC Evolutionary Biology* 7: 32.

Anderson, S., A. T. Bankier, B. G. Barrell, et al. (1981). Sequence and organization of the human mitochondrial genome. *Nature* 290(5806): 457–465.

Barnabas, S., Y. Shouche, and C. G. Suresh. (2006). High-resolution mtDNA studies of the Indian population: Implications for palaeolithic settlement of the Indian sub-continent. *Annals of Human Genetics* 70: 42–58.

Behar, D. M., R. Villems, H. Soodyall, et al. (2008). The dawn of human matrilineal diversity. *American Journal of Human Genetics* 82(5): 1130–1140.

Biesele, M., R. K. Hitchcock, and P. P. Schweitzer (eds.). (2000). *Hunters and gatherers in the modern world: Conflict, resistance and self-determination.* New York: Berghahn Books.

Chen, Y. S., A. Olckers, T. G. Schurr, A. M. Kogelnik, K. Huoponen, and D. C. Wallace. (2000). mtDNA variation in the South African Kung and Khwe – and their genetic relationships to other African populations. *American Journal of Human Genetics* 66(4): 1362–1383.

Cordaux, R., R. Aunger, G. Bentley, I. Nasidze, S. M. Sirajuddin, and M. Stoneking. (2004). Independent origins of Indian caste and tribal paternal lineages. *Current Biology* 14(3): 231–235.

Cordaux, R., N. Saha, G. R. Bentley, R. Aunger, S. M. Sirajuddin, and M. Stonekin. (2003). Mitochondrial DNA analysis reveals diverse histories of tribal populations from India. *European Journal of Human Genetics* 11(3): 253–264.

Cruciani, F., R. La Fratta, B. Trombetta, et al. (2007). Tracing past human male movements in northern/eastern Africa and western Eurasia: New clues from Y-chromosomal haplogroups E-M78 and J-M12. *Molecular Biology and Evolution* 24(6): 1300–1311.

Cruciani, F., P. Santolamazza, P. Shen, et al. (2002). A back migration from Asia to sub-Saharan Africa is supported by high-resolution analysis of human Y-chromosome haplotypes. *American Journal of Human Genetics* 70(5): 1197–1214.

Destro-Bisol, G., V. Coia, I. Boschi, et al. (2004). The analysis of variation of mtDNA hypervariable region 1 suggests that Eastern and Western Pygmies diverged before the Bantu expansion. *American Naturalist* 163(2): 212–226.

Destro-Bisol, G., F. Donati, V. Coia, et al. (2004). Variation of female and male lineages in sub-Saharan populations: The importance of sociocultural factors. *Molecular Biology and Evolution* 21(9): 1673–1682.

Diamond, J., and P. Bellwood. (2003). Farmers and their languages: The first expansions. *Science* 300(5619): 597–603.

Endicott, P., M. T. Gilbert, C. Stringer, et al. (2003). The genetic origins of the Andaman Islanders. *American Journal of Human Genetics* 72(1): 178–184.

Excoffier, L., and S. Schneider. (1999). Why hunter-gatherer populations do not show signs of Pleistocene demographic expansions. *Proceedings of the National Academy of Sciences of the USA* 96(19): 10597–10602.

Friedlaender, J. S., F. R. Friedlaender, F. A. Reed, et al. (2008). The genetic structure of Pacific islanders. *PLoS Genetics* 4(1): e19.

Gonder, M. K., H. M. Mortensen, F. A. Reed, A. de Sousa, and S. A. Tishkoff. (2006). Whole mtDNA genome analysis of ancient African lineages. *Molecular Biology and Evolution* 24: 757–768.

Güldemann, T., and M. Stoneking. (2008). A historical appraisal of clicks: A linguistic and genetic population perspective. *Annual Review of Anthropology* 37: 93–109.

Hammer, M. F., T. M. Karafet, A. J. Redd, et al. (2001). Hierarchical patterns of global human Y-chromosome diversity. *Molecular Biology and Evolution* 18(7): 1189–1203.

Helgason, A., S. Sigureth ardottir, J. Nicholson, et al. (2000). Estimating Scandinavian and Gaelic ancestry in the male settlers of Iceland. *American Journal of Human Genetics* 67(3): 697–717.

Horai, S., K. Hayasaka, R. Kondo, K. Tsugane, and N. Takahata. (1995). Recent African origin of modern humans revealed by complete sequences of hominoid mitochondrial DNAs. *Proceedings of the National Academy of Sciences of the USA* 92(2): 532–536.

Hudjashov, G., T. Kivisild, P. A. Underhill, et al. (2007). Revealing the prehistoric settlement of Australia by Y chromosome and mtDNA analysis. *Proceedings of the National Academy of Sciences of the USA* 104(21): 8726–8730.

Hurles, M. E., J. Nicholson, E. Bosch, C. Renfrew, B. C. Sykes, and M. A. Jobling. (2002). Y chromosomal evidence for the origins of Oceanic-speaking peoples. *Genetics* 160(1): 289–303.

Ingman, M., H. Kaessmann, S. Pääbo, and U. Gyllensten. (2000). Mitochondrial genome variation and the origin of modern humans. *Nature* 408(6813): 708–713.

Jobling, M. A., and C. Tyler-Smith. (1995). Fathers and sons: The Y chromosome and human evolution. *Trends in Genetics* 11(11): 449–456.

Jobling, M. A., and C. Tyler-Smith. (2003). The human Y chromosome: An evolutionary marker comes of age. *Nature Reviews Genetics* 4(8): 598–612.

Kayser, M., S. Brauer, G. Weiss, et al. (2003). Reduced Y-chromosome, but not mitochondrial DNA: Diversity in human populations from West New Guinea. *American Journal of Human Genetics* 72: 281–302.

Kayser, M., O. Lao, K. Saar, et al. (2008). Genome-wide analysis indicates more Asian than Melanesian ancestry of Polynesians. *American Journal of Human Genetics* 82(1): 194–198.

Kelly, R. I. (1995). *The foraging spectrum: Diversity in hunter-gatherer lifeways.* Washington, DC: Smithsonian Institution Press.

Knight, A., P. A. Underhill, H. M. Mortensen, et al. (2003). African Y chromosome and mtDNA divergence provides insight into the history of click languages. *Current Biology* 13(6): 464–473.

Li, J. Z., D. M. Absher, H. Tang, et al. (2008). Worldwide human relationships inferred from genome-wide patterns of variation. *Science* 319(5866): 1100–1104.

Nasidze, I., D. Quinque, I. Udina, S. Kunizheva, and M. Stoneking. (2007). The Gagauz, a linguistic enclave, are not a genetic isolate. *Annals of Human Genetics* 71: 379–389.

Oota, H., B. Pakendorf, G. Weiss, et al. (2005). Recent origin and cultural reversion of a hunter-gatherer group. *PLoS Biology* 3(3): 536–542.

Oota, H., W. Settheetham-Ishida, D. Tiwawech, T. Ishida, and M. Stoneking. (2001). Human mtDNA and Y-chromosome variation is correlated with matrilocal versus patrilocal residence. *Nature Genetics* 29(1): 20–21.

Pakendorf, B. (2007). *Contact in the prehistory of the Sakha (Yakuts): Linguistic and genetic perspectives*. LOT Dissertation Series 170. Utrecht: Landelijke Onderzoekschool Taalwetenschap.

Pakendorf, B., I. N. Novgorodov, V. L. Osakovskij, and M. Stoneking. (2007). Mating patterns amongst Siberian reindeer herders: Inferences from mtDNA and Y-chromosomal analyses. *American Journal of Physical Anthropology* 133(3): 1013–1027.

Pakendorf, B., and M. Stoneking. (2005). Mitochondrial DNA and human evolution. *Annual Review of Genomics and Human Genetics* 6: 165–183.

Pereira, L., V. Macaulay, A. Torroni, R. Scozzari, M. J. Prata, and A. Amorim. (2001). Prehistoric and historic traces in the mtDNA of Mozambique: Insights into the Bantu expansions and the slave trade. *Annals of Human Genetics* 65: 439–458.

Pierson, M. J., R. Martinez-Arias, B. R. Holland, N. J. Gemmell, M. E. Hurles, and D. Penny. (2006). Deciphering past human population movements in Oceania: Provably optimal trees of 127 mtDNA genomes. *Molecular Biology and Evolution* 23(10): 1966–1975.

Poloni, E. S., O. Semino, G. Passarino, et al. (1997). Human genetic affinities for Y-chromosome P49a,f/TaqI haplotypes show strong correspondence with linguistics. *American Journal of Human Genetics* 61(5): 1015–1035.

Quintana-Murci, L., H. Quach, C. Harmant, et al. (2008). Maternal traces of deep common ancestry and asymmetric gene flow between pygmy hunter-gatherers and Bantu-speaking farmers. *Proceedings of the National Academy of Sciences of the USA* 105(5): 1596–1601.

Rosenberg, N. A., and M. Nordborg. (2006). A general population-genetic model for the production by population structure of spurious genotype-phenotype associations in discrete, admixed or spatially distributed populations. *Genetics* 173(3): 1665–1678.

Salas, A., V. Lareu, F. Calafell, J. Bertranpetit, and A. Carracedo. (2000). mtDNA hypervariable region II (HVII) sequences in human evolution studies. *European Journal of Human Genetics* 8(12): 964–974.

Salas, A., M. Richards, T. De la Fe, et al. (2002). The making of the African mtDNA landscape. *American Journal of Human Genetics* 71(5): 1082–1111.

Schmitt, R., S. L. Bonatto, L. B. Freitas, et al. (2004). Short Report: Extremely limited mitochondrial DNA variability among the Aché natives of Paraguay. *Annals of Human Biology* 31(1): 87–94.

Seielstad, M. T., E. Minch, and L. L. Cavalli-Sforza. (1998). Genetic evidence for a higher female migration rate in humans. *Nature Genetics* 20(3): 278–280.

Spielmann, K. A., and J. F. Eder. (1994). Hunters and farmers: Then and now. *Annual Review of Anthropology* 23: 303–323.

Stoneking, M., D. Hedgecock, R. G. Higuchi, L. Vigilant, and H. A. Erlich. (1991). Population variation of human mtDNA control region sequences detected by enzymatic amplification and sequence-specific oligonucleotide probes. *American Journal of Human Genetics* 48(2): 370–382.

Tanaka, M., V. M. Cabrera, A. M. Gonzalez, et al. (2004). Mitochondrial genome variation in Eastern Asia and the peopling of Japan. *Genome Research* 14(10A): 1832–1850.

Thangaraj, K., L. Singh, A. G. Reddy, et al. (2003). Genetic affinities of the Andaman Islanders, a vanishing human population. *Current Biology* 13(2): 86–93.

Tishkoff, S. A., M. K. Gonder, B. M. Henn, et al. (2007). History of click-speaking populations of Africa inferred from mtDNA and Y chromosome genetic variation. *Molecular Biology and Evolution* 24(10): 2180–2195.

Tishkoff, S. A., and K. K. Kidd. (2004). Implications of biogeography of human populations for 'race' and medicine. *Nature Genetics* 36(11): S21–S27.

Tishkoff, S. A., F. A. Reed, F. R. Friedlaender, et al. (2009). The genetic structure and history of Africans and African Americans. *Science* 324(5930): 1035–1044.

Underhill, P. A., G. Passarino, A. A. Lin, et al. (2001a). Maori origins, Y-chromosome haplotypes and implications for human history in the Pacific. *Human Mutation* 17 (4): 271–280.

Underhill, P. A., G. Passarino, A. A. Lin, et al. (2001b). The phylogeography of Y chromosome binary haplotypes and the origins of modern human populations. *Annals of Human Genetics* 65: 43–62.

Vigilant, L., M. Stoneking, H. Harpending, K. Hawkes, and A. C. Wilson. (1991). African populations and the evolution of human mitochondrial-DNA. *Science* 253 (5027): 1503–1507.

Watson, E., K. Bauer, R. Aman, G. Weiss, A. von Haeseler, and S. Pääbo. (1996). mtDNA sequence diversity in Africa. *American Journal of Human Genetics* 59(2): 437–444.

Weiss, G., and A. von Haeseler. (1998). Inference of population history using a likelihood approach. *Genetics* 149(3): 1539–1546.

Wood, E. T., D. A. Stover, C. Ehret, et al. (2005). Contrasting patterns of Y chromosome and mtDNA variation in Africa: Evidence for sex-biased demographic processes. *European Journal of Human Genetics* 13(7): 867–876.

3 Linguistic Typology and Hunter-Gatherer Languages

Balthasar Bickel and Johanna Nichols

3.1   Introduction

It has long seemed plausible that the languages of hunter-gatherer societies might be systematically different from those of food producers. Compared to food-producing societies, hunter-gatherer societies are usually smaller and less complex, with lower population density. They are often based on kinship as a main organizing factor and usually lack large-scale sociopolitical organization with its concomitant traits such as language standardization. (See, however, Donohue and Nichols [2011], other discussion in the same volume, and Moran et al. [2012] for evidence against a correlation of population size with structural complexity in phonology, and Nichols [2009] for grammatical complexity more generally.) Many hunter-gatherer languages may have existed in long-standing conditions of considerable sociolinguistic isolation, a factor known to favor increased structural complexity (Trudgill 2011).[1] Despite the various uncertainties and the changing nature of our understanding of linguistic complexity, it remains worthwhile to raise and test the hypothesis that languages spoken by hunter-gatherer societies are systematically different from those of food producers.

If that could be demonstrated, the consequences for linguistic typology and historical linguistics would be profound. Much cross-linguistic work would need to be redone, and received views on distributions, favored and disfavored feature combinations, and perhaps even constraints and defaults could change. Any linguistic explanation of macroareal skewings of typological variables might be precluded, as continents had (say in 1491) different proportions of hunter-gatherer and non-hunter-gatherer populations, with different and perhaps unknowable demographies and interactions between the types of societies, which means that comparisons of gross frequencies of typological variables across continents would be invalidated in principle. The entire possibility of universals would be called into question.

The vocabularies of hunter-gatherer societies are likely to differ systematically from those of food producers. Their everyday and – especially – technical vocabularies, as well as ritual and poetic language, can be expected to have more and finer distinctions in the realm of activities, entities, species, etc. salient in their specific economies; finer and differently organized terminologies for wild species and their life phases, behavior, etc.; terms for kinds of hunting equipment and their production; and so on, just as their food-producing neighbors will have finer taxonomies for domestic breeds and varieties, processing activities, farm implements, etc. Some constellation of such differences probably does systematically divide hunter-gatherer from food-producing languages, just as some constellation of such differences probably systematically divides the languages of any two cultural or economic types of society, but we are not sure whether such vocabulary differences are better viewed as linguistic or as cultural.[2] More interestingly, as shown in Chapter 4 by Brown, this volume, there may be systematic differences in the very types of nomenclatural systems between hunter-gatherer and food-producing societies. This must, as he notes, have important implications for cognition. We do not know whether differences in terminologies can be expected to have implications for grammar more generally; much work remains to be done, obviously, in this new area. Meanwhile, for present purposes, it is the questions of pure structural type – do the phonetic, phonological, morphological, syntactic, lexical, discourse-structural, pragmatic, etc. typologies of hunter-gatherer languages differ systematically from those of food producers? – that will have profound, even disturbing, implications for grammatical theory and typology if they turn out to be answerable in the affirmative.

Therefore it is important to shed whatever possible light on typological differences (or lack of same) between hunter-gatherer and food-producing societies. Here we use a large database of typological variables to test whether there are such differences.

3.2   Data

We set out to test for differences by looking at frequencies of all available typological variables across all languages for which we had both typological data and information about the dominant food procurement of their speakers' societies. We extracted from the AUTOTYP and WALS databases (Bickel et al. 2017; Haspelmath et al. 2005, respectively) all variables for which we had enough responses across languages (at least 150) and a small enough set of possible responses per variable (between 2 and 4) to make statistical testing straightforward. There are 228 such variables in total. Most of these cover data from between 150 to 694 languages, but a few (22) variables code constructions that can occur more than once per language (e.g., overtly case-marked vs. unmarked agents of transitive verbs, which can occur independently in several different paradigms, subparadigms, and/or constructions per language) and thus have more datapoints, up to more than 13,000. Variables surveyed came from across the entire structural grammar, e.g., phonological and prosodic properties, degrees of fusion of morphemes, positions of morphemes, alignment of various subparadigms, head/dependent marking of various paradigms, number of alienable and inalienable possessive classes, presence and types of inclusive/exclusive oppositions, word order in various phrase types, and others. As we had no specific expectations of whether food procurement type would leave signals in binary or n-ary typological variables, we included multiple versions in the database (e.g., a six-way breakdown of basic word order as well as a binary recoding.)

To control for family and/or geographical bias we also coded languages for language family and area. Specifically, we coded for whether or not languages are spoken inside or outside of the Trans-Pacific macroarea (the Americas, the Pacific coast of Asia, and the Pacific excluding island Southeast Asia) because in previous work (Nichols 1992; Bickel and Nichols 2006) and ongoing work we have found this macroarea to be a distinctive population with its own unique profile of frequencies of many variables. Because this macroarea includes a good number of the surviving hunter-gatherer societies we expect this to be a competing cause affecting the modern distribution of a significant number of typological variables.

Determination as to whether a language was traditionally spoken by hunter-gatherers or food producers was based on Güldemann et al. (Chapter 1, this volume) with some additional information drawn from the Human Relations Area Files (www.yale.edu/hraf), published ethnographic works, consultation with experts, and our own knowledge of some of the cultures.[3]

Map 3.1 shows our coding of languages for food procurement and macro-areal location.

3.3   Methods

We tested each typological variable against the null hypothesis that the type of food procurement has no effect on the distribution of the relevant typology, independently of macroareal location. Statistical testing was performed by step-down comparison of the fit between loglinear models, using a likelihood ratio χ^2 tests with a 5% rejection level (using the anova.glm function in R; R Development Core Team 2011). Specifically, we first compared models including three-way interactions (typology × food procurement × macroarea) versus models including only two-way interactions (typology × food procurement and, independently from this, typology × macroarea). If the difference in fit between the three-way and the two-way models was not significant, any possible two-way interaction would be independent of the other. In these cases, we then tested whether a model that includes a

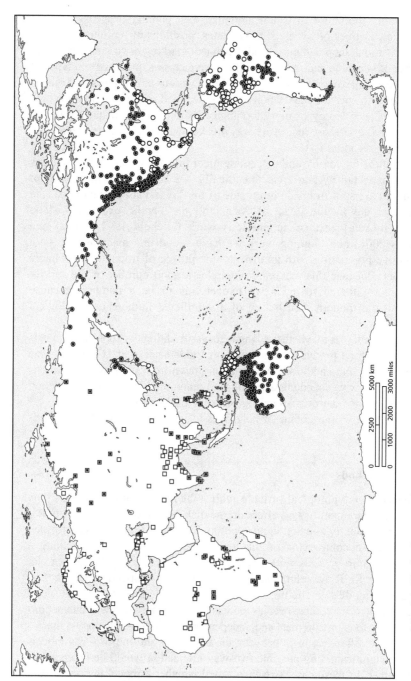

Map 3.1 Black = hunter-gatherers, white = food producers; circle = Trans-Pacific (Americas, Pacific, North Asian Pacific coast), square = elsewhere (Africa, most of Eurasia).

two-way interaction (i.e., a statistical association) between typology and food procurement fits the data significantly better than a model without this inter-action. If this is the case, it suggests that food procurement significantly affects typology independently of macroareal location; i.e., this would constitute statistical evidence for a typological difference between hunter-gatherer and other languages.

A perennial concern in typology is possible confounding effects from the membership of languages in families. In response to this concern, we ran our tests not on raw datapoints (languages or constructions within languages) but on either of two methodological strategies, depending on the amount of data we had for a given typological variable.

First strategy: When there were between 150 and 250 languages, we applied the controlled genealogical sampling algorithm of Bickel (2008) to weed out possible multiplications of the same structures (values of a typological variable) that could plausibly result from shared inheritance instead of from effects from either food procurement type or macroareal location.[4] The algorithm follows the same basic assumptions as Dryer's (1989) and Nichols's (1992) strategy of sampling each family equally, but it is sensitive to the actual distribution of values within families that contain more than one member. We applied the loglinear analysis to the subsample languages suggested by the sampling algorithm.

Second strategy: The genealogical sampling approach is the only one avail-able if the vast majority of families are represented by one language to begin with, and this is necessarily the case with datasets containing fewer than 250 languages. But the approach of taking one language per family can be criticized for always assuming that shared features reflect shared inheritance and that this then would not reflect the effect of some external factor such subsistence type. But shared features can just as well reflect an innovation (early or late but parallel), and furthermore, also when they reflect shared inheritance, this can reflect pressure that favors persistence of a specific feature. When there are more than 250 languages in the data and families are sampled densely, alter-native methods can be applied that overcome this problem. In these cases, we used the Family Bias Method of Bickel (2013).[5] The method estimates statis-tical signals for diachronic biases from their expected synchronic results: if a structure S outnumbers non-S significantly (under binomial or multinomial testing) in a family, a change toward S in this family was more likely than a change away from it (either because S was present in the protolanguage and then was subsequently almost never lost, or because S was not present but was innovated early or often in the family). If there is no significant synchronic preference, by contrast, no signal can be inferred because in this case either there was no diachronic bias toward any structure, or the difference in biases was too small to leave a signal, or the family is too young for a signal to have formed. Using extrapolation methods, signals for diachronic biases can also be estimated for isolates and small families. The loglinear analysis was then applied to the estimates of families being biased toward a given structure in relation to the food procurement type and macroareal location of the family. If a family subsumed diverse food procurement types and macroareal locations, it was split into smaller groups that were homogeneous in these regards.

3.4   Results

For more than 98% of the variables there was no significant difference (*p* >0.05) between hunter-gatherer and other languages; only for 4 of the 228 variables (1.7%) is there a significant difference. Table 3.1 shows the four significant variables: two phonological properties, one morphological, one syntactic, and none with known major implicational correlations with other variables. Table 3.2 is a representative selection of nonsignificant variables, to give a sense of the kinds of properties we tested.

Given the 5% rejection level we assumed, the total of four significant cases is fully within the range of expected statistical error, so the null hypothesis of no typological difference between hunter-gatherer and other languages is not refuted.

3.5   Conclusions

In practical terms, our finding means that, at least for the variables tested here, the languages of hunter-gatherers and food producers can safely be assumed to be, and to have long been, of the same grammatical ilk. That is, the grammatical typology of languages today is not different from what it was in the Paleolithic, and this in turn means that previous typological work taking no account of whether the languages surveyed are spoken by hunter-gatherers or not is still

Table 3.1 *The 4 variables (out of 228) that reached significance in the difference between hunter-gatherer and other languages*

Source	Variable	HG dominant value	HG *p*	*N*
WALS	Velar nasal	Present	0.013	205
Autotyp	Phonologically isolated NEG particle	Present	0.032	151
WALS	Polar question particle	Present	0.035	262
WALS	Uvular consonants	Absent	0.046	219

All the variables happen to be binary presence/absence variables or variables that were recoded as such. HG dominant value = the value of that variable that was dominant in hunter-gatherer languages; HG *p* = significance level for that value (HG vs. non-HG languages); *N* = the number of languages or correlations tested for that value.

Table 3.2 *Selected other variables: illustrative list of variables that were not significantly different for hunter-gatherer languages, chosen for good representation and wide distribution over the kinds of variables tested*

Source	Variable	HG dominant value	HG p	N
WALS	Person marking on adpositions	Absent	0.071	173
WALS	Lateral consonants	Absent	0.082	219
WALS	Tone	Atonal	0.138	205
WALS	Ditransitive "give"	Secondary object	0.155	154
WALS	Syllable structure	Moderately complex	0.160	188
Autotyp	Numeral classifiers	Absent	0.204	159
WALS	"Hand" and "arm"	Different words	0.250	256
WALS	Reduplication	Productive full and partial	0.317	179
Autotyp	Basic locus of marking of S	Head marking	0.384	177
WALS	Order of subject and verb	SV	0.435	371
WALS	Order of object and verb	OV	0.496	419
WALS	Passive constructions	Absent	0.530	171
Autotyp	Dominant head/dependent type	Dependent marking	0.594	931
Autotyp	Minimal/augmented number system	Absent	0.668	213
WALS	Coding of nominal plurality	Some plural marking	0.731	281
Autotyp	Overt possessive classes	Present	0.856	163
Autotyp	Obligatory multiple agreement	Present	0.927	200
WALS	Expression of pronominal subjects	Pro-drop	0.975	213
Autotyp	Overt marking of A	Unmarked	0.997	13105
Autotyp	Noun incorporation	Absent	1.000	173

valid. It is likely that this extends to typological generalizations more generally, although we cannot exclude the possibility that certain aspects of food procurement are still causally related to specific typological patterns. Until such relations are demonstrated, typological generalizations drawn from modern languages can be assumed to be valid for all of the history and prehistory of language (or at least of modern language as we know it, which following Nichols [2011] we are inclined to assume has existed for at least as long as anatomically modern humans, i.e., well over 200,000 years). On the other hand, there are macroareal distributions that have grown, geographically and demographically, mostly in post-Paleolithic times, including much of the human expansion into the Americas and the Pacific. This means that frequencies and distributions, but not principles or defaults or constraints, have changed since the Paleolithic.

NOTES

1. It is true that in the only large area where all societies were hunter-gatherer at contact, namely Australia, there was intense contact and areality; but much of the contact involved language learning by bilingual children and not the absorption of large

numbers of adult learners that simplifies grammars. And in any event the areality is arguably due not to economy or social structure but to the fact that Australia is a closed spread zone (Nichols 2015).

2. See Trudgill (2011: xvii–xxv) for a survey of work on the relation of lexicosemantic properties to cultural and ecological environment.

3. We are grateful to Tom Güldemann for making Güldemann et al. available to us in an early form.

4. The algorithm is implemented in R (R Development Core Team 2011) and available at https://www.comparativelinguistics.uzh.ch/en/software.html. We thank Lukas Wiget for help running our code.

5. The method is implemented in R (R Development Core Team 2011) and available at https://github.com/IVS-UZH/familybias.

References

Bickel, Balthasar. (2008). A refined sampling procedure for genealogical control. *Language Typology and Universals* 61: 221–233.

Bickel, B. (2011). Statistical modeling of language universals. *Linguistic Typology* 15: 401–414.

Bickel, Balthasar. (2013). Distributional biases in language families. In B. Bickel, L. A. Grenoble, D. A. Peterson, and A. Timberlake (eds.), *Language typology and historical contingency: A festschrift to honor Johanna Nichols*. Amsterdam: Benjamins, 415–444.

Bickel, Balthasar, Johanna Nichols, Taras Zakharko, Alena Witzlack-Makarevich, Kristine Hildebrandt, Michael Rießler, Lennart Bierkandt, Fernando Zúñiga, and John B. Lowe. (2017). The AUTOTYP typological databases. Version 0.1.0. https://github.com/autotyp/autotyp-data/tree/0.1.0

Bickel, Balthasar, and Johanna Nichols. (2006). Oceania, the Pacific Rim, and the theory of linguistic areas. In Z. Antić, C.Chang, C. Sandy, and M. Toosarvandani (eds.), *Proceedings of the 32nd Annual Meeting of the Berkeley Linguistics Society. Special Session on the Languages and Linguistics of Oceania.* 3–15.

Donohue, Mark, and Johanna Nichols. (2011). Does phoneme inventory size correlate with population size? *Linguistic Typology* 15(2): 161–170.

Dryer, Matthew S. (1989). Large linguistic areas and language sampling. *Studies in Language* 13: 257–292.

Haspelmath, Martin, Matthew S. Dryer, David Gil, and Bernard Comrie (eds.) (2005). *The world atlas of language structures*. Oxford: Oxford University Press.

Moran, Steven, Daniel McCloy, and Richard Wright. (2012). Revisiting population size vs. phoneme inventory size. *Language* 88(4): 877–893.

Nichols, Johanna. (1992). *Linguistic diversity in space and time*. Chicago: University of Chicago Press.

Nichols, Johanna. (2009). Linguistic complexity: A comprehensive definition and survey. In Geoffrey Sampson, David Gil, and Peter Trudgill (eds.), *Language complexity as an evolving variable*. Oxford: Oxford University Press, 110–125.

Nichols, Johanna. (2011). Monogenesis or polygenesis: A single ancestral language for all humanity? In Maggie Tallerman and Kathleen R. Gibson (eds.),

The Oxford handbook of language evolution. Oxford: Oxford University Press, 558–572.

Nichols, Johanna. (2015). Types of spread zones: Open and closed, horizontal and vertical. In Rik De Busser and Randy La Polla (eds.), *Language structure and environment: Social, cultural, and natural factors.* Amsterdam: Benjamins.

R Development Core Team. (2011). *R: A language and environment for statistical computing.* Vienna: R Foundation for Statistical Computing, www.r-project.org.

Trudgill, Peter. (2011). *Sociolinguistic typology.* Oxford: Oxford University Press.

4 Ethnobiology and the Hunter-Gatherer/Food Producer Divide

Cecil H. Brown

4.1   Introduction

All humans linguistically classify biological organisms. Hunter-gatherers and traditional farmers typically differ with regard to strategies used to do so.

The treatment of two or more distinguishable entities as if they were the same creates a category (Brown 1990a: 17). People develop linguistic categories by assigning the same name or label to different things; for example, an American Robin and a Blue Jay are both included in a category all of whose members are designated by English *bird*. Linguistic categories are "folk" classes when people who speak the same language all or very nearly all agree on the association of a name and category. Folk biological classification refers to folk classes that arise when human groups name plants and animals.

There are two primary types of labels used to categorize biological things: (1) binomial terms and (2) non-binomial terms. A binomial label, as its name suggests, shows two constituent elements: for example, a word for a generic category, i.e., a general class of organisms to which a living thing belongs, e.g., *oak* (*Quercus* spp.), and a modifier, e.g., *white*, as in *white oak* (*Quercus alba*). Categories such as *white oak* and *cutthroat trout* are subgeneric classes. Not all labels that appear to be binomial terms are in fact binomials. For example, English *poison oak*, which designates *Rhus radicans*, consists of a word for a generic class of botanical things, *oak*, plus a modifier, *poison*. *Poison oak*, however, is not formally a binomial because the organism it designates is not an oak.

Poison oak fits into the second nomenclatural category, non-binomial terms. Non-binomial labels typically are monomial terms such as *tree, oak, fish*, and *trout*. But some non-binomials, such as *poison oak*, are polylexemic, having two or more constituent elements each of which has a distinct meaning. Other English examples of non-binomial polylexemic terms include labels such as *Queen Anne's lace, cow-parsnip, false Solomon's-seal*, and *Jack-in-the-pulpit*.[1]

Brown (1985) and Hunn and French (1984) were among the first to recognize a difference in the manner in which hunter-gatherers and farmers name plants and animals. Use of binomial terms in folk biological classification differs significantly in frequency between the two groups. Farmers employ binomial terms for plants and animals to a far greater extent than do hunter-gatherers.

4.2   Early Studies

Hunn and French (1984) reported a dearth of binomial labels in the folk biological classification of speakers of Sahaptin, a hunter-gatherer group of the Pacific Northwest (North America), and pointed out that this is in sharp contrast to the generous use of binomials in classification systems of agriculturalists (such as described in the work of Berlin [1972, 1976] and Berlin et al. [1973, 1974]).

I (Brown 1985) was the first to attempt to quantify this difference by using large comparative samples. In my study, two language samples are developed, one for botanical classification involving thirty-six globally distributed languages, and one for zoological classification involving eleven globally distributed languages. Both samples include all of those languages known to me (around 1985) for which detailed ethnobiological information was available. In both samples, languages spoken by farmers and those spoken by nonfarmers are identified. Agrarian languages, with one exception, include languages spoken by traditional, small-scale agriculturalists. Only one of the farmer languages of the sample is spoken by a people of a nation-state society. Nonfarmer languages include one language spoken by pastoralists as well as those spoken by hunter-gatherers.

For the botanical sample, twenty of the thirty-six languages pertain to nonfarmers and the remaining sixteen to farmers. For the zoological sample, six of the eleven languages pertain to nonfarmers and the remaining five to farmers. For each language of both of samples, the percentage of biological classes labeled binomially is determined. On the average, only 3.6% of plant classes and only 7.6% of animal classes pertaining to nonfarmers are found to be binomially labeled. In striking contrast, farmers on the average are found to have binomial labels for 35% of all plant classes and for 31.6% of all animal classes. These findings indicate that binomial labels are common in the folk biological classification of farmers, but rare in that of hunter-gatherers. In fact, four of the nonfarmer languages of the sample show no binomial labels for plant classes whatsoever and one of these four lacks binomial labels for animal classes as well.

In the 1985 study I concluded that a shift from a nonfarming way of life to agriculture results in an accompanying change from non-binomial to binomial naming of plants and animals. In a later study, I (Brown 2001) developed evidence indicating that when hunter-gatherer people first begin to experiment with farming, they may not employ binomial names. Binomial names apparently emerge as a significant feature of folk biological classification only when an agricultural way of life is fully embraced.

4.3   Folk Classification of Oaks

The 2001 study treats folk biological classification of oaks (*Quercus* spp.) in eighty native languages and dialects of the New World. These languages are distributed from the northern borders of the United States to Costa Rica, a distribution closely matching the natural distribution of oak species through the Americas. Sources for these languages include both bilingual dictionaries and works dedicated to ethnobotany (see Brown [2001] for sources).

Oak naming systems of Amerindian groups vary in two major ways: (1) whether or not they have a generic oak term (GOT) or, in other words, a label for oaks in general that is extended in reference to all or most local oak species, for example, English *oak* (*Quercus* spp.); and (2) whether or not their subgeneric oak terms (SOTs) are binomial, e.g., *white oak* is a binomial term in English designating *Quercus alba*. BOT, short for binomial oak term, is used here to indicate a subgeneric oak class that is binomially labeled.

Tenejapa Tzeltal, a Mayan language spoken by swidden farmers of southern Mexico, and Diegueño, a Yuman language spoken by hunter-gatherers of southern California, offer two examples of systems of oak classification differing significantly from one another with respect to both of these variables. Table 4.1, treating Tenejapa Tzeltal, shows both a GOT and BOTs.

Tenejapa Tzeltal SOTs are all binomials because each entails the compounding of an oak term, in every instance the language's GOT (*hih te'*), with a modifying element (*bac'il*, genuine; *k'eweš*, custard apple; *sakyok*, white-trunked; *čikinib*, armadillo-eared; and *č'iš*, spine).

Table 4.1 *Tenejapa Tzeltal system for the classification and naming of oaks*

Type	Tzeltal term	Scientific referent(s)
GOT	hih te'	*Quercus* spp.
SOT	bac'il hih te'	*Q. peduncularis, Q. rugosa, Q. crassifolia, Q. segoviensis, Q. dysophylla*
	k'eweš hih te'	*Q. polymorpha, Q. rugosa*
	sakyok hih te'	*Q. candicans, Q. crassifolia*
	čikinib hih te'	*Q. acatenangensis, Q. mexicana, Q. sapotifolia, Q. conspersa*
	č'iš hih te'	*Q. corrugate*

Table 4.2 *Diegueño system for the classification and naming of oaks*

Type	Oak term	Scientific referent(s)
GOT	(not present)	*Quercus* spp.
SOT	semtaay	*Q. chrysolepis*
	neshaaw	*Q. douglasi*
	'esnyaaw	*Q. agrifolia*
	'ehwap	*Q. dumosa*
	kuphaall	*Q. kelloggii*

Table 4.3 *Lake Miwok system for the classification and naming of oaks*

Type	Miwok term	Scientific referent(s)
GOT	wajáa'ala	*Quercus* spp.
SOT	jutée'ala	*Q. kelloggii*
	penéel	*Q. chrysolepis*
	múule'ala	*Q. douglasi*
	sáata	*Q. wislizeni*
	hákja'ala	*Q. lobata*
	wátal'ala	*Q. dumosa*

Note. '*ala* designates tree.

The Diegueño system, shown in Table 4.2, lacks both a GOT and binomial SOTs (i.e., BOTs).

SOTs in Diegueño are not BOTS because none are constructions combining a GOT with a modifier.

Some Amerindian systems are intermediate with respect to the strongly contrastive systems of Tenejapa Tzeltal and Diegueño. For example, that of Lake Miwok shown in Table 4.3, a hunter-gatherer language of central California, shows a GOT, but lacks binomial SOTs (i.e., BOTs).

Table 4.4 (an adaption of Table 7.1 in Brown [2001]) is an inventory of oak classification systems in the eighty Native American languages organized by culture area. Within culture areas, languages are grouped according to geographic proximity, involving a more or less north-to-south order. Culture areas are similarly listed, as much as possible, in a north-to-south manner. Noted for each language is (1) whether or not a GOT is present (indicated by the use of + and –), (2) whether or not a BOT is present, and (3) whether or not speakers of the language are traditional agriculturalists (AGR).[2]

Table 4.4 *Inventory of oak naming systems in eighty Native American languages organized by culture area with information on mode of subsistence*

Language (location in italics)	GOT	BOT	AGR
Northwest Coast:			
1. Clallam	−	−	−
Plateau:			
2. Klamath	−	−	−
California:			
3. Karok	−	−	−
4. Chimariko	−	−	−
5. Achumawi	−	−	−
6. Yana	−	−	−
7. Wintu	+	−	−
8. Yuki	+	−	−
9. Patwin	+	−	−
10. Lake Miwok	+	−	−
11. Wappo	−	−	−
12. Nisenan	−	−	−
13. Maidu	−	+	−
14. Plains Miwok	−	−	−
15. Northern Sierra Miwok	−	−	−
16. Central Sierra Miwok	−	−	−
17. Southern Sierra Miwok	−	−	−
18. Chumash (Santa Inez)	−	−	−
19. Tübatulabal	−	−	−
20. Kawaiisu	−	−	−
21. Cahuilla	−	−	−
22. Cupeño	−	−	−
23. Luiseño	−	−	−
24. Diegueño	−	−	−
Baja California:			
25. Kiliwa	−	−	−
Southwest:			
26. Tewa	+	+	+
27. Western Apache	+	−	+
28. Papago-Pima	+	−	+
29. Mountain Pima	−	−	+
30. Nevome	−	−	+
31. Tarahumara	+	−	+
Plains:			
32. Dakota	+	−	+
33. Pawnee	−	−	+
34. Osage	+	−	+
35. Comanche	+	−	−
36. Kiowa-Apache	+	+	−
37. Kiowa	+	−	−
Northeast:			
38. Ojibwa	+	−	+
39. Ottawa	−	+	+

Table 4.4 (*cont.*)

Language (location in italics)	GOT	BOT	AGR
40. Mississaga	–	–	+
41. Algonquin	–	–	+
42. Menominee	+	–	+
43. Fox	+	–	+
44. Maliseet	–	–	+
45. Western Abenaki	–	–	+
46. Natick	+	–	+
47. Delaware	–	–	+
48. Mohawk	–	–	+
49. Onondaga	+	–	+
50. Seneca	–	–	+
Southeast:			
51. Tuscarora	–	–	+
52. Cherokee	–	–	+
53. Creek	+	+	+
54. Alabama	+	–	+
55. Koasati	–	+	+
56. Choctaw	+	+	+
57. Chickasaw	–	–	+
58. Biloxi	+	+	+
59. Ofo	+	+	+
60. Tunica	+	+	+
61. Atakapa	+	–	+
Mesoamerica:			
62. Huichol	–	+	+
63. Tarascan	+	+	+
64. Ixcatec	+	+	+
65. Cuicatec	+	+	+
66. Amuzgo	+	+	+
67. Zapotec (Mixtepec)	–	+	+
68. Zapotec (Mitla)	–	+	+
69. Zapotec (Juárez)	+	+	+
70. Tequistlatec	–	–	+
71. Huave	?	+	+
72. Mixe (Coatlán)	+	+	+
73. Mixe (Totontepec)	+	+	+
74. Tzeltal (Tenejapa)	+	+	+
75. Tzotzil (Zinacantán)	–	+	+
76. Tzotzil (San Andrés)	+	–	+
77. Kekchi	+	+	+
78. Cakchiquel	+	–	+
79. Tzutujil	–	–	+
Lower Central America:			
80. Cabecar	–	–	+

Adapted from Brown (2001).
GOT = generic oak term, BOT = binomial oak term, AGR = traditional agricultural group, + = present, – = absent.

Table 4.5 *Association between BOT and AGR*

		AGR	
		+	−
BOT	+	22	2
	−	30	26

Adapted from Brown (2001).
gamma = 0.81, $p < 0.01$, $N = 80$.

Table 4.6 *Association between GOT and AGR*

		AGR	
		+	−
GOT	+	29	7
	−	22	21

Adapted from Brown (2001).
gamma = 0.60, $p < 0.01$, $N = 79$.

Speakers of 28, or 35% of the languages, are nonagricultural (-AGR), twenty-two of which are native languages of California. Native peoples of California all have HG economies in which collection of acorns is of central importance. Fifty-two, or 65% of the eighty languages, are spoken by farmers who cultivate the traditional Amerindian staple triad of maize, beans, and squash. These are found mainly in the Southwest, Northeast, Southeast, and Mesoamerica culture areas of North America and northern Central America.

Table 4.5, based on information extracted from Table 4.4, cross-tabulates the presence of binomials (+/− BOT) in the eighty languages against language mode of subsistence (+/−AGR). The table attests to a very strongly positive association (gamma = 0.81) that is statistically significant ($p < 0.01$) (if all languages of the sample are independent, which is unlikely): agrarian groups, substantially more than hunter-gatherers, appear to use binomials as labels for subgeneric oak classes. This accords with the finding reported in Brown (1985) discussed earlier.

Table 4.6 cross-tabulates the occurrence of general oak terms (+/− GOT) against language mode of subsistence (+/− AGR). This table attests to another positive relationship (gamma = 0.60) that is statistically significant ($p < 0.01$)

Table 4.7 *Culture area averages*

	GOT	BOT	AGR
California	0.18	0.05	0.00
Southwest	0.67	0.17	1.00
Plains	0.83	0.17	0.50
Northeast	0.39	0.08	1.00
Southeast	0.64	0.55	1.00
Mesoamerica	0.65	0.78	1.00

Adapted from Brown (2001).

(under the condition of language independence): farmers appear to develop generic oak terms more commonly than do nonfarmers. This suggests that groups tend to acquire terms for generic classes of biological things only after becoming farmers.

Table 4.7 presents averages for culture areas of values presented in Table 4.4 For example, the average BOT for California is 0.05, based on the fact that only one of the twenty-two languages of the region shows a general oak term (see Table 4.4). The average BOT for California indicates that very few languages of the region show binomial oak terms compared to, say, Mesoamerica, which has an average BOT of 0.78. Similarly, the average AGR for California of 0.00 indicates that no groups of the area are agricultural, while an average AGR of 1.00 for Mesoamerica indicates that all groups of the area are agrarian. Four areas, the Northwest Coast, the Plateau, Baja California, and Lower Central America, are not included in Table 4.7 because each is represented by only one language (see Table 4.4).

Two of the six culture areas of Table 4.7, California and the Northeast, show average GOTs and BOTs which appear to be significant deviations from corresponding averages associated with the other four culture areas. GOT averages for these areas, respectively 0.18 and 0.39, are substantially smaller than those for others, as are BOT averages at 0.05 and 0.08 respectively for both areas. These differences indicate that languages of California and the Northeast (1) have a greater tendency to lack generic oak terms than Amerindian languages of other regions, and (2) tend to show fewer binomial terms for subgeneric oak classes than languages of other areas.

Agrarian peoples of different areas differ with respect to intensity of agricultural practices. Many groups of the Northeast manifest marginal food-producing economies wherein farming has traditionally been at best only auxiliary to hunting and gathering. Peoples of Mesoamerica show the most thorough dedication to agriculture, with very little supplementary food acquired through other activities. Southeast and Southwest groups are typically somewhere between the extremes represented by the Northeast and Mesoamerica.[3]

The deviation of GOT and BOT averages for California and the Northeast from corresponding averages for other culture areas may relate to area differences in mode of subsistence. Groups of both California and the Northeast differ from peoples of other areas since the latter tend to show either lack of agriculture (California) or only marginal agriculture (the Northeast), while other Amerindian groups are variously more intensely into farming. In addition, California groups are distinctive because for them alone acorns constitute a primary food source.

4.4   Developmental Implications

Correlations between aspects of oak naming and mode of subsistence are suggestive of patterns in the growth and development of oak classification systems. Systems lacking a GOT and those lacking BOTs are more typical of hunting and gathering groups than of farmers whose systems commonly manifest GOTs and BOTs. As a major thrust of human societal development over the last several millennia has been replacement of a foraging way of life with agriculture, the observed correlations suggest that over time classificatory systems have tended to shift from lacking a GOT and BOTs to having these features (cf., Anderson 1991).

Apparently the commencement of such a shift does not necessarily result immediately in the development of GOTs and BOTs. As noted earlier, languages of both California and the Northeast manifest very few GOTs and BOTs compared to Amerindian languages of other regions. With regard to California, this is expected because all groups of the region are nonagricultural. However, this is not predictable for groups of the Northeast who practice agriculture. Among all agrarian groups of the sample (see Table 4.4), people of the Northeast show the most marginal agricultural practices, wherein food production is commonly only auxiliary to hunting and gathering. The mere acquisition of agriculture by a group, then, does not appear to be a sufficient condition for the development of GOTs and BOTs. These may only develop in a system of folk biological classification when people acquire something more than an ancillary interest in farming.

4.5   Conclusion: Explanatory Framework

What are specific factors resulting in the development of GOTs and BOTs with a shift from a hunting-gathering/marginal-farming way of life to one involving full reliance on agriculture? Scholars have proposed explanations for the general increase in binomial terms as groups have replaced foraging with farming (Hunn and French 1984; Brown 1985, 1990b; Berlin 1992; Ellen 1999). Hunn and French (1984: 86–89) review several of these, justifiably rejecting some hypotheses that need not be discussed here. Two accounts, fitting into their category of "evolutionary" explanations, are plausible and deserve attention.

One account, embraced by Hunn and French (1984), and originally by me as well, relates to the number of classes pertaining to a folk system of biological classification. Data first assembled by me (Brown 1985) indicate that the size of such systems is positively correlated with mode of subsistence: hunter-gatherers tend to have systems with much fewer biological classes than those of farmers. Also, the original data seem to indicate that the use of binomial labels is positively correlated with system size: the larger the system, the more binomial labels used. To explain this correlation, Hunn and French (1984) and I (Brown 1985) note that binomial names may be especially useful in helping humans to store and recall large amounts of folk biological knowledge. If so, this helps to explain increase in binomial percentage with augmentation of the size of a system of biological classification. A major problem with this explanation is that it is not clearly the case that systems of hunter-gatherers are always much smaller than those of farmers. Indeed, this was pointed out early by Headland (1985) in direct commentary on Brown (1985).

I now reject the system-size hypothesis in favor of an explanation offered by Berlin (1992: 286). His account involves reference to the process of domestication. Cultivars typically may have been the initial recipients of binomial names. A binomial naming strategy later may become generalized to wild relatives of cultivated plants and animals and, eventually, to other closely similar sets of organisms including both domesticated and wild examples. Berlin points out that domestication involves the manipulation of many new and distinctly different forms of life. As a result, groups acquire a cognitively qualitative difference in the perception of living things as they shift from foraging to farming. They begin to look more closely at nature in general and to become more systematic in their approach to biological things. A major component of this new systematicity is the development of binomial nomenclature and general biological classes, such as English *oak*, first applied to cultivars and, subsequently, to plants and animals in general.[4]

This observation also helps to explain why marginal agriculturalists, such as traditional Amerindian groups of the Northeast, show a dearth of BOTs. Presumably, marginal farmers, compared to groups such as peoples of Mesoamerica who are fully committed to the agrarian enterprise, typically do not have access to a great number and variety of cultivars. In such a circumstance, there would be little or no perceptual motivation, as described by Berlin, for the development of binomial labels for the limited number of domesticated organisms known to them, and even less motivation for binomially naming wild living things such as oaks.

Acknowledgments

I am grateful to Eric Holman and Patrick McConvell for reading and commenting on a draft of this chapter.

NOTES

1. For a more detailed description and categorization of folk nomenclature for plants and animals, consult Berlin (1992).
2. Identification of groups speaking different languages as being or not being traditional farmers follows as closely as possible how the subsistence systems of these groups are commonly characterized in the literature.
3. Plains languages of the sample are spoken by both farmers and hunter-gatherers. Also, some of the California groups, all of which are codified as nonagrarian (see Table 4.4), traditionally cultivate tobacco.
4. In a recent study, Mandaville (2011: 218–228) compiles evidence showing that the folk botanical classification of pastoralists more closely resembles that of hunter-gatherers than that of agriculturalists with respect to number of binomially labeled taxa. This is explained by him as possibly relating to the minimal degree to which pastoralists are typically involved in manipulation of plants compared to farmers.

References

Anderson, Jr., Eugene N. (1991). Chinese folk classification of food plants. *Crossroads* 1: 51–67.

Berlin, Brent. (1972). Speculations on the growth of ethnobotanical nomenclature. *Language in Society* 1: 51–86.

   (1976). The concept of rank in ethnobiological classification: Some evidence from Aguaruna folk botany. *American Ethnologist* 3: 381–399.

   (1992) *Ethnobiological classification: Principles of categorization of plants and animals in traditional societies*. Princeton, NJ: Princeton University Press.

Berlin, Brent, Dennis E. Breedlove, and Peter H. Raven. (1973). General principles of classification and nomenclature in folk biology. *American Anthropologist* 75: 214–242.

   (1974). *Principles of Tzeltal plant classification*. New York: Academic Press.

Brown, Cecil H. (1985). Mode of subsistence and folk biological taxonomy. *Current Anthropology* 26: 43–64.

   (1990a). A survey of category types in natural language. In S. L. Tsohatzidis (ed.), *Meanings and prototypes: Studies in linguistic categorization*. London: Routledge, 17–47.

   (1990b). Ethnozoological nomenclature and animal salience. In Darrell A. Posey et al. (eds.), *Proceedings of the First International Congress of Ethnobiology (Belém, 1988)*. Belém, Brazil: Museu Paraense Emilio Goeldi, 81–87.

(2001). Linguistic ethnobiology: Amerindian oak nomenclature. In Richard I. Ford (ed.), *Ethnobiology at the millennium: Past promise and future prospects*. Ann Arbor, MI: Museum of Anthropology, 111–147.

Ellen, Roy. (1999). Models of subsistence and ethnobiological knowledge: Between extraction and cultivation in Southeast Asia. In Douglas L. Medin and Scott Atran (eds.), *Folkbiology*. Cambridge, MA: MIT Press, 91–117.

Headland, Thomas N. (1985). Comment on Brown (1985). *Current Anthropology* 26: 57–58.

Hunn, Eugene S., and David H. French. (1984). Alternatives to taxonomic hierarchy: The Sahaptin case. *Journal of Ethnobiology* 4: 73–92.

Mandaville, James P. (2011). *Bedouin ethnobotany: Plant concepts and uses in a desert pastoral world*. Tucson: University of Arizona Press.

Part II

Africa

5   Hunters and Gatherers in East Africa and the Case of Ongota (Southwest Ethiopia)

Graziano Savà and Mauro Tosco

5.1   Introduction

Quite a sizeable number of marginal communities are found in[4] East Africa, most notably along and in the proximity of the Rift Valley. Almost everywhere, from Ethiopia to Tanzania, one finds specific occupational outcast groups (usually tanners, blacksmiths, experts in traditional medical and magical practices, and so on), as well as hunting and gathering communities, to which fishermen and bee-keepers must be added.

It is at least convenient (even if not always easy, nor maybe theoretically sound) to draw a separating line between the occupational outcast groups and the hunting and gathering communities on the basis of their ethnic and linguistic affiliation: the former are found by and large *within* a broader ethnic and linguistic community, of which they share typical cultural and sociopolitical traits. On the other hand, hunting and gathering communities may better be considered separate entities; they are (often geographically, but even more culturally) distinct from the neighboring dominating group – to which, of course, they are tightly connected by a complex net of political obligations and economic interests.

Here our interest and our considerations will be strictly limited to the hunting-gathering groups. But even a cursory discussion of all the peoples that fall, one way or another, under this rubric in East Africa seems an impossible task within the limits of a single chapter. Only a few traits that seem common will be discussed:

We wish to gratefully acknowledge the collaboration of Sophia Thubauville (University of Mainz), who accompanied Graziano Savà on a short survey fieldwork in the Ongota village of Muts'e in August 2007 and kindly allowed the authors to include her map of the Ongota history of movements. Graziano Savà's research on Ongota was funded by the Hans Rausing Endangered Languages Documentation Programme. The included data on Ts'amakko come from Savà (2005). This publication is the result of a PhD project financed by the CNWS, University of Leiden. Fieldwork was also supported by the Dutch organization WOTRO. Graziano Savà is greatly indebted to these institutions for their fundamental support. In accordance with Italian academic regulations, we declare that Mauro Tosco is the main author of sections 1 to 4 and of section 10; and that Graziano Savà is the main author of sections 5 to 9.

- Language shift toward the language of a dominating group is widespread: there is evidence (as the present chapter will detail with regard to a specific group in southwestern Ethiopia) that language shift can even be cyclic.
- Ethnic assimilation to a neighboring pastoral community is equally common, although it must not be confused with language shift: a group can either shift its language affiliation without assimilating itself (i.e., without losing its distinctiveness), or retain its language but accept a new ethnic identity.

But it is in regard to the very origin of the hunting-gathering groups that two opposite historical hypotheses have been put forward and still dominate the field. To these we turn in the following section.

5.2   Two Ways of Looking at Hunter-Gatherers

Broadly speaking, the hunter-gatherers of East Africa have been subject to two radically different models of analysis. The first considers them as "relics" – i.e., as the last remnants, a sort of living testimony, of a pristine way of life of hunting and gathering, submerged elsewhere by pastoralism and agriculture. This approach is all the more strengthened when the group in question is not only ecologically, economically, and culturally deviant from the mainstream of the surrounding populations but also linguistically apart. In this view, hunter-gatherers are supposed to be "cultural survivors" precisely because they are, or are considered to be, "linguistic survivors." Their origin, it is claimed, can be traced following a classical genealogical tree, leading from an original starting point all the way down to present times. We call this a top-down model.

Taken to its extreme consequences, a startling example of this approach is Nurse's (1986) reconstruction of the past history of the Dahalo, a group of about 300 people living along the coastal forest strip of northern Kenya, not far from Lamu: traces of Dahalo presence (in the form of possible loans) are traced by Nurse as far as the Central Kenya Highlands. The contrary hypothesis, i.e., that many of them were loanwords *into* Dahalo (while a majority of putative Dahalo loans were probably the product of casual resemblance) was not taken into consideration. The result is a fascinating but utterly unprovable historical reconstruction, where the hunter-gatherers of today are the last representatives of prehistoric groups assimilated by advancing pastoral and agricultural peoples, like the tips of sunken islands.

Of course, there are other, less controversial cases to which a top-down model may apply. In Tanzania, the Hadza and the Sandawe may be instances of long-time ethnic groups united by, inter alia, hunting and gathering as an economic way of life, and stubbornly resisting assimilation. What is certain, on the other hand, is that in many other cases a top-down model, at least in its extreme form, cannot be applied successfully, and a different line of analysis is needed.

The second approach has the hunter-gatherers as marginal groups, and often as former pastoralists who were forced to adopt a despised way of subsistence after having lost their cattle as a result of war or epidemics. Such a view receives further support by the observation that the marginal, outcast groups of East Africa are constantly renewed and enriched through the influx of genetic (and very possibly linguistic) material coming from neighboring peoples: individuals, either men, women, or children, may and often are cast off of their group for a number of reasons, mainly having to do with the infringement of group solidarity and codes (Stiles 1988). There is no single starting point, and a genealogical tree is ill suited to represent the genesis of these groups. This model of analysis can be called "bottom-up."

The two models owe their existence to opposite frames of mind, each of them suiting different interests and methodologies. In a way, they are therefore irreducible to each other. On the other hand, it is well possible to imagine the models as extreme points along a continuum, with extreme and moderate cases. We can imagine, e.g., an original group getting "reinforced" and renovated from time to time through new ethnic and linguistic material.

In this chapter, we will argue that a bottom-up model may better account for the ethnic and linguistic history of the Ongota, and possibly – but certainly not all! – of other hunter-gatherers of East Africa. As detailed in the text that follows, the Ongota have largely replaced their ancestral language with the Cushitic language of their pastoral neighbors, the Ts'amakko, while a bare handful of elders still speak the Ongota language, which is so different from neighboring Cushitic and Omotic languages that it has so far resisted classification. In another radical example of a top-down approach, Fleming (2006) has recently claimed that Ongota represents a separate branch of the Afroasiatic phylum – therefore dating back thousands of years. This hypothesis may be matched at the ethnographic level with the (completely unwarranted) suggestion, found in a travel report from 1896 (Donaldson Smith 1896), that the Ongota are the remnants of an archaic pygmy population of hunter-gatherers.

The Ongota are still fairly unknown – a kind of "new entry" in the world of hunter-gatherer communities – and the problems surrounding their language and past history are very complex indeed. The following sections will present in more detail the Ongota and the ethnolinguistic evidence pointing to their origin.

5.3   The Ongota

The Ongota (known locally mainly as Birale) are a tiny population of about 100 living in southwestern Ethiopia. Their only village, Muts'e, is found along the Weyt'o River, some 35 minutes walking distance from the bridge along the road leading from Konso to the Omo Valley.[1] The village is within the territory of the Ts'amakko (or Tsamai), who speak one of the Dullay varieties of East

Map 5.1 The Ongota and the neighboring peoples mentioned in the text.
(Adapted with changes from: www.southethiopiaresearch.org/.)

Cushitic (Savà 2005). Other neighboring populations are the Gawwada and
other Dullay-speaking groups to the east, the Maale to the north, and the Arbore
to the south (see Map 5.1). All their neighbors speak East Cushitic languages,
except for the Maale, whose language is North Omotic. Additional groups in

contact are the Hamer, the Banna (both South Omotic speakers), the Konso and the Boraana (East Cushitic speakers).

The Ongota are known in the area for their linguistic and ethnographic uniqueness. Their traditional language, called ʔiifa ʕongota, is different from any other language in the area. Actually, it is so different as to be still unclassified, although many proposals have been put forward.

Ongota is also a very endangered language, as the community speaks Ts'amakko for everyday communication. This is also the language taught to children. About ten elders still have a knowledge of the Ongota traditional language (Fleming et al. 1992/93; Savà and Tosco 2000; Fleming 2006).

Ethnographically, the Ongota are described as the only hunter-gatherers in an area characterized largely by the so-called "cattle complex." They practice fishing, hunting, collecting wild plants, as well as apiculture. However, they essentially live on cultivated maize and vegetables and keep some chickens, goats, and sheep. They are also good producers of bananas, which together with honey are marketable goods. Today the Ongota are socially dominated by the Ts'amakko. The influence is so strong that it is hardly possible to find any Ongota cultural trait that is not derived from the Ts'amakko. The two groups intermarry and the Ongota take part in the weekly Ts'amakko market in Weyt'o town.

5.4   The Hunting-Gathering Origins of the Ongota

One may ask why the Ongota are considered hunter-gatherers if they cultivate and have domestic animals. They are not even distinguished by special non-agropastoralist activities, as these are not exclusively Ongota in southwestern Ethiopia. Most of the surrounding people hunt, collect some plants, and produce honey, and, as is well known, hardly any community survives by eating exclusively wild animals and plants; food is always produced from some sort of small-scale agriculture and cattle-keeping. Fishing is the only practice that the Ongota do not share with neighboring peoples; actually, Ongota are the only group for which fish is not a taboo food.

This does not necessarily mean that the Ongota were originally hunter-gatherers and have absorbed alternative forms of food production. Alternatively, they might have had a pastoralist past and for some reason gave up animal husbandry. There are some indications supporting this view. Savà and Thubauville (2010) have found out that older Ongota women have no special knowledge of wild plants. This may help proving that the Ongota are not originally hunter-gatherers. According to Melesse Getu (1997), and as confirmed by the Ongota themselves to Savà and Thubauville in 2006, a massive presence of the tse-tse fly (the biological vector of trypanosomiasis) along the Weyt'o River prevents Ongota from breeding cows. For this reason the only domestic animals the Ongota breed are goats and sheep, beside chickens. This may suggest a bottom-up approach, one in which the Ongota were earlier pastoralists forced to give up cattle-keeping, but also, on the opposite side, the incomplete acculturation of a hunter-gatherer group. The whole story, it will be suggested, is much more complex.

Still, according to Melesse Getu (1997), the presence of firearms in the forest of the Weyt'o River Valley and desertification resulted in drastic impoverishment of fauna and flora. Moreover, the number of fish had decreased during the last years – the main reason being the building of a dam that served the irrigation system of a large cotton farm near the village of Weyt'o and through which few fish could pass. This means that environmental conditions might have posed serious problems for the Ongota if their life was based mainly on hunting and gathering.

The solution to the Ongota dilemma – where do they come from, and what have they been in the past? – might come from the analysis of some, largely unpublished, historical information. In the following paragraphs we will use them to support a bottom-up model for the understanding of the Ongota hunter-gatherer status.

5.5   Internal Evidence: The Myth of the Ongota Origins

The Ongota have a traditional history regarding their origins. This has been recorded, but not published, by Savà and Tosco (2000, 2006). The storyteller was Mole Sagane, the former chief of the community. Until his death in January 2008 he was a respected and charismatic elder and one of the last few speakers of the Ongota traditional language.

The story tells that the original Ongota group was living in the Maale area. They were killing and stealing cattle using sticks with poisoned tips. Apparently, they already were composed of different sections, each one going back to a different people, ranging, for example, from the North Omotic Maale to the South Omotic Banna, to the East Cushitic Borana and Dishina.

They were eventually chased away and forced to move southward along the Weyt'o River. The people started walking along the riverbed and eventually found their way blocked by a large boulder. The people asked the wisest men of each clan how to break it apart. All of them tried their divinations, but to no avail. After the wise men failed, someone suggested asking a small boy to try. They chose one and gave him a rhino's horn. The boy touched the boulder with the horn and it immediately split apart. The Weyt'o River could flow southward and the Ongota could move on.

The Ongota followed the river until its end (the Weyt'o river runs dry somewhere to the South of the Ongota settlement in semidesert areas), where

Table 5.1 *Origin of the Ongota clans*

Clan	Origin
baritta	Boraana
ozbikko	Arbore
ʕamaddo	Gawwada
reegakko	Dishina
hizmakko	Maale, Gabo, Hamar and Boraana

they met the Arbore people. After staying there for some time, they were again forced to move, this time northward, until they settled in the general area where they are found nowadays.

It is interesting to note that the wizards of each section – i.e., of the different peoples – fail to split the boulder, but a child does. One could interpret this as the symbolic expression of a new ethnic identity. Only the Ongota could set the river free, not the original peoples as represented in the tribal sections. The myth, centered as it is on the Weyt'o, may be seen as the Ongota version of the hunter-gatherer topophilia: it certainly symbolizes the strong symbiotic link between the Ongota and the river. While the pastoralists exploit the land beyond the riverbanks, it is the Ongota who really live around and from the river: from it the Ongota get their identity.

From the myth one can see that the Ongota consider themselves a mixture of people coming from surrounding communities. Each Ongota clan retraces its origin from one population, except one that claims four separate connections (Table 5.1).

It is interesting to note that a claimed multiethnic origin is not at all unknown in the area. Further to the west, along the lower course of the Omo, the Dhaasanac have a partially similar story, although the bulk of the Dhaasanac claim to derive from the south and to have submerged a local population of fishermen (Tosco 2007, following and elaborating Sobania 1980). If further research will show that the multiethnic origin has actually an ideological basis in the area, it will be possible to analyze this part of the Ongota myth of the origins as an adaptation of their history to a pattern common among the neighboring pastoralist peoples. This adaptation is also evident from the names of the clans, which are found among the Ts'amakko and the Gawwada (and possibly other groups, although relevant data are missing in this regard).

We have seen that the myth embraces two aspects of the origins of the Ongota: their geographic origin, which is claimed to be strictly local, centered on the Weyt'o River, and their ethnic composition, which is reported as multiethnic from the very beginning. The local geographic origin of the Ongota is compatible with a top-down model (the Ongota as the pristine inhabitants of the area), while the multiethnic origin points to the bottom-up approach. Of course, even the plurality of ethnic origins does not exclude a priori the existence of an original, nuclear group of hunter-gatherers, and the strength of the myth as a proof is further weakened by its not uncommon character. Still, at least two points seem to be clear and cannot be dismissed: the Ongota themselves do *not* consider themselves as the first inhabitants of the area and do *not* see themselves as original hunter-gatherers.

5.6   External Evidence: Old Contacts with the Maale

The Maale are highland pastoralists, living to the north of the Ts'amakko and the Ongota in an area ranging in altitude from about 1,000 to 2,800 meters above sea level (Azeb Amha 2001: 1). The Ongota myth of origin shows that they used to live among the Maale. Other pieces of information confirm this early relation: the Ongota reported to Savà and Thubauville (2006) that they moved often in their (recent?) history. They still remember the names of about thirty settlements they settled and abandoned. The first are located north of their present location, toward the Maale highlands. The present one, Muts'e, is on the Weyt'o River. Before Muts'e the Ongota were living in Aydolle, which is the village visited in 1991 by a few members of the team who authored Fleming et al. (1992). The place lies just some hundred meters from Muts'e toward the forest. A few abandoned huts can still be recognized.

A Maale tradition about the Ongota was collected by Sophia Thubauville in November 2007. Contrary to the Ongota myth of origin, the Maale say that the Ongota were once part of the Maale. To the northeast of the Maale territory there is also a place called Ongo. Maale people still go and dance there to celebrate a good harvest. There is a good memory of the Ongota, and the Maale are proud to know that an offspring of their community can be found some-where along the Weyt'o River.

We also owe a few interesting pieces of information to the American traveler Arthur Donaldson Smith, who visited southwestern Ethiopia at the end of the nineteenth century. The following excerpts of his report are relevant to our discussion:

'We came to a large and warlike tribe called the Arbore, inhabiting half of the valley above Lake Stephanie ... '

[talking about the people that they heard of] They were Burle, Dume, Mali, Borali in succession towards the north, and then the Bunno, Dime, Ario, and Amar to the west (Donaldson Smith 1896: 224).

'Dume, Mali and Borali are pygmies. The Dume conquered the Burle eight years before.' [emphasis ours]

Several populations listed by Donaldson Smith in the preceding quotes and elsewhere can still be found in southwestern Ethiopia. Not so with the Burle, Dume, and Borali. Fleming et al. (1992) proposed connecting the name Borali to Birale, which is the ethnic name presently given to the Ongota by neighboring populations. This would imply, once again, that according to Donaldson Smith the Ongota were living North of the Maale area (referred to as "Mali" by Donaldson Smith). Map 5.2, created by Sophia Thubauville, reconstructs the movement of the Ongota from the Maale area to their present location. Only the

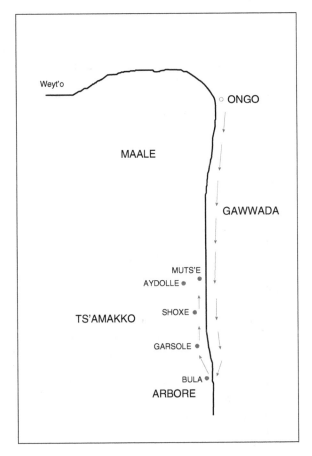

Map 5.2 The movements of the Ongota along the Weyt'o River, according to the Ongota myth of the origins (by Sophia Thubauville).

places that could be localized with the help of Maale and Ongota people are shown.

5.7   The Ongota as a Marginal Group

In contradiction to Fleming's (2006) view, according to which the Ongota were once a much more powerful population in the area (an idea strikingly similar to Nurse's 1986 reconstruction of the Dahalo past in Kenya; see earlier), we believe that the present assimilation of the Ongota to the Ts'amakko and the early affiliation to the Maale are just the two most recent episodes in a long history of Ongota subordinate relations with dominant populations of the area. From each dominant group the Ongota have assimilated cultural traits and linguistic elements.

Similarly, the Boni of the Kenya-Somali border (Tosco 1994) have preserved, with due changes, the South Somali dialect of their previous "masters," the Garre – even though they are politically dominated today by the Oromo. The ethnonym Boni, an adaptation of Somali *boon* "hunters," nowadays widely used in Kenya (Heine 1977), is matched by a parallel denomination as *Waata* among the Oromo and as *Aweer* ~ *Aweera* in the group itself; all these terms simply mean "hunters." All these ethnonyms indicate that, at least since the split from the Somali, one is confronted with an occupational group that is *also* a separate ethnolinguistic entity.

Just south of the Boni, the Dahalo speak a Cushitic language (either of the southern or the eastern branch) but a very limited portion of the vocabulary (approximately fifty words) contains a nasalized dental click (*ŋ/*; cf. Maddieson et al. 1993 for a phonetic analysis of Dahalo), and this may be interpreted as a very old lexical layer: obviously, the very presence of a phonological click in an otherwise orthodox Afroasiatic language may suggest that we are dealing here with the "original" layer, and the only surviving evidence of what was once a Khoisan language. In its turn, this would also be the northernmost relic of the original Khoisan-speaking population of East Africa, prior to the advent in the area of food production (Tosco 1991, 1992). The extreme top-down model expressed by Nurse (1986) and briefly discussed in Section 5.2 seems to follow naturally from such an interpretation. Of course, there is at least a huge obstacle to the whole idea: the very existence of Khoisan as a genetically valid group is today more and more rejected (Güldemann and Voßen 2000).[2]

All these cases indicate that change of linguistic and ethnic affiliation seems indeed to be quite common in the area, for hunter-gatherers and pastoralists alike (cf. Tosco 1998 for an analysis of such changes in terms of the catastrophe theory).

Coming back to the Ongota, it could well be retorted that, as was seen earlier, the Maale consider the Ongota to have been "a part" of their people, which could lend support to the hypothesis that they were actually pastoral peoples driven for unknown reasons to hunting and gathering. But an outcast group is still "part of a people," which in this part of East Africa means being bound by ritual and legal obligations and economic interests, and not by a putative common ethnic origin or linguistic behavior (cf. again Tosco 1998). Similarly, occupational minorities of Ethiopia are still part of an "ethnic group" while being heavily marginalized: indeed, cultural assimilation and subordination to a dominant group distinguish the social history of the outcast groups all over southern Ethiopia (cf. Freeman and Pankhurst 2001), and possibly beyond because the largely unknown outcast groups found among the Somali seem to share a similar history. All these groups are characterized by their skill in handcraft and the power of manipulating clay, iron, and hide give them supernatural attributes. For this reason they are very useful, but despised and feared at the same time. Marriage with an outcast person, for example, is forbidden or at the very least frowned on. The Ongota are not specialized in any handcraft; there is, however at least one indication that in the past they might have been attributed some magical power. During their stay in the South Omo area in 1973 Jean Lydall and Ivo Strecker heard "some interesting news of people called the Birale who live on the east of the Birale mountain, close to the river. The Tsamai refer to them as *hajje*[3] and consider them to be powerful magicians" (Lydall and Strecker 1979: 111). Because they do not keep big herds of cattle and have a strange traditional language of their own, the Ongota are looked on in scorn by the neighboring pastoralist groups (Savà and Tosco 2000: 65). On the other hand, they are allowed to intermarry with the Ts'amakko and the Gawwada. In the context of these ambiguous social relations with their neighbors, the Ongota will most probably decide to abandon for good their status of a socially despised group by starting keeping cattle and becoming a full pastoralist people. They eventually might be accepted as a new Ts'amakko clan, thus completing the assimilation process.

5.8   Ongota: An Unclassified Language

As mentioned earlier, the traditional language of the Ongota, called *ʔiifa ʕongota*, is different from all other languages in the area, which are from the Cushitic and Omotic subgroupings of Afroasiatic and from the Surmic subgrouping of Nilo-Saharan. To explain this uniqueness, the top-down model suggests that the Ongota language is genetically a linguistic isolate spoken by a hunter-gatherer group. Our idea, instead, is that Ongota's complex history of domination by different groups is reflected in the language, with different superimposed strata. The linguistic import of the constant influx, of different individuals, families, and maybe whole sections, resulted in a language that is very deviant form any other language in the area, to the point of being unclassified.

From the morphological point of view, the language is strikingly different. It shows an uncommonly poor and isolating morphology: gender and number have no formal expression on nouns; there are no person and tense verbal suffixes; expression of tense is based on tonal accent change. Moreover, the relatively few grammatical elements have forms not attested in the area: morphological exponents, such as deictic suffixes, determiner suffixes, adjectival endings, and most verbal derivation extensions. Also items belonging to other word classes, such as pronouns, adjectives, adverbs, clitics, and postpositions cannot be etymologically linked to any neighboring group.

One of the most interesting distinctive morphological features is the absence of verb inflection, which is so characteristic of neighboring Cushitic and Omotic languages. The subject is indexed only by preverbal pronominal clitics. Tense is expressed by placing the tonal accent on the rightmost syllable of the verb, in which case the tense is past, or in the preceding one, in order to express non-past tense. The non-past position of the accent in monosyllabic verbs is on the pronominal clitic. This is shown in the following examples.

Example 5.1: Past
(1) *cata   ka=cák*
     meat   I=eat.PAST
     I ate meat

Example 5.2: Non-Past
(2) *cata   ká=cak*
     meat   I=eat.NON-PAST
     I eat/will eat meat

As far as we know, the closest parallel is found in Hamer, a South Omotic language spoken not far from Ongota to the West. Verbs in Hamer are not inflected for the person of the subject, which is indexed by means of preverbal clitics (Cupi et al. 2013). On the other hand, Hamer has a complex system of aspect and tense suffixes, many of which probably derive from old copula elements.

Considering the area in which it is spoken and the typology of neighboring languages, one would also expect Ongota to have a rich nominal morphology. Instead, the language does not show any trace of the complex Cushitic and Omotic system of number and gender. For example, in Ts'amakko a basic noun can be derived for singulative and plurative by means of derivational suffixes: from the noun *kar-o* "dog," one can obtain *kar-itto* "one male dog," *kar-itte* "one female dog," and *kar-re* "dogs." Ongota operates with a simple singular/plural opposition. Plurality, moreover, is either lexicalized (for instance: *ayma* "woman"/ *aaka* "women") or expressed by the word *bad'd'e* "many," following the noun (*kara bad'd'e* "fishes").

There is no published work devoted to comparative Ongota morphosyntax. Some notes are found in Blažek (1991, 2001, 2005), Savà and Tosco (2003), and Fleming (2006). Among the proposals for a classification, Blažek finds similarities in the pronominal series between Ongota and some Nilo-Saharan languages, while Savà and Tosco adopt the more conservative view that Ongota is an East Cushitic language of the Dullay subgroup on the basis of some tone accent similarities in verbs. One should also mention that Aklilu Yilma (p.c.) sees in Ongota's poor morphology an indication that the language is a creolized pidgin. He supports this view with the local legend of the multiethnic origin of the Ongota that we mentioned earlier.

Most of the Ongota comparative studies have focused on lexicon. This is characterized by a mass of Ts'amakko loanwords that entered the Ongota recorded from the last speakers. Among them one could also find words from other Dullay varieties. According to Fleming (2006), however, for the Ts'amakko-like words belonging to some core and cultural lexicon the direction of borrowing could have been the opposite – from Ongota into Ts'amakko.

The proportion of Ts'amakko/Dullay and non-Ts'amakko/Dullay lexicon in Ongota can be calculated using the best comparison of the Ongota lexicon published so far (Blažek 2005): the Ts'amakko/Dullay list consists of 295 parallels, while parallels with neighboring Cushitic (such as Oromo and other East Cushitic languages) and Omotic (such as Hamer and other South and North Omotic languages) adds up to only about fifteen entries each. In his article Blažek considers each classified group of words as a lexical stratum. In his opinion, the oldest has Nilo-Saharan origin; he himself had isolated the similarities with Nilo-Saharan languages in an older paper published only recently (Blažek 2007).

There have been other attempts at Ongota classification by lexical comparison:

- Bender (1994) lists Ongota as "unclassifiable" because, according to his lexicostastistic technique, it shares less than 5% with any other language. However, he later defined Ongota as "hybridized Cushitic" (p.c.).
- Fleming (2006) has proposed that Ongota is Afroasiatic, although *a separate branch* of it, on a par with, say, Cushitic, Berber, or Semitic.
- Ehret (p.c. 2002), on the basis of unpublished comparative work, favors a South Omotic affiliation.

The following section will show why all these proposals are unsatisfactory.

5.9   Traces of Contact in the Ongota Language

The uncertainty on the genetic status of Ongota tells us that the classification of Ongota is a very hard, perhaps unfeasible, task. All the proposed hypotheses are very interesting, but do not provide definite evidence, and all the attempts share the methodological pitfall of not being based on a reconstruction of Ongota. Many similarities and relevant etymologies therefore look very impressionistic and may be put into question (see Savà and Tosco 2007 for a critical appraisal of the reconstructions in Fleming 2006).

Savà and Thubauville (2010) have also tried to classify a corpus of Ongota lexemes. Their aim was not to propose another classification, but to spot the linguistic traces of contact between the Ongota and the groups that they most likely met during their journeys. Their corpus consists of a selection of about 700 Ongota lexical items, much larger than the one used by Blažek. The words come from Savà and Tosco (2000) with some integration from Fleming et al. (1992/93). To accept a borrowing Savà and Thubauville (2010) required a particularly high and unquestionable level of similarity. Whenever possible, the comparisons have been checked against Blažek (2005) and Fleming (2006).

5.9.1   *Ts'amakko Borrowings*

About 200 words are Ts'amakko borrowings. Some of them appear unchanged in Ongota, while others show phonological and morphological adaptation. A few Ts'amakko loanwords that are preserved unchanged are listed in Table 5.2.

Table 5.2 *Ts'amakko borrowings in Ongota*

Ongota and Ts'amakko	Gloss
game	corn
geʔ	to belch
gufaʔ	to cough
kol	to come back, return
komba	beads necklace
malal	to be tired
middo	bracelet
sarba	calf
siibde	bow string
tilile	black kite
laaxko	wooden arrow
palde	iron arrow

Table 5.3 *Vowel length reduction*

Ongota	Ts'amakko	Gloss
dig	*diig*	to pour
bositte	*boositte*	hair of chest

Table 5.4 *Vowel height change*

Ongota	Ts'amakko	Gloss
gunture	*gontore*	eland
merja	*mirja*	kudu

Table 5.5 *Dental assimilation of glottal stop*

Ongota	Ts'amakko	Gloss
moqotte	*muq'oʔte*	frog
oršatte	*oršaʔte*	rhino

Table 5.6 *Nasal change*

Ongota	Ts'amakko	Gloss
kunkumitte	*kumkumitte*	cheek

The phonological makeup of some Ts'amakko words has been slightly changed. Typical adaptations include vowel length reduction, vowel height change, dental assimilation of glottal stop, and nasal change (Tables 5.3–5.6).

In some words, final *a* replaces the Ts'amakko gender suffixes *-o* (M) and *-e* (F) (Table 5.7).

The Ts'amakko singulative suffixes are generally lost in Ongota. In the examples in Table 5.8, a final *a* appears in place of the masculine singulative suffixes *-ko, -akko* and *-atto*.

In Table 5.9 *o* may appear instead of the feminine singulative suffix *-te*.

The example in Table 5.10 shows the deletion of the masculine gender suffix *-ko* and no replacement.

The derivation passive suffixes *-am* has been absorbed in the stem in Table 5.11.

Table 5.7 *Gender suffix replacement in Ongota*

Ongota	Ts'amakko	Gloss
baara	baaro	armpit
irgaʕa	irgaʕo	axe
ħeka	ħeeko	chest
qola	q'ole	animal (domestic)
kirinca	kirince	ankle
kurruba	kurrube	crow, raven

Table 5.8 *Masculine suffix replacement in Ongota*

Ongota	Ts'amakko	Gloss
karawa	karaw-ko	colobus monkey
qoba	q'ob-akko	finger
damʕa	damʕ-atto	giraffe

Table 5.9 *Feminine suffix replacement in Ongota*

Ongota	Ts'amakko	Gloss
ħalo	ħaal-te	calabash cup

Table 5.10 *Suffix loss with no replacement in Ongota*

Ongota	Ts'amakko	Gloss
bor	bor-ko	stomach

Table 5.11 *Suffix absorption in Ongota*

Ongota	Ts'amakko	Gloss
wuyyam	wuyy	to call
	wuyy-am	to be called

Table 5.12 *Internal and final changes in Ongota*

Ongota	Ts'amakko	Gloss
gawarsa	*gawarakko*	bateleur (*Theratopius ecaudatus*)
mirila	*mirille*	cheetah
sayra	*sawro*	dik dik

Table 5.13 *Irregular consonant change in Ongota*

Ongota	Ts'amakko	Gloss
talaħa	*salaħ*	four
luqqa	*lukkale*	chicken

Some borrowings show word internal and final changes (Table 5.12). Irregular consonant change is found in at least two cases (Table 5.13).

5.9.2   Non-Ts'amakko borrowings

Only forty items are considered as borrowings from neighboring languages and language groups. A selection of those with the highest level of similarity with the geographically closest languages is shown in Table 5.14.

Casual lookalikes between unrelated languages can always be found and they can easily get in the way of language comparison; thus, we find at least a couple of similarities with different Nilo-Saharan languages (Table 5.15).

Justifying the presence of these resemblances as due to anything else than other sheer similarity is very difficult because the languages are spoken as far away as the Sudan. Also accepting Blažek's idea that Ongota is originally a Nilo-Saharan language does not make matters much easier, as the languages belong to different Nilo-Saharan subgroups. Moreover, Nilo-Saharan subgrouping, and the very existence of Nilo-Saharan as a linguistic family, are of course a debated matter.

According to Blažek (2005), there are also borrowings from South Cushitic languages. Three of them are particularly interesting (Table 5.16).

Also in this case it is not likely that the Ongota borrowed words from languages spoken as far away as Tanzania; on the other hand, Dahalo could actually be East Cushitic (as argued for by Savà and Tosco 2000), and therefore Ongota might have borrowed from an unknown and closer-to-hand East Cushitic language.

There are other cases in which similarities are shared by more members of a subgroup (Table 5.17).

Table 5.14 *Non-Ts'amakko borrowings in Ongota*

Ongota	Hamer (South Omotic)	Gloss
buusa	*busa*	belly
adab	*atab*	tongue
laɓa	*laɓa*	wide
ooma	*oom*	bow
gaʕ	*gaʔ*	bite
Ongota	**Ari (South Omotic)**	**Gloss**
goola	*goola*	local beer
wanna	*waanna*	good
Ongota	**Maale (North Omotic)**	**Gloss**
naʔa	*naʔi*	child
baliti	*baliti*	forehead
toiti	*toiti*	eldest son
Ongota	**Borana (East Cushitic)**	**Gloss**
arba	*arba*	elephant
meela	*miila*	leg
olla	*olla*	village
Ongota	**Konso (East Cushitic)**	**Gloss**
aama	*ama*	breast
armata	*armayta*	mucus

Table 5.15 *Ongota similarities with Nilo-Saharan languages*

	Nilo-Saharan Language			
Ongota	Mimi	North Mao	Kanuri	Gloss
maara	*maar*	*meri*		boy
itima			*timi*	tooth

Table 5.16 *Ongota borrowings from South Cushitic*

		South Cushitic Languages			
Ongota	Gloss	Dahalo	Iraqw	Burunge	Gloss
c'aʕaw	water	*tl'ááʕa*			river, lake
q'umo	container		*qumi*		traveling gourd
c'aʕa	stone		*tl'aʕa-nu*	*tl'aʕu*	stone

Table 5.17 *Similarities with Oromo dialects, Konsoid and North Omotic languages*

Ongota	Gloss	Oromo of Borana, Waata, Giju, and Macha					Gloss
gaara	mountain	*gara*					mountain
		Konsoid					
		Bussa		**Gidole**			
romini	red	*rooma*		*room/êr-roma*			red, orange, pink
		North Omotic					
		Dizi	**Nayi**	**Sheko**	**Koyra**	**Bench**	
šub	to kill	*šuβo*	*šubo*	*šub*	*šúpe*		to die
						çup/çuk	to slaughter

Table 5.18 *Words with no apparent similarity in other languages*

faʔ	to add
dabaša	baboon
tip	to die
xaʔ	to do
howwa	ear
cak	to eat
naʔ	to give
noqot	to look at
miša	name
axaco	sun
binta	wild animal

Last, we have Ts'amakko loanwords shared by other Dullay dialects; it seems safer to consider all of them borrowed into Ongota through the inter-mediacy of Ts'amakko – also on the basis of the fact that there are no cases of Dullay lexemes in Ongota *not* shared by Ts'amakko.

5.9.3   Unclassified Words

The majority of the words taken into consideration by Savà and Thubauville resist classification, and therefore may suggest an ancient hunter-gatherer group with a yet unknown linguistic affiliation. Some examples of these unaffiliated words are shown in Table 5.18.

5.10   Conclusions

In our opinion, the Ongota myths of origin and the traditions of their northern neighbors, the Maale, seem to lend support to a bottom-up approach, although other historical scenarios are not logically excluded. The main points are:

- The Ongota are the descendants of different peoples – or better, of various sections of peoples – who joined together. The Ongota clan names are in effect the same, apparently, as those found all over the area.
- The Ongota lived originally to the north of their present location, in the territory of the Maale (an Ometo-speaking – i.e., North Omotic – group).
- The Ongota were engaged in stealing cattle at the expenses of the Maale.
- The Ongota forced their way (or were forced to move) southward along the Weyt'o River and have lived in close association with it since then.
- Ongota women do not have any special knowledge of wild plants collection.
- The Ongota cannot keep cattle because of the presence of the tse-tse fly in the area.

The Ongota are presently assimilating to the Ts'amakko pastoralists; recently and still marginally, a few Ongota even bought goats (which nevertheless are not kept in the Ongota village but in Weyt'o town, where several Ongota have been taken residence). From a linguistic point of view, the current terminal state of the Ongota language has been mentioned, while from a cultural point of view the Ongota are certainly hardly distinguishable from their pastoral neighbors. No reliable data on the Ongota economy are available, although economic assimilation to the Ts'amakko has so far been hampered by the absence of cattle, or, in other words, of "hard currency."

The traditional language of the Ongota reflects their contact history. Continuous influence from different languages resulted in a very divergent language with an unusual isolating character and a unique lexicon. The presence of a good number of Ts'amakko loanwords shows the particularly strong relation with the people speaking this language. We assume that the same happened with other groups to which the outcast Ongota were affiliated.

The presence of a fairly substantial number of unclassified words (as seen in Section 5.9.3) yields plausibility to the possibility of an original hunter-gatherer group which came in contact with a number of different peoples and languages, to the point of radically changing its language affiliation. This would make the Ongota resemble a bit both the Dahalo and the Boni of Kenya (discussed in Section 5.7): just like the Dahalo, the Ongota would have preserved a tiny lexical layer of their original language, and just like the Boni they would have shifted their language to that of their dominating language group (the present one – the Ts'amakko – in the case of the Ongota; a former one – Southern Somali Garre – in the case of the Boni). Nothing among the meager available data seems to force such an analysis, and just like for all the other hunter-gatherer groups it is close to impossible to detect the full range of the prehistoric contacts. Weighting the pros and cos of competing models, we opt in the end for a bottom-up approach: it seems to better fit the present situation on a number of counts: the language, the sociology of the Ongota, and their traditions. The simplest (albeit maybe less fascinating) scientific hypothesis remains to project the present state of affairs in the past and to conclude that the Ongota are *not* a remnant hunter-gatherer population. They were originally an outcast community that has been wandering in the area around the Weyt'o River and affiliating itself in the course of time to different dominant pastoralist groups. They are presently attached to the Ts'amakko, but full assimilation is not possible at the moment because the Ongota do not own cattle. The real difference between the Ongota and the pastoralists in the area is the absence of cattle rather than the alleged hunter-gathering lifestyle of the Ongota.

NOTES

1. The Weyt'o River of southwestern Ethiopia (locally called *Dullay, Dullayho,* etc.) is of course not to be confused with the now extinct Weyto language, spoken by hippopotamus hunters in the Lake Tana. It was probably a Cushitic language (Dimmendaal 1989), later superseded by an occupation jargon based on Amharic.
2. We find it mildly ironic that the very name "Dahalo" is considered derogatory by the group itself; the only native alternative seems to be *guħo gʷittso* "little people" (Tosco 1991): certainly not what you would expect for the original, mighty population of the area.
3. *Hajje* in Ts'amakko is the plural form of the noun *hajo*, which indicates a person with magical power.

References

Azeb Amha. (2001). *The Maale language.* Leiden: CNWS.
Bender, Lionel M. (1994). The mystery languages of Ethiopia. In Harold G. Marcus (ed.), *New trends in Ethiopian studies. Papers from the 12th International Conference of Ethiopian Studies.* Lawrenceville, NJ: Red Sea Press, 1153–1174.
Blažek, Václav. (1991). Comparative analysis of Ongota lexicon. Paper presented at the 21st Colloquium on African Language and Linguistics, Leiden.
—— (2005). Cushitic and Omotic strata in Ongota, a moribund language of uncertain affiliation from Southern Ethiopia. *Archiv Orientální* 73: 43–68.

(2007). Nilo-Saharan stratum of Ongota. In Mechthild Reh and Doris L. Payne (eds.), *Advances in Nilo-Saharan Linguistics: Proceedings of the 8th Nilo-Saharan Linguistics Colloquium*, University of Hamburg, August 22–25, 2001. Köln: Köppe, 1–10.

Cupi, Loredana, Sara Petrollino, Graziano Savà, and Mauro Tosco. (2013). Preliminary notes on the Hamar verb. In Marie-Claude Simeone-Senelle and Martine Vanhove (eds.), *Proceedings of the 5th International Conference on Cushitic and Omotic Languages*. Köln: Köppe, 181–195.

Dimmendaal, Gerrit J. (1989). On language death in Eastern Africa. In Nancy C. Dorian (ed.), *Investigating obsolescence: Studies in language contraction and death*. Cambridge: Cambridge University Press, 13–31.

Donaldson Smith, Arthur. (1896). Expedition through Somaliland to Lake Rudolf. *The Geographical Journal* 8: 121–137, 221–239.

Fleming, Harold C., Aklilu Yilma, Ayyalew Mitiku, et al. (1992/93). Ongota or Birale: A moribund language of Gemu-Gofa (Ethiopia). *Journal of Afroasiatic Languages* 3/3: 181–225.

Fleming, Harold C. (2006). *Ongota: A decisive language in Africa prehistory*. Wiesbaden: Harrassowitz.

Freeman, Dena, and Alula Pankhurst (eds.). (2001). *Living on the edge: Marginalised minorities of craftworkers and hunters in southern Ethiopia*. Addis Ababa: Addis Ababa University, Department of Sociology and Social Administration.

Güldemann, Tom, and Rainer Voßen. (2000). Khoisan. In Bernd Heine and Derek Nurse (eds.), *African languages: An introduction*. Cambridge: Cambridge University Press, 99–122.

Heine, Bernd. (1977). Bemerkungen zur Boni-Sprache (Kenia). *Afrika und Übersee* 60: 242–295.

Lydall, Jean, and Ivo Strecker. (1979). *The Hamar of southern Ethiopia. I: Work journal*. Hohenschaftlarn: Klaus Renner Verlag.

Maddieson, Ian, Siniša Spajić, Bonny Sands, and Peter Ladefoged. (1993). Phonetic structures of Dahalo. *Afrikanistische Arbeitspapiere* 36: 5–53.

Melesse Getu. (1997). Local versus outsider forms of natural resources use and management: The Tsamako experience in South-West Ethiopia. In Katsuyoshi Fukui, Eisei Kurimoto, and Masayoshi Shigeta (eds.), *Ethiopia in broader perspective: Papers of the Thirteenth International Conference of Ethiopian Studies (ICES XIII), Kyoto, 12–17 December 1997. Vol. 2*. Kyoto: Shokado, 748–767.

Nurse, Derek. (1986). Reconstruction of Dahalo history through evidence from loanwords. *Sprache und Geschichte in Afrika* 7(2): 267–305.

Savà, Graziano. (2002). Ts'amakko morphological borrowings in Ongota (or Birale). In Christian Rapold and Graziano Savà (eds.), *Proceeding of the 1st International Symposium Ethiopian Morphosyntax in an Areal Perspective. Afrikanistische Arbeitspapiere* 71: 75–93.

(2005). *A grammar of Ts'amakko*. Köln: Köppe.

(2010). The Ongota: A branch of Maale? Ethnographic, historic and linguistic traces of contact of the Ongota people. In Echi Gabbert and Sophia Thubauville (eds.), *To live with others: Essays on cultural neighbourhood in southern Ethiopia*. Köln: Köppe, 213–235.

Savà, Graziano, and Mauro Tosco. (2000). A sketch of Ongota, a dying language of southwest Ethiopia. *Studies in African Linguistics* 29(2): 59–134.

(2003). The classification of Ongota. In M. Lionel Bender, Gabor Takács, and David Appleyard (eds.), *Selected comparative-historical Afrasian linguistic studies in memory of Igor M. Diakonoff.* München: Lincom Europa, 307–316.

(2007). Review article of Fleming (2006). *Aethiopica* 10: 223–232.

Sobania, Neal W. (1980). The historical tradition of the peoples of the Eastern Lake Turkana Basin c. 1840–1925. Unpublished Ph.D. dissertation, University of London, S.O.A.S.

Stiles, Daniel. (1988). Historical interrelationships of the Boni with pastoral peoples of Somalia and Kenya. *Kenya Past and Present* 20: 38–45.

Tosco, Mauro. (1991). *A grammatical sketch of Dahalo, including texts and a glossary.* Hamburg: Buske.

(1992). Dahalo: An endangered language. In Matthias Brenzinger (ed.), *Language death: Factual and theoretical explorations.* Berlin: Mouton de Gruyter, 137–155.

(1994). The historical reconstruction of a southern Somali dialect: Proto-Karre-Boni. *Sprache und Geschichte in Afrika* 15: 153–209.

(1998). "People who are not the language they speak:" On language shift without language decay in East Africa. In Matthias Brenzinger (ed.), *Endangered languages in Africa.* Köln: Köppe, 119–142.

(2007). Something went wrong: On the historical reconstruction of the Dhaasanac verb. In Rainer Voigt (ed.), *From beyond the Mediterranean. Akten des 7. internationalen Semitohamitistenkongresses (VII. ISHaK), Berlin 13. bis 15. September 2004.* Aachen: Shaker, 265–280.

6 Changing Profile When Encroaching on Forager Territory

Toward the History of the Khoe-Kwadi Family in Southern Africa

Tom Güldemann

6.1 Introduction

The history of southern African languages subsumed under "Khoisan" has been subject to a great deal of speculation, which has stemmed in large part from our ignorance about them. In the last two decades, however, our knowledge has grown considerably and a number of earlier views turned out to be misconceptions or at least weak and premature hypotheses, among them the idea of a Macro-Khoisan family. Nevertheless, some insufficiently substantiated claims are still held as conventional wisdom in and outside the field.

This chapter will discuss the linguistic history of the largest lineage subsumed under "Khoisan," the Khoe-Kwadi family, and in so doing will address two frequently encountered assumptions in this research area: (1) that all "Khoisan" lineages in southern Africa are indigenous to the region and (2) that they have always been associated with a forager subsistence. I will present linguistic data relating to these issues and argue instead on account of this and nonlinguistic evidence that the ancestor population giving rise to modern Khoe-Kwadi speaking groups colonized southern Africa relatively recently, and introduced a pastoral mode of life. The extent of diversity found among modern Khoe-Kwadi speakers in terms of linguistic, cultural, and biological traits can be explained as the result of different types of contact with the forager populations that were at the time indigenous to the area. This chapter supplements Güldemann (2008a), addressing in more detail the nonlinguistic aspects of the topic.

I will give a general overview over the non-Bantu languages of southern Africa in Section 6.2 in terms of their genealogical and typological

I am grateful for helpful comments on an earlier draft of this article by Hirosi Nakagawa, Bonny Sands, and Andrew B. Smith. Linguistic abbreviations used are: c, consonant; DIM, diminutive; F, feminine; I, inclusive; IRR, irrealis; INTENS, intensifier; N, nasal; P, plural; S, singular; V, vowel.

classification. On this basis I will go on to discuss in Section 6.3 the linguistic history of the Khoe-Kwadi family, arguing that the available data point to a scenario that is at variance with most previous accounts of the early history of the relevant languages. Section 6.4 will evaluate the hypotheses arrived at on the basis of purely linguistic data in the light of nonlinguistic information about the different modern Khoe-Kwadi speaking groups as well general facts concerning population dynamics in southern Africa.

6.2   The Non-Bantu Languages of Southern Africa

Southern African population history, if viewed from a purely linguistic per-spective, seemed to be a relatively straightforward matter until fairly recently. According to the widely accepted genealogical classification of African lan-guages by Greenberg (1963), only three independent linguistic layers had to be reckoned with: first, the oldest family in the region called "Khoisan"; second, the Bantu family (of the Niger-Kordofanian supergroup), which encroached on the area since ca. 2,000 years BP; and third, a few Indo-European languages such as Portuguese, Dutch, and English, which are associated with European colonization.

Specialists on the indigenous non-Bantu languages have, however, cast doubt on such a simple scenario, because they do not support Greenberg's (1963) classification hypotheses. Neither "Khoisan," which comprises all African click languages other than from Bantu and Cushitic, nor the narrow entity "South African Khoisan" is firmly supported by specialists (see, e.g., Westphal 1971; Traill 1986; Sands 1998; Güldemann 2008b). While "Khoisan" must not be treated as a genealogical unit, more reliable research within the historical-comparative method has established three coherent lineages in southern Africa: Khoe (a.k.a. "Central Khoisan"; see Voßen 1997), Ju (a.k.a. "Northern Khoisan"; see Snyman 1997; Sands 2010), and Tuu (a.k.a. "Southern Khoisan"; see Hastings 2001; Güldemann 2005). First work on higher-order affiliations strongly suggests that two languages not yet considered at the time of Greenberg can be affiliated to these units, leading to two bigger families, Khoe-Kwadi on the one hand (see Güldemann 2004b; Güldemann and Elderkin 2010) and Kx'a on the other hand (see Sands 2010; Heine and Honken 2010). There is even a promising hypothesis about a genealogical relation between Khoe–Kwadi in southern Africa and Sandawe in eastern Africa (see Elderkin 1986; Güldemann and Elderkin 2010).

Hence, whatever future research on southern African non-Bantu languages might reveal, for the time being it is safest to consider no fewer than three independent lineages; they are outlined in Table 6.1 and their approximate distribution is shown in Map 6.1.

Table 6.1 *Independent non-Bantu lineages in southern Africa and internal classification*

Lineages and Branches	Language(s) or Dialects
(1) Khoe-Kwadi	
Kwadi	Single language†
Khoe	
Kalahari	
East	
Shua	Cara, Deti†, ǀXaise, Danisi, etc.
Tshwa	Kua, Cua, Tsua, etc.
West	
Kxoe	Khwe, ǀAni, etc.
Gǀana	Gǀana, Gǀui, etc.
Naro	Naro, Ts'ao, etc.
Khoekhoe	Cape varieties†; !Ora†; Eini†; Nama-Damara; Haiǀom; ǂAakhoe
(2) Kx'a	
Ju (DC)	!Xuun, Juǀ'hoan, etc.
ǂ'Amkoe (DC)	ǂHoan, Sasi, etc.
(3) Tuu	
Taa-Lower Nossob	
Taa (DC)	West !Xoon, 'Nǀoha, East !Xoon, etc.
Lower Nossob	ǀ'Auni†, ǀHaasi†
!Ui	Nǁng (DC); ǂUngkue†; ǀXam† (DC); ǁXegwi†

From a typological perspective, all southern African non-Bantu languages share several diagnostic features and can be grouped together against other languages in Africa and partly on the globe (Güldemann 2013b). Linguistic commonalities across the different lineages are, for example:

(a) phonemic clicks as the backbone of the consonant systems
(b) strongly preferred phonotactic pattern of stems c(c)vcv, or derived c(c)vv and c(c)vn with strong consonants and consonant clusters in the initial c-position
(c) register tone systems different from pitch-accent systems in Bantu
(d) mostly host-final morphology
(e) head-final genitive irrespective of word order elsewhere in clauses and noun phrases
(f) grammatically productive noun compounding, development of nominal suffixes

These and presumably other features are most plausibly interpreted as the reflex of a pre-Bantu linguistic area called by Güldemann (1998) "Kalahari

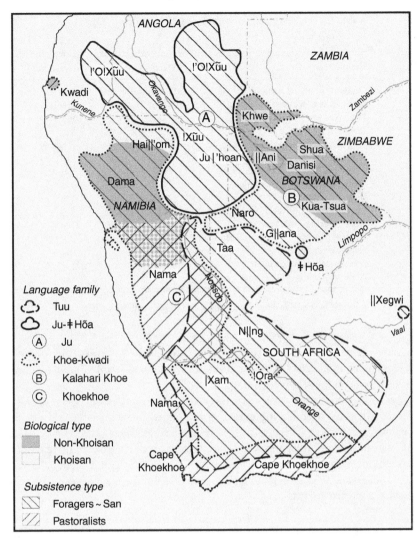

Map 6.1 Non-Bantu populations in southern Africa.

Basin"; this scenario implies a very different conceptualization of what is commonly called "South African Khoisan."

At the same time, there are also considerable differences between the relevant languages. Most importantly, there is a major typological split separating the Khoe-Kwadi family from the other two lineages, Kx'a and Tuu, which

Table 6.2 *Typological comparison between Khoe-Kwadi and Non-Khoe*

Feature	Khoe-Kwadi	Non-Khoe
Object position vis-à-vis verb	Object-verb	Verb-object
Verb position in clause	Final	Medial
Head position in noun phrase	Final	Initial
Preposition	No	Yes
Alignment in pronouns	Accusative	Neutral
Default relational gram	No[a]	Yes
Verb serialization without linker	No	Yes
Verb compounding without linker	No[a]	Yes
Verb derivation	Yes	No
First-person inclusive	No[a]	Yes
Sex gender	Yes	No
Ratio of gender-class vs. agreement-class	< 1	≥ 1
Number marking on noun	Regular	Irregular
Number categories on noun	3	2
Number-sensitive stem suppletion	No	Yes

[a] present in some languages due to language contact with Non-Khoe.

I have previously subsumed under the convenient term "Non-Khoe" (Güldemann 1998, 2013b). Table 6.2 displays a considerable list of features that distinguish the two groups in question.

From a continental perspective there is more to say about Khoe-Kwadi, namely that its overall typological profile shows an exclusive affinity to languages in eastern Africa, as argued by Heine and Voßen (1981) on account of head-final word order, sex gender systems, accusative case alignment, and systems of suffixing verb derivation, and reiterated by Güldemann (2013b). This observation is a first indication that this family may have originated outside southern Africa.

6.3   Linguistic Clues to Early Khoe-Kwadi History

After giving a general outline of the genealogical and typological classification of the non-Bantu languages in southern Africa, I turn to the history of the Khoe-Kwadi family in more detail. As indicated earlier, I argue that this lineage reflects a later layer of colonization in southern Africa and that this expanding population is likely to not have been characterized by a foraging subsistence. What I need to show then is how the modern Khoe-Kwadi speaking groups reached their present location and how they acquired in different ways a number of features – linguistic, cultural, and biological – that make them more or less similar to other clearly indigenous forager groups speaking Non-Khoe languages from Tuu and Kx'a. I will start the historical reconstruction with a discussion of the linguistic data and then go on with a demonstration that individual population profiles and historical scenarios proposed on purely linguistic grounds are largely compatible with the known nonlinguistic facts.

Khoe languages in particular are well known for their complex and unique system of person-gender-number marking and the historical evaluation of this shared feature will play a central role in the following argument. Previous research tended to attribute its most complex manifestations in the modern languages to the oldest proto-stage (Voßen 1997). Central to the present approach is a different hypothesis, viz. that this domain has arguably undergone a gradual restructuring in several steps from a relatively simple stage to more and more complex systems. The data on person-gender-number marking will be accompanied by additional data from lexical comparisons and reconstructions that inform and illuminate the general scenario. As this linguistic argument has been, or is in the process of being, published (Güldemann 2002, 2004a, 2004b, 2006a, 2008a, in press; Güldemann and Elderkin 2010), I only repeat here the central facts, and the reader is referred to the relevant works for more detail. The approach taken here is to work from the most recent events back to earlier processes of change. That is, like peeling an onion, I will try to take off one historical layer after the other in order to arrive at the earliest reachable language state and its likely historical-geographical setting.

6.3.1 From Pre-Khoekhoe to Proto-Khoekhoe

One of the later changes experienced by a Khoe-Kwadi speaking group occurred in the wider Cape region concerning the Khoekhoe branch of Khoe. That is, Güldemann (2006a) argues that the distinct linguistic character of Khoekhoe vis-à-vis its sister branch, Kalahari Khoe, has a likely explanation in terms of a strong substrate of the Tuu family (particularly its !Ui branch), which is older in the area and in whose territory Khoekhoe was entirely included geographically before some groups ventured north and entered Namibia. Under this view, Proto-Khoekhoe is the result of contact of a Pre-Khoekhoe population with the indigenous forager languages of the southernmost region of the wider area.

As mentioned earlier, this general hypothesis can among other things be illustrated with innovations in the system of person-gender-number markers and other pronominal elements (see Güldemann [2002] for a detailed discussion).

Table 6.3 displays the independent pronouns of !Ora, which possesses the most complex system in the entire family. It can be seen that the markers in !Ora,

Table 6.3 *The system of independent complex pronouns in !Ora (Khoekhoe, Khoe)*

Person	Gender						Number
	Common		Feminine		Masculine		
First person			*ti*	*-ta*	*ti*	*-re*	Singular
Second person			*sa*	*-s*	*sa*	*-ts*	
Third person	*ǁ'ãi*	*-'i*	*ǁ'ãi*	*-s*	*ǁ'ãi*	*-b*	
First-person exclusive	*si*	*-m*	*si*	*-sam*	*si*	*-kham*	Dual
First person inclusive	*sa*	*-m*	*sa*	*-sam*	*sa*	*-kham*	
Second person	*sa*	*-khao*	*sa*	*-saro*	*sa*	*-kharo*	
Third person	*ǁ'ãi*	*-kha*	*ǁ'ãi*	*-sara*	*ǁ'ãi*	*-khara*	
First-person exclusive	*si*	*-da*	*si*	*-sē*	*si*	*-tjē*	Plural
First-person inclusive	*sa*	*-da*	*sa*	*-sē*	*sa*	*-tjē*	
Second person	*sa*	*-du*	*sa*	*-sao*	*sa*	*-kao*	
Third person	*ǁ'ãi*	*-n*	*ǁ'ãi*	*-dē*	*ǁ'ãi*	*-ku*	

Bolded: innovation due to Tuu substrate.

as in other Khoekhoe varieties, are morphologically composed of two elements, a set of initial pronominal stems as the base and a set of final grams that are commonly known as PGNs (from "person-gender-number" marker). The very existence of such an elaborate inventory of complex pronouns can be related to local language contact, because the potential substrate languages display productive pronoun modification and hence a tendency to form morphosyntactically complex pronominal expressions (Güldemann 2004a).

When compared to less complex pronominal systems in other Khoe languages two elements in Proto-Khoekhoe cannot be explained by family-internal developments, namely the third-person pronoun base *ǁ'ãi and the first-person exclusive pronoun base *si (boldfaced in Table 6.3). There is, however, a good explanation in terms of language contact: *ǁ'ãi is a grammaticalized instance of an intensifier "self(same)" that is ultimately a loan related to an element of this form and function in !Ui varieties; *si in turn is a borrowing of the Proto-Tuu first-person exclusive pronoun (the elements are illustrated by data from ǀXam and boldfaced in Example 6.1 and Table 6.4, respectively).

Example 6.1

(1) ǀXam (!Ui, Tuu)

   i   *se*   *ǁẽ:i*   *i*   *ǀa*   *ǁk"oen*   (*ǁẽ:i* = [ǁ'ãi])

   1P.I   IRR   INTENS   1P.I   go   look

   ... that we might ourselves go to look. (Bleek 1956: 520)

Table 6.4 *The system of pronouns for participants in ǀXam (ǃUi, Tuu)*

Person	Singular	Plural
First-person inclusive		*i*
First-person exclusive	*ng*	*si*
Second person	*a*	*u*

Bolded: borrowed into Khoekhoe.

A larger set of structural features in Khoekhoe (particularly North Khoekhoe) that I have proposed (Güldemann 2006a) to be induced by Tuu substrate interference is given in the following list (the features under (c), (e), and (h) involve most of the exceptions indicated in Table 6.1 vis-à-vis the general trend in the Khoe-Kwadi family):

(a) comparably small size of consonant inventory, but high phonological load on clicks
(b) lenition of complex egressive stops, loss of velar (affricate) ejective /kx'/
(c) syntactically, rather than semantically triggered marking of participants
(d) similar semantics, morph type, and position of grams marking tense and aspect
(e) lexically complex predicates without segmental linker
(f) clausal pronoun pivot
(g) declarative marker
(h) complex pronouns and inclusive/exclusive distinction (see earlier)

6.3.2   From Pre-Khoe to Proto-Khoe

Another major but earlier historical change to be explained concerning the Khoe-Kwadi family is the emergence of Khoe itself. Connected to this is the development of the elaborate paradigm of PGNs. These were seen in Table 6.3 as the suffixed elements of complex Khoekhoe pronouns, but have a far wider morphosyntactic distribution in Khoe languages as a whole and can be reconstructed as shown in Table 6.5.

As such a system did not characterize the ancestor language Proto-Khoe-Kwadi (see Section 6.3.3), it is necessary to propose a plausible scenario how it emerged from a simpler system in the past, as undertaken by Güldemann (2004b; in press). The major change in the overall process is again the creation of an earlier set of bimorphemic pronominal forms (all duals and first- and second-person plurals in Table 6.5). The dual series in *kho are assumed to be based on a reconstructable noun stem

Table 6.5 *The system of person-gender-number markers in Proto-Khoe*

	Gender			
Person	Common	Feminine	Masculine	Number
First	*ti, *ta			Singular
Second		*sa	*tsa	
Third		*si	*bi	
First	*(kho) -m(u)	*sa -m(u)	*kho -m(u)	Dual
Second	*(kho) -da-o	*sa -da-o	*kho -da-o	
Third	*(kho) -da	*sa -da	*kho -da	
First	*ta -e	*sa -e	*!a -e	Plural
Second	*ta -o	*sa -o	*!a -o	
Third	*nV	*di	*!a -u (> *!u)	

Table 6.6 *The assumed system of pronouns in later Pre-Khoe*

Person	Singular	Plural	Dual
First person	*ti, *ta	*e -!a-e	*(?) -mu
Second person	*sa	*o -!a-o	*o -da-o
Third-person masculine	stem -*(?)-V [front]	stem -*!a-u	*kho -da
Third-person feminine	stem -*sV [front]	stem -**di**	stem -*da

Bolded: innovation due to Kx'a substrate.

"person." The feminine and common forms with the items *ta and *sa (underlined in Table 6.5) are thought to have arisen through analogy from the other complex forms in *kho and *!a in that the initial bases targeted first-person common singular *ta and second-person feminine singular *sa. If one takes away these more recent innovations, one can arguably arrive at a pronoun system similar to that in Table 6.6, which marked gender only in third-person forms.

The full set of changes implied when relating the different systems of Tables 6.5 and 6.6 are outlined in detail by Güldemann (in press). The crucial point in this context is that there are only three elements in the entire paradigm without a family-internal derivation (boldfaced in Table 6.6): first-person plural *e, nonfeminine plural *!a, and third-person feminine plural *di. This is where the second hypothesis about a contact-induced linguistic layer comes into play. I propose that Pre-Khoe spoken further north in southern Africa and encroaching onto the Kalahari Basin integrated

Table 6.7 *The system of pronouns for participants and gender I in Juǀ'hoan (Ju, Kx'a)*

Person	Singular	Plural	Dual
First-person inclusive		*m (ǃá)*	*m (tsá)*
First-person exclusive	*mí*	*è (ǃá)*	*è (tsá)*
Second person	*à*	*ì (ǃá)*	*ì (tsá)*
Third-person human gender I	*ha*	*sì (ǃá)*	*sá*

Parentheses denote optional, but frequent number-specifying modifiers.

a yet earlier input from language contact with local forager groups affiliated with the Kx'a family.

Owing to the phenomenon of pronoun modification that also exists in this family, particularly regarding the feature of number, the contact caused, among other things, the elaboration of PGN marking toward a system with differentiated dual and plural forms in Proto-Khoe. The hypothesis that this was accompanied by the integration of borrowed linguistic material is based on the observation that the assumed substrate languages show markers that are comparable in form and function with the relevant items in Pre- and Proto-Khoe. Compare in this respect Table 6.7 and Example 6.2, which figure the boldfaced elements first-person *e*, plural *ǃa*, and feminine *di* in Juǀ'hoan.

Example 6.2

(2) Juǀ'hoan (Ju, Kx'a)
    *ha-**di***   *ha-ma*   *ha-**di**-ma*
    1-F   1-DIM.S   1-F-DIM.S
    the female one the small one the small female one
                                      (From Güldemann field notes)

6.3.3   Proto-Khoe-Kwadi

A third important point regarding the linguistic history of Khoe-Kwadi is the justification for establishing this family in the first place. While the hypothesis about a genealogical relation between the Khoe family and Kwadi (also known under Kwepe and Kuroka) had been expressed for some time (e.g., Köhler 1981: 469), it was only through a more detailed analysis of Westphal's field notes on Kwadi and its comparison with Voßen's (1997) thorough Proto-Khoe reconstruction that this hypothesis could be substantiated empirically.

Güldemann (2004b) proposed a pronominal proto-system of the minimal-augmented type, based on numerous commonalities of Proto-Khoe and Kwadi

Table 6.8 *The system of pronouns in Proto-Khoe-Kwadi*

Person		−Augmented (or Minimal)	+Augmented
+Speaker/+Hearer	= First + second-person inclusive	*mu	(?)
+Speaker/−Hearer	= First person exclusive	*ti, *ta	(?)
−Speaker/+Hearer	= Second person	*sa	*o or u
−Speaker/−Hearer	= Third person masculine	*stem†-(?)V [front] ‡	*stem†-(?)u ‡
−Speaker/−Hearer	= Third person feminine	*stem†-sV [front] ‡	*stem†-(?)V [front] ‡

(?) without plausible reflex in both Khoe and Kwadi; † elements like deictic *xa (Kalahari Khoe) or generic noun *kho; ‡ also used as gender-number index on nouns.

Table 6.9 *The system of pronouns in Kwadi*

Person	−Augmented or Singular	+Augmented or Plural	Dual
First- + second-person inclusive	(*h*)a-**mu**	(*h*)ina	(*h*)a-**mu**
First-person exclusive	t/i, ta	ala	—
Second person	sa	u	u-wa
Third-person masculine	ha-dɛ	ha-u	ha-wa
Third-person feminine	hɛɛ (< ha-e)	ha-'ɛ	ha-wa

Bolded: Assumed reflexes in Khoe.

in the marking of person, gender, and number. This reconstruction is reproduced in Table 6.8.

It can be seen that this system is quite comparable to that proposed for Pre-Khoe in Table 6.6 of Section 6.3.2 in terms of its structure and the form of the markers, involving half a dozen elements and the vocalic canon in the third-person non-duals (boldfaced in Table 6.8). The major difference is that the Pre-Khoe paradigm would have changed already from the minimal-augmented system reconstructed in Table 6.8 to one with a genuine category of dual, exploiting the inherited first-person dual inclusive *mu and a suffix *da for second and third persons.

Table 6.9 shows the reported pronoun system of Kwadi; it is similar to that of Pre-Khoe in Table 6.6 and of Proto-Khoe-Kwadi in Table 6.8 regarding the markers (boldfaced in the table) as well as their categorial organization. As there are two duals formed by the suffix -wa in addition to the first-person dual inclusive (*h*)amu, the system can be analyzed as still being on the threshold from a minimal-augmented one to one with three number categories: singular, dual, and plural. Note that the functionally identical elements *da of Proto-Khoe and -wa of Kwadi are arguably cognate.

Table 6.10 *Selected lexical correspondences between Kwadi and Khoe*

Kwadi	Proto-Khoe (unless otherwise stated)
goe- 'cow, cattle'	*goe 'cow, cattle' (Kalahari West)
guu- 'sheep'	*gu 'sheep'
ha 'to come'	*ha 'to come'
pa- 'to bite'	*pa 'to bite'
pi-/ bi- 'milk, breast'	*pi 'milk, breast'
kho- 'person'	*khoe 'person'
kõ 'to go'	*!ũ, *kũ 'to go' (Kalahari East)
kuli- 'year'	*kudi, also kuri 'year'
kum (also *kũŋ*) 'to hear'	*kum 'to hear' (Kalahari)
kxo- 'skin, fur'	*kho, also kxo 'skin, fur'
kx'a 'to drink'	*kx'a 'to drink'
kx'ami- 'mouth'	*kx'am 'mouth'
k"o- [= /kx'o/] 'male'	*kx'ao 'male'
k"o- [= /kx'o/] 'meat'	*kx'o 'to eat (meat)'
mh(u) 'to smell'	*mm (Kalahari), *ham (Khoekhoe) 'to smell'
se 'to grasp, take'	*se 'to grasp, take'
so- 'medicine'	*tso, *so 'medicine' (Khoekhoe)
tame- 'tongue'	*dam 'tongue'
tumu- 'throat', also 'to swallow'	*dom 'throat'
thõ, thũ 'illness'	*thũ 'pain'
thwii [< /thu-/] 'night'	*thu 'night'
ǀui 'one'	*ǀui 'one'
ǀ'o- 'blood'	*ǀ'ao 'blood'

The genealogical hypothesis of a Khoe-Kwadi family is based not only on this grammatical evidence. Güldemann and Elderkin (2010) give additional support from lexical data. Table 6.10 illustrates this point with a list of selected and fairly straightforward correspondences in basic vocabulary items.

6.3.4   Toward the External Genealogical Relationship of Khoe-Kwadi

The linguistic evidence regarding the history of the Khoe-Kwadi family has not yet been exhausted. Several authors, in particular Elderkin (1986, 1989), have raised the question about a possible genealogical relation between the Khoe family in the south and the isolate language Sandawe in eastern Africa; if Khoe is a branch of the larger family Khoe-Kwadi, this hypothesis must, of course, involve this older lineage. In any case, its relevance for the present topic should be clear: if one group of the non-Bantu languages of southern Africa turns out to have a relative in far eastern Africa, the traditional assumption that all these languages share the same time depth in the area can no longer be maintained.

I have already pointed out in Section 6.2 that there is indeed a clear typological affinity of Khoe-Kwadi to languages in eastern Africa. Moreover, Güldemann (1999) has argued that shared diagnostic traits in word order and sound structure can even be identified in some geographically intervening Bantu languages that then deviate from the general trend in this family. This observation points toward the existence of a Pre-Bantu substrate that once bridged the synchronic geographical gap between Khoe-Kwadi and Sandawe.

Once the modern linguistic patterns in Khoe are seen as the potential result of innovation within the new areal context of southern Africa, the focus of investigation would have to shift toward the older structures in Proto-Khoe-Kwadi. And indeed, the pronoun systems involved under this approach reveal a closer relationship to Sandawe than would have been possible in a direct comparison of Sandawe and Proto-Khoe. This has been discussed by Güldemann and Elderkin (2010).

Table 6.11 gives the pronoun system of Sandawe, which displays a structural similarity to that of Proto-Khoe-Kwadi in Table 6.8 as well as several potential cognates (boldfaced in Table 6.11). These data do not yet prove a genealogical relationship, but they are concrete and thus more promising evidence than that which has hitherto been invoked for an alleged "Khoisan" family as a whole.

Comparing vocabulary among Sandawe, Kwadi, and Khoe also yields an ambiguous picture, which is complicated by the very limited material available for Kwadi. Surely, there are salient differences in lexical structure, but remarkably not necessarily between Sandawe and Kwadi. For example, it is rather Sandawe and Kwadi together that show a relatively low proportion of click words in the lexicon and thus differ from the Khoe family, which overall shows a considerably higher amount of such lexemes (in many languages more than 50 percent). Also, the typical southern African phonotactic root pattern (see

Table 6.11 *The system of Sandawe pronouns*

Person	Singular	Plural
First person	*tsi*	*sũ:*
Second person	*hapu*	*sĩ:*
Third-person masculine	*he-we*	*he-so*
Third-person feminine	*he-su*	*he-so*

Bolded: Assumed reflexes in Khoe-Kwadi.

Table 6.12 *Potential cognates between Sandawe and Khoe involving clicks*

Sandawe	Proto-Khoe (unless otherwise stated)
kéké 'ear'	*ǂàé 'ear'
kṹ: 'red hot coals'	*ǂòm̀ (*ǂùm̀) 'charcoal'
tlíné 'to build'	*ǁaũ 'to fence'
tlôkù̧ (*-kù̧* causative) 'to pour'	*ǁóé 'to lie down'
ǀ'ã̂:kí 'to fight'	*ǀ'ãã̂ 'to fight'
ǀ'íné 'to be ripe'	*ǀ'ání 'to ripen'
ǀ'ô 'to sleep'	*ǀ'óm̀ 'to sleep'
ǃŏ: 'to get', *ǃŏ:kí* 'to meet'	*ǃóá 'to meet' (NKk+N)
ǃó:mé 'to fill'	*ǃóm̀ '(to be) heavy'
ǃwǎ: 'place, opportunity'	*ǃˣáì 'place, matter' (NKk+N)
ǀă: 'leaf'	*glana * glãã̂, 'leaf, grass'
ǀã̂:tímà 'fly (musca)'	*glani 'fly'
ǁèẃ 'buffalo'	*ǁáò 'buffalo'
ǀwê: 'eye'	*ǂˣáí 'eye, (to wake up)'
ǀ'ã̂:kị̧: 'above'	*ǂ'ám̀(ki) 'top (of)'
ǀ'ĕ: 'to see'	*ǂ'áń 'to know'

Ka = Kalahari Khoe; N = Naro; (N)Kk = (Namibian) Khoekhoe.

Section 6.2) can be reconstructed to Proto-Khoe, while it is not attested in this strict form in Sandawe. Kwadi also deviates in this respect; but this fact is hard to interpret, because it could reflect an older situation or be the result of language contact and death.

Nevertheless, Tables 6.12 and 6.13 demonstrate that there also exist lexical affinities between Sandawe in eastern Africa and Khoe-Kwadi in southern Africa (see Güldemann and Elderkin [2010] for further discussion).

Table 6.12 shows probable correspondences between words involving clicks between Sandawe and Proto-Khoe; given the very restricted click inventory of Kwadi (Güldemann 2013a), it should not come as a surprise that this language is hardly ever involved in potential correspondences of this kind. In the comparisons of words without clicks given in Table 6.13 Kwadi does, however, show good candidates for cognates and some items link in fact all three units.

The pattern of a relatively higher amount of shared words without clicks may not be coincidental: under the hypothesis of a strong Kx'a substrate in Pre-Khoe (see Section 6.3.2), it can be hypothesized that this contact situation is also responsible for an increase in click words that then could not be reconstructed back to Proto-Khoe-Kwadi. Different lexical loan strata in Khoe languages, first from Kx'a and later from Tuu, compounded by the problem of historically younger, but geographically widespread borrowing from

Table 6.13 *Potential cognates between Sandawe, Kwadi, and Khoe not involving clicks*

Sandawe	Kwadi	Proto-Khoe (unless otherwise stated)
hàká 'four'		*haka 'four'
hàwé 'to draw water'		*hàdè 'to fetch (water), pick'
hìmé 'to smell'	*mh(u)* 'to smell'	*mm (Ka),*ham (Kk) 'to smell'
k'é: 'to cry'		*kx'àí 'to cry'
k'úts^hè 'raw'		***kx'òrà** 'raw' (NKk+N)
k'àwà?é 'ferment, turn sour'		*kx'àú 'bitter'
pĕ: 'to put (singular object)'	*pɛ* 'to put'	
síé 'to take'	*se* 'to take'	*séè 'to take, grasp' (Ka)
tím 'to swallow'	*tumu* 'to swallow, throat'	*tóm̀ 'to swallow'
t^hŭ: 'darkness'	*thwii* (< /thu-/) 'night'	*t^hùú 'night'
t^hìm 'to cook'	*sẽ* (also *Ɵẽ*) 'to cook'	*tsã̂(i) 'to cook' (Ka)
t^hĕ: 'tree'	*tʃhi-* 'tree'	
ts^hô 'excrement'		*tsuu 'excrement'
tsĕ: 'head'	*tshẽ* 'head'	

Ka = Kalahari Khoe; N = Naro; (N)Kk = (Namibian) Khoekhoe.

prestigious Khoekhoe varieties into many forager languages, might in fact account largely for the vocabulary that is shared across southern African non-Bantu languages. While these have traditionally been invoked as evidence for "Khoisan" as a language family, they could turn out to reflect different layers of contact phenomena among the three linguistic lineages involved. A first exploration of "Pan-Khoisan" vocabulary in the domain of body parts by Güldemann and Loughnane (2012) is fully compatible with this line of thinking.

6.3.5 *Linguistic Evidence for the Reconstruction of Proto-Khoe-Kwadi Culture*

Lexical data also throw light on another question, namely which cultural type most likely characterized the population that spoke the earliest reconstructed language state of the Khoe-Kwadi family. The most common current assumption is that all southern African non-Bantu lineages are originally associated with a foraging subsistence and only a small group at the northern fringe of the Kalahari Basin, the ancestors of the Khoekhoe, adopted a pastoral mode of life through contact with another population colonizing the wider area from the north (Elphick 1977; Ehret 1982, 1998: 82–5, 212–22).

Table 6.14 *Proto-Khoe reconstructions atypical for a foraging subsistence*

Form	Meaning	Page number in Voßen (1997)
*nǃubu	'to churn, (shake)'	427
*ǀãu	'to fence in'	430
*ǀkx'ao ~ *ts'ao	'to milk in container'	466
*gu	'sheep'	483
*ǀ'an(i)	'to dwell, build'	508

The first important point is that the Kwadi, whose language appears to be close to Proto-Khoe-Kwadi and thus the most conservative in the family, are reported to have possessed a culture involving animal husbandry (Estermann 1959; Guerreiro 1971). This cannot be reconciled easily with a generalized foraging origin of Khoe-Kwadi speakers, unless one assumes again the same scenario of a cultural shift.

What then about Proto-Khoe culture? The primary data source to address this question from a linguistic angle is Voßen's (1997) extensive reconstructions involving several hundred lexical items (Voßen 2007 is a more recent summary of the lexical domain at issue here). Tables 6.14 and 6.15 show that these data cast doubt on the assumption that Proto-Khoe speakers pursued a stone-age foraging subsistence; they suggest instead a food-producing culture. While the linguistic facts have been known for a long time (cf. Voßen 1984; Köhler 1986), their implications for a general historical reconstruction have never been taken into account appropriately.

Table 6.14 shows that Proto-Khoe speakers – not just the Khoekhoe pastoralists in the Cape and their direct ancestors – are likely to have had a partly sedentary life style and been familiar with domesticated animals, just like the Kwadi. Given that there is only a proto-form for "sheep," but not for "cattle" (see Voßen 1997: 478), animal husbandry seems to have been based on small stock.

Sets of lexical proto-forms that are atypical for an ancient stone-age culture, but confined to individual Khoe subgroups, are possibly even more significant. While such proto-forms as *ǃhana "field, garden" and *ǃhada "(cattle) kraal" (Voßen 1997: 434, 503) may not be too surprising for Khoekhoe pastoralists, those restricted to Kalahari Khoe as displayed in Table 6.15 are quite unexpected, because the relevant groups are today all characterized by a predominantly foraging subsistence. This reiterates the apparent contradiction between historical linguistic data and modern facts from cultural anthropology.

Given that some lexical reconstructions in Table 6.15 even indicate a form of small scale agriculture, it is also significant that Köhler (1986)

Table 6.15 *Proto-Kalahari Khoe reconstructions atypical for a foraging subsistence*

Form	Meaning	Page number in Voßen (1997)
*kom(a)	'bellows' (Kxoe and Shua)	424
*ǀhada	'field, garden'	434
*ǀhao	'hoe, (plough)/ to plough'	446
*tsxom	'to milk in the mouth'	466
*kada	'kraal'	503
*ǁ'ae	'settlement'	508

shows the Kalahari Khoe language Kxoe to possess a considerable compo-nent of agricultural vocabulary that cannot be explained by borrowing from Bantu. As Bantu is widely associated with the introduction of agriculture to the area, the relevant terms in Kalahari Khoe, some of them with clicks, must even more raise the suspicion about a pre-Bantu population with food production.

6.4   Toward a History of the Khoe-Kwadi Family

6.4.1   *The General Population Profile of Non-Bantu Language Groups in Southern Africa*

I have presented in Section 6.3 linguistic evidence that suggests several important points regarding the history of the largest southern African lan-guage family subsumed under "Khoisan." First, it is possible to identify several historical layers in the development of person-gender-number mark-ing. These layers correlate with a geographical pattern: the more a linguistic subgroup deviates from the most conservative language state of Khoe-Kwadi the further south it is located. This observation can in turn be related to proposed situations of contact with indigenous languages of the respec-tive areas, namely Kx'a in the north and center of the Kalahari Basin and Tuu in its southern parts up to the southern tip of the continent. Second, Khoe-Kwadi has a clear linguistic leaning to eastern Africa from a typological and possibly even genealogical perspective. Third and finally, the linguistic reflexes of the earlier language states of the family do not necessarily indicate an origin in a pristine forager population, but could well have been associated with a food-producing subsistence. In the following I will relate these linguistic findings to facts concerning the nonlinguistic popula-tion profile of the relevant southern African groups and some other aspects of the early history of the area.

The first step to this end is a brief nonlinguistic characterization of the peoples speaking Non-Khoe languages. In Section 6.2 I have mentioned the considerable degree of linguistic-typological homogeneity of this grouping that comprises two different language families. The historical significance of this observation is unclear: the Non-Khoe unity could result from areal convergence over a long time span or it could spring from a very old common ancestor language that cannot yet be demonstrated by accepted linguistic methodology. Whatever the final answer to this question, the speakers of Non-Khoe languages also display a considerable amount of homogeneity in nonlinguistic terms. First, they are consistently foragers (called traditionally "San" in southern Africa) and this culture shows continuity with the earlier archaeological records in the relevant area. Second and just as important is the fact that there is also a common genetic-biological trait across Non-Khoe. Human populations show a phylogeny in mitochondrial DNA lineages that allows one to distinguish three major population profiles in Africa, two of which have a very biased geographical distribution (Soodyall and Jenkins 1998; Chen et al. 2000; Pickrell et al. 2012). The first two groups are geographically restricted regional populations confined to Africa and involve the most ancient genetic lineages.

(a) "Pygmy" in central Africa
(b) "Khoisan" in southern Africa
(c) Other African (traditionally often called "Negro") and the rest of the world

It is important in this respect that the term "Khoisan" was originally coined by Schultze (1928) for a purely anthropo-biological entity. Apparently, this phenotypical observation has genetic correlates. As this connotation of "Khoisan" is the only one with a clear empirical substance, the term without quotation marks will from now on be used in this nonlinguistic sense. The important fact for the present topic is that Non-Khoe groups consistently show the strongest affiliation with these genetic Khoisan traits (and lack the typical features of pygmies). Taking the linguistic, cultural, and genetic facts together, it can be concluded that groups speaking Kx'a and Tuu languages are relatively homogeneous in showing a clear profile of old and local southern African population traits.

This general observation stands in striking contrast to the groups speaking Khoe-Kwadi languages. Consider first that this family is the largest non-Bantu lineage in southern Africa with considerable internal sub-branching (cf. Table 6.1) and the widest geographical range (cf. Map 6.1); this itself suggests the importance of processes of historical expansion and accompanying divergence. This is indeed corroborated by a high degree of internal differentiation in terms of all basic population features considered here.

Table 6.16 *Population diversity among major Khoe-Kwadi speaking groups*

	Group	Language (group)	Subsistence	Biology
1	Kwadi	Kwadi	Pastoralists	Other African
2	Dama	Namibian Khoekhoe, formerly distinct	Khoekhoe clients < ?	Other African
3	Northeastern Kalahari Khoe	Kxoe, Shua, Tshwa	"San"	Other African
4	Hailom, ǂAakhoe	Distinct Namibian Khoekhoe varieties	"San"	?Khoisan + other African
5	Southwestern Kalahari Khoe	Naro, Glana	"San"	Khoisan
6	Pastoral Khoekhoe	Khoekhoe	Pastoralists	Predominantly Khoisan

Linguistically speaking, although Khoe-Kwadi is a clear genealogical language group and thus involves by all means a shorter time depth than Non-Khoe, it is as a whole structurally as diverse as, or even more diverse than, Non-Khoe, irrespective of the ultimate historical nature of that unit. In cultural-ethnological terms, Khoe-Kwadi speakers comprise historically not only foragers a.k.a "San" but also pastoralists. Finally, Khoe-Kwadi groups differ tremendously in genetic-biological profile and this can, like some part of the linguistic differentiation, be correlated with a kind of geographical cline: while the groups in the north and northwest show a clear affiliation with non-Khoisan groups subsumed here under "other African," the groups further south have a far stronger Khoisan profile; notably the southernmost pastoral Khoekhoe display in spite of their strong phenotypical Khoisan appearance an important non-Khoisan component. The overall diversity among groups speaking Khoe-Kwadi languages is summarized in a simplified form in Table 6.16 (cf. also Map 6.1).

6.4.2   *Toward the Precolonial Historical Sequence in Southern Africa*

Based on the foregoing information I will try in this section to place the different non-Bantu groups in the general population sequence of southern Africa. As a baseline for the present purpose, one can make a simplified distinction between three major precolonial population layers according to the archaeological and historical records (Deacon and Deacon 1999; Mitchell 2002). These are, in chronological order:

I. Various stone age cultures, based on hunting and gathering
II. Late Stone Age culture from about 2,000 years BP, based on sheep pastoralism (only partial correlation with first pottery)

III. Iron age culture from a few centuries later, based on agriculture and pastoralism, slightly later than II.

In interpreting this cultural sequence, most research has so far started from two assumptions, viz. about (a) a considerable linguistic homogeneity across non-Bantu groups in southern Africa (a.k.a. "Khoisan") and (b) their generalized original association with a foraging subsistence. Consequently, the earliest hunting-gathering phase is coupled with "Khoisan" as a whole, while all food-producing layers were usually tied in one way or another to the Bantu expansion. However, the first food-producing phase under (II) in particular posed considerable problems, because the archaeological records as well as its most direct modern reflex in the form of early Khoekhoe pastoralism lack essential ingredients of a Bantu population profile. The solution to this was the assumption that local foraging non-Bantu groups "borrowed" pastoralism from Bantu at the northern fringe of the Kalahari Basin and then expanded across the region further south. This hypothesis largely ignored an essential problem, namely that foragers, at least in southern Africa, have not been shown to shift easily to a food-producing subsistence and its important regalia in ideology and social structure (Smith 1990, 1996, 2005a, 2005b; Barnard 2002, 2007).

Based on more reliable linguistic data and the historical interpretation proposed in Section 6.3, I will develop a different scenario on pre-colonial southern African population history. It will become clear that this overlaps considerably with Westphal's (1963, 1980) ideas, but importantly is now backed up by better linguistic evidence. It is based on the plausible possibility to associate the three linguistic groups identified above, Non-Khoe, Khoe-Kwadi, and Bantu, with the three basic population layers just outlined.

The speakers of Non-Khoe languages (comprising Tuu and Kx'a) constitute the oldest southern African population cluster under (I). This cluster, tied together by a long areal and/or genealogical relationship, can be reconstructed to have been characterized originally by (a) a Khoisan genetic profile, (b) forager subsistence, and (c) considerable linguistic homogeneity. Taking aside the changes arising in the later contact with incoming populations, this general profile can still be discerned for these groups today.

Second and most importantly in the present context, the Khoe-Kwadi family is proposed to be the modern linguistic reflex of the new cultural sequence under (II), which marks the introduction of food production into this part of Africa from about 2,000 years BP on (Smith 2005a). That is, early Khoe-Kwadi speakers can with some probability be linked to pastoralism, with a particular focus on sheep (the role of cattle remains unresolved), because the word *gu "sheep," can be reconstructed for the entire family (see Section 6.3.5) and this word has been borrowed widely into Bantu languages whose animal husbandry focused more on cattle and goats (see, e.g., Westphal 1963: 253–6). Khoe-Kwadi herders spread relatively rapidly from a general northern direction throughout southern Africa, eventually up to the southernmost area of the Cape. It is important to consider at this point the general importance of climatic dynamics for regional population changes. That is, the advent and expansion of pastoralism in southern Africa coincided with a precipitation peak in summer rainfall areas around 3,000–2,000 years BP which in turn lead to a far more humid Kalahari and an extension of surface water, forests, etc. around 2,500–1,500 years BP (Denbow 1986). Hence, the pastoral spread of early Khoe-Kwadi groups would not have had to skirt the vast dry interior of today. Following Smith (1996) and pace Elphick (1977), in spite of intensive and geographically wide and diverse contacts between incoming pastoral groups and indigenous forager populations, the different modes of life can be shown to have remained distinct in both historical and modern times. In summary, at the earliest historical stage, the original population initiating the above change is assumed to have (a) possessed a non-Khoisan genetic profile, (b) subsisted at least on small-stock pastoralism, and (c) spoken an early chronolect of Khoe-Kwadi. All these population characteristics are compatible with or even specifically suggest an ultimate origin of Khoe-Kwadi in eastern Africa.

The final arrival of the iron-age culture based on a more diversified economy happened only slightly later. This event can be associated without much controversy with the last population layer under (III) that emerged in connection with the Bantu expansion. For the later history of Non-Khoe and Khoe-Kwadi groups, this meant their large-scale obliteration as distinct entities, except for the interior Kalahari Basin and adjacent dry areas in the west and south. This can largely explain that Khoe-Kwadi speaking groups, just like Non-Khoe groups, give today the impression of relic populations. Also, if the genealogical link between Khoe-Kwadi and eastern African Sandawe is real, the Bantu expansion would have obliterated the likely earlier geographical connection between them (see Oliver and Fagan [1978: 376] for such a hypothesis, which at the time was linguistically entirely unsubstantiated, however). To put it differently in the context of the present scenario, modern Khoe-Kwadi as a whole can be characterized as a geographically marginalized remnant reflex of an earlier population spread supplanted by a later population spread.

6.4.3   *A Scenario of Khoe-Kwadi Expansion and Diversification*

When speaking here of a "population," it should be clear that this refers first of all to a group in more or less specific space and time. As soon as the term refers to a more abstract classificatory category historical change and diversification come into play. Hence, the relation between the features of a reconstructed population and any type of modern group can be mediated only indirectly by means of individual historical processes. As is well known, these can change a population profile tremendously in one or more features. For the present purpose, this means to show how the earlier Khoe-Kwadi profile reconstructed in the previous section gave rise to the great diversity displayed by the relevant modern groups outlined in Section 6.4.1.

Before doing this, it should, however, be taken into account that it will provide only a tiny part of the entire history of Khoe-Kwadi groups in southern Africa. It is important to keep in mind that Bantu groups encroached onto the wider area only slightly later and obliterated previous populations as distinct entities. One clear indication of this claim has already been given, namely that Bantu groups all over southern Africa must have been confronted with sheep pastoralism of the Khoe-Kwadi type, because a reflex of the reconstructed Khoe-Kwadi form *gu "sheep," is found widely as a borrowing in areas where we no longer have clear evidence for the presence of the donor culture itself. Thus, it is very probable that Khoe-Kwadi had a wider geographical distribution in the past and other such groups existed at least in Zimbabwe and the eastern parts of Botswana and South Africa where they gave way to incoming Bantu.

The present reference parameter is the linguistic genealogical classification of the area at issue. It is therefore also important to recall another point: there are two ways how a certain recently attested ethnic group may have come to speak a language of a particular family, here Khoe-Kwadi, namely by language maintenance or by language shift. This means that the following perspective is first of all how an abstract LINGUISTIC entity has changed and, so to speak, spread over population types identified by other criteria.

Accordingly, I can start from the different linguistic layers in the Khoe-Kwadi family identified in Section 6.3 and, if relevant, their associated types of contact interference argued for on linguistic and topological grounds. For this purpose, I summarize the reconstructed events of linguistic divergence and convergence processes in this family in the schema of Figure 6.1.

The first major event was the arrival of a Pre-Khoe-Kwadi population in the northern periphery of southern Africa. As mentioned earlier, this stands a good chance to be related historically to groups in eastern Africa (cf. Section 6.3.4 for the linguistic evidence). A likely point of immigration would be somewhere close to the wider area where Zambia, Zimbabwe, Botswana, and Namibia border on each other, because this seems to be the best staging point for explaining the location of modern related languages. The historical state after the arrival but before the subsequent dispersal would coincide with the linguistically assumed chronolect Proto-Khoe-Kwadi (cf. Section 6.3.3).

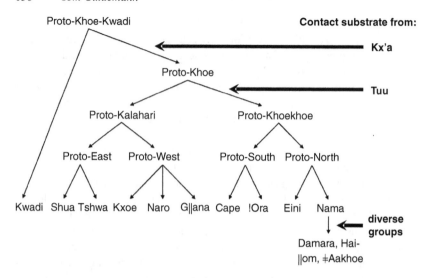

Figure 6.1 Proposed historical development of the Khoe-Kwadi family.

In a second important step, a Pre-Kwadi group expanded westwards into southern Angola and eventually became separated from the rest of the family, most likely through language replacement in the intermediate areas. Comparing the population profile of the historically attested Kwadi with that assigned to early Khoe-Kwadi speakers in Section 6.4.2 it can be seen that it remained relatively unchanged.

This is not the case with the Pre-Khoe who expanded south into the northern Kalahari. Because of the linguistic Kx'a substrate in Proto-Khoe proposed in Section 6.3.2, I assume a period of intensive contact with local foragers. On account of their geographical location modern groups speaking Kalahari Khoe languages could be expected to be the most direct reflex of an early stage of Khoe. However, if comparing them to the reconstructed early Khoe-Kwadi profile, these must have changed considerably.

This becomes clear from the internal diversity in Kalahari Khoe, because there is an important cline in this linguistic unit from a "northeastern" to a "southeastern" cluster. Speakers of the northeastern cluster roughly comprising Kalahari Khoe East as well as the Kxoe group of Kalahari Khoe West have been observed to appear more non-Khoisan than Khoisan in terms of phenotype (hence their common designation, "Black Bushmen"). Moreover, although being mostly foragers in the recent past, they show various ethnographic features that are atypical for the more ancient foraging tradition in southern Africa (see Cashdan 1986). The major difference of the modern northeastern

Kalahari Khoe to my early Khoe-Kwadi profile is their foraging subsistence. The other southeastern cluster comprising in particular such groups as the Naro and Glui of Kalahari Khoe West has a quite different profile: these are overall close in biological and cultural terms to Non-Khoe; the puzzling point here is that they speak Khoe instead of Non-Khoe languages.

However, these contradicting facts can be fitted into a plausible history. Regarding the last-mentioned southwestern cluster my hypothesis is a language shift by local groups of Non-Khoe foragers to a Khoe language under maintenance of their ethnic and cultural autonomy; this would fully explain their modern population profile. Recent genetic studies such as Pickrell et al. (2012) are indeed compatible with this hypothesis. While the exact location and date of the shift as well as processes subsequent to it remain unclear, the most plausible historical scenario would in my view run parallel to the history of such forager groups as the central African Pygmies and the Philippine Negritos after coming in contact for the first time with food-producing groups. This hypothesis would suggest a time when the early pastoral Khoe economy was still viable in the wider area.

Today most locations where Kalahari Khoe languages are spoken either do not support a pastoral subsistence or have become dominated sociopolitically by Bantu speakers. This leads to my hypothesis regarding the other cluster of Kalahari Khoe in the north and east. I have pointed out in Section 6.4.2 that the spread of pastoralism, arguably through Pre-Khoe immigration, coincided with wetter conditions in the Kalahari Basin; it is just as important to recognize that this phase was followed by desiccation and environmental deterioration, leading eventually to the modern conditions in the Kalahari in which traditional forms of pastoralism are difficult or even impossible. Because the Bantu spread closely followed the supposed Khoe spread, the Khoe in the interior were "trapped" between the re-desertifying Kalahari and its north(east)ern fringes occupied in the meantime by Bantu, as argued convincingly by Denbow (1986). In an admittedly very simplified way, there would have been two basic options for these Khoe pastoralists in the long term. One would be to amalgamate with Bantu groups, the evidence for which would have to be sought among the Bantu of the area in the form of a Khoe substrate. The second solution would be to adopt a forager economy.

The reflex of this second scenario turns out to be far more visible under the present hypothesis in that it can be associated with the so-called "Black Bushmen." In the present terms they should be viewed as the pastoral Khoe of the northern parts of the Kalahari Basin who first interacted intimately with local foragers and then reverted to a foraging economy when pastoralism was no longer viable. This would explain the linguistic Non-Khoe substrate as well as the genetic Khoisan admixture. Note that this "devolution" theory is not a new idea (cf. Köhler 1960: 76–7; Nurse and Jenkins 1977; Cashdan 1986:

174–5); new, however, is its explicit association with non-Bantu groups – in the past these "Khoisan" peoples had to be viewed by default as ultimately indigenous foragers.

The assumed cultural shift is not without potential traces of the earlier identity. First, as mentioned, some cultural features of northeastern Kalahari Khoe groups are not typical for the local forager tradition and can be assumed to continue Khoe-Kwadi traits. Second, when European explorers contacted these groups for the first time in northeastern Botswana some were in fact herding peoples (cf. Livingstone 1851: 23–4, 1858), although the significance of this fact is admittedly difficult to evaluate, given their long previous contact with neighboring Bantu.

I will now turn to the profile of the Khoekhoe further south. I assume that Khoe pastoralists could successfully traverse the wider area during the wetter climatic phase so that some groups – among them the Pre-Khoekhoe – expanded into regions south of the Kalahari. Here and on their way they first of all encountered foragers speaking Tuu languages. As argued by Güldemann (2006a), this contact changed the profile of the Pre-Khoekhoe tremendously. Linguistically, it caused the emergence of Proto-Khoekhoe that is characterized by a heavy Tuu substrate as outlined briefly in Section 6.3.1. Genetically, it implied socially upward, and thus unilateral gene flow, and led to far more extensive Khoisan admixture. Since Schultze (1928), this has been the motivation for early and modern scholars to regularly lump the Khoekhoe together with other non-Bantu groups in biological terms. Culturally, it further increased their subsistence component of hunting and gathering, making them the see-mingly only pastoral group in Africa that could be entirely independent of any exchange with agricultural food producers. The exact trajectory of the spread of this Khoe fraction and its geographical extent in the past remain unclear. It should in fact not be implied that the colonization of these southernmost parts must be tied to a single group and a single point in time; it cannot be excluded that there were different waves. However, it is certain that the Khoe spread reached the Cape area and gave rise to the different groups of pastoral Khoekhoe in South Africa, which, it must be stated, are linguistically quite homogeneous. With the re-desertification of the Kalahari as well as with the southward spread of Bantu peoples the earlier geographical link between other equally diversifying Khoe languages was interrupted, leading to the modern picture of two geographically separate branches of the family: Kalahari Khoe and Khoekhoe.

The last major historical shift concerning modern Khoe-Kwadi speaking groups, namely the expansion of a subgroup of pastoral Khoekhoe, the Nama, and Orlam, from south of the Orange River northward into Namibia is the reason why both Khoe branches are today in contact with each other. This spread seems to have occurred from the seventeenth century on and was eventually checked by

Table 6.17 *Assumed history of major Khoe-Kwadi speaking groups*

	Group	Language	Subsistence	Biology
1	Kwadi	Maintenance	Maintenance of pastoralism	Maintenance of non-Khoisan profile
2	Dama	Shift to Khoekhoe from ?Khoe-Kwadi	?	Maintenance of non-Khoisan profile
3	Northeastern Kalahari Khoe	Maintenance with Non-Khoe substrate	Shift to foraging	Maintenance of non-Khoisan profile
4	Hailom, ǂAakhoe	Shift to Khoekhoe from Non-Khoe + ?	Maintenance of foraging	?
5	Southwestern Kalahari Khoe	Shift to Khoe from Non-Khoe	Maintenance of foraging	Maintenance of Khoisan profile
6	Pastoral Khoekhoe	Maintenance with Non-Khoe substrate	Maintenance of pastoralism	"Relative" shift to Khoisan profile

their encounter of another pastoralist group encroaching on Namibian territory from the north, the Bantu-speaking Herero (Vedder 1934; Budack 1986). The Nama-Orlam migration led to yet other types of population contact and, owing to the prestige of the incoming herder language, to the widespread linguistic Khoekhoeization of indigenous groups. Their original languages cannot always be identified securely because of the scarcity of linguistic data. In southern Namibia they can be assumed to have spoken Tuu languages (cf. Güldemann 2006b). In northern Namibia at least some groups subsumed today under Hailom and ǂAakhoe may have spoken Ju varieties (cf. Werner 1906). A particularly enigmatic case is posed by the Damara, many of which were Nama clients, who possess a genetic non-Khoisan profile very different from that of the early Nama. It is possible but so far not supported by robust evidence that the Damara are remnants of the western thrust of the early Khoe-Kwadi expansion and thus do have a closer historical link to the Kwadi, as hypothesized by Ehret (1982: 169–70). All Namibian nonpastoralist groups shifting to Khoekhoe seem to have been involved in the socially upward, unilateral gene flow that affected the Namibian pastoral Khoekhoe (see inter alia Soodyall and Jenkins 1992: 321).

My hypotheses for reconciling the population profile of the major Khoe-Kwadi speaking groups of the recent past with that of the early Khoe-Kwadi speakers who are supposed to have been non-Khoisan pastoralists are summarized in Table 6.17.

6.5   Conclusions

This chapter has traced the history of Khoe-Kwadi, the largest family subsumed under the spurious "Khoisan" lineage, by discussing its external and internal relations and proposing historical scenarios of how the different modern subgroups came into being. The linguistic argument relied heavily on evidence from pronoun systems and their historical evaluation. This shows their potential importance for research on both nonapparent genealogical relationships as well as areal contact, provided the proposed associations involve both the matching of individual elements in form and function and the typologically plausible changes from one system to another.

The results of the linguistic analysis in conjunction with the evaluation of nonlinguistic evidence provide a very different perspective on the history of this part of the African continent. I argue against the common assumptions that (a) Khoe-Kwadi is an old lineage in southern Africa and that (b) all its speakers were originally foragers. I propose instead that the Proto-Khoe-Kwadi population colonized southern Africa relatively recently as a pastoralist group and was thus responsible for the first introduction of food production into this region. That is, not all populations lumped together under "Khoisan" have entirely emerged in southern Africa and represent "pristine" foragers.

The differences to the supposed early Khoe-Kwadi as well as the great internal diversity that modern groups display in cultural, biological, and linguistic terms are explained by the complex dynamics of interacting populations that involved in particular the intimate contact between incoming Khoe-Kwadi groups with foragers indigenous to the respective area: either a Khoe-Kwadi group changed its population profile in one or more major aspects under the new conditions it was in (in particular, language change through borrowing and shift-induced substrate interference, cultural reorientation and shift, and genetic admixture) or entire groups of different linguistic affiliation shifted to a Khoe-Kwadi language. This can resolve the paradox that modern groups which today constitute the Khoe-Kwadi family are in many ways more heterogeneous than the Non-Khoe groups that do not form a family (or at best form a family that is far older).

This historical scenario, if substantiated in future research, is also relevant for early population history in general. It would provide a quite dramatic case of an areal "blending-in" of a colonizing population to the extent that it has traditionally been classified as "indigenous" to its present area. What is of prime importance in the context of this book is the strong influence of indigenous foragers on incoming food producers, involving in particular a heavy linguistic substrate in the colonizing layer. This possibility should be considered in other areas of the world and might warrant a different perspective on the emergence of local and even more global macroareal population profiles.

What remains to be determined in this respect is to what extent the Khoe-Kwadi case can be generalized. It must be taken into account that it involves two quite specific constellations, namely contact of foragers with

(a) the FIRST wave of food-producers and who (b) were primarily PASTORALISTS rather than agriculturalists. Future research on other relevant cases must show whether one or both of these conditions make it particularly likely that foragers can have a major impact on a colonizing food-producing population.

References

Barnard, Alan. (2002). The foraging mode of thought. In Henry Stewart, Alan Barnard, and Keiichi Omura (eds.), *Self- and other images of hunter-gatherers.* Senri Ethnological Studies 60. Osaka: National Museum of Ethnology, 5–24.

(2007). From Mesolithic to Neolithic modes of thought. In Alasdair Whittle and Vicki Cummings (eds.), *Going over: the mesolithic-neolithic transition in north-west Europe.* Proceedings of the British Academy 144. London: The British Academy, 5–19.

Bleek, Dorothea F. (1956). *A Bushman dictionary.* American Oriental Series 41. New Haven, CT: American Oriental Society.

Budack, Kuno F. R. (1986). Die Klassifikation der Khwe-khwen (Naman) in Südwestafrika. In Rainer Voßen and Klaus Keuthmann (eds.), *Contemporary studies on Khoisan,* Vol. 1: *Quellen zur Khoisan-Forschung 5.* Hamburg: Helmut Buske, 107–143.

Cashdan, Elizabeth. (1986). Hunter-gatherers of the northern Kalahari. In Rainer Voßen and Klaus Keuthmann (eds.), *Contemporary studies on Khoisan,* Vol. 1: *Quellen zur Khoisan-Forschung 5.* Hamburg: Helmut Buske, 145–180.

Chen, Yu-Sheng, Antonel Olckers, Theodore G. Schurr, et al. (2000). mtDNA variation in the South African Kung and Khwe and their genetic relationships to other African populations. *American Journal of Human Genetics* 66(4): 1362–1383.

Deacon, Hilary J., and Janette Deacon. (1999). *Human beginnings in South Africa: uncovering the secrets of the stone age.* Cape Town/ Johannesburg: David Philip.

Denbow, James R. (1986). After the flood: A preliminary account of recent geological, archeological and linguistic investigations in the Okavango region of northern Botswana. In Rainer Voßen and Klaus Keuthmann (eds.), *Contemporary studies on Khoisan,* Vol. 1: *Quellen zur Khoisan-Forschung 5.* Hamburg: Helmut Buske, 181–214.

Ehret, Christopher. (1982). The first spread of food production to southern Africa. In Christopher Ehret and Merrick Posnansky (eds.), *The archeological and linguistic reconstruction of African history.* Berkeley: University of California Press, 158–181.

(1998). *An African classical age: eastern and southern Africa in world history, 1000 B.C. to A.D. 400.* Charlottesville: University Press of Virginia.

Elderkin, Edward D. (1986). Diachronic inferences from basic sentence and noun phrase structure in Central Khoisan and Sandawe. In Franz Rottland and Rainer Voßen (eds.), Tagungsberichte des Internationalen Symposions "Afrikanische Wildbeuter", *Sankt Augustin, Januar 3–5, 1985,* Vol. 2: *Sprache und Geschichte in Afrika 7.* Hamburg: Helmut Buske, 131–56.

(1989). *The significance and origin of the use of pitch in Sandawe.* PhD thesis, Department of Language and Linguistic Science, University of York.

Elphick, Richard. (1977). *Kraal and castle: Khoikhoi and the founding of white South Africa.* New Haven, CT: Yale University Press.
Estermann, Carlos. (1959). Os habitantes do Namibe: observação prévia. *Portugal em Africa* 16: 322–330.
Greenberg, Joseph H. (1963). *The languages of Africa.* Bloomington: Indiana University Press.
Guerreiro, Manuel Viegas. (1971). Vida humana no deserto de Namibe: Onguaia. *Finisterra* 6(11): 84–124.
Güldemann, Tom. (1998). The Kalahari Basin as an object of areal typology: A first approach. In Mathias Schladt (ed.), *Language, identity, and conceptualization among the Khoisan. Quellen zur Khoisan-Forschung 15.* Köln: Rüdiger Köppe, 137–169.
    (1999). Head-initial meets head-final: Nominal suffixes in eastern and southern Bantu from a historical perspective. *Studies in African Linguistics* 28(1): 49–91.
    (2002). Die Entlehnung pronominaler Elemente des Khoekhoe aus dem !Ui-Taa. In Theda Schumann, Mechthild Reh, Roland Kießling, and Ludwig Gerhardt (eds.), *Aktuelle Forschungen zu afrikanischen Sprachen: Sprachwissenschaftliche Beiträge zum 14.* Afrikanistentag, Hamburg, 11–14. Oktober 2000. Köln: Rüdiger Köppe, 43–61.
    (2003). Complex pronominals in Tuu and Ju, with special reference to their historical significance. *Afrika und Übersee* 86: 1–25.
    (2004a). Complex pronominals in Tuu and Ju, with special reference to their historical significance. *Afrika und Übersee* 87: 79–103.
    (2004b). Reconstruction through 'de-construction': The marking of person, gender, and number in the Khoe family and Kwadi. *Diachronica* 21(2): 251–306.
    (2005). Tuu as a language family. In Tom Güldemann, Studies in Tuu (Southern Khoisan). University of Leipzig Papers on Africa, Languages and Literatures 23. Leipzig: Institut für Afrikanistik, Universität Leipzig, 11–30.
    (2006a). Structural isoglosses between Khoekhoe and Tuu: The Cape as a linguistic area. In Yaron, Matras, April McMahon, and Nigel Vincent (eds.), *Linguistic areas: Convergence in historical and typological perspective.* Hampshire: Palgrave Macmillan, 99–134.
    (2006b). The San languages of southern Namibia: Linguistic appraisal with special reference to J. G. Krönlein's N|uusaa data. *Anthropological Linguistics* 48(4): 369–395.
    (2008a). A linguist's view: Khoe-Kwadi speakers as the earliest food-producers of southern Africa. In Karim Sadr and François-Xavier Fauvelle-Aymar (eds.), *Khoekhoe and the earliest herders in southern Africa.* Southern African Humanities 20, 93–132.
    (2008b). Greenberg's "case" for Khoisan: The morphological evidence. In Dymitr Ibriszimow (ed.), *Problems of linguistic-historical reconstruction in Africa.* Sprache und Geschichte in Afrika 19. Köln: Rüdiger Köppe, 123–153.
    (2013a). Phonetics and phonology: Kwadi. In Rainer Voßen (ed.), *The Khoesan Languages.* London: Routledge, 87–88.
    (2013b). Typology. In Rainer Voßen (ed.), *The Khoesan languages.* London: Routledge, 25–37.

(in press). Person-gender-number marking from Proto-Khoe-Kwadi to its descendents: A rejoinder with particular reference to language contact. In Voßen, Rainer and Christa König (eds.), Patterns of linguistic convergence in Africa. Frankfurter Afrikanistische Blätter 27. Köln: Rüdiger Köppe. Retrieved from: www.iaaw.hu-berlin.de/de/region/afrika/afrika/linguistik/mitarbeiter/1683070/dokumente/khoe-kwadi-pronoun-contact

Güldemann, Tom, and Edward D. Elderkin. (2010). On external genealogical relationships of the Khoe family. In Matthias Brenzinger and Christa König (eds.), *Khoisan languages and linguistics: Proceedings of the 1st International Symposium January 4–8, 2003, Riezlern/Kleinwalsertal. Quellen zur Khoisan-Forschung 24*. Köln: Rüdiger Köppe, 15–52.

Güldemann, Tom, and Robyn Loughnane. (2012). Are there "Khoisan" roots in body-part vocabulary? On linguistic inheritance and contact in the Kalahari Basin. In Tom Güldemann, Gary Holton, Robyn Loughnane, and Laura Robinson(eds.), *Methodology in linguistic prehistory*. Language Dynamics and Change 2, 2, 215–258.

Haacke, Wilfrid H. G. (2002). *Linguistic evidence in the study of origins: The case of the Namibian Khoekhoe-speakers* (inaugural lecture). Windhoek: University of Namibia.

Hastings, Rachel. (2001). Evidence for the genetic unity of Southern Khoisan. In Arthur Bell and Paul Washburn (eds.), *Khoisan: Syntax, phonetics, phonology, and contact*. Cornell Working Papers in Linguistics 18. Ithaca, NY: Cornell University, 225–246.

Heine, Bernd, and Henry Honken. (2010). The Kx'a family: A new Khoisan genealogy. *Journal of Asian and African Studies* 79: 5–36.

Heine, Bernd, and Rainer Voßen. (1981). Sprachtypologie. In Bernd Heine, Thilo C. Schadeberg, and Ekkehard Wolff (eds.), *Die Sprachen Afrikas*. Hamburg. Buske, 407–444.

Jenkins, Trefor. (1988). The peoples of southern Africa: Studies in diversity and disease. Raymond Dart Lectures 24. Johannesburg: Witwatersrand University Press.

Köhler, Oswin. (1960). Sprachkritische Aspekte zur Hamitentheorie über die Herkunft der Hottentotten. *Sociologus* 10(1): 69–77.

(1981). Les langues khoisan, Section 1: présentation d'ensemble. In Jean Perrot(ed.), *Les langues dans le monde ancien et moderne, prèmière partie: Les langues de l'afrique subsaharienne*. Paris: CNRS, 455–482.

(1986). Allgemeine und sprachliche Bemerkungen zum Feldbau nach Oraltexten der Kxoe-Buschleute. In Franz Rottland and Rainer Voßen (eds.), Tagungsberichte des Internationalen Symposions "Afrikanische Wildbeuter," *Sankt Augustin, Januar 3–5, 1985*, Vol. 2: Sprache und Geschichte in Afrika 7. Hamburg: Helmut Buske, 205–272.

Livingstone, David. (1851). Second visit to the South African Lake Ngami. Extract of letter from Rev. Dr. Livingston, under Date Kolobeng, 24th August, 1850. *Journal of the Royal Geographical Society of London* 21: 18–24.

(1858). *Missionary travels and researches in South Africa*. New York: Harper and Brothers.

Mitchell, Peter. (2002). *The archaeology of Southern Africa*. Cambridge: Cambridge University Press.

Nurse, George T., and Trefor Jenkins. (1977). Serogenetic studies on the Kavango peoples of south west Africa. *Annals of Human Biology* 4(5): 465–78.

Oliver, Roland, and Brian M. Fagan. (1978). The emergence of Bantu Africa. In J. D. Fage (ed.), *The Cambridge history of Africa*, Vol. 2: *From c. 500 BC to AD 1050*. Cambridge: Cambridge University Press, 342–409.

Pickrell, Joseph K., Nick Patterson and Chiara Barbieri (2012). The genetic prehistory of southern Africa. *Nature Communications* 3, Article 1143. Retrieved from: www .nature.com/ncomms/journal/v3/n10/full/ncomms2140.html

Rottland, Franz, and Rainer Voßen (eds.). (1986). Tagungsberichte des Internationalen Symposions "Afrikanische Wildbeuter", *Sankt Augustin, Januar 3–5, 1985*, 2 vols. Sprache und Geschichte in Afrika 7. Hamburg: Helmut Buske.

Sands, Bonny E. (1998). Eastern and southern African Khoisan: Evaluating claims of distant linguistic relationships. Quellen zur Khoisan-Forschung 14. Köln: Rüdiger Köppe.

   (2010). Juu subgroups based on phonological patterns. In Matthias Brenzinger and Christa König (eds.), *Khoisan languages and linguistics: Proceedings of the 1st International Symposium January 4–8, 2003, Riezlern/Kleinwalsertal*. Quellen zur Khoisan-Forschung 24. Köln: Rüdiger Köppe, 85–114.

Schultze, Leonhard. (1928). *Zur Kenntnis des Körpers der Hottentotten und Buschmänner*. Jena: G. Fischer.

Smith, Andrew B. (1990). On becoming herders: Khoikhoi and San ethnicity in southern Africa. *African Studies* 49: 50–73.

   (1996). Khoi/San relationships: Marginal differences or ethnicity. In Pippa Skotnes (ed.), *Miscast: negotiating the presence of the Bushmen*. Cape Town: University of Cape Town Press, 249–251.

   (2005a). Origins and spread of African pastoralism. *History Compass 3*, AF 187: 1–7.

   (2005b). The concepts of 'Neolithic' and 'Neolithisation' for Africa? *Before Farming* 1, article 2: 1–6. Retrieved from: https://online.liverpooluniversitypress.co.uk/loi/bfarm

Snyman, Jan W. (1997). A preliminary classification of the !Xũũ and Žu|'hõasi dialects. In Wilfrid H. G. Haacke and Edward D. Elderkin (eds.), *Namibian Languages: Reports and Papers*. Namibian African Studies 4. Köln: Rüdiger Köppe, 21–106.

Soodyall, Himla, and Trefor Jenkins. (1992). Mitochondrial DNA polymorphisms in Khoisan populations from Southern Africa. *Annals of Human Genetics* 56: 315–324.

   (1998). Khoisan prehistory: The evidence of genes. In Andrew Bank (ed.), *The Proceedings of "The Khoisan Identities and Cultural Heritage Conference*," organized by the Institute for Historical Research, University of the Western Cape, held at the South African Museum, Cape Town, July 12–16, 1997. Cape Town: Infosource, 374–382.

Traill, Anthony. (1986). Do the Khoi have a place in the San? New data on Khoisan linguistic relationships. In Franz Rottland and Rainer Voßen (eds.), Tagungsberichte des Internationalen Symposions "Afrikanische Wildbeuter", Sankt Augustin, Januar 3-5, 1985, vol. 1. Sprache und Geschichte in Afrika 7(1): 407–430.

Vedder, Heinrich. (1997 [1934]). *Das alte Südwestafrika: Südwestafrikas Geschichte bis zum Tode Mahareros 1890*. Windhoek: Namibia Wissenschaftliche Gesellschaft.

Voßen, Rainer. (1984). Studying the linguistic and ethno-history of the Khoe-speaking (central Khoisan) peoples of Botswana, research in progress. *Botswana Notes and Records* 16: 19–35.

(1997). *Die Khoe-Sprachen: Ein Beitrag zur Erforschung der Sprachgeschichte Afrikas.* Quellen zur Khoisan-Forschung 12. Köln: Rüdiger Köppe.

(2007). Languages of the desert ... and what they can tell us about the economic history of southern Africa. In Wilhelm J. G. Möhlig, (ed.), *Cultural change in the prehistory of arid Africa.* Sprache und Geschichte in Afrika 18. Köln: Rüdiger Köppe, 175–185.

Voßen, Rainer (ed.). (2013). *The Khoesan languages.* London: Routledge.

Voßen, Rainer, and Klaus Keuthmann (eds.). (1986). *Contemporary Studies on Khoisan,* 2 vols. Quellen zur Khoisan-Forschung 5. Hamburg: Helmut Buske.

Werner, H. (1906). Anthropologische, ethnologische und ethnographische Beobachtungen über die Heikum- und Kungbuschleute, nebst einem Anhang über die Sprachen dieser Buschmannstämme. *Zeitschrift für Ethnologie* 38(3): 241–68.

Westphal, Ernst O. J. (1963). The linguistic prehistory of Southern Africa: Bush, Kwadi, Hottentot, and Bantu linguistic relationships. *Africa* 33: 237–265.

(1971). The click languages of southern and eastern Africa. In Thomas A. Sebeok (ed.), *Linguistics in Sub-Saharan Africa.* Current Trends in Linguistics 7. The Hague/ Paris: Mouton, 367–420.

(1980). The age of "Bushman" *languages* in southern African pre-history. In Jan W. Snyman (ed.), *Bushman and Hottentot Linguistic Studies* (papers of seminar held on July 27, 1979). Miscellanea Congregalia 16. Pretoria: University of South Africa, 59–79.

Part III

Tropical Asia

7   Hunter-Gatherers in South and Southeast Asia: The Mlabri

Jørgen Rischel

7.1   Introductory Survey

The Indian subcontinent and mainland Southeast Asia are two vast expanses of land, which to a considerably extent are taken up by fertile valleys or lowlands. There have been sedentary groups of food producers for millennia over much of this area.

The traditional inhabitants of the Indian subcontinent speak Dravidian and Mundaic languages except that the mountainous regions to the north are in part inhabited by speakers of Tibeto-Burman languages. Millennia ago, however, the Aryans spread over much of the Indian subcontinent with the result that the Indo-European language family is now the dominant one.

As for Southeast Asia, the dominant language family used to be Mon-Khmer, a highly differentiated language family which belongs to Austroasiatic together with Mundaic. In the far south, Malay languages are dominant. To the north and west, languages of the Sino-Tibetan phylum have a long history as well, mostly languages of the Tibeto-Burman family. Only a thousand years ago wet-rice cultivators speaking Tai migrated down from China and ended up being the dominant population in the central lowlands.

Although most of the populations whose languages belong to these large families have a long tradition as food producers, there are – or used to be – scattered groups of hunter-gatherers both in South and Southeast Asia (in the following these will be referred to as hunter-gatherers no matter whether they still adhere to the foraging lifestyle or have now switched to farming or paid labour).

There are at least two places in this part of the world in which hunter-gatherers seem to have preserved the language or languages they spoke at the time of their first migration to the area. One is Nepal, i.e. the extreme north of the Indian subcontinent, and the other the Andaman Islands off the western shore of Burma.

The linguistic isolate Kusunda used to be spoken by forest-bound people in central Nepal. The Kusunda language was long thought to be extinct but David

Watters worked with a single speaker in 2004. Watters found that although surrounding languages are ergative, this is a nominative-accusative language (Watters, 2006).

The hunter-gatherers on the Andamans are Negritos. Three languages are known in greater or lesser detail: Jarawa, Onge and Great Andamanese. Jarawa and Onge form a language family, South Andamanese. Great Andamanese, spoken in the north, is the remnant of a gamut of languages that used to be spoken by several different tribes and were to some extent mutually intelligible; it is reported to have loans from several of these, including Aka-cari, Aka-Bo, Aka-kede and Aka-Jeru, languages situated from the northernmost fringes and southwards (Abbi 2006). The languages mentioned so far have no proven ties to languages outside the Andamans. There is a further language, Sentinelese, which is spoken by an isolated tribe that lives on a separate island and still resists contact with outsiders; the classification of their language is an open question.

The time depth of the presence of Negritos on these islands is open to debate. It has been suggested that they are remnants of the pre-Neolithic population of Southeast Asia and may represent the first migration of modern humans to Southeast Asia, i.e. possibly as much as 75,000 years ago. Recent genetic studies suggest long-term isolation. On the other hand, it now seems that the islands could have been connected to Burma as recently as 5,000 years ago so that migration across a land bridge could have happened that late in time.

All other hunter-gatherer groups in South and Southeast Asia speak languages that belong to the same language families as those of the food-producing groups.

On the Indian side there are records of hunter-gatherers mainly in the central region. In the interior of Sri Lanka (Ceylon), however, there is a now decimated autochthonous population, the Vedda, who lived as hunter-gatherers when the Singhalese colonized the island less than 3,000 years ago, but later switched to swidden farming. Their traditional language (which has now almost suc-cumbed to the main languages of the island: Singhalese and Tamil) is related to Singhalese. The interesting question is how much their presence antedates that of the Aryans, and further, what language they originally spoke.

In India proper a number of populations speak Munda languages (Mundaic being one main branch of Austroasiatic, Mon-Khmer the other). Some of these are traditionally hunter-gatherers, e.g. the Juang and Birhor, but most, e.g. the Sora, Mundari and Santali, are sedentary food producers. Their linguistic prehistory has been reconstructed back at least 3,500 years. Although it was formerly taken for granted that the Munda groups were hunter-gatherers at that early time and that some of the groups later switched to farming, a fairly recent

study (Zide and Zide 1976) shows the presence in Proto-Mundaic of vocabulary related to agriculture, involving rice and cabbages and a few other plants.
The authors conclude that

> If we judge by the linguistic evidence, the reverse seems to have been the case; the
> primitive Juang and Birhor are probably atypical, being examples of reversion from a
> more complex culture to a simpler one. (Zide and Zide 1976, pp. 1295–6)

Switching now to Southeast Asia, the Malayan Peninsula presents the most
complex picture. There is an ethnic multitude of forest-bound foragers, some
groups speaking so-called Aslian languages belonging to Mon-Khmer whereas
others speak languages related to Malay. Some of the hunter-gatherers are
Negritos and others not; this division according to physical-anthropological
criteria does not coincide with the major linguistic boundaries. The Aslian
languages have been definitively classified (by Benjamin 1976) into North,
Central and South Aslian. North Aslian languages are spoken (mostly) by
Negritos, Central and South Aslian mostly by non-Negritos.

The non-Negritos on this part of the Malayan Peninsula have been classified into two groups on the basis of their physical appearance plus local
administrative divisions. Those of the so-called Senoi groups, who all
speak Aslian languages, are farmers. The rest, the Proto-Malays, are farmers
or hunter-gatherers, or they are fishers. One of the most thoroughly studied
groups are the so-called sea-gypsies, the Moken, who have developed a
lifestyle bound to their boats all the year round.

As for the Negritos, those speaking North Aslian languages (with one
exception) have until very recently all been nomadic hunter-gatherers migrating in such a way that they got into mutual contact. Their languages therefore
form a mesh in terms of shared vocabulary (Benjamin 1976: 74).

The history of Mon-Khmer in this area has been reconstructed some 3,500
years back in time. Food-producing has a long history in the area; and it is an
interesting question how far back in time there was a duality of farmers and
hunter-gatherers speaking fairly closely related languages. It makes sense to
assume that the Negritos were originally all hunter-gatherers and spoke one or
more now lost languages which were replaced wholesale – without culture shift
– by Austroasiatic (Mon-Khmer) and Austronesian (Malay) languages more
than three millennia ago, i.e. a situation reminiscent of that of the Pygmies in
Africa. Because some of the non-Negrito groups are hunter-gatherers, it makes
sense to suggest that cultural reversion has happened in those cases.

Another hunter-gatherer area is the Nicobar Islands in the Andaman Sea, for
a long time notorious for their uninviting climate. The hunter-gatherer groups
there speak Nicobarese, which has been classified alternatively as a separate
branch of Austroasiatic or as Mon-Khmer; in any case, Nicobarese branched

off very early. It is not known how or when the speakers of Nicobarese came to the islands.

There are no records of such groups in the central part of Southeast Asia but in the inner parts of Vietnam there are several highlander groups that are part-time hunters and gatherers although they are sedentary. The least known and perhaps most interesting are the hunter-gatherers in the remote northernmost part of Vietnam, close to the border with Laos. These groups – Arem, Ruc, Maliêng, Mày, and Sách – number fewer than 2,000 persons in total. They were made sedentary in 1954 but before that they lived in the deep mountain forests, refusing contact with outsiders. They wore clothes made of bark and lived as hunter-gatherers most of the year, but they did intermittent swidden farming, with rice and corn as crops, during three months of the dry season. The language of one of these groups, Ruc, has been studied in some detail and turned out to be a Vietic language of the Mon-Khmer family, i.e. it is rather closely related to Vietnamese.

Finally, there are three small groups around the northernmost Thailand-Laos border who speak lexically divergent but structurally almost identical varieties of the same language, Mlabri. This language belongs to the Mon-Khmer family although certain features of its grammar suggest a weak link to Sino-Tibetan.

As the hunter-gatherer languages of South and Southeast Asia are for the most part fairly closely related to languages spoken by sedentary groups, in some cases even to languages spoken by urbanized societies, the question has been raised repeatedly whether some of these groups may have an unknown past record as sedentary food producers who at some point performed a cultural reversion, switching to hunting or (particularly) gathering. Socio-economically, a change from food production to gathering is not difficult to envisage. The fertile areas became densely populated, and some ethnic groups supplemented their income as food producers by making excursions into the forest so as to gather edible roots, honey, etc. or hunting or fishing. This is still done on a considerable scale in mountain villages in Southeast Asia. The transition to full-time foraging is not that big a leap, especially not if it went through an intermediate stage in which the annual cycle comprised both foraging and swidden farming, as in the case of the aforementioned Vietnamese groups.

The transition from a food-producing to a gathering lifestyle was undoubt-edly not just a kind of retreat but a way to preserve and even re-establish the ethnic identity and integrity of the group. Still, tiny ethnic groups may sometimes have felt directly threatened by larger groups, who monopolized the land. Some individuals may have been physically expelled from their mountain villages and forced to move into the forest. As will be argued in the text that follows, it is conceivable that the forest-bound lifestyle of a group such as the

Mlabri, the speakers of the Mlabri language, is in part due to a combination of such factors. That would explain why the Mlabri were until recently notoriously shy and afraid of people they did not know, and why their only strategy up to this day has been to hide instead of making any attempts to keep outsiders away.

The Mlabri language and its speakers occupy a unique position in the discussion of such cultural regression. That is because a paper by a group of biologists (Oota et al. 2005) provides mitochondrial and other DNA evidence suggesting that the group was founded not more than some 800 years ago (maybe as little as 500 years ago), that the founders involved one or at most two women, who were of villager descent, and that the male founders likewise had genetic affinity to villager populations of the area. The remainder of this chapter concentrates on Mlabri, viewed from a comparative linguistic perspective. By way of conclusion, a scenario is sketched which might reconcile the biological and the linguistic evidence.

7.2   A Case Study: The Mlabri Language

7.2.1   Mlabri and Tin

Mlabri material culture strikes me as a typical survival culture, with an absolute minimum of tools and with a glaring absence of such a basic technology as pottery. What little handicraft and manufacturing of tools they do have is apparently shared with mountain villagers of the area. I think all of that is consistent with the assumption of a cultural reversion, as suggested by the *PLoS* paper.

The question, then, is: what villager group may have been involved? The *PLoS* paper points to the Tin or Lua' group as possible ancestors of the Mlabri (with reference to earlier papers by me). Tin speak two closely related languages belonging to the Khmuic branch of Mon-Khmer, like Kammu. The Tin are peasants living in the high mountains of the region on both sides of the northern border between Thailand and Laos, just like the Mlabri. The Tin, like nearly all Austroasiatic groups of mainland Southeast Asia, were probably villagers eating rice as their staple food since time immemorial. There are faint traces of a dual lifestyle, as villagers and as hunter-gatherers, in the Mlabri language. For example, the standard expression for 'eating' is either 'to eat rice' (as it is in most Southeast Asian languages) or 'to eat tubers' (which is a forest phenomenon).

As for a possible genetic bond between the Mlabri and the Tin, it is interesting that the Tin are the only ethnic group with which the Mlabri themselves feel some bond. Still, the Mlabri consider them a quite distinct ethnic group.

The *PLoS* paper refers to a Tin story according to which a boy and a girl were expelled from a Tin village but survived in the forest and had offspring, thus creating the Mlabri tribe by a founder event. I have heard the contents of that story in slightly different versions, and I have heard it in two different Tin villages speaking two mutually unintelligible varieties of Tin: Prai and Mal, respectively. That suggests that the story may antedate the bifurcation of Tin into two languages and thus be several centuries old, although I have not had occasion so far to study the distribution of the story over the Tin area.

We can hardly draw any historical conclusions from such oral traditions. In my view, the most significant aspect of the story about the boy and the girl is the attitude it conveys. By telling it the Tin people explicitly recognize the Mlabri as their remote relatives. As the Mlabri are at the absolute bottom of the social scale, and the Tins are just above them (with sporadic attempts to climb the social ladder), there would be no reason for the Tins to point to such a low-prestige connection unless it had some factual background.

That is probably as far as one can stretch the evidence furnished by oral traditions. Mlabri folklore differs from anything else that I know of in the area. That suggests that Mlabri spiritual culture has sprung from a different source than that of the Tins.

The lexical discrepancies across both Tin and Mlabri are suggestive of a high degree of innovation in these languages. That is not necessarily true of Mon-Khmer in general. The lexicon of Kammu is surprisingly homogeneous across a vast area with a population approaching half a million; population density in itself has obviously played a major role in reducing variability, whereas the fairly small Tin population and the tiny Mlabri population have split up into lexically divergent speech communities. That is conspicuous in the case of the two Tin languages, Mal and Prai, which for lexical reasons exhibit little mutual intelligibility although the separation between them may date back only a few centuries, and the same happened maybe a century ago with lexical polarization among the three varieties of Mlabri.

Back in 1989, when I first wrote about the Mlabri-Tin connection I found that the Khmuic stratum in Mlabri must reflect a pre-stage of Tin, possibly a common ancestor language, which I called (and still call) 'Tinic'. I have since found Mlabri to be crucial for the adequate reconstruction of the earliest history of Tin. That does not mean that most of the words in Mlabri are Tinic; on the contrary the Tinic words make up only a minor fraction of the total vocabulary but a significant one.

The trickiest problem is syllable number. In addition to monosyllables Mlabri has a proliferation of so-called sesquisyllabic word forms consisting of a presyllable plus a main syllable. In Tin, on the contrary, the great majority of words are monosyllabic. It is often apparent that this is due to loss of structure and structure simplification.

Among the Khmuic languages I have examined (which unfortunately do not include Tâyhat for lack of sufficient data) there was only one that resembled Tin by greatly favouring monosyllables, namely the little-known language Phong. Mlabri and the remaining three reference languages, Kammu, Khabit and Ksiing Mul, all agree on having comparable inventories of monosyllabic and sesquisyllabic words. The wordforms in more than one syllable that we find in Mlabri may in many instances stem from Tinic.

Then again, many of the presyllables I would like to posit for Tinic appear to have been lost without any trace whatsoever in Tin (like in Phong), along with loss of morphology. All of this makes it more complicated to do comparative etymological work on Mlabri and Tin, and some of the resulting lexical comparisons look less convincing at first glance.

In contrast, the most convincing regularities are found in monosyllables with initial stop consonants. They involve *consonant mutation*, and that constitutes one of the important criteria for time depth when one makes lexical comparisons between Mlabri and Tin or Kammu.

Tin has undergone a complex mutation, which typologically resembles the Germanic sound-shift (Grimm's law). Its mechanism is quite different from devoicing in Kammu, both historically and typologically. In Tin one can observe that

I.   Old voiceless stops became aspirated.
IIa. Plain voiced stops were devoiced in absolutely initial position.
IIb. Plain voiced stops remained voiced elsewhere.

There is ample evidence for the regularity of the consonant mutation in Tin, with such changes as /b/ · /p/, /g/ · /k/, /p/ · /pʰ/ and /k/ · /kʰ/.

Mlabri and Tin have drifted apart to a surprising extent. The full extent of these changes can be appreciated only by meticulous comparison with more conservative Mon-Khmer languages.

As for phonological differences between Mlabri and Tin, the development of vowels is particularly tricky. More often than not, one observes that vowel qualities differ moderately between Mlabri and Tin, either in terms of aperture or in terms of front-back tongue position, but the pattern is anything but clear. The same is sometimes true of vowel length, which is unstable in Mlabri.

An additional source of complication is that Mlabri often has an open syllable when the syllable in Tin is terminated by glottalization, and vice versa. At present, I simply have to accept fluctuations in vowel quality and length *and* syllable-final phonation when searching for look-alikes between Mlabri and Tin.

Several wordforms, such as the numeral '2', /bɛːr/, have /ɛː/ in Mlabri as against /aː/ in Kammu. At first sight that seems suggestive of irregular vowel raising /aː/ · /ɛː/ in Mlabri, but because the very same words have a diphthong

/ia/ in Tin the behaviour of the vowel should be seen from a Tinic perspective. That makes perfect sense because we already know of a process of mono-phthongization /ia/ · /ɛ:/ that affects Mon-Khmer words in°/ia/ in Mlabri. My suggestion, then, is that Mlabri /ɛ:/ from Mon-Khmer /a:/ is the result of a two-step process: the old Mon-Khmer vowel°/a:/ had become /ia/ in Tinic, and thus it could undergo monophthongization into /ɛ:/ in Mlabri. The question why the old vowel /a:/ sometimes but not always diphthongized in Tinic need not be addressed here.

If Tin and Mlabri agree on the quality of the initial stop as voiceless unaspirated *or* as aspirated, then that is hard evidence for some scenario of borrowing. The word may be a shared, recent borrowing from a Tai language, or it may be a borrowing from Tin into Mlabri which happened *after* the consonant mutation in Tin. In either case, the word is invalid in genetic comparison. If, on the contrary, Tin and Mlabri differ on an otherwise similar wordform in that only Tin shows mutation, then that is hard evidence for an old lexical affinity at the level which I call Tinic, or even before that.

As a consequence of the diagnostic value of consonant mutation I decided to restrict my sample of Mlabri monosyllables so as to include *only words in plain initial stops that mutate in Tin.*

After searching for etymologies across all these words I decided to limit the sample even further, namely to Mlabri monosyllables in labial and velar stops, i.e. /b p g k/, because of specific complications with dentals and palatals.

All of these operations reduced the number of words but made the totality of remaining words more diagnostic.

The definitive sample includes not only words in single initial stops but also words in initial clusters of *stop + sonorant.*

I decided to stick to core vocabulary with tangible and well-defined mean-ings and with non-expressive phonological form (to the very limited extent that the last-mentioned criterion could be applied), so I stripped the provisional sample of four categories of words, namely

1. Function words
2. Proper names
3. Words attested only in fixed expressions
4. Non-domestic terminology

What does it take for Mlabri wordforms to be safely regarded as Tinic? Systematic agreement with Tin is not a sufficient criterion for Tinic prove-nance. One must always consider the possibility that such wordforms are not *specifically* affiliated with Tin but are shared more widely among Northern Mon-Khmer languages. The only practical way I could test that was to check, for each word, whether I could retrieve it in Kammu as well (the short word lists of other Khmuic languages were rarely of much help). If many of the Mlabri words occurred also in Kammu that might suggest extensive borrowing, considering that Kammu is spoken very widely across Northern Laos and adjacent regions (its speakers form the largest ethnic group there with a thousand times as many speakers as Mlabri).

Of the Khmuic words in /b̪/ and /g̈/, 62% satisfy my criteria for claiming that they were shared with Tin at a Tinic level, and that percentage rises to 83% if we include words that are formally ambiguous over two kinds of etymology: they may be old Tinic words or loans from Kammu. If we look at Khmuic words in /p/ and /k̠/ the percentages are halved: they are only 35% and 41%, respectively.

The percentages I have quoted are just meant to illustrate that there is a certain incidence of shared lexicon in Mlabri and Tin. What is more important is that words in initial stops are diagnostic of a specific family relationship between Mlabri and Tin, and that the phonological correspondences are fairly straightforward if one compares Mlabri with reconstructed Proto-Tin. A corollary of this Tinic bond is that the Mon-Khmer appearance of Mlabri is hardly due to very extensive lexical borrowing from Kammu. A working hypothesis, then, is that *Mlabri and Tin are sister languages that have drifted apart very rapidly.*

7.2.2   Non-Tinic Lexical and Structural Features of Mlabri

In spite of the considerable lexical impact of Tinic on Mlabri there are several lexical items in the Mlabri language which suggest that there existed an 'Early Mlabri' language before the Tinic connection. Although some of the Early Mlabri words agree with an origin of Mlabri as a distinct Khmuic branch, there are other words which are suggestive of old contact with another branch of Northern Mon-Khmer, namely Palaungic.

Interestingly, this is confirmed by morphology. Tin has only rudiments of morphology, and comparison with Phong (another Khmuic language) shows that the causative formation by prenasalization on stops, e.g. /ᵐbəl/ 'kill', is hardly of the same origin as the Mlabri prefix /pɑ̝/, e.g. /pɑ̝buɪl/ (which was my assumption until recently). Mlabri morphology is simple with respect to pre- and infixation, but there are some suffixes with very restricted distribution which definitely point away from Khmuic.

Some aspects of Mlabri grammar even suggest an early bond with Sino-Tibetan languages, though there is no basis for positing an origin entirely outside Mon-Khmer.

7.2.3   Semantic Categorizations and 'World View'

As stated earlier, the material culture of the Mlabri has the appearance of a survival culture. The most visible criteria in their selection of material culture are being able to procure food or interchangeable goods, being able to erect shelters at short notice and being mobile by virtue of having an absolute minimum of outfit. That does not tell us much about the relative likelihood of the three scenarios that could in theory account for the recent history of the Mlabri (over a millennium at most): (1) a bottleneck situation: decimation and 'regrowth' of a hunter-gatherer population, (2) a founder event involving villagers only (cultural reversion) and (3) an ethnic fusion, i.e. a combination of scenarios.

Switching to language and spiritual culture, one is struck by the degree to which they share characteristics with ethnic groups elsewhere that have been hunter-gatherers for probably many millennia, in particular the much publicized Pirahã of the Amazon. Like their language and culture, the language and culture of the Mlabri have features which seem difficult to reconcile with Chomskyan ideas about universal grammar and about a universal basis of cognition.

By way of introduction, it can be stated as conspicuous characteristics of the Mlabri that they are disinterested in life outside their own whereabouts, and that they are reluctant to respond to any kind of hypothetical or artificial situations. The 'unsophisticated' Mlabri are not even interested in looking at documentaries featuring their own kinsmen. I experienced that once when there was such a documentary on the TV, and I naïvely brought some Mlabri to look at it in the nearest town. After a few moments they turned their back on the TV screen with remarks to the effect that "This is what we see at home every day!"

Their native zoology and botany is geared to highlighting the discrimination of animals and plants that are useful or harmful at the expense of those that are irrelevant. Accordingly, they have terms for species of snakes, monkeys, frogs, cicadas and so on but no cover terms; on the other hand they have only one term for 30 or more butterfly species. Also other semantic taxonomies are geared to the useful.

Taking the categorization of colours, for example, the Mlabri do not distinguish colours in a way that even remotely resembles divisions within the gamut of colours in the rainbow. Their apprehension seems to reflect the importance of colours in nature, as when they have a term for deep, saturated red which at the same time refers to ripeness of fruits, and another term that encompasses almost the whole spectrum of colours but refers only to insipid, non-saturated colours such as those of unripe fruits or fresh plant stems. There is also a term for dark hues and a term for the light yellow colour of the sky. As a consequence, one speaker named different parts of his jacket by means of different colour names depending on the degree of incident light, and on the other hand he lumped together many different colours of raincoats by using one colour term for all of them. He spoke Northern Thai fairly well, and when I asked how he would distinguish colours using that language instead I was told that he would of course then name the raincoats differently, as the colours were different. He saw no paradox in all that; "That is the way my language is!" he explained.

Taking numerals, it is so that the Mlabri know the numerals up to 10 in their own language as a nursery rhyme. One numeral, 'four', is used as an indefinite quantifier meaning 'several', and a few of the numerals are used as components in complex kinships terms. Only the numerals for 'one' and 'two', however, are used as numerical quantifiers, and in that function the Mlabri numeral has been more or less replaced by the corresponding Thai/Lao numeral. It is possible to quantify a trinity of things as well, namely by means of a fixed expression that can be translated as 'two N additional'. Otherwise, no quantification by means of numerals is done, not even if one asks, for example, how many children a person has; they must be counted by pointing. If the present Mlabri population were solely the result of a founder event involving villagers less than a millennium ago, this kind of primitive mathematics would be somewhat surprising.

Some Mlabri know the low numerals in Northern Thai, and they then willingly state precise numbers of items, such as their children, in that language. Again, the mathematics is an intrinsic property of their language which does not prevent them from seeing the world as composed of discrete numbers of items.

To mention one more 'primitive' feature of Mlabri, there is, to my knowledge, no way of making distributive statements. I once gave a simple instruction when handing out bags: "There is one bag per person!" and the senior Mlabri present explained that to the others by shouting in Mlabri, "One person one bag, one person one bag." It is worse if one needs to explain a complex daily operation (such as shifting bandages on wounds). It is then perfectly possible to say "Do so-and-so every day!" in Northern Thai if that language is understood, but I have heard such an instruction passed on in Mlabri by referring to the daily cycle: "The sun rises and sets, and you do so-and-so; the sun rises and sets, and you do so-and-so," etc., repeated a number of times.

As for language as such, the Mlabri have a split attitude towards their own language. On the one hand they know that it is ridiculed and has a very low status because it does not even possess an orthography. On the other hand, when asked in an environment with no unpleasant interferences they may admit that they consider themselves to be the *real* human beings, and their language to be the *real* language. Many years ago a Mlabri, who took interest in my tape recordings of his speech and had listened to the playback, suggested that when I came back to my own place I would broadcast the Mlabri language on the radio worldwide, and soon all of mankind would pick it up and start speaking Mlabri. As for the Mlabri themselves, everybody speaks it as the first language, and children up to a certain age are monolingual. Several women are likewise virtually monolingual although that is changing rapidly. Thus, Mlabri is not an endangered language in the short run (though there is an obvious danger of the ethnic group as such being eventually extinct). There have been deliberations to extend a minority language revitalization program in Thailand so as to comprise the Mlabri. What is needed instead is to give them a chance to keep the language functional to the same extent as it is now.

Switching to Mlabri cosmology, that is a topic which provides clear evidence of the retention or construction of a strong ethnic identity. Although the Mlabri share the Flood myth, which is found also with other groups in Southeast Asia, they have a myth about a separate cataclysmic event (which is not and cannot be expected to be in any well-defined chronological order with the Great Flood). That cataclysmic event is described as a red liquid (or 'soup') which swept across the ground and left it swidden, all humans being burnt into skeletons. The cultural hero of the Mlabri, Trlegerk, collected the clean bones in a cloth and resurrected them as human beings of various ethnicities, whereas filthy remains were revived as repulsive beings: worms and the like. According to one account, Trlegerk collected the bones in a pen with wooden sides; bones that remained inside became villagers whereas those that spilled over became forest-bound people.

Another interesting aspect of the cataclysm is that after a while, a pigeon flew over the barren soil and was shot down. It had both rice and maize grains in its crop. These were sown, and when the plants came up the next year their crops were sown again, and so on. After a few years people had the possibility of growing crops for their consumption. Obviously, this is suggestive of a food-producing past, but most interestingly, the two kinds of crops are exactly those grown by the part-time hunter-gatherers in northernmost Vietnam (see Introduction). The story may be of considerable age; it need not postdate the presence of maize in Southeast Asia because it may originally have referred to another type of crop, though maize is now strongly dominant as a highland crop in the area where the Mlabri live.

According to Mlabri cosmology, the inhabitable areas of this world consti-tute three layers. One is underground and has water; there are no humans of our kind down there. Another layer is the ground on which we live. A third layer is constituted by the sky, which is apparently envisaged as a shell with vegetation on the upper side. A cataclysmic event (separate from the brown-soup catastrophe) happened once when the sky fell down and rested on one side so close to the earth that people could not walk fully upright. According to one story there was a man who took advantage of this, having a wife on earth and another wife on the upper side of the sky. Trlegerk took offense and pushed the sky into place, thereby forcing the man with the lascivious behaviour to live with only one wife.

Although comparative studies are called for, it is my immediate impression that such cosmological myths are rather unique in the area in which the Mlabri now live. As for the origin of humans, the Trlegerk story tells about a revival but it is another question where human beings originally came from. One Mlabri told me that the various ethnic groups first came out of separate holes in the ground (it was not specified whether they emanated from the underground world). Among other ethnic groups of the area, however, the stories are quite different. A widespread myth tells about birth out of a giant gourd.

The Mlabri have created their own, supernatural reason for adhering stubbornly to forest life: the spirits take offense if the Mlabri grow any kind of crops or raise any kind of animals (except for the omnipresent dogs). It is different if they are used (exploited) as cheap labour by mountain villagers; this has been happening for many decades now, and the spirits apparently tolerate that. Within the last couple of decades the Mlabri in Thailand have been subjected to acculturation; along with that some have been persuaded to make small attempts to grow or raise something as their own property. Although that is a blow to their traditional culture, of course, it is my impression that they still feel that there is something left which defines them as Mlabri, in particular the language. The Mlabri in Laos engage in barter trade with neighbouring villagers but scattered attempts to make them leave the forest temporarily in order to work outside it have had no success so far. Recently, the Lao government adopted a policy of no interference. These few Mlabri have more of their integrity left than the Mlabri in Thailand, but it is evidently only a matter of time.

Finally, it deserves mention that the Mlabri have a kinship terminology which is complex and still poorly understood. What is clear so far is that it does not encompass more than three generations and that it lumps together two kinds of consanguineal relatedness of the second order (strictly ascending/descending order, as between grandparents and grandchildren, and more indirect relatedness, as between parents' siblings and their nephews and nieces). Referring to one's younger kinspeople, one can thus use a term which refers to one's own children, versus another term which refers indiscriminately to grandchildren and nephews and nieces. These possibilities of lumping groups of kinspeople have a functional reason, of course. As for the shallow chronological depth of the kinship terminology, the explanation may be the very most straightforward one: considering the small size of the population it would be hard to find spouses within one's ethnic group if the kinship system could impose more rigid criteria in terms of incest taboos than the extant system invites. Intermarriage with persons outside one's own group is, or was until very recently, considered totally out of the question.

7.2.4   A Hypothetical Scenario Reconciling Biological and Linguistic Evidence

In spite of lack of evidence it makes sense now to sketch a fairly plausible history of the Mlabri and their language. Let us assume that more than a millennium ago there was a fairly numerous and active ethnic group, the ancestors of the Mlabri (on the male side), who lived partly by foraging in the forest, partly by activities in the open land such as trade of meat, wax, etc. for other goods. They would have to be at least bilingual; many, at least among the grown-up men, would be trilingual. The relevant languages in northernmost Southeast Asia would belong to Sino-Tibetan and to Mon-Khmer. There might even be intermarriages across ethnic and cultural barriers. The eventual outcome was a language whose lexicon was of general Mon-Khmer appearance, whereas its syntax on some points resembled Sino-Tibetan.

Assuming that the 'original' mother-tongue of the Mlabri was a Mon-Khmer language, the impact from Sino-Tibetan might be due to extensive use of another language for communication outside the domestic environment, i.e. extensive bilingualism. Again, however, one would expect lexical, not just syntactic impact. There may have been a strong social bond within the group which was instrumental in the preservation of native vocabulary without mixing it up extensively with the extraneous vocabulary.

The conclusion is that Early Mlabri was a Northern Mon-Khmer language, possibly constituting a branch of its own but with lexical and morphological affinities to Palaungic; it seems to have had some syntactic affinity to Sino-Tibetan.

Later, the Mlabri experienced another early encounter with outsiders: Tai-speaking newcomers to the area. They continued their external contacts including barter trade, and that readily explains the presence of such words as /bɛːŋ/, 'costly', in Ancient Thai form in Mlabri.

Eventually, the Mlabri must have been considered an unwanted section of the population. Maybe the number of individuals roaming the northern Thailand-Laos border area was indeed decimated by the Northern Thais, as suggested by a Mlabri myth, and a few survivors took refuge in the deep forest. That was where they encountered a few ethnic Tin, including one or at most two girls according to the biologists' findings (as said earlier, the Tin myth suggests that there was just one girl and also a boy).

These few individuals then founded the ethnic group anew, with the result that the language had a lexical influx of Tin words, mostly belonging to domestic vocabulary rather than being related to hunting. There was no perceptible influence on Mlabri grammar; it was taken over wholesale from Early Mlabri.

In the first centuries after that the Mlabri population grew to more or less its present size but they stuck to a minimum subsistence as hunter-gatherers, perhaps because the collective memory of previous near-eradication transformed into a constant fear of outsiders, particular of lowlanders (a fear put into system by developing a belief into the spirits strictly banning interaction with outsiders).

The historical progression in the account above is admittedly speculative but to the best of my conviction not implausible. It accounts for all the linguistic observations and for the myths as well, both those of the Mlabri and those of the Tin. It suggests that the hunter-gatherer lifestyle of the Mlabri was a means of survival, and that is consistent with the finding that their material culture is on the one hand minimalistic and on the other hand characterized by tools and techniques that are used also by other locals if they camp in nature or go hunting.

References

Abbi, Anvita. (2006). Reconstructing pre-colonization knowledge-base of ecological environment and sociolinguistic practices of Andamanese. Paper given at the Hunter-Gatherer Workshop, Max Planck Institute of Evolutionary Anthopology, Leipzig, August 2006.

Benjamin, Geoffrey. (1976). Austroasiatic subgroupings and prehistory in the Malay Peninsula. *Austroasiatic Studies* I: 37–128.

Bernatzik, Hugo A. (2005). *The spirits of the yellow leaves. The enigmatic hunter-gatherers of northern Thailand.* (Originally 1938 and 1958; new edition by Jørgen Rischel). Bangkok: White Lotus Press.

Boeles, J. J. (1963). Second expedition to the Mrabri of North Thailand. *JSS* 51, 2: 133–160.

Nguyên Phú Phong, Trân Trí Dõi and Michel Ferlus. (1988). *Lexique Vietnamien-Ruc-Français.* Paris: Université de Paris VII, Sudestasie.

Oota, H., B. Pakendorf, G. Weiss, et al. (2005). Recent origin and cultural reversion of a hunter-gatherer group. *PLoS Biology* 3(3): e71.

Rischel, J. (1995). *Minor Mlabri: A hunter-gatherer language of northern Indochina.* Copenhagen: Museum Tusculanum Publishers.

Rischel, J. (2000). The dialect of Bernatzik's (1938) 'Yumbri' refound? *Mon-Khmer Studies* 30: 115–122.

Rischel, J. (2005). Preface (p. xi), Introduction (pp. xiii–xxxviii), Appendix (pp. 135–172, i.e. a detailed analysis of Bernatzik's Mlabri word list of 1938), and Selected Bibliography (pp. 173–175) to Bernatzik 2005.

Watters. David. (2006). Notes on Kusunda grammar: A language isolate of Nepal. *Himalayan Linguistics Archive* 3:1–182.

Zide, Arlene R. K. and Norman H. Zide. (1976). Proto-Munda cultural vocabulary: Evidence for early agriculture. *Austroasiatic Studies* II: 1295–1334.

8 Foraging and the History of Languages in the Malay Peninsula

Niclas Burenhult

8.1 Introduction

The hunter-gatherer groups of Southeast Asia represent a diverse range of adaptations (Sather 1995; Morrison and Junker 2002; Rischel, Chapter 7). The so-called Negritos of the Andaman Islands, the Malay Peninsula and the Philippines have attracted particular attention because of long-standing claims that they represent traces of pre-agricultural Southeast Asia (Bellwood 1997).[1] Research on Andaman and Philippine prehistory has tended to maintain at least some components of this view. Research on Malayan prehistory, however, has in recent decades taken a different course, proposing that the local Semang foragers represent a physical and economic adaptation in response to Neolithic and later events (Rambo 1988; Fix 1995). This perspective developed alongside a general revisionist trend in anthropology which questioned the notion of hunter-gatherers as static relics of prehistory. The Malayan argument, inspired by a complex local situation of language-culture-biology relations, relied heavily on historical-linguistic reconstruction of the Aslian branch of Austroasiatic (Aslian languages are spoken by most aboriginal groups in the Malay Peninsula, including all of the Semang foragers). Recent genetic studies cast doubt on this Malayan perspective, suggesting instead a robust connection between the Semang foragers and the local pre-Neolithic population (Hill et al. 2006; Oppenheimer 2011).

In the present chapter I review the Malayan debate and, in light of new genetic and linguistic insights, outline a reinterpretation of the linguistic prehistory of the Malay Peninsula. Issues of language history, contact, change and shift are set against a proposed niche of hunting-gathering, in an effort to explain the current language identities and characteristics of the Semang foragers.

8.2 The Malayan Case: A Background

8.2.1 The Languages

Today's linguistic situation in the Malay Peninsula is shaped by the successive historical arrival of several language families: Austroasiatic, Austronesian, Tai,

164

Sinitic, Dravidian and Indo-European. While the latter four entered the scene only within the last few hundred years, the peninsular history of Austroasiatic and Austronesian goes further back. Austroasiatic, and its peninsular manifestation 'Aslian' (see further in the text that follows), is believed to have been introduced several thousand years ago from the north by the first agriculturalists in the peninsula. Austronesian was probably present early on too, but the ancestor of its current representatives, various Malayic dialects, is likely to have arrived from overseas (possibly Borneo) about 1,500 years ago (Collins 2006).

The Austroasiatic languages of the peninsula form a genetically and geographically distinct branch called Aslian (from Malay *asli*, 'original'), now spoken mainly in small pockets in the interior of Peninsular Malaysia and Isthmian Thailand. Early lexicostatistics (Benjamin 1976a) and historical phonology (Diffloth 1975, 1979) both produced an Aslian family tree consisting of three sub-branches: Northern, Central and Southern Aslian (cf. Figure 8.1). According to this classification, the Northern branch includes languages such as Kensiw, Kentaq, Jahai, Menriq, Batek and Ceq Wong,[2] spoken in scattered areas of southern Thailand and northern Peninsular Malaysia as far south as central Pahang. The Central branch is spoken in a fairly continuous area of interior Peninsular Malaysia, comprising the uphill portions of the states of Perak, Kelantan and Pahang. Its members are Semai, Temiar, Lanoh, Semnam and Jah Hut. The Southern branch is spoken in parts of the Peninsular Malaysian states of Terengganu, Pahang, Selangor, Negeri Sembilan and Johor. Its languages are Semaq Beri, Temoq, Semelai and Mah Meri. However, the tripartite family tree is not unquestioned. Subsequent reappraisals of Jah Hut have been proposed on phonological grounds (Diffloth and Zide 1992: 139), suggesting it is better viewed as an independent fourth branch of Aslian, a result supported by our own recent phylogenetic modelling of lexical diversification (Dunn et al. 2011). Importantly, however, all sub-branches of Aslian still await detailed historical reconstruction, as extensive lexical data are lacking for most of the languages.

While the Austroasiatic identity of Aslian is unquestionable, its languages display features which are atypical of other Austroasiatic branches (Matisoff 2003). Its geographical location has spared it from the areal trends of monosyllabism and isolating morphology typical of the mainland, preserving, for example, intricate and productive morphological processes and paradigms. Influence from Austronesian languages, Malay in particular, has further consolidated its atypical characteristics. Malay has also permeated the Aslian lexicon, as seen in a number of loanwords, also for basic vocabulary like 'blood', 'moon', 'snake', 'star' and 'stone' (Benjamin 1976a).

Aslian phonemic systems are rich, especially as far as vowel distinctions are concerned, some Central Aslian languages having 30 or more distinctive vowel

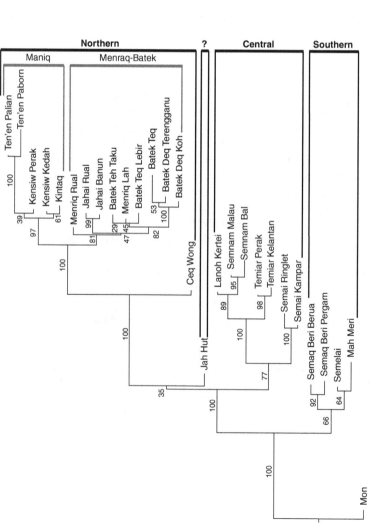

Figure 8.1 Aslian family tree, rooted on Mon (from Dunn et al. 2011). This is a maximum clade credibility tree, summarizing the 750 post-burn in trees of the Bayesian phylogenetic tree sample with branch length equal to the median length of all congruent branches found in the sample. Numbers on the branches indicate percentage of the tree sample supporting each bifurcation (for details, see Dunn et al. 2011). While broadly reproducing the earlier proposed clades of Aslian genealogy, the phylogenetic aspect of this study also reveals that the three major clades show very unequal rates of lexical divergence: Southern Aslian is the most conservative branch; Central Aslian shows a bit more divergence; and most of Northern Aslian is contained within a clade which is highly divergent externally, but which has low internal diversity, suggesting a recent diversification. It is the Northern Aslian languages spoken by Semang foragers which show great external divergence whereas the geographic and cultural outlier Ceq Wong comes out as an early and conservative split.

nuclei (Benjamin 1976b; Burenhult and Wegener 2009). The rich morphology is most evident in derivational categories applied to verbs (e.g. nominalization, aspect and Aktionsart and valency-changing distinctions) and nouns (e.g. unitization and verbalization). Such derivation is achieved through combined processes of partial reduplication and affixation, typically prefixes and infixes. A range of inflectional and modal clitics and particles adds to the complex morphological picture. Aslian languages also have elaborate paradigms of deictic distinctions, such as pronouns and demonstratives. Aslian syntax shows variable word order and different strategies of argument permutation. Case-marking of arguments is achieved by means of prefixes or proclitics. Alignment types vary between languages, with ergative, accusative and stative-active systems all being in evidence. The word class known as 'expressives' is widely attested in Aslian. (For detailed grammatical information the reader is referred to e.g. Benjamin 1976b; Diffloth 1976; Kruspe 2004; Burenhult 2005). Aslian lexicons are rich, monolexemic forms encoding fine semantic detail in domains such as anatomy, biology and physiography (Burenhult 2006, 2008; Kruspe 2010). Yet, as already noted, Aslian languages engage in extensive lexical borrowing from Malay.

Benjamin (1980, Semang, Senoi, Malay: culture-history, kinship, and consciousness in the Malay Peninsula. Unpublished manuscript; Benjamin 1985, 2004) proposes a broad connection between the three Aslian sub-branches and three distinct societal groupings of their speech communities. Thus, Northern Aslian is associated with the nomadic foragers known ethnographically as the Semang (see further in Section 8.2.2), characterized e.g. by a loose and egalitarian band structure and a patrifocal descent system. Central Aslian is associated with the semi-sedentary swidden horticulturalists known as Senoi, who display an egalitarian tribal structure and cognatic descent groups. Southern Aslian, finally, is spoken by groups of so-called Aboriginal Malays, collectors-traders with ranked tribal societies and a Malay-type matrifocal descent system.[3] Benjamin's societal classification is based primarily on the specific institutionalized kinship regimes of these groups, such as marital patterns and kin-avoidance rules. Other societal and economic features map more or less well onto these categories, forming more general and less robust patterns of language-culture connection. Benjamin points to some significant exceptions to the generalization. For example, ethnolinguistic groups such as Jah Hut, Ceq Wong, Semaq Beri and Lanoh cannot be straightforwardly assigned to any of the three societal types, but rather display a mix of features, not least as far as the subsistence system is concerned. Moreover, the linguistic subgroupings contain mismatches, such as Ceq Wong, which is Northern Aslian but spoken by people who are not Semang foragers, or Lanoh and Semnam, who display some forager characteristics but speak Central Aslian languages. Finally, the Aboriginal Malay societal tradition embraces not only speakers of Southern Aslian languages, but also several aboriginal groups who do not speak Aslian languages at all but Austronesian (Malay) dialects.

The present linguistic ecology of Aslian is one of marginalization, retreat and endangerment. Malay dialects and Standard Malay form a powerful Austronesian majority which exerts influence on the Aslian languages and spreads at their expense. Several indigenous groups who now speak dialect forms of Malay, such as the Jakun and the Temuan, are assumed to have been Aslian-speaking until recently (Benjamin 2012). Several Northern Aslian varieties in northwestern Peninsular Malaysia are known to have been replaced geographically by Malay dialects in the past 100 years. But patterns of expansion, decline and extinction are also evident within the Aslian group itself (Burenhult 2005; Burenhult and Wegener 2009). For example, Central Aslian Temiar (with about 15,000 speakers) is currently spreading northwards, assimilating smaller relatives and pushing at least two varieties of Lanoh to the brink of extinction. The official number of speakers of Aslian languages varies between approximately 150 (Menriq) and 30,000 (Semai).

8.2.2   The Foragers

The hunter-gatherers of the Malay Peninsula are referred to ethnographically as the Semang. This is a cultural label which is defined in terms of a nomadic, foraging economy and associated societal features (Benjamin 1985). For a long time, however, observers have maintained that there is a close connection between this cultural constellation and the physical features of its bearers. The purportedly short stature, dark skin and curly hair of the Semang led early anthropologists to classify them physically as 'Negritos' (see e.g. Schebesta 1952), a term which to some extent is still used. It is also used to refer to physically similar hunter-gatherer populations in the Andaman Islands and the Philippines. The cultural and physical characteristics of the Semang are generally considered to set them apart from other aboriginal groups in the peninsula, such as the semi-sedentary Senoi swiddeners, or the collecting-trading-based Aboriginal Malay. As noted, Semang, Senoi and Aboriginal Malay form three broadly defined cultural entities. Together they are referred to in Malaysia as the *Orang Asli* (a Malay term meaning 'original people') in anthropological as well as Malaysian administrative practice. This term is a fairly recent invention, coined for official purposes following Malaysian independence in 1957 to distinguish the many diverse aboriginal groups from the politically dominant Malay-speaking Muslim majority population.

The Semang inhabit the rainforests of the peninsula's northern interior, forming a string of scattered groups from Trang and Pattalung provinces of

Isthmian Thailand in the north to central Pahang state, Peninsular Malaysia, in the south. The current total number of individuals can be estimated at approximately 4,000–4,500, distributed over some 8 or 10 ethnolinguistic groups. Some of these groups inhabit lowland rainforest areas along major waterways such as the Perak and Kelantan Rivers, but others are found in more mountainous regions. According to historical records, Semang groups had a much wider distribution only 100–200 years ago, occupying also coastal areas of Perak, Penang and Kedah states, Peninsular Malaysia (for a recent overview of sources, see Nagata 2006; for information on the groups in Thailand, see Hamilton 2006).

Traditionally, the Semang live in groups of about 15 to 50 people. Temporary camps of lean-tos or huts are inhabited for a few days to several weeks or months (sometimes even years), depending on the sustenance circumstances. The economy is based on foraging in a broad sense. Hunting, fishing and gathering form the subsistence backbone. But the Semang also make occasional swiddens, collect rainforest products for trade with outsiders and seize any opportunity to engage in wage-labour, if such activities are considered to be economically advantageous at the time. Nowadays many Semang are permanently settled in resettlement villages established by the Malaysian and Thai governments, but some groups in both countries still pursue a mobile existence.

As elucidated by Benjamin (1980, 1985), Semang society enforces this mobile lifestyle, social structures encouraging dispersal and flux in space, time and human relations. The conjugal family is the only persisting social unit, and bands and camps consist of several such families which coexist on a voluntary basis. Strict cross-sex in-law avoidance rules apply, the filiative bias is patrifocal, and residence is virilocal. Semang society is egalitarian, and there is a moral obligation to share food with other members of a camp (van der Sluys 2000). For detailed accounts, see e.g. Schebesta (1952), Endicott (1979), Lye (1997) and Dallos (2003).

Without exception, all Semang groups speak languages of the Aslian branch of Austroasiatic. As noted in Section 8.2.1, this is a feature they share with other minorities in the Malay Peninsula, including all Senoi groups and some Aboriginal Malay groups (Map 8.1). Their society and/or physical features therefore do not correlate with a separate linguistic origin. As also noted, however, there is a connection between the Semang and one particular sub-branch of Aslian, the Northern one. This connection holds for all Semang groups except some of those inhabiting the Perak Valley, who speak a language referred to as Lanoh, which belongs to the Central Aslian sub-branch (see further in the text that follows). Furthermore, Ceq Wong, the southernmost Northern Aslian language (western Pahang state), is spoken by about 300 people who are *not* considered to belong to the

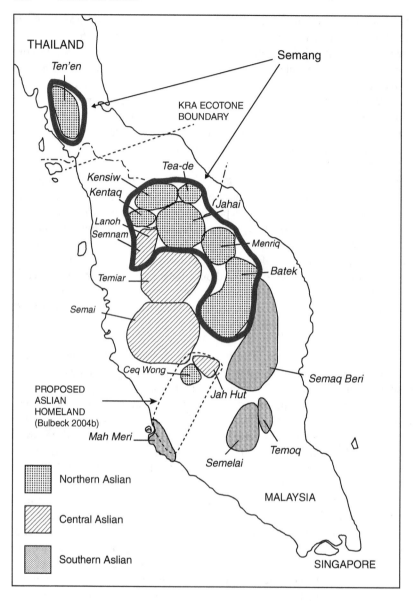

Map 8.1 Map of the Malay Peninsula showing the approximate
distribution of Aslian languages and sub-branches (according to the
traditional tripartite classification) and their relationship to the cultural label
'Semang'. Language distribution is adapted from Benjamin (1976a).

Semang societal tradition. I will return to these linguistic-cultural mismatches in Section 8.3.

On lexical and phonological grounds, the Northern Aslian languages spoken by the Semang can be divided into two groups (Benjamin 1976a; Dunn et al. 2011). One group comprises most of the languages and dialects on the Thai side of the border, such as Ten'en, Kensiw and Tea-de, as well as Kensiw and Kentaq in Malaysia. These varieties will here be referred to generically as Maniq (from their word for human being, *mani?* or *mni?*). The extinct varieties once spoken along the northwest coast of Peninsular Malaysia probably also belonged to this group. The other group is found predominantly in Malaysia and comprises three languages: Jahai, Menriq and Batek. While Jahai and Menriq share a term for human being (*mnra?*), the Batek term is the same as the ethnonym (*batɛk*). In what follows, this group will be referred to as Menraq-Batek.

The Central Aslian-speaking Semang of the Perak Valley are referred to generically as Lanoh in administrative and scientific practice. Not all Lanoh refer to themselves as Lanoh, however, at least not traditionally. Several groups with distinct ethnonyms are known, Lanoh being one and restricted to upstream dialects which are nearly extinct. Present-day downstream groups call themselves Semnam (Burenhult and Wegener 2009; cf. Benjamin 1976a).[4]

8.2.3   The Histories

Several models of prehistory have been proposed to account for the currently observable physical, cultural and linguistic diversity in the Malay Peninsula. These models are broadly classified to represent either an 'indigenist' perspective, in which local development is foregrounded, or a 'diffusionist' perspective, which places emphasis on the influx of features from outside (cf. Fix 1995: 313–314; Bulbeck 2004b: 366–369). Extreme versions of diffusionism (e.g. Carey 1976) have early precursors such as Skeat and Blagden (1906), who posited successive waves of migration into the peninsula to account for the present-day aboriginal categories. This is popularly known as the 'layercake model' (cf. Winstedt 1961). Extreme versions of the indigenist perspective (e.g. Solheim 1980) posit unbroken local continuity in the physical, cultural and linguistic development of all of the peninsula's indigenous groups, at least since the early Holocene.

The diffusionist perspective is today represented mainly by models which posit a close connection between the spread of agriculture and the expansion of language families, the so-called Farming/Language Dispersal Hypothesis. This school of thought, famously represented by Renfrew's 1987 reappraisal of Indo-European prehistory, was pioneered in the East and Southeast Asian context by Bellwood (1985, 1997, 2004, 2005). The origin and spread of the

Table 8.1 *Semang ethnolinguistic groups in Thailand and Malaysia*

Ethnolinguistic group	Language subgroup	Aslian sub-branch	Location	Sociolinguistic situation
Ten'en	Maniq	Northern	Langu and Thungwa districts of Satun province, Palian district of Trang province, and Paborn district of Pattalung province, Thailand	Several scattered groups, possibly still largely nomadic; number of speakers is unknown.
Kensiw			Thanto district of Yala province, Thailand; Baling district of Kedah state, Malaysia	Thailand group settled in one village, number of speakers is unknown; Malaysian group settled in one village and numbers 232 speakers; occasional speakers in semi-nomadic mixed Kensiw-Jahai groups along the border.
Kentaq			Hulu Perak district of Perak state, Malaysia	Settled in one village, 157 speakers; close contacts with Kensiw, which is very closely related.
Tea-de			Wean and Srisakorn districts of Narathiwat province, Thailand	Situation unknown; groups possibly still largely nomadic; may be identical to a group referred to by the Jahai as *Idɛk*, in which case Tea-de is in contact with Kelantan Jahai.
Jahai	Menraq-Batek		Hulu Perak district of Perak state and Jeli district of Kelantan state, Malaysia; Srisakorn district of Narathiwat province and Betong district of Yala province, Thailand	Several settled, semi-nomadic and nomadic groups, with particular concentrations around Lake Temengor in Perak and Sungai Rual in Kelantan; while the Thailand figure is unknown, the number of speakers in Malaysia is 1,843; in Perak largely co-settled with Temiar, and in Kelantan with Menriq.
Menriq			Gua Musang, Jeli and Kuala Krai districts of Kelantan state, Malaysia	Settled in three villages along the middle portion of the Kelantan river and one village in Jeli district; only in two of these locations do speakers refer to themselves as Menriq; in the other two they refer to themselves as Batek *Tɔh*; total number of speakers can be estimated at 250–300; one group is co-settled with Batek *Deʔ*, another with Jahai.

Batek		Gua Musang district of Kelantan state, Lipis and Jerantut districts of Pahang state, and Hulu Terengganu and Besut districts of Terengganu state, Malaysia	Several settled, semi-nomadic and nomadic groups, divided into at least four distinct dialects (Batek *Deʔ*, Batek *Tɛʔ*, Batek *Nɔŋ*, and Batek *Tanim*); the number of speakers is 1,255, although this figure is likely to include some 100 speakers of Menriq who nevertheless refer to themselves as Batek; co-settled with Menriq in one location in Kelatan, and with Semaq Beri in one location in Terengganu; Batek *Tanim* is sometimes referred to as Mintil.
Lanoh	Lanoh	Hulu Perak district of Perak state, Malaysia	Extinct or near-extinct varieties on the Perak River above Grik, including Yir, Jengjeng (*Jŋjĕŋ*) and *Bnraʔ*; remembered (but not actively spoken) by a handful of scattered individuals assimilated by the Temiar.
	Central		
Semnam		Hulu Perak district of Perak state, Malaysia	Settled groups along the Perak River below Grik, totalling about 350 speakers; main group of ca. 250 speakers settled in one village west of the Perak, remaining ones co-settled with the Temiar in two villages east of the Perak; a closely related dialect Sabüm, spoken until recently in the Grik basin, is now extinct.

Thailand data are based on Phaiboon (2006); Malaysia data from Kedah, Perak and Kelantan are from a survey conducted by the author 2004–2006; Pahang and Terengganu information draws on Lye (1997, 2004, personal communication) and Kruspe (personal communication); population figures are from 2003 and have been obtained from the website of the Center for Orang Asli Concerns (www.coac.org.my).

region's major language families (Austronesian, Austroasiatic and Sino-Tibetan) are here linked to the appearance and expansion of Neolithic communities. In the Malayan context, the arrival of Austroasiatic is linked to the first spread of agriculture from the north and a proposed population influx some 4,000–5,000 years ago (Bellwood 1993, 1997). The model fits well with calibrations of the time-depth of Austroasiatic, where the Aslian branch is suggested to have come into existence around that time (Diffloth 2005: 79; Dunn et al., 2013). The Semang, like other 'Negrito' hunter-gatherer groups in Southeast Asia, are viewed as a marginalized remnant population, i.e. physical and cultural descendants of the pre-agricultural Pleistocene and early Holocene inhabitants, who have carried on with their hunting-gathering lifestyle. The fact that the Semang speak Aslian languages closely related to those of their neighbours is seen as evidence of a language shift in the hunter-gatherer populations owing to intense interaction with the incoming agriculturalists (for a parallel scenario in the Philippines, see e.g. Reid 1987, 1994; Headland and Reid 1989; and in equatorial Africa, see Bahuchet, 2012).

The currently dominant version of the indigenist paradigm builds ulti-mately on Benjamin's (1980, 1985) characterization of the present-day Semang, Senoi and Malay as distinct yet complementary societal and eco-nomic traditions. Scholars from several disciplines have corroborated this as a model to be projected into the past with data from anthropology (Rambo 1988), archaeology (Bulbeck 1996, 2004a, 2004b) and human biology (Fix 1995, 2002). The traditions, the associated language groups and the physical features of their bearers are considered to have evolved in parallel from a common origin. By most accounts, this origin is traced to the first appearance of agriculture and Austroasiatic languages in the peninsula, acknowledged to have been introduced from the north. This original Proto-Aslian-speaking culture is suggested to have had diverse subsistence strategies, including swiddening, foraging and collecting, and to have been represented by a ranked tribal society (see e.g. Bulbeck 2004b: 378). The subsequent devel-opment involved specialization in response to contacts and trade with (pre-dominantly Austronesian-speaking?) coastal communities (cf. Junker 2002), resulting in the tripartite cultural divisions currently observed. Following Bulbeck (2004b), I will here refer to this paradigm as the Orang Asli Ethnogenesis Hypothesis.

Thus, according to this view, the Semang represent an economic specia-lization which crystallized out of a proto-culture whose subsistence was not primarily based on foraging. Setting out from the Aslian linguistic tree, Bulbeck (2004b: 376, building on Benjamin 1985, cf. Rambo 1988) explains the peninsular hunter-gatherers as those descendants of the proto-culture who retained its foraging component but lost its focus on swiddening and collecting. In the process, they developed egalitarianism, a specific kinship system and a band-based society. Linguistically, these developments are argued to be closely connected to the Northern Aslian sub-branch, although the Lanoh (Central Aslian) have gone through similar developments. Furthermore, Fix (1995) argues that some of the genetic characteristics of the Semang can be explained as adaptations in response to a change to a society with attributes such as nomadism, low population density and forest habitat.[5] Also, Bulbeck (2004b) points to the lack of archaeological evidence for a connection between today's Semang and the pre-Neolithic hunter-gatherers of the peninsula.[6]

This view of the Semang as a wholly Neolithic and post-Neolithic adaptation connects to a general revisionist trend within anthropology in recent decades to view present-day hunter-gatherers not as isolated relics of the pre-agricultural way of life but as adaptations characterized by considerable dependence on neighbouring non-hunting-gathering communities (Lewin 1988; Bower 1989; Headland and Reid 1989; Stiles 1992; Spielmann and Eder 1994). Tropical foragers have received particular attention in this respect, following claims that tropical rainforests are unable to sustain populations with a 'pure' hunter-gatherer economy (Headland 1987; Bailey et al. 1989; Headland and Bailey 1991).[7]

Recent advances in the field of human biology provide a refined and conciliatory picture of peninsular population history, supporting elements of both diffusionism and indigenism. On bioarchaeological grounds, Bulbeck and Lauer (2006) propose a complex interplay between the influx of foreign population elements and local physical continuity and diversification. Genetic studies (Hill et al. 2006; Oppenheimer 2011) propose similar complexity. Analysing mitochondrial DNA in Southeast Asian populations, the Hill et al. study is the first to address the genetic characteristics of each traditional aboriginal grouping in the Malay Peninsula (Semang, Senoi, Aboriginal Malay) in a wider Southeast Asian perspective. In brief, the results show that all three groups have undergone considerable genetic drift, but that phylogeographic traces nevertheless remain of the ancestry of their maternal lineages. These indicate that Semang, Senoi and Aboriginal Malay all carry mtDNA haplogroups with a deep history in the peninsula, probably 50,000–60,000 years, but they do so to varying degrees. These haplogroups are most evident in the Semang, which appear to have experienced only minor subsequent gene flow from outside the peninsula. They are also evident in the Senoi, who nevertheless also carry haplogroups which can be positively traced to an origin in Indochina within the last 7,000 years. The Aboriginal Malay are more diverse, with mid-to-late-Holocene haplogroups originating from Island Southeast Asia and also, unexpectedly, a haplogroup originating in late Pleistocene Indochina.

Although several aspects of the peninsula's genetic history have yet to be charted in detail (including paternal haplogroups), the Hill et al. (2006) study sheds light on issues of core concern to the debate. It suggests that today's Semang are the most direct descendants of the local Pleistocene inhabitants, supporting in some respects the idea that they represent traces of an earlier population in the process of being replaced (as proposed by e.g. Bellwood 1997a). In fact, it implies a robust connection between present-day foraging and a locally ancient and relatively unmixed genetic presence. However, it also suggests that other groups, the Senoi in particular, can trace part of their genetic ancestry to the same local population, and another part to populations from the north, probably arriving with agriculture and Austroasiatic languages. This points to early intermarriage between locals and newcomers and a pattern of intermixing linked to the adoption of an agricultural economy by parts of the local population (cf. Bellwood 1993, 1997). These results run counter to the early 'layer cake' models, as they show that the Semang, Senoi and Aboriginal Malay cannot be viewed as non-mixing strata of immigrants. Nevertheless, they support the diffusionist standpoint in showing that indigenousness, in the sense of local genetic continuity, comes in degrees. Accordingly, they also throw considerable doubt on some components of the indigenist Orang Asli Ethnogenesis paradigm, especially those hypotheses which posit local and recent genetic differentiation to account for present-day physical variation (e.g. Rambo 1988; Fix 1995, 2002). Contrary to these hypotheses, the Hill et al. (2006) study discloses that the Orang Asli do not all descend from a single ancestral population and that local antiquity of haplogroups differs within the Orang Asli constellation. In response to these conclusions, Fix (2011) proposes a new model of Malayan population history involving continuous small-scale gene flow from outside the peninsula.

A puzzling aspect of peninsular prehistory is the archaeological horizon referred to as the Hoabinhian. This was characterized by a forager economy with an industry of flaked cobble artifacts and was distributed across much of Southeast Asia during the early Holocene, c. 10,000 years ago (Bellwood 1979: 64–71; Bulbeck 2003). In the peninsular context, it is sometimes associated with the ancestors of the Semang, but this is refuted on craniometric grounds by Bulbeck (2004a). Hill et al. (2006) similarly rule out a Semang-Hoabinhian connection and, as we have seen, instead link the Semang to a more ancient colonization event. At the same time, they identify an influx of distinct mtDNA haplogroups (present mainly in Aboriginal Malays) around 10,000 years ago from northern Indochina and tentatively link these to a Hoabinhian expansion into the Malay Peninsula. Thus, a hunter-gatherer expansion originating from the north may have occurred several thousand years before the Neolithic immigration, complicating Bellwood's (1997) simpler scenario of agricultur-alists mixing with hunter-gatherers in the mid-Holocene. It is noteworthy that this Hoabinhian genetic influx seems to have by-passed the local ancestors of the Semang (and the Senoi), who were obviously present in the peninsula but for whom there is still no separate archaeological evidence (cf. Bulbeck 2004b; see further in Section 8.3.1).

Setting out from the insights of human biology, especially the Hill et al. (2006) study, the following section outlines a corresponding model for the historical circumstances and course of linguistic events among the hunter-gatherers of the peninsula.

8.3 The Linguistic History of Foraging in the Peninsula: A Reinterpretation

Previous models of peninsular prehistory tended to treat linguistic history as analytically intertwined with, if not inseparable from, cultural and biological history. The Farming/Language Dispersal Hypothesis obviously builds on the idea that the three are intimately connected. While this may be relevant in a macro-context, close examination at the local level has proven it difficult to find a clear correlation between the spread of farming and a particular linguistic affinity. Indeed, in some cases language spread through agricultural expansion is likely to have been the exception and not the rule (Bulbeck 2004b: 368). The Orang Asli Ethnogenesis Hypothesis presumes an even closer relationship between linguistic, cultural and biological history, and it does so on the basis of a model of contemporary societal constellations which itself does not have tools of historical reconstruction but relies heavily on historical linguistics. As we have seen, this hypothesis is vulnerable to analyses which are based on such tools (especially genetics) and, accordingly, has problems reconciling them.

A reasonable first step in reinterpreting peninsular linguistic prehistory is therefore to acknowledge that language, culture and biology are analytically distinct entities and that their historical development may or may not converge. Thus, figuratively, different historical processes can run both parallel and crosswise in relation to each other. Such a standpoint allows us to introduce models into the picture which handle lateral processes, such as cultural borrowing and language shift (see further in Section 8.3.2). Focusing on the linguistic history of the Semang, the suggestions made in the following sections build on the idea that such intersecting of distinct processes is a major mechanism in historical development and change. First, however, I should restate some general conclusions about peninsular prehistory which are reasonably well established and which are prerequisites of the scenarios outlined in the following:

1. All language families currently represented in the peninsula have been introduced from outside; Austroasiatic probably has the most ancient

presence and is likely to have been introduced from the north around 4,000–5,000 years ago with the spread of agriculture into the peninsula.

2. Peninsular populations can trace their local genetic ancestry far back into the Pleistocene (perhaps 50,000 years), but they differ as to the degree of subsequent intermixing with extra-peninsular populations; the Semang show a particularly close association with the local Pleistocene ancestral population.

3. The currently observable cultural variation in the peninsula is the result of a complex set of processes of diversification and complementary specialization going back to the arrival of agriculture; there is little archaeological evidence for cultural continuity going further back than that.

8.3.1   The Semang-Pleistocene Connection: A New Slant on Forager Prehistory in the Peninsula

The recently exposed genetic connection between the present-day Semang and a local ancestral Pleistocene population provides evidence of the diachronically most extended and geographically most stable continuity in the prehistory of the Malay Peninsula. Yet, as we have seen, there is little archaeological evidence of this connection and instead plenty of evidence showing that the ethnographically observable Semang developed their material culture through interaction with surrounding non-foragers, such as blowpipes and iron tools (Bulbeck 2004b). There is no technological continuity associated with the genetic continuity. The only obvious (but implied) cultural connection is the more abstract economic frame of hunting-gathering as such. It will therefore be proposed here that hunting-gathering has represented a continuously available, rewarding and constantly occupied subsistence niche from the Pleistocene until the present, and that this niche has served as a refuge for the locally ancient maternal lineages since foreign lineages and farming entered the peninsula during the Holocene. The exact mechanisms preventing external lineages from entering this proposed niche can only be speculated on, but it could be suggested that its mobile lifestyle and low population density have inhibited the influx of individuals from demographical settings characterized by sedentism and higher population density.[8]

Note in this context that gene flow in the opposite direction appears to happen more easily, as suggested by the presence of the ancient local haplogroups in today's Senoi agriculturalists, proposed to represent a mix of local and foreign populations (Hill et al. 2006). Arguably, individuals and perhaps whole groups from the hunting-gathering niche have had no problem leaving the niche, settling down and assuming an agricultural economy (a process still in evidence today). In doing so, they have exposed themselves more to intermixture with foreign lineages.

Importantly, this scenario of a hunting-gathering refuge explains the survival of ancient local lineages without suggesting that the carriers of those lineages are isolated relics who stubbornly hold on to an unchanged pre-agricultural way of life, unwilling to intermix with their farming neighbours. On the contrary, it implies that the local lineages remain largely unmixed thanks to a continuously worthwhile subsistence mode which non-hunter-gatherers are unable or unwilling to enter.[9] Thus, genes and subsistence mode coincide not because they are inherently connected, but because a demographical asymmetry prevents external forces from taking them apart. Incidentally, this view of hunter-gatherers as economic and genetic success stories also contrasts with the revisionist models of hunter-gatherers, which tend to picture them as marginalized products of surrounding economies, unable to support themselves without food produced by their agricultural neighbours (see the body of work cited in Section 8.2.3). It also challenges revisionism in proposing that present-day hunting-gathering as such (although not necessarily particular cultural manifestations of it) can have pre-Neolithic roots.

One might wonder whether there is something that makes the Malay Peninsula especially suitable for such continuous hunting-gathering. Endicott and Bellwood (1991) show that the Malayan rainforest is rich enough in food resources to support populations which subsist solely on hunting and gathering, disproving claims that tropical rainforests are unable to sustain such populations (Headland 1987; Bailey et al. 1989). A particularly rich environment is to be found in the so-called Kra ecotone, an area stretching across northern Peninsular Malaysia and southern Isthmian Thailand which represents a zone of transition between the wet evergreen rainforests to the south and the drier and semi-evergreen forests to the north (Whitmore 1984). The zone contains animal and plant species characteristic of both types of environment, resulting in exceptional biological diversity. Benjamin (1985: 243–244, 261–262) suggests that the Kra ecotone has been influential in the development of Semang culture and especially the extreme nomadism exhibited by the more northerly groups. So, as far as environmental clues are concerned, the Kra ecotone may be a potential candidate also as a stable host habitat of the continuously worthwhile hunting-gathering niche proposed here.

The relationship between the Semang-Pleistocene connection and the Hoabinhian horizon of the early Holocene is unclear. As noted in Section 8.2.3, Hoabinhian expansion into the peninsula appears to have by-passed the local population genetically, and the archaeological record provides few indications of a link between the Hoabinhian and the Semang. This would seem to indicate that distinct forager traditions existed at the same time during the early Holocene and that the hunting-gathering niche proposed here resisted outside influence long before the arrival of agriculture. Yet the relationship between human biology and culture during this period is little known, and one could imagine scenarios in which populations carrying the ancient local hap-logroups did incorporate Hoabinhian elements without necessarily mixing with newcomers (cf. Bulbeck 2003 on this point).

On this account of forager history in the peninsula, Semang culture is the current occupant of the hunting-gathering niche. As has been argued by proponents of the indigenist paradigm, the societal and material characteristics of this particular cultural scheme are likely to have developed in response to the economic and social upheavals that occurred in the peninsula from the mid-Holocene and onwards, including the arrival of agriculture, increased trade[10] and the use of metal. Major technological advances would have included the introduction of iron tools (such as jungle knives) and blowpipes (with an associated shift of focus from terrestrial to arboreal game). In this respect, the models of Benjamin (1985), Bulbeck (2004b) and others propose plausible detailed scenarios of the appearance and development of Semang culture. Unlike these models, however, the present work explicitly proposes that Semang cultural genesis occurred in a hunter-gatherer framework which was already in place. Thus, Semang culture is viewed primarily as a significant modification of the hunting-gathering niche, rather than as a full-scale and novel adaptation.

The hunting-gathering niche postulated here is a tentative hypothetical attempt to explain the close genetic connection between the Semang and the local Pleistocene population. It is still in need of corroboration, for example with models of archaeology and demography (which is beyond the scope of the present study). The linguistic scenarios outlined in the text that follows rely mainly on the validity of the Semang-Pleistocene connection itself and not on that of the proposed causal niche. As will become clear, however, the niche turns out to be analytically helpful in explaining some of the linguistic phenomena at issue.

8.3.2   *Austroasiatic in the Peninsula: Processes of Spread*

The exact circumstances of the establishment and spread of Austroasiatic in the peninsula are far from clear. However, the association with the arrival of agriculture and at least some population movement from the north is now reasonably well established. It is also fairly safe to posit that its introduction involved the common ancestor of all of the peninsula's present-day Austroasiatic languages, Proto-Aslian. We know nothing of the languages which were certainly spoken in the peninsula at the time Austroasiatic arrived. Early attempts to link Semang vocabulary to the distinct Andamanese languages (the so-called Proto-Negrito Hypothesis, cf.

Trombetti 1923; Bloch 1952; Zide and Pandya 1989) cannot be substantiated on present evidence.[11]

On archaeological and linguistic grounds, Bulbeck (2004b: 377) proposes that a Proto-Aslian speaking colony developed in the south-central west of the peninsula (in today's Selangor and western Pahang). With Northern, Central and Southern Aslian languages (as well as Jah Hut) all represented, this area currently displays the greatest linguistic density of the Aslian geographic range. Our own phylogeographic analysis of basic vocabulary points to the easternmost extreme of this area, the slopes of Gunung Benom in present-day Pahang, as the most likely homeland (Dunn et al. 2013). This colony would also have been the locus of early elements of agriculture and genetic lineages originating north of the peninsula. Already from its start, it is likely to have had an indigenous component, e.g. by assimilation of local hunter-gatherers through intermarriage, or the adoption of the new economy by whole groups of locals. The indigenous component probably also involved elements of resource use, resulting in a mixed proto-economy (cf. Bulbeck 2004b: 378). For demographic reasons, the new mixed economy, lineages and language quickly got the upper hand and came to dominate the subsequent course of events. As proposed in Section 8.3.1, however, a narrow but worthwhile hunting-gathering niche of pure nomadic foraging remained a refuge for unmixed indigenous genetic lineages. But at some point the new language group got a foothold here too.

The significant indigenous component in this course of events makes it clear that we have to take into consideration the phenomenon of *language shift*, that is, the process through which a population abandons a language in favour of another (Gal 1979; Dorian 1981; Brenzinger 1992; Fase et al. 1992).[12] In this context it is useful to distinguish some general social settings in which language shift and language death can occur. What is common to all such settings is a situation of language contact, an obvious prerequisite of shift. They are also characterized by some degree of asymmetry between the languages in contact, one being more dominant than the other. The fastest and perhaps most common type of language replacement occurs in a situation of assimilation in which speakers of a Language A intermarry with speakers of a more dominant Language B, the offspring growing up speaking the dominant language. In situations of extensive intermarriage the weaker language can be eradicated in a generation or two. This situation can be observed currently among the Lanoh, where extensive intermarriage with speakers of dominant Temiar has led to the extinction of several Lanoh dialects. It is also a possible scenario for the early introduction of Austroasiatic by immigrants who intermarried with locals.

A different type of setting involves a situation in which a distinct population speaking Language A adopts a dominant Language B without extensive intermarriage and assimilation. The shift is driven by intense and asymmetrical interaction, and Language B is 'imported' to handle certain linguistic domains for which Language A is less functional. The complementary distribution of domains then changes gradually, so that Language B replaces Language A in domain after domain until Language A is entirely abandoned and dies (Sasse 1992). The shift is complete when adults transmit only Language B to the next generation.

One can imagine a variety of intermediate types of setting, in which, for example, a distinct population speaking Language A adopts the economy of a population speaking Language B without immediately adopting their language. However, the shift of economy can pave the way for more extensive patterns of contact and intermarriage and ultimately language replacement. Moreover, the change in lifestyle is likely to be associated with the introduction of new linguistic domains for which Language B is more useful, exposing the community to a more rapid shift in the complementary, domain-bound use of languages from A to B.

The particular socio-cultural circumstances of each case of language shift determine to what extent the winning language goes through structural and lexical change as it is passed on to new speakers (Weinreich 1979: 109; Thomason and Kaufman 1988: 110–146). Key factors in this respect are the manner, extent and duration of exposure to the new language, patterns of its actual usage and values associated with it and the age at which exposure takes place. For example, children who grow up in constant, enduring and amicable contact with native speakers of the new language (not to mention children who receive the new language from one native-speaking parent) are more likely to end up speaking a version of it which is closer to the original than unenthusiastic adult language learners with limited exposure. Linguistic residues from the lost language, so-called substratum influence or interference, are therefore more likely to occur in the latter case. Importantly, however, all such cases of language shift involve the acquisition of the bulk of the grammar and lexicon of the new language. The acquired language as a whole still reflects its genetic background, in spite of the fact that it has been passed on to a new population (Thomason and Kaufman 1988: 146). Indeed, identifying structural and lexical evidence for the abandoned language in it is frequently difficult (Thomason and Kaufman 1988: 110–115). Thus, in the case of Aslian spread for example, the language varieties produced through shifts under varying socio-cultural circumstances would all go through systematic (albeit different) changes and always be recognizable as descendants of Proto-Aslian. Reconstruction of linguistic development (e.g. historical phonology) will have no problem establishing an historical continuity in such development, in spite of the fact that this historical process sometimes cross-cuts population history. Accordingly, we cannot expect to easily identify traces of the languages that have disappeared.

Variable socio-cultural circumstances of language assimilation and shift, such as the ones outlined earlier, are likely to have played an important part in the spread and diversification of the whole Aslian language group (Dunn et al. 2013). Unfortunately, most of them are untraceable with our current tools of historical inquiry. But merely acknowledging that language shift may have been a natural, common and significant mechanism in Aslian history is of conceptual help in trying to understand the relationship between language, society and biology in the peninsula.

8.3.3   The Northern Aslian Problem

Comparative phonology, lexicostatistics and phylogenetic analysis of lexical diversification all show that Northern Aslian (NA) forms a well-defined sub-branch of Aslian. It is generally thought to have branched off early from Proto-Aslian (Diffloth 1975; Benjamin 1976a; Dunn et al. 2011). However, our recent phylogeographic analysis suggests NA may not have separated from its closest relatives Central Aslian and Jah Hut until much later, during the Late Neolithic and Early Metal Age, c. 1,800–2,500 years ago. Phonologically, its branching off was characterized by the loss of length distinction in vowels as well as some fairly dramatic vowel changes, e.g. a change from Proto-Aslian (and Proto-Mon-Khmer) */a:/ to */i/ or */e/. The cognate pairs in Table 8.2 contrast NA forms (from Menriq) with equivalents in Central Aslian (from Semnam), which has retained the vowel of Proto-Aslian.

Preliminary comparison based on the two NA languages for which there is extensive grammatical data available, Jahai (Burenhult 2005) and Ceq Wong (Kruspe et al. 2014), suggests that NA also displays typological characteristics which set it apart from the rest of Aslian. These include the presence of bilabial fricatives, morphological processes which delete presyllables of roots, an

Table 8.2 *Northern and Central Aslian cognate pairs*

Northern Aslian (Menriq)	Central Aslian (Semnam)	Gloss
jʔiŋ	jʔa:ŋ	bone
lntik	lnta:k	tongue
haliʔ	sla:ʔ	leaf
jliʔ	jila:ʔ	thorn
jim	ya:m	to cry
mniʔ	mna:ʔ	smell

accusative tendency in case-marking and a comparatively indistinct class of expressives.[13] If these observations turn out to be correct, it is likely that such typological features were present also in Proto-NA.[14] At any rate, the particularities of NA suggest that the branching off of Proto-NA involved several significant linguistic developments pertaining to lexicon, phonology and grammar.

NA is usually presented as intimately connected with the Semang foragers (Benjamin 1985; Bulbeck 2004b). In the Orang Asli Ethnogenesis Hypothesis, for example, the spread of NA is by and large explained in the context of a forager adaptation. NA Ceq Wong, spoken by non-Semang in a small area isolated from the rest of NA, presents a challenge in this respect. Not only are its present speakers culturally different from other NA speakers; it is also distinct in that its proto-language split off from the rest of NA at an early stage, possibly 1,500-2,000 years ago (Dunn et al. 2013; cf. Bulbeck 2004b: 375–376). A wholesale association of NA with Semang foraging would entail that Proto-NA coincided with the origin of Semang culture, and that Ceq Wong represents an exception and (perhaps early) divergence from the NA-forager connection. Ceq Wong would have to be considered to have made an exodus from the Semang sphere.

But the NA-Semang near match, and the currently peripheral status of Ceq Wong, may falsely conceal a different historical reality. First, the present-day Ceq Wong have a mixed economy which is thought to be typical of the society in which Aslian originated (Bulbeck 2004b). Thus, they can be viewed as conservative descendants of the Proto-NA-speaking society. Second, one valid correlation which *can* be made is that between NA-speaking Semang and that branch of NA which is made up of the Maniq and Menraq-Batek language groups (referred to henceforth as MMB). As far as the linguistic identity of the original Semang culture is concerned, Proto-MMB would therefore seem to be a better candidate than Proto-NA. This is in line with Bulbeck's model, which suggests that Ceq Wong is that NA language which has experienced the least societal modifications since Proto-Aslian, whereas the rest of NA has experienced a shift to a foraging focus, nomadism and band structure. Our own recent lexical analyses, which confirm the conservative status of Ceq Wong, also show that the MMB clade has undergone exceptional lexical divergence from the rest of Aslian, including Ceq Wong (Dunn et al. 2011; Burenhult et al. 2011; see Figure 8.1). This is a clear indication that it is the later branching off of MMB (and not NA as a whole) which is associated with the Semang societal setting. It should be kept in mind that Ceq Wong-type situations may have been more dominant historically. It is likely that there were additional languages or even whole branches of NA, now extinct, which were not spoken by Semang foragers. For all we know, Proto-MMB may initially have been a tiny offshoot from an impressive NA tree. It is unwise to assume a rigid historical connection between the Semang and NA as a whole.

How is this scenario to be related to the hunting-gathering niche proposed in Section 8.3.1? The obvious answer is that Proto-MMB represents the most likely first entry of Aslian into the niche. This would involve the importation by hunter-gatherers of a NA language from a neighbouring community (cf. Bahuchet 2012). This language subsequently replaced the previous language(s) through shift as it spread throughout the niche, and it diversified into the distinct subgroups and languages observable today. The language contact and asymmetry required for such a shift to occur are likely to be closely connected to the social and material changes associated with the development of Semang culture. Arguably, trade and imported novel technologies such as metal formed an impetus for the introduction or development of language domains in which the NA language proved functional (e.g. a trade lingua franca, handicraft or hunting jargon or song texts) and from which it eventually infiltrated other domains of the language. The shift may initially have been restricted to part of the niche's population. But once it got a foothold, its spread throughout the niche may have been easy and rapid, considering the social, geographical and linguistic flux typical of today's Semang communities. The most likely timing of this Aslian intrusion into the niche is some time during the Metal Age, possibly c. 1,500 years ago (Dunn et al. 2013).

The hunting-gathering niche may also be helpful in explaining the current association between Semang and NA. If we accept that NA initially developed in a non-forager context, and that Ceq Wong represents a rare trace of a state of affairs which was once more typical of NA, the niche gives the impression of not only having absorbed NA but also largely preserved it. In doing so, it has consolidated linguistic and cultural categories to a point where Semang has become almost synonymous with NA. In a situation analogous to the genetic one (see Section 8.3.1), language and subsistence mode coincide not because they are inherently connected, but because the niche has been good at preventing external forces from taking them apart.

It is interesting that the branching off of Proto-NA seems to have been a linguistically more dramatic event than that of Proto-MMB. This may point to differences in the socio-cultural circumstances surrounding the events. One could speculate that the birth of Proto-NA involved the acquisition of Aslian by an indigenous hunter-gatherer group which settled down and assumed the lifestyle of the Proto-Aslians. Perhaps, contact patterns of a restricted kind led it to develop a very distinct version of Aslian, whose peculiar features were carried down to all its linguistic descendants. The later branching off of Proto-MMB involved the acquisition of NA by a population which retained its foraging economy, and may have been shaped by a more intense and enduring contact situation, e.g. with an extended period of bilingualism. The contact-oriented nature of Semang society may indeed be the reason why NA made its way into the hunting-gathering niche with such ease. Incidentally, today's

Semang are frequently described as skilled multilinguals (Burenhult 2005: 7; Benjamin 2012).

Bulbeck (2004b: 379–386) proposes three alternative geographical scenarios for the spread of Aslian (cf. Benjamin 1976a: 82–89, 1997: 98–105). In all three, NA spread involves northward movement from the Proto-Aslian homeland. There are obvious pitfalls in the geographical interpretation of language spread, owing not least to our limited knowledge of the social circumstances of each spread event, as well as our lack of knowledge of related languages which are certain to have existed but disappeared without a trace. Accepting the idea proposed here of a late language shift involving Proto-MMB in the hunting-gathering niche, however, we can at least postulate that the shift occurred where NA abutted geographically on the habitat of the niche. A tentative suggestion is the Kra ecotone mentioned in Section 8.3.1. Possibly, NA and its associated culture spread northward from the Proto-Aslian homeland until it reached this northerly area, which may have been especially gainful for a hunting-gathering economy. Faced with the successful niche, the genes and basic economy associated with the NA expansion failed to spread any further, but language did. NA outside the niche subsequently gave way to other branches of Aslian (especially Central Aslian), retreated southward and survived only in the form of Ceq Wong. The descendants of Proto-MMB ended up being the thriving but geographically marooned main manifestation of NA, eventually branching up into the subgroups and languages in evidence today. Attractively, this scenario need not posit a great deal of movement on the part of Proto-MMB and its descendants, the region where NA was adopted being confined to the band across the peninsula where Semang have been recorded in historical times.

8.3.4   Hunter-Gatherer Language Interaction

Semang linguistic history is further complicated by the second exception to the forager-NA connection: the cluster of dialects known generically as Lanoh, spoken along portions of the middle and upper Perak River. This is a Central Aslian (CA) language, closely related to Temiar, one of the main languages of the Senoi cultural sphere. Yet it is spoken by people who display several Semang attributes, such as a 'Negritoid' appearance, a band-based society and conjugal families as the basic social units of production. Also, their subsistence is based on nomadic foraging, at least historically. Their descent system, on the other hand, is shared with the Senoi rather than with the Semang (Benjamin 1985: 251; 2012; Dallos 2003).

Lanoh and Temiar are considered to have diverged from a common ancestor some 1,000–1,500 years ago (Bulbeck 2004b: 375–376) or later (Dunn et al. 2013). The question is then how this development is to be related to the bigger picture of Aslian-Semang relationships. A plausible explanation is that Lanoh represents another adoption of Aslian by the Semang, a sort of second linguistic intrusion into the hunting-gathering niche. This may have been an event parallel to the shift to NA discussed in Section 8.3.3, in the sense that different sections of the niche adopted different Aslian sub-branches. Or it may have happened after NA had spread throughout the niche, in which case a section of NA-speaking Semang shifted to a CA language. The latter alternative is more realistic, considering that Proto-MMB branched off at an earlier point in time than Proto-Lanoh did. Again, asymmetrical interaction can account for the shift, evidenced possibly also by some Senoi-like societal features among the Lanoh.

In spite of this NA/CA partition of the forager sphere, MMB and Lanoh share some linguistic features which are not encountered in other Aslian settings. The sociolinguistic characteristics of Semang society form one such feature (Benjamin 1976a: 74–76, 1980: 4, 1985: 234–235, 2001: 111). The mobile lifestyle of the Semang, manifested in their system of intermarriage between individuals of widely dispersed bands, as well as in their pattern of group disintegration and regrouping into new constellations in response to changing subsistence conditions, is linked to particular patterns of individual language use. A speaker may move through several linguistic environments throughout his or her lifetime, which leads to a high rate of idiolectal change. At the same time, the diverse linguistic origins of members of a band also lead to marked variation in the language use of different speakers. Benjamin (2001: 111) discusses NA in terms of a mesh-like relation between language varieties which is idiolectal as much as it is dialectal. Consequently, it is not always easy to identify clear-cut language boundaries. Lanoh and MMB form a continuum of such linguistic interaction and, in the sociolinguistic sense, represent a unitary linguistic constellation.[15]

There is also lexical evidence for such a Semang language constellation. In the study by Dunn et al. (2011), Neighbor-Net clustering methods are used to consider synchronic similarities in basic vocabulary among 27 Aslian varieties representing the three sub-branches. The analysis draws on the coding of the reflex of each basic meaning as a potential cognate at the Proto-Aslian level. Thus, there is no a priori recognition of the established sub-branches, and possible intra-Aslian loans are included in the analysis. The resulting clustering patterns confirm that vocabulary similarities are first and foremost associated with the established historical sub-groupings. Further to this, however, the patterns show that significant vocabulary similarities are associated with the cluster of languages comprising MMB and Lanoh. That is, in spite of their different sub-branch identities, MMB and

Lanoh have a traceable amount of basic vocabulary in common which is not shared with the rest of Aslian.[16] A follow-up study drawing on both lexicostatistics and Bayesian phylogenetic inference provides further evidence of considerable secondary lexical exchange between Lanoh and all of the MMB branch, unparalleled in the rest of the Aslian setting (Burenhult et al. 2011). Apparently, secondary contact and borrowing within the forager constellation have made its languages lexically more similar than what would be expected on traditional historical grounds (cf. Benjamin 1976a). The results are summarized in Figure 8.2.

There is less evidence for parallel similarities in grammar (perhaps stemming partly from the fact that detailed grammatical data is still lacking for many of the languages). However, at least one morphemic category present in both MMB and Lanoh has yet to be discovered elsewhere in Aslian. This is a causative infix surfacing in some MMB languages as <*ri*> and in Semnam (a Lanoh variety) as <*yi*> (the *y* in the latter is an expected reflex, given the lack of a phoneme /r/ in Semnam). The following examples from Jahai and Semnam exemplify the two manifestations: Jahai *kribis*, 'to kill', from *kbis*, 'to die'; Semnam *kyibəs*, 'to kill', from *kbəs*, 'to die'. Another candidate is plural inflection in human nouns by means of an infix <*ra*> in some MMB languages and a corresponding <*ya*> in Semnam, as in the following examples: Jahai *krajɨh*, 'boys', from *kjɨh*, 'boy'; Semnam *kyalooʔ*, 'older siblings', from *klooʔ*, 'older sibling'. However, this infix is also present in a northern variety of Semaq Beri, a Southern Aslian language (Burenhult et al. 2011), which probably borrowed it from NA Batek.

The small number of unique shared typological features notwithstanding, MMB and Lanoh behave in some important respects as a linguistic unit. Thus, the foragers exhibit linguistic interaction patterns determined by their mobile lifestyle, and their lexicon and grammar are shaped in part by this interaction. The hunting-gathering niche once again proves to be helpful, this time providing the framework for specific linguistic mechanisms of internal contact and exchange.

8.4   Conclusions

One's view of prehistoric processes depends ultimately on how one ontologizes the research question in the first place. A conceptual basis of macro-areal language/subsistence correlations (as in the Farming/ Language Dispersal Hypothesis) will result in interpretations of prehistory different from those arrived at with a basis represented by a local contemporary constellation of heterogeneous groups (as in the Orang Asli Ethnogenesis Hypothesis). Both, of course, provide important insights.

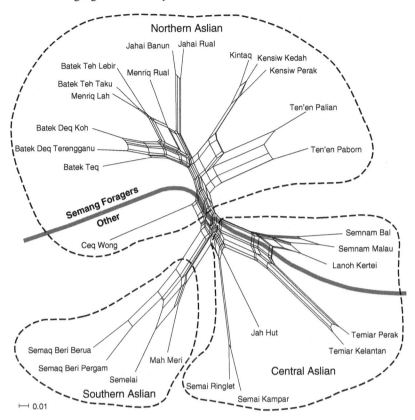

Figure 8.2 Neighbor-Net graph of Aslian basic vocabulary, based on reflexes of 160 basic meanings in 27 Aslian language varieties (from Dunn et al. 2011). The words of each language are coded as members of potential cognate sets. The Neighbor-Net graph represents binary splits of this data (split by whether or not they have reflexes of a particular cognate set) as a series of parallel lines; thus the parallelograms in the graph show two conflicting divisions of the data. Longer lines show splits supported by more words; where the graph has the form of an (unrooted) tree we can say that the data is treelike (i.e. has low levels of conflict). The method measures language similarity without a priori recognition of established sub-branches, and the network should therefore not be regarded as a 'family tree'. The clustering shows that there is a pattern of lexical commonality which corresponds to the Northern Aslian subbranch of Aslian, represented here by varieties of Batek, Menriq, Jahai, Kensiw, Kentaq and Ceq Wong. However, it also shows that there is a conflicting pattern of commonality which excludes Ceq Wong but includes the Central Aslian languages Lanoh and Semnam. This pattern coincides with the Semang forager societies.

The present work sets out from yet another conceptual basis: deep local continuity. Recognizing the diachronically and locally most stable elements in Malayan prehistory (as evidenced by genetics) as a workable starting point, it sets historical processes, especially linguistic ones, against a continuous niche of hunting-gathering, currently occupied by the Semang forager tradition. While still exploratory, the approach proves useful in that it calls attention to some linguistic issues of potential significance to models of peninsular prehistory. Thus, it (1) addresses the role of language shift in the history of Aslian languages, (2) calls into question the customary equation between the Semang foragers and the Northern sub-branch of Aslian, and (3) presents linguistic indications that the Semang sphere represents a unit of distinct language interaction. From the point of view of linguistics, any future pursuit of these and other questions relies on further grammatical and lexical description of the understudied and endangered Aslian languages, comprehensive reconstruction of the historical phonology of Aslian sub-branches and careful typological comparisons of structural and semantic features in Aslian.

Unlike most models of peninsular prehistory, the approach taken here treats the Semang foragers as the centrepiece of inquiry. This follows from their particular connection with locally ancient genetic lineages. Their current combination of cultural, biological and linguistic features is seen as the result of an interplay between distinct historical processes, deep economic and genetic ancestries merging with more recent cultural and linguistic ones. Consequently, the Semang are viewed as neither isolated relics, nor recent 'by-products', but as a successful blend of old and new. It has been suggested here that the economic niche of hunting-gathering has been the crucial stable feature in this development. While this remains to be confirmed, it is clear that the deep local signal of the foragers of the Malayan rainforest hints at a continuity which seems difficult to reconcile with the revisionist view of the history of hunting and gathering.

Acknowledgements

I am grateful to the editors for inviting this contribution to the volume. The original version was written in 2006–2007, and revisions and updates were made in 2014. The ideas developed here are inspired by exchanges with several scholars on the Orang Asli, including Dee Baer, Geoffrey Benjamin, David Bulbeck, Alfred Daniels, Bob Dentan, Gérard Diffloth, Alan Fix, Nicole Kruspe and Lye Tuck-Po. For additional input I am grateful to Michael Dunn, Nick Evans, Marianne Gullberg, Gunter Senft and Thomas Widlok. Special thanks to Dee Baer, Peter Bellwood, David Bulbeck, Alan Fix, Tom Güldemann and Nicole Kruspe for commenting on earlier drafts of the chapter. Research was supported by the Max Planck Society, a European Community

Marie Curie Fellowship, a Volkswagen Foundation DoBeS grant and a Swedish Research Council project grant.

NOTES

1. From now on I will avoid the term 'Negrito' as far as possible. While it is still a largely uncontroversial label (especially in the Philippine context), its use as a cover term for Andamanese, Malayan and Philippine hunter-gatherers is unfortunate because it is based on superficial similarities. There is little evidence, least of all linguistic, that the three groups share a recent common origin.

2. The spelling of the ethnonym and language *Ceq Wong* (which in previous literature is usually rendered as *Chewong*) follows Kruspe (2009).

3. 'Aboriginal Malay' is a term used frequently to distinguish these groups from the Muslim Malay majority, but Benjamin himself prefers to include them in a more general 'Malay' societal pattern.

4. The relationship between foraging and linguistic subgrouping is further complicated by Semaq Beri, a Southern Aslian language spoken by a group of c. 2,300 people with a clear focus on foraging, although they are not included in the Semang societal grouping. Benjamin (1976a, 1985) treats their nomadism as a deviation from the defined cultural-linguistic division (collector-trader Southern Aslian), proposing that the Semaq Beri are 'secondarily nomadic'. They currently coexist with Semang neighbours (Batek) and may have developed mobile forager characteristics in response to this contact. Such a scenario is supported to some extent by our own studies of lexical diversification (Burenhult et al. 2011).

5. In one of our conversations, Geoffrey Benjamin once referred to Fix's original proposal as one of 'Negritoisation'. I have not come across this term in print, but it illustrates well the contrast between Fix's paradigm and the traditional view of 'Negritos' as physical relics.

6. Throughout his extensive work, Benjamin himself has always more or less explicitly left the door open for deeper hunter-gatherer continuity and the adoption of Austroasiatic (see e.g. Benjamin 1976a: 82–83, 1985: 235, 1997: 100–101, footnote 21, 2002: 34–37).

7. Endicott and Bellwood (1991) challenge these claims in the Malayan context, and Porter and Marlowe (2007) question the general association of hunter-gatherers with marginal habitats.

8. For genetic indications of this in the Semang of southern Thailand, see Fucharoen et al. 2001.

9. The Semaq Beri (speakers of a Southern Aslian language with a focus on foraging) may be a recent and unusual exception in the Malayan context (Burenhult et al. 2011).

10. Benjamin (1985: 244, 261) specifically mentions the Satingphra trade-and-civilization complex of the Isthmian east coast, which arose around 2,000 years ago, and its associated trade routes, as a pivotal factor in the development of Semang culture.

11. The assumed connection is based ultimately on the alleged physical and cultural similarities between these populations (see e.g. Cooper 1940). Genetic evidence disproves any specific recent shared ancestry between hunter-gatherer groups in the Malay Peninsula, the Andaman Islands and the Philippines (Hill et al. 2006: 2488). There is similarly no reason to expect a shared linguistic origin. However, for a

different kind of linguistic connection between Austroasiatic and Andamanese, see Chapter 9 by Blevins, this volume.

12. To the extent that it has been considered at all, a language shift to Austroasiatic in the peninsula has in previous work been addressed only in terms of a "palaeo-sociolinguistic problem" restricted to the Semang and, as such, an obstacle to models proposing a distinct and locally ancient origin of them (Benjamin 2002: 35).

13. Expressives form a distinct word class in many Southeast Asian languages (Diffloth 1972). They are similar to the 'ideophones' of the Africanist and Americanist descriptive traditions.

14. I am grateful to Nicole Kruspe for her input regarding these features in Ceq Wong. As far as the bilabial fricatives are concerned, syllable-final voiceless ones are well attested in Maniq and Menraq-Batek languages (Bishop 1996: 23; Burenhult 2005: 28; Phaiboon 2006: 208). In Ceq Wong a syllable-initial variant has been recorded by Kruspe, but only in some speakers. She also reports a single instance of a syllable-final bilabial fricative in one Semaq Beri (Southern Aslian) narrative, the only such example found outside Northern Aslian.

15. Present-day Lanoh has a limited pattern of interaction mainly with Kentaq and Kensiw. Historically, however, it was also in direct contact with Kayen (a Maniq variety spoken in Selama, now extinct) and Jahai (Schebesta 1928; Burenhult, field notes).

16. It is important to point out that cognate forms can (and often do) exist in other Aslian languages. What makes MMB and Lanoh stand out as a unit is a particular pattern of association of certain Aslian forms with some specific basic meanings. In other words, it is the mapping of form and meaning, not the presence or absence of forms in languages, which accounts for the similarities. Therefore we cannot automatically regard the similarities as potential effects of lexical influence from a non-Austroasiatic substratum, or other types of extra-Aslian borrowing.

References

Bailey, Robert C., Genevieve Head, Mark Jenike, Bruce Owen, Robert Rechtman, and Elzbieta Zechenter. (1989). Hunting and gathering in tropical rain forest: Is it possible? *American Anthropologist* 91(1): 59–82.

Bellwood, Peter. (1979). *Man's conquest of the Pacific: The prehistory of Southeast Asia and Oceania*. New York: Oxford University Press.

Bellwood, Peter. (1985). *Prehistory of the Indo-Malaysian archipelago*. Sydney: Academic Press.

Bellwood, Peter. (1993). Cultural and biological differentiation in Peninsular Malaysia: The last 10,000 years. *Asian Perspectives* 32: 37–60.

Bellwood, Peter. (1997). *Prehistory of the Indo-Malaysian archipelago*. Honolulu: University of Hawaii Press.

Bellwood, Peter. (2004). The origins and dispersals of agricultural communities in Southeast Asia. In Ian Glover and Peter Bellwood (eds.), *Southeast Asia: From prehistory to history*. Abingdon/New York: RoutledgeCurzon, 21–40.

Bellwood, Peter. (2005). Examining the farming/language dispersal hypothesis in the East Asian context. In Laurent Sagart, Roger Blench and Alicia Sanchez-Mazas (eds.), *The peopling of East Asia: Putting together archaeology, linguistics and genetics*, Abingdon/New York: RoutledgeCurzon, 17–30.

Benjamin, Geoffrey. (1976a). Austroasiatic subgroupings and prehistory in the Malay Peninsula. In Philip N. Jenner, Laurence C. Thompson and Stanley Starosta (eds.), *Austroasiatic studies, Part I*. Honolulu: The University Press of Hawaii, 37–128.

Benjamin, Geoffrey. (1976b). An outline of Temiar grammar. In Philip N. Jenner, Laurence C. Thompson and Stanley Starosta (eds.), *Austroasiatic studies, Part I*. Honolulu: The University Press of Hawaii, 129–188.

Benjamin, Geoffrey. (1985). In the long term: Three themes in Malayan cultural ecology. In Karl L. Hutterer, A. Terry Rambo and George Lovelace (eds.), *Cultural values and human ecology in Southeast Asia*. University of Michigan: Center for South and Southeast Asian Studies, 219–278.

Benjamin, Geoffrey. (1997). Issues in the ethnohistory of Pahang. In Nik Hassan Shuhaimi bin Nik Abd. Rahman, Mohamed Mokhtar Abu Bakar, Ahmad Hakimi Khairuddin and Jazamuddin Baharuddin (eds.), *Pembangunan arkeologi pelancongan negeri Pahang*. Pekan: Muzium Pahang, 82–121.

Benjamin, Geoffrey. (2001). Orang Asli languages: From heritage to death? In Razha Rashid and Wazir Jahan Karim (eds.), *Minority cultures of peninsular Malaysia: Survivals of indigenous heritage*. Penang: Academy of Social Sciences,101–122.

Benjamin, Geoffrey. (2002). On being tribal in the Malay world. In Geoffrey Benjamin and Cynthia Chou (eds.), *Tribal communities in the Malay world: Historical, cultural and social perspectives*. Singapore: Institute of Southeast Asian Studies, 7–76.

Benjamin, Geoffrey. (2004). The Malay world as a regional array. Paper presented at the International Workshop on Scholarship in Malay World Studies: Looking Back, Striding Ahead, Leiden, the Netherlands, 26–28 August, 2004.

Benjamin, Geoffrey. (2012). The Aslian languages of Malaysia and Thailand: An assessment. *Language Documentation and Description* 11: 136–230.

Bishop, Nancy M. (1996). A preliminary description of Kensiw (Maniq) phonology. *Mon-Khmer Studies* 25: 227–253.

Bloch, Jules. (1952). L'Andaman. In Marcel Cohen (ed.), *Les langues du monde*. Paris: Société linguistique de Paris, 512–521.

Bower, Bruce. (1989). A world that never existed: Re-assessing hunter-gatherers. *Science News* 135(17): 264–266.

Brenzinger, Matthias (ed.). (1992). *Language death: Factual and theoretical explorations with special reference to East Africa*. Berlin/New York: Mouton de Gruyter.

Bulbeck, F. David. (1996). Holocene biological evolution of the Malay Peninsula aborigines (*Orang Asli*). *Perspectives in Human Biology* 2: 37–61.

Bulbeck, F. David. (2003). Hunter-gatherer occupation of the Malay Peninsula from the Ice Age to the Iron Age. In J. Mercader (ed.), *The archaeology of tropical rain forests*. New Brunswick, NJ: Rutgers University Press, 119–160.

Bulbeck, F. David. (2004a). Indigenous traditions and exogenous influences in the early history of Peninsular Malaysia. In Ian Glover and Peter Bellwood (eds.), *Southeast Asia: From prehistory to history*. London: RoutledgeCurzon, 314–336.

Bulbeck, F. David. (2004b). An integrated perspective on Orang Asli ethnogenesis. In Victor Paz (ed.), *Southeast Asian archaeology: Wilhelm G. Solheim II Festschrift*. Quezon City: The University of the Philippines Press, 366–399.

Bulbeck, F. David and Adam Lauer. (2006). Human variation and evolution in Holocene Peninsular Malaysia. In Marc Oxenham and Nancy Tayles (eds.), *Bioarchaeology of Southeast Asia*. Cambridge: Cambridge University Press, 133–171.

Burenhult, Niclas. (2005). *A grammar of Jahai*. Canberra: Pacific Linguistics.

Burenhult, Niclas. (2006). Body part terms in Jahai. *Language Sciences* 28: 162–180.

Burenhult, Niclas. (2008). Streams of words: hydrological lexicon in Jahai. *Language Sciences* 30: 182–199.

Burenhult, Niclas and Claudia Wegener. (2009). Preliminary notes on the phonology, orthography and vocabulary of Semnam (Austroasiatic, Malay Peninsula). *Journal of the Southeast Asian Linguistics Society* 1: 283–312.

Burenhult, Niclas, Nicole Kruspe and Michael Dunn. (2011). Language history and culture groups among Austroasiatic-speaking foragers of the Malay Peninsula. In Nick Enfield and Joyce White (eds.), *Dynamics of human diversity: The case of mainland Southeast Asia*. Canberra: Pacific Linguistics, 257–275.

Carey, Iskandar. (1976). *Orang Asli: The aboriginal tribes of Peninsular Malaysia*. Kuala Lumpur: Oxford University Press.

Collins, James T. (ed.). (2006). *Borneo and the homeland of the Malays*. Kuala Lumpur: Dewan Bahasa dan Pustaka.

Cooper, John M. (1940). Andamanese-Semang-Eta cultural relations. *Primitive Man* 13(2): 29–47.

Dallos, Csilla. (2003). Identity and opportunity: Asymmetrical household integration among the Lanoh, newly sedentary hunter-gatherers and forest collectors of Peninsular Malaysia. Doctoral thesis. McGill University: Department of Anthropology.

Diffloth, Gérard. (1972). Notes on expressive meaning. In P. M. Peranteau, J. N. Levi and G. C. Phares (eds.), *Papers from the Eighth Regional Meeting, Chicago Linguistic Society*. Chicago: University of Chicago Press, 440–447.

Diffloth, Gérard. (1975). Les langues mon-khmer de Malaisie: classification historique et innovations. *Asie du sud-est et monde insulinde* 6(4): 1–19.

Diffloth, Gérard. (1976). Jah-Hut: An Austroasiatic language of Malaysia. In Nguyen Dang Liem (ed.), *South-east Asian linguistic studies*, Vol. 2. Canberra: Pacific Linguistics, 73–118.

Diffloth, Gérard. (1979). Aslian languages and Southeast Asian prehistory. *Federation Museums Journal (new series)* 24: 2–16.

Diffloth, Gérard. (2005). The contribution of linguistic palaeontology to the homeland of Austro-Asiatic. In Laurent Sagart, Roger Blench and Alicia Sanchez-Mazas (eds.), *The peopling of East Asia: Putting together archaeology, linguistics and genetics*. Abingdon/New York: RoutledgeCurzon, 77–80.

Diffloth, Gérard and Norman Zide. (1992). Austro-Asiatic languages. In William Bright (ed.), *International encyclopedia of linguistics*, Vol. 1. New York/Oxford: Oxford University Press, 137–142.

Dorian, Nancy C. (1981). *Language death: The life cycle of a Scottish Gaelic dialect*. Philadelphia: University of Pennsylvania Press.

Dunn, Michael, Niclas Burenhult, Nicole Kruspe, Sylvia Tufvesson and Neele Becker. (2011). Aslian linguistic prehistory: A case study in computational phylogenetics. *Diachronica* 28(3): 291–323.

Dunn, M., Kruspe, N. and Burenhult, N. (2013). Time and place in the prehistory of the Aslian languages. *Human Biology* 85: 383–400.

Endicott, Kirk. (1979). *Batek Negrito religion: The world-view and rituals of a hunting and gathering people of Peninsular Malaysia*. Oxford: Clarendon.

Endicott, Kirk M. and Peter Bellwood. (1991). The possibility of independent foraging in the rain forest of Peninsular Malaysia. *Human Ecology* 19(2): 151–185.

Fase, Willem, Koen Jaspaert and Sjaak Kroon (eds.). (1992). *Maintenance and loss of minority languages*. Amsterdam: John Benjamins.

Fix, Alan G. (1995). Malayan paleosociology: Implications for patterns of genetic variation among the Orang Asli. *American Anthropologist* 97(2): 313–323.

Fix, Alan G. (2002). Foragers, farmers, and traders in the Malayan Peninsula: Origins of cultural and biological diversity. In Kathleen D. Morrison and Laura L. Junker (eds.), *Forager-traders in South and Southeast Asia*. Cambridge: Cambridge University Press, 185–202.

Fix, Alan G. (2011). Origin of genetic diversity among Malaysian Orang Asli: An alternative to the demic diffusion model. In Nick Enfield and Joyce White (eds.), *Dynamics of human diversity: The case of mainland Southeast Asia*. Canberra: Pacific Linguistics, 277–291.

Fucharoen, G., S. Fucharoen and S. Horai. (2001). Mitochondrial DNA polymorphisms in Thailand. *Journal of Human Genetics* 46(3): 115–125.

Gal, Susan. 1979. *Language shift: Social determinants of linguistic change in bilingual Austria*. New York: Academic Press.

Hamilton, Annette. (2006). Reflections on the 'disappearing Sakai': A tribal minority in southern Thailand. *Journal of Southeast Asian Studies* 37(2): 293–314.

Headland, Thomas N. (1987). The wild yam question: How well could independent hunter-gatherers live in a tropical rain forest ecosystem? *Human Ecology* 15: 463–491.

Headland, Thomas N. and Robert C. Bailey (eds.). (1991). Human foragers in tropical rain forests [special issue of *Human Ecology* 19(2)].

Headland, Thomas N. and Lawrence A. Reid. (1989). Hunter-gatherers and their neighbors from prehistory to the present. *Current Anthropology* 30(1): 43–66.

Hill, Catherine, Pedro Soares, Maru Mormina, et al.(2006). Phylogeography and ethnogenesis of Aboriginal Southeast Asians. *Molecular Biological Evolution* 23(12): 2480–2491.

Junker, Laura L. (2002). Southeast Asia: Introduction. In Kathleen D. Morrison and Laura L. Junker (eds.), *Forager-traders in South and Southeast Asia*. Cambridge: Cambridge University Press, 131–166.

Kruspe, Nicole. (2004). *A grammar of Semelai*. Cambridge: Cambridge University Press.

Kruspe, Nicole. (2009). Loanwords in Ceq Wong, an Austroasiatic language of Peninsular Malaysia. In Martin Haspelmath and Uri Tadmor (eds.), *Loanwords in the world's languages: A comparative handbook of lexical borrowing*. Berlin: Mouton de Gruyter, 659–685.

Kruspe, Nicole. (2010). *A dictionary of Mah Meri, as spoken at Bukit Bangkong*. Honolulu: University of Hawai'i Press.

Kruspe, Nicole, Niclas Burenhult and Ewelina Wnuk. (2014). Northern Aslian. In Paul Sidwell and Mathias Jenny (eds.), *Handbook of the Austroasiatic languages*. Leiden: Brill, 419–474.

Lye Tuck-Po. (1997). Knowledge, forest, and hunter-gatherer movement: The Batek of Pahang, Malaysia. Doctoral dissertation. University of Hawai'i: Department of Anthropology.

Lye Tuck-Po. (2004). *Changing pathways: Forest degradation and the Batek of Pahang, Malaysia*. Lanham, MD: Lexington Books.

Matisoff, James A. (2003). Aslian: Mon-Khmer of the Malay Peninsula. *Mon-Khmer Studies* 33: 1–58.

Morrison, Kathleen D. and Laura L. Junker (eds.). (2002). *Forager-traders in South and Southeast Asia*. Cambridge: Cambridge University Press.

Nagata, Shuichi. (2006). Subgroup 'names' of the Sakai (Thailand) and the Semang (Malaysia): A literature survey. *Anthropological Science* 114: 45–57.

Oppenheimer, Stephen. (2011). MtDNA variation and southward Holocene human dispersals within mainland Southeast Asia. In Nick Enfield and Joyce White (eds.), *Dynamics of human diversity: The case of mainland Southeast Asia*. Canberra: Pacific Linguistics, 81–108.

Phaiboon Duangchan. (2006). The Northern Aslian languages of southern Thailand. *Mon-Khmer Studies* 36: 207–224.

Porter, Claire C. and Frank W. Marlowe. (2007). How marginal are forager habitats? *Journal of Archaeological Science* 34: 59–68.

Rambo, A. Terry. (1988). Why are the Semang? Ecology and ethnogenesis of aboriginal groups in Peninsular Malaysia. In A. Terry Rambo, K. Gillogly and Karl L. Hutterer (eds.), *Ethnic diversity and the control of natural resources in Southeast Asia*. Ann Arbor: University of Michigan Press, 19–35.

Reid, Lawrence A. (1987). The early switch hypothesis: Linguistic evidence for contact between Negritos and Austronesians. *Man and Culture in Oceania* 3: 41–59.

Reid, Lawrence A. (1994). Unravelling the linguistic histories of Philippine Negritos. In Tom Dutton and Darrell T. Tryon (eds.), *Language contact and change in the Austronesian world*. Berlin/New York: Mouton de Gruyter, 443–475.

Renfrew, Colin. (1987). *Archaeology and language: The puzzle of Indo-European origins*. London: Jonathan Cape.

Sasse, Hans-Jürgen. (1992). Theory of language death. In Matthias Brenzinger (ed.), *Language death: Factual and theoretical explorations with special reference to East Africa*. Berlin: Mouton de Gruyter, 7–30.

Sather, Clifford. (1995). Sea nomads and rainforest hunter-gatherers: Foraging adaptations in the Indo-Malaysian archipelago. In Peter Bellwood, James J. Fox and Darrell Tryon (eds.), *The Austronesians: Historical and comparative perspectives*. Canberra: Department of Anthropology, Research School of Pacific and Asian Studies, Australian National University, 229–268.

Schebesta, Paul. (1928). *Among the forest dwarfs of Malaya*. Kuala Lumpur: Oxford University Press.

Schebesta, Paul. (1952). Die Negrito Asiens: Geschichte, Geographie, Umwelt, Demographie und Antropologie der Negrito. Vienna: St. Gabriel Verlag.

Skeat, Walter William and Charles Otto Blagden. (1906). *Pagan races of the Malay Peninsula*. 2 vols. London: Macmillan and Co. (Reprint: 1966, London: Frank Cass)

Solheim, Wilhelm G. (1980). Searching for the origins of the Orang Asli. *Federations Museum Journal* 25: 61–75.

Spielmann, Katherine A. and James F. Eder. (1994). Hunters and farmers: Then and now. *Annual Review of Anthropology* 23: 303–323.

Stiles, Daniel. (1992). The hunter-gatherer revisionist debate. *Anthropology Today* 8(2): 13–17.

Thomason, Sarah G. and Terrence Kaufman. (1988). *Language contact, creolization, and genetic linguistics*. Berkeley: University of California Press.

Trombetti, Alfredo. (1923). Elementi di glottologia. Volume pubblicato a spese della cassa di risparmio in Bologna. Bologna.

van der Sluys, Cornelia M. I. (2000). Gifts from the immortal ancestors: Cosmology and ideology of Jahai sharing. In Peter P. Schweitzer, Megan Biesele and Robert K. Hitchcock (eds.), *Hunters and gatherers in the modern world: Conflict, resistance and self-determination.*New York: Berghahn, 427–454.

Weinreich, Uriel. (1979) [1953]. *Languages in contact: findings and problems*. The Hague: Mouton.

Whitmore, T. C. (1984). *Tropical rain forests of the Far East*. Oxford: Clarendon.

Winstedt, Richard O. (1961). *The Malays: A cultural history*, 6th edition. London: Routledge and Kegan Paul.

Zide, Norman and Vishvajit Pandya. (1989). A bibliographical introduction to Andamanese linguistics. *Journal of the American Oriental Society* 109(4): 639–651.

9 Linguistic Clues to Andamanese Prehistory: Understanding the North-South Divide

Juliette Blevins

9.1 An Introduction to Languages and Peoples of the Andaman Islands

The Andaman Islands are a cluster of more than 200 islands in the Bay of Bengal between India and Myanmar (Burma) (see Map 9.1).

They were once home to a range of hunter-gatherer societies, who are best known from the descriptions of Man (1883) and Radcliffe-Brown (1914, 1922). These writers, along with the Andamanese themselves, split the population of the Andamans into two primary language/culture groups, the 'Great Andaman Group' and the 'Little Andaman Group' (Radcliffe-Brown 1922: 11). The Great Andaman Group inhabits the northern and central reaches of the islands and its members speak approximately 10 different closely related languages (Aka-Cari, Aka-Bo, Aka-Kora, Aka-Jeru, Aka-Kede, Aka-Kol, Oko-Juwoi, A-Pucikwar, Akar-Bale, and Aka-Bea). The Little Andaman Group, or Ongans, inhabit Little Andaman Island and the southern reaches of the main island chain, and speak three or four closely related languages (Onge, Jarawa, Jangil, and perhaps Sentinelese). It is this north-south divide in language/culture between the Great Andaman Group and the Little Andaman Group that the title of this chapter refers to.

Map 9.2 shows the approximate locations of these tribes and their speakers in the mid-1800s based on nineteenth-century government officer reports.

Jangil has not been spoken for more than a hundred years, and today there are no more than 40 speakers of 'Great Andamanese'. Most describe modern Andamanese as a 'mixed language' or koine, involving a melange of the once 10 distinct languages, with dominant features of Aka-Jeru (Abbi 2006: 20–22). Most Great Andamanese speakers are bilingual in Andamani Hindi, and little remains of their hunter-gatherer lifestyle. In contrast, Onge, Jarawa, and Sentinelese are still spoken, and these tribes still live primarily a hunter-gatherer lifestyle (Sreenathan 2001; Weber 2006).

The indigenous people of the Andaman Islands, including all speakers of Jarawa and Onge, are 'Negritos' – a descriptive term for dark-skinned

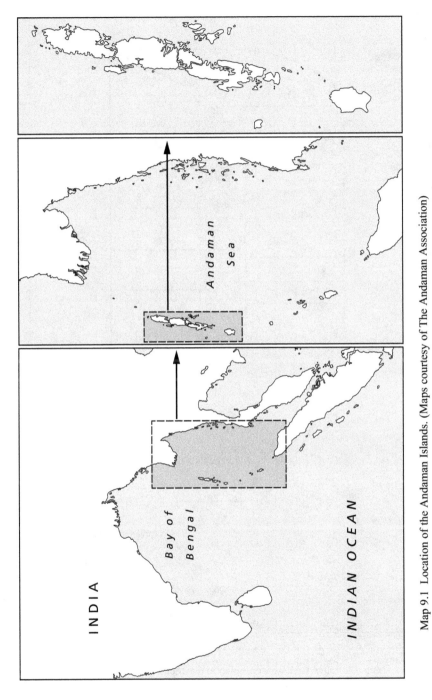

Map 9.1 Location of the Andaman Islands. (Maps courtesy of The Andaman Association)

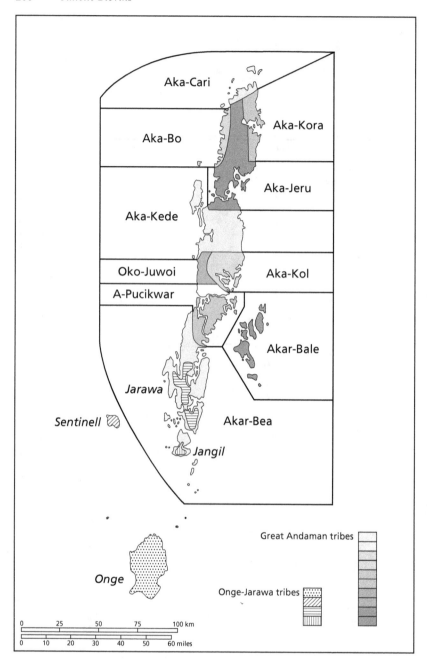

Map 9.2 Tribal territories occupied in the 1860s. (Maps courtesy of The
Andaman Association)

frizzy-haired people of insular and mainland Southeast Asia, usually of short stature. Negrito hunter-gatherer populations are found in the Philippines, and in peninsular Malay and Thailand. In both the Philippines and mainland Southeast Asia, Negritos are thought to represent populations which predate the influx of Austronesian and Austroasiatic speaking populations respectively (see Chapter 10 by Reid, this volume; Chapter 8 by Burenhult, this volume; Weber 2006).

Ethnologies of the Andamanese include Man (1883) and Radcliffe-Brown (1922), with recent archaeological studies summarized in Cooper (2002), and a wide range of earlier work summarized in Weber (2006). The Andamanese appear to represent a pre-Neolithic hunter-gatherer society and many culture features are shared across the north-south divide. There is no evidence of agriculture. Stone flake tools were used, but wood, shells, and bones (including sting-ray barbs) were preferred as points. There is also no evidence of fire-making. Prior to the introduction of matches in the nineteenth century, the Andamanese had no means of making fire. They kept hearth fires burning, carried resin torches through the forest, and buried smoldering logs for future use. The Andamanese manufactured rudimentary rafts, dugout log canoes, and single outriggers, but none of their craft were built for long sea voyages. Shelters, made of wood and woven palm leaves, included small temporary huts, put together quickly while hunting; semi-permanent individual family houses; and more solid large communal shelters. Clay cooking pots are made by all groups, though shapes differ across the north-south divide. The most involved technology may be that of the bow and arrow: bow size and shape distinguishes the northern and southern groups, and all tribes have at least four distinct arrow types. Another flourishing technology is the production of head, neck, and waist ornaments from flowers and plant fibers. Ceremonial practices shared across the north-south divide include long specialized fasts associated with initiation, the ceremonial use of red-ochre and animal fat as body paint, and the exhumation of human bones, which are made into ornamental necklaces.

The physical world inhabited by the Andamanese is rich and varied. The flora and fauna of the islands include thousands of plant species, with a wide range of hardwood trees, palms, bamboos, tubers, canes, and orchids. There is an abundance of reptiles, including snakes, salt water crocodiles, monitor lizards, turtles, small lizards, and geckos. The jungles are home to wild pigs, megapodes, a myriad of other birds, as well as a dozen species of indigenous mammals, including shrews, bats, and a palm civet. Coastal waters and inlets are home to dugongs, hundreds of fish species, crustaceans, and mollusks. Dogs live on the islands, but were introduced only in about 1858, with dramatic effects on the hunt. Prior to their introduction, wild pig hunts represented a special challenge, with pig jaws hung as trophies, and special initiation ceremonies for a young man's first successful hunt. With dogs, however, the hunt was easier, and the value and prestige associated with prize game fell. The jungles are also home to many bee species, and the Andamanese gather honey regularly during the dry seasons. They have good knowledge of a range of plants useful as bee repellents, and refer to seasons by the flowers in blossom from which bees collect nectar.

With this flora and fauna, it may not be surprising to find that populations are divided into 'coastal' and 'inland' groups. Each Andaman language has a term for this division. For example, in Aka-Bea, coast-dwellers are *ar-yoto* (lit. 'one who uses large nets and harpoon lines'), while inland people are *erem-taga*, 'jungle dwellers'; in Onge coast dwellers are *əm-bela-kwe* ('person-seacoast-stay'), while forest dwellers are *əŋ-gea-kwe* ('person-land-stay'). Coastal groups tend to excel in turtle hunting, using their acute hearing to shoot turtles in the darkness. Inlanders, on the other hand, are referred to by coast-dwellers as 'deaf', as they lack this particular skill, but show great talent in hunting pigs and other game in the dense jungles.

Linguistic work on languages of the Andamans has been primarily descriptive. Research until approximately 1988 is summarized in the annotated bibliography of Zide and Pandya (1989). Weber (2006) and Blevins (2007) summarize most work done since that time. For Great Andamanese, the most detailed descriptions are Portman's (1887) *Manual of the Andamanese Languages,* Portman's (1898) *Notes on the Languages of the South Andaman Group of Tribes*, Temple's (1903) grammatical and comparative notes, and Man's (1923) *Dictionary of the South Andaman Language* (Aka-Bea). Reconstructions of Great Andamanese in the text that follows are based on these sources, unless noted otherwise.

Many researchers assume that the Great Andamanese languages and the Ongan languages are distantly related based on geographic proximity, as well as cultural and racial similarities. Radcliffe-Brown's (1922: 14) remarks on this topic are representative of this view:

The identity of the flora and fauna of the Little Andaman with those of the Great Andaman and the shallowness of the strait between the islands suggests that at no very remote period they have been united by a continuous land connection. Whether or not this connection existed at the time when the islands were first peopled, it is at any rate reasonable to suppose that the original ancestors of the present Andamanese had one language and one culture. Once the Little Andaman was peopled, the strait between it and the Great Andaman seems to have acted as an effective barrier, to keep the two divisions of the race apart for many centuries. During this period of this separation each division followed its own line of development, with the result that there arose the considerable difference of language and culture that now exist.

However, little firm comparative linguistic evidence has been put forth to support a family relationship between the Great Andamanese and Ongan languages (Blevins 2007: 158–159; Abbi 2008). In recent comparative work on Onge and Jarawa, Blevins (2007) reconstructs a basic Proto-Ongan vocabulary, and suggests a relationship, not with Great Andamanese, but with Proto-Austronesian. In Section 9.2 preliminary Proto-Great Andamanese reconstructions are proposed, based on application of the comparative method to available descriptions. Section 9.3 compares aspects of this preliminary Proto-Great Andamanese vocabulary with features of Proto-Ongan, and suggests early culture differences in sea- versus land-based hunting and gathering. The linguistic differences across the north-south divide are further explored in Section 9.4. Here, a range of Proto-Great Andamanese reconstructions are shown to resemble Proto-Austroasiatic forms. A northern Proto-Austroasiatic adstrate would contrast with a southern Austronesian adstrate, and would support independent linguistic prehistories for the two groups as well.

Before turning to the comparative data, a note is in order concerning contact between the Andamanese and 'outsiders', as many have the inaccurate impression of the Andamanese as one of the most isolated hunter-gatherer groups on earth. Though the Andamanese have traditionally been hostile to outsiders, there is no question that many different travellers have visited the archipelago. Archaeological evidence dates sea trade between India and Thailand across the Bay of Bengal to at least 2,000 years ago; an Arab travelogue of the ninth century describes the Andamanese; and there is extensive evidence that Malaysian, Burmese, and Nicobarese took Andamanese slaves, and collected edible swift's nests and sea-slugs from their coasts and offshore waters (Cooper 2002: 8–31). In addition, Blust (1994) suggests that the outrigger was invented only once in human history, by speakers of Austronesian languages, either in Taiwan or in the northern Philippines. He goes on to suggest that the Andamanese acquired the outrigger by contact with the Nicobarese, who themselves had contact with Austronesian speakers. Despite this evidence of contact, the hostility of Andamanese to outsiders (prior to the establishment of the penal settlement at Port Blair) appears to have resulted in little mixing with visitors, for the simple reason that few visitors who stepped ashore seemed to survive (Cooper 2002: 8–31). The external relationships suggested between Proto-Great Andamanese and Proto-Austroasiatic in the text that follows, or between Proto-Ongan and Proto-Austronesian by Blevins (2007), then, are not easily attributed to contact in situ. They may, however, be taken to reflect potential prehistoric contact zones or family homelands from which migrations to the Andamans took place.

9.2   Proto-Great Andamanese Reconstructions

There has been little past work on the diachronic phonology of the Great Andamanese languages, though Temple (1903) provides a good starting point for comparative phonology and morphology. This is likely because the phonologies of the languages are so similar that little was felt to be needed, apart from listing cognate sets (see, e.g. Temple 1903: 116). Usher (2006), whose primary interest appears to be long-distance comparison, begins by saying "The reconstruction of Proto-Great Andamanese ... is well underway" (p. 295), but contains no comparative data from Great Andamanese languages, and only five reconstructed Proto-Great Andamanese morphemes, four being monosegmental pronominal prefixes (see Table 9.19).

I will try to fill this gap by (in some cases, trivial) application of the comparative method to available data from Great Andamanese languages, most of which comes from Portman (1887, 1898), Temple (1903), and the more detailed Aka-Bea dictionary of Man (1923), including appendices. Interpreting historical sources on these languages is not always straightforward. Temple and Man adopt a transcription system recommended by A. J. Ellis which is narrow in its treatment of vowel quality, and criticize Portman for not following suite. However, many of the quality contrasts Man and Temple transcribe appear to be non-contrastive. In presenting Great Andamanese data in the text that follows, I have taken the liberty of 'normalizing' transcriptions to reflect my phonemic analysis of the languages as having a simple five vowel /i u e o a/ system. In terms of the original symbols used by Man and Temple, their vowel symbols with diacritics are represented here by the same vowel symbol without a diacritic. Other than this, the only differences in transcription are my writing of /ŋ/ for 'ng', the velar nasal, and /c/ for 'ch', a voiceless palatal affricate. With the exception of /c/, /j/, the voiced palatal affricate, and /y/, the voiced palatal glide, all symbols are those of the International Phonetic Alphabet.

9.2.1   Sound Correspondences and the Lexicon

The Great Andamanese languages have similar phonological systems. Portman (1887) provides wordlists from (north to south): Aka-Cari (his Aka Chariar), Aka-Kede, A-Pucikwar (his Aka Bojigiab), and Aka-Bea (his Aka Bia-da), while Man's (1923) dictionary of Aka-Bea provides more extensive phonetic, phonological, morphological, and lexical material on this southernmost Great Andamanese language which borders Ongan languages to the south. All of these languages appear to have oral and nasal stops at bilabial, alveolar/dental, and velar points of articulation. All languages have palatal affricates, and all lack oral fricatives (though Temple 1903: 116 notes that Bojigyab /c/ is palato-dental and tends to *t*, and that the *ch* of Bea tends in Bojigyab to become *s*'). In addition, all languages have sonorants /l r w y/, and all appear to have a contrast between voiced and voiceless stops /p t k/ and /b d b/ in non-final position. Syllable structure in these languages is relatively simple, with V, CV,

Table 9.1 *Great Andamanese consonant correspondences*

Proto-Great Andamanese	*p	*b	*m	*w	
Aka-Cari	p	b	m	w,ø	
Aka-Kede	p	b	m	w	
A-Pucikwar	p/ø	b	m	w	
Aka-Bea	p/b/ø	b	m	w	
Proto-Great Andamanese	*t	(*d)	*n	*l	*r
Aka-Cari	t	d	n	l	r
Aka-Kede	t	d	n	l,y,ø	r
A-Pucikwar	t	d	n	l	r
Aka-Bea	t,d	d	n	l	r
Proto-Great Andamanese	*c	*ɲ	*y	*k	*ŋ
Aka-Cari	c	ɲ	J	k	ŋ
Aka-Kede	c	ɲ	J	k	ŋ
A-Pucikwar	c	ɲ	y	k,c	ŋ
Aka-Bea	c,j	ɲ	y	k,g	ŋ

VC, and CVC syllables in evidence. Words may end in vowels or consonants, and the majority of unaffixed stems are monosyllabic or disyllabic. Stress is transcribed by Man (1923) for Aka-Bea and does not appear to be predictable, although final syllable stress is rare: compare *'rata*, 'sea water'; *'jabag*, 'bad'; and *ya'ba*, 'a little'.

Although Portman, Temple, and Man all transcribe a wealth of vowel qualities, there is, as noted earlier, little evidence for more than a five way /i u e o a/ contrast, with allophonic variation, especially in unstressed position. The most variable reflexes occur where, I hypothesize, Proto-Great Andamanese had a schwa, or a consonant cluster split by vowel insertion. Consonantal sound correspondences in Table 9.1 are based on the comparative data discussed in the text that directly follows.

Reflexes of Proto-Great Andamanese *p are stable (Table 9.2), with the exception of CVVC forms, where final *p appears to be lost in the southern languages. Note also that Aka-Bea shows variable voicing of *p word-finally, as it does for all inherited voiceless stops. This final voicing can be attributed to regressive assimilation in the context of the suffix /-da/, which generally follows substantives, adjectives, and adverbs when they are not followed by a post-position or in construction, and the verbal suffix /-ŋa/ (Man 1923: 5). Regressive voice assimilation has resulted in many stems being analyzed with final voiced obstruents, e.g. Aka-Bea *log* 'channel' < *luk (cf. Aka Bojigiab, Aka Kede, Aka Chariar *luk*), while others, such as /bulap/ (9.2d), are recorded with voiceless and voiced variants of final stops.

Table 9.2 *Correspondences for Proto-Great Andamanese *p (initial, medial, and final)*

Proto-Great Andamanese	Gloss	Aka-Bea	Aka-Bojigiab	Aka-Kede	Aka-Chariar
a. *por	bamboo, cane	por	por	por	por
b. *pila	tusk, tooth	pili/ca	pila, pela	pile	pile
c. *ɲipə	sandfly	ɲipa	ɲipa	ɲipo	ɲipo
d. *bələp	to weep, mourn	bulap, bulab	bilap	bilip	bilup
e. *rərəp	anvil	rarap	rarap	rorop	rorop
f. *cuəp	fasten	co	ca	cup	cop
g. *kap	cheek	-ab-	kap	kap (Aka-Juwai)	

Table 9.3 *Correspondences for Proto-Great Andamanese *b (initial and medial only)*

Proto-Great Andamanese	Gloss	Aka-Bea	Aka-Bojigiab	Aka-Kede	Aka-Chariar
a. *ba	mother-of-pearl	ba	Ba	ba	ba
b. *bələp	to weep, mourn	bulap, bulab	bilap	bilip	bilup
c. *betmə	rope, cord	betma	betmo	betmo	
d. *burəin	hill, mountain	boroin	burin	burin	burain
e. *cabiə	seaweed	cabya	cabia	cabia	cabio

Proto-Great Andamanese *b and *m are also stable, as shown in Table 9.3 and Table 9.4. Note that *b is not reconstructable for word-final position.

Proto-Great Andamanese *w occurs mainly in initial position, though at least one clear example of medial *w is found in *cowai, 'clam' (Table 9.5 h). No final *w is reconstructable at this point. This phoneme is also relatively stable, though in Aka-Chariar the reflex of initial *w is sometimes zero.

Proto-Great Andamanese *t occurs in initial, medial and final position (Table 9.6). As with *p, voiced variants are found finally in Aka-Bea. There is also sometimes initial voicing in Aka-Bea when the next consonant in the word is voiced: Proto-Great Andamanese *tu '1sg', Aka-Bea *do-la* 'I'; Proto-Great Andamanese *tomə, 'flesh, meat', Aka-Bea *dama*. There is no evidence of *t palatalization before *i: Proto-Great Andamanese *tire, 'boy'; Aka-Bojigiab *tire*, Aka-Kede *tira*, Aka-Chariar *tire*. Finally, notice that while /rt/ clusters can occur word-medially in Aka-Bea and

Table 9.4 *Correspondences for Proto-Great Andamanese *m (initial, medial, and final)*

Proto-Great Andamanese	Gloss	Aka-Bea	Aka-Bojigiab	Aka-Kede	Aka-Chariar
a. *muən	dirt, matter, pus, brains	mun	min	mine	mine
b. *mulə	egg	molo	mula	mulo	mulu (Jero)
c. *təmə	flesh, meat	dama	toma	tomo	-tomo
d. *yom	make, work	yom	yom	yom	jom
e. *yəm	rain, rain water	yum	—	jem	—

Table 9.5 *Correspondences for Proto-Great Andamanese *w (initial and medial only)*

Proto-Great Andamanese	Gloss	Aka-Bea	Aka-Bojigiab	Aka-Kede	Aka-Chariar
a. *waic	splash	wij, wej	waic	waic	ec
b. *waka	lobster	waka	waka	waka	oka (Jero 'prawn')
c. *wat	fin	wat, wad	wat	wat	et
d. *werə	to open	were	were	wero	ero
e. *wət	bat, flying fox	wot, wod	wat	wot	wot
f. *wal	lightning	wol/oij 'star'	wal	wai	wai
g. *wolo	adze	wolo	wolo	wo	olo
h. *cowai	clam	cowai	cowai	cowai	cowai

Aka-Bojigiab, the same clusters are split by vowel epenthesis in Aka-Kede and Aka-Chariar in reflexes of Proto-Great Andamanese *artəm, 'ancient, old'. Reflexes of intervocalic *t appear as voiced /d/ sporadically in all Great Andaman languages; if this is predictable, further conditions remain to be discovered.

Though all Great Andaman languages appear to have a contrast between /t/ and /d/, it has a low functional load, and may be due to (1) voicing of *t in Aka-Bea as noted above in assimilation with adjacent voiced sounds; (2) sporadic lenition of *t > d in all languages, as just noted; or (3) borrowing of words with [d]. For example, from Proto-Great Andamanese *kiter, 'coconut', we find Aka-Bea jeder (1), and Aka Chariar, Jeru kider (2); and from *torup, 'to flip', we find Aka-Bea dorop, Aka Kede dorup, but Aka Chariar torup. In Table 9.7 I include all cognate sets where *d might be reconstructed for Proto-Great Andamanese, but the set is quite small, and *d may not be a

Table 9.6 *Correspondences for Proto-Great Andamanese *t (initial, medial, and final)*

Proto-Great Andamanese	Gloss	Aka-Bea	Aka-Bojigiab	Aka-Kede	Aka-Chariar
a. *talak	whetstone	talag	talak	toku	taluko
b. *tei	blood	ti, tei	tei	teyi	tei (Jero)
c. *tɔi	bone	ta	ta	tuwe	toi
d. *artəm	ancient, old	artam	artam	aratom	aratom
e. *lotə	enter; wear	loti	lote	lota	-lota
f. *kət	think, understand	gad	kot	kot	kot
g. *lat	afraid, fear	lat, lad	lat	yat	lat

Table 9.7 *Correspondences for Proto-Great Andamanese *d (initial, medial, and final)*

Proto-Great Andamanese	Gloss	Aka-Bea	Aka-Bojigiab	Aka-Kede	Aka-Chariar
a. *dəp	unripe	ti/ripa	dop	dop	dop
b. *dadi	sail, sailing ship	dadi	dadi	dadi	rali
c. *cuəd	to go	jud, juru	cid	cid	cid

proto-phoneme. For *cud, the Aka-Bea *juru* is glossed by Man (1923) as 'go on a voyage', while *cita*, 'to sail', is provided by Portman for Aka Kede and Aka Chariar. If these forms are all cognate, then the correct reconstruction may be *cut, with the sporadic voicing noted above, as well as further lenition of /d/ to /r/ in Aka-Bea.

Proto-Great Andamanese *n is also found in initial, medial and final position (Table 9.8). The proto-phoneme and its reflexes show a strong co-occurrence with other sonorants within the morpheme, though there are one or two exceptions, such as *pon, 'crab'. Generally, *n continues unchanged. The only exception found so far is Aka-Bea *bad* < *pon, 'crab'. Here, the sound change is most likely assimilatory in the context of the common /-da/ suffix, with a change of pre-Aka Bea *ban-da > bad-da 'crab'. Dental/ alveolar *n contrasts with palatal *ɲ and velar *ŋ in all positions, including before *i: compare *nili, 'shrill' with *ɲipə, 'sandfly', and *ŋilip, 'a cold, nasal mucus'.

Proto-Great Andamanese *l is also found in initial, medial and final position (Table 9.9). The lateral has lenited to /y/ or zero in Aka-Kede.

Table 9.8 *Correspondences for Proto-Great Andamanese *n (initial, medial, and final)*

Proto-Great Andamanese	Gloss	Aka-Bea	Aka-Bojigiab	Aka-Kede	Aka-Chariar
a. *neu	pulse	nu	neu	neu	neu
b. *nili	shrill	nili	nili	nili	nili
c. *inə	water	ina	ena	ine	ino
d. *un ke	to leave	on ke	un-eke	un-i	un-i
e. *burəin	hill, mountain	boroin	burin	burin	burain
f. *marən	soot	marin	maran	maron	maron
g. *len	to repair	len/yi	len	yen	len
h. *muən	dirt, matter, pus, brains	mun	min	mine	mine
i. *pon	crab (big, edible)	bad	pon	pon	pon

Table 9.9 *Correspondences for Proto-Great Andamanese *l (initial, medial, and final)*

Proto-Great Andamanese	Gloss	Aka-Bea	Aka-Bojigiab	Aka-Kede	Aka-Chariar
a. *lat	afraid, fear	lat, lad	Lat	yat	lat
b. *len	to repair	len/yi	len	yen	len
c. *luk	channel	log	luk	luk	luk
d. *lotə	enter; wear	loti	lote	lota	-lota
e. *pila	tusk, tooth	pili/ca	pila, pela	pile	pile
f. *pulia	mist	pulia	pulia	poia	–
g. *talak	whetstone	talag	talak	toku	taluko
h. *wolo	adze	wolo	wolo	wo	olo
i. *pil	corpse, dead	pil	pil	pil	pil
j. *teil	mosquito	teil	teil	teil	teil
k. *wal	lightning	–	wal	wai	wai

Proto-Great Andamanese *r is found in initial, medial and final position (Table 9.10), and has /r/ reflexes in all languages, where /r/ is a rhotic approximant.

Proto-Great Andamanese *c is found in initial, medial and final position Table 9.11, and has /c/ reflexes in all languages. In Aka-Bea, as already mentioned, voiced reflexes are found word-finally (9.11i, k, l), and when the following consonant in the word is voiced (9.11h). Non-high vowels preceding /c/ have undergone diphthongization (*a > ai, *e > ei, etc.), though it is unclear whether this is a feature of Proto-Great Andamanese,

Table 9.10 *Correspondences for Proto-Great Andamanese *r (initial, medial, and final)*

Proto-Great Andamanese	Gloss	Aka-Bea	Aka-Bojigiab	Aka-Kede	Aka-Chariar
a. *raic	broth, watery juice	raij	reic	raic	raic
b. *rau	to bore	reu	reu	ro	ro
c. *rim	resin	rim	rim	rem	rem
d. *romə	to howl	romo	roma	romu	romu
e. *tire	young boy	dere	tire	tira	tire
f. *korə	hand	koro	kora	koro	kora
g. *artəm	ancient, old	artam	artam	aratom	aratom
h. *werə	to open	were	were	wero	ero
i. *kor	middle	–	kor	kor	kor
j. *kider	coconut	jeder	ceter	kiter	kider
k. *mucur	to smile	mujur	moicar	moijur	moicur

Table 9.11 *Correspondences for Proto-Great Andamanese *c (initial, medial, and final)*

Proto-Great Andamanese	Gloss	Aka-Bea	Aka-Bojigiab	Aka-Kede	Aka-Chariar
a. *cabiə	seaweed	cabya	cabia	cabia	cabio
b. *cowai	clam	cowai	cowai	cowai	cowai
c. *cuəd	to go	jud, juru	cid	cid	cid
d. *cuəm	abscess, wound	cum	cim	e/cem	e/cem
e. *cuiɲ	odour	cuiɲ	cuiɲ	cuiɲ	cuɲ
f. *cup	basket	job	cop	cup	cup
g. *bəicə	break to pieces	paica	boice	boica-	boicu-
h. *muicur	to smile	mujur	moicar	moijur	moicur
i. *pəic	pot, vessel	buj	pait	paic	baic
j. *paic	hair	pic	paic	paic	paic
k. *raic	broth, watery juice	raij	reic	raic	raic
l. *waic	splash	wij, wej	waic	waic	ec

or a set of parallel developments in the daughter languages. Where possible, I reconstruct this feature for Proto-Great Andamanese, though it is clearly predictable there, and reflects earlier monophthong + palatal stop sequences.

Proto-Great Andamanese does not appear to have had a voiced palatal stop *j. In modern languages, /j/ is either a voiced reflex of *c, or a strengthening of *y, the palatal glide, in initial position (Table 9.13).

Table 9.12 *Correspondences for Proto-Great Andamanese *ɲ (initial, medial, and final)*

Proto-Great Andamanese	Gloss	Aka-Bea	Aka-Bojigiab	Aka-Kede	Aka-Chariar
a. *ɲipə	sandfly	ɲipa	ɲipa	ɲipo	ɲipo
b. *kaiɲer	rough	eɲer,-reɲi	kaiɲer	kaiɲer	kaiɲir
c. *cuiɲ	odour	cuiɲ	cuiɲ	cuiɲ	cuɲ

Table 9.13 *Correspondences for Proto-Great Andamanese *y (initial only)*

Proto-Great Andamanese	Gloss	Aka-Bea	Aka-Bojigiab	Aka-Kede	Aka-Chariar
a. *yar-	prepare	yar-	yar-	jor	jor
b. *yarə	canoe (of this wood)	yere	yara	jaru	jeru
c. *yitə	tattoo; write	yiti	yiti, yite	jito	jido
d. *yiw	earthquake	yu-	yiwe	jiwu	jiwu
e. *yom	make, work	yom	yom	yom	jom
f. *yulə	a sail; shadow	yolo	yulu	jule	julu
g. *yəm	rain, rain water	yum	–	jem	–

The palatal nasal *ɲ is reconstructable for initial, medial and final positions (Table 9.12).

Proto-Great Andamanese *y is reconstructable for initial position only. In Aka-Chariar and Aka-Kede, *y is strengthened to /j/ (Table 9.13). Recall that in Aka-Kede, synchronic /y/ is often the reflex of Proto-Great Andamanese *l. Forms like Aka-Kede /yom/, 'work' (9.13e), show that /y/ can also be the result of borrowing from neighboring languages where *y is reflected as /y/.

Proto-Great Andamanese *k is reconstructable in initial, medial, and final position. In initial position it is relatively stable, though in a few instances, *k-loss may be in evidence (e.g. 9.12b). Aka-Bea shows voicing of *k > g intervocalically (9.14g), in addition to the final voicing triggered by following voiced suffix-initial consonants (9.14i, j), and the anticipatory voicing when the next consonant is voiced (9.14b). In two sets, there is evidence of velar palatalization, where *ki > ci (9.14k, l). Since Aka-Bojigiab is the only language that has palatal reflexes in both sets, I assume velar palatalization took place in this language only, and that palatal forms spread via contact with other tribes.

Table 9.14 *Correspondences for Proto-Great Andamanese *k (initial, medial, and final)*

Proto-Great Andamanese	Gloss	Aka-Bea	Aka-Bojigiab	Aka-Kede	Aka-Chariar
a. *kəiɲ	arise, awake	geiɲ-, geɲ-,	koiɲe	koiɲe	koiɲ
b. *kət	think, understand	gad	kot	kot	kot
c. *kor	middle	—	kor	kor	kor
d. *korə	hand	koro	kora	koro	kora
e. *koi	new	goi	kui	kui	koi
f. *kmuəl	rainy season	gumul	kimil	kimil	kimil
g. *brukə	reef (of rocks)	boroga	buruke	burko	burku
h. *kukal	to stop	gugl/i	kukat	kukal	—
i. *talak	whetstone	talag	talak	toku	taluko
j. *luk	channel	log	luk	luk	luk
k. *kider	coconut	jeder	ceter	kiter	kider
l. *teki	put down	tegi	teic	teici	teici

Table 9.15 *Correspondences for Proto-Great Andamanese *ŋ (initial, medial, and final)*

Proto-Great Andamanese	Gloss	Aka-Bea	Aka-Bojigiab	Aka-Kede	Aka-Chariar
a. *ŋ-	2 person	ŋ-	ŋ-	ŋ-	ŋ-
b. *ɲilip	a cold, mucus	ɲilip	ɲilip	ɲilip	–
c. *ŋoto	swim	–	ŋata	ŋoto	ŋoto
d. *biɲə	mindful; ask	–	biɲa	biɲi	biɲi
e. *leŋri	smooth	leŋeri	liŋeri	leŋri	leŋre
f. *pəŋ	mouth; cave; well	baŋ	poŋ	poŋ	poŋ
g. *təŋ	above, over; tree	taŋ	taŋ-, toŋ	toŋ	toŋ

Proto-Great Andamanese does not appear to have had a voiced velar stop *g. In modern languages, /g/ is usually a voiced reflex of *k, and has the widest distribution in Aka-Bea, owing to the obstruent voicing processes already discussed.

Proto-Great Andamanese *ŋ is reconstructable in initial, medial, and final position, though medial cases may turn out to be final (as yet, unanalyzed) multimorphemic items. It is reflected as /ŋ/ in all attested Great Andaman languages (Table 9.15). All second-person pronominal forms, singular and plural, begin with reflexes of *ŋ-, which appears to be a general second-person marker.

Table 9.16 *Some Great Andamanese vowel correspondences (V = vowel copy)*

Proto-Great Andamanese	*i	*u	*a	*e	*o	*ə	*ai	*uə
Aka-Cari	i,e	u	a	e	o	o,V	ai	i
Aka-Kede	i	u	a	e	o	o,V	ai	i
A-Pucikwar	i	u	a	e	o	a,V	ai	i
Aka-Bea	i	u,o	a	e	o	a,V	ai,e,i	u

Vowel correspondences for the Great Andamanese languages are some-what more difficult to systematize. A first attempt at correspondences is shown in Table 9.16, with most sets in Tables 9.2–9.15 conforming to these. Vowels which vary widely across the languages are assumed to be phonologizations of earlier schwa: in neutral contexts, this is usually con-tinued as /o/ in the northern languages and as /a/ in the southern languages, but it is also often subject to assimilation of neighboring consonants and/or vowels.

9.2.2   Aspects of Proto-Great Andamanese Morphology

A notable feature of all Great Andamanese languages is the systematic use of a limited range of body part stems or prefixes that serve to delineate semantic properties of the prefixed base. In some languages, like Aka-Bea, the use of these prefixes is systematic and ubiquitous for body parts. In others, like Aka-Kol, prefixes are absent on the majority of words. Some Aka-Bea examples are given in Table 9.17, following Man (1923: 6–8), who quotes Dr. A. J. Ellis's 1882 Presidential Address to the Philological Society.

Reconstruction of the full body part prefix system is beyond the scope of this paper. However, based on the available limited wordlists, preliminary recon-structions in Table 9.18 are proposed, with extremely rough glosses. In some cases, the prefixes may be cognate with body-part roots. For example, Proto-Great Andamanese prefix *ab- associated with humans, the body, and the flesh, may ultimately be cognate with Proto-Great Andamanese *kap, 'cheek', while Proto-Great Andamanese *ig-, 'eye/face area' may be related to the root of Aka Bojigiab *ir-kadig*, 'eye'. The prefix *aka- relating to the mouth, and by extension to language, may have its source in Proto-Great Andamanese *payaka*, 'lips' (cf. Aka-Kol *payaka*, 'lips'). While many aspects of the prefix system have yet to be analyzed, the absence of a full-blown system in Aka-Kol appears to be due to the recent development of the system, rather than its near total loss within Aka-Kol.

Table 9.17 *Aka-Bea body part prefixes*

	Root:	*beriŋa*	*jabag*	*lama*
Prefix/class		good	bad	to miss, fail
ab-	human/body	*a-beriŋa*	*ab-jabag*	*ab-lama*
		good person	bad person	a duffer in turtle hunt
aka-	mouth/voice	*aka-beriŋa*	*aka-jabag*	*aka-lama*
		nice taste	bad taste	one who uses wrong word
un-	hand/foot	*un-beriŋa*	*un-jabag-*	*un-lama*
		clever	stupid	one who misses striking an object with hand or foot
ig-	eye	*ig-beriŋa*	*ig-jabag-*	*ig-lama*
		sharp-sighted	dull-sighted	one who fails to see/find an object
ot-	head/heart	*ot-beriŋa*	*ot-jabag-*	*ot-lama*
		virtuous	evil	one who is senseless

Table 9.18 *Proto-Great Andamanese body part prefixes (cf. Man 1923: Appendix VI)*

Proto-Great Andamanese	Gloss	Aka-Bea	Aka-Bale	Aka-Bojigiab	Aka-Juwai
a. **ab-*	human/body/flesh	ab-	o/ab-	ab-	a-
b. **ar-*	leg area	ar-	o/ar-	ar-	ra-
c. **aka-*	mouth area	aka-	o/aka-	o-	o/oka-
d. **oŋ-*	hand/foot area	oŋ-	o/oŋ-	oŋ-	oŋ-
e. **ig-*	eye/face area	ig-, i-	ig-	ir-	i-
f. **ot-*	head/heart area	ot-	oat-	ota-	ota-
g. **oto-*	waist only	oto-	oto-	oto-	–

Though Temple (1903: 119–20) suggests a similar prefix system for Onge and Jarawa, more recent work on the language does not support this (Blevins 2007). For example, Temple suggests *ik-, ig-, i-* as referring to 'cheek, ear', but this appears to be a misparsing of Jarawa *-ikwa, -ikwagu* 'ear', Onge *-ikwage* 'ear'. Though body part terms do often have complex internal morphological structure, there is no sign of a system similar to that outlined in Table 9.17.

Preceding these body part prefixes in Great Andamanese languages are pronominal prefixes marking person and number. Again, reconstruction of the full pronominal system is not yet possible, but available evidence suggests the mono-consonantal prefixes shown in Table 9.19. The reconstructions in Table 9.19 differ from Usher (2006: 298) in the following ways: they are based on the cognate sets shown; no aspirated proto-phoneme *t^h* is

Table 9.19 *Proto-Great Andamanese Pronominal prefixes*

	Proto-Great Andamanese	Aka-Bea	Aka-Bale	Aka-Bojigiab	Aka-Juwai	(Proto Ongan)
1sg	*t-	d-	t-	t-	t-	(*m-)
1pl	*m-	m-	m-	m-	m-	(*et-)
2	*ŋ-	ŋ-	ŋ-	ŋ-	ŋ-	(*ŋ-)

proposed for Proto-Great Andamanese; first-person singular is *t- with an unaspirated dental/alveolar stop; and a third-person plural *n- is not reconstructed.

The pronominal prefix system is one of the few places where Proto-Great Andamanese and Proto-Ongan comparisons are fruitful, as shown by the last column in Table 9.19. However, given the mono-consonantal status of the Proto-Great Andamanese reconstructions, and the mismatch of number in first-person forms, chance resemblances cannot be ruled out.

9.3   Northern Coast-Dwellers, Southern Inlanders

As noted earlier, all Andaman tribes appear to be divided into 'coastal' and 'inland' groups, with coast-dwellers hunting and gathering primarily in and along the sea, and inlanders subsisting more on forest flora and fauna. Coastal groups specialize in turtle and dugong hunting, while inlanders once took pride in their pig-hunting prowess. A striking feature of the available Great Andamanese comparative data is the number of cognate sets relating to the sea and its resources, as shown in Table 9.20 (see Man 1923: 187–188 for identification of Aka-Bea shellfish).

One interpretation of the semantic richness in this area of Proto-Great Andamanese vocabulary is that the Great Andamanese were primarily and originally sea-oriented hunter-gatherers, with jungle foraging and hunting secondary, or a later development. This interpretation receives some support from archeological evidence. The Andamans are dotted with middens – cultural deposits consisting primarily of shell, but also of faunal remains, pottery, and bone and stone artifacts (Cooper 2002). The word for kitchen-midden in Aka-Bea is *bud-l'artam*, 'encampment of ancient times'. To date, the oldest carbon-dates are from the Chauldari Midden (South Andaman Island, in traditional Aka-Bea territory) (Cooper 2002: 51). Here, uncalibrated radiocarbon dates obtained from charred and uncharred shells at 4.5 meters depth are dated at 2,280 ± 90 BP (Cooper 2002: 47–94). During the early phase of occupation at this

Table 9.20 *Sea-related cognate sets in Great Andamanese*

Proto-Great Andamanese	Gloss	Aka-Bea	Aka-Bale	Aka-Bojigiab	Aka-Juwai
i. Sealife					
*ba	mother-of-pearl, scallop	ba, be	ba	ba	ba
*cabiə	seaweed	cabya	cabia	cabia	cabio
*cer	skate, ray	cir	ce	ce	cet
*coaR	porpoise	coag	coa	cua	coa
*cowai	clam, *Tridacna crocea*	cowai	cowai	cowai	cowai
*kaibaic	saltwater shrimp	kaibij	kebit	kebait	kebait
*pioto	eel	pioto	pioto	pioto	biota
*pon	crab, large, edible	bad	pon	pon	pon
*waka	lobster, crayfish	waka	waka	waka	oka
*wat	fin	wat, wad	wat	wat	et
*taur	hawks bill turtle	tau	tare	toro	toro
*telem	cowrie shell	telim	telem	telem	etelem
*toiɲ	oyster	toiɲ	toin	tuin	toin
ii. Seascape					
*bərukə	rocky reef; shore cliffs	boroga	buruke	burko	burku
*curə	sea	juru	cire	ciro	ciro
*korə	coast; shore	gora	kori	kori	koro
*luk	channel (navigable by boats)	log	luk	luk	luk
*tai-be	coral reef	taibe	taibi	tebe	–
iii. Sea Voyaging					
*carək	outrigger canoe	carig/ma	carok	carok	carok
*cər	current, riptide	car/at	car/at	cor/ie	cor/ea
*dadi (?)	sail, sailing ship	dadi	dadi	dadi	rali
*raic	bale out	raic, raij	raic	weic	je/raic
*rok	canoe	roko	ro	ro	ro/a
*yulə	a sail; shadow	yolo	yulu	jule	julu

midden just over 2,000 years ago, shell remains are mostly from species that live in rocky shores and estuaries, while approximately 700 years later, there is evidence of a shift to bivalves from mudflats. In addition, shells (especially Cyrena), were, and continued until Man's time, to be used as knives, scrapers, and spoons; Nautilus shells were used as drinking vessels, and arrowheads were made from shaped valves of *Perna eppiphium, Tridacna species*, and stingray barbs.

Additional evidence for sea-based subsistence in the north comes from an aspect of lexical semantics. In Aka-Bea, *yat-* is the general word for 'fish' and 'food', suggesting fish as the basic or unmarked food type. The same is true for Aka Kede *tai jeu*, 'fish; food'.

Table 9.21 *Diversity in Onge and Jarawa sea-related terms*

Sea-related	language	lexeme(s)
conch	Onge	cenegili
	Jarawa	otahonaw, inotaindom
hermit crab	Onge	toɲewe
	Jawara	tahodkale
jelly fish	Onge	kele
	Jawara	toote toote
prawn	Onge	ɲaɲa
	Jawara	yewe
sea	Onge	iŋe, kwatannaŋe, balame
	Jawara	tomaya
turtle	Onge	narelaŋe, takwatoa
	Jawara	ukela
fish	Onge	coge
	Jawara	napo

The rich Proto Great Andamanese terminology associated with the sea contrasts with preliminary Proto-Ongan reconstructions (Blevins 2007). While there is no lexical resource on Onge or Jarawa to match Man's work on Aka-Bea, Onge, and Jarawa wordlists show surprisingly diverse terms for the sea, and creatures in it, as illustrated in Table 9.21. As a consequence, it is difficult to reconstruct sea fauna for Proto-Ongan. In contrast, words associated with inland hunting and gathering are reconstructable for Proto-Ongan, including PIG, HONEY, FRUIT/SEED, FOREST, and PATH/TRAIL (Blevins 2007). With respect to this last meaning, note the proposed semantic contrast between Proto-Great Andamanese *luk*, 'channel, strait; path, trail, road', where the path in question can be through water or land, and Proto-Ongan *icele*, 'path, road', which is unattested in reference to waterways.

Finally, in contrast to the northern languages mentioned, Onge *coge*, 'fish', and Jarawa *napo*, 'fish', are not general words for food. They refer only to fish.

A working hypothesis is that these aspects of the Proto-Great Andamanese and Proto- Ongan lexicons reflect prehistoric aspects of culture. The Great Andamanese tribes were originally hunter-gatherers who made primary use of sea resources, while the southern Ongan tribes appear to have had a terrestrial orientation before their separation, which accounts for the reconstructable nature of these terms in contrast to sea fauna.

This proposed difference in resource use is consistent with an interesting aspect of tool distribution in the Andamans. The bow and arrow was used by all Andamanese tribes, and was historically the most important hunting weapon for them (Radcliffe-Brown 1922: Appendix A). Based on careful comparison of bows from the Onge/Jarawa and Great Andamanese tribes, Radcliffe-Brown

(1922: Appendix A) suggests that 'Little Andaman' (Onge/Jarawa) bow represents the oldest form in the Andamans, with Aka-Bea and other southern Great
Andaman bows derived from these, and the North Andaman bows, in turn,
derived from those of the southern tribes. After the bow and arrow, the most
important weapon for the Great Andamanese was the harpoon, used for hunting
dugong, turtle, porpoise, and large fish (Radcliffe Brown 1922: 441–443).
Harpoons were not used by the Onge or Jarawa, and though Radcliffe-Brown
believes harpoons are of relatively recent origin in Great Andamanese culture
(Radcliffe Brown 1922: 441–443), an alternative is that old harpoons with shell
points were replaced with iron barbs once iron became available.

9.4   A Linguistic North-South Divide

Nearly every linguist that has compared the languages of the Great
Andamanese tribes with Onge and Jarawa has come to the same conclusion:
the language groups do not appear to be related (for a recent summary, see
Blevins 2007). One notable exception is Temple (1903: 120), who says, on the
topic of 'Proof of the Identity of Önge-Jarawa with the other Groups':

> Among an untutored people, so long isolated even from the other Andamanese, one would
> hardly look for many roots now in common with them, but the following, which occur in
> such short lists as those available, sufficiently establish a common origin for the family.

Once mistranscriptions, false cognates, and loans are identified in Temple's
comparative word list of 10 items, one is left with little more than chance
resemblances (though Table 9.19 shows more fruitful comparisons). Even so,
Temple's remarks in the foregoing are still relevant to any comparison one
might make between languages of the Andamans, and between these languages
and other language families.

9.4.1   The South: Proto-Ongan and Proto-Austronesian

In this light, results of a recent study comparing Proto-Ongan with Proto-
Austronesian are surprising. Blevins (2007) proposes more than 80 cognate
sets including Proto-Ongan and Proto-Austronesian reconstructions. Regular
sound correspondences are established, basic vocabulary is reconstructed, and
morphological and distributional evidence is used to support a hypothesis of a
distant genetic relationship between Proto-Ongan and Proto-Austronesian.
  Though the evidence is consistent with ancient borrowing, one strong argument against this is the existence of bare CVC roots in Proto-Ongan which do
not appear alone in Proto-Austronesian. Examples are shown in Table 9.22.
  If cognates of Proto-Austronesian CVC roots are reconstructable for Proto-
Ongan, they cannot be due to contact or borrowing, since they are not attested as

Table 9.22 *Bare monosyllabic roots in Proto-Ongan, and Proto-Austronesian cognates*

	Proto-Ongan	Proto-Austronesian
SMOKE	*bel	*qe/bel
MAT	*kam	*Si/kam
TREE TRUNK; LOG	*taŋ	*ba/taŋ (Proto-Malayo-Polynesian)

free morphemes in any attested or reconstructed Austronesian language. The simplest hypothesis is that they are inherited from a shared mother language, Proto-Austronesian-Ongan. The most problematic aspect of this hypothesis is geographical: although Austronesian languages are spoken very close to the Andamans, in Sumatra and the southern Malaysian peninsula to the south/south-east, linguistic and archaeological evidence point to an Austronesian homeland in southeast China, from where a first migration took Proto-Austronesian speakers across the Formosa strait to present day Taiwan (Bellwood 1985; Blust 1985).

Even if one does not accept the hypothesis that similarities between Proto-Ongan and Proto-Austronesian are due to direct inheritance, most would agree that they defy chance. The only alternative is that, at some period in prehistory, there was sustained contact between speakers of Ongan languages and speakers of Austronesian languages, and that this led to contact-induced change, including lexical borrowing. Under either hypothesis, there was some point in prehistory during which the ancestors of present-day Onge and Jarawa speakers were interacting with speakers of ancient Austronesian languages.

It is possible that Proto-Great Andamanese once showed the same lexical and morphological similarities with Proto-Austronesian that are reconstructed for Proto-Ongan. Of the CVC roots in Table 9.22, at least one may have a Proto-Great Andamanese CVC cognate: *təŋ, 'tree; above', as reconstructed in Table 9.15. However, when basic vocabulary and morphology are compared, Proto-Great Andamanese shows only three to four potentially shared lexemes with Proto-Austronesian and no shared morphology, while Proto-Ongan shows more than 100 cognate sets, including cognate bound morphemes. In contrast, as shown in the text that follows, an initial comparison of Proto-Great Andamanese with neighboring language families shows striking resemblances, not with Proto-Austronesian, but with Austroasiatic languages.

9.4.2   The North: Proto-Great Andamanese and Proto-Austroasiatic

The preliminary Proto-Great Andamanese reconstructions in the foregoing allow us to assess potential external relationships between Proto-Great Andamanese and other language families. In this area, the most fruitful comparisons I have found to date, as just noted, are with Austroasiatic languages, and possibly, with Proto-Austroasiatic itself. In the following, I present a list of preliminary comparisons, which, together, may suggest an Austroasiatic adstrate in Great Andamanese.

The Austroasiatic language family can be seen to surround the Andaman Islands. It includes languages of India and Bangladesh to the north and west, languages of mainland Southeast Asia to the east, and languages of the Nicobars to the south. While the subgrouping of Austroasiatic is disputed, we follow Diffloth (2005) in recognizing three basic subgroups: Munda, Khasi-Khmuic, and Nuclear Mon-Khmer (including Nicobarese)(cf. Diffloth 1968, 1979; Benjamin 1976).

The cognate sets that follow are organized alphabetically by English gloss of the Proto-Great Andamanese reconstruction. In all cases in which only part of a word is compared, a slash separates the relevant root from the rest of the word. For Great Andamanese languages, pre-root body part prefixes and post-positions are not included for most roots compared. Great Andamanese data are taken from the sources already noted. Austroasiatic data are primarily from Shorto's (2006) Mon-Khmer Comparative Dictionary (MKCD). When reconstructions or data are taken from that source, they are followed by the cognate set number they appear in. Reconstructions or attested forms on which reconstructions are based are written in bold, and all Proto-Great Andamanese reconstructions in this section are based on attestations from at least three Great Andamanese languages. Other relevant comparanda are in non-bold italics. If Shorto's reconstruction is based on lexical material from at least two of Diffloth's three subgroups of Austroasiatic (Munda, Khasi-Khmuic, and Nuclear Mon-Khmer), then it is identified as 'Proto-Austroasiatic'. Other reconstructions are simply labeled as Proto-Mon-Khmer, following Shorto's original practise. Shorto's reconstructions are preceded by double asterisks, and my own by single asterisks. The reader is referred to Shorto (2006) for criteria on which his reconstructions are based. Finally, additional Nicobarese data have been taken from Man (1889) (abbreviated M) and from Whitehead (1925) (abbreviated W). Notes on the cognate sets are set directly below each set in smaller point-size.

[1] **ADZE**

Proto-Great Andamanese *****wolo**.

Aka-Bea **wolo-**; A-Pucikwar **wolo-**; Aka-Kede **wo** (<*woo<*wolo); Aka-Cari **olo**

Proto-Austroasiatic ******wəl** 'to turn; to dig or cut round, hew, dig out' [MKCD: 1794]

(all major subgroups except Munda)

Car **hul** 'to hew, cut into' [W: 90] (cf. Car *ul, uu* 'to dig' [W: 308]); Nicobarese -**hola** in **oal-hola** 'scoop a canoe, trough, etc.' [M: 183] (cf. *oal, ol*, 'inside, interior' [M: 183]); Khmer **vìəl** 'to dig or cut round, to enlarge [hole]'); Riang-Lang **vəl** 'to stir round and round'.

Shorto's gloss is 'to turn'. However, given the data here, semantics might include 'to dig or cut round, hew, dig out', as one would with an adze. An anonymous reviewer notes that this comparison may be compromised by potential sound-symbolism associated with twisting/turning actions.

[2] AFRAID, FEAR.

Proto-Great Andamanese *lat.

    Aka-Bea **-lat-**; A-Pucikwar **lat**; Aka-Kede **yat**; Aka-Cari **lat**;

Proto-Austroasiatic **[c]laat** 'frightened' [MKCD: 1086]

    (Khmer, Katuic, North Bahnaric, Palaungic).

[3] FORBID, OBSTRUCT, KEEP FROM.

Proto-Great Andamanese *kənə.

    Aka-Bea **-kana-**; A-Pucikwar **kono**; Aka-Kede **kono**; Aka-Cari **kono**;

Proto-Austroasiatic **ghaŋ** 'to obstruct, prevent, forbid' [MKCD: 785]

    (Khmer, Katuic, South Bahnaric, Khasi).

The words in Great Andamanese are glossed by Portman (1887) as 'anchor', though Man (1923) clarifies that this transitive verb in Aka-Bea means 'forbid', with the full term for 'anchor' meaning, literally, 'forbid (canoe) to drift'.

[4] ANCIENT, OLD.

Proto-Great Andamanese *ar təm.

    Aka-Bea **ar tam**; A-Pucikwar **ar tam**; Aka-Kede **ara tom**; Aka-Cari **ara tom**

Proto-Austroasiatic **triəm** 'old' [MKCD: 1395]

    (cf. Proto-Austroasiatic *ram, *raam 'decay, age, perish' [MKCD: 1086])

Proto-Austroasiatic *tram 'aged, of long ago, ancient'

    NIC **tiram** 'long ago; formerly, in those days; in the earliest times; once upon a time, formerly' [M: 208]; Khasi *iap* **tram** 'to wither'.

Metathesis relates the *rt and *tr clusters. Note that within the Great Andamanese languages, there is evidence of metathesis where *rt clusters are involved. Compare Aka-Bojigiab *ar-bot*, Aka-Juwai *ra-bot* 'hip'; Aka-Bojigiab *ar-cog*, Aka-Juwai *ra-cok*, 'leg'; Aka-Bojigiab *ar-kata*, Aka-Juwai *ra-kata*, 'loin', etc.

[5] BALE OUT.

Proto-Great Andamanese *raic < *rac

    Aka-Bea **raic, raij-**; A-Pucikwar **raic**; Aka-Kede **weic**; Aka-Cari **je/raic**

Proto-Austroasiatic **raac** 'sprinkle' [MKCD: 837]

Compare, in particular, Shan **hăt** 'to dash [water]; to bale'; Mon **sat** 'to bale'; Santali **areɛɟ'** 'to bale out'.
Compare Proto-Austroasiatic ****saac**, 'to bale out' [MKCD: 872].

[6] **BASKET.**
Proto-Great Andamanese ***cup.**

Aka-Bea **job**; A-Pucikwar **cop**; Aka-Kede **cup**; Aka-Cari **cup**;
Proto-Austroasiatic ****ckuup, **ckuəp**, etc. 'to cover' [MKCD: 1237].
Semantic comparison may appear more distant than it is, given reflexes like Mon *kap*, 'to catch with a fish-basket'. Compare FASTEN, ADJOIN.

[7] **BAT, FLYING FOX.**
Proto-Great Andamanese ***wat.**

Aka-Bea **wot, wod**; A-Pucikwar **wat**; Aka-Kede **wot**; Aka-Cari **wot**;
Proto-Mon-Khmer ***wət**

Proto-South Bahnaric ****[w]ət** 'kind of bat' [MKCD: A81b] (Stieng **uət** 'small kind of bat frequenting houses'; Biat **wɔt** 'kind of bat')
Semang **ka:/wed** 'flying fox'

[8] **BELT, BAND, SLING.**
Proto-Great Andamanese ***ciəp.**

Aka-Bea **cip** 'sling or band made by women from bark which is worn like a sash over one shoulder by women, and sometimes by men, when carrying infants'; A-Pucikwar **ca**; Aka-Kede **cup**; Aka-Cari **cup**

Proto-Austroasiatic ****cuup, **cuəp, **ciəp** 'to put on, to wear' [MKCD: 1244].
In Nicobarese this stem is used with specific reference to a woman's waistcloth. The lack of clothing makes this one of the few functional items worn by the Andamanese.

[9] **BLIND.**
Proto-Great Andamanese ***tapə.**

Aka-Bea **tapa**; A-Pucikwar **tapa**; Aka-Kede **topo**; Aka-Cari **taba**;
Proto-Mon-Khmer ***[j]ɗaap** 'to pass hand along' [MKCD: 1262]
The semantic association is between blindness and the act of touching, feeling, groping (cf. Khmer **stì:əp** 'to touch, feel, stroke, grope for'.) Shorto relates the proto-form above to **1042 *[j]ɓat** &c. 'to feel, grasp' by metathesis. See also ****tɓə?** 'touch, feel' [MKCD: 124].

[10] **PUS; DIRT; MATTER; BRAINS.**
Proto-Great Andamanese ***muən.**

Aka-Bea **mun-**; A-Pucikwar **mina**; Aka-Kede **mine**; Aka-Cari **mine**;

Proto-Austroasiatic **muən 'pimple' [MKCD: 1186].
Add Central Nicobarese mõ 'mucus; albumen (of egg)' [M: 179]

[11] CANOE.
Proto-Great Andamanese *rok.

Aka-Bea roko (generic); A-Pucikwar ro; Aka-Kede ro; Aka-Cari ro;
Proto-Mon-Khmer **ɗuk 'boat, canoe' [MKCD: 336].

CAVE (see MOUTH [23])

[12] CHANNEL OF WATER, STRAIT; PATH; ROAD.
Proto-Great Andamanese *luk.

Aka-Bea log; A-Pucikwar luk; Aka-Kede luk; Aka-Cari luk;
Proto-Austroasiatic **ruŋ,**ruuŋ,**ruəŋ 'channel, river' [MKCD: 668]
Cf. also Jahai rkruk (< /ruk/) 'to go along a watercourse' (Burenhult 2005)
Proto-Mon-Khmer **luk, **luuk 'to have a hole in' [MKCD: 430]
based on Mon, Katuic, Nicobaric
Proto-Mon-Khmer **ruŋh 'hole, hollow' [MKCD: 666].

[13] CLAY, POWDER.
Proto-Great Andamanese *buə.

Aka-Kede pua 'clay; earth'; Aka-Cari bua 'clay; earth'
Proto-Austroasiatic **buəh 'ash, powdery dust' [MKCD: 2034].
Ochreous clay was dried and baked to a powder by the Andamanese, then mixed with animal fat and applied to people, weapons, utensils, etc. for ceremony and ornamentation.

[14] COUNT, TO.
Proto-Great Andamanese *lap.

Aka-Bea lap; A-Pucikwar lop; Aka-Kede lup; Aka-Cari lub;
Proto-Austroasiatic **rap 'to count' [MKCD: 1271]
(Mon, Khmer, South Bahnaric, Khmuic).

[15] CURRENT; TO FLOW.
Proto-Great Andamanese *cuər.

Aka-Bea car/at; A-Pucikwar car/at; Aka-Kede cor/ie; Aka-Cari cor/ea
Proto-Austroasiatic **cuər 'to flow, to pour' [MKCD: 1597].
Austroasiatic glosses include the meanings 'current' and 'flow through channel'.

[16] **DIGGING STICK.**
Proto-Great Andamanese *lakə.

Aka-Bea **laka** [Man 1923: 179]

Proto-Austroasiatic **lak 'to hoe' [MKCD: 418].

[17] **EGG.**
Proto-Great Andamanese *mulə.

Aka-Bea **molo**; A-Pucikwar **mula**; Aka-Kede **mulo**; Aka-Cari **mulu** (Jero)

Proto-Austroasiatic **muul, **muəl, etc. 'round' [MKCD: 1772].

[18] **FASTEN, ADJOIN.**
Proto-Great Andamanese *cuəp.

Aka-Bea **co**; A-Pucikwar **ca**; Aka-Kede **cup**; Aka-Cari **cop**;

Proto-Austroasiatic **bcuup, **bcuəp, etc. 'to adjoin, adhere' [MKCD: 1245].

[19] **FISHING NET, HAND NET.**
Proto-Great Andamanese *kut.
Aka-Bea **kud**

Proto-Austroasiatic **kuut 'to tie, to knot' [MKCD: 959].
(Munda, Bahnaric, Central Aslian, Khmer)

[20] **FLY (INSECT, BITING).**
Proto-Great Andamanese *ɲipə 'sandfly'.
Aka-Bea **ɲipa**; A-Pucikwar **ɲipa**; Aka-Kede **ɲipo**; Aka-Cari **ɲipo**;
Proto-Khmero-Vietic **jɔɔp 'horsefly' [MKCD: 1247]
(Katuic, Bahnaric)
Proto-Mon-Khmer **jnjaap 'to flutter' [MKCD: 1249]
(Mon, Khmer)

[21] **HILL, MOUNTAIN.**
Proto-Great Andamanese *burə/in.
Aka-Bea **boroin**; A-Pucikwar **burin**; Aka-Kede **burin**; Aka-Cari **burain**
Proto-Austroasiatic **bruuʔ 'hill' [MKCD: 182]
Kuy **bru:**; Sora **bəru:-n, baru:-n**; Kharia **biru**.

[22] **JUICE, WATERY; BROTH.**
Proto-Great Andamanese *raic < *rac
Aka-Bea **raic, raij-, rac**; A-Pucikwar **raic**; Aka-Kede **weic, waic**; Aka-Cari **je/raic**

Proto-Austroasiatic **raac 'sprinkle (liquid)' [MKCD: 837].

[23] MOUTH; CAVE; OPENING.
Proto-Great Andamanese *pəŋ.

Aka-Bea baŋ; A-Pucikwar poŋ; Aka-Kede poŋ; Aka-Cari poŋ;
Proto-Austroasiatic **paaŋ 'mouth, opening' [MKCD: 605].
In Great Andamanese languages, the same stem means 'to dig', perhaps, literally 'make opening, make hole'.

[24] NECK.
Proto-Great Andamanese *loŋə.

Aka-Bea loŋo; A-Pucikwar loŋo; Aka-Kede yoŋo; Aka-Cari loŋo;
Proto-Austroasiatic **tluŋ, **tluuŋ, **tluəŋ 'throat' [MKCD: 744].
Central Nicobarese reflexes mean 'neck'.

[25] ODOUR.
Proto-Great Andamanese *cuiɲ < *cuɲ.

Aka-Bea cuiɲ, ciɲ; A-Pucikwar cuiɲ; Aka-Kede cuiɲ; Aka-Cari cuɲ;
Proto-Mon-Khmer **jʔuuɲ, **jhuuɲ 'to smell, sniff' [MKCD: 887].

[26] PERSPIRATION. (see also [28])
Proto-Great Andamanese *gum/er.

Aka-Bea gumer; A-Pucikwar kimer; Aka-Kede kir; Aka-Cari kirme (with metathesis)
Proto-Austroasiatic **gmaʔ 'rain' [MKCD: 141].

[27] POT, SMALL VESSEL.
Proto-Great Andamanese *bəic < *bəc.

Aka-Bea buj; A-Pucikwar paic; Aka-Kede paic; Aka-Jeru pec (Colebrooke 1795) Aka-Cari baic
Proto-Mon-Khmer **buəc 'kind of small vessel' [MKCD: 826].
This form appears to have been borrowed from Aka-Bea into Ongan: compare Onge, Jarawa *bucu* 'cooking vessel, pot', which does not show the otherwise regular sound change of *bu > u (Blevins 2007).

[28] RAINY SEASON. (see also [26])
Proto-Great Andamanese *gum/əl.

Aka-Bea gumul (cf. yum, 'rain)'; A-Pucikwar kimil; Aka-Kede kimil; Aka-Cari kimil
Proto-Austroasiatic **gmaʔ 'rain' [MKCD: 141].
(Katuic, Khmuic, South Aslian, Munda)

[29] **RUB, TO, WIPE.**
Proto-Great Andamanese *cət.
Aka-Bea **jit**; A-Pucikwar **cot**; Aka-Kede **cet/o**; Aka-Cari **cet/or**;
Proto-Austroasiatic ****juut** 'to wipe' [MKCD: 994].
Proto-Austroasiatic ****gsuut** 'to rub' [MKCD: 1102].

[30] **SAIL (n.).**
Proto-Great Andamanese *yulə.
Aka-Bea **yolo**; A-Pucikwar **yulu**; Aka-Kede **jule**; Aka-Cari **julu**;
Proto-Austroasiatic ****yo[o]l** 'to oscillate'
(based on Khmer, Katuic, North Bahnaric, Khmuic). Note especially:
Khmer **yò:l** 'to oscillate, ripple, wing', Bahnar **ju:l** '[large object]
swinging')
Proto-Austroasiatic ****syuul, **syuəl** 'to fly through the air' [MKCD: 1783]
(based on Khmer, Palaungic, Mon, Bahnaric).
No cognates are known in Nicobarese.

[31] **SWEEP, TO.**
Proto-Great Andamanese *tbuj.
Aka-Bea **buj**; A-Pucikwar **bij**; Aka-Kede **tibij**; Aka-Cari **tibel**;
Proto-Austroasiatic ****tpəs, **tpuəs** 'to sweep' [MKCD: 1916].

[32] **TUSK, TOOTH.**
Proto-Great Andamanese *pila.
Aka-Bea **pili/ca**; A-Pucikwar **pila, pela**; Aka-Kede **pile**; Aka-Cari **pile**
Proto-Austroasiatic ****plaaʔ** 'blade, edge' [MKCD: 215]
Proto-Austroasiatic ****mlaʔ** 'tusk, ivory' [MKCD: 225].
Boar's tusks were used by the Andamanese for planing wood, and were greatly
valued. When used in this way, the inner edge of the tusk was sharpened with a
Cyrena shell, making a sharp edge.

[33] **WINK, TO.**
Proto-Great Andamanese *ne/mil, *ne/mal.
Aka-Bea **ne/mil**; A-Pucikwar **ne/mil**; Aka-Kede **na/mal**
Proto-Austroasiatic ****məl, **mil**, etc. 'to watch (for)' [MKCD: 1773]
cf. Khmer **rə/muɪl** 'to steal a glance'

Table 9.23 *TR/TVR correspondences*

Proto-Austroasiatic	Proto-Great Andamanese	Glosses
*bruuʔ	*burə/in	hill
*gmaʔ	*gumə/l	rain/rainy season; sweat
*plaaʔ	*pila	blade, edge/tusk, tooth

Table 9.24 *CVR/CVRə correspondences*

Proto-Austroasiatic	Proto-Great Andamanese	glosses
*wəl	*wolə	hew/adze
*muul	*mulə	round/egg
*yo[o]l	*yulə	oscillate/sail (n.)

Table 9.25 *Correspondences in pre-palatal diphthongs*

Proto-Austroasiatic	Proto-Great Andamanese	glosses
*raac	*raic (<*rac)	sprinkle/bale out
*jhuuɲ	*cuiɲ (<*cuɲ)	smell, sniff/odour
*buəc	*bəic (<*bəc)	small vessel, pot
*pac, *puuc	*pəic (<*pəc)	chisel/dugout canoe

In addition to straightforward vowel and consonant correspondences, there are several notable aspects of these proposed comparison sets. First, where Proto-Austroasiatic shows*TRVʔ, T an obstruent and R a sonorant, a vowel of variable quality is often found in Proto-Great Andamanese. Examples from the foregoing sets are repeated in Table 9.23.

Second, some Proto-Austroasiatic *CVR words, where R is a sonorant, correspond to vowel-final forms in Proto-Great Andamanese, as shown in Table 9.24.

Finally, Table 9.25 shows correspondences between diphthongs preceding final palatals in Proto-Great Andamanese and diphthongs or monophthongs in Proto-Austroasiatic. The apparent shift of Proto-Great Andamanese *a > ai and *u > ui before palatals is parallel to sound changes that have taken place in many Austroasiatic languages/subgroups, including Khasi, Lawa, and Central Nicobarese. For example, reflexes of Proto-Austroasiatic *kac, 'to pluck, break off, cut' [MKCD: 800] include Modern Khmer *kac*, Kuy *kac*, Sre *kac*, but Khasi *keit*, Central Nicobarese *-kaic-*. While this could be seen as an accidental parallel development, it could also be viewed as an instance of drift, where related languages show certain predispositions for certain types of sound change. Note also that the phonotactic of final palatal nasals itself is rare cross-linguistically.

An initial impression is that within the Proto-Great Andamanese lexicon, the nouns most likely to show resemblances to Austroasiatic forms are basic verbs, objects made and used by the Andamanese, and the natural resources necessary to make these objects. Perhaps owing to the nature of the Andamanese bodypart prefix system, few body parts are included in these preliminary sets. However, [23] MOUTH, CAVE is a perfect sound/meaning match, including the semantic range over mouth/hole/opening of body and mouth/hole/opening of earth, land.

Recall that Proto-Great Andamanese reconstructions in Section 9.2 are based only on lexemes attested in three or more Great Andaman languages, and that lexical data on all languages but Aka Bea is limited to at most 600–800 words per language. Despite these handicaps, preliminary comparison of Proto-Great Andamanese reconstructions with Proto-Austroasiatic, and Austroasiatic languages more generally, yields some striking similarities and correspondences. Given the dearth of comparative data, future Proto-Great Andamanese reconstructions will need to be based, in large part, on internal reconstruction of Aka-Bea – the only language for which extensive lexical and grammatical material is known.

9.5   Summary and Discussion

Many earlier researchers seem to believe that because the Great Andamanese and Little Andamanese share an archipelago, are all Negritos, and share numerous culture traits, that their languages ultimately descend from the same mother tongue. However, there are numerous geographically defined culture areas in the world which span unrelated languages or language groups. A well-studied case involving hunter-gatherers is the culture area of north-western California, traditionally inhabited by the Karuk, Yurok, Wiyot, Hupa, and Tolowa tribes. Historically these tribes shared numerous belief systems, ceremonial customs, and hunter-gatherer technologies (Kroeber 1925). Nevertheless, comparative linguistic study shows that the five languages represent three distinct language families: Algic (Yurok, Wiyot), Athabaskan (Hupa, Tolowa), and Karuk (isolate). A priori, there is no reason to believe that the Andaman culture area should be any different, and the preliminary comparative evidence in the foregoing suggests it is not.

Comparative work on the Great Andamanese languages suggests a prehistoric north-south divide culturally and linguistically. Preliminary reconstructions of Proto-Great Andamanese show many sea-related terms, suggesting sustained ocean-side hunting and gathering. Proto-Ongan lacks depth in this semantic field, with predominance of forest plants and animals, suggesting a more land-based subsistence. External linguistic comparisons between Proto-Great Andamanese and Proto-Austroasiatic are fruitful: cognates are in evidence, and preliminary sound correspondences can be formulated. This external connection contrasts with recent work on Proto-Ongan, which appears to contain an identifiable Austronesian adstrate.

These observations lead us to question the generally held view, outlined by Radcliffe-Brown in the foregoing, that the north-south divide is a recent one, and that both populations descend from a single group in situ, with a break-up of northern and southern groups solidified by the geographic barrier of the strait between Little Andaman and Great Andaman. A different prehistoric scenario seems possible, and indeed necessary, if the distinct Austroasiatic and Austronesian adstrates are to be accounted for. Perhaps speakers of Proto-Great Andamanese and Proto-Ongan arrived in the Andamans by distinct migrations, perhaps even by different routes, from the north and south respectively? Or maybe, as alluded to earlier, Proto-Great Andamanese and Proto-Ongan are descended from a common mother tongue, but an ancient population split combined with extensive contact between Proto-Great Andamanese speakers and speakers of Austroasiatic languages has overwritten much of their shared history?

While the preliminary nature of the foregoing linguistic proposals must be stressed, they illustrate the many ways that comparative linguistics can inform models of hunter-gatherer prehistory, from hypotheses regarding sea versus land resource use, to mapping of prehistoric language contact zones. As comparative work on Andaman languages progresses, a firmer basis for evaluating these hypotheses should emerge.

References

Abbi, Anvita. (2006). *Endangered languages of the Andaman Islands.* Munich: Lincom Europa.

Abbi, Anvita. (2008). Is Great Andamanese genealogically and typologically distinct from Onge and Jarawa? *Language Sciences* (22 April 2008).

Bellwood, Peter. (1985). *Prehistory of the Indo-Malaysian Archipelago.* Sydney: Academic Press.

Benjamin, Geoffrey. (1976a). Austroasiatic subgroupings and prehistory in the Malay Peninsula. In P. N. Jenner et al. (eds.), *Austroasiatic Studies,* Oceanic Linguistics Special Publications No. 13. Honolulu: University of Hawaii Press, 37–128.

Blevins, Juliette. (2007). A long lost sister of Proto-Austronesian? Proto-Ongan, mother of Jarawa and Onge of the Andaman Islands. *Oceanic Linguistics* 46: 154–198.

Blust, Robert. (1985). The Austronesian homeland: A linguistic perspective. *Asian Perspectives* 20: 46–67.

Blust, Robert. (1994). The Austronesian settlement of mainland Southeast Asia. In Karen L. Adams and Thomas John Hudak (eds.), *Papers from the Second Annual Meeting of the Southeast Asian Linguistics Society.* Tempe, AZ: Program for Southeast Asian Studies, Arizona State University, 25–83.

Colebrooke, R. H. (1795). On the Andaman Islands. *Asiatic Researches* 4: 385–395.

Cooper, Zarine. (2002). *Archaeology and history: Early settlements in the Andaman Islands.* Oxford: Oxford University Press.

230   *Juliette Blevins*

Dif/loth, Gérard. (1968). Proto-Semai phonology. *Federation Museums Journal* (new series), 13: 65–74.

Diffloth, Gérard. (1979). Aslian languages and Southeast Asian prehistory. *Federation Museums Journal* 24: 3–16.

Diffloth, Gérard. (2005). The contribution of linguistic palaeontology and Austroasiatic. In Laurent Sagart, Roger Blench, and Alicia Sanchez-Mazas (eds.), *The peopling of East Asia: Putting together archaeology, linguistics and genetics*. London: RoutledgeCurzon, 77–80.

Kroeber, A. L. (1925). *Handbook of the Indians of California*. Bureau of American Ethnology, Bulletin 78. Washington, DC: Government Printing Office.

Man, E. H. (1883). On the aboriginal inhabitants of the Andaman Islands. *Journal of the Anthropological Institute* 12: 69–116, 327–434.

Man, E. H. (1889). *A dictionary of the Central Nicobarese language*. Bombay: British India Press.

Man, E. H. (1923). *Dictionary of the South Andaman language*. Bombay: British India Press.

Portman, M. V. (1887). *Manual of the Andamanese languages*. Calcutta: Office of the Superintendent of Government Printing. [Reprinted in 1992 by Manas Publications, Delhi.]

Portman, M. V. (1898). *Notes on the languages of the South Andaman group of tribes*. Calcutta: Office of the Superintendent of Government Printing.

Radcliffe-Brown, A. R. (1914). Notes on the languages of the Andaman Islands. *Anthropos* 9: 36–52.

Radcliffe-Brown, A. R. (1922). *The Andaman Islanders: A study in social anthropology*. Cambridge: Cambridge University Press.

Shorto, Harry. (2006). *A Mon-Khmer comparative dictionary*. Paul Sidwell (ed.). Pacific Linguistics 579. Canberra: Research School of Pacific and Asian Studies, the Australian National University.

Sreenathan, M. (2001). *The Jarawas: Language and culture*. Anthropological Survey of India. Calcutta: Government of India.

Temple, Richard C. (1903). *The Andaman and Nicobar Islands*. Report on the Census. Census of India, 1901. Volume III. Calcutta: Office of the Superintendent of Government Printing, India.

Usher, Timothy. (2006). Great Andamanese reconstruction underway: A condensed handout with tentative remarks on Papuan and Australian vis-avis external language families. *Mother Tongue: Journal of the Association for the Study of Language Prehistory* XI: 295–298.

Weber, George. (2006). *The Andamanese*. www.andaman.org/BOOK/text.htm.

Whitehead, Rev. G. (1925). *Dictionary of the Car-Nicobarese language*. Rangoon: American Baptist Mission Press.

Zide, Norman, and Vishvajit Pandya. (1989). A bibliographical introduction to Andamanese linguistics. *Journal of the American Oriental Society* 109: 639–651.

10 Historical Linguistics and Philippine Hunter-Gatherers

Lawrence A. Reid

10.1 Hunter-Gatherer Groups in the Philippines

In addition to the Negrito groups, who are traditionally all hunter-gatherers, there is one non-Negrito hunter-gatherer group reported for the Philippines who were also traditionally hunter-gatherers. These are the Tasaday, a group of formerly cave-dwelling Manobo, first reported in the early 1970s and frequently portrayed in the popular press as a hoax. The linguistic evidence for the authenticity of the Tasaday as a distinct ethnolinguistic group is irrefutable and has been dealt with in various articles (Reid 1992, 1996, 1997, 2018). This is the only case known in the Philippines where a formerly food-producing population is known to have acquired a hunter-gatherer subsistence secondarily, probably brought about by a small number of people escaping to the forest within the last 200–300 years, to avoid some catastrophic epidemic. In recent years, the group has intermarried with neighboring farmers and has again adopted a farming lifestyle supplemented by gathering of forest products. Their similarity in many respects to the Mlabri of Laos and Thailand has been commented on in Reid (1997: 193–195). The Tasaday will not be discussed further in this chapter. Appendix 10.1 provides a listing of the known Negrito groups still speaking languages distinct from their non-Negrito neighbors in the Philippines, and Map 10.1 identifies the general locations where these Negrito languages are still spoken. It should be noted that the various Ayta groups in western Luzon are fairly closely related to one another, and that in the Bicol region of southeastern Luzon the Manide and Rinconada Agta have a number of distinct dialects.[1] The same is true also of Atta and the Dumagat and other Agta groups of the eastern coastal areas of Luzon.

This chapter was originally presented to the symposium on Historical Linguistics and Hunter-Gatherer Populations in Global Perspective, Max Planck Institute for Evolutionary Anthropology, Leipzig, August 10–12, 2006, and was first published in *Piakandatu ami Dr. Howard P. McKaughan*, edited by Loren Billings and Nelleke Goudswaard, pp. 234–260. Manila: Linguistic Society of the Philippines and SIL Philippines, 2010. This is a slightly revised version of that paper. A more up-to-date view of the relationship between Negritos and their non-Negrito neighbors may be found in Reid (2013).

The names of Negrito groups that are of most interest, however, are those that reflect Proto-Malayo-Polynesian (PMP) *qaRta 'Negrito'; these terms include Agta, Atta, Arta, Alta, and Ayta, with the variant medial consonant depending on the reflex of the *R protophoneme.[2] These names are of interest because the majority of Negrito groups use them to refer to themselves and to distinguish themselves from so-called farming lowlanders.[3] Furthermore, it is the specific reflex of *R in each of these languages that provides an important clue to the subgrouping relationship that each language has to other languages of the Philippines (Reid 1987).

There are several points of contention regarding the foregoing reconstruction. Zorc (1979: 8) has reconstructed Proto-Philippines *qaGta? 'Negrito, black person', while Blust (1972) reconstructed PAn *qa(R)(CtT)a 'outsiders, alien people'.[4] The questions concern (a) whether the form is reconstructible with a medial consonant cluster or not, (b) whether the form had a final glottal stop or not,[5] and (c) what the form actually meant.

Drawing on data from the Samal,[6] Indonesian, and Oceanic languages that show only a single medial consonant and no final glottal stop, Blust concluded that a medial cluster could not be securely reconstructed, in that "languages that reflect this root with an intervocalic stop either do not permit consonant clustering at all or limit it to homorganic prenasalization" (Blust 1972: 169). He claims that the final glottal stop was innovated in one of the Central Philippine languages and spread to its neighboring languages, giving such forms as Bikol *agta?* 'Negrito person', and Cebuano *agta?* 'large supernatural black creature living in caves, trees, and empty houses who likes to play tricks on people, to kidnap them, and has a cigar in his mouth, also sometimes applied to 'Negritos' (Wolff 1972), which reflect a final glottal stop. But note Tagalog *agta* 'Negrito' and Western Bukidnon Manobo *agta* 'a kind of chicken which is black; in folk tales, black people', neither of which has a final glottal stop.[7] Northern Philippine languages provide no evidence because a final glottal stop was regularly lost in those languages.

Reflexes of *qaRta, with the medial cluster, occur throughout Philippine languages, including both central and southern Philippines. The names Ita or Aeta are also used for some groups that have a *y* reflex of *R, and are probably developments of the term Ayta, a form that has been borrowed widely into other Philippine languages as well, such as Maranao *aita?* 'Negrito-mountain people with kinky hair and small stature' (McKaughan and Macaraya 1967: 7).

The names of other groups who identify themselves as Negrito, such as the Ati groups of northern and southern Panay, and the Ata groups of Negros, may be irregular reflexes of the same name, but are more likely to be exonyms adopted by the groups to refer to themselves, based on one of the linguistic features that the group uses that differentiates them from their farming neighbors. Thus the language of Samar-Leyte is called Waray, as *waray* is their term for the negative existential 'there is none', which in most of the other Bisayan languages is *walay*. The forms *ti and *ta are demonstrative bases reconstructible to very early proto-languages in the Philippines. The former generally has the meaning 'that (remote)'. Zorc (1974: 589) notes, however, that in a few languages, specifically the Central Luzon group and Iraya of Northern Mindoro, *ti* is the base for demonstratives denoting nearness. Likewise the use of *ta* as a base denoting remoteness is found only in Kapampangan (a Central Luzon language) and in some of the Northern Mindoro languages. Neighboring languages in Northern Mindoro show completely opposite uses of these bases; thus for 'that (yonder)', Tadyawan has *ata*, and Alangan has *ati*.

Inati, the language of the Ati of Panay, shows the shifted meanings of both demonstratives that occur in the Central Luzon and Northern Mindoro languages. Namely, *ti* occurs in demonstratives indicating 'this (either near speaker, or near speaker and addressee)', whereas *te* (a reflex of *ta) occurs in the demonstrative indicating 'that (remote)' (Pennoyer 1986–87: 15–16). It is possible then that at least the Ati name is not etymologically related to PMP *qaRta at all, but reflects the particular developments that occurred in the demonstrative system of this language, which distinguishes it from its neighbors.[8]

There is one other group who call themselves Ata. They are a medium-sized group, 26,653 in 2000 according to the Ethnologue (Eberhard et al. 2019), who live in central Mindanao. However, they do not identify themselves as Negrito but as Manobo and are not primarily hunter-gatherers. Given the relatively widespread distribution of Negrito groups in Luzon and parts of the Visayas, and the fact that there is only one extant Negrito group speaking a language distinct from its neighbors in Mindanao (the Mamanwa), it is probable that other Negrito groups are now completely assimilated into Manobo, and perhaps other language families in Mindanao, accounting not just for the remnant Ata name, but also for the relatively darker skin and curly hair of many Manobo people, especially the Tigwa and Matigsalug groups who are linguistically fairly closely related to the Ata Manobo. This is supported by the fact that the term *agtaʔ* is found in Manobo folktales, to refer to dark-skinned people and by extension even for a chicken with black feathers (Elkins 1968), and is used in Sarangani Manobo as a verb meaning 'to chase, to pursue, to hunt small game' (DuBois 1974). In Tausug, one of the Central Philippine languages, but spoken in the Sulu archipelago in the south of the Philippines, the term also occurs in legends to refer to 'a short, black antagonistic, ill-looking woman, evil-minded but wise' (Hassan et al. 1994). Both terms – Ata 'Manobos of Libuganon, Kapugi, Langilan, Kapalong; Ata of Davao' and *agtaʔ*, 'a person with black skin, a Negrito; used in folklore' – are found in Dibabawon Manobo (Forster and Barnard 1976: 9, 23).

Blust (1972) attempts to justify his reconstruction of the meaning of the form as 'outsider, alien people' instead of the meaning 'slave' that had earlier been proposed by Dempwolff (1938), both of which meanings appear in various languages. Some languages have the meaning 'man' but this gloss is rejected by Blust for the reconstructed form because of the conflict with the much more widely occurring form, reconstructed as PAn *Cau. He considers that Negrito groups that now use reflexes of his Proto-Malayo-Polynesian (PMP) *qaRta have adopted the term applied to them by non-Negrito groups. I find this scenario highly unlikely, in that Negrito groups, until probably relatively recently, have carefully maintained their own identity, and still reject the wide range of derogatory names by which outsiders call them. A far more likely scenario is that those groups in which the gloss of the term is 'man, human being' have assimilated Negritos into their group and have replaced a reflex of PAn *Cau with the term that the Negritos used for themselves.

10.2   Time Depth of First Interaction between Negrito and Non-Negrito Groups

The Negrito groups are considered to be the earliest inhabitants of the Philippines. We know this from an examination of the archaeological evidence that clearly places the earliest movement of Neolithic peoples from Taiwan around 4,000 years ago.[9] Pottery from Torongan and Sunget in the Batanes Islands between Taiwan and Luzon has been dated to between 3600 and 3000 BP, and Taiwan jade dated to c. 3500 BP has been recovered from an archaeological site at Nagsabaran in the Cagayan Valley of northern Luzon (Bellwood et al. 2003; Bellwood and Dizon 2005). We assume that prior to the first movement of an Austronesian-speaking group from Taiwan, the Philippines was probably occupied by maybe several hundred or more separate groups, with widely disparate languages, not unlike the distribution patterns of peoples in New Guinea. Very early human skeletal remains from the Tabon Caves have been dated at more than 50,000 BP, and a possibly human toe bone from the Peñablanca Caves in Cagayan Province has recently been dated at more than 70,000 BP. Genetic evidence (the occurrence of unique alleles) suggests that the Negrito groups in Mindanao may have been separated from those in Luzon for 20–30,000 years (Omoto 1981).

Prior to the arrival of Austronesian-speaking people into the northern Philippines from Taiwan, it is probable that the Negrito groups occupied coastal areas, as they still do in northeastern Luzon, and also broad river valleys, such as that of the Cagayan River, subsisting off the readily available shell fish, the remains of which form extensive shell middens along the Cagayan River, and exploiting the animal and vegetable products widely available in the largely undisturbed grasslands and forests that filled the valleys.

Blust (2005) speculates that from the initial Austronesian settlement of the Philippines (his Proto-Malayo-Polynesian) for perhaps a thousand years of agricultural expansion and language differentiation, the pre-Neolithic Negrito populations remained in their "exclusive preserve" (2005: 54), the mountainous interior regions of the Philippines, apparently having no contact at all with Austronesians. He speculates that they were also probably hardly affected at all during his "First Extinction" (2005: 39–41), a period during which he claims the expansion of one particular Austronesian-speaking group, in a competition between agricultural groups for the same territory, eliminated all of the diversity that had developed in the previous millennium, and became the parent (his Proto-Philippines) of all of the languages currently spoken in the Philippines and parts of Northern Sulawesi. It was only subsequent to these events, he believes, that meaningful contact was established between the Negrito hunter-gatherers in their "remote mountain areas" (2005: 41) and the Austronesian-speaking farming populations that resulted in the loss of the Negritos' inherited languages and their adoption of Austronesian languages.

It is inconceivable to me that the Negritos would have chosen to live in such remote mountain areas, rather than in the valleys and seashores where food supplies would have been far more abundant and readily obtainable. Bellwood refers to them as "traditionally forest and coastline hunters and gatherers" (1985: 72). There is considerable archaeological evidence to support this claim, notably the extensive shell middens near Lal-lo and other sites along the lower Cagayan River in northern Luzon. The lower levels of these midden sites date to 5000 BP, at least a thousand years prior to the Austronesians' arrival in the area, while the upper levels date to 4000 BP (Paz 1999: 154). There are also pre-Neolithic remains in cave-sites in the area. Furthermore, the so-called Dumagat Negritos along the eastern coast of northern Luzon, have long been associated with the ocean and river valleys that drain the eastern slopes of the Sierra Madre, the mountain chain that separates the Cagayan Valley from the Pacific coast (see Section 10.5 for a fuller discussion of these groups), while the name of the Mamanwa Negrito group in Mindanao means 'people of the forest' (Miller and Miller 1976: 17). Blust's isolationist view runs counter to recent scholarship which demonstrates that interethnic trade has been the pattern of contact between hunter-gatherers and farmers since Holocene times and that claims of isolation have usually been shown to be mythological (Headland and Reid 1991).

I have claimed instead that contact with Negritos must have occurred soon after the first arrival of the Austronesian-speaking migrants, and that they developed a pattern of interaction with Negritos that resulted in the loss of the Negritos' original languages in favor of the language of the group that they were interacting with. Their adaptation to the remote mountain areas must have gradually come as the expanding agriculturalists took over the Negritos' traditional hunting and gathering sites in the lower altitudes for farming, and conflict between the groups motivated them to move to more remote areas to avoid the farmers.

We know that the first Austronesian-speaking migrants into the Philippines were a technologically advanced group compared to the Negritos. They were not only weavers and pot-makers; we know also that they were agricultural-ists with a long history in Taiwan of rice and millet agriculture (Blust 1995, 1976). That they brought rice with them is clear not only from the linguistic evidence of reconstructed forms for Proto-Austronesian, such as for the rice plant, for harvested and cooked rice, rice husk, and mortar and pestle (reflexes of which are found throughout the Philippines), but also from the very early date available for a rice husk (3400 BP ±125), recovered in Andarayan in the northern Cagayan River Valley (Snow et al. 1986). That the Negritos must have survived on a diet of relatively insufficient carbohy-drates (perhaps accounting for their short stature) has been discussed in various places (e.g., Headland and Reid 1989, 1991), and probably relatively soon after the Austronesian-speaking migrants arrived, developed a taste for rice, satisfying as it did some of their nutritional needs. Early migrants would not have been numerous, and it would have been to the advantage of the in-migrating Austronesians to develop a good relationship with the Negrito bands they certainly must have encountered, or they would have been slaughtered.

A pattern of interaction between the two groups probably developed in the very early stages of contact, whereby the Negritos assisted the in-migrants with felling of forest trees and preparation of swiddens for dry rice cultivation, and ultimately of pond-field development for wet rice, a pattern that has persisted into historical times.

10.3   Patterns of Interaction with Farming Groups

Although Negrito populations in the Philippines all now speak Austronesian languages that are relatable to the languages of the farming groups with whom they interact, the degree of that relationship varies widely. Reid (1987) explores the question of what this variation implies for the prehistoric interaction between the groups and presents a number of possible scenarios to account for the different types of relationship between them. Four possible scenarios are discussed, each of which will be outlined in the following sections.[10]

10.3.1   The Relatively Recent Hypothesis

It is conceivable that the language shift to an Austronesian language took place relatively recently in cases where total assimilation has taken place and no record is left of the prior language, or in cases such as the Atta dialect of Pamplona which is said to share 91% of its basic vocabulary with its closest neighbor, Ibanag. But given the same facts, it is possible that these same groups could have lost their original languages thousands of years ago, and by maintaining continual intimate contact with their neighbors shared in all the changes in the dominant language community, a hypothesis that is discussed next.

10.3.2   The Relatively Remote-with-Continual-Contact Hypothesis

Evidence for continual contact over an extended period is found when one considers the large number of Spanish loanwords in Atta. Certainly the Negrito groups didn't have the kind of contact with Spanish that would have brought about such large-scale borrowing, whereas the Ibanag did have, resulting in a massive influx of Spanish loanwords into their language. The Atta, because of their continual and intimate contact with Ibanag, at least since the early Spanish period in the Philippines, have borrowed many of these forms into their own language.

10.3.3   The Relatively Remote-with-Cyclic-Contact Hypothesis

This hypothesis proposes that a group of Negritos could have learned their first Austronesian language at a remote period, subsequently withdrawn from their neighbors, resulting in normal language split, and then at a later date reestablished intimate contact with them, resulting in extensive borrowing from them or even replacement of their Austronesian language. Linguistically, it would be difficult to distinguish between this situation and the preceding one, where contact had not been broken for an extended period. It is probable, however, that some of the Negrito languages of the east coast of northern Luzon fit this scenario.

Some of these appear to be quite closely related to one another, others of which are considerably different. Magaña (2003: 242–243) claims that "the total population of Agta ..., as of the year 2000 is 1,828 [... in] ninety-nine villages grouped as bands in twenty-seven barangay ... in the five municipalities [Palanan, Divilican, Maconacon, San Mariano, and Dinapigue] of the NSMNP [Northern Sierra Madre Natural Park]." This number does not include the Dupaningan Agta found in numerous bands along the coasts and valleys to the north, in eastern Cagayan Province as far north as Palaui Island, just off the northern shore of Luzon.

The most closely related set of languages are Dupaningan Agta in eastern Cagayan Province, the Palanan Agta in Isabela Province, and Casiguran Agta in Aurora and Quirino Provinces, which share from about 70% of basic vocabulary in the case of Dupaningan Agta and Casiguran Agta, to 87% in the case of Palanan Agta and Casiguran Agta (Headland 1975, based on the 372 wordlist of Reid 1971).

Each of these languages has a *g* reflex of *R, a feature that is shared with the Northern Cordilleran languages such as Ibanag, Itawis, and Yogad that are spoken in the Cagayan Valley to the west of the Sierra Madre range. Casiguran Agta is the best-described of these languages, and has a number of features that make it look very conservative. It has been grouped as a Northern Cordilleran language (Tharp 1974: 101), primarily on the basis of its *g* reflex of *R, yet it does not share in several other phonological innovations that characterize other members of that group, such as *ǝ to *a* and gemination of a single root-medial consonant following its reflex of *ǝ. McFarland's (1980: 66) subgrouping agrees with Tharp's in placing the Agta languages of northeastern Luzon in a group coordinate with other Northern Cordilleran languages.

Apart from a large influx since the 1960s of immigrant groups of farmers speaking languages of the Cagayan Valley and the Cordillera Central, there are two non-Negrito languages spoken on the east coast of northern Luzon: Kasiguranin and Paranan. Casiguran Agta and Palanan Agta both share a considerable number of lexical and grammatical features with these languages (respectively), a fact that I investigate more fully in Section 10.5.

The facts seem to support the hypothesis of this section, that the Negrito groups learned the language of their non-Negrito neighbors at a fairly remote period, certainly long enough ago for the present differentiation among the Negrito groups to have taken place, and also long enough ago for the changes to have taken place that now distinguish these languages from the languages of the farmers in the area.

Because of the paucity of information available for Palanan and Dupaningan Agta, examples are given here only for Casiguran Agta.[11] These changes are of two types, those that are probably innovations in the Negrito languages not shared by their neighboring farmers, and those that are probably innovations in the language of their neighbors that are not shared by the Negrito languages. Of the first type, Casiguran Agta has changed the old PMP *di locative preposition, which is still found in Paranan, from marking only singular nouns to marking only plural nouns. (The forms *to* and *ta* are now used in Casiguran Agta to mark singular locative common nouns.) Casiguran Agta has extended the function of *di* to include also nominative and genitive (Headland and Headland 1974).[12]

Of the second type, Casiguran Agta retains unreduced forms of the completed aspect of the reconstructed Proto-Malayo-Polynesian verbal

Table 10.1 *The development of verbal prefixes*

PMP	Casiguran Agta	Paranan
*m\<in\>aR-	*minag-*	*nag-*
*m\<in\>aN-	*minaN-*	*naN-*
*m\<in\>a-	*mina-*	*na-*

prefixes (Table 10.1). In Proto-Malayo-Polynesian, verbs were marked as completed aspect, or past tense, by infixing *\<in\> following the first consonant (*m-), of the verbal prefixes. Paranan, and all other Northern Cordilleran languages (as well as Ilokano, and the non-Negrito Central and Southern Cordilleran languages), have subsequently reduced these infixed forms by deleting the first two segments, thus setting up an *m-/n-* nonpast/past paradigm.

The evidence, then, fairly clearly points to a very early contact with Austronesian speakers in the area that was probably near the place where Austronesians first entered the Philippines (assuming that they came south from Taiwan). This contact has apparently been maintained over thousands of years in a cyclic fashion, allowing for normal language differentiation as well as continuing diffusion of features, primarily lexical items from Paranan, Kasiguranin, and other linguistic groups, such as Ilokano and Tagalog, with which they have from time to time associated, while maintaining features of the early Austronesian language that they first acquired.

10.3.4 The Relatively Remote-with-Cyclic-Contact-with-a-Different-Language Hypothesis

A much more interesting hypothesis, because it is potentially more revealing of the prehistoric situation, is that a Negrito group learned its first Austronesian language at some remote date, and then lost contact with its neighbors, either because they themselves moved, or – as appears to be more likely – their non-Negrito neighbors were driven off by other expanding non-Negrito populations. Subsequently the Negritos established contact with another language group, such as the in-migrating group, being affected to a greater or lesser degree by the nature of this contact.

One would expect that in a situation such as this, some evidence would remain of the original language that had been learned. For example, the sound shifts that characterized the original Austronesian language would be found in at least the basic vocabulary of this Negrito language, and there would be an identifiable body of vocabulary that would appear to be borrowed from the

Table 10.2 *Examples of the* y *reflex of PAN* *R *in Sinauna Tagalog*

PMP	Sinauna Tagalog	Gloss
*?ikuR	*?ikuy*	tail
*?uRat	*?uyat*	vein
*ba?əRu	*ba?yu*	new
*bəR?at	*ba?yat*	heavy
*buRəw	*buyaw*	drive away
*hiRup	*?iyup*	sip
*Ruaŋ	*paywaŋ*	gap

The form *buyaw* is from the Infanta Dumagat dialect of ST.

language or languages with which later contact had been maintained. One might also expect to find features of morphology and syntax that agree more closely with those of the language family with which it was first associated than with the language with which it was subsequently associated. In the following sections I will discuss two languages, the nature of which can be explained by a hypothesis of this sort.

10.3.4.1 Sinauna Tagalog   Literally 'ancient Tagalog', Sinauna Tagalog (ST) is (or was) spoken in and around Tanay, Rizal Province, in the middle of a Tagalog-speaking area (Santos 1975). A close dialect of the language, spoken just across the Sierra Madre range around the town of Infanta, Quezon Province, has been called Infanta Dumagat. Another dialect, referred to as Remontado Dumagat, is said to still be spoken. The Sinauna Tagalog identified themselves as Tagalogs. The younger people all speak Tanay Tagalog. The language of the older people, now deceased, was not Tagalog, although it was heavily larded with Tagalog words. However, their language retained a number of features that clearly indicate that their language is genetically part of the Central Luzon group (which includes the non-Negrito Sambal languages of Botolan and Tina, as well as Kapampangan), much farther to the north, and is not most closely related to Tagalog at all. These features include a number of basic lexical items having a *y* reflex of PMP *R (Table 10.2). This is the regular reflex in the Central Luzon languages, whereas the regular Tagalog reflex is *g*.

Table 10.3 presents forms that illustrate the regular ST reflex of PAn *ə. As in the other Central Luzon languages, it is *a*, whereas in Tagalog, the regular reflex is *i*.

A cursory comparison of some of the verbal affixation in ST, Kapampangan, and Tagalog (Table 10.4) shows that the ST forms agree

Table 10.3 *Examples of the a reflex of PAN *ə in Sinauna Tagalog*

PMP	Sinauna Tagalog	Gloss
*ʔənəm	ʔaʔnam	six
*ʔətut	ʔaʔtut	fart
*ʔutək	ʔutak	brain
*bəRʔat	baʔat	heavy
*buək	buak	hair
*ŋipən	ŋipan	tooth

Table 10.4 *Comparison of Sinauna Tagalog verb affixation*

Tense/Aspect	Sinauna Tagalog	Kapampangan	Tagalog
Present	mag-	mag-	mag-
Progressive	mina:g-	ma:g-	nagCV:-
Past	mig-	mig-, meg-	nag-
Future	magCV-	mag-	magCV:-

CV stands for consonant-vowel reduplication, with: representing vowel length.

more closely with Kapampangan than with Tagalog. Both ST and Kapampangan use a change in vowel (*a* to *i*) to distinguish past tense from present. In addition, ST and Kapampangan retain *m*-initial forms for all tenses. Although this is a retention from the protolanguage and therefore of little value for establishing a subgrouping relationship, it is apparent that ST does not participate in the innovations that resulted in the *n*-initial forms found in Tagalog.

It is significant that the full, unreduced forms of the completed aspect of PMP verbs (Table 10.1) were apparently also continued into Proto-Central Luzon. In some of the Central Luzon languages the pattern of reduction was generally different from that in the languages in the north of Luzon, the third and fourth segments being deleted, resulting in an <a> / <i> nonpast/past paradigm. Botolan Sambal (Antworth 1979), on the other hand, has reduced its perfective affixes in the same way, as did Paranan, as well as most of the other languages of Luzon. The <a> / <i> nonpast/past paradigm also occurs in Mamanwa, a Negrito language in northeast Mindanao, but not as far as I have been able to discover in other East Mindanao languages. In Maranao, only the medial *n* was deleted, setting up an <a> / <ia> nonpast/past paradigm (Reid 1987: 50).

Sinauna Tagalog, however, alone among the Central Luzon languages, still maintains the unreduced form in part of its verbal paradigm, as can be seen in

Table 10.5 *Central Luzon and Tagalog nominative pronouns*

	Sinauna Tagalog	Kapampangan	Botolan Sambal	Tagalog
1sg	saku	ʔaku	hiku	ʔako
2sg	siʔika	ʔika	hika	ʔikaw
1,2sg	siʔitadaw	ʔikata	hita	kata
3sg	siʔya	ʔiya	hiya	siya
1pl	siʔkami	ʔikami	hikayi	kami
2pl	siʔkamu	ʔikayu	hikawu	kayo
1,2pl	siʔtamu	ʔitamu	hitamu	ta:yo
3pl	sira	ʔila	hila	sila

Table 10.4, distinguishing it again from the other members of that family, and giving evidence that ST's ancestors learned their language from their non-Negrito neighbors at a very early period in the development of the Central Luzon language family.

If we now look at free nominative pronouns for ST, Kapampangan, Botolan Sambal, and Tagalog (Table 10.5), we see that ST shares at least one innovation with the Central Luzon family that is not shared by Tagalog, that is, loss of the final *w* from the second-person singular (2sg) form. Similarly, ST does not share in the innovation reflected in the Tagalog first-person inclusive plural (1,2pl) form, which changed PMP *=tamu into =*ta:yo*.

It is of interest also to note that ST maintains features that were probably present in Proto-Central Luzon, but have been subsequently lost in all other Central Luzon languages. Inspection of these forms shows Kapampangan suffixing its pronominal bases to a personal noun specifier *ʔi*, and Botolan Sambal instead suffixing them to *hi* from *si. Sinauna suffixes its pronominal bases to either *siʔi* or *siʔ*, apparently reflecting an earlier system in which a sequence of personal noun specifiers (*si and *ʔi) were the forms to which pronominal bases became encliticized and later suffixed.

An alternate hypothesis, that Kapampangan actually reflects the original form of the personal noun specifier and that it was replaced by *si after the dispersal of the family, is also possible. Under this hypothesis, the evidence would suggest that ST is more closely related to Botolan Sambal than to Kapampangan (Himes 2012).

It is clear from the foregoing evidence that ST is indeed a Central Luzon language. Its geographic location, in the middle of a Tagalog-speaking area, could be the result of either a northward in-migration of Tagalog speakers, or a southward shift in the hunting range of the Negritos. It is probable that in this case it is the Negritos who have retained their traditional foraging areas and it is their earlier Central Luzon speaking neighbors who migrated north under the pressure of in-migrating Tagalogs from Marinduque and Mindoro in the Central Philippines (Zorc 1993; Gonzalez 2005: 94).

Evidence that the Tagalogs are the latecomers to this area is considerable, and is generally accepted by linguists. Zorc writes, "When the Tagalogs first migrated to Southern Luzon, they came in contact with various Northern Philippine languages such as Kapampangan, Sambal, and (later?) Pangasinan. Through centuries of contact, trade, and intermarriage, these languages were displaced by Tagalog or moved north" (1979: vii). The geographical extent of this early language with which the Ayta Negritos can be associated has been suggested by Zorc (1974). He has presented a number of features in the languages of Mindoro, including *R to *y*, that appear to be probable shared innovations with the Central Luzon group and possibly with Bashiic in the far north, indicating that at least the northern languages of Mindoro are probably more closely related genetically to these northern groups than they are to the other languages of the Central Philippines.

10.3.4.2 The Alta Languages   There are two Alta languages spoken by Negritos over a fairly wide area of the Sierra Madre from eastern Nueva Ecija to the boundary of Aurora and Nueva Vizcaya Provinces north of Maria Aurora. The Northern and Southern Alta languages are very different from one another, and are not mutually intelligible. The only published materials for Northern Alta are Vanoverbergh (1937), who refers to the language as Baler Negrito, and Reid (1991); the latter also provides the only published data on Southern Alta. For the purposes of this chapter, I will restrict my discussion of these Negrito languages to Northern Alta.

Although the Northern Alta live in the same general area (the Baler River Valley and environs) as the Southern Ilongot, who speak a language of the Southern Cordilleran family, their primary contacts, especially in the Dingalan area and in Nueva Ecija are with speakers of Tagalog. Consequently, most Northern Alta are bilingual in this language. This contact has continued for long enough that the language shows a considerable number of Tagalog borrowings. There appears to have been considerable contact also between Northern Alta and other Negrito groups, especially those speaking dialects of the Umiray Dumaget language (as in Section 10.3.5.2) who are scattered down the eastern coast of Luzon.

The genetic relationship of the Alta languages, however, is probably with the South-Central Cordilleran languages. These include Kalinga, Bontok, and Ifugao (Central Cordilleran), and Pangasinan, Ibaloi, and Ilongot (Southern Cordilleran). The Alta languages are the only extant Negrito languages to be related to this group. Their genetic relationship is indicated by their *l* reflex of *R, the reflex also found in the South-Central Cordilleran languages (Table 10.6). All of these languages, including Alta, also share an innovation

Table 10.6 *Examples of the* l *reflex of PAN* *R *in Northern Alta*

PMP	Northern Alta	Gloss
*qaRta	*?alta*	man
*()duR	*?adul*	thunder
*baqəRu	*bulu*	new
*bahaR	*bal*	loincloth
*diRus	*dilus*	bathe
*huRas	*?ulas*	wash
*kaRat	*?alat*	bite
*niuR	*niyul*	coconut
*saNdiR	*saŋgil*	lean
*taRaqinəp	*tale:nip*	dream
*wiRi	*?awilih*	left hand

in the system of verbal prefixes. The reflex of the Proto-Philippine intransitive verb prefix *maR- in these languages should be *mal-. Instead, all show a reflex of *man-.

There are several very conservative features of Northern Alta that suggest that these Negritos switched to speaking an Austronesian language at a quite remote time. These features are as follows. Two of the lexical items cited in Table 10.6 have been replaced in all of the other Central and Southern Cordilleran languages. These are the words for 'coconut' and 'dream'. Only in Northern Alta are these terms preserved with an *l* reflex of *R, the way they must have been pronounced in Proto-South-Central Cordilleran. Northern Alta, like other Negrito languages discussed earlier, also maintains unreduced forms of the completed aspect of verbal prefixes. All other Central and Southern Cordilleran languages have reduced them to *n*-initial forms.

The other conservative aspect of Alta is its pronominal system. The pronouns of Northern Alta do not reflect innovations that have occurred in all of the other languages of this subgroup. Table 10.7 compares the free nominative pronouns of Northern Alta with the forms reconstructed for Proto-Southern Cordilleran, Proto-Central Cordilleran, and Proto-Northern Luzon (also called Proto-Cordilleran), the parent of all the Cordilleran languages – including Northern Cordilleran, not otherwise mentioned here (Reid 1974, 1979; Tharp 1974). For instance, Northern Alta does not share in the loss of final *-w from the second-person singular (2sg) form, as have all other Central and Southern Cordilleran languages. Neither does Northern Alta share in the loss of the penultimate syllable *mu from the second-person plural (2pl) form, as have all other Central and

Table 10.7 *Nominative pronouns in Northern Alta and other Cordilleran languages*

	AltN	P-SCo	P-CCo	P-SCCo	P-NLzn
1sg	si?ən	siyak	sakən	siyakən	siyakən
2sg	si?aw	si?ika	sik?a	si?ika	si?ikaw
1,2sg	si?e:ta	si?ikita	da?ita	si?ikita	si?ikita
3sg	siya	siya	siya	siya	siya
1pl	si?ami	si?ikami	dakami	si?ikami	si?ikami
2pl	si?am	si?ikayu	dakayu	si?ikayu	si?ikamuyu
1,2pl	si?e:tam	si?ikitayu	dataku	si?ikita()	si?ikitam
3pl	sidda	si?ida	da?ida	si?ida	si?ida

Southern Cordilleran languages. Northern Alta instead lost the final three segments of the original pronoun. Furthermore, Northern Alta does not share in either of the innovations that occurred in the pronominal formatives marking first-person inclusive plural (1,2pl). In Southern Cordilleran the original form became =*tayu*; in Central Cordilleran it became =*taku*. In Northern Alta the form is =*tam*, a reflex of the form reconstructed for Proto-Northern Luzon (Reid 2009).

There is also an innovation that took place in the genitive pronoun set of Southern Cordilleran languages that is not shared by Northern Alta. In these languages the third-person singular (3sg) genitive pronoun *=na is replaced by =*tu*. Alta retains =*na*, the form that is reconstructed for Proto-Northern Luzon. Northern Alta is also different from the South-Central Cordilleran languages, in that its locative personal pronouns are attached to the locative case-marking preposition *di*, like the Agta languages already described, rather than with a reflex of *ka-ni. Ivatan (spoken in Batanes Province) is the only non-Negrito language in the north that has locative personal pronouns case-marked with *di*.

It seems likely then that the Alta languages are the only languages to retain pronominal forms that were probably present in Proto-Meso-Cordilleran, the immediate parent of Proto-South-Central Cordilleran and Proto-Alta. A diagram showing the relationships among the Northern Luzon languages is listed in Appendix 10.2.

10.3.5 The Relatively Remote-with-Little-Subsequent-Intimate-Contact Hypothesis

The most interesting hypothesis would be that a Negrito group switched languages at a remote period, as a result of intimate contact with one of the early Austronesian protolanguages in the Philippines, then went its own way, without subsequent intimate contact with that language or any subsequent daughter languages of the protolanguage, perhaps until the historical period. Such groups would appear to be isolates, difficult to subgroup with other Philippine languages, and would potentially have great value for determining which features were present in the proto-language. Such groups would probably have led relatively isolated lives in peripheral geographic areas with low population density, and like languages in other relic areas, would have retained features of the parent language that may have been lost in the more innovative languages of its immediate relatives.

Although there are several Negrito groups that perhaps fall into this category in that their languages appear to be very different from the languages of their immediate neighbors, and it is difficult to unambiguously group them with any other subgroup, they nevertheless show considerable lexical influence from local non-Negrito groups. This is to be expected, as within the historical period, at least, each of these groups has maintained close ties with their non-Negrito neighbors. In the following sections, three such groups – the Arta, the Umiray Dumaget of Luzon, and the Inati of Panay – will be discussed.

10.3.5.1 Arta   The Arta are a very small group of Negritos living along the Addalem River in the proximity of Aglipay and Maddela, Quirino Province, in northeastern Luzon. As of 1987, only about a dozen remaining speakers of the language could be found. They are generally referred to by local non-Negritos as Dumagats and assumed to be speakers of the same language as the Casiguran Agta, some of whom also live in the area (Reid 1989).

An examination of the Arta reflexes of Blust's (1981) reconstructions of 200 basic lexical items indicates that Arta retains only 26.9% (51/189), almost 8% fewer than any other Philippine language for which similar scores have so far been calculated.

Arta, as its name implies, has the reflex *r* for *R (Table 10.8). The only other language in Luzon with an *r* reflex for *R is Ilokano, suggesting the possibility that Arta may be most closely related genetically to Ilokano. However, Arta shares no other innovation with Ilokano and even though the language now exhibits a large number of borrowings from Ilokano, as it does also from other languages in the Cagayan Valley such as Yogad and Itawis, and Negrito languages of the east coast of Luzon, it appears not to subgroup with any of them. Arta has a fairly large percentage of unique lexical items, and some unique (for the area) phonological changes, including a zero reflex of both PMP *?, *q and *k, and a vowel-harmony rule not

Table 10.8 *Examples of the* r *reflex of PAN* *R
in Arta

PMP	Arta	Gloss
*qaRta	arta	man
*qəRəs	aras	worm
*quRat	urat	vein
*()duR	adur	thunder
*baqəRu	buru	new
*dapuR	dupuran	hearth
*diRu	diru	soup
*huRas	uras	wash
*kaRat	uarat	bite
*taRaŋ	taraŋ	rib

found elsewhere in the northern Philippines (Reid 1989). Further evidence for the aberrant nature of this language is found in the numeral system. It has unique forms for the numerals 'one' and 'two', *si:paŋ* and *tallip*, respectively, and is the only Philippine language to use the term for 'person' as the numeral 'twenty', thus *si:paŋ a arta*, 'twenty', *tallip a arta*, 'forty', and *lima arta*, 'one hundred' (literally, 'five people').

Arta, like other Negrito languages discussed in the foregoing, also retains unreduced forms of the completed-aspect verbal affixes (Table 10.1). As can be seen from Appendix 10.2, it is an isolate among the Northern Luzon (or Cordilleran) languages.

10.3.5.2 Umiray Dumaget   Umiray Dumaget is the Negrito language spoken in Umiray, Quezon Province, and in several other localities along the coast of Dingalan Bay and the Polillo Islands, reaching to Aurora, Nueva Ecija, Bulacan, and Rizal provinces as well. Although heavily influenced by Tagalog, it has a number of features that distinguish it from other languages in the area. It has a *g* reflex of *R, but does not appear to be closely related to any presently spoken non-Negrito language with the same reflex. It has generally been linked to the Agta languages along the coast to the north of it – Casiguran Dumagat, and Palanan – with which it shares some features. However, Reid (1994b) suggests that Umiray Dumaget is not a Cordilleran language but rather that it is relatable to Bikol, a Central Philippine language. Himes (2002: 275) writes:

While the evidence from phonological changes and the pronominal system does not compel us to favor one subgrouping over the other, the lexical data do show that DgtU [Umiray Dumaget] is most closely related to the Central Philippine

Table 10.9 *Nominative pronouns in Umiray Dumaget, Paranan, and Casiguran Agta*

	Umiray Dumaget	Paranan	Casiguran Agta
1sg	*iʔako*	*sikən*	*sakən*
2sg	*iʔaw*	*siko*	*siko*
1,2sg	*ikita*	*sikita*	*sikita*
3sg	*iʔeya*	*siya*	*siya*
1pl	*ikami*	*sikami*	*sikame*
2pl	*ikamo*	*sikam*	*sikam*
1,2pl	*ikitam*	*sikitam*	*sikitam*
3pl	*ida*	*hidi*	*side:*

languages. Culturally, we can infer that DgtU results from very early contact between the non-Austronesian-speaking Negrito population and speakers of that variety of Central Philippines that evolved into Tagalog, Bikol, and the Bisayan languages.

The Umiray Dumaget pronouns are similar to those found in Palanan and in the other Agta languages of northeast Luzon (Table 10.9), but show that Umiray did not share in an innovation in the third plural (3pl) form that characterizes Casiguran and Palanan, and it shows either a different pattern of reduction of the *siʔi personal noun specifier element in the parent language of this group (Umiray has only an *i*), or else it retains a reflex of an original *ʔi and never participated in the *si replacement that appears in Paranan and Casiguran. (Compare the pronominal features discussed earlier for Sinauna Tagalog and the Central Luzon languages.)

The case-marking systems of Umiray Dumaget and the other languages of the east coast of Luzon are unlike those of other Philippine languages (Reid 1978). The device for marking plurality in a common-noun phrase in Umiray is similar to that still found in Ivatan and in a few other languages such as Ibanag: the form of the third-person plural (3pl) pronoun immediately follows the pluralized noun. Paranan and most other Philippine languages, including Tagalog, place a (non-pronominal) plural marker between the case marker and the head noun. Addition of a plural form following the head noun was possibly a feature that was present in the parent language of the Philippines, but that has been lost in most of the extant languages. (See Reid and Liao 2004: 473–477.)

10.3.5.3 Inati   Inati of Panay (Pennoyer 1986–1987), although surrounded by Bisayan languages (part of the Central Philippine subgroup), shows no evidence that these are the languages with which it is most closely related genetically. It appears to have a unique reflex of *R, with about a dozen forms showing *d* for *R, whereas Bisayan languages have *R to *g*. It also appears likely that the inherited reflex of *ə was *a*, like the Central Luzon languages, not *u* as in the Bisayan languages (e.g., PMP *liqəR > *li?ad*, 'neck'; *yakən > *yakan*, 'mine'; *bəkən > *bakan,* 'negative') with *a > *e* in some environments (e.g., PEF *Ramut > *yemət*, 'root', an interesting instance of *R becoming *y*). However, the reflex of the transitive suffix *-ən is *-in*.

This language also shows a semantic reversal of the demonstratives *ti* and *ta* that also occurred only in some of the Central Luzon languages (including Sinauna Tagalog). In the Sogodnin dialect of Inati, *o* appears as a nominative common-noun marker, a form that elsewhere occurs with this function only in Ivatan.

There can be no question that the ancestors of the Inati learned their language prior to the settlement of the Visayas by the people now speaking so-called Bisayan languages. Unfortunately the language has undergone so many changes that it is difficult to see which, if any, Philippine group it is genetically most closely related to.

An examination of the other Negrito languages of the Philippines, in light of the linguistic evidence discussed earlier – particularly the various Ayta languages of the Zambales mountain range, the Batak of Palawan, and the Mamanwa of northeast Mindanao – may shed further light on the kinds of relationships these peoples have had with their non-Negrito neighbors in prehistoric times.

10.4   Substratum Questions

Although there are no clear cases of substratal elements in non-Negrito languages of the Philippines, one paper has been published that attempted to look for possible remnants of pre-Austronesian forms in the Negrito languages (Reid 1994a). The extremely long period of differentiation among the Negrito languages prior to the arrival of the Neolithic Austronesian-speaking population would suggest that there would have been little in common between the languages of remotely separated Negrito bands, such as those in Mindanao and northern Luzon. However, groups within the same area would undoubtedly have maintained periodic contact with each other, and the languages may well have been close enough to enable communication to take place. With this operating assumption, the available lexical material for Negrito groups in Luzon was searched for forms that were shared by Negrito groups, but for which no apparent cognate had been found in any Austronesian language.

Table 10.10 *Radical phonological change in Northern Alta*

P-NLzn	AltN	Gloss
*ʔabak	ʔabdəʔ	body
*ʔigat	ʔigdət	eel
*taba	tabdə	fat
*lagaʔan	lagdən	light weight
*ʔugat	ʔugdət	root
*babaʔi	dəbdi	woman

A considerable number of unique terms were found, some of which were fairly widely shared among contiguous groups, with some shared also with noncontiguous groups, but that did not have comparable forms in Austronesian languages. A fairly substantial number of them are part of the environment in which Negritos presumably lived and that tend to be culture-specific (e.g., abaca, rattan, sugarcane, coconut, betel leaf, rat, snake, buffalo, deer, dog, locust, crocodile, butterfly, termite, ant, mosquito), or secret language (e.g., vagina, penis). Such forms are suggestive of a contact language, in which basic vocabulary had been replaced with forms borrowed from the Austronesian language with which contact had been established, but so-called native cultural vocabulary was retained.

A further set of forms in the Negrito languages consists of look-alikes of forms in Austronesian languages, but with radical phonological and/or semantic change. Typically only the initial syllable of the Austronesian form was retained, or the Austronesian forms were systematically modified, as in Northern Alta in which terms with second syllables originally consisting of a voiced stop plus /a/ sequence have /d/ inserted before the second vowel, which is reflected as /ə/, as in Table 10.10 (Reid 1994a: 52–56).

Such terms would have hindered, rather than enhanced, communication with the Negritos' Austronesian neighbors, and suggest that after the loss of their original language such forms developed as part of a secret language and became linguistic markers of group identity.

10.5   Creole Questions

The data examined in the previous section suggest that the Negrito languages may have passed through a period of creolization, with subsequent decreolization as a result of thousands of years of intermittent interaction with Austronesian languages. There are, however, two Austronesian languages that provide evidence that they also may have begun as creoles. These are the languages Paranan and Kasiguranin mentioned in Section 10.3.3. Relatively little data are available from either of these languages. For Kasiguranin, there is a short wordlist published in Vanoverbergh (1937). The pronouns, case markers, and verb affixation of this language are almost identical to those of Tagalog. Lexically, however, Kasiguranin is very similar to its neighboring Negrito dialects – sharing, for example, 77% of its basic vocabulary with Casiguran Agta versus only 52% with Tagalog (Headland 1975). Although McFarland (1980) groups it with the Negrito languages, it seems to be the language of a group speaking an early Tagalog language that moved into the Casiguran Valley and was influenced by the Negritos in the area, a view first proposed by Vanoverbergh, who comments, "Here, however, instead of losing the language they [the Negritos] had borrowed from their conquerors, they partly imposed it on their masters and brought into being a Casiguran dialect" (Vanoverbergh 1937: 11).

Paranan, on the other hand, although showing considerable influence from Tagalog, with 45% shared vocabulary (Headland 1975), clearly retains case markers and pronouns that are very conservative. Specifically, it appears to be the only language in Luzon that still retains a *di* locative preposition for common noun phrases, e.g., *di bilay* 'to the house', alongside proper noun locations, such as *di Manila* 'to Manila' (Finkbeiner 1983: 6). Although *di* occurs in many languages with various other case-marking functions and occurs widely as the initial formative of locative adverbs and demonstratives, it is as a locative preposition that it is reconstructible for Proto-Malayo-Polynesian.

Although speakers of Paranan are now restricted to the geographical area around the town of Palanan, there is clear evidence that a wide area of northeastern Luzon was once occupied by people speaking a language that also had a *di* locative preposition. Nearly all of the old place names in this area have an initial *di* formant. Interestingly, these place names are mostly found within the present ranges of the Negrito groups being discussed in this section.

That the eastern coast of Luzon has been occupied by non-Negritos for thousands of years is supported by archaeological evidence (Peterson 1974). Excavations at Dimolit, a site in the Palanan Bay area, uncovered the postholes of house structures that are without doubt remains of an Austronesian settlement in the area, with pottery and grain-reaping knives. Peterson claims that the area was probably occupied between 2500 and 1500 BC. The present-day Paranans are perhaps the last linguistic survivors of that settlement.

Both Kasiguranin and Paranan, then, exhibit characteristics of having been relexified as a result of intimate contact with one or more of the Negrito languages in the area.

10.6   Conclusion

This chapter has covered a number of fairly disparate themes with reference to the relationship between Philippine hunter-gatherers and their neighbors. Currently, probably none of the Philippine Negrito groups are pure hunter-gatherers. All have begun, with greater or less success, to introduce horticultural practices into their daily activities. This has primarily been the result of the massive loss of primary-forest cover through logging activities and the accompanying degradation of the environment and loss of game and other forest products that were the main source of livelihood of the hunter-gatherers.

Increasing intermarriage with non-Negrito groups, education, and incorporation into the social fabric of mainstream Philippine society is resulting in the rapid loss of the relatively few remaining Negrito languages in favor of the major languages of their neighbors: Ilokano, Tagalog, Bikol, and Cebuano.

Despite the general lack of in-depth information about the languages the Negritos have been speaking since soon after the arrival of Austronesian-speaking migrants into the Philippines from what is now Taiwan, sufficient detail is available to enable us to make at least the following claims.

1. The very conservative nature of the verbal morphology and the case-marking systems of a number of these languages implies that contact with the in-migrating farmers was established relatively soon after their first arrival in the country.
2. The contact was probably of an intimate sort – that is, Negritos and farmers living together in the same communities – with the children playing together and perhaps learning each other's languages.
3. Pidgins probably developed, with creoles forming within a generation or two.
4. The Austronesian-speaking farmers were probably the dominant group on the basis of their technological know-how rather than their dominant numbers.
5. The Negritos were treated as serfs, working with the farmers to establish rice fields and being paid with part of the harvest. They probably also traded forest products for rice.

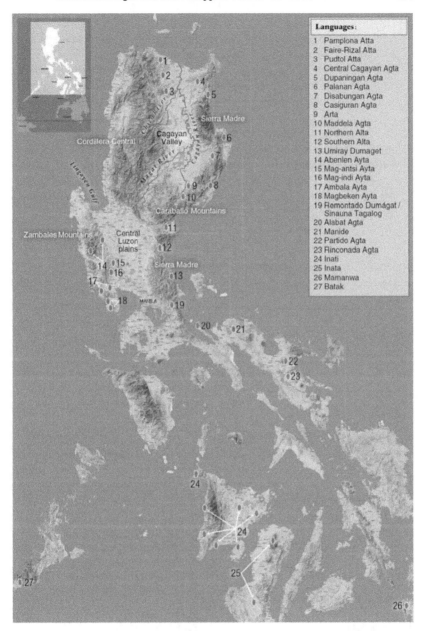

Map 10.1 Map of Negrito languages of the Philippines

6. The relationship with farmers was intermittent. Conflict or other causes resulted in the separation of the groups, leading to the development of dialects and eventually separate languages.
7. The separation of the groups was not necessarily complete. Trading probably continued either with their former working partners or with other Austronesian groups when the former group moved away or were replaced by farmers speaking another language.
8. Until relatively recently, within the historical period, many (if not most) Negrito groups were careful to maintain their own identity, distinguishing themselves from their neighbors by developing distinctive linguistic emblems, by calling themselves by a reflex of *qaRta, 'Negrito person', and having a distinct term for all non-Negrito people.

Appendix 10.1 *Negrito languages spoken in the Philippines*

Language name	Location
Batak	Palawan
Mamanwa	Northeastern Mindanao
Ati	Panay, Negros
Ata	Northern Negros
Atta	Pamplona, western Cagayan Province, Luzon
Atta	Faire-Rizal, western Cagayan Province, Luzon
Atta	Pudto, Apayao Province, Luzon
Abenlen Ayta	Tarlac Province, Luzon
Mag-antsi Ayta	Zambales, Tarlac, and Pampanga provinces, Luzon
Mag-indi Ayta	Zambales and Pampanga provinces, Luzon
Ambala Ayta	Zambales, Pampanga, and Bataan provinces, Luzon
Magbeken Ayta	Bataan Province, Luzon
Northern Alta	Aurora Province, Luzon
Southern Alta	Quezon Province, Luzon
Arta	Aglipay, Quirino Province, Luzon
Agta	Central Cagayan Province, Luzon
Dupaningan Agta	Eastern Cagayan Province, Luzon
Agta	Palanan and Divilacan, Isabela Province, Luzon
Agta	San Mariano-Disabungan, Isabela Province, Luzon
Agta	Casiguran, northern Aurora Province, Luzon
Agta	Maddela, Quirino Province, Luzon
Agta, Umiray Dumaget	West-central Luzon
Agta	Alabat Island, Quezon Province, Luzon
Rinconada Agta	Camarines Sur Province, Luzon
Manide Agta	Camarines Norte, western Camarines Sur Province, Luzon

Appendix 10.2 *Subgrouping of Northern Luzon languages*

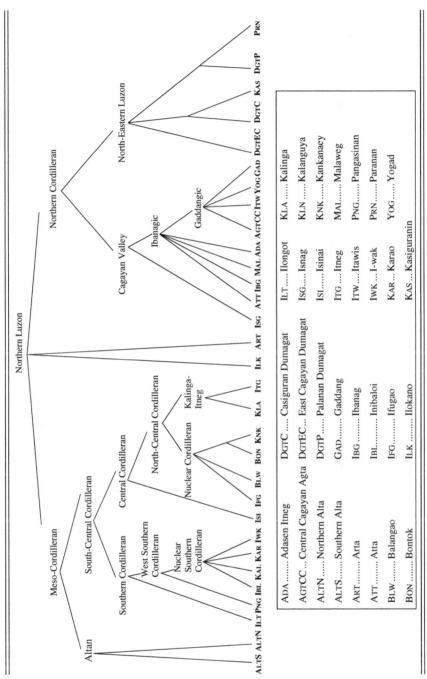

ADA........ Adasen Itneg	DGTC..... Casiguran Dumagat	ILT...... Ilongot	KLA ..... Kalinga
AGTCC... Central Cagayan Agta	DGTEC... East Cagayan Dumagat	ISG...... Isnag	KLN ..... Kalanguya
ALTN..... Northern Alta	DGTP..... Palanan Dumagat	ISI....... Isinai	KNK..... Kankanaey
ALTS...... Southern Alta	GAD....... Gaddang	ITG ...... Itneg	MAL...... Malaweg
ART........ Arta	IBG .... Ibanag	ITW..... Itawis	PNG...... Pangasinan
ATT........ Atta	IBL.......... Inibaloi	IWK..... I-wak	PRN...... Paranan
BLW .... Balangao	IFG.......... Ifugao	KAR... Karao	YOG...... Yogad
BON .... Bontok	ILK .... Ilokano	KAS ... Kasiguranin	

NOTES

1. Headland (2002:26) also contains a table said to list thirty-three Negrito languages still spoken in the Philippines. A few problems exist with that table. First, only thirty-two groups are actually listed; second, two of the languages (Agta of Villaviciosa, Abra Province; Agta of Dicamay, Jones, Isabela Province) are listed as extinct. Lobel (2013), suggests that several others in the Headland list may also no longer be spoken. These include Agta of Isarog, Camarines Sur Province (listed by Headland as nearly extinct), and the so-called Ayta of Sorsogon Province. Sinauna Tagalog (not listed by Headland) may also be extinct, although its close dialect, Remontado Agta, with which it is equated in the Ethnologue (Eberhard et al. 2019), may still be spoken. Although there are large numbers of people identified as Negrito throughout the Bicol and Visayan areas, there are relatively few who still speak a language distinct from that of their neighbors. Lobel claims, moreover, that the groups that he has visited are no longer nomadic; all have lost their traditional lifestyle and live year-round in houses. Manide and Rinconada Agta are Lobel's terms (pers. comm., 20 June 2006).

2. The following transcriptions (shown in italics) used in this paper represent deviations from the International Phonetic Alphabet (in square brackets): *y* [j], *j* [dʒ]; in addition, *N* (and *N) is a place-assimilating nasal consonant; capital letters in reconstructions (i.e., in forms preceded by an asterisk) – C, G, R, and T – are conventional symbols used in Austronesian historical linguistics, the exact phonetic values of which are often not fully agreed upon. In addition, a preceding equals sign indicates that the form is an enclitic. Finally, the following special abbreviations are used in this paper. AltN: Northern Alta, BP: before present (more precisely before AD 1950), PAN: Proto-Austronesian, P-CCo: Proto-Central Cordilleran, PMP: Proto-Malayo-Polynesian, P-NLzn: Proto-Northern Luzon (=Proto-Cordilleran), P-SCo: Proto-Southern Cordilleran, P-SCCo: Proto-South-Central Cordilleran. The empty parentheses in tables 6 through 8 indicate that some phonetic material was probably present in this position, but its reconstruction is uncertain. And an asterisk preceding an italicized form indicates an unattested modern form.

3. The Central Cagayan Agta refer to Ilokano people as *ugsin*. The Casiguran Agta call the non-Negrito Kalinga near San Mariano, Isabela, *ugdin* (Tom Headland pers. comm. April 9, 2010). The Dupaningan Agta call Ilokanos *ogden* (Robinson 2012), while the Alta refer to non-Negritos as *uldin*. These terms appear to be reflexes of a form *ʔuRtin, which is also reflected in Atta *ujojjin* 'red', giving an interesting insight into the possible reason for the name. The in-migrating Austronesians (from Taiwan) were apparently perceived as having red skins. The Arta call a non-Negrito person *agani*, which appears to be cognate with Ilokano *agáni* 'to harvest rice; one who harvests rice' (Reid 1971, 1994b).

4. Given Blust's more recent views on higher-level subgroups in Austronesian, and the lack of any Formosan cognate, the reconstruction should only be made as far back as his Proto-Malayo-Polynesian. Zorc's *G and Blust's *R both represent what was probably a velar fricative /ɣ/ (or perhaps uvular /ʁ/) in the parent language, and since PAN *C, *t, and *T are all reflected as *t outside of Taiwan, there is no need to reconstruct a set of ambiguous phonemes as the second consonant of the cluster. In addition, Blust's two uses of parentheses in *qa(R)(CtT)a serve differing functions. The first parentheses imply that the data are insufficient to definitively reconstruct *R in that position, while

the second set implies that the data are insufficient to be definitive about which of the three – *C, *t, or *T – was the proto-sound in that position. Blust's most recent reconstruction is PMP *qaRta (Blust and Trussel Ongoing).

5. Although a few Philippine languages (Tboli, Agutaynen, and Kalamianen) show /k/ as a reflex of PEF *q, the usual reflex in Philippine languages is glottal stop.

6. Samal is a Sama-Bajaw language spoken in the southern Philippines, but is not a Philippine language. The Sama-Bajaw languages are now classified as belonging to the Barito family of languages of southeast Kalimantan (Blust 2005:45).

7. For Maranao, McKaughan and Macaraya also give *ate?* 'chicken with black feather and flesh, person who is dark brown to black' (1967:31); and *agta?* 'witch, demon-black' (1967:5).

8. Jason Lobel (pers. comm., 12 July, 2006) suggests the possibility that although the languages are very dissimilar, the language names Inati and Inata are related, in that Pennoyer notes that the Ati of Northwest Panay call their language Inete (where e [ɛ] is a reflex of both *a and *ə). Pennoyer (1986–87:7) also notes that he recorded three variations of the name of the group: Ati, Ete, and Ata.

9. Peter Bellwood states, "We have a new site, Reranum Cave, right at the northern end of Itbayat. It has red slipped ware and some sherds of fine-cord marked pottery, a classic type in Taiwan around 4500–4000 BP. We also have dates of 4000 BP from Torongan Cave also on Itbayat. As a matter of interest, we also know the site of Anaro on Itbayat was involved in manufacturing *lingling-o* [ear rings] of Taiwan jade around 2000–1500 years ago" (pers. comm., 7 May, 2006).

10. Much of the information in these sections previously appeared in Reid (1987).

11. A grammar of Dupaningan Agta has recently been published (Robinson 2012), but is not considered here.

12. Headland and Headland use the terms oblique, topic, and attributive (for my locative, nominative, and genitive, respectively).

References

Antworth, Evan L. (1979). A grammatical sketch of Botolan Sambal. *Philippine Journal of Linguistics Special Monograph* 8. Manila: Linguistic Society of the Philippines.

Bellwood, Peter. (1985). *Prehistory of the Indo-Malaysian archipelago*. Sydney: Academic Press.

Bellwood, Peter, and Eusebio Dizon. (2005). The Batanes archaeological project and the "out-of-Taiwan" hypothesis for Austronesian dispersal. *Bulletin of the Indo-Pacific Prehistory Association* 1(1): 1–36.

Bellwood, Peter, Janelle Stevenson, Atholl Anderson, and Eusebio Dizon. (2003). Archaeological and palaeoenvironmental research in Batanes and Ilocos Norte Provinces, northern Philippines. *Bulletin of the Indo-Pacific Prehistory Association* 11: 141–161.

Blust, Robert. (1972). Note on PAN *qa(R)(CtT)a 'outsiders, alien people'. *Oceanic Linguistics* 11(2): 166–171.

(1976). Austronesian culture history: Some linguistic inferences and their relations to the archaeological record. *World Archaeology* 8(1): 19–43.

(1981). Variation in retention rate among Austronesian languages. *Paper presented to the Third International Conference on Austronesian Linguistics*, Bali, Indonesia.

(1995). The prehistory of the Austronesian-speaking peoples: A view from language. *Journal of World Prehistory* 9(4): 453–510.

(2005). The linguistic macrohistory of the Philippines: Some speculations. In Hsiu-chuan Liao and Carl R. Galvez Rubino (eds.), *Current issues in Philippine linguistics and anthropology: Parangal kay Lawrence A. Reid*. Manila: Linguistic Society of the Philippines and SIL Philippines, 31–68.

Blust, Robert, and Steve Trussel. *Ongoing. Austronesian comparative dictionary*. www.trussel2.com/ACD/.

Dempwolff, Otto. (1938). *Austronesisches Worterverzeichnis: Vergleichende Lautlehre des austronesischen Wortschatzes 3*. Beihefte zur Zeitschrift für Eingeborenen-Sprachen 19. Berlin: Dietrich Reimer.

DuBois, Carl D. (1974). Sarangani Manobo dictionary. Unpublished computer printout. Library of SIL Philippines.

Eberhard, David M., Gary F. Simons, and Charles D. Fennig (eds.). 2019. *Ethnologue: Languages of the World*. Twenty-second edition. Dallas, Texas: SIL International. Online version: http://www.ethnologue.com.

Elkins, Richard E. (1968). *Manobo-English dictionary*. Oceanic Linguistics Special Publication 3. Honolulu: University of Hawaii Press.

Finkbeiner, Marianne. 1983. Paranan lessons. Lesson 8. Manuscript. Library of SIL Philippines.

Forster, Jannette, and Myra Lou Barnard. (1976). Dibabawon-English dictionary with English-Dibabawon index. Unpublished typescript. Library of SIL Philippines.

Gonzalez, Andrew. (2005). Contemporary Filipino (Tagalog) and Kapampangan: Two Philippine languages in contact. In Hsiu-chuan Liao and Carl R. Galvez Rubino (eds.), *Current issues in Philippine linguistics and anthropology: Parangal kay Lawrence A. Reid*. Manila: Linguistic Society of the Philippines and SIL Philippines, 93–114.

Hassan, Irene U., Seymour A. Ashley, and Mary L. Ashley. (1975/1994). *Tausug-English dictionary: Kabtangan iban maana*, 2nd edn. Sulu Studies 6). Jolo, Sulu: Notre Dame of Sulu College; Manila: Summer Institute of Linguistics, 1st edn. Sulu Studies 4. Jolo, Sulu: Coordinated Investigation of Sulu Culture; Manila: Summer Institute of Linguistics.

Headland, Thomas N. (1975). Report of eastern Luzon language survey. *Philippine Journal of Linguistics* 6(2), 47–54.

(2002). Why Southeast Asian Negritos are a disappearing people: A case study of the Agta of eastern Luzon, Philippines. In Thomas N. Headland and Doris E. Blood (eds.), *What place for hunter-gatherers in millennium three?* Publications in Ethnography 39. Dallas, TX: SIL International and International Museum of Cultures, 25–39.

Headland, Thomas N., and Janet D. Headland. (1974). *A Dumagat (Casiguran)-English dictionary*. Pacific Linguistics C–28. Canberra: Department of Linguistics, Research School of Pacific Studies, Australian National University.

Headland, Thomas N., and Lawrence A. Reid. (1989). Hunter-gatherers and their neighbors from prehistory to the present. *Current Anthropology* 30(1), 43–51.

(1991). Holocene foragers and interethnic trade: A critique of the myth of isolated hunter-gatherers. In Susan A. Gregg (ed.), *Between bands and states*. Carbondale: Southern Illinois University Press, 333–340.

Himes, Ronald S. (2002). The relationship of Umiray Dumaget to other Philippine languages. *Oceanic Linguistics* 41(2): 275–294.

(2012). The Central Luzon group of languages. *Oceanic Linguistics* 51(2): 490–537.

Lobel, Jason W. (2013). Philippine and North Bornean languages: Issues in description, subgrouping, reconstruction. Ph.D. dissertation, University of Hawai'i.

Magaña, Delia S. (2003). The Agta foragers in the Northern Sierra Madre Natural Park: Ancestral domains in theory and practice. In Jan van der Ploeg, Andres B. Masipiqueña, and Eileen C. Bernardo (eds.), *The Sierra Madre mountain range: Global relevance, local realities.* Tuguegarao City: Golden Press, 241–257.

McFarland, Curtis D. (1980). *A linguistic atlas of the Philippines.* Study of Languages and Cultures of Asia and Africa Monograph Series 15. Tokyo: Tokyo University of Foreign Studies.

McKaughan, Howard P., and Batua A. Macaraya. (1967/1996). *A Maranao dictionary.* Honolulu: University of Hawai'i Press. 2nd edn, Manila: De La Salle University Press and Summer Institute of Linguistics.

Miller, Jeanne, and Helen Miller. (1976). *Mamanwa grammar.* Language Data: Asian-Pacific Series 8. Huntington Beach, CA: Summer Institute of Linguistics.

Omoto, Keiichi. (1981). The genetic origins of the Philippine Negritos. *Current Anthropology* 22(4): 421–422.

Paz, Victor J. (1999). Neolithic human movement to island Southeast Asia: The search for archaeobotanical evidence. *Bulletin of the Indo-Pacific Prehistory Association* 18(2): 151–157.

Pennoyer, F. Douglas. (1986–1987). Inati: The hidden Negrito language of Panay, Philippines. *Philippine Journal of Linguistics* 17(2), 18(1): 1–36.

Peterson, Warren E. (1974). Summary report of two archaeological sites from northeastern Luzon. *Archaeology and Physical Anthropology in Oceania* 9(1): 26–35.

Reid, Lawrence A. (1971). *Philippine minor languages: Word lists and phonologies.* Oceanic Linguistics Special Publication 8. Honolulu: University of Hawaii Press.

(1974). The Central Cordilleran subgroup of Philippine languages. *Oceanic Linguistics* 13(1–2): 511–560.

(1976). *Bontok-English dictionary.* Pacific Linguistics C–36. Canberra: Department of Linguistics, Research School of Pacific Studies, Australian National University.

(1978). Problems in the reconstruction of Proto-Philippine construction markers. In S. A. Wurm and Lois Carrington (eds.), *Second International Conference on Austronesian Linguistics: Proceedings*, Vol. 1. Pacific Linguistics C–61. Canberra: Department of Linguistics, Research School of Pacific Studies, Australian National University, 33–66.

(1979). Towards a reconstruction of the pronominal systems of Proto-Cordilleran, Philippines. In Nguyen Dang Liem (ed.), *South-east Asian linguistic studies*, Vol. 3. Pacific Linguistics C–45. Canberra: Department of Linguistics, Research School of Pacific Studies, Australian National University, 259–275.

(1987). The early switch hypothesis: Linguistic evidence for contact between Negritos and Austronesians. *Man and Culture in Oceania.* Tokyo: Japanese Society for Oceanic Studies 3 (special issue), 41–60.

(1989). Arta, another Philippine Negrito language. *Oceanic Linguistics* 28(1): 47–74.

(1991). The Alta languages of the Philippines. In Ray Harlow (ed.), *VICAL 2: Western Austronesian and contact languages: Papers from the Fifth International Conference on Austronesian Linguistics.* Auckland: Linguistic Society of New Zealand, 265–297.

(1992). The Tasaday language: A key to Tasaday prehistory. In Thomas N. Headland (ed.), *The Tasaday controversy: An assessment of the evidence.* Washington, DC: American Anthropological Association, 180–193.

(1994a). Possible non-Austronesian lexical elements in Philippine Negrito languages. *Oceanic Linguistics* 33(1): 37–72.

(1994b). Unraveling the linguistic histories of Philippine Negritos. In Thomas E. Dutton and Darrell T. Tryon (eds.), *Language contact and change in the Austronesian world.* Trends in Linguistics: Studies and Monographs 77. Berlin: Mouton de Gruyter, 443–475.

(1996). The Tasaday tapes. *In Pan-Asiatic linguistics: Proceedings of the 4th International Symposium on Languages and Linguistics*, January 8–10, 1996, Vol. 5. Salaya, Thailand: Institute of Language and Culture for Rural Development, Mahidol University, 1743–1766.

(1997). Linguistic archaeology: Tracking down the Tasaday language. In Roger Blench and Matthew Spriggs (eds.), *Theoretical and methodological orientations: Archaeology and language 1.* One World Archaeology 27. London: Routledge, 184–208.

(2009). The reconstruction of a dual pronoun to Proto-Malayo-Polynesian. In Bethwyn Evans (ed.), *Discovering history through language. Papers in honour of Malcolm Ross.* Canberra: Pacific Linguistics, 461–477.

(2013). Who are the Philippine Negritos? Evidence from language. *Human Biology* 85(1–3): 329–358.

(2018). Tasaday: Their current situation. Paper presented to the 12th International Conference on Hunting and Gathering Societies, Universiti Sains Malaysia, July 23–27, 2018.

Reid, Lawrence A., and Hsiu-chuan Liao. (2004). A brief syntactic typology of Philippine languages. *Language and Linguistics* 5(2): 433–490.

Robinson, Laura C. (2012). *Dupaningan Agta: Grammar, vocabulary, and texts.* Canberra: Pacific Linguistics.

Santos, Pilar C. (1975). Sinauna Tagalog: A genetic study examining its relationship with other Philippine languages. MA thesis, Ateneo de Manila University, Quezon City.

Snow, Bryan E., R. Shutler, D. E. Nelson, J. S. Vogel, and J. R. Southon. (1986). Evidence of early rice cultivation in the Philippines. *Philippine Quarterly of Culture and Society* 14(1): 3–11.

Tharp, James A. (1974). The Northern Cordilleran subgroup of Philippine languages. *Working Papers in Linguistics* 6(6): 53–114.

Vanoverbergh, Morice. (1937). *Some undescribed languages of Luzon.* Publications de la Commission d'Enquête Linguistique 3. Nijmegen: Dekker and van de Vegt.

Wolff, John U. (1972). *A dictionary of Cebuano Visayan*, 2 vols. Data Paper 87. Ithaca, NY: Southeast Asia Program, Cornell University.

Zorc, R. David. (1974). Internal and external relationships of the Mangyan languages. *Oceanic Linguistics* 13(1–2): 561–600.

(1979). *Core etymological dictionary of Filipino*, fascicle 1. Batchelor, Northern Territory, Australia: Public Domain.

(1993). The prehistory and origin of the *Tagalog* people. In Øyvind Dahl (ed.), *Language–a doorway between human cultures: Tributes to Dr. Otto Chr. Dahl on his ninetieth birthday.* Oslo: Novus, 201–211.

11 Hunter-Gatherers of Borneo and Their Languages

Antonia Soriente

11.1 Hunter-Gatherers in Borneo

Borneo, the third largest island in the world, is divided into three countries: Malaysia, Indonesia, and Brunei Darussalam. It is located in the center of Southeast Asia and is transversed by the Equator. Despite its considerable landmass of 746,000 km^2, it has an overall population of around 15 million ethnically diverse people, of which (mostly former-)hunter-gatherers constitute a very small minority of about 25,000 people (see Kaskija 2017) scattered across Brunei Darussalam; the Sarawak State of Malaysia; and the North, East, West, and Central Kalimantan Provinces of Indonesia. This diverse group of people live mainly in 30 clusters and occupy (or used to occupy) the rainforest hills of the central part of Borneo at the headwaters of the main rivers in difficult interior terrain below 1,000 m. This land use pattern is due to their dependence on *Eugeissona utilis*, a sago palm from which their staple food is extracted and which grows only below this elevation. In addition to this carbohydrate source, they exploit a wide range of resources by hunting wild animals, gathering wild plant foods, and fishing. They have no domesticated plants or any animals except for dogs and they engage in commercial relationships with settled groups to trade forest goods such as game, camphor, resin, wild rubber, and woven rattan goods in exchange for metal, cloth, salt, and tobacco. It is important to stress that certain elements are common to all these Bornean hunter-gatherer groups in that their subsistence economies not only are based on harvesting sago palm but that they also share an ideological core

An earlier version of this chapter was presented at the SEALS 16 (South East Asia Linguistic Society) conference held in Jakarta in 2006 and at ALLL 3 (3rd Conference on Austronesian Languages and Linguistics) conference held in London in 2007. I gratefully acknowledge the help of Bernard Sellato, who gave me access to much of his material, shared with me his views on Borneo hunter-gatherers, and made valuable comments on the paper. I also extend my gratitude to Miyako Koizumi and Rajindra Puri, who gave me insightful input on general issues related to the Penan Benalui people, Jayl Langub, who provided me with comments, information and a list of hunter-gatherer groups in Borneo. The discussions and the comments by Tom Güldemann on previous versions of this chapter were valuable too.

that is quite unlike that of farmers – a feature common to many hunter-gatherers described in other contributions to this volume.

Nowadays most of the hunter-gatherers in Borneo have settled down except for few individuals in Sarawak. More than a century ago, groups such as the Bukat and Kereho chose to relinquish their way of life under the pressure of colonial powers, and in the last two or three decades nearly all the hunter-gatherer groups have increasingly diversified their livelihoods. This diversification affects how we classify them in terms of the HRAF categories.[1] For instance, while in the 1960s it was estimated that 70–80% of all Penan in Sarawak were still nomadic (Brosius 1992), most of the nomadic hunter-gatherer groups today follow a more settled way of life. In fact, some of them have done so to such an extent that they have even forgotten their nomadic origin.[2] Today there are probably no more than a few hundred "genuine" hunter-gatherers in Borneo[3] (Brosius 1992; Sellato and Sercombe 2007: 7; Kaskija 2017), and most of the other former hunter-gatherers survive through swidden rice agriculture, cash crop cultivation, and wage labor. Nevertheless, they continue to hunt and gather. Although they farm in the same way as their agricultural neighbors, they are neither as committed nor as proficient. Moreover, their agricultural neighbors still see them as hunter-gatherers and they continue to perceive themselves as still directly connected with their hunting and gathering tradition. Thus their traditions continue and socially and culturally they are seen as distinct from their neighbors in terms of identity.

Seen in a wider geographic perspective, the Borneo hunter-gatherers have much in common culturally, socially, and economically with other groups of hunter-gatherers scattered in peninsular and insular Southeast Asia despite the geographical distance between them. In addition to the hunter-gatherers in Vietnam, Thailand, Malaysia, and the Philippines, (some of which are discussed elsewhere in this book), Southeast Asia is, or was, home to a number of other distinct groups of forest hunter-gatherers (Endicott 1999; Sellato and Sercombe 2007: 2). In Indonesia, the Moluccas are home to the Huaulu and the Maneo of Seram and the Tugutil of Halmahera, who combine horticulture with exploitation of wild resources such as sago palm, game, and fish; they live in settled villages. The same applies to the Toala' and the Sinalutan Lauje of Sulawesi. The Kubu living in Sumatra have a foraging tradition, speak an Austronesian language, and are phenotypically similar to the Malays. They number 15,000 people and are historically considered remnants of an Austronesian group that specialized in foraging to resist domination by local Malay kingdoms (Endicott 1999: 279). In addition, it is important to consider hunter-gatherers relying on maritime resources. Borneo's eastern coastline and offshore islands are home to scattered communities of maritime nomads, of whom the best known are the Bajau Laut (or Sama Dilaut). Thus whereas these sea nomads traditionally earned a living off the sea, the nomads of interior Borneo have traditionally lived off wild resources in the humid tropical rainforest. In total it is estimated that until recently there were as few as 50,000 nomadic peoples in Southeast Asia.[4]

Sellato and Sercombe (2007: 3) point out that these communities display many similarities: they are based on egalitarian social organization, have autonomous nuclear families grouped in small-sized bands, and are usually scattered widely over areas far from large settlements. Their basic technological kit, including a digging stick, a harpoon, a pike, and a blowpipe and/or bow-and-arrow, as well as baskets, mats, and carrying nets, has allowed them to exploit wild resources available in their natural environment so that they often attained self-sufficiency in spite of their historical lack of metal. Finally, although they have lived in relative isolation, most eventually established trade relations with their settled neighbors. If one were to hypothesize a common origin for all these Southeast Asian hunting and gathering groups, it must be kept in mind that they are divided phenotypically into Negrito and Mongoloid populations and that their languages belong to two separate language families, that is, Austroasiatic (specifically Mon-Khmer) and Austronesian (Sellato and Sercombe 2007).

11.2   Terminology and Inventory of Hunter-Gatherer Groups in Borneo

Needham (1954: 73) stated, regarding the problematic terminology for forager groups in Borneo, "In the ethnographic literature on Borneo, one of the most recurring confusions has lain in the term 'Punan'. In Sarawak this has been compounded by the appearance of the term 'Penan'. . . .. The inconsistencies and contradictions that have surrounded these terms contribute to one of the major ethnographic problems of Southeast Asia." That is, 'Penan' and 'Punan' are terms used indiscriminately to refer to most hunter-gatherers in Borneo. Most of the ethnonyms of hunter-gatherer groups are composed of these two terms followed by the name of the region where they are (or were) located. Owing to their continuous migration across large areas, they are also prone to assume different ethnonyms – a problem evident since the earliest work done by ethnographers who erroneously referred to a given group by different names, following the way other settled groups such as Kayan and Kenyah refer to it. This and the lack of salient autonyms have made it difficult to study them in a historical perspective.

'Penan' is traditionally used to refer to nomadic people and their languages in Sarawak and covers many units that are classified into two main groupings, Western Penan and Eastern Penan; the respective languages are considered distinct within the range of mutual intelligibility[5]. Eastern Penan is spoken in the Baram and Limbang District in Sarawak and in one village in Brunei,[6] while Western Penan is spoken in the Belaga, Baram, and Bintulu Districts in Sarawak.[7] This term also applies today to some groups spread in Kalimantan such as the Penan Benalui. As already mentioned, most of the Penan have settled down, except for a mere 295 individuals in 8 locations along the Tutoh, the Magoh and the Adang Rivers in Sarawak who are still nomadic. The distinction between Eastern and Western Penan, originally advanced by Needham (1954), is still used today with reference to Sarawak groups but is insufficient to account for the large variety of groups and their languages.

'Punan' is used today in Kalimantan for people with nomadic hunter-gatherer habits in general but also for the settled Punan Ba, the Punan Aput, the Punan Batu, and the Punan Busang, whose languages are allegedly unintelligible to the speakers of other Penan languages (Brosius [1992], e.g., notes that Punan Ba and Punan Aput have only 25% cognate percentage with Penan languages). In addition, the foraging and sedentary Punan groups do not seem to recognize a common ancestry and differ in many aspects of custom, language, and social organization. Thus, the Punan Ba have no tradition of having been nomadic and belong to the Kajang peoples (see Hudson 1978). Apparently, Penan people in Sarawak do not like being called Punan, even though Kayan agriculturalists routinely call them by this when speaking English or Malay. (See Thambiah [2007] for a detailed description of the concept 'Punan' and its different meaning according to context.)

'Punan' and 'Penan' are not part of the lexicon of the groups to which these terms refer. In many of the languages of the agriculturalists (mainly Kenyah) the term *punan* means 'snatch away.' According to the Kenyah speakers, 'to snatch away and fight over something' is a common feature of the 'less civilized' and poor Punan people. In Punan Aput there is a word *punan* that means 'roaming around' but this is not attested in other Pnan languages. Punan is also the name of a river in Sarawak where the Punan Ba were locatedIn Penan Benalui the derived word *pe-naan* means 'to be of the same kind,' probably meaning that they come from the same place or referring to the fact that the Penan are an egalitarian society. Okushima (2008) stated that the term Penan is a Kayanic term that originally meant 'someone who brings rice souls from deep forest' or 'forest spirits' though later the term came to refer to hunter-gatherers or in general to old allies who brought practical benefits such as game or other forest products. In any case, none of the etymologies can be considered certain.

Nevertheless, not all the nomadic groups refer to themselves as Punan or Penan. Thus, the Bukat, Lisum, and Beketan in the upper Mahakam and Tabang of today's East Kalimantan Provinces as well as the Kereho have always referred to themselves by these names, without adding the term Punan.

Besides Punan in East and North Kalimantan and Penan in Sarawak, other common terms of reference are Ot ('upriver people') in Central Kalimantan, Ukit in West Kalimantan and Sarawak, and Tau Utan in West Kalimantan. Other even more generic exonyms have also come to be applied to Borneo hunter-gatherers. While Orang Ulu ('upriver people') has emerged in Malaysia, in Indonesia the term Dayak (from *daya* 'upriver') is mostly preferred.

The exonym Dayak is particularly ambiguous because it includes anyone who does not speak a Malay variety and/or follows the Islamic religion. The dichotomy Malay versus Dayak simplifies a very diverse and complex cultural network on the part of non-Malay peoples, embracing a population of 3 million from several dozens of distinct ethnic groups whose origin, language, and customs may be fundamentally different. However, this usage, which arose in colonial times, has been embraced today by Malay and Dayak alike. While the term Dayak at one time carried a negative connotation, this is no longer usually the case but rather evokes the unity of different peoples sharing a similar perspective about life and political interests. While the many different Penan and Punan groups may quite often be lumped together under the generic concept of Dayak, Punan has come to contrast with the specific sense of Dayak as settled or itinerant farming people living upriver, as stated by Sellato and Sercombe (2007: 7).

To prevent ambiguity in the use of the terms Punan, Penan, and 'Borneo nomads,' Sellato and Sercombe (2007: 30) have chosen to use the term 'Pnan' to refer in general to foraging groups of Borneo, whether in Sarawak, Brunei, or Kalimantan; whether they are now still nomadic, semi-nomadic, or completely settled; and regardless of the use of their past or present ethnonyms (autonyms or exonyms). This includes groups that have never referred to themselves as either Penan or Punan. Sellato and Sercombe justify this choice because the term Pnan highlights the common past and present way of life and the idea these people have of themselves as opposed to the agriculturalists, their feeling of sharing a common identity. In this chapter I adopt this definition when referring in a general way to hunter-gatherer groups in Borneo, but I still employ the current ethnonym when referring to a specific group.

Despite the confusion of names and affiliations, Sellato and Sercombe (2007) tentatively proposed the existence of eight major groups of Borneo hunter-gatherers, based on available ethnohistorical data and apparent linguistic affinities. Table 11.1 presents this basic classification compared to the one proposed by Ethnologue (Simons and Fennig 2018) and provides, whenever available, information on group size and contact population.[8] It is worth noting

Table 11.1 *An inventory of Pnan groups in Borneo*

Autonym	Exonym, alternate names	Location	Group size	Contact population	Name and code in Ethnologue
(1) Bukat-Beketan		East and North Kalimantan (Mahakam, Tabang area, Apo Kayan, West Kalimantan (Kapuas), several settlements in Sarawak (Belaga)			
Bukat	Punan Bukat/Ukit/ Ot, Bhuket	Upper Mahakam	1,000	Aoheng	*Bukat* (bvk)
					Ukit (umi)
Lisum	Punan Lisum		500	Kenyah	
Punan Long Top	Punan Oho'/ Punan Hu'		73	Kenyah	
Beketan	Punan Beketan, Begetan, Bukitan		500	Iban, Kenyah	*Bukitan* (bkn)
Lugat				Iban	
(2) Punan Aput-Busang-Merah-Kohi		Sarawak, East and North Kalimantan			
Punan Aput	Punan Haput		1000	Kenyah	*Punan Aput* (pud)
Punan Busang	Punan Vuhang, Punan Tekalet, Punan Nuo		153	Kayan, Kenyah	
Punan Merah	Punan Serata, Punan Kohi, Punan Langasa, Punan Nya'an		100	Busang, Bahau	*Punan Merah* (puf)
Sihan[a]	Sian	Sarawak (Rejang)	300	Kajang/ Kayan	Sian (spg)

Table 11.1 (*cont.*)

Autonym	Exonym, alternate names	Location	Group size	Contact population	Name and code in Ethnologue
(3) Western Penan		Sarawak (between the Baram and the Balui Rivers), and North Kalimantan	6,000		all subsumed under *Western Penan* (pne) without distinction of individual ethnolinguistic groups
Penan Benalui	Punan Benalui, Penan Menalui, Punan Badeng	North Kalimantan	450	Kenyah	
Penan Silat	Western Penan	Sarawak	800	Kenyah	
Penan Geng	Penan Belaga, Western Penan	Sarawak	2,100	Kenyah	
Penan Apau	Western Penan	Sarawak		Kayan, Kenyah	
Penan Niah		Sarawak			
Lusong Seping	Penan Lusong	Sarawak		Kenyah	
Penan Lanying					
Penan Nyivung Jelalong				Cebop/Sebop	
Penan Bunut	Penan Jelalong		720	Kayan, Kenyah	
(4) Eastern Penan		Sarawak (east of the Baram River), Brunei (on the Belait River)	12,000[b]	Kayan, Kenyah	All subsumed under *Eastern Penan* (pez) without distinction of individual ethnolinguistic groups
Penan Selungo	Penan Serongo, Eastern Penan			Kenyah, Kayan	
Penan Sukang	Penan Belait, Eastern Penan		56	Kenyah	

Group	Alternative names	Location	Population	Language affiliation	Code
Penan Apoh	Eastern Penan		315	Kenyah, Berawan	
Penan Selaan	Eastern Penan		384	Kenyah, Berawan	
Penan Magoh	Eastern Penan		460		
(5) Punan Tubu'-Malinau-Mentarang		Malinau Regency, North Kalimantan, especially on the upper part of the Tubu' river and in the resettlement camp Respen Tubu'			
Punan Tubu'	Tuvu'	North Kalimantan	3,700	Merap, Abai, Tebilun	*Punan Tubu (ptu)*
Punan Sekatak	Punan Dulau / Punan Berusu'/Bulusu'		280	Berusu'	
Punan Semeriot	Punan Lunang / Punan Berusu'/Bulusu'		135	Berusu'	
Punan Merap	Punan Malinau,			Merap	*Punan Merap (puc)*
Punan G. Solok P. Bengalun				Merap	
Punan Mentarang	Punan Tubu'			Tidung / Tebilun	
(6) Punan Kelai-Segah		Berau Regency, East Kalimantan			
Punan Kelai			800	Ga'ai	
Punan Malinau^c	Punan Segah, Pnaan		80	Ga'ai	
Punan Segah			600	Ga'ai	
Punan Long Yiin			100	Segai, Ga'ai	
Punan Batu	Punan Kelai, Punan Segah			Segai	*Sajau Basap (sjb)*
Basap	Orang Darat, Dayak			Segai	*Sajau Basap (bdb)*

Table 11.1 (cont.)

Autonym	Exonym, alternate names	Location	Group size	Contact population	Name and code in Ethnologue
(7) Müller-Schwaner		Müller and northern Schwaner mountain range and along the Mahakam and upper Kapuas at the border between West and East Kalimantan	5,000		
Kereho	Punan Kerého, Punan Keriau			Aoheng, Kayan, Mandai	*Kereho* (xke)
Uheng	Punan Bungan			Kayan, Aoheng	
Hovongan				Kayan, Long Gelat, Aoheng	*Hovongan* (hov)
Seputan				Aoheng, Seputan, Ot Danum	
Kereho	Olo Ot Nyawong, Punan Penyabung	Upper Barito (Kalimantan)			
Busang					
(8) Punan Murung-Ratah		Along the border of East, South, and Central Kalimantan			
Punan				Long-Gelat, Busang, Murung	
Murung				Bahau, Modang	
Punan Ratah					
Other[d]					
Punan Berun		East Kalimantan		Kayan, Merap	
Punan Benyaung		East Kalimantan		Kayan, Merap	
Punan Lasan		East Kalimantan		Kayan, Merap	
Punan Bahau		East Kalimantan		Kayan	
Punan Batu 1		Sarawak		Kayan	Punan Batu 1 (pnm)

[a] An overview of the Sihan ethnoscape can be obtained in Kato, 2017.

[b] Figures provided by Ian MacKenzie (p.c. 2018). See Bruno Manser Fund (2017), a series of 23 maps containing data of 63 Penan villages, a very important documentation of Penan culture.

[c] Punan Malinau, also known as Ma' Pnaan or Punan Segah, is a homonym with the Pnan groups found in the Malinau Regency in North Kalimantan belonging to the Punan Tubu' subgroup, to which is not related at all. The name Malinau is the name of a river that is found in different areas of the island. As a matter of fact, Punan Malinau is an ethnonym of two different groups.

[d] In the definition 'Other' are included single communities whose affiliation is not clear due to lack of information and data.

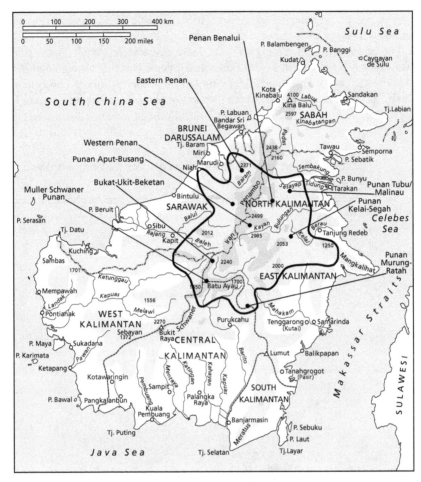

Map 11.1 Approximate location of hunter-gatherers in Borneo (Sercombe and Sellato 2007: 4).

that not all the hunter-gatherers listed in the table are represented in Ethnologue, that some have a different affiliation and others do not fall into any of the eight groups. Map 11.1 shows the geographical locations of these groups.

Looking at Table 11.1, one can notice the considerable heterogeneity among the Borneo hunter-gatherers. For example, their group size varies widely from a mere 30 to 50 people, as in the case of the bands on the Magoh river in Sarawak or the Sukang of Brunei, to around 4,000, as with the Punan Tubu' dialects in the Malinau District in today's North Kalimantan Province. Scholars do not even agree on whether all groups recorded in Table 11.1 represent former nomadic foragers, as is the case of the Basap.

The languages of Pnan groups also do not represent a coherent linguistic unit (Brosius 1992; Sellato 1993: 51). This is also reflected in their current linguistic classification according to the 21st Edition of Ethnologue (Simons and Fennig 2018), as given in Table 11.2, which displays only the Pnan languages according to their respective groupings of the North Borneo phylum and omitting the

Table 11.2 *Genealogical classification of Pnan languages according to the Ethnologue*

North Borneo (93)
  [1] Melanau-Kajang (12)
    Kajang (7)
      Bukitan [bkn] (A language of Indonesia)
      Kajaman
      Lahanan
      Punan Batu 1 [pnm] (A language of Malaysia)
      Sekapan
      Sian [spg] (A language of Malaysia)
      Ukit [umi] (A language of Malaysia)
    Melanau (5)
  [2] North Sarawakan (41)
    Berawan-Lower Baram (8)
    Bintulu (1)
    Dayic (6)
      Murutic (12)
    Kayan-Kenyah (25)
      Kayanic (17)
        Kayan Proper (8)
        Modang (2)
          Modang
          Segai [sge] (A language of Indonesia)
        Müller-Schwaner 'Punan' (6)
          Aoheng [pni] (A language of Indonesia)
          Hovongan [hov] (A language of Indonesia)
          Kereho [xke] (A language of Indonesia)
          Punan Aput [pud] (A language of Indonesia)
          Punan Merah [puf] (A language of Indonesia)
          Bukat [bvk] (A language of Indonesia)
        Murik Kayan (1)
      Kenyah (6)
        Kenyah, Mainstream [xkl] (A language of Indonesia)
        Upper Pujungan (2)
        Kayanic Kenyah (3)
          Kenyah, Wahau

Table 11.2 (*cont.*)

Long Wat [ttw] (A language of Malaysia)
Sebop [sib] (A language of Malaysia)
Penan (2)
Penan, Eastern [pez] (A language of Malaysia)
Penan, Western [pne] (A language of Malaysia)
Punan Tubu (1)
Punan Tubu [Puj] (A language of Indonesia)
[3] Rejang-Sajau (5)
Basap [bdb] (A language of Indonesia)
Burusu [bgr] (A language of Indonesia)
Penan, Bah-Biau [pna] (A language of Malaysia)
Punan Merap [puc] (A language of Indonesia)
Sajau Basap [sjb] (A language of Indonesia)
[4] Sabahan (35)

Note: Pnan languages are in bold font; Non-Pnan languages relevant for the discussion are in italic.

branches that are not relevant to Pnan. Note also that according to this classification, like the ones that appeared in previous editions of Ethnologue (see, e.g., Gordon 2005), Pnan languages belong to three of the four branches of the North Borneo phylum, that is, Melanau-Kajang, North Sarawakan, and Rejang-Sajau. Nevertheless this classification is not accepted among all specialists (cf., e.g., Sellato and Sercombe's [2007] exclusion of Bukat from the Müller-Schwaner Punan group and the definition of a Bukat–Beketan–Lisum group (Sellato and Soriente 2015).

The Ethnologue classification still poses some problems because, it includes languages such as Bukitan, Sian (Sihan), and Ukit within the Kajang though they should be in separate branches. The Bukat now in the Müller-Schwaner 'Punan, should become a branch by itself including Bukat, Beketan and Lisum (see Sellato and Soriente 2015), whereas the Müller-Schwaner 'Punan' should be reduced to include only Aoheng, Hovongan, and Kereho. At the same time the Punan Aput, Punan Busang and Sihan could become a different branch[9].

Other problems are posed by the Rejang Sajau group because it includes languages from other branches like Burusu, which is actually a Sabahan language (Murutic), and Punan Merap, which is related to Punan Tubu'.[10] Conversely, the Modang subgroup within the Kayanic branch should include Punan Kelai/Segah, a language that, though spoken by hunter-gatherers, is indeed Kayanic.[11] Within the Kenyah subgroup, Kayanic Kenyah includes language such as Long Wat and Sebop that should be put together with Penan since they share many similarities.

Table 11.3 *Pnan and Dayak compared*

Pnan hunter-gatherers	Dayak farmers
Seminomadic	Settled
Hunter-gatherers	Agriculturalists
Sago eaters	Rice eaters
Egalitarian	Stratified
Single dwelling in the forest	Longhouse along rivers
Seen as culturally "inferior"	Seen as "culturally superior"
20–50 people	300 and more
No organized political structure	Organized political structure where aristocrats have political, religious, and social roles
Bilingual in the language of the settlers	Never learn the language of nomads
Use of avoidance terms	Reduced use of avoidance terms

11.3   Differences between Foraging Pnan and Sedentary Dayak

It is generally understood that the Pnan have had prolonged contact with settled Dayak groups. This is particularly the case for the Müller–Schwaner groups, the Lisum, and the Punan Busang who were all in different ways vassals of the Kayan; the Western and Eastern Penan, who were in contact with the Kayan, Kenyah, and Kelabit; and the Beketan, who interacted with the Iban. The result of this contact has been an overlap and mixture of linguistic and cultural features between both types of groups. In spite of this, a number of nonlinguistic features distinguish the forest nomads from their settled neighbors. They live far upstream in the mountainous interior, where they inhabit climax rainforests and are continually on the move. There are also essential cultural features that distinguish the Pnan and Dayak, as presented in Table 11.3.

The hunter-gatherers of Borneo have an egalitarian society, as do most hunter-gatherers. This social structure has in turn affected the way in which they interact with the settled populations whose societies are notably different in this respect. For instance, with Kenyah agriculturalists, who have a strongly stratified society, there used to be essentially little intermarriage, like the few recent cases of Penan–Kenyah couples in Sarawak; the few reported cases involve marriages of Penan Benalui women with not well-off Kayan or Kenyah men. Similarly, the Bukat and Kayan rarely intermarry. Hence, hunter-gatherer communities are often monoethnic and self-contained cultural and genetic groups. This is not the case, however, with other groups of hunter-gatherers such as the Beketan, who have intermarried with their agricultural Iban neighbors, because these are egalitarian by nature and easily integrate outsiders.

Intermarriages between groups who were not enemies are reported too (Lisum-Merah, Beketan-Tubu).[12]

In the case of integration into stratified farming communities, the farmers even claim to own the Pnan. In this asymmetric relation, the Pnan are obliged to collect forest goods for the settled aristocrats. For example, the Punan Batu were "owned" by the Sultan just like the caves from which they gathered their resources. The Punan Malinau and the Punan Merap are considered to be vassals of the Merap, just as the Penan Benalui are said to be the vassals of the Badeng Kenyah with whom they have always traded forest goods. However, while some groups have become closely associated with farming groups within asymmetric relations of prestige and trade, some other groups are considered to be free, meaning that they have no patron–client relation. That is, the history of relations between Pnan and agriculturalists does not conform to a single pattern except for the commonalities of hierarchy, ownership, and labor relations. Lastly, the Pnan people have never practiced head hunting but were instead the victims of head hunting raids by the by the Iban, the Kayan, and the other agriculturalists. So the agricultural populations did not invade the land of hunter-gatherers by means of open warfare, but rather pushed them into the remaining pockets of remote forest through their demographic expansion.

The hierarchical relations are also reflected in linguistic facts. Most of the Pnan languages have absorbed elements from the Kayan, Kenyah, Iban or Murutic languages, whereas the reverse does not hold. Linguistic exogamy, that is, the acquisition of a Pnan language by a non-Pnan spouse, has begun to occur only recently. In general, there has not been intermarriage between Pnan groups nor have other networks been established. Only the Seputan, Kereho, Hovongan, and Aoheng, who have no history of conflict and can understand each other, have social networks sustained by intermarriage. For the Pnan peoples as a whole, it was only after 1994 that they began to develop social networks with each other. This was mainly due to the creation of the Association of Pnan People (*Yayasan Adat Punan*) in Kalimantan, and in following subsections like the most recent one *Yayasan Adat Punan Borneo* established in 2018, in an effort to preserve Pnan cultural traditions. The people in this association come from very diverse groups but yet they feel associated by the more or less same social structure and social habits. Nevertheless, it is important to emphasize that there has never been a lingua franca and that all power relations are dictated by their relevant patrons.

All in all, these forest dwellers are in effect an underclass and their sense of inferiority has been compounded over the last decades by the increasing loss of territory as the region has been deforested and developed.[13] They constitute minority groups and/or comprise the poorest sector of the settled population.

For example, the Penan Benalui, who have been living for the last decades in close association with a Badeng Kenyah village first and a Bakung Kenyah village later, consider themselves to be at the bottom of the social scale with no chance of changing this situation. They are not given access to jobs outside of the area and still prefer to live on gathering and trading forest products, as is also the case of the Punan Tubu' (see Klimut and Puri 2007). Accordingly, the Pnan consider their patrons' languages more prestigious and they are fully cognizant of the fact that they have a pronounced tendency to borrow linguistic material from their agricultural patrons.

One important question that has been asked is whether hunter-gatherer substrates can be identified in other linguistic populations that are known to have incorporated hunter-gatherer populations. So far, there are no known cases of this for the Kenyah, Kayan, Busang, and Bahau, which are all stratified agricultural societies in North, East, and West Kalimantan. In contrast, the Iban, who are egalitarian, have assimilated the Beketan Lugat.

11.4   The Debated Origin of Borneo Hunter-Gatherers

The origin of Borneo forager groups is highly controversial, and the discussion is complicated by the fact that the simple opposition between hunter-gatherers and agriculturalists is itself problematic because the various subsistence systems in the area rather form a continuum involving rice agriculture, sago and tuber cultivation, forest foraging, hunting, and fishing. The history of hunter-gatherers of this region, as of Southeast Asia in general, is usually modeled within two evolutionary frames. One is that they have always foraged in the forest, originally independently from agriculturalists (Von Heine Geldern 1946; Nicolaisen 1976a, b). Alternatively they represent devolved farmers (Hoffman 1986) or farmers who once depended on a mixed economy and became specialized on forest resources, thereby abandoning the agricultural option (see Bellwood 1999; Endicott 1999).

In spite of the many empirical uncertainties in this historical debate, some basic themes have by now been established on the ground that a sharp dichotomy between food producing and foraging economies might not have existed (see Sather 1995). First, most of the languages of the nomadic groups in Borneo seem to be more or less related to each other (Hudson 1978; Sellato 1993); certainly, they all speak languages of the Austronesian family. Second, there are considerable cultural similarities between the Pnan and the local agriculturalists. Third, all the forest hunter-gatherer groups are phenotypically largely similar to the Mongoloid stock of agriculturalists.

Many scholars have observed the gradual shift of hunter-gatherers toward a more sedentary life and the strong cultural and linguistic similarities of some agriculturalists with nomadic groups. Hence, Hose and McDougall (1912: 193) speculated that these settled people were nomads who adopted a sedentary life, and consequently that modern hunter-gatherers are remnants of an earlier Pan-Borneo culture. Later, Urquhart (1958: 206), and more recently, Whittier (1973: 22) and Brosius (1988: 84), even proposed that the settled Kenyah, long-time dedicated swiddeners, are derived from nomadic Penan, who opted for a sedentary existence two or three centuries ago. It can be disputed, though, how the idea of an earlier Pan-Borneo culture arises out of the sedentarization of foragers. The same thing could have happened with previous diverse forager populations.

Hoffman (1986) favored the idea that hunter-gatherer populations in Borneo are earlier agriculturalists who devolved to specialize on forest resources, which would make trade the primary force for driving modern foragers into their niche specialization. Bellwood (1999) developed a partly different argument: modern foragers are Austronesians who respecialized in basing their economy on sago to serve their subsistence needs when they entered the rainforest. This is based in particular on the current lack of archaeological evidence for settlement of the forest before 4000 BC, which is debatable as an argument, because the lack of evidence for small hunter-gatherer groups in dense tropical rainforest cannot be taken as proof that such populations did not exist. Hoffman and Bellwood also focus on the general observation that nomads and agriculturalists have linguistic affinities and ethnic associations but give a different historical explanation. Clearly, many questions revolve around whether each Pnan group is more similar to its neighboring settled group or to other Pnan groups, or conversely whether at all the foragers were diverse populations before any contact with the agriculturalists.

Linguistic data have been put forward partly to support the latter approach but these cannot be viewed as conclusive. Blust (1974: 248), using a selection of words from three Eastern Penan groups in Sarawak (Long Labid, Long Merigan, and Long Lamai), lumped the two language groups, Penan and Kenyah, together and posited that his lexical evidence pointed to a cultural reversion of agricultural populations. Blust (1976a) argued in a similar fashion that the original Austronesians were settled populations with grain crops, pigs, dogs, etc. and that parts of these populations turned to the forest to become hunter-gatherers for economic reasons (cf. Hoffman 1986).

Sellato (1993, 2002) proposes an alternative Borneo history, suggesting that hunter-gatherers might have a different origin from sedentary agriculturists – an idea not widely accepted by other scholars. In also viewing them to have been subject to a general trend from hunting-gathering to farming practices, he assumes that prior to the Austronesian expansion to Borneo the island was inhabited by "non-Mongoloid" hunter-gatherers who spoke non-Austronesian languages. Instead of believing that these populations became extinct when the Austronesian people arrived on Borneo, he considers it more likely that they adapted to varying degree to these early Austronesian immigrants; these may also not have been full agriculturalists but brought with them a mixture of fishing, horticulture, and wild-plant collection (see also Bellwood 1999: 287) As Sather (1995) well explains, foraging economies existed in Island Southeast Asia, including Borneo, long before the spread of Austronesian. When these agriculturalists arrived, they entertained with the foragers various networks of symbiotic exchange and underwent different levels of transformation including assimilation and adaptation. The partial similarity between nomadic foraging and sedentary agricultural peoples may have developed when certain forms of horticulture together with new hunting-gathering techniques gradually spread inland until after the middle of the second millennium A.D. Sellato argues that Pnan societies have an individualistic, opportunistic and secular ideology which allows them to easily adopt cultural, religious, linguistic, and technological elements from other groups. This arguably could have resulted in a culture with an inner ideological core and an outer borrowed layer of linguistic and technological elements (Sellato 2002: 108). In order to investigate the history of Pnan and to go beyond the current evidence, Sellato poses such questions as: What is the ancient history of the Pnan? What distinguishes Pnan culture from that of the agriculturalists? What elements are specific to Pnan culture? Is there a substratum in Pnan languages that is not attested in the agriculturalists' languages?

Sellato assumes that at least for some nomadic groups the common pattern has been progressive language replacement by a food producer language and that the substratum of a previous pre-Austronesian language is still evident. On the one hand, Sellato (2002: 118–119) cited lexical borrowings as evidence: some Pnan languages share items for 'rice', 'pig', 'chicken', and 'iron' with the agriculturalists' languages, hypothesizing that the Pnan borrowed them together with the associated technology. On the other hand, he proposed three lexical items for the common hunter-gatherer substratum, which are not found in the languages of the main agricultural groups and for which no Austronesian root has been reconstructed: *kelovi* 'child', *kan* 'to give', and *kavo* 'to die'. These words are thought to be of critical symbolic significance and to constitute evidence for a cultural and linguistic substratum uniting hunter-gatherer societies. Two of these items, *kan* and *kavo*, are likely to be related to parallel items in Land Dayak (or Bidayuh) languages. Adelaar (1995), noting a few striking phonological and lexical similarities between some of the Land Dayak languages of Borneo and Aslian languages in Peninsular Malaysia, suggested that Land Dayak possibly underwent a shift from Aslian to Austronesian or that both Aslian and Land Dayak had a common substraturm from a third language. The connection between Borneo and Aslian and consequently with Austroasiatic has led Sellato (2007: 15) to propose a remote common linguistic non-Austronesian substratum among hunting-gathering groups of Borneo. More recently, on the same line, Blench (2010) looked for more consistent examples of lexical evidence that link Borneo to Austroasiatic in an effort to show the remarkably fragmented nature of the Austroasiatic phylum (see also Sidwell and Blench, 2011).

In general, Sellato and Sercombe (2007: 15) concluded that "the original languages could have been overwhelmed by Austronesian languages." Likewise, the Austronesians could have absorbed the less numerous auto-chthonous pre-Austronesians, with the result that nomadic groups started to resemble farmers biologically. Note in this respect that Sellato (1993)and Sellato and Soriente (2015) assumed that these foraging Austronesians, equipped with the superior neolithic tool kit, successfully competed with a low-density Australoid population and finally submerged it phenotypically and linguistically. However, one Seputan subgroup of the Müller Mountains, claims that a part of their forefathers (the Mangan) were short people with dark skin and curly hair; indeed, some of the Seputan still display to a certain extent these features. Some archaeologic excavations in the Müller mountains might well revive the old polemic on the existence of "Negritoes" in Borneo. The resulting, predominantly Mongoloid populations, the ancestors of today's Punan, have persisted in remote regions as subsistence foragers equipped with polished quadrangular stone axes until not so long ago.

Since a scenario of absorption and language shift by foragers, rather than devolution by agriculturalists, is recurrently attested outside Borneo (cf. the Veddah in Sri Lanka, the Negritos in the Philippines, the Pygmies in Central Africa, and the San in southern Africa), it is indeed also plausible for Borneo. Nevertheless, both pre-Austronesian genes and languages should have left traces, which may one day be more fully revealed. The most reliable features for investigating these issues are possibly genetic markers, in particular, for determining whether in the distant past there was language shift on the part of hunter-gatherers from a non-Austronesian to an Austronesian language, which is not obviously reflected in current linguistic and nonlinguistic evidence. Unfortunately, population genetic data for Pnan are scanty and unanalyzed, and historical reconstruction is compromised by the fact that they are small groups with a history of continuous migrations. So it does not seem possible at our present state of knowledge to decide conclusively for any single hypothesis about the origin of Borneo's Pnan. Moreover, instead of an either–or model, a more balanced perspective would allow for the possibility that two or more of the foregoing scenarios coexisted on the island across space and time. We can conclude with Kaskija (2017) that considering the ambiguous boundaries and the complex features characterized by linguistically, socially, and culturally hetherogenous categories of the hunter-gatherers, an opposition between hunter-gatherers and agriculturalists is not so relevant since the relations between the two groups are much more fluid and that a simple picture of hunter-gatherers in Borneo cannot be put forward.

11.5   The Penan Benalui as a Linguistic Case Study

The Penan Benalui are a group of semisettled people originally inhabiting Usun Apau, a mountain area of Central Borneo in the rainforest at about 500 meters above sea level. Traditionally, they were completely self-sufficient, but they also interacted with farmers to trade and obtain protection from raids. This group of hunter-gatherers migrated from Usun Apau around 1890 and followed a group of settled groups, the Badeng Kenyah on the Lurah River, a tributary of the Bahau in East Kalimantan (see Puri [2005] for a description of the Penan Benalui regarding anthropology, history, and social relationship with their neighbors). Nowadays they live in seven communities and are not always in contact with each other: Long Bena (52 people) and Long Belaka (165 people) on the Lurah River, Long Lame (a.k.a. Long Lame Baru) (190 people), Long Sungai Taket (population included in Long Lame), on the Bahau River, and other villages of settled Kenyah people in the Pujungan regency such as Long Uli (42 people) and Pujungan (2 persons) (see Maps 11.2 and 11.3).

It is difficult to classify the Penan Benalui according to the HRAF categories because there is a range of economic practices that are employed in different communities to varying degrees, thus complicating the use of clearcut classification systems. It could be said that prior to 1960 they were all primarily foragers, but have since then begun to settle down and involve themselves with agriculture, gardening, and even some wage labor. In the village of Long Lame, now closest to the agriculturalists' village, traditional sharing values and practices are under threat because of markets for fish and meat. In the upriver village the influence of the Kenyah farmers has meant a very successful engagement with swiddens and gardening. According to Koizumi et al. (2012), who undertook a qualitative food survey at Long Belaka, 50% of their starch consisted of rice cultivated in the village, 30% of their rice was bought from outside, other starch cultivated in the village totaled 18%, and wild sago constituted only 2% of their starch. As regards meat, almost 100% was hunted. For vegetables, 30% were gathered and 70% cultivated. In addition, in the village of Long Bena, when rice was unavailable, the inhabitants relied entirely on wild sago. This shows that the hunter-gatherer livelihood is still a critical aspect of their lives. Prior to 1965 they fell into category 1 (foragers) but at present a difference has to be made between the villages upriver and downriver. In the uppermost village of Long

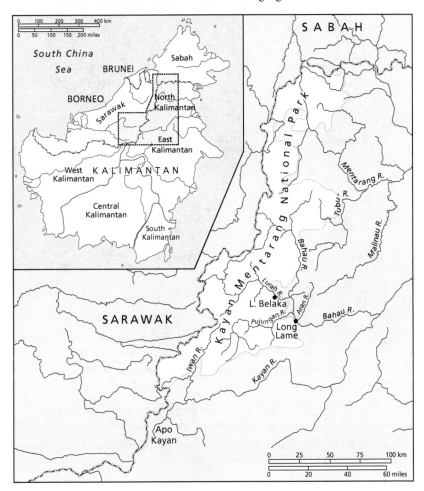

Map 11.2 The location of the Penan Benalui in East Kalimantan (Puri 2005: 44).

Bena they can be classified in categories 1, 2, and 4. In Long Belaka and Long Lame they fall into category 4.

The Penan Benalui language is spoken by almost 450 people and has been considered a member of Western Penan comprising also the Penan Geng, Penan Silat, and Penan Apau in Sarawak between the Baram and the Balui Rivers (Brosius 1999). According to Penan Benalui speakers, Penan Silat is quite similar. Eastern Penan languages are spoken in Sarawak and Brunei and are considered slightly different in vocabulary and phonetics. Data from

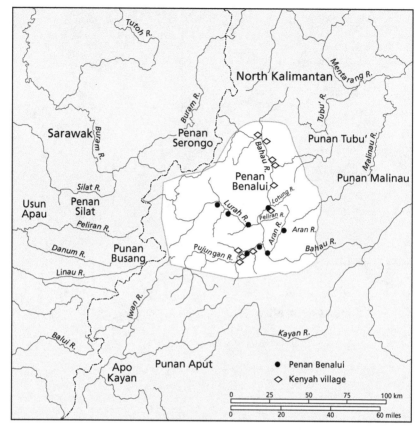

Map 11.3 The distribution of some Pnan groups around the watershed of
the Lurah River (Puri 2005: 46).

a collection of stories in Eastern and Western Penan varieties put together
by Langub (2001) seem to confirm this fact, but no thorough research has
been carried out. The Penan Benalui are a very small group that has lived for
many years separated from groups in Sarawak, apparently speaking sister
languages.

They are generally bilingual, speaking the language of the settlers they are in
contact with, namely the Badeng Kenyah, with whom they have historical
relations; today with the Bakung, the Kenyah people living next to the Penan
Benalui village; and the Uma' Lasan Kenyah, the majority people in the district
capital of Long Pujungan. They are claimed to speak the language of any settled
neighbor and are always defined by Kenyah as multilingual. This sociolinguistic picture can be interpreted as a consequence of their mobility, the small

number of speakers, the lack of any lingua franca that could allow them to communicate, and their adaptability to change. Today, with the spread of Indonesian as a national language, Penan Benalui also communicate with non-neighboring Kenyah in Indonesian, and this also is the language used with other Pnan as demonstrated during the first cross-Pnan meeting held in Malinau in 2002.

Unfortunately, full linguistic descriptions of Penan varieties are nearly nonexistent and the few published materials have almost exclusively focused on the Eastern and Western Penan languages of Sarawak so that previous comparative work has always been based on very limited material. Typically, a mere 100 to 200 words have been used to compare the language of a Penan group with the language of a settled group. While such limited data have shown clear similarities between these groups, this result is provisional considering the small database. Moreover, no specific work has been carried out on the languages of other nomadic groups in Borneo, nor has there been any comparative research. I attempt here to review what information does exist and lay the groundwork for more substantial future research in this area.

The linguistic materials that exist today are as follows. Blust (1974) provided comparative data on three Eastern Penan varieties for classification purposes. Hudson (1978), using a few items of an Eastern Penan variety placed it within the Kenyah subgroup. Clayre (1996) provided scattered data on Penan for morphosyntactic analysis. Brosius (1992), without providing any linguistic data, discussed the relationship of Western Penan to Eastern Penan and to certain Dayak communities; he stated that more than 80% of Western Penan vocabulary was shared by Eastern Penan and other languages such as Cebop (or Sebop), Lirong, Long Wat, Seping, and Bah Mali, whereas the relationship with Badeng Kenyah and Lepo' Aga Kenyah (Mainstream Kenyah) was only around 50%. Brosius also compiled a Western Penan wordlist (n.d.). An unpublished dictionary of Cebop[14] (closely related to Penan) was produced in Sarawak[15]. A collection of Western and Eastern Penan folk stories was compiled by Langub (2001). A Punan Tuvu' dictionary was published by Dollop Mamung (1998) and a revised and expanded version accompanied by a collection of stories and grammatical notes came out in 2015 (see Césard et al. 2015). Recent work by Sercombe (2002, 2006) has provided a more detailed description of Penan Sukang (Eastern Penan) whereas a dictionary and some oral narratives have been stored in the ELAR archive of endangered languages at SOAS (see Sercombe 2018). Finally, the dictionary produced by Mackenzie (2006) and other lexicographic materials, as well as stories and legends of the Eastern Penan are accessible in MacKenzie's webpage in www.rimba.co m/penindexf/penindex.html. Documentation of Penan Malinau/Segah, on

Punan Aput and Punan Semeriot is currently in progress. A language documentation project on Sihan in Sarawak is being carried out by Peter Puxon (see Puxon 2018).

Regarding the relation between Eastern and Western Penan, Brosius (1992) stated that despite their many phonetic and lexical differences, the two are mutually intelligible, estimating a cognate percentage of 82%. This view is not always shared by Penan people themselves. Asked about the similarities with Eastern Penan languages, the Penan Benalui state that they can understand part of what is said but in general they cannot communicate. The same is reported by Sercombe (2006: 6) and Mackenzie (2006), who worked extensively on Eastern Penan.

Needham (1954: 73) first proposed a classification of Sarawak Penan languages within the Kenyah family. Although his view has been shared by many other scholars (Blust 1974; Brosius 1992, 1999; Sercombe 2002, 2006), it is not at all straightforward, as the Kenyah and Penan can barely communicate with each other.

Blust (1974, 2007, 2010) has proposed a subgroup Kenyah within the North Sarawak group (see Table 11.4) that includes both Kenyah proper and Penan. Involving data from three Eastern Penan villages in Sarawak, he classified Sarawak Kenyah into two main branches, Highland and Lowland Kenyah, whereby Penan belongs to the Lowland Kenyah together with Sebop, Long San, and Long Wat. Blust (1974: 248) overstated his case that there were no strong linguistic reasons to distinguish the three Eastern Penan languages from Kenyah. He stated that both quantitative and qualitative

Table 11.4 *The internal subgrouping of the North Sarawak group (Blust 2010)*

A. BINTULU: Bintulu
B. BERAWAN-LOWER BARAM
1. BERAWAN: Long Terawan, Batu Belah, Long Teru, Long Jegan
2. LOWER BARAM: Belait, Miri, Dali', Narum, Lelak, Lemeting, Kiput
C. KENYAH
1. HIGHLAND KENYAH: Long Anap, Long Atun, Long Jeeh, Long Moh, Òma Lóngh, Lebu' Kulit, etc.
2. LOWLAND KENYAH: Long Ikang, Long San, Long Sela'an, Long Dunin, Long Wat, Sebop, various Penan communities
D. DAYIC
1. MURUTIC: Long Semado, etc.
2. KELABITIC: Bario, Long Lellang, Long Napir, Long Seridan, Pa' Dalih, Long Banga' (Sa'ban), Long Terawan (Tring)

evidence indicated that the closest external relations of the Penan were with settled Kenyah groups.

Similarly, language atlases such as Wurm and Hattori's (1984) and Moseley and Asher's (1994) list Punan and Penan languages within the Kenyah branch of the Kayan–Kenyah subgroup, and all the editions of Ethnologue until the 15th (see Gordon 2005), repeat the same pattern.

Similarly, Hudson (1978), using lexicostatistics, placed Penan languages within his Kenyah cluster of the Kayan–Kenyah languages. Subsequently, Soriente (1997), commenting on the relationship of Penan Benalui and Kenyah, speculated that the apparent lexical similarities between the two languages derived exclusively from borrowing by the foragers from the agriculturalists and not from a direct relationship. Although Penan Benalui is related to Kenyah languages found along the Bahau River and its tributaries, it is a distinct language – an observation based on the method of dialectometry. Hence, Soriente (1997) proposed that the similarities were in fact due to a process of 'Kenyahization' of the Penan people. Sercombe (2002) argued that this Kenyahization would have had to take place in a quite uniform way throughout all Central Borneo where Kenyah groups are distributed and, because this was unlikely, reclaimed the traditional view that the Penan languages belong to the Kenyah subgroup because of the strong ethnolinguistic links between different communities of Penans.

11.6   A Linguistic Comparison of Penan Benalui and Kenyah

The purpose of the remainder of this chapter is to evaluate linguistic evidence from Penan Benalui and engage the debate about its genealogical classification. I argue that previous conclusions were arrived at on the basis of insufficient data. I myself can also only present a linguistic comparison between Penan Benalui and other Kenyah languages. In so doing, I will compare Penan Benalui with Badeng Kenyah (the language of its closest agricultural group), Lebu' Kulit (a Kenyah variety of the Kayanic branch), Uma Leken (a Kayan dialect) and Proto-Kenyah – all this before the background of Proto–Austronesian (PAN) reconstructions.[16]

These comparisons question the classification of Penan Benalui as a Kenyah language. My phonological analysis points to a subgrouping of Penan Benalui with Kayanic. A superficial lexical comparison suggests a Kenyah grouping, but many lexical items are not shared with Kenyah but with other related languages such as Cebop, Mboh (both classified as Kenyah in Ethnologue but indeed quite divergent from Kenyah), and other Penan languages. It appears then that Kayanic Kenyah (with Cebop, Mboh, Long Wat, and Long Tap, subsumed in the literature under Lowlands Kenyah), is a link between

Kenyah and Penan; and Penan, comprising Eastern and Western, represents a linguistic branch of its own.

11.6.1 Phonology

Without giving a detailed description of the phonology of Penan Benalui, the main differences between Penan Benalui and Badeng are examined. As far as consonants are concerned, *β*, *d/r*, *j*, and *h* are discussed as well as the lack of gemination and prenasalized stops. These phonological changes set Penan Benalui off from Badeng.

Tables 11.5 and 11.6 illustrate some of the similarities between Penan Benalui, Kenyah, and Kayan varieties. They show that they are indeed descendants of the same Kayan-Kenyah language family (Soriente 2004, 2008). In addition, it is significant that the phonological changes shared by Penan Benalui and the other languages, namely the reflexes of PAN *b, *d, and *j, show certain key differences between Penan and non-Penan languages.

Table 11.5 shows that Penan Benalui shares many lexical items with Kayan and Kenyah but does not share the same phonological change with Badeng and other Usun Apau Kenyah varieties in which there is a split of PAN *b in *b/p* (see *buSek 'hair' vs. *tebuq 'sugarcane'). In the medial position, *b is reflected as *β*. This voiced bilabial fricative, occurring generally in medial position in complementary distribution with *b*, is absent in Badeng and other Usun Apau Kenyah languages but appears in the Kayanic language Lebu' Kulit and the Kayan language Uma Leken,

Table 11.5 *Reflexes of PAN *b*

Penan Benalui	Gloss	Badeng (Kenyah)	L. Kulit (Kayanic)	Proto-Kenyah	U. Leken (Kayan)	PAN
bulun	hair	*bulu*	*buləw*	**bulu	*bulo?*	*bulu
(ka:n)/mabuy, baβuy	bearded pig	*babuy*	*baβuy*	**babuy	*baβuy*	*babuy
uβəy	cassava	*ubi*	*uβəy*	**ubi	*uβe*	*qubi
bəlaβow	rat	*bəlabaw*	*bəlaβaw*	**bəlabaw	*laβaw*	*labaw
pipin	lip	*bibe*	*siβe*	**bibe	*siβeh*	*biRbiR
butih	calf of the leg	*bət:e*	*bət:i*	**bət:i	*bətih*	*bitiqis
bok	hair	*puk*	*buk*	**buk	*bok*	*buSek
baβay	above	*mbow*	*mompaw*	*mbaw	*ho?baw*	*babaw
tubəu	sugarcane	*təp:u?*	*təβəw*	*təb:u	*təβo*	*tebuq

Table 11.6 *Reflexes of PAN *d and *j*

Penan Benalui	Gloss	Badeng (Kenyah)	L. Kulit (Kayanic)	Proto-Kenyah	U. Leken (Kayan)	PAN
murip	live	*modip*	*murip*	**mudip	*murip*	*quDip
urəu	grass	*a'ot*	*urəu*	**udu	*uru*	*udu
(*uɲit*)	nose	*ndoŋ*	*ntoŋ*	**ndoŋ	*uruŋ*	*ijuŋ
parey	paddy	*padey*	*parey*	**padey	*pare*	*pajey
(*kə*)*bara*	inform	*bada*	*baraʔ*	**bada	*bara*	*bajaq
siran	when	*midan*	*miran*	**(m)idan	*hiran*	*(q)ija(ŋ)
ŋaran	name	*ŋadan*	*ŋaran*	**ŋadan	*aran*	*ŋajan
padi/tadin	y. brother	*sadin*	*sarin*	** (s)adi(n)	*harin*	*Sua(ŋ)ji
bura	foam	*buda*	*bura*	**buda	*lurək*	*bujaq
puɪdun	gall bladder	*pət:u*	*pəd:əw*	**pədu	*pəru*	*qapəju

although there are also a number of occurrences in which *b* occurs in intervocalic position.

The Penan Benalui word *mabuy* 'bearded pig', occurring next to the expected *baβuy* (and *maβuy*), is explained as a direct borrowing from Kenyah varieties where the reflex of intervocalic *b* is *b*, like in Badeng, whereas the reflex *m > b* and vice versa *b > m* in initial position is very frequent, like in the case Menalui > Benalui, Badeng > Madeng. In fact, in Penan Benalui the common way to refer to the bearded pig is *ka:n*, which is the root for food and is also used to refer in a generic way to any animal. The bearded pig is the main protein source for those Penan Benalui who depend on hunting. The same might have happened to the word *tuɪbəu* 'sugarcane' that should have been *təβəw*. It is noticeable to stress that in Penan Benalui there occurs a doublet *təbu* (again with the unexpected medial labial stop) to refer to gingers. (The Penan Benalui word *pipin* 'lip' is unexplained and may be borrowed from another source.)

There are a few cases of *β* in initial positions like *βi* 'uncle', and *βai* 'village people' as opposed to *bai* 'riverbank'. The two words are obviously related because they both refer to the geographical position close to the riverbank. The village people are called *βai* exactly because their village is generally located by the river. The existence of this doublet is one piece of evidence that Penan Benalui has been subject to extensive contact. While *bai* is clearly Kenyah, the origin of *βai* and *βi* is unclear because the bilabial fricative tends to occur only in the medial position. Thus I conclude that these words must have been borrowed from other sources where the bilabial fricative can occur in an initial position like in Kenyah Oma Longh word *βi* 'mother'.

Table 11.6 shows that the reflexes of PAN intervocalic *d and *j merged as *d* in Badeng, and as *r* in Lebu' Kulit, Uma Leken, and Penan Benalui – yet another sign for the difference of Penan Benalui from Kenyah and its similarity to Kayanic and Kayan. The words for 'gall bladder' *puudun* and for 'younger brother' *padi/tadin* have the unexpected reflex of *j for *d*, suggesting that they have been directly borrowed from Badeng.

Other changes considered to be diagnostic for the classification of Penan Benalui outside of the Kenyah subgrouping are for the consonants, the lack of the voiceless palatal affricate *c*, the occurrence of *h* in final position, the absence of both gemination and prenasalized stops; and for vowels, the quality of the central vowel that occurs as *ɯ*, the reflex of PAN *-a in *ɯ:*, and the diphthongization of PAN final *i and *u.

While the voiceless obstruents *p*, *t*, and *k* have their voiced counterparts *b*, *d*, and *g* in Penan Benalui, the opposition is missing in the case of the voiced palatal stop: *j* does not have a voiceless counterpart *c* (except in borrowed words like *camat* 'district head'). This gap in the phonological inventory does not occur in Usun Apau Kenyah (see, e.g., Badeng *can* 'ladder' and *ja* 'that'), but is present in Kayan, Kayanic, Cebop, and Mboh.

In the case of *h*, it occurs in Penan Benalui only in the final position in words like *duah* 'two', *jah* 'one', *puɲah* 'already', *butih* 'calf of the leg'. In Usun Apau Kenyah it is absent, but it occurs in Cebop and Mboh, and in Kelabit, Kayanic, and Kayan.

In Penan Benalui no gemination of consonants occurs after the central vowel *ə*, a common feature of Kenyah languages. In Kenyah consonant gemination occurs after the central vowel *ə* (-CC/-əC-). This is probably due to the different value of the medial vowel that is much higher and can retain stress.[17] In this regard, compare *buti* 'calf of the leg' in Table 11.5.

In Penan Benalui there is no occurrence of prenasalized stops *mb*, *nd*, *ŋg*, and *nj*, a feature of the Usun Apau Kenyah and Kayanic languages. Compare the languages in Table 11.7.

Penan Benalui vowels are largely the same as in Kenyah except for the central vowel. The reflex of Proto-Kenyah **ə is in Penan Benalui *ɯ* (central

Table 11.7 *Correspondence of Proto-Kenyah **NC*

P. Benalui	Gloss	Badeng	Proto-Kenyah
ba	forest	*mba*	**mba
kələβit	shield	*kələmbit*	**kələmbit
mo-jam	able	*mə-njam*	**njam

Table 11.8 *Reflex of Proto-Kenyah **ə*

P. Benalui	Gloss	Badeng	Proto-Kenyah
puudun	gall bladder	*pət:u*	**pət:u
buut:i	calf of the leg	*bət:i*	**bət:i

Table 11.9 *Reflex of Proto-Kenyah **a*

P. Benalui	Gloss	Badeng	Proto-Kenyah
amuu	father	*ama-y*	**ama
akuu 'rattan'	vine	*aka*	**aka
buu 'water'	flood	(*suŋay*) 'water, river'	**suŋay
buuʔ	unhusked rice	*baaʔ*	**baaʔ
duu	blood	*daa*	**daa

Table 11.10 *Final diphthongs in Penan Benalui*

P. Benalui	Gloss	Badeng	Proto-Kenyah
lakəy	man/male	*laki*	**laki
asəw	dog	*asu*	**asu
paləw	sagu being hit	*palu*	**palu

high vowel) that has as its allomorph ə. The central high vowel is generally pronounced and transcribed as <e> or also <o> in the medial position. See, for instance, Penan Benalui *puuŋah* 'already' (pronounced as *pəŋah* or *poŋah*).

Another typical feature of Penan Benalui is the reflex of PAN final *a in *uu*: (generally transcribed as <ee>) (Table 11.9).

Penan Benalui diphthongs occur in final position as reflexes of Proto-Kenyah **u and **i. We find this feature in Lebu' Kulit but also in Cebop, Mboh, and, according to Blust (2003), in Kiput (Table 11.10).

In conclusion, it seems that Penan Benalui, despite the many lexical similarities, comprises features that do not point to a common origin with Kenyah. Some of these features suggest a grouping with Kayan (lenition of intervocalic *b*, occurrence of *h* in final position, the reflex *r* of PAN *d and *j). Others suggest that Penan Benalui should be grouped on its own as some of its peculiar features are absent in Kayan and Usun Apau Kenyah, such as the absence of intervocalic gemination after *ə*, the absence of prenasalized stops, the absence of the phoneme *c*, the reflex *uu:* of PAN *a in the final position, and the occurrence of *uu*.

11.6.2   Grammar

There are at least two grammatical features relevant for the classification of Penan Benalui. First, it does not have pronominal suffixes except for the third-person singular clitic *-n* on body parts like in *pipin* 'lips'; *bulun* 'body hair'; *ulun* 'head'; *silun* 'nail'; *matən* 'eye'; *paan* 'thigh' and terms of address, *nən* 'mother' and *mən* 'father'. These lexemes with the agglutinated *-n* are frozen forms, which is evidence for the hypothesis that these words were borrowed from Kayan, where the process is mostly employed, indicating inalienable possession (see Blust 1977: 42). In Kenyah varieties where *n*-suffixation is at work only for a few lexical items, speakers can distinguish between first- and second-person possessives, like *matak'* my eyes,' *matam* 'your eyes' in Lebu' Kulit.

The verbal morphology of Penan Benalui is very similar to that of Kenyah and Kayan in terms of morphotactics (only prefixes) and paradigmatic structure. Kenyah and Penan Benalui share the same prefixes: *(me)N-* for actor orientation, *me-* for stative (in a few cases also for iterative), *pe-* for reciprocal, causative/benefactive and intransitive (and as nominalizer), and lastly *ke-* for future and irrealis. However, the undergoer voice in Penan Benalui is expressed through the infix *-en-*, as in Example 11.1, which is absent in Kenyah and Kayan. It is realized as an infix *-en-* in roots with initial *p*, *t*, *s*, and *k*; and as *n-* in monosyllabic roots and roots beginning with *n* (see Soriente 2013).[18]

Example 11.1

sangep	*senua*	*man*	*tulat*	*akeu*
sangep	\<en>sua	(a)ma(i)=n	tulat	akeu
dress	\<UV>buy	father=3POSS	divide	1SG

'The dress was bought by father for me'

A parallel undergoer voice sentence in Badeng, as in Example 11.2, is quite different from the foregoing Penan Benalui structure in employing the common Kenyah particle *uban* 'trace' (corresponding to *en* in Kayan; see Soriente 2013).

Example 11.2

sapai	*uben*	*amai*	*meli*	*makéq*
sapai	uben	amai	N-beli	(ku)ma=kéq
dress	AG	father	AV-buy	for=1SG.POSS

'The dress was bought by father for me'

Nevertheless, Example 11.3 of Penan Benalui, where the undergoer voice is not expressed morphosyntactically but only by constituent order, might be interpreted as the result of influence of a Badeng Kenyah structure illustrated in Example 11.4.[19]

Example 11.3

padikéq	*tinen/nen*	*moru*
padi=kéq	tina=n	N-poru
younger.sibling=1SG.POSS	mother=3SG.POSS	AV-bathe

'The younger brother is bathed by mother'

Example 11.4 (Badeng Kenyah)

sadin	*(uban)*	*uwéq*	*ndo*
sadi-n	uban	uwéq	ndo
younger.sibling-3SG.POSS	AG	mother	bathe

'The younger brother is bathed by mother'

Numeral constructions in Penan Benalui also differ partly from those in languages of food producers. While the numerals themselves are mostly shared with Kenyah (as also most languages of other nomadic groups), the construction based on the numeral *jap* 'ten', which actually means 'to count', is unique. Other Kenyah languages and many other nomadic languages use for 'ten' the Austronesian word *pulu*. The addition construction with *jap* in Penan Benalui for the numerals from ten to twenty is syntactically different, as it is formed by placing the number from one to nine after *jap*; for example, 'eleven' is *jajap jah*. In Kenyah languages the unit is followed by the word *sue?* 'more, plus' preceding the numeral 'ten', as in Badeng *ca? sue? pulo* which is literally 'one plus ten'.[20] For the record, the Penan Benalui quantifier *pinu:* 'many' is related to the Kayan word *pina*, not to Kenyah *kadu*.

It is also noteworthy that a number of grammatical elements have a different form in or are even entirely unique to Penan Benalui. For example, the pronouns for second-person singular *kaau*, first-person plural *ulu*, and second-person plural *kah* seem to have a different unexplained vowel. The third person plural pronoun *iru:* is indifferently used to refer to the pronoun or to the generic term for 'person', instead of the common Kenyah word *kəlunan*. Among the demonstratives a semantic reversal has taken place with the demonstratives *ni* and *ti*, as found in other Kenyah languages such as Lebu' Kulit, where the n-form is the proximal and the t-form the distal demonstrative; in Penan Benalui these are *eet* 'this' and *een* 'that'. Locative prepositions like *la?* 'in' and *toŋ* 'at' do not occur in Kenyah, where they are expressed by *ko?* and *tə* respectively. Aspectual markers are also different in Penan. While the complete action marker in Kenyah varieties is *lepa?*, in Penan Benalui it is *puŋah*, which occurs in Kelabit and in Punan Malinau/Segah as well. *Laruy*

Table 11.11 *Penan Benalui grammatical words not shared by Kenyah*

Gloss	P. Benalui	Badeng	L. Kulit	Proto-Kenyah
First plural inclusive	*ulu*	*ilu*	*iləw*	**ilu
Second plural	*kah*	*ekam*	*ikam*	**ikam
Second singular	*kaau*	*iko*	*iku?*	**iku?
already	*puŋah*	*ləpa*	*ləpək*	**ləpa
at	*la?*	*ka*	*ko?*	**ko?
don't (prohibitive)	*amai*	*aien*	*ɲən*	
how	*kənah*	*kombin*	*ɲumpe*	**kumbin
if	*daun*	*bok*	*bok*	**bok
in	*toŋ*	*tə*	*tə*	**tə
in the middle of	*laruy*	*dalow*	*daləw*	**dalaw
not (verb/adjective negation)	*iəŋ*	*nta*	*mpəy*	**mbi
that	*een*	*ji*	*iti*	**iti
this	*eet*	*ja*	*ini*	**ini
want (volition, future)	*ju?*	*uba?*	*ova*	**uba?
what	*emah*	*inu/iu*	*inəw*	**inu
where	*səmah*	*kəŋge*	*ko? mpəy*	**kəmbi

'still' is opposed to *daleaw* in Kenyah to indicate imperfective aspect. To indicate the immediate future the marker *ju?* 'want' is employed while in Kenyah it is *uba?* 'want'. Function words for questions and negation in Penan Benalui are also mostly different from Kenyah.[21] A summary of the different forms of grams is given in Table 11.11.

In conclusion, while most parts of the morphosyntactic system seem to favor a classification of Penan Benalui with Kayan and Kenyah, the occurrence of the *-en-* infix and the use of a number of grammatical elements seem to suggest that Penan Benalui should be classified as a separate branch from Kenyah and Kayan.

11.6.3   *Lexical Structure*

Comparing the lexicons of Kenyah and Penan Benalui we find many cognates and regular sound-meaning correspondences (see Tables 11.5 and 11.6). There are, however, a number of loanwords in Penan Benalui from Kenyah related to a sedentary lifestyle, as in the foregoing discussion of words retaining Kenyah *b* in medial position and of *d* instead of *r* in medial position. Besides the words *mabuy* 'bearded pig' and *təbu* 'sugarcane'

Table 11.12 *Penan Benalui lexemes not shared by Kenyah*

Gloss	P. Benalui	Badeng	L. Kulit	Proto-Kenyah
ants	*kətuɲan*	*sanəm*	*sanam*	**sanam
arm	*ləʔəp*	*ləŋən*	*ləŋən*	**ləŋən
bearcat	*pasuy*	*ketan*		
bearded pig	*ka:n*	*babuy*	*babuy*	**babuy/kan
big	*ja:u*[24]	*bio*	*jau*	**biyuʔ
black	*padəŋ*	*saləŋ*	*saləŋ*	**saləŋ
cat's eye fruit	*jilən*	*isaw bala*	*isaw*	**isaw
chicken	*dək*	*iyap*	*iyap*	**yap
chilli	*suman*	*səbe*	*səde*	**səb:e
clouded leopard	*duraʔ*	*kule*	*kule*	**kule
come	*tuey*	*ney*	*nay*	**nay
dragonfly	*təkoɲit*	*səkibet*		
eleven	*jap jah*	*caʔ sueʔ pulo*	*se sui pulu*	**sa sue pulo
fear	*mədə*	*takut*	*takut*	**takut
fire	*porok*	*apuy*	*apuy*	**apuy
fish	*bətolu*	*atok*	*booŋ*	**atok
foot	*gəm*	*takət*	*takət*	**takət
forest rambutan	*sagup*	*mbui luan*		
gingers	*təbu*	*lia*	*lia*	**lia
green pidgeon	*kuni*	*punay*	*punay*	**punay
house fly	*pikət*	*laŋaw*	*laŋaw*	**laŋaw
iron wood	*təw*	*bəleyen*	*bəliən*	**bəlian
laugh	*mala*	*gəra*	*pətawe*	**tawa
leaf monkey	*buwi*	*tutuk*		
look for subsistence	*mapun*	*naw*	*naw*	**naw
Mangifera pajang	*paɲin*	*alim*	*alim*	**alim
many	*pinu:*	*kado*	*kaduʔ*	**kaduʔ
Nephelium rambutan	*məw*	*abuŋ*	*avuŋ*	**abuŋ
nose	*uɲit*	*ndoŋ*	*ntuŋ*	**nduŋ
person/they	*iru:*	*kəlonən*	*kəlunan*	**idakelunan
porcupine	*borək*	*bəkia*		
rain	*tu:*	*ojan*	*usan*	**ujan
rattan	*laku:*	*uwey*	*uwai*	**uway
real	*mun*	*lan*	*lan*	**lan
red durian	*lai*	*dian bala*	*dian bala*	**diyan
rib	*sawi*	*usuk*	*usuk*	**usuk

Table 11.12 (*cont.*)

Gloss	P. Benalui	Badeng	L. Kulit	Proto-Kenyah
salak	*sum*	*salak*	*salak*	**salak
scorpion	*duyuŋ*	*lepa busuŋ*		
shoulder	*posun*	*liʔip*	*liʔip*	**liʔip
sleep	*pəgən*[25]	*londo*	*luntu*	**lundu?
stomach	*bori*	*batək*	*batək*	**batək
sun/day	*laŋit*	*daw*	*daw*	**daw
ten	*jə-jap*	*pulo*	*pulu*	**pulu
tobacco	*sigup*	*jakoʔ*	*jakoʔ*	**jako
walk	*məlakaw*	*maset*	*masat*	**asat
water/river	*bɯː*	*suŋay*	*suŋay*	**suŋay

already discussed, another borrowing is *umuː* 'home', cognate with the correspondent Badeng word *oma* 'home' which started to be used since the Penan settled down, and *lamin* a term used to refer to the traditional Penan shelter. *Lamin* is definitely a loanword because the same word occurs in all the Kenyah languages in the meaning of 'longhouse', something that was not found anywhere among Pnan people until very recently).[22] *Gula* 'sugar' is also a borrowed word because it does not display the usual vowel -*ɯː* in final position as a reflex of final -*a*. The word *camat* 'head district' is definitely a recent loanword, as it is the only word with *c* in initial position. Other words that may have been borrowed earlier display a Penan phonology like *sukup* 'enough' (from Indonesian/Malay *cukup*). The word *lopu* 'village' is definitely a word borrowed from Badeng because the regular reflex would be *b* in the medial position so that one would expect *ləbu* or *ləβəw*. Other borrowings such as *ubaʔ* 'want', *uyan* 'do', *tabat* 'medicine', and the locative preposition *ke* seem to occur alongside such genuine Penan words as *juʔ* 'want', *manəw* 'do', *toŋ* 'at'.

As opposed to this, Table 11.12 presents a list of Penan Benalui lexemes that are not shared by Kenyah but in some cases occur in other ethno-linguistic groups like the Kayan, for instance. The table displays the words in Penan Benalui as compared to the correspondent word in two Kenyah languages, Badeng and Lebu' Kulit, followed by a Proto-Kenyah reconstruction, when possible. The empty spots in the table indicate that either the information was not available or that no reconstruction was possible. The words belong to such different lexical domains as verbs, body parts, plants, and animals.[23] Many common words such as 'day,' 'moon,' 'rain,' and 'water' do not match, and the same is the case with common verbs such as 'sleep,' 'walk,' 'come,' 'fear,' and the color 'black' and a great number of cultural and ethnobiological terms.

It is significant that among the names for body parts, the word for 'shoulder' in Penan Benalui, *posun*, is not cognate with the Kenyah *liʔip*. Penan Benalui has a cognate in *ləʔəp*, but it refers to the arm. This constitutes a semantic widening. The word for 'foot' *gəm* (shared also by Cebop, Mboh, and Kelabit) seems to have experienced a semantic shift from the root that means 'to hold with arms' to 'foot,' probably shifting from the meaning of 'upper limb' to 'lower limb.' Another example is *uŋit* 'nose' which is also found in languages of other nomadic groups but has no correspondence in Kenyah.

The more specific one gets the more differences one finds. In comparison to Kenyah, Penan Benalui has a much richer system of necronyms, or death names (names or titles given to persons on the death of a close relative) (Brosius 1995).[26] Moreover, because of the religious belief that all sentient living things possess a soul, the Penan Benalui focus on the interaction of spirits and souls. Consequently they have a rich, poetic, and articulated language with avoidance terms in order to keep malevolent forces away. Brosius (1999: 315), who studied Western Penan, stated that death is attracted by reference to the death of any being and therefore any mention in this respect should be avoided.

For a similar reason the Penan are also careful not to use an animal's real name when discussing hunting, so that the animal is not alerted. For instance, in Penan Benalui most avoidance names refer to animals, for example, *ɲakit* is used instead of *baŋat* 'gray leaf monkey,' *uyəm* instead of *modok* 'pigtail macaque,' *ŋoyəu* instead of *kuyat* 'longtail macaque,' *balu bulun* instead of *telau* 'deer,' *payəp* instead of *lagu* 'sambar deer'.[27] Agriculturalists do not have these avoidance terms.

In the field of ethnobiology (see Puri 2001), based on a list of 164 plant names, Penan Benalui and Kenyah share an average of 70% of cognate roots (a sample of 110 animal terms yielded a cognate percentage of 65%).[28] The ethnobiological study of the Penan Benalui by Koizumi and Momose (2007) analyzed the use, classification, and nomenclature of wild plants, specifically seeking an answer to the question of whether hunter-gatherers have less knowledge of wild organisms than subsistence farmers. This was triggered by a controversial article by Berlin (1992) that compared ethnobiological classifications among subsistence farmers and hunter-gatherers. Berlin argued that most hunter-gatherers had virtually no knowledge of specific taxa and that they are less aware of the biological differences between closely related organisms and recognize the usefulness of fewer wild organisms and plants.

While it can be expected that hunter-gatherers know less about cultivated plants and domesticated animals, Koizumi and Momose (2007) found it unlikely that they would know less about wild organisms. Exploring this issue in a detailed study, they pointed out that comparisons should be made between people living in similar natural environments with similar species diversity, as this affects the number of taxa in a folk biological classification. They used two comparative frameworks to take into account the population diversity of Borneo in general, and the diversity among different groups of hunter-gatherers and agriculturalists in particular, regardless of the high number of biological species found there. In doing so, they employed interlanguage comparisons (between hunter-gatherer and agricultural societies living under similar environmental conditions) and intralanguage comparisons (between people engaging in different subsistence activities).

Although the knowledge of useful wild plants and their classification and nomenclature among the Penan Benalui and the Bornean farmers are very similar, the nature of this knowledge is different, as is expected when considering their different cultural preferences. The Penan Benalui had a much more limited knowledge pertaining to food plants than did the agriculturalists, who used more wild plants to enrich their diets. Conversely, the Penan Benalui could name more sago palm species and more fruit species. In the field of medicine, the Penan Benalui knew a smaller number of species for medicines, perhaps because there is a higher incidence of illnesses in settled populations. In addition, they also had a more limited language relating to the use of plants for religious and magic purposes. As Shimeda (1996) has pointed out for the Western Penan, however, this can be explained by the fact that voice is the prime means to communicate with spirits. Moreover, they know many alternative plants for technical uses though they usually use the most favorable species.

The use of the forest by Penan Benalui is closely related to plant collection, and they are also attentive to signs of animals, such as bitten fruits and footprints, and these extralinguistic factors provide critical data that need to be considered rather than merely comparing word lists for species and their uses. In summary, the Penan Benalui use of wild plants was mostly practical and supported by broad and general knowledge of plants and the forest. They have elaborate techniques to use plants for subsistence, especially for sago processing. The broad knowledge of the Penan Benalui about wild plants also could be seen in their plant classification system. The Penan Benalui classified plants mostly to the species level, so we can expect that they have as many or more taxa of wild plants than farmers in the neighboring areas. Moreover, Penan Benalui systems of classification and nomenclature of plants were similar to those of subsistence farmers across the world.

In conclusion, as Koizumi and Momose (2007) pointed out, the Penan Benalui hunter-gatherers have both general knowledge and a detailed classification of forest plants whereby their knowledge of plants is largely simple and differs significantly from that of the farmers. It is significant that the process of acquiring this knowledge appears to be more or less dependent on personal experience rather than through any form of instruction. Lastly, as hunter-gatherers and agriculturalists have very different systems of knowledge pertaining to their distinct lifestyle, they have different classifications of plants resulting from specific subsistence systems, local flora, nomenclature patterns, and histories, and for this reason one must be very careful when comparing the knowledge systems of such groups.

11.7 Discussion and Conclusions

All languages dealt with here are grouped under a subgroup, Kayan-Kenyah, which comprises Kenyah, Kayan, Kayanic, and Penan. Blust (1974, 2007) has proposed a North Sarawakan bigger language group and more recently a Greater North Borneo group (Blust 2010) (see Table 11.4). Recall that although Blust's general theory is compelling, it is acceptable only with some reservations; notably, his vowel deletion hypothesis cannot accommodate the some Kayan varieties and his idea that the close relationship between Kayan and Kenyah is mostly due to contact is not substantiated by the empirical evidence. Also, in Blust (2010) the North Sarawak group (with Kenyah and Penan as part of it) does not include Kayan, which is considered instead part of 'Other Borneo.' Up to now the predominating linguistic affiliation of the Penan is with the Kenyah subgroup as proposed by both linguists and nonlinguists (Needham 1954; Blust 1974, 1998, 2007, 2010; Hudson 1978; Brosius 1992; Sercombe 2002). If it is true that Penan shares a number of similarities with Kenyah languages, its close relationship with Kayan cannot be denied. In fact Blust (2002: 30) stated that "Kenyah preceded the Kayan in the Usun Apau region and elsewhere in the upper courses of the main rivers in Borneo. The Kayan probably began to migrate upriver from a geographically more compact region within five to six centuries." Historical and cultural data do not support this claim, as Blust refers to a period dating back hundreds of years or more for which there is no historical trace whatsoever. On the contrary there are strong cultural and historical relationships between the groups of people inhabiting a wide area in the highland of Central Borneo (see Whittier 1973 and Rousseau 1988). Furthermore, it has been established that the Kayan originated in the Apau Kayan region (Rousseau 1988: 23, 257), which they left as the Kenyah moved in. The Kenyah, together with other related groups like some Kajang, originally lived in Usun Apau, as did groups of Penan. It is thus difficult to prove that their linguistic relationship is due only to long-term contact. The Kayan, Kenyah, and Penan languages share a high number of lexical innovations but a number of phonological innovations are also shared between Kayan and Kayanic languages such as Lebu' Kulit, proper Kayanic, Mboh, and Penan. The exclusive similarities displayed by Penan, Cebop, and Mboh, being more closely related to each other, may lead one to interpret these as a group. The speakers of these languages, the Cebop and the Mboh, settled on the Baram, whereas the Penan continued their wandering in the upper part of the rivers.

Regarding in particular Penan Benalui, the previous section has demonstrated that it is indeed related historically to Kenyah and Kayan as well as to other languages spoken in North Borneo, such as for example Kelabit, but that the particular Kenyah affiliation is problematic. According to Soriente (2004, 2008), the Kenyah languages include three quite distinct branches, Mainstream or Usun Apau Kenyah (also called Highland Kenyah by Blust (1974, 1998, 2007, 2010), and Upper Pujungan Kenyah and Kayanic Kenyah (including Lebu' Kulit and its sister languages such as Uma' Timai, Uma' Pawa', Uma' Kelep, called Lowland Kenyah by Blust). The Usun Apau Kenyah branch has a high number of speakers and distinct varieties, while the Upper Pujungan branch is much smaller. Penan Benalui shares a significant number of lexical items with Kenyah, particularly the Usun Apau varieties, involving many cognates and regular sound–meaning correspondences, but also phonologically is closer to the Kayanic section. At the same time, there are a number of semantic shifts in all the vocabulary in addition to a number of dubious correspondences. Nevertheless, the overall analysis of the phonology, morphology, and lexicon shows that Penan Benalui is quite distinct and unintelligible to most Kenyah and Kayan speakers. Accordingly, it is reasonable to propose that the part of the primarily lexical similarities between Penan Benalui and other Kenyah varieties may be the result of contact. All in all the previous classification of Penan languages as belonging to the Kenyah branch, as proposed for Eastern Penan varieties by previous authors, is not supported.

Penan Benalui also shows features of other languages that are spoken by culturally and linguistically different groups such as the Kayan and the Kelabit. It is important to recall in this respect that the linguistic Kenyah affiliation of a number of other small sedentary groups, who define themselves ethnically as Kenyah and do not recognize a foraging past, is also controversial. This concerns such groups in Sarawak as the Kiput and the Berawan as well as the Cebop, whose language is very similar to Western Penan (see Needham 1954, and Soriente's notes [n.d.]); the Mboh, whose language is very divergent from the main group of Kenyah dialects; and finally the groups in Long Wat on the Apoh and Long Tap on the

Tutoh. I have proposed in Soriente (2004) that some such languages, notably the Lebu' Kulit branch, Cebop, and Mboh, should be separated from Kenyah and grouped as Kayanic within Kayan–Kenyah.

It is these Kayanic languages that display the greatest linguistic similarity with Penan Benalui, notably in the phonology. Moreover, the Western Penan variety is as closely related to the Cebop and Lirong languages in the Tinjar and the Long Wat on the Apoh as to Eastern Penan (cf. the cognate percentage of 82% between Western Penan and Cebop). Finally, Eastern and Western Penan languages share a considerable number of phonological, morphological, and structural similarities despite the fact that their speakers are scattered over large areas and have been in contact with different groups of agriculturalists. According to Brosius (1992), Eastern and Western Penan are even mutually intelligible, in spite of existing phonetic and lexical differences. These linguistic similarities are supported by what we know of the history of these people: the Penan, Cebop, Lirong, Long Wat, and Badeng were long in close proximity along the Seping, Peleran, and Danum Rivers until shortly before the turn of the twentieth century. It is thus possible that all these languages, including Penan Benalui, are genealogically more closely related. I thus hypothesized in Soriente (2004) that Penan Benalui is part of the Kayanic branch. (Recall that it is even possible that such settled groups as the Cebop, Mboh, Long Wat, and Long Tap used to be hunter-gatherers themselves but assimilated earlier to the Kenyah. This affinity might have been the reason why these linguistically closely related Penan groups came to be labeled as Kenyah, too.)

If a North Sarawak language family is accepted, then there is no strong reason to remove Kayan from the grouping. By including Kayan varieties within the family, the linguistic position of some Kenyah languages with Kayanic features can be justified, as can that of Penan Benalui. Penan Benalui is most probably a member of this North Sarawak family but together with other languages nowadays in Sarawak (what Blust 2007, 2010 has defined Lowland Kenyah) represents a branch of the Kayan–Kenyah subgroup. Unfortunately one cannot speculate any further on such matters, as no thorough study on other Eastern and Western Penan languages or on other related languages like Cebop and Mboh has been carried out as of yet.

However, after gathering additional material, it has become clear to me that Kenyah and Kayanic features are both relevant in Penan Benalui. At the same time, a number of facts described in Section 11.6 show that Penan Benalui is neither a Kenyah nor a Kayan language. Hence, Penan is for the time being better understood as a branch of its own within the Kayan-Kenyah subgroup (Soriente 2008) of North Sarawakan (Blust 1974, 1998, 2010). More extensive research on these and other Western or Eastern Penan languages might show a higher or lower level of similarity with other languages in Northern Borneo.

Returning to the general problem of the origin of the Borneo hunter-gatherers and their languages, while the linguistic facts strongly suggest a common origin with the languages of agriculturalists this is not conclusive evidence that the modern hunter-gatherers are merely the result of devolution from agricultural ancestors. Instead, to a certain extent the opposite could be the case, namely that populations which are now agriculturalists were once hunter-gatherers, as proposed by Whittier (1973), Brosius (1988), and Rousseau (1990). The genealogical relation between the languages of foragers and food producers may very well result from a yet earlier process in which hunter-gatherer populations slowly or abruptly abandoned their original language in favor of the Austronesian language of the then closest agricultural group. However, the scattered lexical similarities between different Pnan groups that may hint at a concrete pre-Austronesian hunter-gatherer substrate population from which also Penan Benalui developed are still quite restricted and it is necessary to look for more common elements in all the relevant languages.[29] Only a systematic and detailed study, which takes all possible historical processes including language contact into account, can shed more light on this hypothesis.

Apart from a necessary reevaluation within the frame of comparative linguistic studies, molecular anthropological surveys of hunter-gatherer and non–hunter-gatherer populations of Borneo will also be indispensable; in particular, only the combination of these two fields can detect cases of language shift. Clearly, in order to unravel the linguistic history of Borneo, a more complex model is needed, a model involving such different scenarios as split of languages, long-term contact with convergence, language shift, as well as changes of cultural patterns. It is extremely unlikely that the traditional linguistic model focusing on divergence processes as well as the simple opposition of "continuity" versus "devolution" are sufficient.

It is worth making clear that whether pre-Austronesian foragers have a common origin or not is independent of the assumption about a substratum that shifted to Austronesian. It is as well possible that pre-Austronesian foragers could have been heterogeneous. Despite the fact that there is very little evidence for the forager substratum, nevertheless given the many precedent cases worldwide for prehistorically foragers language shift under maintenance culture, the hypothesis is strong and very simple. If we can assume that Borneo was settled by humans before the arrival of the Austronesians, it is likely that these pre-Austronesian foragers shifted their languages to Austronesian languages instead of hypothesizing that these pre-Austronesian were wiped out.

Abbreviations

1 2 3	personal pronouns
AV	actor voice
AG	agentive marker
DET	determiner
NOM	nominalizer
PAN	Proto-Austronesian
POSS	possessive
SG	singular
UV	undergoer voice

NOTES

1. HRAF are the Human Resources Area Files, which classify the primary livelihood of various groups into nine distinct categories based on caloric sources (foraging, farming, herding, etc.); whether a group is sedentary or not; the size of the group, etc.

2. For instance, the Lisum and Beketan have been relocated and now live in areas inhabited by other settlers in Sungai Lunuk, a resettlement village close to Muara Tubo' in Tabang town district, though we do not have detailed information on the specifics of how this came about. In addition, the Penan Niah have been forced by their patrons to guard the caves in this area, as is the case for the Punan Batu and Basap in the coastal areas of Sangkulirang. In these coastal instances, however, it is uncertain to what degree these people are remnants of mixed slave populations (see Sellato 2018).

3. Communication with few Penan people and some scholars involved in the study of Penan issues such as Jayl Langub and Ian Mackenzie confirm this data. Actually only eight household of Eastern Penan groups still maintain a real nomadic life-style. Very few are defined semi settled and the majority are basically settled and can be considered as former hunter-gatherers.

4. The review of the literature on Southeast Asia hunter-gatherers and Borneo is very general and does not expect to cover the many issues related to the anthropology of nomads despite the fact that it addresses various historical debates like the one about Penan versus Punan or that of devolution. What is really relevant to stress is that variation frequently occurs, especially because of contact with different farming groups. Additional data on Southeastasia hunter-gatherers can be found in Winzeler (2011).

5. This view is not shared by all the speakers nor by all the scholars. Ian Mackenzie, for instance, who undertook extensive research among the Eastern Penan considers Eastern and Western Penan to be mutually unintelligible. This point will be discussed later in Section 11.5.

6. The figures for Eastern Penan are about 12,000 people located in about 80 locations east of the Baram in Sarawak and one on the Belait River in Brunei (Penan Sukang) and include small groups of hunter-gatherers (Penan Selungo, Penan Apoh), of whom only a few are still nomadic or semisettled. In particular, 135 people in three locations are semisettled and 295 individuals in 8 locations on the Magoh

and Adang River are nomadic. The semisettled Eastern Penan communities are located in the Upper Tutoh River, in Long Taha (47 individuals) and in Ba' Marong (27) and on the Kuba'an River, in Long Tah (33) and in Ba' Madamut (55). The nomadic groups on the Magoh River are Ba' Magoh (39), Ba' Tepen (56), Ba' Puak (50), Ba' Bareh (39), and Ba' Ubong (48). The nomadic Penan on the Adang River are Ba' Ureu (12) and Ba' Lepang (24). It is important to stress that these figures are provisory and were obtained through discussion with several community members, scholars, and stakeholders. Unfortunately a real census has never been carried out but the recent publication of community maps by the Bruno Manser Fund (2017) has highly contributed to a better knowledge of the distribution of these people. Both the semisettled and the nomadic groups interact with the Kelabit neighbors.

7. Western Penan includes about 6,000 individuals spread in 44 locations.

8. The column listing Pnan groups includes both known groups and single communities whose affiliation is not clear. Also, the column on population figures is rather incomplete, and comes from information obtained from published and unpublished sources and is therefore provisory. Contact groups, historically, are probably more varied than those listed. In short, such a detailed table with many empty cells just tells us how fragmentary our knowledge of those groups and their languages is.

9. Currently research on Punan Sihan language is being carried out by Peter Puxon for an ELDP-SOAS language documentation project and some data on Punan Aput are being collected by Antonia Soriente.

10. Information obtained during fieldwork carried out in the Punan Tubu' community showed that Punan Merap ethnonym refers to the Punan Tubu' people who interacted with the Merap (Kayanic). A superficial survey and sociolinguistic interviews confirmed the fact that this is just a variant of Punan Tubu'

11. A study of Punan Malinau/Segah or was carried out by Soriente in 2009–2011. Preliminary findings demonstrate that, though very idiosyncratic, this language behaves like languages of the Kayanic subgroup.

12. Sellato (p.c. 2013).

13. However, according to Sellato (2007: 71), certain Pnan groups are at least nominally some of the largest landowners in Kalimantan. Numbering ca. 6,000 persons, they have formal jurisdiction over areas amounting to almost 25,000 km^2, all or most of it upland forests holding much sought-after trade products.

14. Also referred to as Sebop, Sibop or Chebop in the literature and generally listed as Kenyah though it is much more similar to Western Penan than it is to Kenyah.

15. Clement Langet Sabang compiled a dictionary of Cebop.

16. Apart from the IPA, the following special symbols are used for Proto-Austronesian: *S for an alveolar sibilant, *R for an alveolar or uvular trill, *C for an alveolar affricate, and *q for a pharyngeal stop.

17. Probably this is not the main reason, as stress is in general very light (see also Sercombe 2006: 10).

18. In some Kenyah varieties some roots display a frozen <-en>- infix but the usual undergoer voice is not explicitly expressed in Kenyah (see also Clayre 1996: 80 and Clayre 2014). In Òma Lóngh Kenyah an involuntary passive with the prefix ten- is employed. The same prefix does not seem to be productive in other Kenyah varieties on which I have collected extensive data, like Lebu' Kulit or Lepo' Tau, Lepo' Ma'ut, or Bakung. The infix is recorded in Eastern Penan by Sercombe

(2006: 13) and Clayre (1996, 2014). The same undergoer voice system is found in Cebop that despite being classified as Kenyah displays features very similar to Western Penan. The infix also occurs in Kiput (in the Lower Baram) to unambiguously distinguish passive-perfective verbs from the infix that refers to transitive and intransitive verbs (Blust 2003: 11 and as Clayre (1996: 81) also notices is common in Sabah languages. According to her the infix <in>, a direct descent of PAN * seems to be lost in the languages of North-Central Sarawak.

19. For a more detailed description of Voice in some languages of Northeastern Borneo, see Soriente (2012).

20. The same way to indicate numerals from ten to twenty with the use of the 'plus' lexeme is shared by Kayan and Kayanic, including Punan Malinau/Segah, whereas the juxtaposition system of ten followed by the numerals from one to nine is followed by other Pnan languages like Punan Tubu'.

21. Aspect markers and negators are very diverse in the other Pnan languages like Punan Tubu' and Ma' Pnaan. The marker for perfective is *bəlum* for Punan Tubu' and *ŋa* for Ma' Pnaan, both meaning 'finished,' whereas for imperfective Punan Tubu' employs the spatial expression *an luaŋ* 'in the middle'. Negators too are very different: *ovi?* and *maliŋ* for Punan Tubu' and *ana* and *mbai* for Ma' Pnaan.

22. Resettled groups of Pnan in Sarawak live nowadays in longhouses, but this was not the case in the past.

23. Though it was very tricky to elicit names of plants and animals because some informants confuse species and genus. The words provided here were counter-checked with the list of ethnobiological terms compiled by Puri (2001).

24. The lexeme *jau* corresponds to the same word in Kayan for 'big.'

25. The Kenyah cognate is Proto-Kenyah **megen that means 'to lay down.

26. It is indeed true that in the last field trips in Long Lame (2009), the village established next to the Badeng Kenyah settlement, only few elders were able to remember all the necronyms.

27. Koizumi's notes and p.c. 2009.

28. Puri (2005: 15–22) highlights the importance of knowledge relating to hunting as a central component of the cultural ethos of Penan Benalui. An unexplored and potentially productive comparative analysis of Penan languages could well emerge from looking into the differences in the animal domain.

29. The words considered by Sellato (2002) of critical importance, as evidence of a cultural and linguistic substratum uniting all the hunter-gatherers societies, as exposed in Section 11.4, are not part of the Penan Benalui lexicon. On the other hand they are found in the other groups of Pnan of Table 11.1, the Bukat, the Punan Tubu', and the Beketan-Lisum.

References

Adelaar, K. Alexander. (1995). Borneo as a cross-roads for comparative Austronesian linguistics. In P. Bellwood, J. J. Fox, and D. Tryon (eds.), *The Austronesians: Historical and comparative perspectives*. Canberra: Australian National University, Department of Anthropology, Research School of Pacific and Asian Studies, 75–95.

Bellwood, Peter. (1999). Archaeology of Southeast Asian hunters and gatherers. In Richard B. Lee and Richard Daly (eds.), *The Cambridge encyclopaedia of hunters and gatherers*. Cambridge: Cambridge University Press, 284–288.

Berlin, Brent. (1992). *Ethnobiological classification: Principles of categorization of plants and animals in traditional societies*. Princeton, NJ: Princeton University Press.

Blench, Roger. (2010). Was there an Austroasiatic presence in island SE Asia prior to the Austronesian expansion? *Bulletin of the Indo-Pacific Prehistory Association* 30: 133–144.

Blust, Robert. (1974). *The Proto-North Sarawak vowel deletion hypothesis*. Unpublished PhD thesis, University of Hawai'i.

(1976a). Austronesian culture history: Some linguistic inferences and their relations to the archaeological record. *World Archaeology* 8(1): 19–43.

(1976b). A third palatal reflex in Polynesian languages. *Journal of the Polynesian Society* 85: 339–358.

(1977). Sketches of the morphology and phonology of Bornean languages 1 Uma Juman (Kayan). *Papers in Borneo and Western Austronesian linguistics* 2: 7–122.

(1998). The position of the languages of Sabah, in Bautista, L.S. PAGTANÁW. *Essays on Language in honor of Teodoro A. Llamzon*. Manila: The Linguistic Society of the Philippines.

(2002). Formalism or phoneyism? The history of Kayan final glottal stop. In K. Alexander Adelaar and Robert A. Blust (eds.), *Between worlds: Linguistic paper in memory of David John Prentice*. Pacific Linguistics, 29–37.

(2003). *A short morphology, phonology and vocabulary of Kiput, Sarawak*. Pacific Linguistics, 546.

(2007). Òma Lóngh Historical Phonology. *Oceanic Linguistics* 46: 1–53.

(2010). The Greater North Borneo Hypothesis. *Oceanic Linguistics* 49(1): 44–118.

Brosius, J. Peter. (1988). A separate reality: Comments on Hoffman's "The Punan: Hunters and gatherers of Borneo." *Borneo Research Bulletin* 20(2): 81–106.

(1992). *The axiological presence of death: Penan Geng death-names*. PhD thesis, University of Michigan.

(1995). Signifying bereavement: Form and context in the analysis of Penan death-names. *Oceania* 66(2): 119–146.

(1999). The Western Penan of Borneo. In Richard B. Lee, and Richard Daly (eds.), *The Cambridge encyclopaedia of hunters and gatherers*. Cambridge: Cambridge University Press, 312–316.

Bruno Manser Fund. (2017). *Mép tana'suket asen lu'. Penan Community maps*. Basel: Bruno Manser Fund and Keluan.

Césard, Nicolas, Antonio Guerreiro, and Antonia Soriente, eds. (2015). *Petualangan Unjung dan Mbui Kuvong. Sastra lisan dan Kamus Punan Tuvu' dari Kalimantan*. Jakarta: EFEO and KPG Gramedia.

Clayre, Beatrice. (1996). The changing face of focus in the languages of Borneo. In Hein Steinhauer (ed.), Papers in Austronesian Linguistics 3. Pacific Linguistics A-84, 51–88.

(2014). A preliminary typology of the languages of Middle Borneo. In Peter Sercombe, Michael Boutin and Adrian Clynes (eds.), *Advances in research on Linguistic and cultural practices in Borneo* (Memorial volume in honor of Peter Martin). Phillips: Borneo Research Council, 123–152.

Endicott, Kirk M. (1999). Introduction: Southeast Asia. In Richard B. Lee and Richard Daly (eds.), *The Cambridge encyclopaedia of hunters and gatherers*. Cambridge: Cambridge University Press, 275–283.

Gordon, Raymond G. (ed.) (2005). *Ethnologue: Languages of the world*, 15th ed. Dallas: SIL International. www.ethnologue.com

Heine-Geldern, Robert Von. (1946). Research on Southeast Asia: Problems and suggestions. *American Anthropologist* 48: 149–175.

Hoffman, Carl L. (1986). *The Punan: Hunters and gatherers of Borneo*. Studies in Cultural Anthropology, 12. Ann Arbor: University Microfilms International Research Press.

Hose, Charles and William McDougall. (1912). *The Pagan tribes of Borneo: A description of their physical, moral and intellectual condition with some discussion of their ethnic relations*. 2 vols. London: Macmillan.

Hudson, Alfred B. (1978). Linguistic relations among Bornean peoples with special reference to Sarawak: An interim report, in Sarawak: Linguistics and Development Problems. Williamsburg, VA: College of William and Mary, Department of Anthropology. *Studies in Third World Societies* 3: 1–44.

Kaskija, Lars. (2017). Devolved, diverse, distinct? Hunter-gatherer research in Borneo. In V. T. King, Z. Ibrahim and N. H. Hassan (eds.), *Borneo studies in history, society and culture*. Singapore: Springer, 125–158.

Kato, Yumi. (2017). Perceptions of the Iban in the Sihan Ethnoscape. *Ngingit* 9: 49–58.

Klimut, K. A. and R. K. Puri. (2007). The Punan from the Tubu' river, East Kalimantan: A native voice on past, present, and future circumstances. In Peter Sercombe and Bernard Sellato (eds.), *Beyond the green myth: Borneo's hunter-gatherers in the 21st century*. Copenhagen: Nias Press., 110–134.

Koizumi, Miyako, Dollop Mamung and Patrice Levang. (2012). Hunter-gatherers' culture, a major hindrance to a settled agricultural life: The case of the Penan Benalui of East Kalimantan. *Forests, Trees and Livelihoods* 21(1): 1–15.

Koizumi, Miyako and Momose Kuniyasu. (2007). Penan Benalui wild-plant use, classification, and nomenclature. *Current Anthropology* 48(3): 454–459.

Langub, Jayl. (2001). Sukét: Penan folk stories. Sukét Penan, Kota Samarahan: Universiti Malaysia Sarawak, Institute of East Asian Studies, Oral Literature Series, 2.
(2003)

Mackenzie, Ian. (2006). *Dictionary of Eastern Penan*. Ms. Soriente www.rimba.com

Mamung, Dollop. (1998).*Kamus Punan-Indonesia. Bah Ngguh Punan Tufu'. Kamus Bahasa Punan Tubu'*. Samarinda: Pusat Kebudayaan dan Alam Kalimantan.

Moseley Christopher and R. E. Asher. (eds.). (1994). *Atlas of the world's languages*, London: Routledge.

Needham, Rodney. (1954). Penan and Punan. *Journal of the Royal Asiatic Society, Malaysian Branch* 27(1): 73–83.

Nicolaisen, Johannes. (1976a). The Penan of Sarawak: Further notes on the neo-evolutionary concept of hunters. *Folk* 18: 205–236.

(1976b). The Penan of the seventh division of Sarawak: Past, present and future. *Sarawak Museum Journal* 24(45): 35–61.

Okushima, Mika. (2008). Ethnohistory of the Kayanic peoples in Northeast Borneo (Part 2): expansion, regional alliance groups, and Segai disturbances in the colonial era. *Borneo Research Bulletin* 39.

Puri, Rajindra K. (2001). *Bulungan thnobiology handbook*. Bogor: CIFOR.

(2005). *Deadly Dances in the Bornean rainforest*. Leiden: KITLV Press.

Puxon, Peter. (2018). *Documentation of Sihan, an endangered language of Borneo*. London: SOAS, Endangered Language Archive. https://elar.soas.ac.uk/Collection/MPI1104004.

Rousseau, Jerome. (1988). *Central Borneo: A bibliography*. Special Monograph n. 5. Kuching: Sarawak Museum.

(1990). *Central Borneo: Ethnic identity and social life in a stratified society*. Oxford: Clarendon Press.

Sather, Clifford. (1995). Sea nomads and rainforest hunter-gatherers: Foraging adaptations in the Indo-Malaysian archipelago. In Peter Bellwood, James J. Fox and Darrell Tryon (eds.), *The Austronesians: Historical and comparative perspectives*. Canberra: Department of Anthropology, Research School of Pacific and Asian Studies, Australian National University, 229–268.

Sellato, Bernard. (1993). The Punan question and the reconstruction of Borneo's culture history. In V. H. Sutlive Vincent Jr. (ed.), *Change and development in Borneo*. Williamsburg, VA: Borneo Research Council, 47–82.

(2002). *Innermost Borneo: Studies in Dayak cultures*. Paris: SevenOrients, and Singapore: Singapore University Press.

(2007). Resourceful children of the forest: The Kalimantan Punan through the twentieth century. In Peter Sercombe and Bernard Sellato (eds.), *Beyond the green myth: Borneo's hunter-gatherers in the 21st century*. Copenhagen: Nias Press, 61–90.

(2018). Hunter-gatherers and the slave trade in coastal eastern Borneo, 18th–19th c. Paper presented at the Eleventh Conference on Hunting and Gathering Societies (CHAGS 11), at USM, Penang Malaysia.

Sellato, Bernard and Peter Sercombe. (2007). Introduction. In Peter Sercombe and Bernard Sellato (eds.), *Beyond the green myth: Borneo's hunter-gatherers in the 21st century*. Copenhagen: Nias Press, 1–49.

Sellato, Bernard and Antonia Soriente (2015). The languages and peoples of the Müller Mountains: A contribution to the study of the origins of Borneo's nomads and their languages. *Wacana* 16(2): 339–354.

Sercombe, Peter. (2002). *Linguistic continuity and adaptation among the Penans of Brunei Darussalam*. PhD thesis, Universiti Kebangsaan Malaysia.

(2006). The Eastern Penan language of Borneo. In Chong Shin et al. (eds.), *Reflections in Borneo Rivers: Essays in honour of Professor James T. Collins*. Pontianak: Stain Press, 1–34.

(2018). *A dictionary of Eastern Penan*. London: SOAS, Endangered Languages Archive. https://elar.soas.ac.uk/Collection/MPI1171473.

Shimeda, Takashi. (1996). *Koe no chikara (Power of voice)*. Tokyo: Koubundou.

Sidwell Paul and Roger Blench. (2011). The Austroasiatic Urheimat: The Southeastern Riverine Hypothesis. In Nick J. Enfield (ed.), *Dynamics of human diversity: The case of mainland Southeast Asia*. Canberra: Pacific Linguistics 627, 1–30.

Simons, Gary F. and Charles D. Fenning, eds. (2018). *Ethnologue: Languages of the world*, 21st ed. Dallas, TX: SIL International. www.ethnologue.com.

Soriente, Antonia. (1997). The Kenyah isolects of Long Pujungan district in North-east Kalimantan. In C. Ode', and W. Stokhof (eds.), *Proceedings of the Seventh*

International Conference on Austronesian Languages. Amsterdam: Rodopi, 713–738.

(2004). *A classification of Kenyah varieties in Sarawak and Kalimantan.* PhD thesis, Universiti Kebangsaan Malaysia.

(2008). The classification of Kenyah languages: A preliminary statement. *Journal of the SEAsian Linguistics Society.* 14(2). www.JSEALS.org

(2013). Undergoer voice in Borneo: Penan, Punan, Kenyah and Kayan languages. In *NUSA: Linguistic studies of languages in and around Indonesia, Vol. 54.* Voice variation in Austronesian languages of Indonesia: 175–203.

Thambiah, Shanty. (2007). The emergence of the ethnic category Bhuket: Diversity and the collective hunter-gatherer identity in Borneo. In Peter Sercombe and Bernard Sellato (eds.), *Beyond the green myth: Borneo's hunter-gatherers in the 21st century.* Copenhagen: Nias Press, 91–109.

Urquhart, Ian A. N. (1958). Nomadic Punans and Pennans. *Sarawak Gazette* 30 November, 205–207.

Winzeler, Robert L. (2011). *The peoples of Southeast Asia today: Ethnography, ethnology and change in a complex region.* Plymouth: AltaMira Press.

Whittier, Herbert L. (1973). *Social organization and symbols of social differentiation: an ethnographic study of the Kenyah Dayak of East Kalimantan.* PhD thesis, Michigan State University. Ann Arbor: University Microfilms.

Wurm, Steven A. and Shiro Hattori, eds. (1984). *Language atlas of the Pacific area.* Pacific Linguistics C-66.

Part IV

New Guinea and Australia

12 The Linguistic Situation in Near Oceania before Agriculture

Malcolm Ross

12.1 Introduction

Near Oceania consists of mainland New Guinea, the Bismarck Archipelago (New Britain, New Ireland and Manus), Bougainville and the Solomon Islands. I divide Near Oceania into two regions which are distinct in terms of their linguistic history. The first region is mainland New Guinea. The second consists of the Bismarcks, Bougainville and the Solomon Islands, which I refer to collectively as Northwest Island Melanesia. All the larger islands of Near Oceania are mountainous, and the highlands cordillera of the island of New Guinea, with peaks up to nearly 5,000 m, is particularly significant in the region's settlement history (see Map 12.1).

Two modern political boundaries cut across the region. The western half of mainland New Guinea is part of Indonesia, while the eastern half, together with the Bismarcks and Bougainville, forms the independent state of Papua New Guinea. The Solomon Islands are also an independent state.

Are there hunter-gatherers in Near Oceania today? Were there any at European contact? The conventional answer is 'no' (Rosman and Rubel 1989: 27), but recent scholarship has questioned this with regard to New Guinea (Roscoe 2005). An answer is dependent on one's definition of 'hunter-gatherer', but a linguistically useful answer also requires a diachronic context, as it seems that some of the communities that may be eligible for the label of 'hunter-gatherer' or 'forager' have adopted their current lifestyle fairly recently in the island's long settlement history. For this reason, a substantial portion of this chapter is devoted to sketching the diachronic context of foragers and their languages before I turn in Section 12.5 to their alleged present-day representatives.

12.2 The Settlement History of Near Oceania

As Map 12.2 shows, Near Oceania is bounded to the west by Wallacea, a collection of islands located in deep seas, and to the east by sea crossings of

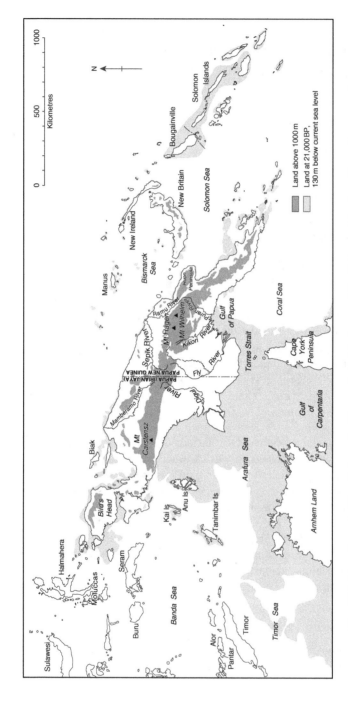

Map 12.1 Near Oceania: New Guinea, the Bismarck Archipelago and the Solomon Islands, with contiguous regions.

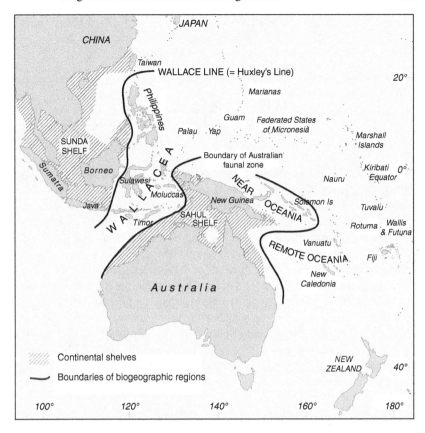

Map 12.2 Major biogeographic regions of Island SE Asia and the Pacific: Sundaland, Wallacea, Near Oceania, and Remote Oceania.

350 km or more to the nearest islands of Remote Oceania, namely the Santa Cruz group and Vanuatu. At the time of the Last Glacial Maximum at 21,000 BP, New Guinea was joined to Australia and together they formed the land mass known as Sahul. Sumatra, Borneo and Java were part of the extension of the Asian continent known as Sundaland. Bougainville, Choiseul, Santa Isabel and Guadalcanal formed a single island known as Greater Bougainville (Map 12.1).

The prehistory of Near Oceania is conveniently divided into four periods (BP = before present):

1. Before 21,000 BP: settlement during the Pleistocene, before the Last Glacial Maximum

2. 21,000–12,000 BP: the late Pleistocene, after the Last Glacial Maximum
3. 12,000–3,300 BP: early and mid-Holocene
4. From 3,300 BP until European contact (1870–1965)

The Pleistocene was the period of the great Ice Ages, beginning around 1.8 million years ago and ending with the Younger Dryas, a short cold period (roughly 13,400–12,000 BP) which followed a major retreat of the ice.

By 21,000 BP, the end of Period 1, Sahul and all of Near Oceania had been settled except perhaps the islands beyond Greater Bougainville. This settlement entailed sea crossings, with gaps of 70 km in Wallacea, of 180 km from New Ireland to Greater Bougainville and 200 km to Manus. These sea crossings obviously required considerable seamanship. We have no way of knowing how many such crossings there were, but there is no evidence of regular traffic across these gaps during Periods 1 and 2, nor indeed until the arrival of Austronesian-speaking seafarers at the end of Period 3 around 3,300 BP.[1] Because of the phylogenetic diversity of New Guinea languages, it has sometimes been claimed that there must have been numerous migrations from Sundaland across Wallacea to New Guinea, but the diversity is readily attributable to the immense time depth of settlement, together with forms of socio-economic organisation in which societies were always small and were not economically interdependent (Nettle 1999: 72–73). It seems likely that as the sea level gradually rose after 21,000 BP (Chappell 2005: 527–528), sea crossings, which had been few, declined almost to zero. We cannot exclude multiple migrations, but there is no obvious linguistic or archaeological evidence for them.

The limited archaeological evidence suggests that the most significant socio-economic development in NW Island Melanesia during Period 2, the late Pleistocene, was a gradual shift from mobile foraging bands to foraging sedentism. There are indications that animal and plant species were deliberately imported into New Ireland and Manus. Spriggs (1996, 1997: 31–34, 61) interprets this as the beginning of what he calls wild-food production, i.e. the deliberate tending of the forest environment by selective weeding or clearing and by transplanting, without the permanent clearing of the forest which is entailed in agriculture and which significantly alters the productivity patterns of the environment. In all probability similar developments were occurring in New Guinea. In the lowlands this included the initial domestication of the sago palm. Indeed, foraging sedentism persists among a number of New Guinea communities that depend on the sago palm for their starch intake. One may infer, however, that such lifestyles occurred only in the coastal lowlands. In Period 1, the grasslands of the central New Guinea Highlands were home to megafauna, and there is archaeological evidence of seasonal hunting and collecting (Evans and Mountain 2005), but the winter climate would have been too severe for foraging. Early in Period 2, around 18,000 BP, as the climate began to warm up, the highland grasslands were replaced by dry land rain forest, principally *Nothofagus* (the 'southern beech'), creating an environment impossible for foragers except close to the forest edge (Sillitoe 2002).

The early Holocene (Period 3), around 9,000 BP, saw the beginnings of agriculture in the New Guinea Highlands (but apparently not in NW Island Melanesia),[2] with the cultivation of taro (*Colocasia esculenta* and bananas [Golson 1977]). By 6,000 BP there had been a significant spread of agriculture along the cordillera, certainly westward and presumably eastward too (Hope and Haberle 2005). By world standards this was an early agricultural beginning, but this is not surprising in view of the closeness of New Guinea to the Equator and the consequently mild Highland climate of the early Holocene. Both taro and banana are lowland crops, and it is reasonable to infer that they were deliberately transported to the Highlands,[3] and indeed provided the mechanism for Highlands settlement as forests were cleared and gardens planted. New Guinea geography suggests that domestication (the control of reproduction) and early cultivation are likely to have occurred first in the northern lowlands, the more so as the Sepik and Ramu Rivers then emptied into an 'inland sea' and the coastline accordingly approached the northern foothills of the cordillera far more closely than it does today. The inland sea reached its greatest extent around 6,000 BP (see Map 12.3),[4] and the speculative inference that its expansion pushed lowland populations to conquer upland territory is rather tempting. During this period, too, the distribution of sago stands was probably extended by human intervention (Klappa 2006).

The 3,300 BP boundary between Period 3 and Period 4 represents the arrival from the west of Austronesian agriculturalists in Near Oceania (see Map 12.4). There are Austronesian languages of the Eastern Malayo-Polynesian group in the west of New Guinea around the Bird's Head and Cenderawasih Bay, but we have no archaeological evidence to date their arrival. We can be reasonably certain, however, that speakers of the language immediately ancestral to Proto-Oceanic, itself the ancestor to all the Austronesian languages of Oceania, arrived in the Bismarcks around 3,300 BP. Early Oceanic speakers rapidly colonized NW Island Melanesia and moved beyond it to Santa Cruz, Vanuatu, New Caledonia, Fiji, Tonga and Samoa. Later they occupied Micronesia and the rest of Polynesia, and also gained toeholds on the offshore islands and coasts of New Guinea itself. Our confidence about this history is based on a widely accepted correlation of the Proto-Oceanic language with the archaeologically salient Lapita culture (Pawley 2008). Proto-Oceanic marks the beginning of a remarkable linguistic tale (Pawley 2005), but one that it is not relevant to tell here.

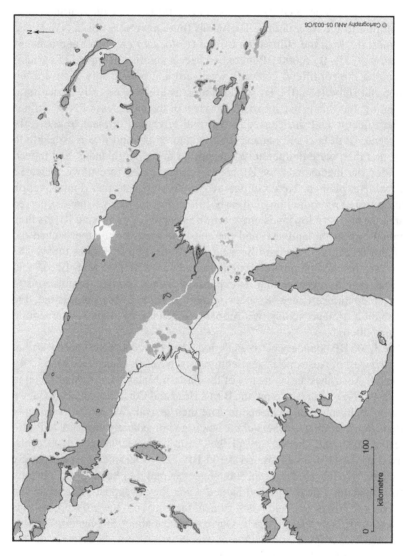

Map 12.3 New Guinea shoreline at 6,000 BP (after Chappell 2005, Swadling and Hide 2005).

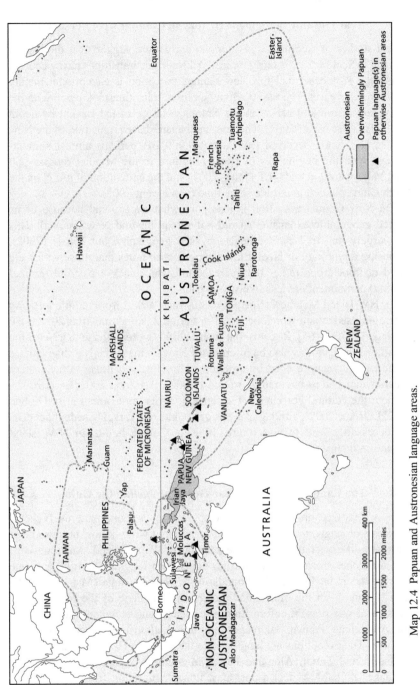

Map 12.4 Papuan and Austronesian language areas.

12.3   Near Oceanic Settlement History in Comparative Perspective

Recent studies of Neolithic transitions to agriculture suggest that the history outlined in Section 12.2 is fairly typical. All Neolithic transitions have occurred during the Holocene, and the New Guinea transition is exceptional mainly insofar as it is early. The world's first Neolithic transition took place with the cultivation of rye and barley in the Natufian culture of the Levant by about 10,400 BP (Bar-Yosef 2002). The taro-and banana-based transition of the New Guinea Highlands occurred from about 9,000 BP, perhaps almost simultaneously with the beginnings of rice agriculture in the Middle Yangtze and Huai Valleys around 8,500 BP (Jones 2002) and the cultivation of millet on the North China plain at about the same time (van Driem 2002).

The New Guinea transition is also somewhat exceptional because of its limited geographic expansion (it did not spread beyond New Guinea). This was largely due to New Guinea's physical geography, but Harris (2002), proposing a typology of Neolithic transitions, also notes that those which are based on root crops rather than cereals and which lack a pastoral (animal herding) component are less likely to expand.

For NW Island Melanesia Spriggs reconstructs a shift from mobile foraging to foraging sedentism which occurred in Period 2, sometime after 20,000 BP (Spriggs 1997: 61–65). It seems that such a shift is a prerequisite to a Neolithic transition, and can thus also be inferred for New Guinea. The Natufian culture of the Levant was preceded by a period of foraging sedentism in the eastern Sahara which had its beginnings around 18,000 BP (Barker 2002; Ehret 2002). Without the cultural correlates of sedentism, agriculture cannot arise (Cohen 2002; LeBlanc 2002), although, as Spriggs points out, foraging sedentism does not necessarily lead to agriculture. In New Guinea it did; in NW Island Melanesia it apparently did not.

12.4   The Language Map of Near Oceania: Peeling the Onion

Today's Near Oceania language map displays some striking patterns. It shows two kinds of language: Papuan and Austronesian. I write 'kinds' because there is a sharp difference between the denotations of 'Papuan' and 'Austronesian'. The Austronesian languages form an undisputed language family, and one which extends far beyond the boundaries of Near Oceania (Map 12.4). The term 'Papuan', on the other hand, labels any language of the New Guinea region that was present before European contact and is neither Austronesian nor Australian. Papuan languages are found almost exclusively in Near Oceania. The exceptions are languages to the west: on Halmahera in northern Wallacea, and Timor, Alor and Pantar in southern Wallacea. The southern languages probably reflect a post-agricultural emigration from New Guinea

(Pawley and Hammarström 2017: 76–78). The history of the north Halmahera languages is less clear, but they are related to languages of the Bird's Head (Voorhoeve 1987). Papuan languages otherwise manifest no known relationship with any language outside Near Oceania (despite Greenberg's 1971 proposed Indo-Pacific grouping).

There is no linguistic evidence that all Papuan languages are related to each other. If we include isolates and small phylic groups, Map 12.5 shows twenty-two seemingly unrelated phylogenetic units in New Guinea. The Papuan languages in NW Island Melanesia provide another eight such units (Map 12.6) (Ross 2001, 2005). New Guinea thus has the greatest phylogenetic linguistic diversity on Earth (Nettle 1999: 116–117, who notes that New Guinea also has the greatest language diversity, i.e. the largest number of different languages in a geographic area). I have suggested elsewhere that there is some evidence of a deep phylogenetic relationship among some Papuan groups. I return to this in Section 12.7.

The language map reflects the socio-economic history of Near Oceania and the effects of the different transitions to agriculture in New Guinea and in NW Island Melanesia. Given that the focus of this chapter is on the languages of foragers, and that the latter were presumably more widespread earlier rather than later in that history, I will look at major events in reverse chronological order, peeling off the layers of the onion in order to reveal what aspects of the map reflect forager speech communities.

The most recent significant event in this context was the arrival of Austronesian agriculturists around 3,300 BP. Their advent in Near Oceania was part of their rapid spread from Taiwan into the northern Philippines, and thence southwards into the Indo-Malaysian archipelago and eastwards to New Guinea and the Bismarck Archipelago. According to Bellwood and Hiscock (2005), settlement from the northern Philippines to the Bismarcks took only about nine centuries, from around 4,400 to 3,500 BP. It appears that the immigrants passed along the north coast of New Guinea by skipping from offshore island to offshore island, so that their first significant settlements were in the Bismarcks (Pawley 2008). The reason for this is easy to infer: New Guinea had long since undergone its own Neolithic transition, leaving little space for new arrivals. The Bismarcks, on the other hand, lie in NW Island Melanesia, which had apparently not moved beyond foraging sedentism: the arriving Austronesians, whose language soon became Proto-Oceanic, brought Neolithic transition to the Bismarcks. The effect of this on the language map was the displacement of Papuan languages in much of NW Island Melanesia (Map 12.6) as indigenous foraging populations intermarried with the new arrivals (Hurles 2002) and shifted to an agricultural lifestyle. Today the map of NW Island Melanesia is filled by Oceanic Austronesian languages, interspersed by a scattering of Papuan isolates and tiny groups. Only in the

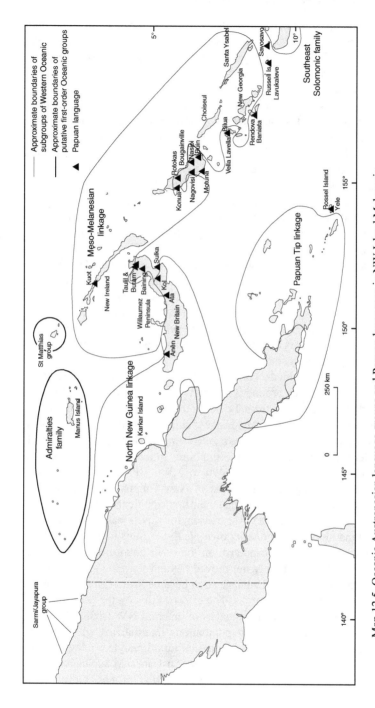

Map 12.5 Oceanic Austronesian language groups and Papuan languages in NW Island Melanesia.

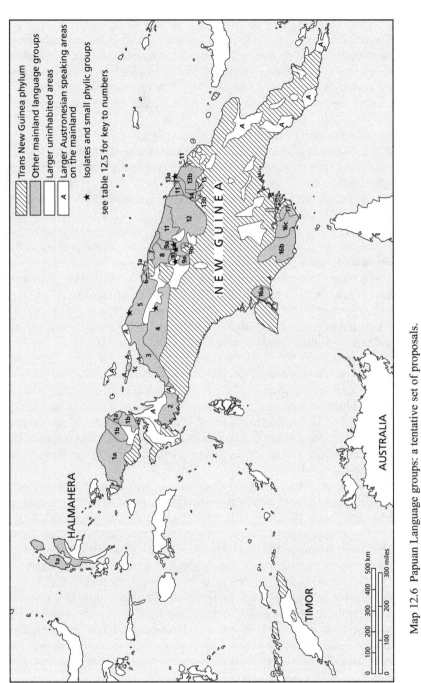

Map 12.6 Papuan Language groups: a tentative set of proposals.

mountainous interiors of eastern New Britain and Bougainville do we find small groups of contiguous Papuan languages. There is no evidence of a phylogenetic relationship among the eight groups, but there are typological indicators that the Papuan languages of NW Island Melanesia formed a linguistic area at the time of their first contact with Austronesian speakers, and their length separation from one another has not eliminated these typological signals (Ross 2001; Dunn et al. 2002).

The language map of New Guinea (Map 12.5) looks very different. Here, Austronesian languages are hardly a significant feature. We now know that it took until 2,600 BP for Austronesian-speaking communities to be established along the south coast of New Guinea (David et al. 2011; Skelly et al. 2014), and that Austronesians probably occupied the offshore islands along the north coast from 1,600 ± 100 BP in the east to about 1,200 BP in the Schouten Islands further west (Lilley 1999: 28; Lilley 2000:177, 187; 2007). The reasons for the slow speed of Austronesian settlement on mainland New Guinea are probably rather complex, but one of them was certainly the presence of well-established Papuan-speaking communities. As I noted earlier, it is possible that agriculture on part of the north coast predates its appearance in the Highlands: it had been there since perhaps 10,000 BP. In other coastal areas a shift to agriculture would have been much later, probably after 6,000 BP, but this date is still much earlier that the first arrival of Austronesian speakers around 3,300 BP.

Where the map of NW Island Melanesia reflects the Neolithic transition brought by the Austronesians, the map of New Guinea displays the much earlier home-grown agriculture of the Highlands, with its beginnings around 9,000 BP. Much of Map 12.5 is occupied by the Trans New Guinea (TNG) family,[5] and it is reasonable to infer that it reflects the spread of agriculture along the cordillera, across the Ramu-Markham divide into the mountains of the Huon Peninsula, and down the valleys of the cordillera's southern flank towards the coast.

On this interpretation, the TNG family is an instance of farming-driven language dispersal as predicted by Bellwood and Renfrew's 'farming/language dispersal hypothesis' (Renfrew 1991, 1992, 2000, 2002; Bellwood 1997, 2001, 2002), according to which the expansion of many (but of course not all) of the world's larger language families is attributable to a Neolithic transition. I suggested earlier that Highlands agriculture may have begun somewhere to the south of the Sepik-Ramu inland sea. The archaeological evidence is consonant with this, as the oldest signs of agriculture have been found at Kuk in the Western Highlands Province. The linguistic evidence is also compatible with this suggestion, as *ceteris paribus* we would expect the Proto-TNG homeland to be located in the TNG family's area of greatest internal phylogenetic diversity, and this is roughly what we find: the putative homeland area lies within the area of greatest diversity (Ross 2005: 34).

The monolithic nature of the TNG family stands on Map 12.5 in stark contrast to the utter heterogeneity of the large region along the north coast and the small regions on the south coast near the Torres Strait which are occupied by languages belonging to twenty-three apparently separate phylogenetic units. Comparison with Map 12.1 reveals that the northern region is the whole lowland region to the north of the cordillera, minus a small area at its eastern end that is occupied by the Madang subfamily of TNG languages. The small regions near the Torres Strait occupy some of the areas which lie furthest from the southern flank of the cordillera. As these regions were evidently not reached by TNG speakers, one may infer that they represent pre-agricultural languages. That is, their phylogenetic diversity reflects a diversity that characterized the languages of New Guinea at the Pleistocene/Holocene transition around 12,000 BP.

The uneven distribution of phylogenetic groups in New Guinea raises two important questions:

1. Was the Pleistocene diversity of the northern and southern regions characteristic of the whole of New Guinea before the spread of the TNG family?
2. Why did the TNG family spread so far south of the cordillera but hardly at all to its north?

The answer to Question 1 is rather straightforward. As I noted earlier, at the Pleistocene/Holocene transition the Highlands were covered in dry land rain forest. This must have been a very poor foraging environment and would have been too cold for permanent habitation, afflicted by frequent winter frosts. It is probable that agriculture itself brought continuous settlement to the Highlands. Before that time, the cordillera would have effectively been a blank on the language map.

The answer to the second half of Question 2 was also adumbrated earlier. If the shores of the inland sea were the locus of the earliest cultivation of taro and bananas, then they would also have been relatively densely populated and therefore unavailable to the Highlands agriculturists. We know from the distribution of stone pestles and mortars that there was significant early interaction between Sepik-Ramu and Highlands peoples (Swadling and Hide 2005), but the subsequent expansion of the inland sea itself would have wiped out relevant archaeological evidence. Today, the high population density of what was once the inland sea is sustained by the lesser yam (*Dioscorea esculenta*), but its introduction postdates the introduction of taro to the Highlands. The assumption of relatively dense population around the inland sea is thus based on inference rather than direct evidence. The inland sea area, however, is only a small part of the northern region of diversity. A glance at Map 12.7, showing the locations of present-day sago-dependent sedentary foragers (see Section 12.5), tells us that many of these communities are located

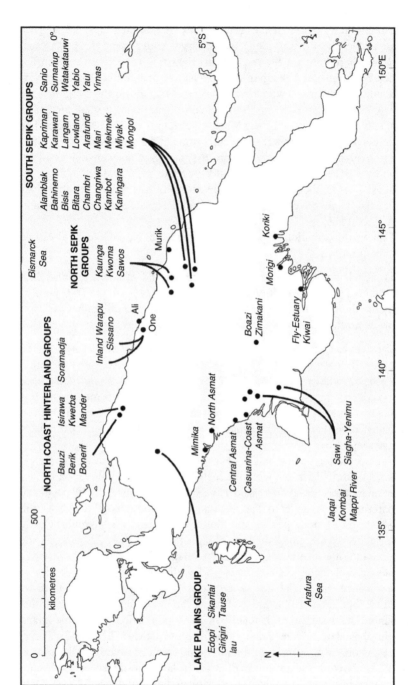

Map 12.7 The hunters and gatherers of New Guinea. (Adapted from Roscoe 2002.)

in the northern region to the west of the former inland sea. That is, the environments they occupy are largely swampy and unsuitable for agriculture. Allen (2005) showed that the Sepik Valley, immediately to the west of the inland sea, is divided into small areas which are suitable for intense agriculture (today based on the lesser yam) and larger swampy areas supporting extensive stands of sago palms. He proposed that earlier attempts to account for the history of the Sepik Valley in terms of large movements of people should be revised in the direction of much smaller movements of people who learned to adapt to the various environments in which they found themselves. Thus, Highland agriculturists seeking new territories in the lowlands to the north of the cordillera could well have finished up as sago-dependent foragers.

There is no evidence known to me that Highland agriculturists did seek new territories to the north of the cordillera, but, assuming that TNG speakers were initially farmers, there is clear evidence that some of their descendants finished up as sago-dependent foragers south of the cordillera. There is probably no single story which will explain why TNG speakers have occupied so much of the southern lowlands, but some significant partial explanations can be given. The most important is that, as Map 12.3 shows, a large portion of southwest New Guinea sank below sea level between 8,000 and 6,000 BP, and has only gradually become accessible to human habitation in the ensuing millennia. If this area displayed Pleistocene phylogenetic diversity before 8,000 BP, those languages have been lost, and their place taken by languages of the Asmat subfamily of TNG, many of whose speakers are today sago-dependent foragers. To the southeast of the area of inundation, on the northern shore of the Torres Strait, are speakers of South Central Papuan and Eastern Trans-Fly languages (Ross 2005: 30), which may be a remainder of a more widespread region of Pleistocene diversity that was neither inundated by the sea nor, because of its distance from the cordillera, occupied by TNG speakers. Further east around the Gulf of Papua, the lowland coastal strip is much narrower and more accessible from the cordillera. According to the map, this strip, which consists of river deltas, is today TNG-speaking, but it is worth noting that the TNG subfamilies include the Kiwai and Eleman groups, which are only tentatively attributable to TNG.

12.5   Are There Foragers in Present-Day Near Oceania?

I remarked in the introduction to this chapter that the conventional negative answer to this question has itself recently been questioned. One's answer is dependent on one's definition of 'hunter-gatherer'.

As I noted earlier, in Period 2 (the late Pleistocene) there was a gradual shift from mobile foraging bands to foraging sedentism (Section 12.2), and variants of foraging sedentism have persisted in various parts of the world without evolving into agriculture (Section 12.3). One such variant is represented by sago-dependent communities in New Guinea. According to Roscoe (2002, 2005) these are the only candidates for the label 'hunter-gather' or 'forager' in Near Oceania, and he argues that because they are completely dependent for starch on wild sago-palm stands and do not till the soil, they are appropriate candidates for the label. This position, however, depends on a two-category division into foragers and agriculturists. If one follows Groube (1989) and Spriggs (1996, 1997) in making a three-way categorization into mobile for-agers, foraging sedentism and farmers, then the sago-dependent communities in New Guinea clearly fall into the second category, practicing what Spriggs calls 'wild-food production'.

These communities, shown in Map 12.3, borrowed from Roscoe (2005), depend on the wild sago palm (*Metroxylon sagu*) for starch and usually con-sume no cultivated foods. Roscoe suggests that there may be up to a hundred such groups in New Guinea. They vary in the amount of sago-tending work that they do: some communities plant and tend the palms, while others just clear the underbrush around wild palms. In all cases, however, starch is collected by washing the pith of the trunk and drying it as sago flour, and Ohtsuka (1985) finds that sago gathering and processing is just as complex technologically as agriculture. The palms, incidentally, also provide leaves for roofing thatch, while the sago grub (*Rhyncosphorus ferringinlus papuanus*) is cooked and is a minor protein source.

By way of placing sago-dependent communities in context, it is worth noting that some sago-dependent communities also have small gardens (Guddemi 1992, Allen 2005), while some agricultural communities rely on sago in times of famine. Thus there is a cline from entirely sago-dependent groups to occasional sago-users. In any case, even intensive agriculturalists in New Guinea traditionally practised some foraging, with differing patterns on the coast and inland. Men hunt birds and animals or go fishing at sea, and women gather seafood on the reef at low tide, trap fish in rivers and collect greens in the forest. Tending large fruit trees (but not necessarily planting them) is also common practice. We can therefore say that sago-dependent communities are at one extreme on a cline of New Guinea traditional societies which more usually have mixed forager/agriculturalist economies.

If we re-examine the regions of phylogenetic diversity (Map 12.5) in the light of Roscoe's map of sago-dependent communities (Map 12.7), clear patterns emerge. Table 12.1 lists the communities named on the map,[6] together with the phylogenetic group to which they belong and any available grammar or dictionary.[7] As Roscoe uses accepted language names for the groups, assigning them to phylogenetic groups is straightforward. The phylogenetic groups are those presented in Ross (2005).[8]

Table 12.1 *Foragers of New Guinea, according to Roscoe (2005)*

Family/language	Subfamily	Grammar	Dictionary
Sepik			
Kaunga (Yelogu)	Ndu	(Laycock 1965)	
Sawos (Malinguat)	Ndu	(Laycock 1965)	
Kwoma (Washkuk)	Nukuma	Kooyers 1974	Bowden 1997
Alamblak	Sepik Hill	Bruce 1984	
Bahinemo	Sepik Hill		
Bisis	Sepik Hill		
Bitara (Berinomo)	Sepik Hill		
Kaningara	Sepik Hill		
Kapriman	Sepik Hill	Sumbuk 1999	
Mari	Sepik Hill		
Sanio (Saniyo-Hiyewe)	Leonhard Schultze	(Lewis 1972a, b)	
Ramu-Lower Sepik			
Chambri	Lower Sepik		
Karawari (Tabriak)	Lower Sepik		
Murik	Lower Sepik	Schmidt 1953	
Yimas	Lower Sepik	Foley 1991	
Kambot (Ap Ma)	Ramu	Wade 1984	
Langam	Ramu		
Mongol	Ramu		
Yaul	Ramu		
Arafundi			
Lowland Arafundi	—		
Yuat			
Changriwa	—		
Mekmek	—		
Miyak	—		
Oceanic Austronesian			
Ali	Schouten		
Sissano	Schouten		
Torricelli			
One	Wapei		
Skou			
Inland Warapu	Skou	Corris 2006	
East Cenderawasih Bay			
Bauzi	—	(Briley 1996)	
Tor			
Berik	—	(Westrum 1976, 1988)	(Westrum et al. 1986)
Bonerif [almost extinct]	—		
Mander [almost extinct]	—		
Isirawa			
Isirawa	—	(Erickson and Pike 1976, Oguri and Cochran 1976, Oguri 1976, 1985)	

Table 12.1 (*cont.*)

Family/language	Subfamily	Grammar	Dictionary
Kwerba			
Kwerba	—	(de Vries and de Vries 1997)	
Lakes Plain			
Girigiri (Kirikiri)	West Tariku		
Edopi	Central Tariku		
Iau	Central Tariku	(Bateman 1986)	
Sikaritai	East Tariku		
Extended West Papuan?			
Tause	—		
Trans New Guinea			
Mimika (Kamoro)	Asmat	Drabbe 1953, Voorhoeve 1980	
North Asmat	Asmat	Voorhoeve 1980	
Causaurina Coast Asmat	Asmat	Voorhoeve 1965, 1980	
Kombai	Awyu-Dumut	de Vries 1993	
Sawi (Sawuy)	Awyu-Dumut		
Siagha-Yenimu	Awyu-Dumut		
Boazi	Marind	Edwards-Fumey 2006	
Jaqai (Yaqai)	Marind		
Mappi River	Marind		
Zimakani	Marind		
Perhaps Trans New Guinea			
Fly Estuary Kiwai	Kiwai	Ray 1932	
Morigi	Kiwai		
Koriki (Purari)	—		
Unknown			
Soramadja	?		

A consequence of Roscoe's use of language names is that he perhaps inflates the number of sago-dependent societies, sometimes naming closely related neighboring groups separately, when the linguistic boundary between them is perhaps not as clear as the nomenclature makes it look. To examine the consequences of this in detail, however, would require data that are not available to me.

The languages are listed in Table 12.1 starting at the eastern end of their extent on the north coast and working anticlockwise around the coast as far as the Gulf of Papua. I have ordered languages belonging to the same local group together. As we would expect in the light of Section 12.5, all the languages on or near the north coast (from the Sepik family in the east to the Extended West Papuan family in the west) belong to families located in the northern region of diversity, and it is quite likely that in general terms they reflect the late

Pleistocene situation: sedentary foragers whose languages display phenomenal phylogenetic diversity. By 'in general terms', I mean that the situation of diversity among sedentary foraging societies probably characterized the late Pleistocene; I assume that there has been an ongoing process of phylogenetic groups splitting and disappearing in the past 12,000 years, and that today's languages cannot tell us anything specific about the languages of the late Pleistocene. This assumption is supported by the fact that three Austronesian languages appear in Table 12.1, their speakers apparently having switched from agriculture in the face of an environment that encouraged dependence on sago.

All the sago-dependent communities south of the cordillera, however, speak TNG or possible TNG languages. As the discussion earlier indicates, those in the west represent communities of TNG speakers who moved down to the new coastline after the sea had receded, adapting their lifestyle to their new environment.

At least some of the listed languages further east around the Gulf of Papua speak languages of doubtful TNG provenance, here labeled 'Perhaps Trans New Guinea'. This means that at the moment the evidence points towards their belonging genealogically to the TNG family, but less convincingly so than for most of the member subfamilies of TNG. It is possible that these language groups will turn out not to belong to the TNG family, in which case they reflect a situation, and perhaps a history, similar to that of the northern region of diversity. It is also possible that they reflect contact between TNG and non-TNG languages. This is a topic in urgent need of research.

12.6   Concluding Thoughts

Whether we count New Guinea's sago-dependent communities as hunter-gatherers or not is a matter of definition. It seems likely, however, that in general terms the languages of the sedentary foragers of the northern region of New Guinea reflect an amazing phylogenetic diversity that was already present at the end of the Pleistocene. The diversity is attributable to the immense time depth of settlement and to the socio-economic features of New Guinea communities. Most New Guinea societies (agricultural as well as forager) were traditionally parochial, i.e. the inhabitants of a village owed no allegiance to anyone outside the village, although they might well be tied to their neighbors by kin networks. The village was also an economically independent unit, with few or no economic relationships to other villages. These, according to Nettle (1999: 72–73), are the conditions in which linguistic diversity flourishes. A concomitant of this kind of socio-economic organization is that the authority structure within the village is a weak gerontocracy, such that there is little or no enforcement of linguistic norms, and languages can change fast.

Whether the few remaining non-TNG groups on the south coast and the questionably TNG groups on the Gulf of Papua also reflect the late Pleistocene situation is a question that has yet to be answered even tentatively.

Although few Papuan languages survive in NW Island Melanesia, it is noteworthy that on the two larger islands with several Papuan languages, namely New Britain and Bougainville, there are signs of considerable pre-Austronesian diversity, in that even among the few survivals we find two phylogenetically unrelated groups on each island. This is hardly conclusive evidence, but it suggests that foraging sedentism may also have been accompanied by extreme phylogenetic diversity in NW Island Melanesia.

If I am right that the diversity of at least the New Guinea northern region languages is attributable to time depth, then I am at least allowing the inference that non-TNG families may be phylogenetically related, but at a time depth too great for us to detect their relationships. As we are looking at diversification which has been going on since before 12,000 BP (!), we would be unlikely to find conventional evidence of relationship. What we might just find, however, is bound morphology. I have found just one piece of such evidence, pointing to a possible relationship between two TNG subfamilies in the putative Proto-TNG homeland area (Chimbu-Wahgi and South Engan) and three non-TNG families in the northern region of diversity (Sepik, Torricelli and Senagi). The proto-language of each group displays a contrast between *-m* 'plural' and *-p* 'dual' (Ross 2005: 48). If this pattern is preserved in two TNG subfamilies and three non-TNG families, then one might infer that it occurred in Proto-TNG and has been lost in most TNG subgroups and perhaps in other non-TNG families.

I would have liked to finish this chapter with some generalizations about the typology of languages in New Guinea's northern region of diversity and in NW Island Melanesia, but I am unable to offer any (see Donohue, Chapter 13). In the case of NW Island Melanesia, relevant research has been done. Dunn et al. (2002) find signs of seemingly *Sprachbund*-like features in the Papuan languages of NW Island Melanesia that have resisted the influence of Austronesian contact, but they are insufficient to allow precise inferences. Terrill (2002) studies one such feature, nominal classification, and finds that it varies from language to language to such a degree that the only inferences she can make are either that it reflects a phylogenetic relationship so far back in time that its signals have disappeared or that it reflects an ancient *Sprachbund*. As for the languages of the sedentary foragers of New Guinea, comparative study of the available grammars and dictionaries listed in Table 12.1 is a project that awaits a researcher, but the descriptive coverage is sparse and patchy.

NOTES

1. For a historical summary and references, see Pawley (2008).
2. This is also about the time that rising sea levels cut off New Guinea's direct land access to Australia, but the relationship between this event and the beginnings of agriculture is indirect: both reflect climate change.
3. However, Denham (2002) argues that taro spread naturally to the Highlands.
4. Map 3 is reproduced from Chappell (2005: 528), with the inland sea added in accordance with a map provided by Swadling and Hide (2005: 290).
5. Several versions of the Trans New Guinea family have appeared in the literature, and their story is told by Pawley (2017: 23–29).The version represented in Map 12.5 is presented in Ross (2005).
6. I have removed one language, Waropen, from Map 7, as its speakers are agriculturists (Mark Donohue, pers. comm.).
7. I list descriptions that are detailed enough for sound typological work, and dictionaries that would allow thorough lexical comparisons. Works in parentheses probably do not meet these criteria. The reader of Carrington's (1996) linguistic bibliography will find a good many entries that I have not mentioned here: many are brief descriptions of certain features of a given language or are anthropological in subject matter.
8. Many of the languages are located in or around the Sepik Valley, for which Foley (2005) provides a detailed reanalysis. The groups identified for this area by Ross (2005) are the same as Foley's. The term 'Extended West Papuan' is marked with a question mark, as its integrity is questionable.

References

Allen, Bryant J. (2005). The place of agricultural intensification in Sepik foothills prehistory. In Andrew Pawley, Robert Attenborough, Jack Golson and Robin Hide (eds.), *Papuan pasts: Cultural, linguistic and biological histories of Papuan-speaking peoples*. Canberra: Pacific Linguistics 572, 585–623.

Barker, Graeme. (2002). Transitions to farming and pastoralism in North Africa. In Peter Bellwood and Colin Renfrew (eds.), *Examining the farming/language dispersal hypothesis*. Cambridge: MacDonald Institute for Archaeological Research, University of Cambridge, 151–162.

Bar-Yosef, Ofer. (2002). The Natufian culture and the early Neolithic: Social and economic trends. In Peter Bellwood and Colin Renfrew (eds.), *Examining the farming/language dispersal hypothesis*. Cambridge: MacDonald Institute for Archaeological Research, University of Cambridge, 113–126.

Bateman, Janet. (1986). *Iau verb morphology*. NUSA: Linguistic Studies of Indonesian and Other Languages in Indonesia 26. Jakarta: Universitas Katolik Indonesia Atma Jaya.

Bellwood, Peter. (1997). Prehistoric cultural explanations for the existence of widespread language families. In Patrick McConvell and Nicholas Evans (eds.), *Archaeology and linguistics: Aboriginal Australia in global perspective*. Melbourne: Oxford University Press,123–134.

(2001). Early agriculturalist population diasporas? Farming, languages and genes. *Annual Review of Anthropology* 30: 181–207.

(2002). Farmers, foragers, languages, genes: The genesis of agricultural societies. In Peter Bellwood and Colin Renfrew (eds.), *Examining the farming/language dispersal hypothesis*. Cambridge: MacDonald Institute for Archaeological Research, University of Cambridge, 17–28.

Bellwood, Peter and Peter Hiscock. (2005). Australia and the Austronesians. In Christopher Scarre (ed.), *The human past*. London: Thames and Hudson, 264–305.

Bellwood, Peter and Colin Renfrew. (eds.). (2002). *Examining the farming/language dispersal hypothesis*. Cambridge: MacDonald Institute for Archaeological Research, University of Cambridge.

Bowden, Ross. (1997). *A dictionary of Kwoma: A Papuan language of north-east New Guinea*. Canberra: Pacific Linguistics C-134.

Briley, David. (1996). Four grammatical marking systems in Bauzi. *Pacific Linguistics* A 85: 1–131.

Bruce, Les. (1984). *The Alamblak language of Papua New Guinea (East Sepik)*. Canberra: Pacific Linguistics C-81.

Carrington, Lois. (1996). *A linguistic bibliography of the New Guinea area*. Canberra: Pacific Linguistics D-90.

Chappell, John. (2005). Geographic changes of coastal lowlands in the Papuan past. In Andrew Pawley, Robert Attenborough, Jack Golson and Robin Hide (eds.), *Papuan pasts: Cultural, linguistic and biological histories of Papuan-speaking peoples*. Canberra: Pacific Linguistics 572, 525–539.

Cohen, Mark Nathan. (2002). The economies of late pre-farming and farming communities and their relation to the problem of dispersals. In Peter Bellwood and Colin Renfrew (eds.), *Examining the farming/language dispersal hypothesis*. Cambridge: MacDonald Institute for Archaeological Research, University of Cambridge, 41–47.

Corris, Miriam. (2006). *A grammar of Barupu: a language of Papua New Guinea*. PhD thesis, University of Sydney.

David, Bruno, Ian J. McNiven, Thomas Richards, Sean P. Connaughton, Matthew Leavesley, Bryce Barker and Cassandra Rowe. (2011). Lapita sites in the Central Province of mainland Papua New Guinea. *World Archaeology* 43: 576–593.

Denham, Tim. (2002). Archaeological evidence for mid-Holocene agriculture in interior New Guinea: A critical review. *Archaeology in Oceania* 38: 159–176.

Drabbe, Peter. (1953). *Spraakkunst van de Kamoro-taal*. The Hague: Martinus Nijhoff.

van Driem, George. (2002). Tibeto-Burman phylogeny and prehistory: languages, material culture and genes. In Peter Bellwood and Colin Renfrew (eds.), *Examining the farming/language dispersal hypothesis*. Cambridge: MacDonald Institute for Archaeological Research, University of Cambridge, 233–249.

Dunn, Michael, Ger Reesink and Angela Terrill. (2002). The East Papuan languages: A preliminary typological appraisal. *Oceanic Linguistics* 41: 28–62.

Edwards-Fumey, Deborah. (2006). *The Verb Subject Prefix in Kuni*. Lizentiatsarbeit, Universität Bern.

Ehret, Christopher. (2002). Language family expansions: Broadening our understandings of cause from an African perspective. In Peter Bellwood and Colin Renfrew (eds.), *Examining the farming/language dispersal hypothesis*. Cambridge: MacDonald Institute for Archaeological Research, University of Cambridge, 163–176.

Erickson, Carol J. and Evelyn G. Pike. (1976). Semantic and grammatical structures in an Isirawa narrative. In Ignatius Suharno and Kenneth L. Pike (eds.), *From Baudi to Indonesian.* Jayapura: Cenderawasih University and Summer Institute of Linguistics, 63–93.

Evans, Benjamin and Mary-Jane Mountain. (2005). Pasin bilong tumbuna: Archaeological evidence for early human activity in the highlands of Papua New Guinea. In Andrew Pawley, Robert Attenborough, Jack Golson and Robin Hide (eds.), *Papuan pasts: Cultural, linguistic and biological histories of Papuan-speaking peoples.* Canberra: Pacific Linguistics 572, 363–386.

Foley, William A. (1991). *The Yimas language of New Guinea.* Stanford, CA: Stanford University Press.

——— (2005). Linguistic prehistory in the Sepik–Ramu basin. In Andrew Pawley, Robert Attenborough, Jack Golson and Robin Hide (eds.), *Papuan pasts: Cultural, linguistic and biological histories of Papuan-speaking peoples.* Canberra: Pacific Linguistics 572, 109–144.

Golson, Jack. (1977). The making of the New Guinea Highlands. In J. H. Winslow (ed.), *The Melanesian environment.* Canberra: Australian National University Press, 45–56.

Greenberg, Joseph H. (1971). The Indo-Pacific hypothesis. In Thomas A. Sebeok (ed.), *Current trends in linguistics,* Vol. 8. The Hague: Mouton, 807–871.

Groube, L. M. (1989). The taming of the rain forests: A model for Late Pleistocene forest exploitation in New Guinea. In David R. Harris and G. C. Hillman (eds.), *Foraging and farming: The evolution of plant exploitation.* London: Unwin Hyman, 292–317.

Guddemi, Phillip. (1992). When horticulturalists are like hunter-gatherers: The Sawiyano of Papua New Guinea. *Ethnology* 31: 303–314.

Harris, David R. (2002). The expansion capacity of early agricultural systems: A comparative perspective on the spread of agriculture. In Peter Bellwood and Colin Renfrew (eds.), *Examining the farming/language dispersal hypothesis.* Cambridge: MacDonald Institute for Archaeological Research, University of Cambridge, 13–34.

Hope, Geoffrey S. and Simon G. Haberle. (2005). The history of the human landscapes of New Guinea. In Andrew Pawley, Robert Attenborough, Jack Golson and Robin Hide (eds.), *Papuan pasts: Cultural, linguistic and biological histories of Papuan-speaking peoples.* Canberra: Pacific Linguistics 572, 541–554.

Hurles, Matthew. (2002). Can the hypothesis of language/agriculture co-dispersal be tested with archaeogenetics? In Peter Bellwood and Colin Renfrew (eds.), *Examining the farming/language dispersal hypothesis.* Cambridge: MacDonald Institute for Archaeological Research, University of Cambridge, 299–309.

Jones, Martin. (2002). Issues of scale and symbiosis: unpicking the agricultural 'package.' In Peter Bellwood and Colin Renfrew (eds.), *Examining the farming/language dispersal hypothesis.* Cambridge: MacDonald Institute for Archaeological Research, University of Cambridge, 369–377.

Klappa, Stefanie. (2006). Sago and the settling of Sahul: How present patterns of plant use may illuminate subsistence prehistory. In *Proceedings of the IVth International Congress of Ethnobotany* (ICEB 2005). Istanbul: Yeditepe University Press.

Kooyers, Orneal. (1974). Washkuk grammar sketch. In Richard Loving (ed.), *Grammatical studies in three languages of Papua New Guinea.* Workpapers in Papua New Guinea Languages 6. Ukarumpa: Summer Institute of Linguistics, 5–74.

Laycock, D. C. (1965). *The Ndu language family (Sepik District, New Guinea).* Canberra: Pacific Linguistics C-1.

LeBlanc, Steven A. (2002). Conflict and language dispersal: Issues and a New World example. In Peter Bellwood and Colin Renfrew (eds.), *Examining the farming/ language dispersal hypothesis*. Cambridge: MacDonald Institute for Archaeological Research, University of Cambridge, 357–365.

Lewis, Ronald K. (1972a). Sanio-Hiowe paragraph structure. *Pacific Linguistics* A 31: 1–9.

Lewis, Sandra C. (1972b). Sanio-Hiowe verb phrases. *Pacific Linguistics* A–31:11–22.

Lilley, Ian. (1999). Too good to be true? Post-Lapita scenarios for language and archaeology in West New Britain–North New Guinea. *Bulletin of the Indo-Pacific Prehistory Association* 18: 25–34.

(2000). Migration and ethnicity in the evolution of Lapita and post-Lapita maritime societies in northwest Melanesia. In Sue O'Connor and Peter Veth (eds.), *East of Wallace's Line: Studies of past and present maritime cultures of the Indo-Pacific region*. Modern Quaternary Research in Southeast Asia 16. Rotterdam: Balkema, 177–195.

Lilley, Ian. (2007). The evolution of Sio pottery: Evidence from three sites in north-eastern Papua New Guinea. In Jim Specht and Val Attenbrow (eds.), *Archaelogical studies of the Middle and Late Holocene, Papua New Guinea*. Records of the Australian Museum: Technical Reports 20. Sydney: Records of the Australian Museum.

Nettle, Daniel. (1999). *Linguistic diversity*. Oxford: Oxford University Press.

Oguri, Hiroko. (1976). Form and meaning in the Isirawa noun phrase. *Irian* 5: 85–103.

(1985). Isirawa clauses. *Pacific Linguistics* A 63: 139–154.

Oguri, Hiroko and Anne M. Cochran. (1976). Complexity in Isirawa verbs. In Ignatius Suharno and Kenneth L. Pike (eds.), *From Baudi to Indonesian*. Jayapura: Cenderawasih University and Summer Institute of Linguistics, 177–191.

Ohtsuka, Ryutaro. (1985). The Oriomo Papuans: Gathering versus horticulture in an ecological context. In V. N. Misra and Peter Bellwood (eds.), *Recent advances in Indo-Pacific prehistory: Proceedings of the international symposium held at Poona, December 19–21, 1978*. New Delhi: Oxford and IBH, 343–348.

Pawley, Andrew. (2005). The chequered career of the Trans New Guinea hypothesis: Recent research and its implications. In Andrew Pawley and Robert Attenborough (eds.), *Biological histories of Papuan-speaking peoples*. Canberra: Pacific Linguistics 572, 67–107.

(2007). Recent research on the historical relationships of the Papuan languages, or, What can linguistics add to the stories of archaeology? In Jonathan Friedlaender (ed.), *Population genetics, linguistics, and culture history in the Southwest Pacific: A synthesis*. New York: Oxford University Press, 36–59.

Pawley, Andrew. (2008). Where and when was Proto Oceanic spoken? Linguistic and archaeological evidence. In Yury A. Lander and Alexander K. Ogoblin (eds.), *Language and text in the Austronesian world: Studies in honour of Ülo Sirk*. Studies in Austronesian Linguistics 06. Munich: Lincom Europa, 47–71.

Pawley, Andrew, Robert Attenborough, Jack Golson and Robin Hide (eds.) (2005). *Papuan pasts: Cultural, linguistic and biological histories of Papuan-speaking peoples*. Canberra: Pacific Linguistics 572.

Pawley, Andrew and Harald Hammarström (eds.) (2017). The Trans New Guinea family. In Bill Palmer (ed.), *The languages and linguistics of the New Guinea area: A comprehensive guide*. The World of Linguistics 4. Berlin: De Gruyter Mouton, 21–195.

Ray, Sidney H. (1932). *A grammar of the Kiwai language, Fly Delta, Papua, with a Kiwai vocabulary by E. Baxter Riley*. Port Moresby: E. G. Baker, Government Printer.

Renfrew, Colin. (1991). Before Babel: Speculations on the origins of linguistic diversity. *Cambridge Archaeological Journal* 1: 3–23.

(1992). World languages and human dispersals: A minimalist view. In John A. Hall and Ian C. Jarvie (eds.), *Transition to modernity*. Cambridge: Cambridge University Press, 11–68.

(2000). At the edge of knowability: Towards a prehistory of languages. *Cambridge Archaeological Journal* 10: 7–34.

(2002). 'The emerging synthesis': The archaeogenetics of farming/language dispersals and other spread zones. In Peter Bellwood and Colin Renfrew (eds.), *Examining the farming/language dispersal hypothesis*. Cambridge: MacDonald Institute for Archaeological Research, University of Cambridge, 3–16.

Roscoe, Paul. (2002). The hunters and gatherers of New Guinea. *Current Anthropology* 43: 153–162.

(2005). Foraging, ethnographic analogy, and Papuan pasts: Contemporary models for the Sepik–Ramu past. In Andrew Pawley, Robert Attenborough, Jack Golson and Robin Hide (eds.), *Papuan pasts: Cultural, linguistic and biological histories of Papuan-speaking peoples*. Canberra: Pacific Linguistics 572, 555–584.

Rosman, Abraham and Paula J. Rubel. (1989). Stalking the wild pig: Hunting and horticulture in New Guinea. In Susan Kent (ed.), *Farmers as hunters: The implications of sedentism*. Cambridge: Cambridge University Press, 27–36.

Ross, Malcolm. (1988). *Proto Oceanic and the Austronesian languages of western Melanesia*. Canberra: Pacific Linguistics.

(2001). Is there an East Papuan phylum? Evidence from pronouns. In Andrew Pawley, Malcolm Ross and Darrell Tryon (eds.), *The boy from Bundaberg: Studies in Melanesian linguistics in honor of Tom Dutton*. Canberra: Pacific Linguistics, 301–321.

(2005). Pronouns as a preliminary diagnostic for grouping Papuan languages. In Andrew Pawley, Robert Attenborough, Jack Golson and Robin Hide (eds.), *Papuan pasts: Cultural, linguistic and biological histories of Papuan-speaking peoples*. Canberra: Pacific Linguistics 572, 15–66.

Schmidt, Joseph. (1953). *Vokabular und Grammatik der Murik-Sprache in Nordost-Neuguinea*. Micro-Bibliotheca Anthropos 3.

Sheppard, Peter J. and Richard Walter. (2006). A revised model of Solomon Islands culture history. *Journal of the Polynesian Society* 115: 47–76.

Sillitoe, Paul. (2002). Always been farmer–foragers? Hunting and gathering in the Papua New Guinea Highlands. *Anthropological Forum* 12: 45–76.

Skelly, Robert, Bruno David, Fiona Petchey and Matthew Leavesley. (2014). Tracking ancient beach-lines inland: 2600-year-old dentate-stamped ceramics at Hopo, Vailala River region, Papua New Guinea. *Antiquity* 88: 470–487.

Spriggs, Matthew. (1996). Early agriculture and what went before in Island Melanesia: continuity or intrusion. In David R. Harris (ed.), *The origins and spread of agriculture and pastoralism in Eurasia*. London: University College London Press, 524–537.

(1997). *The Island Melanesians*. Oxford: Blackwell.

Suharno, Ignatius and Kenneth L. Pike (eds.). (1976). *From Baudi to Indonesian.* Jayapura: Cenderawasih University and Summer Institute of Linguistics.

Sumbuk, Kenneth Memson. (1999). *Morphosyntax of Sare.* PhD thesis, University of Waikato, New Zealand.

Swadling, Pamela and Robin Hide. (2005). Changing landscape and social interaction: looking at agricultural history from a Sepik–Ramu perspective. In Andrew Pawley, Robert Attenborough, Jack Golson and Robin Hide (eds.), *Papuan pasts: Cultural, linguistic and biological histories of Papuan-speaking peoples.* Canberra: Pacific Linguistics 572, 289–327.

Terrill, Angela. (2002). Systems of nominal classification in East Papuan languages. *Oceanic Linguistics* 41: 63–88.

Voorhoeve, C. L. (1965). *The Flamingo Bay dialect of the Asmat language.* Verhandelingen van het Koninklijk Instituut voor Taal-, Land-en Volkenkunde 46. Leiden: KITLV Press.

(1980). *The Asmat languages of Irian Jaya.* Canberra: Pacific Linguistics B-64.

(1987). Worming one's way through New Guinea: The chase of the peripatetic pronouns. In Donald C. Laycock and Werner Winter (eds.), *A world of language: Papers presented to Professor S. A. Wurm on his 65th birthday.* Canberra: Pacific Linguistics C-100, 709–727.

de Vries, James and Sandra de Vries. (1997). An overview of Kwerba verb morphology. *Pacific Linguistics* A 87: 1–35.

de Vries, Lourens. (1993). *Forms and functions in Kombai, an Awyu language of Irian Jaya.* Canberra: Pacific Linguistics B-108.

Wade, Martha L. (1984). *Some stratificational insights concerning Botin (Kambot), a Papuan language.* MA thesis, University of Texas at Arlington.

Westrum, Peter N. (1976). Preliminary analysis of Berik clause and clause root types. In Ignatius Suharno and Kenneth L. Pike (eds.), *From Baudi to Indonesian.* Jayapura: Cenderawasih University and Summer Institute of Linguistics, 145–152.

(1988). A grammatical sketch of Berik. *Irian* 16: 133–181.

Westrum, Peter N., Susan Westrum, Paulus Sowenso and Deetje Songkilawan. (1986). *Ol unggwanfer Berik olem/Perbendaharaan kata bahasa Berik/Berik vocabulary.* Publikasi khusus bahasa-bahasa daerah B, 1. Jayapura: Universitas Cenderawasih and Summer Institute of Linguistics.

13   Language, Locality and Lifestyle in New Guinea

Mark Donohue

13.1   Introduction

This chapter is intended to problematize the label 'hunter-gatherer', and to point out that, in the New Guinea area at least, we *can* identify linguistic differences between hunter-gatherer societies and their more agriculturally oriented neighbours. This is not to say that there is a hunter-gatherer 'linguistic type', merely to claim that there are differences between hunter-gatherer populations and their agriculturalist neighbours in this region.

Rather than presenting a detailed examination of the literature, or even an overview of 'hunter-gatherer' languages and societies in New Guinea (see Chapter 12 by Ross, this volume, drawing on Roscoe 2002), I shall examine three case studies which examine the contrast between hunter-gatherers and agriculturists: first, the case of neighbouring related languages with different lifestyle profiles, one society being one that can be characterized as 'hunter-gatherer' and one not, and second the case of unrelated languages in a similar area and with similar lifestyles one 'hunter-gatherer' and one not. The final case study is of a highland group that retains a foraging lifestyle that was common during the last ice age, but which has largely been replaced with intensive agricultural practices In short, I will, briefly, check for typological similarities and links between lifestyle and language, through the connecting factor of locality.

The following geographic terms will be used: **New Guinea**: the island of that name, abbreviated to NG; **Papua**: the western half of NG, previously (variously) known as Irian Jaya, West Nieuw Guinea, Dutch New Guinea, and sometimes (incorrectly) West Papua (this region is currently administered by Indonesia); **Papua New Guinea**: the eastern half of NG, an independent nation since 1975; **highlands**: the central cordillera running across the centre of the island from east to west; **South coast**: everything south of the highlands; **Mamberamo, Sepik, Digul**: riverine areas shown on Map 13.1.

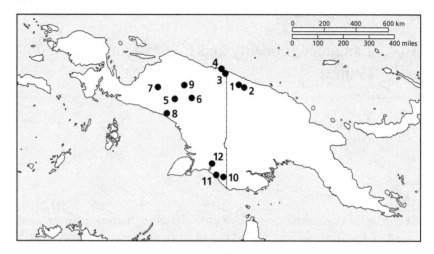

Map 13.1 New Guinea and the languages and areas referred to in the text.
1: One; 2: Olo; 3: Skou; 4: Tobati; 5: Damal; 6: Lani; 7: Auye; 8: Kamoro; 9:
Doutai, Airo; 10: Kanum; 11: Morori; 12: Marind.

13.2   New Guinea

The area known as 'New Guinea' is located just south of the equator, on the
edge of several geographic zones: arguably the very edge of Asia, or the southwestern fringe of the Pacific. It was, until relatively recently (approximately
8,000 years ago) the northern edge of the Sahul continent that is now split
between New Guinea and Australia. It is, in short, difficult to characterize in
terms of better-known larger 'areas'; the most accurate characterization is that
it forms an area, or areas, of its own. It is not an exceptionally large island: the
area (and shape) is approximately similar to a slice from Sicily to Denmark,
including Italy, Austria, Switzerland and Germany.[1] On the other hand, it is
geographically *incredibly* diverse, with some of the most rugged mountain
terrain, and most impenetrable lowland swamp, found anywhere on the planet.
By all accounts New Guinea is home to the most linguistically diverse population of people on the planet, both in terms of number of languages (there are
more than 1,000) and number of genetic entities (thought to be somewhere
between 15 and 50); none of these genealogical families have relatives outside
the New Guinea area.

  The division that has most concerned linguists is that between the
Austronesians, a seafaring culture that arrived in the area from the west at
most 3,800 years ago; and the *Papuans*, a cover term for a diverse range of
peoples speaking not necessarily related languages; 'Papuan' can best be
thought of as shorthand for 'non-Austronesian (but in the vicinity of New

Guinea [and not from Australia])'. Phenotypically there is great diversity in peoples, and along the coast the Austronesians have, in most cases, been assimilated to the Papuan 'type', indicating a long period of contact. The cultural conservatism typical of Melanesian languages is sometimes confused by many recent social movements.

13.2.1   Locality

The different geographic zones of New Guinea have a major impact on the lifestyles of the majority of people living in them. The *Highlands* see human habitation up to 4,500 m, and historically even higher. The inhabited parts of the highlands are mostly large open valleys, under intense agriculture, with forested mountaintops. There are some exceptions; the Star Mountains have small, high separate valleys, and the Carstensz highlands are a series of connected high plateaux used as hunting grounds, with lower (±2,500 m) valleys. The *coastal* strip contains both Austronesian and Papuan populations, though there is little evidence of a settled Papuan presence before the coming of the Austronesians (coastal areas have been in use for at least 20,000 years, but only in a foraging sense, with no evidence of permanent settlements or specialized utilization). The coastal societies typically show more hierarchical social organization than in the interior of NG. A *riverine* area, the Sepik basin, is the only river system that really qualifies as a distinct 'zone' extending any distance inland; otherwise river populations tend not to utilize the river as a trade resource, and typically lived away from the banks. Other non-coastal populations can be termed *'bush'* or *'interior'* peoples, and they are best characterized socially as not participating in the long-distance trade that characterizes coastal populations, and not (or only peripherally) trading with highland communities. The *islands* both to the west and the east of the mainland of NG show special instances of 'coastal' populations in most cases, with even the more inland populations showing substantial differences from the highland or interior populations on the mainland.[2]

13.2.2   Lifestyle

Most NG groups cultivate some crops, either as agriculture or as domiculture; in the lowlands, the crop of choice is sago, a palm tree which takes six to eight years to reach maturity, but which requires only irregular maintenance during that time. This, plus the low calorie yield that results, means that high population densities are impossible in most areas. In the highlands the main crop is sweet potatoes, which require drier soil for successful cultivation, and which are labor-intensive, but which yield a much greater number of calories per hectare cultivated. Across NG people eat taro, if it is available, as it can grow in wet soil which is ubiquitous, either naturally or through modification of the landscape to extend swamps (e.g., Denham et al. 2003). Animal husbandry is widely practiced in both the highlands and the coastal zones; the bush areas have less intensive animal husbandry, and nowhere is full-scale pastoralism the norm, even in those few savanna areas in the south that would permit it.

The question of hunter-gatherer lifestyles in New Guinea is contentious. While Roscoe (2002) presents a recent overview of the islands, there are many assertions in that article that could, and should, be contested. Other relevant literature includes Bailey et al. (1989), Barrau (1959), Etkin (1994), Hames (1983), Headland (1987), Headland and Bailey (1991), Jenkins and Milton (1993), Klappa (2006), Morren (1977), Ohtsuka (1983), Spriggs (1993), Stahl (1989), Swadling and Hide (2006), Ulijaszek and Poraituk (1993), Watson (1965) and Yen (1974, 1991).[3]

13.2.3   Language

The linguistic diversity of the region is overwhelmingly concentrated in north-central New Guinea, and (to a much lesser extent) in the far south; most highland areas appear to have (relatively) recently seen the loss of a lot of diversity in the center and east; considerable population movement from the highlands into the south has similarly reduced earlier diversity.

13.3   North-Central New Guinea

I shall present two brief case studies, one involving two related languages, One and Olo, and one involving two languages in a heavy contact situation, Skou and Tobati. Both of these pairs contain one group that can be considered to be more of a 'hunter-gatherer' population than the other, despite living in adjacent territories, and following near-identical material cultures.

13.3.1   One and Olo

Both One and Olo are Torricelli languages, with Olo being the immediate eastern neighbour of One, which is itself the westernmost Torricelli language. My sources for Olo are McGregor and McGregor (1982); Staley (1994, 1995, 1996, nd.) and my own field notes. For One, I refer to Crowther (2001), Donohue (2000, 2006), Donohue and Crowther (2005), Laycock (1975a), Sikale et al. (2002), and unpublished field notes taken by Crowther or Donohue.

13.3.2   One

One is the westernmost Torricelli language, spoken in the eastern Bewani Mountains. This area has the highest rainfall in northern NG (averaging 5,500 mm per year), the lowest life expectancy (42 years for men, and 38 years for women) and the highest infant mortality rate (±40%, based on a village survey). Dense primary rainforest covers the whole area, except for the riverbeds and scree slopes on the highest mountains (Mt. Tiw: 2,000 m). My experience is peculiar to the village of Molmo, located in the Pibi Valley, and its outstations. This valley is in the center of the One range, and while details do not generalize to every One village, Molmo is not atypical for the small settlements of the region.

Settlement   Settlement patterns are such that all adults own several parcels of land in the valley; houses contain nuclear families; and houses can be occupied for as little as one year before a family moves on to a new location and builds a new house. Aggregations of houses do not necessarily carry over from one settlement area to another, though there are only a few cases of families living completely alone, mostly involving multiple wives.

Plant Consumption   All families maintain a number of inherited sago swamps, though often these are neglected for years at a time; such neglect can lead to other village members disputing the custodianship of the land, and acquiring it. Taro is planted, but not regularly weeded or tended; attempts to stop wild pigs rampaging are half-hearted at best; and plantings are not maintained from one year to another. Green vegetables (*tulip, aibika*) are gathered from the wild; they are not planted or tended, but are found scattered in the bush.

Meat Consumption   Meat is not frequently consumed in any form, not due to lack of desire, but because the region is lacking in plentiful in animal species. All meat sources are eaten when available; even small (±20 cm) snakes are eaten when caught, as well as frogs, beetles, grubs, various rats and land crabs (though pig, wallaby, fish, cassowary, crocodile and couscous are the preferred meats). No animal husbandry is practiced, beyond the keeping of immature cassowaries as pets.[4] Male hunting is treated as an activity with communal rewards; any successful hunt will be subject to claims based on (in approximately decreasing order of validity): kin relationship; marriage relationship; possible influence of the recipient in the future; help in carrying the animal back to the village or prior debt; ownership of land on which the animal was shot; and claims of previously wounding the animal (for large animals such as pigs and cassowaries, which are frequently wounded days before their final death).

Female hunting is treated as a mainly nuclear family-oriented activity; the only successful prosecuted claims on such animals that I am aware of have been based on the claimant having an immediate kin relationship with the successful hunter, and/or assistance rendered on the trip on which the food was acquired.

All of these features are common in the north-coast lowlands, but are somewhat extreme in the poor soil and rugged hills of the eastern Bewani Mountains.

13.3.3   Olo

Olo is a large language, spoken in a number of varieties by more than 10,000 people immediately east of One, but in a comparative rain shadow, so the land is dry enough to support sweet potato; this crop, with its much greater calorie yield, results in a *much* higher population density, and a wider spread of that population. As a result of this population, land ownership is under more pressure, and relationships both between groups and between a group and its land is much more localized. Limited animal husbandry is practised, and settlements are more permanent and larger than One ones.

Plant Consumption   All families maintain a number of sago swamps, together with sweet potato and vegetable gardens; vegetable surpluses are frequent, and are sold in local towns such as Lumi and Yangguganok.

Meat Consumption   As mentioned earlier, limited animal husbandry is practiced. This combined with the tighter local social relations, means that there is a steadier supply of animal protein into most people's diet. Both hunted meat and kept animals are frequently consumed, though reptiles and amphibians are not favoured, and hunting is an activity with communal rewards, again a result of the tighter local relationships.

13.3.4   Summary

The preceding sections have demonstrated that One culture is much more a hunter-gather culture than is Olo, despite the two languages being relatively closely related. Some examples of lexical correspondences between the two languages are shown in Table 13.1; there are of course many words which do not show such close correspondences, but these items indicate that the shared Torricelli heritage of One and Olo is substantial.

The pronominal prefixes of the two languages are shown in Table 13.2; as can be seen, the first person forms match very closely, while the second and

Table 13.1 *Sample lexical correspondences*

	One	Olo
'dog.SG'	pala	pele
'fire'	weila ('hot')	weli
'garden'	mouli	liom
'moon'	anina	anene
'tooth'	nala	nelpe
'water'	fola	tepel

Table 13.2 *Pronominal prefixes in One and Olo compared*

One (no gender)				Olo			
	Sg	du	Pl		sg	du	pl
1	k-	f-	m-	1	k-	w-	m-
2	y- / w-	p-	p-	2	Ø-	y-	y-
3m	y- / w-	n-	n-	3 m	l-	t-	p-
3f				3f	n-	m-	p-

third person forms in One can be derived from the Olo ones by assuming a loss of the dual: plural and gender contrasts, and an anticlockwise movement of the retained pronominal forms, most likely initiated by a politeness shift causing the second person plural *y-* to be used with singular reference; thus, 2PL -> 2SG; 3PL -> 2PL; and finally 3SG -> 3PL. The *w-* can be reconstructed to an earlier stage of Torricelli as a 3SG prefix, but is not reflected in Olo, while in One the *y-* and *w-* have generalized as 2/3SG prefixes, and become lexically specified.

A large number of other similarities hold between the languages: they both show SVO order, a feature of the Torricelli languages and one that is highly unusual in New Guinea; they both show the remnants of an old classification system (more completely attested in related languages to the east such as Arapesh), marked by suffix on the a noun and on some adjectives (and, in the more conservative Olo, on numerals as well); they both show a single series of stops at bilabial, alveolar and velar places, and they both show agreement on the verb by monoconsonantal nominative prefix (which is, however, an areal feature found across a number of languages along the north coast of New Guinea and to its west).

There are, however, a large number of significant differences, some of which are shown in Table 13.3.

Table 13.3 *Typological differences between One and Olo*

One	Olo
N and modifier unordered in NP	N Modifier order in NP
limited, optional number concord in the NP	Obligatory number/gender concord in the NP
S and PRED unordered in nonverbal clauses	S PRED order in nonverbal clauses
no velar nasal	(non-initial) velar nasal
Only one phonemic liquid	Two phonemic liquids
Stress contrastive on verbs only	Stress not contrastive

Table 13.4 *Typological features of One and the north-central New Guinea area*

One linguistic feature	Other languages in NCNG
N, Modifier order?	N Modifier order
Concord in the NP?	(not generally)
Order in nonverbal clauses?	S PRED
Velar nasal?	No velar nasal
Liquids?	Two liquids
Stress/tone?	Stress/tone contrastive

Can any of One's features be ascribed to outside contact? To answer these questions, we must know what the normal feature settings for languages in the area of New Guinea are? Table 13.4 addresses the features shown in Table 13.3 from an areal perspective; *italics* indicate a setting that is normal for this area regardless of linguistic affiliation, and so can be considered to be areal.

Some of the features that characterize One, as opposed to Olo, are typical in the NCNG area, but many, including the more unusual ones, are not. The provenance of these features is thus not easily explained, either through genetic inheritance or through appeal to areal influence.

13.3.5   Skou and Tobati

Unlike One and Olo, Skou and Tobati are not related languages: Skou is the westernmost language of the Greater Skou family, and its speakers have a relatively shallow history of settlement on the coast, while Tobati is the easternmost member of the Humboldt Bay subgroup of Oceanic, and as such is a member of the far-flung Austronesian family. While this family is not indigenous to New Guinea, all the evidence suggests that the ancestors of the Tobati people have been in occupation of the Humboldt Bay area for a much greater period than the Skou people have been their coastal neighbours. The languages are immediate neighbors, and frequent marriage partners (sources used for these languages are: Donohue [2002a, 2002b, 2002c, 2003, 2005, 2006, 2007, 2008], Cowan 1952a, 1952b; Galis 1955; Laycock 1975b; Purba et al. 2003; Ross 1980, 1988; Thomas [1941/1942]; Voorhoeve 1971).

Settlement   Both Skou and Tobati are coastal settlements, Tobati inside Humboldt Bay, Skou just to the east of the bay. There is moderate rainfall, and predominantly sandy soil except in Entrop, the traditional sago grounds for the Tobati. Housing is by nuclear family, though houses are built and owned by entire clans; settlements are fixed. In terms of land ownership we can see differences: in Tobati: land is owned by the clan, while in Skou land is owned by patrilines within clans.

Plant Consumption   Taro and various wet-earth tubers are planted on the edges of villages in Skou, but these plantings are not maintained against wild pigs; wild tubers are gathered from hill-tops, but because these are dry-earth tubers they're not favoured. Coconuts and pandanus are collected and eaten, especially coconuts. By contrast, Tobati and Enggros did not cultivate tubers, but trade for them with both Skou and other traditionally bush people such as the Sentani.[5] Green vegetables (*tulip, aibika*) are gathered from the wild by Skou people; they are not planted or tended, but are found scattered in the bush. Tobati and Enggros people traditionally cultivated leafy vegetables by the side of their sago swamps.

Meat Consumption   Skou people fish in season, and also have traditionally hunted in the forest to their villages' south; hunted meat is mostly kept within the families of the hunting group, unless someone can talk them out of it. Tobati/Enggros people fish year-long, and occasionally traded for bush meat from their neighbours before being caught up in urbanization.

13.3.6 Summary

Skou is much more accurately characterized as being a hunter-gather culture than is Tobati. When we examine linguistic characteristics of the two languages, we can sort the data into shared characteristics, and points of difference. These are summarized in Tables 13.5–13.7.

Many of the features that identify Skou can be explained by reference to inheritance from its Proto Western Skou ancestor, or areality, in that it is a language of north-central New Guinea.

The absence of a velar nasal is clearly expected in Skou; both the area in which Skou is found, and the family to which it belongs, lack phonemic velar

Table 13.5 *Linguistic features that are shared between Skou and Tobati*

Feature	Areal?
Nominative agreement prefixes on verbs	Yes
Few voicing contrasts	Yes
No velar nasal or voiced velar stop	Yes

Table 13.6 *Linguistic features that differentiate between Skou and Tobati*

Skou	Tobati
SOV order	OSV order
Remnants of an old classification system, marked by prefix	No classification
Few fricatives	Many fricatives
(Optional) ergative case	No case
Contrastive tone	No contrastive tone or stress
Relic object agreement ablaut	Productive object agreement suffixes

Table 13.7 *Features of Skou in an areal and genealogical perspective*

	Other languages in NCNG	Other Western Skou languages
Clausal order?	SOV	SOV
Classification	*(not generally)*	No
Ergative case	*(not generally)*	*(not generally)*
Fricatives?	(inconclusive)	(inconclusive)
Velar nasal?	*No velar nasal*	*No velar nasal*
Liquids?	Two liquids	One liquid
Stress/tone?	*Stress /tone contrastive*	*Stress /tone contrastive*

Table 13.8 *Typological differences between Damal and its neighbouring languages*

	Word order	V agr.	NP case?	Tone?	Vowels?	Nasal C	Nasal V
Damal	APV/SV	p-V-a V-p-a	erg, abs	tone	5	ŋ	±nasal
Lani	APV/SV	x-p-V-a	erg	(tone)	5, 7	m n	—
Auye	APV/SV	p-V-a	erg	tone	5	m n	—
Kamoro	APV/SV	V-a-p	—	(tone)	5	—	—
Doutai	APV/SV	V	erg	tone	5+2	—	—

Table 13.9 *Free pronouns in Auye, Damal and Lani compared*

	Auye		Damal		Lani		Ross's TNG	
	sg	Pl	sg	pl	sg	pl	sg	pl
1	anii	inii	ã	(j)enoŋ	an	nit	*na	*ni
2	aa	ikii	ã	enoŋ	kat	kit	*ga	*ki
3	waa	okoo	ã	nuŋ	at	it	*[y]a	*i

	Auye		Damal		Lani		Pawley's TNG	
	sg	Pl	sg	pl	sg	pl	sg	nsg
1	-a	-e	-õɓo	-õɓo	-i	-o	-in	-uL / -un
2	-e	-ea	-te	-oŋo	-in	-ot	-an	-iL / –
3	-i / -a	-ea	-ke	-ke	-e	-(w)a	–	–

Note: The two forms in the last columns on the bottom row represent different dual and plural forms; there are no reconstructed third-person forms.

nasals. While Proto-Oceanic, a language ancestral to Tobati, did have a velar nasal, and while etyma reflecting these velar nasals are not uncommon in Oceanic languages, Tobati has changed away from this conservative model.

13.3.7   Damal and the Western Highlands

Damal is the language of approximately 15,000 people living in seven southern and two northern valleys encircling the Kemabu plateau. To the south the valleys drop off to the swampy lowlands that are inhabited by the Kamoro people, and which quickly fade into the Arafura sea. The northern, western and eastern borders of the Damal range consist of highland valleys and peaks ranging from 1,000 m to 4,000 m above sea level; the Kemabu plateau in the middle lies between 4,000 m and 4,500 m above sea level, with peaks and glaciation above 4,800 m. The highland plateau are spread out over several hundred square kilometers and are unsuitable for cultivation; they are, however, used for hunting, with parties travelling for up to 10 days through the area, camping in rock shelters and hunting the small rats and marsupials that can be found there.

While most, if not all, reports of hunter-gatherer societies in New Guinea describe sago-cultivators of the lowlands, Damal at least should be considered at being a hunter-gatherer society, despite being a highland society which practises tuber cultivation. The Damal (also known as Amungme, Uhunduni, Enggipiloe) do plant and consume taro, but not intensively; further, they do not regularly construct fences to protect their gardens from wild pigs and other animals. While most families will keep one or two pigs at any one time, these animals are almost invariably consumed as part of ceremonial feasts (such as the *wigogo*), and do not constitute a serious supplement to the meat that is obtained through hunting. This lifestyle is in sharp contrast to that of other highland groups of the area, which tend to be sweet-potato cultivators and which keep fenced-in domestic pigs. The contrast is most obvious in the Ilaga Valley in the north-east of the Damal range, where Lani speakers from the east have been encroaching in historical times, with a more agricultural lifestyle and widespread animal husbandry. While the Lani, the westernmost Dani group, are a distinctly highlands population, the Damal enjoy trade with the Kamoro lowlanders to their south to a degree not found with more 'purely' highland cultures. Further, while the Dani peoples settle in different and distinct separate valley populations, typically showing linguistic differentiation whenever a significant range or ridge is crossed, the Damal are much more linguistically uniform despite covering a similar expanse. This is due to the ongoing practice of hunting on the high plateau, and the social acceptance and frequency of the *hai*, by which an individual receives a calling to follow the spirit world (for spiritual or material benefits, or both), and can wander widely within (and, since the Dutch colonial presence began to be felt in the area and widespread warfare largely died down, without) the nine valleys and their uplands that constitute Damal territory.

In many respects Damal shows the typological profile typical of a non-coastal language in New Guinea, in having agreement for two arguments on the verb, lexical tone and an ergative case, but it differs in terms of the placement of the agreement markers, and in terms of phonological traits such as the treatment of nasalization and the presence of a marked absolutive case.

Unlike most of the languages in at least the central and eastern highlands, Damal cannot be considered to be a Trans New Guinea language. The only lexical item that can be related to Pawley's (1999) reconstructions for Trans New Guinea is mõ 'taro', which transparently resembles the reconstruction *mV 'taro'. Examining the free pronouns in Damal and nearby languages, we can see that while Lani, a Dani family language spoken immediately east of Damal, transparently reflects all of Ross' (2005) reconstructions, and while Auye, a Wissel Lakes languages found to the north-west, has a number of good candidates for cognacy, none of the Damal pronouns (which are tonally distinct) are plausible reflexes of the Proto Trans New Guinea forms. Examining the reconstructions for bound subject suffixes we can see that there is some cognacy in Lani, but none at all in Auye or Damal.[6]

As mentioned earlier, the Lani share a range with the Damal, both being found in the Ilaga Valley and with the recent appearance of Lani in the Beoga Valley as well. Comparing these two languages for a range of features, we arrive at Table 13.10.

Table 13.10 *Damal and Lani compared*

	Damal	Lani	Comments
1. Stops	p ɓ t ɗ dʒ k kʷ	p t kʷ q	Damal patterns with the languages to its west
2. Fricatives	—	—	
3. Sonorants	l	l	
4. Nasal vowels?	All 5	None	Damal shows complexity
5. Syllable pitches	High, low, fall	High, fall	Damal shows complexity
6. Lexical clusters	None	NC	Damal is simpler
7. Core case	Ergative, absolutive	Ergative	Damal shows complexity
8. Oblique case	Locative	Locative, ablative, oblique	Damal is simpler
9. Agreement	Suffix S, A and P	Prefixal P, suffixal S, A	
10. Classification	None	None	
11. Word order	S O obl V	S O obl V	
12. Valency change	None	None	

As can be seen in the preceding tables, Damal differs from its nearest neighbour in many phonological ways, but is less distinctive morphosyntactically, except in the realm of case marking.

13.4   Summary: The hunter-Gatherer Influence on Linguistic Type

Can we generalize across the case studies presented here? The patterns observed for differences between agriculturalists and hunter-gatherers in the three New Guinea studies are shown in Table 13.11, where those patterns cannot be attributed to areal or inherited norms. Thus, for instance, although Skou has suffixal P agreement relics, this is normal in north-central New Guinea, and so has not been counted here. Similarly, Damal has only one liquid phoneme, but this is normal for the western highlands area in which it is spoken. The table also includes notes from cases in the Lakes Plains to the north-west of the central cordillera and the Wasur region in the far south; there are undoubtedly many more areas of contact that could be examined (see Roscoe 2002 for a recent assessment of hunter-gatherer groups in New Guinea).[7]

It is clear that the only traits that distinguish hunter-gatherer populations from agriculturalist neighbours are the absence or reduction of number concord in the NP, and the existence of a small fricative system. The fact that the first of these traits is a negative trait reduces its value dramatically, but recall that the only features listed in Table 13.11 are those for which a neighbouring agriculturalist group has a different setting; thus, while there is no NP concord in Damal, there is (limited) concord in neighbouring Lani. The fact that the

Table 13.11 *Distinguishing features compared across different hunter-gatherer populations*

		Hunter-gatherers	Language(s)	... but not
1.	Configurationality	Non-configurational NP	One	Skou, Damal, Airo, Kanum
		Non-configurational IP	Kanum	One, Skou, Damal, Airo
2.	Number concord	Less	One, Damal	—
3.	Liquids	Only one	One	Skou
4.	Suprasegmentals	Complex	One, Skou, Damal, Airo	Kanum
5.	Fricatives	Few (2 or less)	One, Skou, Kanum	—
6.	Case marking	Ergative	Skou, Kanum	One
7.	P agreement	Suffixal	Damal	(Airo), Kanum
8.	Nasal C	Few	Damal	One
9.	Nasal V	Present	Skou, Damal	One, (Airo), Kanum
		Absent	–	

hunter-gatherer groups in the mini-survey here all show small fricative systems is unlikely to be significant in absolute terms: the average number of fricatives present in a non-Austronesian language of New Guinea is 2.3 per language, so the fact that the hunter-gatherer groups show two or fewer fricatives is not particularly striking, apart from the fact that, as mentioned earlier, these features are ones that distinguish the hunter-gatherer group from its neighbours. While Skou, with two fricatives (f h) is not unusual (apart from the lack of a /s/), the more agricultural neighbours speak languages with between three and six fricative phonemes; similarly, Kanum has no contrastive fricatives, while Marind has five (f v s z fi).[8] There are, in short, no linguistic features in the survey here that show consistent settings one way or another for agriculturalists or for hunter-gatherers. This does not mean that there are no linguistic correlates of the hunter-gatherer lifestyle.

13.5   Conclusion: The Hunter-Gatherer Contrast

From the examination of these test cases we have seen that there is not a consistent linguistic relationship between lifestyle and locality. While there is no 'hunter-gatherer' linguistic type, at least not in the languages of New Guinea, we CAN consistently identify differences between more hunter-gatherer type populations and more agricultural populations, albeit not consistent differences. The character of these differences is not the same for all areas; that is to say, the 'directionality' of difference is not consistent across different areas. The commonality we can claim for hunter-gatherers lies only in the fact that they show at least one easily identified linguistic difference with any agriculturalist neighbours that they have. There are numerous complexities involved in determining these differences; local areal trends need to be investigated, and ideas about the typology of the languages and their relatives must be clear before micro-variation between languages spoken by people with different lifestyles within these areas can be accurately interpreted.

In some cases these differences might be described as being due to contact or substratal influences, but the fact that there are typological differences between 'hunter-gatherers' and their more agricultural neighbours implies that some of the differences observed should be ascribed to a lifestyle difference. It might be that some of the hunter-gatherer populations represent a linguistic type that was prevalent in the area before the agricultural expansion that spread through the highlands of New Guinea and which transformed the demographics of the area (Diamond and Bellwood 2003).

NOTES

1. Or, in North American terms, the area of California, Nevada, Idaho and Oregon.
2. The terms used here are translations of the Tok Pisin or Malay words in use in New Guinea to describe different ethnic macro-groups: highlands: *hailans/pegunungan*; coastal: *nambis/pantai*; riverine: *bilong wara / sungai*; bush: *bus/pedalaman*; islands: *ailans/pulau*.
3. There are undoubtedly many more relevant works. Since this main direction of this chapter is primarily linguistic, I make no apologies for not reviewing the anthropological literature in detail.
4. These are killed before they become big enough to be a significant contribution to the diet; even a medium-sized cassowary can easily kill a small child.
5. Because all of the garden lands of the Tobati have been taken over for the urban development of Entrop and parts of Abepura, and all non-marine food is now purchased from shops, reference to Tobati practice is in the past tense.
6. The reconstructions in Pawley (1999) are largely based on languages from the extreme north-east of New Guinea, and may turn out not to be relevant for the more western languages discussed here.
7. Note that there are many more areas in New Guinea in which a contrast between more and less settled societies corresponds to a difference in linguistic structure. In the Lakes Plains area that lies to the north-west of the main cordillera there are strong differences between the highland fringe and the more northerly populations, and between land and water populations (the latter living exclusively on canoes, coming ashore only to hunt and gather). These social divisions correspond to a difference between the presence of stricter configurationality and ergative case on the fringe, and the use of extensive auxiliaries with 'loose' NP configurationality and minimal inflection as the languages become more northern, and more 'water-based'. In the far South Coast we can see differences between the more settled Marind and the more hunter-gatherer Kanum people, with the Morori as a 'mediator' culture. Marind is a

configurational and classifying language, while Kanum is extensively nonconfigurational, and does not have a confirmed linguistic classification.

8. Damal also has no phonemic fricative phonemes, but its neighbors are similarly lacking in fricatives, showing that the lack of fricatives is an areal feature of the western highlands. This might represent ancient substratal influence from languages related to Damal in the area (since relatives of the Wissel Lakes and Dani family languages that are further from Damal tend to show phonemic fricatives), but it would take substantial further research to establish this point.

References

Bailey, R. C., G. Head, M. Jenike, B. Owen, R. Rechtman and E. Zechenter. (1989). Hunting and gathering in tropical rain forest: Is it possible? *American Anthropologist* 91: 59–82.

Barrau, J. (1959). The sago palms and other food plants of marsh dwellers in the South Pacific Islands. *Economic Botany* 13: 151–162.

Cowan, H. K. J. (1952a). Een toon-taal in Nederlandsch Nieuw Guinea. *Tijdschrift Nieuw Guinea* 12(1–6): 55–60.

(1952b). De Austronesisch-Papoea'se taalgrens in de onderafdeling Hollandia (Nieuw Guinea). *Tijdschrift Nieuw Guinea* 13: 133–143, 161–177, 201–216.

Crowther, Melissa. (2001). All the One language(s): Comparing linguistic and ethnographic definitions of language in New Guinea. Thesis, Department of Linguistics, University of Sydney.

Denham, T., S. G. Haberle, C. Lentfer, R. Fullagar, J. Field, M. Therin, N. Porch and B. Winsborough. (2003). Origins of agriculture at Kuk Swamp in the highlands of New Guinea. *Science* 301: 189–193.

Diamond, Jared and Peter Bellwood. (2003).Farmers and their languages: The first expansions. *Science* 30: 597–603.

Donohue, Mark. (2000). One phrase structure. In Keith Allan and John Henderson (eds.), *Proceedings of ALS2k, the 2000 Conference of the Australian Linguistic Society*. University of Melbourne. www.arts.monash.edu.au/ling/archive/als2000/proceedings.html.

(2002a). Tobati. In John Lynch, Malcolm Ross and Terry Crowley (eds.), *The Oceanic languages*: Richmond: Curzon Press, 186–203.

(2002b). Which sounds change: Descent and borrowing in the Skou family. *Oceanic Linguistics* 41(1): 157–207.

(2002c). Reanalysis and word order change in Tobati. Paper presented at the Fifth International Conference on Oceanic Languages. Australian National University. Canberra, 15 January 2002.

(2003). Agreement in the Skou language: A historical account. *Oceanic Linguistics* 42(2): 479–498.

(2005). Configurationality in the languages of New Guinea. *Australian Journal of Linguistics* 25(2): 181–218.

(2006). Negative grammatical functions in Skou. *Language* 82(2): 383–398.

(2007). Lexicography for your friends. In Diana Eades, John Lynch and Jeff Siegel, (eds.), *Language description, History and Development: Linguistic Indulgence in*

Memory of Terry Crowley. Creole Studies Library 30. Amsterdam: John Benjamins, 395–405.

(2008). Complex predicates and bipartite stems in Skou. *Studies in Language.* 32(2): 279–335.

(2012). Argument structure and adjuncts: Perspectives from New Guinea. In Z. Antic et al. (eds.), *Proceedings of the 32nd Annual meeting of the Berkeley Linguistic Society (Theoretical Approaches to Argument Structure).*

Donohue, Mark and Melissa Crowther. (2005). Meeting in the middle: Interaction in North-Central New Guinea. In Andrew Pawley, Robert Attenborough, Jack Golson and Robin Hide (eds.), *Papuan pasts: Cultural, linguistic and biological histories of Papuan-speaking peoples*: Canberra: Pacific Linguistics, 167–184.

Etkin, Nina. (1994). The Cull of the Wild. In Nina Etkin (ed.), *Eating on the wild side: The pharmacologic, ecologic, and social implications of using noncultigens.* Tucson: The University of Arizona Press.

Galis, K. W. (1955). Talen en dialecten van Nederlands Nieuw Guinea. *Tijdschrift Nieuw Guinea* 16(1–6): 109–118, 134–135, 161–178 (especially part III, p. 164: Skou wordlist).

Hames, R. (1983). Monoculture, polyculture, and polyvariety in tropical forest swidden cultivation. *Human Ecology (Special Issue)* 11: 13–34.

Headland, T. N. (1987). The wild yam question: How well could independent hunter-gatherers live in a tropical rain forest ecosystem? *Human Ecology* 15: 463–491.

Headland, T. N. and R. C. Bailey. (1991). Introduction: Have hunter-gatherers ever lived in tropical rain forest independently of agriculture? *Human Ecology (Special Issue)* 19: 115–122.

Jenkins, Carol and Katharine Milton. (1993). Food resources and survival among the Hagahai of Papua New Guinea. In C. M. Hladik, A. Hladik, O. Linares, H. Pagezy, A. Semple and M. Hadley (eds.), *Tropical forests, people and food: Biocultural interactions and applications to development.* Man and the Biosphere Series Vol. 13. UNESCO Publications, 281–293.

Klappa, Stefanie. (2006). *Fallow farming: Exploring subsistence in Krisa, far northwest Papua New Guinea, and beyond.* PhD thesis, University of Canterbury.

Laycock, D. C. (1975a). The Torricelli Phylum. In S. A. Wurm (ed.), *New Guinea area languages and language study*, Vol. 1: *Papuan languages and the New Guinea linguistic scene.* Canberra: Pacific Linguistics C-38, 767–780.

(1975b). Sko, Kwomtari, and Left May (Arai) phyla. In S. A. Wurm (ed.), *New Guinea area languages and language study*, Vol. 1: *Papuan languages and the New Guinea linguistic scene.* Canberra: Pacific Linguistics C-38, 849–858.

McGregor, Donald E. and Aileen R. F. McGregor. (1982). *Olo language materials.* Canberra: Pacific Linguistics D-42.

Morren, G. E. B. (1977). From hunting to herding: pigs and the control of energy in montane New Guinea. In T. P. Bayliss-Smith and R. Feachem (eds.), *Subsistence and survival: Rural ecology in the Pacific*: New York: Academic Press, 273–315.

Ohtsuka, R. (1983). *Oriomo Papuans: Ecology of Sago eaters in lowland Papua.* Tokyo: University of Tokyo Press.

Pawley, Andrew. (1999). Some Trans New Guinea phylum cognate sets. MS, Department of Linguistics, Research School of Pacific and Asian Studies, Australian National University.

Purba, Theodorus T., Yulini Rinantanti, Budi Rahayu and Tri Handayani. (2003). *Morfologi dan sintaksis Bahasa Tobati*. Jayapura: Universitas Cenderawasih.

Roscoe, P. (2002). The hunters and gatherers of New Guinea. *Current Anthropology* 43: 153–162.

Ross, Malcolm D. (1980). Some elements of Vanimo, a New Guinea tone language. *Papers in New Guinea linguistics* No. 20. Canberra: Pacific Linguistics A-56, 77–109.

(1988). *Proto Oceanic and the Austronesian languages of western Melanesia*. Canberra: Pacific Linguistics C-98.

(2005). Pronouns as a preliminary diagnostic for grouping Papuan languages. In Andrew Pawley, Robert Attenborough, Robin Hide and Jack Golson (eds.), *Papuan pasts: Cultural, linguistic and biological histories of Papuan-speaking peoples*. Canberra: Pacific Linguistics, 15–66.

Sikale, John, Melissa Crowther and Mark Donohue. (2002). *Silla palla Molmo miri* [Molmo One dictionary]. Sandaun Province Department of Education and the University of Sydney.

Spriggs, M. (1993). Pleistocene agriculture in the Pacific: why not? In M. A. Smith, M. Spriggs and B. Fankhauser (eds.), *Sahul in review: Pleistocene archaeology in Australia, New Guinea and Island Melanesia*. Occasional Papers in Prehistory. Canberra: Australian National University, Department of Prehistory, Research School of Pacific Studies, 137–143.

Stahl, A. B. (1989). Plant-food processing: Implications for dietary quality. In D. R. Harris and G. C. Hillman (eds.), *Foraging and farming: The evolution of plant exploitation*: London: Unwyn Hyman, 171–194.

Staley, William E. (1994). Theoretical implications of Olo verb reduplication. *Language and Linguistics in Melanesia* 25: 185–190.

(1995). *Reference management in Olo: A cognitive perspective*. PhD thesis, University of Oregon.

(1996). The multiple processes of Olo verb reduplication. *Language and Linguistics in Melanesia* 27: 147–173.

n.d. *Dictionary of the Olo language, Papua New Guinea*. Vanimo: Small print run by Mark Donohue.

Swadling, Pamela and Robin Hide. (2006). Changing landscape and social interaction: Looking at agricultural history from a Sepik–Ramu perspective. In Andrew Pawley, Robert Attenborough, Jack Golson and Robin Hide (eds.), *Papuan pasts: Cultural, linguistic and biological histories of Papuan-speaking peoples*: Canberra: Pacific Linguistics, 289–327.

Thomas, K. H. (1941/1942). Notes on the natives of the Vanimo coast, New Guinea. *Oceania* 12: 163–186.

Ulijaszek, S. J. and S. P. Poraituk. (1993). Making Sago in Papua New Guinea: Is it worth the effort? In C. M. Hladik, A. Hladik, O. Linares, H. Pagezy, A. Semple and M. Hadley (eds.), *Tropical forests, people and food: Biocultural interactions and applications to development*. Man and the Biosphere Series Vol. 13. UNESCO Publications, 271–280.

Voorhoeve, C. L. (1971). Miscellaneous notes on languages in West Irian. *Papers in New Guinea Linguistics* No. 14. Canberra: Pacific Linguistics A-28, 47–114.

Watson, J. B. (1965). From hunting to horticulture in the New Guinea Highlands. *Ethnology* 4: 295–309.

Yen, D. E. (1989). The domestication of environment. In D. R. Harris and G. C. Hillman (eds.), *Foraging and farming: The evolution of plant exploitation*: London: Unwyn Hyman

(1991). Domestication: The lessons from New Guinea. In A. Pawley (ed.), *Man and a half: Essays in Pacific anthropology and ethnobiology in honour of Ralph Bulmer*: Auckland: The Polynesian Society, 558–569.

14 Small Language Survival and Large Language Expansion on a Hunter-Gatherer Continent

Peter Sutton

14.1 Introduction

The population sizes of Australian Aboriginal language-affiliated groups that can be reconstructed for the period of initial British colonization vary enormously. To establish this range with more precision than has been done in the past, here I analyse those cases in which the number of constituent estate-holding groups per language-territorial group has been recorded (see Appendix). Put simply, an estate group in this sense is a country-owning set of kin that is also, and *ipso facto*, a language-owning descent group. In Australian tradition, language varieties are not owned through being spoken, but on the basis that they who own a particular territory thus also inherit its linguistic identity, which was laid down at creation (Sutton 1978:17, Sutton and Palmer 1980; Rumsey 1993; Sutton 1997b). People spoke not only their own languages but also those of others, but the fact of distinct linguistic identity was not thereby blurred by multilingualism. This is very like the distinction between being Spanish and speaking Spanish. While only some people are Spanish, many more speak Spanish.

There are a few areas of Australia where numbers of estate groups per linguistic variety range from as low as between 1 and 5 (Appendix). The figures then range upwards, with a large proportion of the documented cases numbering between 5 and 25 estate groups per linguistic variety, followed by a smaller number of cases where linguistic varieties were held by scores of estate groups, as in the cases of Yir-Yoront (34 estate groups), Guugu-Yimithirr (32 estate groups) (both Cape York Peninsula), Ngarinyin (68 estate groups, north-west Australia), Djab Wurrung (41 estate groups), and Gunditjmara (58 estate groups) (both south-eastern Australia).

At the upper demographic extreme, but where a descent-group estate land tenure model is inappropriate or where local group structures have been insufficiently recorded, are languages like Western Desert (central Australia) or Wiradjuri (south-eastern Australia), whose owners numbered in the several thousands at colonization. Western Desert, its dialectal diversity much reduced post-conquest to a set of communalects (Hansen 1984; Sutton 2010), remains vibrant. It has a number of named varieties (e.g. Dixon 2002: xxxvii lists 16, but there were many more; see Nancy Munn's field data in Sutton 2010). The vastly spread language Wiradjuri (mostly on the Western Plains of New South Wales) went under a single indigenous rubric but with dialectal variations (Krzywicki 1934: 317) and is now moribund if undergoing a degree of revival. Such cases as these, where numbers of component subgroups are not reliably described, I have omitted from the tables in the Appendix because they cannot be subjected to the same kind of analysis as the others.

This chapter explores three main questions:

1. What sociological conditions of this hunter-gatherer population allowed language-owning groups to persist at such extremely low numbers as we find repeatedly in different parts of the Australian continent?
2. Were the 'large' languages numbering in the many hundreds and thousands of owners (and more speakers), which were a minority of the languages considered here, cases of recent expansion due to population replacement, or perhaps diffusion – in other words, was relative smallness the norm, and relative largeness a manifestation of ruptured geopolitical equilibrium?
3. If Australian language population sizes have tended to cycle though long phases of diminution through diversification, followed by replacement-events that created large-population languages in their stead during periods of demographic disturbance or language shift, is this model also able to suggest a hypothesis as to what triggered the cataclysmic, continentally impactful Pama-Nyungan expansion of the mid-Holocene period? I will deal with these questions in the same order.

14.2   Language Group Size in Australia

Aboriginal language groups are usually described as collectivities of smaller groups, commonly referred to as estate-owning groups. These were not, as is often assumed, bands (camping groups) but structural formations whose memberships persisted regardless of the often scattered geographical distribution of their affiliate members. Aboriginal linguistic territories, such as 'Yidinji country' or 'Kuku Yalanji country', are correspondingly described as being collectivities of estates whose owners share the same language affiliation. One such arrangement, in a report based on painstaking long-term field work including extensive site-mapping, has been portrayed by Chris Anderson as shown in Figure 14.1.

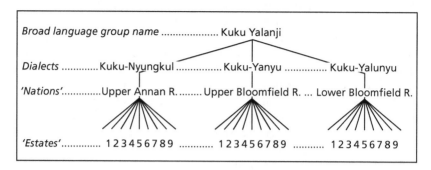

Figure 14.1 Nested groupings, south-east Cape York Peninsula. (Based on Anderson 1984: 91.)

While this kind of model and others like it works over much of Australia, it does not work in the Western Desert (Map 14.1), where the use of the descent group/estate model has been found more than once to be inapplicable,[1] and it is doubtful that south-eastern Australia was uniform on this question, although we shall probably never know for sure as that region has undergone cataclysmic cultural change since colonization (re Western Desert on this see Sutton 2015). But for much of Australia, especially in regions remote from urban centers it has been quite widely possible to obtain information on the social and territorial subgroups of a linguistic group or territory.

The Australian 'tribe' in the sense of a linguistic-territorial unit has often been said to have numbered, at colonization, on average about 500 people.[2] The linguist R. M. W. Dixon adhered to this figure in earlier publications on Australian languages (e.g. 1980:18) but has more recently omitted it (Dixon 2002). He has written in 2002 that at colonization there were probably around a million Aboriginal people divided into about 700 'political groups' which are commonly referred to as tribes, which were linguistic and territorial units (Dixon 2002:3). This would yield an average of 1,429 people per tribe, three times the once popular figure. Such an average would, if correct, stand in some contrast with the widely distributed occurrence of very small linguistic groups, as well as much larger ones, implied by the data in the Appendix. Many of the very small groups are in fact linguistic isolates at the level of a grammarian's definition of a language.

Dixon has also estimated that on linguistic rather than geopolitical criteria there were probably in the range of 230 to 300 languages spoken in Australia at colonization, in the sense that a linguist distinguishes a language from a dialect (Dixon 2002:7). At an assumed population of 1,000,000 this would yield

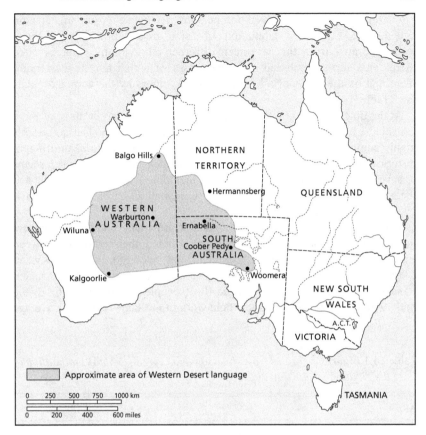

Map 14.1 Western Desert language (from Glass 1997).

average figures of 3,333 to 4,348 persons per grammarian's language. These figures are surprisingly large.

I prefer a more ethnographically precise way to approach the question. This is to examine the number of estate-holding groups within each 'tribe', as recorded by reliable ethnographic sources, and multiply it by some kind of reliable average estate group population figure, or range of figures. This is an evidentially grounded way to proceed but it requires a great deal of dataon estate group numbers.

We have vastly more data on the number of estate groups per linguistic variety than we have on estate groups population sizes. My rough estimations of populations here are based on the assumption of a range of 25 to 50 people per estate group is deliberately a little on the high side of those figures we do have for persons per estate group.

Average figures were given for persons per estate group in Peterson and Long's (1986:69) tabulation of 'size distribution of patrilineal groups' drawn from the seventeen different ethnographic sources cited there. This survey included seventeen cases of which ten, at least, were identified by the name of a linguistic group, others by the names of areas (see Table 14.1).

At the time of recording the estate groups would in many or most of these cases have been diminished by the impacts of colonization. The question is highly complex, given that epidemics hit Australian populations at different historical periods in different regions (e.g. smallpox 1780–1870, which seems to have left some large regions untouched including Cape York Peninsula and the south-west of Western Australia, see Campbell 2002: 85, 106, 137, 164, 192; Butlin 1993:115).

There is also the reverse factor of population growth beyond the old numbers due to modern conditions: the Warlpiri doubled their numbers between European contact and 1976 (Peterson and Long 1986:68). In 1926–29 when Lloyd Warner did his field work among Yolngu people in north-east Arnhem Land patrilineal estate groups averaged 40–50 people (Warner 1958:16). By the mid 1970s, when Ian Keen did his field work in the same region, the average

Table 14.1 *Figures extracted from Peterson and Long's (1986:69) tabulation of 'size distribution of patrilineal groups'*

AREA	DATE	APPROX AVERAGE SIZE
Worora	c. 1912	15.5
Yolngu	1976	45.3
Wik	1977	20.2
Yiryoront	1933–35	11.1
Thayorre	1972	28.8
Blyth River	1958–60	15.5
Port Keats	1950	27.5
Groote Island [sic]	1929	16.3
Borroloola	1977	28.8
Bentinck Island	1942	15.5
Kurintji	1982	11.5
Alyawarra	1971–72	13.5
"Utopia"	1920	75.5
"Warlmanpa"	1981	46.2
Warlpiri	1979	38.3
Willow[r]a	1980	43.6
Kurnai	1879	31.5
AVERAGED AVERAGES		363.7 ÷ 17 = 21.4

membership of the same entities had risen only slightly to about 55 (Keen 1994:66). Note that both Yolngu and Warlpiri are in the Peterson and Long list above.

One consequence of the punctuated spread of epidemiological and other factors in post-conquest Aboriginal depopulation is that we cannot be sure which populations had recovered their old numbers by the time of anthropological records and which were still highly depleted. It is for these reasons of uncertainty that I suggest working with an estimated average of 25–50 people per estate group for the purpose of reconstructing language group sizes at colonization.

I have collated numbers (not populations) of constituent estate groups for about 150 Aboriginal linguistic varieties in the tables in the Appendix. The first section of the Appendix deals with north-west Cape York Peninsula, and I will draw on that section here for discussion.

In the northern Paman example, at least 31 estate groups belonging to 14 named language varieties were distributed among 5, possibly 6 grammarians' languages (Sutton 2001:460). At 25–50 people per estate group that gives a total estimated population range of 775–1550, an average of 55–111 people per named linguistic variety, and an average of 155–310 people per distinct grammarian's language. Clearly this is a region with very small languages in both the named variety sense and the grammarians' sense.

In the Wik case, in the sub-region immediately to the south of the northern Paman languages, we have a coastal and pericoastal pattern of small languages and an inland pattern of big ones, in the senses both of populations and geographical extents of linguistic territories. Here an average of 25 people per estate yields a figure of 506 average per grammarians' language, and of course double that (1,012) if we use the higher assumption of 50 people.

As the Wik and northern Paman areas are abutting, they reflect the fact that regional differences of language size are not based *simply* on effective rainfall, and yet one can also see at times a regional ecological logic to the way language is subdivided culturally. Smallness of language in Australia suggests, usually, not merely relative richness of resources but also long-term stability and a normative multilingualism that was integral to the conduct of relationships between closely related people. Indeed this was the case in this region of Cape York Peninsula.

Estate-holding groups were or are typically exogamous. That is, their members usually married members of other such groups (a few cases of estate group endogamy are recorded). Members of the same language group but a different estate group could commonly marry each other, but they could also marry members of estate groups from different language groups, in widely varying percentages. This significant linguistic group exogamy was the case whether or not the languages involved were deeply different or dialects of a single grammarian's language (Sutton 2013a, b). The smaller the language group the fewer potential spouses who could be found within one's own language-identity group, and in any case a preference for marrying a person of one's own language was not by any means universal among Aboriginal people and indeed has not been reported to be widespread. For the smallest language groups all marriages could be interlingual (e.g. Wik Ep, Cape York Peninsula, Sutton 1978) where all members of the same generation were unmarriageable (e.g. classed as siblings, or of one exogamous moiety where such a structure existed).

It is a common error, especially among archaeologists, to equate Aboriginal estate groups with bands, and language-owning groups with speaker-communities. This badly confuses the structural with the behavioral. In a region like Cape York Peninsula most camps, unlike estate groups, would have been polyglot in composition, given the high ranges of linguistic exogamy in that population prior to the 1970s (Sutton 2013b). In a census of still-nomadic bands in the western part of this region in the early 1930s the anthropologist Lauriston Sharp found that at least two distinct languages were represented in every bush camp (Sharp 1958: 3; Sharp's raw data are tabulated at Sutton 2003: 70).

Estate groups were small sets of closely related people, most often (but not always) recruited on a presumptive principle of shared patrilineal descent. These patriclans, as they are sometimes called, were typically unified under the emblems of certain totems, and they held title to land and waters by a timeless mythic charter, referred to in the languages by a vast multiplicity of terms, and usually referred to now in English as the 'Dreaming', 'History' or 'Story', depending on region. In this mythic chartering it is not infrequently recorded that the particular form of speech of the founding Beings for each estate group was the one peculiar to that place and that group. Many regions have mythic 'discovery figures' who traverse the country at the beginning of the world and implant or discover each language in its own particular area as they move from place to place (for case material see Sutton 1997b). Thus each language was inherent in the soil, rocks and creeks of a particular location, and in the bodies and spirits of estate group members. In some regions each small estate group within the larger language group received its characteristic accent from its founding totemic ancestor. For these religious reasons the sub-dialect of an estate group may 'sound' like a particular ancestral way of talking. So while several hundred people may label their common language as, say, Wik-Mungkan, at a lower order of specificity, namely the patriclan or estate group level, only a few dozen people may also name their dialect as e.g. '*Wik Korr*' 'Brolga Language'. Only some Wik-Mungkan estate groups have Brolga Totem. These are 'patrilects', in David Nash's terminology (Nash 1990).

14.3   Equilibrium

This religious basis for landed identity and linguistic identity is essential to the common but by no means universal story of long-term stability or equilibrium in Aboriginal linguistic geography, and to the cultural motivation for linguistic self-distinction. It may be regarded as a form of localized linguistic totemism.

Most writers agree that Aboriginal people did not, ideologically at least, countenance the acquisition of land by invasion or theft, and have little mythology or old oral history that countenances or provides any charter for human migrations. The linguistic geography of Australia indeed gives a general impression of tremendous stability. As a continent Australia stands in stark contrast with the Americas, for example, where representatives of particular linguistic stocks can be found scattered over vast distances as a result of demographic shifts, and where heroic legends of tribal movement and conquest may be part of memory culture, as in the Nass River area of the Pacific Northwest for example (Sterritt et al. 1998).

In recent decades comparative work has shown Australia to be largely made up of something like linguistic tectonic plates, very few of which show any particular relationship with distant neighbours that might be evidence of migration or of separation by immigration. The cases of Yolngu Matha in northeast Arnhem Land, and Yanyuwa in the Gulf Country (Map 14.2), which are isolated outliers of Pama-Nyungan, and that of Djamindjungan on the coast and Jingiluan to its east (Harvey 2008), separating distant linguistic relations rather like the situation of Finnish and Hungarian, are the exception, not the rule. In vast areas such as Cape York Peninsula (Paman languages) and the Lake Eyre region of central Australia, it is clear that not only do all the languages have a common ancestry, but none are inliers, and none are outliers (Hale, Kenneth L. Linguistic evidence for long-term residence of the Wik-speaking peoples in their present location in Cape York Peninsula: part I, lexical diversity [1997, unpublished manuscript]; Hale, Kenneth L. Linguistic evidence for long-term residence of the Wik-speaking peoples in their present location in Cape York Peninsula: part II, morphosyntax [1997, unpublished manuscript]; Bowern 2001: 246, 254). This strongly suggests in situ efflorescence.

We should not take smallness of language populations to be a reflection of social closure between their speakers. The small languages of any Aboriginal region were, in general, internal features of the regional society, not markers of its boundaries. The clearest exceptions to this generalization are island languages such as Tiwi (Hart and Pilling 1960) and Kayardild (Evans 1995: 24–27). Systematic multilingualism within a population could mean that both structural convergence and lexical and phonological diversification could proceed within the same population's linguistic repertoires.

This appears to have been the case in the Princess Charlotte Bay region of Cape York Peninsula. This is a *Sprachbund* phenomenon.

14.4   Punctuation

But there have been episodes of punctuation amidst this general picture of equilibrium. The picture that emerges, with few exceptions, is that the Pama-Nyungan family of languages (Map 14.2) 'exploded' over some period in the mid-to-late Holocene, rapidly replacing previous languages, and thus reducing dramatically what we can assume was a far greater linguistic diversity that preceded it over about five-sixths of the Australian mainland and nearby islands. I should mention here that R. M. W. Dixon (2002: 44–54) does not accept 'Pama–Nyungan' as a genetic subgroup and indeed in that work does not index it under names of linguistic groups but in a general subject index and as an 'idea' (2002: 733). Australianist linguists overwhelmingly disagree with Dixon on this and continue to work with 'Pama-Nyungan' as a genetic subgroup, as I do here.

At certain early stages in this cataclysmic event of Pama-Nyungan spread there may have been a single large Pama-Nyungan language with some dialect diversity or a cluster of Pama-Nyungan languages possibly number-ing in the hundreds or low thousands of owners and speakers. The spread of the daughter-languages of this group most likely happened in stages, given that the internal structure of Pama-Nyungan is lumpy rather than evenly graduated across two-dimensional and comparative linguistic space (Bowern and Atkinson 2012). The daughter languages in many regions seem to have settled down more or less to a state of relative stability, and grammatical, lexical and phonological diversifications proceeded in situ.

Other regions were less stable. One example is the relatively recent expan-sion of the low-diversity Maric subgroup of Pama-Nyungan, most likely from a coastal origin at about where Mackay now stands in Queensland, spreading quickly inland to both north-west and south-west (see map at Dixon 2002: 682). Maric dialects were identified by many different dialect names. A similar region of low linguistic diversity covering a large well-watered area is the south-west of Western Australia where, between Mullewa, Esperance and the sea there were many named dialects forming a single if varied language now called Nyungar. Estimates of this population at conquest range from 12,000 (Radcliffe-Brown 1931:689) to 6,000 (Berndt 1979:81) – either way the figures are extreme by Australian standards generally. Language groups with high estimated numbers at contact also included Kalkatungu 2–3,000 (north Queensland, Krzywicki 1934:515), Baakandji 3000 (NSW ibid.:516), Gamilraay 6–7,000 (NSW ibid.:517), and Wiradjuri 'several thousand' (NSW ibid.). For the other end of the spectrum, where language groups could have as few as 1–5 component estate groups, and thus estimated owner-

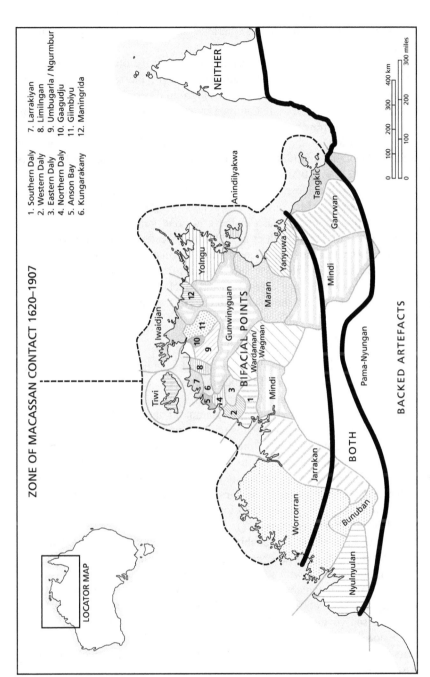

ZONE OF MACASSAN CONTACT 1620–1907

1. Southern Daly
2. Western Daly
3. Eastern Daly
4. Northern Daly
5. Anson Bay
6. Kungarakany
7. Larrakiyan
8. Limilngan
9. Umbugarla / Ngurmbur
10. Gaagudju
11. Giimbiyu
12. Maningrida

LOCATOR MAP

NEITHER

Anindilyakwa

Tiwi

Iwaidjan

Yolngu

Gunwinyguan

Maran

Yanyuwa

Tangkic

Garrwan

Mindi

BIFACIAL POINTS

Wardaman/
Wagman

Mindi

Worrorran

Jarrakan

Bunuban

Nyulnyulan

BOTH

Pama-Nyungan

BACKED ARTEFACTS

0   100   200   300   400 km
0   100   200   300 miles

Map 14.2 Mid-Holocene lithic expansion zones (bifacial points vs. backed artefacts vs. both vs. neither) mapped onto non–Pama-Nyungan languages (hatched) and the Asian contact zone 1620–1907.

numbers ranging from 25–50 to 125–250, see e.g. Cobourg Peninsula (Northern Territory) and Princess Charlotte Bay (Cape York Peninsula) in the Appendix.

The cases of low linguistic diversity across populations numbering in the thousands would, on the model I advance here, be the result of only recent centuries, not millennia, of dialect and subgroup diversification and language spread. They seem to be more common in the temperate zone and away from the coasts, but there is no definitive pattern.

The expansion of the Western Desert language from the north-west of Western Australia down into central and southern Australia similarly appears to be younger than 2,000 years and its south-eastern extremity, where dialect diversity is extremely low, appears to have been established within very recent centuries (Map 14.1; McConvell 1996; see also Smith 2005). While there was a significant population increase in the arid zone generally beginning about 1500–1000 years ago (Smith et al 2008), the Western Desert arid zone sub-region stands out as showing the most recent linguistic and demographic spread by comparison with arid zone sub-regions of stable diversity such as the Pilbara, the Arrerntic area centred on the MacDonnell Ranges, the majority of Lake Eyre Basin, and the inland stretches of the Murray-Darling Rivers.

14.5   Pama-Nyungan Expansion

My focus here is on the unresolved question of what triggered the expansion of Pama-Nyungan from the mid-Holocene onwards (see O'Grady and Tryon 1990; McConvell and Evans 1997).

My hypothesis is basically this. Beginning at about 5,000 years BP in the south, gradually moving northwards until about 3,800 years BP, there was an explosion in the production of microliths, small stone tools that were used, among other things, for the barbs on spears used in human combat. This archaeological evidence of small tool expansion cuts out at the southern edge of the non-Pama-Nyungan languages zone, north of which a parallel but distinct microlith production explosion had been taking place about the same time (Hiscock 2002; see Map 14.2).

The coincidence of this set of shifts in technology with the achieved limits of Pama-Nyungan (Map 14.2) expansion may be no coincidence, especially if it can be found matched with some other pattern with which both fit. It is worth considering Asian contact in this context. The period of the mid-Holocene was not only the start of Pama-Nyungan expansion but also the era in which extensive sea voyaging by Austronesian peoples in the south Pacific began (Bellwood 1995). The arrival of the dingo or Asian dog in Australia by 3,800 years ago (Corbett 1995) suggests to many that contact with Asians occurred at least at this period. The best documented contact between Aboriginal

Australians and Asians in the historic past is, however, much more recent: that with the people known as Macassans. Their annual visits to north Australia for trepang (sea slugs) and some other commodities were facilitated by the north-west monsoon which enabled them to sail down to Australia's north, and at the end of the season they could return home on the south-east trade wind. Their contact zone extended from the Kimberley coast in the west to the Wellesley islands area in the east (Macknight 1976; Map 14.2).

Now we come to the most speculative part of my hypothesis. If the Austronesians had made contact several millennia earlier along the same sea coastsas did the later Macassan visitors, is it possible that this may have imparted relative epidemiological immunity to the Aboriginal peoples of those coasts? In turn this would, if true, suggest that the remaining populations of the Australian continent were far more susceptible to exogenous epidemic disease. Were they to have been severely or largely reduced by epidemic disease, the scenario would then exist for a replacement spread of both population and, in its wake, language. The catastrophic demographic effects on Aboriginal people of epidemic disease introduced from the Indonesian archipelago in the eighteenth and nineteenth centuries are well known (Campbell 2002; Hiscock 2008: 12–17). These may not have been the first such events.

As a consequence of the foregoing scenarios I propose that serious consideration be given to the possibility that the Pama-Nyungan expansion may have been triggered, above all else, by a catastrophic population collapse outside the non-Pama-Nyungan zone, due to epidemic disease introduced by Asian contact.

Whatever the trigger or triggers for that massive replacement event, and whatever the relationship between genetic (DNA) replacement or continuity versus linguistic shift, it is clear that the modern descendants of speakers of Proto-Pama-Nyungan have proceeded, over and over again, towards ever more microscopic language-variety-owning populations. To this problem I now return.

14.6   The Mystery of Small Languages

It is clear from the large number of very small Australian languages reconstructible at contact that these were not merely cases of languages that were about to disappear due to depopulation. This stands in some contrast with the more general picture worldwide (Table 14.2), where it is often a fair assumption that the smallest languages are evidence of a more general process of mass linguistic extinctions.

Joseph Birdsell (1953) put forward a model in which Australian tribal territory size varied proportionately to effective rainfall, including the unearned benefits of accumulated drainage. At the level of the named or 'tribal' speech varieties there is much to recommend this model. But when we look at linguistic diversity in the grammatical, lexical and phonological senses, the

Table 14.2 *Worldwide language speaker estimates*

Population range	No. of Lgs	Per cent	No. of speakers	Per cent
100,000,000 to 999,999,999	8	0.1	2,301,423,372	40.20753
10,000,000 to 99,999,999	75	1.1	2,246,597,929	39.24969
1,000,000 to 9,999,999	264	3.8	825,681,046	14.42525
100,000 to 999,999	892	12.9	283,651,418	4.95560
10,000 to 99,999	1,779	25.7	58,442,338	1.02103
1,000 to 9,999	1,967	28.5	7,594,224	0.13268
100 to 999	1,071	15.5	457,022	0.00798
10 to 99	344	5.0	13,163	0.00023
1 to 9	204	3.0	698	0.00001
Unknown	308	4.5		
TOTAL	**6,912**	**100.0**	**5,723,861,210**	**100.00000**
Lgs with under 1 k speakers	**1,927**	**27.88**	**470,883**	**0.0822**
Lgs with over 10 m speakers	**83**	**1.2**	**4,548,021,301**	**79.25722**

Source: Gordon (2005).

correlation is nowhere near so neat. In Table 14.3 I have listed the geographic regions covered by my sample of linguistic varieties in the Appendix in order of average population size per variety. Similar environmental regimes seem to be scattered through the different figures.

There are wet tropical areas such as eastern Cape York Peninsula and well-watered temperate regions such as the south-west of Western Australia where linguistic diversity is very low, much lower than, for example, in the Arandic (Arremtic) region of the arid zone centred on Alice Springs. What these instances suggest is that the various regions were caught, at colonization, at different points in a hitherto perennial cycle of regionally specific processes, in which some language types expanded and replaced others, only to settle down and pursue long periods of more or less uninterrupted geopolitical equilibrium and in situ diversification. Models suggesting constant rates of linguistic diversification, as opposed to extremely jerky ones, would seem on this basis to be unsustainable.

Finally, if we look at Table 14.4, it is clear that regional averages below 10 estate groups per linguistic variety, at least at the level of the ethnically identified tribe, constitute more than half the sample of regions.

14.7   Conclusion

It was by no means the exception that, given the socio-cultural conditions of the past including a pervasive religious basis for small group distinction, different Aboriginal speech varieties, many of them technical linguistic isolates, many of

Table 14.3 *Geographic regions and average number of estate groups per language variety*

Language areas	Average number of estates per named (usually) language variety
Lower Murray Pericoastal (temperate)	1.4
Northern Paman (monsoonal)	2.4
Croker Island – Cobourg Peninsula region (monsoonal)	4.0
Port Keats/ Moyle River area (Barber) (monsoonal)	4.0
Wik coastal and pericoastal (monsoonal)	4.2
North-east and Eastern Arnhem Land (monsoonal)	4.7
Timber Creek area (monsoonal)	4.7
Eastern Princess Charlotte Bay (monsoonal)	4.7
Alligator Rivers region (monsoonal)	4.7
Atherton Tableland (monsoonal)	5.0
Rockhampton coastal district (subtropical)	5.0
Roper River region (monsoonal)	5.0
North Central Queensland (monsoonal)	6.0
Northern NSW (subtropical)	6.0
South-east Queensland (subtropical)	6.7
Darling River (temperate arid zone)	6.7
Western Princess Charlotte Bay (monsoonal)	7.0
Central Victoria (Barwick) (temperate)	7.6
Middle Murray River (temperate arid zone)	8.0
Rose River region (monsoonal)	9.0
Daly River area (monsoonal)	9.2
Eastern Cape York Peninsula (monsoonal)	9.3
Port Jackson NSW (subtropical)	10.0
Upper Victoria River region (monsoonal)	11.0
Western Nullarbor Plain (temperate arid zone)	12.0
Central Australia: Arrerntic (arid zone)	12.9
South-west Queensland (arid zone)	14.0
Groote Eylandt (monsoonal)	14.0
Dampier Land (monsoonal)	14.5
Wik inland (monsoonal arid zone)	15.5
Gulf Country (monsoonal)	15.5
North-central Arnhem Land (monsoonal)	15.5
Wellesley Islands region (monsoonal)	15.7
Gippsland (temperate)	19.0
West Kimberley[3] (monsoonal)	19.6
Western and Central Victoria (Clark) (temperate)	20.2
Mitchell-Edward Rivers (monsoonal)	21.0
Pilbara (arid zone)	22.5
Lower Murray Coastal (temperate)	26.3
South-east Cape York Peninsula (monsoonal)	29.0
Western Victoria (Lourandos) (temperate)	32.2
Total (41)	**465.7 ÷ 41 = 11.36**

Table 14.4 *Proportions of regional size averages*

Average estates per language	No. of regional averages in range	Subtotals	Subtotals as % of total
1.4–4.9	9		
5.0–9.9	13	1–10 average estates: 22	53.7
10.0–14.9	7		
15.0–19.9	6	10–20 average estates: 13	31.7
20.0–24.9	3		
25.0–29.9	2	20–30 average estates: 5	12.2
30.0–34.9	1		
35.0–39.9	0	30–40 average estates: 1	2.4

them sister dialects, were able to survive with owner/identifier numbers in only the scores to low or mid hundreds. While multilingualism typically added numbers of non-owner speakers to the tally for each variety, the resulting total numbers of speakers would still be modest by world standards.

While no one would suggest a return to hunting and gathering as a way of preserving today's thousands of endangered languages worldwide, this Australian example shows that, given appropriate and stable socio-cultural and ideological conditions, languages are not automatically endangered by their smallness.

APPENDIX ESTATE/LANGUAGE DATA FOR ABOUT 150 CASES OF AUSTRALIAN LINGUISTIC VARIETIES

Note: Omitting cases of duplication (chiefly involving the western Victorian figures from Ian Clark and Harry Lourandos, see end of table), the number of estate groups listed in the sample below comes to about 1500. At 25 people per group the theoretical population of the sample area would have been 37,500. At 50 people per group the theoretical population of the sample area would have been 75,000. Assuming that the sample area is about ten per cent of mainland Australia and covers a fairly representative range of ecological zones (Map 14.3), an estate group average of 25–50 would result in a highly hypothetical total figure of 375,000 to 750,000 mainland Aboriginal people at 1788.

This upper figure is surprisingly close to that of White and Mulvaney (1987) whose estimate was 750,000 to 800,000. It is consistent with Mulvaney and Kamminga (1999:69) whose conclusion as to the Aboriginal population of 1788 was a best estimate of 'some hundreds of thousands, perhaps at most three-quarters of a million' (750,000). Lourandos (1997:38) agreed with Butlin (1993) that the figure should be 'closer to one million, or at least around 900,000. In a careful revision of Butlin's data and with added argument about the role of chickenpox in reducing the Aboriginal population, Hunter and Carmody (2015:136) have come to a 'preferred estimate' of 800,000 people at 1788. Alan Williams has used 4575 radiocarbon dates from archaeological sites to derive a population curve for Australia over the last 50,000 years. This resulted in a population estimate at 1788 of 770,000 to 1.1 million (Williams 2013). These estimates, now clustering about 750,000 to a million, are well in excess of Radcliffe-Brown's estimate that the original Australian population had been 'certainly over 250,000, and quite possibly, or even probably, over 300,000' (1930:696).

Map 14.3 Sample areas.

Named linguistic varieties	Estates
Cape York Peninsula	
Western Cape York Peninsula, broader 'Wik' region:[4]	
Northern Paman: Port Musgrave (source: Thomson 1934)	
Tjungundji	9
Northern Paman: from Love River north to Weipa Peninsula[5] (sources: Sutton et al. 1990; Sutton 1997a)	
Adithinngithigh	1
Alngith	2
Anathangayth	1
Andjingith	8 [plus 2 possibles]
Arrithinngithigh	1
Latumngith	1
Linngithigh	4
Mamangathi[6]	1
Mbiywom	4 [plus 2 possibles]
Ndra'ngith	2
Ndrangith	1
Ngkoth	1
Paach (Wik Paach)	4
Total	**31 [plus 4 possibles]**
Average	**2.38 [–2.69]**
Wik subgroup, coastal and pericoastal:	
Wik subgroup: northern coastal[7] (source: Sutton et al. 1990)	
Wik-Alken/Wik-Elkenh[8]	6
Wik-Ngatharr	4
Wik-Ngathan	8
Wik subgroup: northern pericoastal[9] (source: Sutton et al. 1990)	
Wik-Ep/Wik-Iit	4
Wik-Keyenganh	1
Wik-Me'enh	5 [plus 1 possible]
Wik subgroup: southern (mainly coastal and pericoastal)[10] (source: Sutton et al. 1990)	
Kugu-Mangk	2
Kugu-Muminh	7
Kugu-Mu'inh	6
Kug-Ugbanh	3
Kug-Uwanh	3
Kugu-Yi'anh	1
Coastal and pericoastal combined:	
Total	**50 [plus 1 possible]**
Average	**4.16 [–4.25]**
Wik subgroup: inland[11] (sources: Sutton et al. 1990; Sutton 1997a; Smith 2001)	
Wik–Mungkan	12 [plus 1 possible]
Wik–Iiyanyi/Wik–Iiyeyn/Wik[Kugu-]–Iiyanh/Mungkanhu[12]	19 [plus 2 possibles]
Inland:	
Total	**31 [plus 3 possibles]**
Average	**15.5 [–17.0]**

(*cont.*)

Named linguistic varieties	Estates
Mitchell–Edward Rivers region (sources: Taylor 1984; Sharp 1937; Alpher 1991)	
Thaayorre	8
Yir–Yoront	34
Total	**42**
Average	**21**
Eastern Cape York Peninsula (sources: Chase 1980, 1984; Thompson 1976)	
Kuuku–Ya'u	10+?
Uutaalnganu	12+?
Umpila	6+?
Total	**28+?**
Average	**9.3–?**
Western Princess Charlotte Bay (source: Bruce Rigsby personal communication)[13]	
Lamalama	24[14]
Rimanggudinhma	2
Umbuygamu	3
Umpithamu	1
Ayapathu	5[15]
Total	**35**
Average	**7.0**
Eastern Princess Charlotte Bay (source: Sutton 1993)	
Marrett River Language	3
Flinders Island Language	8
Barrow Point Language	5
Red Point Language[16]	3
Total	**19**
Average	**4.75**
South-east Cape York Peninsula: Bloomfield River (source: Anderson 1984) *Kuku-Yalanji Dialect and 'nation cluster':*	
Kuku–Nyungkul (Upper Annan River)	9
Kuku–Yanyu (Upper Bloomfield River)	8
Kuku–Yalunyu (Lower Bloomfield River)	9
Total Kuku–Yalanji	**26**
South-east Cape York Peninsula: Hopevale area (source: Haviland and Haviland 1980)	
Guugu Yimithirr	32
Total Kuku–Yalanji + Guugu Yimithirr	**58**
Average	**29.0**
Queensland Other than Cape York Peninsula	
Wellesley Islands and adjacent mainland (sources: McKnight 1999; Tindale 1962; Evans 1995)	
Lardil	31[17]
Yangkaal	6[18]
Kaiadild	8–12[19]
Total	**45–49**
Average	**15.0–16.3 [say 15.7]**
Yukulta	?
Atherton Tableland (source: Dixon 1972)	
Mamu	5

(*cont.*)

Named linguistic varieties	Estates
North Central Queensland (source: Tindale 1974)	
Ilba	6
Rockhampton coastal district, Queensland (source: Flowers 1881 [1910])	
Ku-in-murr-burra[20]	7
Ningebal	5
Tarumbal	4
Warrabal	4
Total	**20**
Average	**5.0**
South-east Queensland (sources: Tindale 1974; Mathew 1910)	
Dalla	5
Kabi and Wakka combined	15[21]
Total	**20**
Average **(5+15 divided by 3)**	**6.66**
South-west Queensland (sources: Wells 1893; Luise Hercus personal communication)	
Karangura	14 (13?)
Northern Territory	
Upper Victoria River region (source: Merlan 1994)	
Wardaman	11
Gulf country (source: John Bradley personal communication)	
Yanyuwa	14[22]
Garrwa	16–18[23]
Total	**30–32**
Average	**15.0–16.0**
North-central Arnhem Land (sources: Hiatt 1965; McKay 2000)	
Gidjingali	19[24]
Ndjébbana	12
Total	**31**
Average	**15.5**
North-east and Eastern Arnhem Land (sources: Waters 1989; Heath 1978a, 1980a, b; Schebeck 1968 via Tindale 1974[25]; cf. Schebeck 2001); entries in brackets are drawn from Zorc (1986)	
Djinang	7 (7)
Dhangu[26]	6 (6)
Djangu	2 (2)
Nhangu	8 (7)
Dhuwala	7 (5 or 8)
Dhuwal	8 (8 or 10)
Dhay'yi	2 (2)
Dhiyakuy[27]	3 (2+)
Ritharrngu	4
Totals	**46 (or 39 or 44)**
Average	**5.1 (or 4.3 or 4.8) (say 4.7 overall)**
At the level of technically defined languages:	
Dhangu-Djangu	8

(*cont.*)

Named linguistic varieties	Estates
Dhuwala-Dhuwal-Dhay'yi	17 (or 15 or 20 depending)

Rose River region (sources: Heath 1980d, 1982, personal communication; Biernoff 1979)

Nunggubuyu	9 (11)[28]

Roper River region (sources: Heath 1978b, 1980c, 1981; Merlan 1983; Brett Baker personal communication)

Ngandi	5
Wandarang	6
Marra	3–6[29]
Ngalakgan	8
Mangarrayi	7
Alawa	5–7
Total	**65**
Average	**5.0**

Groote Eylandt (source: Waddy 1988)

Anindilyakwa	14

Croker Island – Cobourg Peninsula region (sources: Nicolas Peterson and Nicholas Evans personal communications)

Marrgu	6[30]
Ilgar	1[31]
Garig	?
Iwaidja	5[32]
Total	**12**
Average	**4.0**

Alligator Rivers region (source: Mark Harvey personal communication)

Amurdak	8
Ngaduk	2
Gaagudju	4

Three mutually intelligible varieties collectively known as

Giimbiyu	5
Erre	1
Mengerrdji	1
Urningangk	3
Total	**19**
Average	**4.75**

Daly River area (sources: Sutton and Palmer 1980; Duelke 1998:45 and personal communication)

Malak Malak	11[33]
Madngele	5
Nganggiwumirri	5[34]
Nganggikurunggurr	6
Total	**37**
Average	**9.25**

Port Keats/ Moyle River area (source: Kim Barber personal communication)

Murrinypatha	7
Murrinykura	3[35]
Maringar	6

(*cont.*)

Named linguistic varieties	Estates
Magatige	2
Marridjabin	2
Marriamu	4
Total	**24**
Average	**4.0**
[cf. Port Keats area (source: Falkenberg 1962: 24)	
Mari'ngar [Maringar]	7^{36} [possible others omitted]
Murin'bata [Murrinypatha]	11
Magati'ge [Magatige]	2
Mari'djäbin [Marridjabin]	5
Total	**25**
Average	**6.25]**
Timber Creek area (source: Mark Harvey personal communication)	
Nungali	6
Jaminjung	5^{37}
Ngaliwurru	3^{38}
Total	**14**
Average	**4.7**
Central Australia: Arrerntic (sources: Strehlow 1965; Moyle 1983; Koch and Koch 1993; Jenny Green personal communication; John Morton personal communication)	
Western Arrernte (Aranda)	10^{39}
Northern Arrernte	$9–10^{40}$
Alyawarra	$9–15^{41}$
Kaytetye	$15–21^{42}$
Anmatyerr	15^{43}
Total	**58–71**
Averages	**11.6–14.2 (say 12.9)**
Western Australia	
West Kimberley (source: Blundell 1975)	
Worora	18
Worora (Worora subgroup)	11^{44}
Aridjarami (Worora subgroup)	3
Winyawidjagu (Worora subgroup)	4
Umi:da	4
Unggarangi	5
Unggumi	3^{45}
[Ngarinyin (westernmost estates only)	18]
Source: Alan Rumsey personal communication:	
Ngarinyin	68
Total	**98**
Average	**19.6**
Dampier Land (source: Bagshaw 2001)	
Bardi	24
Jawi	5
Total	**29**
Average	**14.5**

(*cont.*)

Named linguistic varieties	Estates
Pilbara (source: Radcliffe-Brown 1913)	
Kariyarra (Kariera)	20–25 [say 22.5]
Western Nullarbor Plain (source: Bates 1985)	
Mirniny	12+[46]
South-East Australia	
Northern NSW (source: Tindale 1974)	
Ngaku	6
Darling River (sources: Cameron 1885; Tindale 1974)	
Barindji	8
Barkindji	7
Maraura	5
Total	**20**
Average	**6.7**
Murray River (source: Clark 1990)	
Wembawemba	8+[47]
Port Jackson NSW (source: Tindale 1974)	
Eora	10
Lower Murray River (source: Berndt and Berndt 1993)	
Pericoastal:	
Marunggulindjeri	2
Naberuwolin	1
Potawolin	2
Walerumaldi	2
Malganduwa	1
Wonyakaldi	1
Wakend	1
Total	**10**
Average	**1.43**
Coastal:	
Yaraldi	38
Tangani	27[48]
Ramindjeri	14[49]
Total	**79**
Average	**26.33**
Gippsland (Victoria) (source: Howitt 1904)	
Tribe: Kurnai (single language, with dialectal varieties)	
'Kurnai Clans' (geographical subgroups) and no. of their 'divisions' (estates):	
Krauatungalung	4
Brabralung	5
Brayakaulung	4
Brataualung	3
Tatungalung	3
Total	**19**
Average	**3.8**

(cont.)

Named linguistic varieties		Estates
Central Victoria (source: Barwick 1984; compare Clark source below)[50]		
Bunurong[51]		6
Woiwurung		6
Taungurong		9
Ngurai-illam-wurrung		3
Wathaurung[52]		14
Total		**38**
Average		**7.6**
Western and Central Victoria (source: Clark 1990; compare Lourandos below)		
Dhauwurd wurrung (Gundidjmara)		59
Dialects:[53]		
Wulu wurrung	14	
Gai wurrung	6	
Gurngubanud	4	
Dhauwurd wurrung	11	
Big wurrung	14	
Average	**9.8**	
Djab wurrung		41
Djadja wurrung		16
Djargurd wurrung		12
Gadubanud language		5
Girai wurrung		21
Gulidjan language		4
Jardwadjali language		37
Wada wurrung		25
Wergaia language		20
East Kulin language		25
Bun wurrung	6	
Daung wurrung	9	
Ngurai-illam wurrung	3	
Woi wurrung	7	
Barababaraba language		8
Wadiwadi language		2
Wembawemba language		8
Total		**283**
Average		**20.2**
Western Victoria (source: Lourandos 1977[54]; cf. Clark above)		
Manmeet (Gunditjmara)		58
Tjapwurong		33
Wathaurung		21
Kirrae		16
Bunganditj (Glenelg Area)		33
Total		**161**
Average		**32.2**

NOTES

1. See our literature survey of models of Western Desert local organization and our own conclusions in Sutton and Vaarzon-Morel (Yulara anthropology report, Part 1. [unpublished manuscript, for Central Land Council, Alice Springs 2003: 124–198, 228–271]), and Sutton (2015).

2. For example, Radcliffe-Brown (1930: 693), Birdsell (1953: 198, 206), Dixon (1980: 18). Krzywicki (1934: 63) suggested the average as a range of between 300 and 600 persons. Hiatt (1968) referred to 500 as 1 of the 'magic numbers' of Aboriginal demographic history.

3. An extreme example of how far averages can be from individual scores, which in this case are 3, 4, 5, 18 and 68.

4. The area covered here is from the Embley to Edward River, inland to Rokeby and Meripah, thus including both the Wik subgroup proper (Archer to Edward) and those northern Paman languages south of Embley River to the Archer – there are more northern Paman varieties north of there but I do not have the requisite data. Inland Wik varieties beyond this region have also been excluded here, e.g. Pakanh, Ayapathu, but see further below.

5. Of these varieties, Alngith, Linngithigh and Ndra'ngith are dialects of a single language (Hale 1966: 175). Relations between the others are either not as yet ascertained, or they are distinct varieties not close enough to any known other to be regarded as dialects of one language (Hale 1966: 175) Ngkoth, Arrithinngithigh and Mbiywom are clearly distinct from the nearest other sampled languages Ndra'ngith, Alngith and Linngithigh.

6. According to Hale Mamngayth (Mamangathi) is one of three virtually identical dialects subsumed under the title Awngthim (1966: 165). According to Crowley, Mamangathi is referred to as one of several 'groups' speaking the Awngthim language, and the implication is that these were exogamous estate groups rather than dialect groups per se (Crowley 1981: 150). The data I have seen suggest that the name Mamangathi (Mamngayth, Mamangithigh etc. depending on the language in which it is being named) at least also functioned as the name of a linguistic variety, and was not just a estate group name.

7. These varieties are dialects of a single linguist's language, although Wik-Ngathan is clearly distinct from the others in a number of morphosyntactic and lexical ways and unlike the other varieties does not engage in synchronic initial-dropping and certain other complexities.

8. Some say this is the same as Wik-Ngatharr, others keep the two names distinct, but they are very similar or virtually identical varieties in any case. Wik-Ngatharr appears to be the Wik-Mungkan name for the variety self-named Wik-Elkenh.

9. These varieties are dialects of a single linguist's language.

10. These varieties are dialects of a single linguist's language.

11. These varieties are dialects of a single linguist's language.

12. Pakanh and Ayapathu mainly fall outside the study area in this case, but there are two estates affiliated to each variety in my own data. For these plus five more Ayapathu estates see later under Western Princess Charlotte Bay.

13. The estates and members of these estate groups have now passed wholly or in part to the contemporary language-named 'Lamalama tribe' (Rigsby and Hafner 1994).

14. This needs some refinement; identification of some patriclan varieties is less than certain, and some are also identified as Koko Warra – dual affiliations may be present; some varieties were more distantly related and in at least one case was not identified as Lamalama but as 'like Flinders mob' (Bruce Rigsby personal communication).

15. These are the Ayapathu groups with estates at or near Princess Charlotte Bay. This is a Wik variety which also straddles the inland of the Peninsula and there are two estates recorded with Ayapathu affiliation in the inland. Combined, the figures come to 7.

16. The status of Red Point is unclear because of the paucity of available linguistic materials, but the others are certainly different languages on formal linguistic criteria.

17. This figure is from McKnight (1999: 82); Memmott (1983: 43) has 29 Lardil countries reconstructed to c. 1914. See also Trigger (1987).

18. Tindale (1974: 170) lists three named 'hordes' and one unnamed.

19. According to Tindale (1962) there were eight 'dolnoro'. In Evans (1995: 19) this is supported by a statement that there were eight patrilineal estates. However, Nicholas Evans has done much more intensive work in the area and now considers Tindale's version an 'inordinate rigidification' of the situation and notes that in his own field notes Tindale gives 'a different carve-up'. A figure of 8 to 12 is 'a reasonable estimate of the number of main groups, with the caveat that calling them 'estates' exaggerates the degree to which boundaries and membership were really fixed, and 'site portfolios' might be a better term . . ..' People from certain localities could be referred to by using the compass points (northerners etc.) but such usage was loose, given there were more locality groups than points of the compass. The origin case could be added to 'big name sites' to derive a way of talking about locality groups, e.g. Rukuthiwaanda jardi 'the Rukuthi mob', but 'little name sites' might also be employed in this way [of parallel kinds of groups? Individuals?] (N. Evans personal communication).

20. Ku-in-murr = a plain, so this may not be a linguistic designation. The 20 subgroups listed in Roth (1910: 89–90 and Pl. XXVI) and referred to here look like a mixture of geographical epithets (mountain-belonging-to, Townshend Island-belonging-to, big river-belonging-to etc.) and totemic ones (sand fly-belonging-to, green-headed ant-belonging-to, sickness/retching-belonging-to etc.).

21. Mathew considered 'communities' named after some feature of themselves or their country and whose names ended in *-bora* (*-barra*) were apparently more numerous among the Kabi than any other tribe known to him (1910: 129). The Kabi countries were coastal, the Wakka ones inland, which may account for the greater density of country-named groups associated with Kabi.

22. At least 12 estates are seen as 'full Yanyuwa'; one on the east is described as Yanyuwa/Garrwa mixed and one on the west is described as Yanyuwa/Marra mixed.

23. Bradley's information would suggest there are at least 16 to 18 Garrwa estates, but this is complicated by the fact that in the east some say that the named speech variety Kundirri with which part of the area is associated is 'rough eastern Garrwa' while others say it is a separate language (John Bradley personal communication).

24. Gidjingali, technically *Gu-jingarliya* 'it with tongue', is the single joint self-designation of the two dialects *Gun-narta* and *Gun-narda* (Glasgow 1994: 7). According

to Glasgow (1994: 7) *Gun-narta* is the dialect of the An-barra 'regional tribe' from the mouth of the Blyth River, and *Gun-narda* is the dialect of the Martay 'regional tribe' from the east side of the Blyth. Their eastern neighbours called these two 'regional tribes' *Burarra*, and this now is the official name of their language. A third close dialect is called *Gun-nartpa*, which is also self-described as *Gu-jarlabiya* 'it moves along'. This variety is that of the Mu-golarra (or Mukarli) 'regional tribe' of the Cadell River (Glasgow 1994: 7). Hiatt refers to entities such as An-barra and Martay as 'communities'. The Gidjingali communities he described were constituted primarily by 19 land-owning units which in turn were made up of 28 patrilineal groups (1965: 18–19). But whereas Glasgow cites only two 'regional tribes' as falling under this *Gu-jingarliya* rubric, Hiatt cites four, the others being Marawuraba (Mu-rrawurrpa) and Maringa. Glasgow (1994: 551) says that Mu-rrawurrpa is a regional tribe speaking the Martay dialect, and Maringa is a regional tribe from east of Cape Stewart speaking the Yanyangu dialect (1994: 472). This Maringa, however, must be a different one from Hiatt's as the latter is from west of Cape Stewart. Hiatt's Maringa community was made up of four land-owning units comprised of seven named patrilineal groups including Gamal and Bindarara (Bindararr). Bagshaw (1995: 123), on the other hand, says that the Gamal, Bindararr and Ngurruwula estate-owning groups comprise the Gulala regional group. (Meehan 1982: 14 and Jones 1985: 187 likewise show Gulala in the area where Hiatt's map had Maringa.) More recently, Bagshaw (1998:165 and personal communication) advises that the term Gulala, also pronounced Gulalay, means 'mangrove seedling' and is most accurately applied only to the Gamal and Ngurruwula estate groups. The same three estate-owning groups, i.e. Gamal, Bindararr and Ngurruwula, are also grouped together and known as Walamangu on the different basis that they share a single song-series called Wulumungu (*sic*, 1998:164). However, Gamal and Bindararr are primarily identified with the Burarra (Gu-jingarliya) language and Ngurruwula with the Yan-nhangu (Yanyangu) language, although all three estate-owning groups may also be referred to as Yan-nhangu in certain contexts (Bagshaw 1995: 124, 1998: 164). Note that all four of Hiatt's Gidjingali 'communities' had core members belonging to both patrimoieties (1965: 19). Bagshaw's regional groups are the same, with the exception of Gulala (y), all of whose estate-owning groups are Yirritjinga moiety (1995: 123, 1998: 164). Hiatt's listing of 'communities' (1965: 19) describes them as 'Gidjingali', but this was the name for their language rather than for themselves. They had no name for themselves as a group and referred to themselves collectively as 'we', the use of the name Gidjingali being used of them by Hiatt 'for the sake of convenience' (1965: 1). But Hiatt went on to explain that one of the Anbara community patrilineal groups, Galamagondija, had once been comprised exclusively of people whose primary language was Nagara. By 1960 it had 18 members whose primary language was Gidjingali and 7 whose language was Nagara, the latter regarding themselves as belonging to the Nagara community rather than the Anbara one. The patrilineal groups Galamagondija, Garabam and Milingawa collectively made up the Djunawunja estate-owning unit. Galamagondija comprised a combination of Gidjingali and Nagara people, Garabam people spoke Nagara, and Milingawa people spoke Gidjingali. There is thus no neat sense in which estate-owning units as wholes were subsets of 'communities'. There is also no neat sense here in which all the members of an estate-owning unit constituted a subset of the membership of a single language group, given that some of the former were of more than one linguistic identity.

25. The differences between this list and the published version of Schebeck (2001) are slight and probably have no bearing on the outcome here.

26. Frances Morphy (1983: 3–4) regards Dhangu-Djangu and Dhuwala-Dhuwal-Dha'yi as a single language in each case.

27. Morphy (1983: 3) cites Zorc as setting up a Yolngu subgroup described as 'Ritharrngu (Dhiyakuy)', although the two are separately represented in Tindale (1974). '"Dhiyakuy" is not recognized by the Ritharrngu people' (Zorc 1986: 79).

28. Heath (1980d: 5) lists 4 'core Nunggubuyu-speaking clans'. Heath (1982: 392) has 9 Nunggubuyu estate groups (presumably including the 'non-core' ones as well as the four core ones). Biernoff (1979: 153) has 10 Nunggubuyu estate groups but one of these (Magurri) is the name of a subclan of Murungun according to Heath (1982: 392). Heath (ibid.) shows a map of 11 'clan centres' which are presumably akin to what are generally known as estates, two of which are Murungun (one just 'Murungun', the other 'Murungun, Maguri subclan'), and two of which are Numamurdirdi (Num-barwar and Bingarawu subclans respectively). Thus it would appear there are 11 countries identified with Nunggubuyu at this level of resolution.

29. Heath (1981: 3) has three, as also do Bern *et al* (1980), but Brett Baker has argued (personal communication) that the area between Bing Bong and Limmen Bight was probably also Marra, at least in earlier times, and this is an area that would have had about three or four estates given existing local patterns.

30. This is probably a maximum and the modal figure may have been more like four (N. Peterson personal communication).

31. The islands of Grant, Lawson and McCleur and lesser islands of the group 'probably formed one estate' (N. Peterson personal communication). This is consistent with the observation that here probably would never have been more than about 20 primary speakers (i.e. owners) of Ilgar (N. Evans personal communication).

32. It is 'probably possible to say that there were five groups (Agalda, Majunbalmi, ... Ngaynjaharr, and two Murran estates)' (N. Peterson personal communication).

33. About 40 sites were mapped, among 250 or so, which were identified as to linguistic affiliation but not as to estate. Most of these were Malak Malak sites (see Sutton and Palmer 1980: 114–121). It is possible that the number of estates was a few more in both cases than appears here.

34. Stanner (1979: 85–86) lists 26 *dede* ('countries'; *dede* also refers to sites and camps) for Nangiomeri (Nganggiwumirri), but Duelke's research has led her to conclude that this list includes sites within countries as well as names of countries, which accounts for her lower figure.

35. These three estates are sometimes also referred to as being Murrinypatha, and one is also in some circumstances said to be Djamandjung (Kim Barber personal communication). Mark Harvey also supplied the same figure for this language (personal communication).

36. Here I also include three 'half Mari'ngar' estates as amounting to a score of 3; two of the same estates also counting as 2 under Murin'bata and 1 under Mari'djäbin.

37. In his 1934–35 survey Stanner listed 32 Jaminjung *yagbali* (places, localities, camps, countries) with which particular totemic beings were associated but did not apparently cluster them into estates (Stanner 1979: 77–78).

38. 'There are probably other Ngaliwurru estates.' (M. Harvey personal communication). In his 1934–35 survey Stanner listed 51 Ngaliwurru *ngurayik* (places, localities) with which particular totemic beings were associated but did not cluster them into estates (Stanner 1979: 68–70).

39. Strehlow (1965).

40. John Morton (personal communication) lists nine Northern Arrernte estates, with some uncertainty as to whether a tenth area is part of another estate or an estate in its own right.

41. Moyle (1983) has 9; Jenny Green (personal communication) lists 15.

42. Koch and Koch (1993) have 21 Kaytetye countries. Jenny Green (personal communication) lists 15.

43. Jenny Green (personal communication) lists 15.

44. One of these estates (Malanduma) was subdivided into three major sub-estates owned by three named lineages (Blundell 1975: 87).

45. One estate was Unggumi and Ngarinyin 'mixed' and thus appears numerically under each language name here.

46. Bates (1985: 41–43) names and describes 12 coastal estates for the Mirniny area, but there are other inland estates mentioned in her various works which invite further investigation.

47. These eight Wembawemba estates are located in Victoria, but there would have been many more in the eastern two thirds of Wembawemba country, now located in N. S. W. (see Hercus 1992).

48. This figures includes eight recorded by other scholars but not by the Berndts themselves.

49. I have omitted the one estate shown under the linguistic variety called 'Lower Kona or Kaurna' because the whole named language area was not included by the Berndts in that case.

50. Scholars such as Barwick (1984) and Clark (1990), meticulous as they clearly have been, are limited by the abundance and quality of their colonial-era source materials. Data from the remoter parts of Australia are usually more recent and based on the work of professional researchers and are thus generally more reliable.

51. Bunurong, Woiwurung, Taungurong and Ngurai-illam-wurrung were apparently dialects of one language (Walsh 1981–83, Barwick 1984: 125). Many complications are glossed over here. For example, one of the estates (Wurundjeri-Willam) had a three-way subdivision into 'tracts' (Barwick 1984: 122–124).

52. Lourandos (1977: 207) estimated there were 21 Wathaurung 'bands', of which only seven names appear to be the same as those of Barwick's 14 Wathaurung 'clans'. A number of the differences here are probably attributable to the multiple sources of group names, but note that Clark (1990) has 25 'clans' for this language.

53. Nine estates are shown by Clark as having a location unknown and do not appear on his map, and 18 appear on the map with a query (1990: 54–55). Doubts about the location of estates whose whereabouts are approximately known become of more significance when trying to plot them onto subdivisions of Dhauwurd wurrung country into the five dialect areas proposed by Clark (1990: 54).

54. Lourandos (1977) refers to the named country holding small groups as 'bands' but it is apparent from the text that these names refer to enduring tenure units, not to camps of mixed composition.

References

Alpher, Barry. (1991). *Yir-Yoront lexicon: Sketch and dictionary of an Australian Language*. Berlin: Mouton de Gruyter.

Anderson, Christopher. (1984). *The political and economic basis of Kuku-Yalanji social history*. PhD thesis, University of Queensland.

Bagshaw, Geoffrey. (1995). Comments on north-central Arnhem Land section of map by Stephen Davis. In Peter Sutton (ed.), *Country: Aboriginal boundaries and land ownership in Australia*, Canberra: Aboriginal History Monographs, 122–124.

—— (1998). Gapu dhulway, gapu maramba: Conceptualization and ownership of saltwater among the Burarra and Yan-nhangu peoples of Northeast Arnhem Land. In N. Peterson and B. Rigsby (eds.), *Customary marine tenure in Australia*. Sydney: Oceania, 154–177.

—— (2001). Anthropologist's supplementary report. Submission to the Federal Court in the Bardi/Jawi native title application WC95/48.

Barwick, Diane E. (1984). Mapping the past: An atlas of Victorian clans 1835–1904. *Aboriginal History* 8: 100–131.

Bates, Daisy M. (1985). *The native tribes of Western Australia* (ed. I. White). Canberra: National Library of Australia.

Bellwood, Peter. (1995). Austronesian prehistory in south-east Asia: Homeland, expansion and transformation. In P. Bellwood, J. J. Fox and D. Tryon (eds.), *The Austronesians: Historical and comparative perspectives*. Canberra: Australian National University, 103–118.

Bern, John, Jan Larbalestier and Dehne McLaughlin. (1980). *Limmen Bight Land claim*. Darwin: Northern Land Council.

Berndt, Ronald. (1979). Aborigines of the South-west. In R. M. Berndt and C. H. Berndt (eds.), *Aborigines of the West: Their Past and Present*. Perth: University of Western Australia Press, 81–89.

Berndt, Ronald and Catherine Berndt (with J. E. Stanton). (1993). *A world that was. The Yaraldi of the Murray River and the Lakes, South Australia*. Melbourne: Melbourne University Press at the Miegunyah Press.

Biernoff, David. (1979). Traditional and contemporary structures and settlement in eastern Arnhem Land with particular reference to the Nunggubuyu. In M. Heppell (ed.), *A black reality: Aboriginal camps and housing in remote Australia*. Canberra: Australian Institute of Aboriginal Studies.

Birdsell, Joseph Benjamin. (1953). Some environmental and cultural factors influencing the structuring of Australian Aboriginal populations. *American Naturalist* 87: 171–207.

Blundell, Valda. (1975). *Aboriginal adaptation in northwest Australia*. PhD dissertation, University of Wisconsin, Madison.

Bowern, Claire. (2001). Karnic classification revisited. In J. Simpson, D. Nash, P. Austin and B. Alpher (eds.), *Forty years on: Ken Hale and Australian languages*. Canberra: Pacific Linguistics, 245–261.

Bowern, Claire and Quentin Atkinson. (2012). Computational phylogenetics and the internal structure of Pama-Nyungan. *Language* 88: 817–845.

Butlin, Noel George. (1993). *Economics and the Dreamtime: a Hypothetical History* Cambridge: Cambridge University Press

Cameron, A. L. P. (1885). Notes on some tribes of New South Wales. *Journal of the Royal Anthropological Institute* 14: 357.

Campbell, Judy. (2002). *Invisible invaders: Smallpox and other diseases in Aboriginal Australia 1780–1880*. Melbourne: Melbourne University Press.

Chase, Athol Kennedy. (1980). *Which way now? Tradition, continuity and change in a North Queensland Aboriginal community*. PhD thesis, University of Brisbane.

Chase, A. K. (1984). Belonging to country: Territory, identity and environment in Cape York Peninsula, northern Australia. In L. R. Hiatt (ed.), *Aboriginal landowners*. Sydney: Oceania, 104–128.

Clark, Ian D. (1990). *Aboriginal languages and clans: An historical atlas of Western and Central Victoria, 1800–1900*. Clayton (Victoria): Department of Geography, Monash University.

Corbett L. (1995). *The dingo in Australia and Asia*. Sydney: University of NSW Press. http://australianmuseum.net.au/Dingo#sthash.Mrywv8aG.dpuf

Crowley, Terry. (1981). The Mpakwithi dialect of Anguthimri. In R. M. W. Dixon and B. J. Blake (eds.), *Handbook of Australian languages*, Vol. 2.Canberra: Australian National University Press, 146–194.

Dixon, R. M. W. (1972). *The Dyirbal language of North Queensland*. Cambridge: Cambridge University Press.

(1980). *The languages of Australia*. Cambridge: Cambridge University Press.

(2002). *Australian languages*. Cambridge: Cambridge University Press.

Duelke, Britta. (1998). *" ... Same but Different ... " Vom Umgang mit Vergangenheit. Tradition und Geschichte im Alltag einer Nordaustralischen Aborigines-Kommune*. Köln: Rüdiger Köppe Verlag.

Evans, Nicholas D. (1995). *A grammar of Kayardild, with historical-comparative notes on Tangkic*. Berlin: Mouton de Gruyter.

Falkenberg, Johannes. (1962). *Kin and totem: Group relations of Australian Aborigines in the Port Keats District*. Oslo: Oslo University Press.

Flowers, W. H. (1881 [1910]). Sketch map of the Rockhampton and surrounding Coast District, showing the main tribal boundaries. Plate XXVI in W. E. Roth (ed.), *North Queensland Ethnography Bulletin* No. 18 (*Records of the Australian Museum* 8(1): 79–106, 1910).

Glasgow, Kathleen. (1994). *Burarra – Gun-nartpa dictionary with English finder list*. Darwin: Summer Institute of Linguistics Australian Aborigines and Islanders Branch.

Glass, Amee D. (1997). *Cohesion in Ngaanyatjarra discourse*. Berrimah (Northern Territory): Summer Institute of Linguistics.

Gordon, Raymond G. (ed.) (2005). *The Ethnologue*, 15th edn. Dallas, TX: SIL International.

Hale, Kenneth L. (1966). The Paman group of the Pama-Nyungan phylic family; appendix to XXIX. In G. N. O'Grady and C. F. and F. M. Voegelin (eds.), *Languages of the World: Indo-Pacific Fascicle 6 (= Anthropological Linguistics* 8(2): 162–197.

(1997a). Linguistic evidence for long-term residence of the Wik-speaking peoples in their present location in Cape York Peninsula: part I, lexical diversity. Unpublished manuscript.

(1997b). Linguistic evidence for long-term residence of the Wik-speaking peoples in their present location in Cape York Peninsula: part II, morphosyntax. Unpublished manuscript.

Hansen, Kenneth C. (1984). Communicability of some Western Desert communilects. In J. Hudson and N. Pym (eds.), *Language survey*. Work Papers of SIL AAB, B 11). Darwin: Summer Institute of Linguistics, 1–112.

Hart, Charles W. M. and Arnold R. Pilling. (1960). *The Tiwi of North Australia*. New York: Holt, Rinehart and Winston.

Harvey, Mark. (2008). *Proto Mirndi: A discontinuous language family in northern Australia*. Canberra: Pacific Linguistics.

Haviland, John B. and Lesley Haviland. (1980). 'How much food will there be in heaven?': Lutherans and Aborigines around Cooktown before 1900. *Aboriginal History* 4: 119–149.

Heath, Jeffrey. (1978a). *Linguistic diffusion in Arnhem Land*. Canberra: Australian Institute of Aboriginal Studies.

(1978b). *Ngandi grammar, texts, and dictionary*. Canberra: Australian Institute of Aboriginal Studies.

(1980a). *Dhuwal (Arnhem Land) texts on kinship and other subjects with grammatical sketch and dictionary*. Sydney: Oceania.

(1980b). *Basic materials in Ritharngu: Grammar, texts and dictionary*. Canberra: Pacific Linguistics.

(1980c). *Basic materials in Warndarang: Grammar, texts and dictionary*. Canberra: Pacific Linguistics.

(1980d). *Nunggubuyu myths and ethnographic texts*. Canberra: Australian Institute of Aboriginal Studies.

(1981). *Basic materials in Mara: Grammar, texts and dictionary*. Canberra: Pacific Linguistics.

(1982). *Nunggubuyu dictionary*. Canberra: Australian Institute of Aboriginal Studies.

Hercus, Luise A. (1992). *Wembawemba dictionary*. Canberra: The author.

Hiatt, Lester R. (1962). Local organisation among the Australian Aborigines. *Oceania* 32: 267–286.

(1965). *Kinship and conflict: A study of an Aboriginal community in Northern Arnhem Land*. Canberra: Australian National University.

(1968). The magic numbers '25' and '500': Determinants of group size in modern and Pleistocene hunters [discussion section]. In R. B. Lee and I. De Vore (eds.), *Man the hunter*. Chicago: Aldine, 245–246.

Hiscock, Peter. (2002). Pattern and context in the Holocene proliferation of backed artefacts in Australia. In R. G. Elston and S. L. Kuhn (eds.), *Thinking small: Global perspectives on microlithization.* Arlington, VA: American Anthropological Association, 163–177.

(2008). *Archaeology of ancient Australia.* London: Routledge.

Howitt, Alfred William (1904). *The native tribes of south-east Australia.* London: Macmillan.

Hunter, Boyd and John Carmody. (2015). Estimating the Aboriginal population in early colonial Australia: The role of chickenpox reconsidered. *Australian Economic History Review 55*: 112–138.

Jones, Rhys. (1985). Ordering the landscape. In Ian Donaldson and Tamsin Donaldson (eds.), *Seeing the first Australians.* pp. Sydney: George Allen and Unwin,181–209.

Keen, Ian. (1994). *Knowledge and Secrecy in an Aboriginal Religion* Oxford: Clarendon Press.

Koch, Grace (comp. and ed.) and Harold Koch (transl.). (1993). *Kaytetye country: An Aboriginal history of the Barrow Creek area.* Alice Springs: Institute for Aboriginal Development.

Krzywicki, Ludwik. (1934). *Primitive society and its vital statistics.* London: Macmillan.

Lourandos, Harry. (1977). Aboriginal spatial organization and population: South-western Victoria reconsidered. *Archaeology and Physical Anthropology in Oceania* 12: 202–225.

(1997). *Continent of Hunter-Gatherers: New Perspectives in Australian Prehistory* Cambridge: Cambridge University Press.

Macknight, Campbell C. (1976). *The voyage to Marege: Macassan Trepangers in northern Australia.* Melbourne: Melbourne University Press.

Mathew, John. (1910). *Two representative tribes of Queensland, with an inquiry concerning the origin of the Australian race.* London: T. Fisher Unwin.

McConvell, Patrick. (1996). Backtracking to Babel: The chronology of Pama-Nyungan expansion in Australia. *Archaeology in Oceania* 31:125–144.

McConvell, Patrick and Nicholas Evans. (1997). *Archaeology and linguistics: Aboriginal Australia in global perspective.* Melbourne: Oxford University Press.

McKay, Graham. (2000). Ndjébbana. In R. M. W. Dixon and B. J. Blake (eds.), *Handbook of Australian languages*, Vol. 5. Melbourne: Oxford University Press, 154–354.

McKnight, David. (1999). *People, countries, and the rainbow serpent.* Oxford: Oxford University Press.

Meehan, Betty. (1982). *Shell bed to shell midden.* Canberra: Australian Institute of Aboriginal Studies.

Memmott, Paul. (1983). Social structure and use of space amongst the Lardil. In Nicolas Peterson and Marcia Langton (eds.), *Aborigines, land and land rights.* Canberra: Australian Institute of Aboriginal Studies, 33–65.

Merlan, Francesca. (1983). *Ngalakan grammar, texts and vocabulary.* Canberra: Pacific Linguistics.

(1994). *A grammar of Wardaman: A language of the Northern Territory of Australia.* Berlin: Mouton de Gruyter.

Morphy, Frances. (1983). Djapu, a Yolngu dialect. In R. M. W. Dixon and Barry J. Blake (eds.), *Handbook of Australian languages*, Vol. 3. Canberra: Australian National University Press, xxiv, 1–188.

Moyle, Richard. (1983). Songs, ceremonies and sites: The Agharringa case. In N. Peterson and M. Langton (eds.), *Aborigines, land and land rights.*Canberra: Australian Institute of Aboriginal Studies, 66–93.

Mulvaney, Derek John and John Peter White. (1987). How many people? In Derek John Mulvaney and John Peter White (eds.), *Australians to 1788.* Sydney: Fairfax, Syme and Weldon Associates, 114–119.

Mulvaney, Derek John and Johan Kamminga. (1999). *Prehistory of Australia.* St Leonards (Sydney): Allen and Unwin.

Nash, David. (1990). Patrilects of the Warumungu and Warlmanpa and their neighbours. In Peter Austin, R. M. W. Dixon, Tom Dutton and Isobel White (eds.), *Language and history: Essays in honour of Luise A. Hercus.* Canberra: Pacific Linguistics, 209–220.

O'Grady, Geoffrey N. and Darrell T. Tryon (eds.) (1990). *Studies in comparative Pama-Nyungan.* Canberra: Pacific Linguistics.

Peterson, Nicolas with Jeremy Long. (1986). *Australian Territorial Organization*: A Band Perspective. Sydney: Oceania Monographs.

Radcliffe-Brown, Alfred Reginald (1913). Three tribes of Western Australia. *Journal of the Royal Anthropological Institute* 43: 143–194.

(1930). Former numbers and distribution of the Australian Aborigines. In John Stoneham (ed.), *Official year book of the Commonwealth of Australia.* Melbourne: Government Printer, 687–696.

Rigsby, Bruce (1980). Land, language and people in the Princess Charlotte Bay area. In N. C. Stevens and A. Bailey (eds.), *Contemporary Cape York Peninsula.* Brisbane: Royal Society of Queensland, 89–94.

(1992). The languages of the Princess Charlotte Bay region. In T. Dutton, M. Ross and D. Tryon (eds.), *The Language Game: Papers in Memory of Donald C. Laycock.* Canberra: Pacific Linguistics, 353–360.

(1997). Structural parallelism and convergence in the Princess Bay languages. In P. McConvell and N. Evans (eds.), *Archaeology and Linguistics: Aboriginal Australia in Global Perspective.* Melbourne: Oxford University Press, 169–178.

Rigsby, Bruce and Diane Hafner. (1994). *Lakefield National Park land claim, claim book.* Cairns: Cape York Land Council.

Roth, Walter Edward (1910). Social and individual nomenclature. *North Queensland Ethnography Bulletin 18.* Records of the Australian Museum 8 (1), Sydney.

Rumsey, Alan. (1993). Language and territoriality in Aboriginal Australia. In M. Walsh and C. Yallop (eds.), *Language and culture in Aboriginal Australia.* Canberra: Aboriginal Studies Press,191–206.

Schebeck, Bernhard. (2001). *Dialect and social groupings in northeast Arnheim [sic] Land*. Munich: Lincom Europa.

Sharp, R. Lauriston. (1937). *The social anthropology of a totemic system in North Queensland, Australia*. PhD thesis, Harvard University.

(1958). People without politics. In V. F. Ray (ed.), *Systems of political control and bureaucracy*. Seattle: University of Washington Press, 1–8.

Smith, Benjamin R. (2001). *Wik native title supplementary anthropological overview: Pastoral lease areas*. The Wik Peoples – Native Title Determination Application QC94/3.

Smith, Mike. (2005). Desert archaeology, linguistic stratigraphy, and the spread of the Western Desert Language. In P. Veth, M. Smith and P. Hiscock (eds.), *Desert peoples: Archaeological perspectives*. Malden, MA: Blackwell.

Smith M. A., A. N. Williams, C. S. M. Turney and M. L. Cupper. (2008). Human-environment interactions in Australian drylands: Exploratory time-series analysis of archaeological records. The Holocene 18: 389–401.

Stanner, William Edward Hanley (1979). *Report on field work in North Central and North Australia 1934–35*. Canberra: Australian Institute of Aboriginal Studies [Microfiche No 1].

Sterritt, Neil J., Susan Marsden, Robert Galois, Peter R. Grant and Richard Overstall (1998). *Tribal boundaries in the Nass Watershed*. Vancouver: UBC Press.

Strehlow, Theodore George Henry (1965). Culture, social structure, and environment in Aboriginal Central Australia. In R. M. Berndt and C. H. Berndt (eds.), *Aboriginal man in Australia. Essays in honour of Emeritus Professor A. P. Elkin*. Sydney: Angus and Robertson, 121–145.

Sutton, Peter. (1978). *Wik: Aboriginal society, territory and language at Cape Keerweer, Cape York Peninsula, Australia*. PhD thesis, University of Queensland.

(1993). *Flinders Islands & Melville National Parks land claim*. Cairns: Cape York Land Council.

(1997a). *Wik native title: Anthropological overview*. Cairns: Cape York Land Council.

(1997b). Materialism, sacred myth and pluralism: Competing theories of the origin of Australian languages. In F. Merlan, J. Morton and A. Rumsey (eds.), *Scholar and sceptic: Australian Aboriginal studies in honour of L. R. Hiatt*. Canberra: Aboriginal Studies Press, 211–242, 297–309.

(2001). Talking language. In Jane Simpson, David Nash, Mary Laughren, Peter Austin and Barry Alpher (eds.), *Forty years on: Ken Hale and Australian languages*. Canberra: Pacific Linguistics, 453–464.

(2003). *Native title in Australia: An ethnographic perspective*. Cambridge: Cambridge University Press.

(2010). Linguistic identities in the eastern Western Desert: The Tindale evidence. In Brett Baker, Ilana Mushin, Mark Harvey and Rod Gardner (eds.), *Indigenous language and social identity: Papers in honour of Michael Walsh*. Canberra: Pacific Linguistics, 43–66.

(2013a). Comment on Denham's 'Beyond fictions of closure in Australian Aboriginal Kinship.' *Mathematical Anthropology and Cultural Theory: An International Journal* 5(5):1–5. http://hdl.handle.net/2440/89092.

(2013b) Cross-comment on Denham's 'Beyond fictions of closure in Australian Aboriginal Kinship.' *Mathematical Anthropology and Cultural Theory: an International Journal* 5(6):1–6. http://hdl.handle.net/2440/89093.

(2015). Norman Tindale and native title: His late appearance in the Jango case. In Amy Roberts and Kim McCaul (eds.), *Norman B. Tindale's Research Legacy and the Cultural Heritage of Indigenous Australians.* Special issue of the *Journal of the Anthropological Society of South Australia* 39: 26–72.

Sutton, Peter, David Martin, John von Sturmer, Roger Cribb and Athol Chase. (1990). *Aak: Aboriginal estates and clans between the Embley and Edward Rivers, Cape York Peninsula.* Adelaide: South Australian Museum.

Sutton, Peter and Arthur B. Palmer. (1980). *Daly River (Malak Malak) land claim.* Darwin: Northern Land Council.

Sutton, Peter and Petronella Vaarzon-Morel. (2003). *Yulara anthropology report, Part 1.* Unpublished report. Word-processed 309pp plus 9 substantial appendices and 16 maps; for Central Land Council, Alice Springs.

Taylor, John C. (1984). *Of acts and axes: An ethnography of socio-cultural change in an Aboriginal community, Cape York Peninsula.* PhD thesis, James Cook University of North Queensland.

Thompson, David A. (1976). A phonology of Kuuku-Ya'u. In Peter Sutton (ed.), *Languages of Cape York.* Canberra: Australian Institute of Aboriginal Studies, 213–235.

Thomson, Donald Fergusson (1934). Notes on a hero cult from the Gulf of Carpentaria, north Queensland. *Journal of the Royal Anthropological Institute* 64: 217–235.

Tindale, Norman B. (1962).Geographical knowledge of the Kaiadilt people of Bentinck Island, Queensland. *Records of the South Australian Museum* 14: 259–296.

(1974). *Aboriginal tribes of Australia: Their terrain, environmental controls, distribution, limits, and proper names.* Berkeley: University of California Press.

Trigger, David S. (1987). Inland, coast and islands: traditional Aboriginal society and material culture in a region of the southern Gulf of Carpentaria. *South Australian Museum Records* 21: 69–84.

Waddy, Julie A. (1988). *Classification of plants and animals from a Groote Eylandt Aboriginal point of view.* 2 vols. Darwin: North Australia Research Unit, Australian National University.

Walsh, Michael (comp.) (1981–83). Map 20: Western part of Australia. In S. A. Wurm and S. Hattori (eds., and T. Baumann, cartography). *Language atlas of the Pacific Area. Part 1: New Guinea area, Oceania, Australia.* Canberra: Pacific Linguistics for the Australian Academy of the Humanities in collaboration with the Japan Academy.

Warner, William Lloyd. (1937 [1958]). *A Black Civilization: A Social Study of an Australian Tribe.* New York: Harper and Brothers.

Waters, Bruce E. (1989). *Djinang and Djinba: A grammatical and historical perspective.* Canberra: Pacific Linguistics.

Wells, F. H. (1893). The habits, customs, and ceremonies of the Aboriginals on the Diamantina, Herbert, and Eleanor Rivers, in east Central Australia. *Australasian*

Association for the Advancement of Science Report of the 5th Meeting, 1893: 515–522.

Williams, Alan N. (2013). A new population curve for prehistoric Australia. Proceedings of the Royal Society B 280: 20130486. http://dx.doi.org/10.1098/rspb.2013.0486.

Zorc, R. David. (1986). *Yolngu-Matha dictionary*. Darwin: School of Australian Linguistics.

15 Language and Population Shift in Pre-Colonial Australia

Non-Pama-Nyungan Languages

Mark Harvey

15.1 Introduction

This chapter considers the evidence relating to significant shifts in land-language affiliations in Australia. In particular, it examines the issue of whether the evidence favors an analysis of significant shifts as atypical phenomena, arising from an infrequent co-occurrence of causal factors, or whether significant shifts should be analyzed as standard phenomena, arising from a more common co-occurrence of causal factors. I will show that the evidence favors the second alternative, and that significant shifts in land-language affiliations should be analyzed as a standard possibility within the long term diachrony of hunter-gatherer societies.

As discussed in the introduction to this volume, much of the current research on the expansion of widespread language families has focused on expansion involving agriculturalists. Diamond and Bellwood (2003) posit a causal connection between the innovation of agriculture and language spread. Once innovated in a particular area, agriculture can support a much greater population than the previous hunter-gatherer economy. This greater population occupies not only the areas where the innovation occurred, but also expands into areas occupied by hunter-gatherer populations. The languages spoken by the agriculturalists also spread their range, roughly in tandem with the population spread.

This model does not account for all widespread language families, as there are a number of widespread families which are not historically associated with agriculture (Campbell 2003: 50). The proposed causal link between the geographical spread of languages and significant population increase is not in fact necessarily limited to agriculture. In a foraging economy, if there was a quantum increase in the efficiency of foraging techniques, then this would support a significant population increase, which would in turn support language spread.

Wichmann (2010) proposes a model which can include a range of prehistoric modes of production with differing productivity outputs. He proposes that there is a correlation between variations in the 'density' of language families and different, prehistoric modes of production. Wichmann defines 'density' as follows.

$$\text{Density} = \frac{\text{Number of languages in a family}}{\substack{\text{Minimal number of centuries since break-up of the} \\ \text{proto-language as determined by glottochronology}}}$$

Wichmann states that his algorithm does not depend on assent to the claims of glottochronology. Rather, he states that time depths as determined by glottochronology are the best available stand-in for measures the rate of lexical differentiation. Further, lexical differentiation is, in turn, the best available stand-in for measures of 'differentiation' generally between languages.

The 'density' algorithm is therefore intended ultimately to measure the number of languages in a family as against the rate of linguistic differentiation between the members of that family. Wichmann proposes that language families diachronically associated with higher output modes of production show a higher numerical value for 'density' than language families diachronically associated with lower output modes of production.

Wichmann, following Nettle (1999a, b), proposes that this follows from the fact that the rate of linguistic differentiation is greater in small communities, based on lower output modes of production, than in larger communities, based on higher output rates of production. The constructed example in Table 15.1 illustrates the operation of the density algorithm.

Wichmann's calculations of 'density' appear to have a wide applicability. However, Wichmann himself categorizes the languages of Australia as a significant problem for his theory, as they show a high 'density' figure, regardless of how this is calculated.

This naturally raises the issue of what kind of an exception is the Australian data. One possibility is that it is an unusual exception resulting from a very rare concurrence of the relevant factors. If this is the case, then Wichmann's hypothesis might require only comparatively minor modification. However, another possibility is that the Australian data constitute a more significant

Table 15.1 *Density algorithm operation*

Fam memb.	Lang speaker num.	Rate of differentiation	Density
8	All large, based on agriculture	Lower because of large communities, say '1'	8
8	All small, based on hunter-gatherer	Higher because of small communities, say '2'	4

exception resulting from a highly probable concurrence of the relevant factors. In this case, Wichmann's hypothesis would require more significant modification.

I suggest that the second alternative is better supported by the evidence. The first point to note is that Australia was the only continent where hunter-gatherer modes were the sole modes of production. It was the only continent where populations using hunter-gatherer modes of production did not coexist or compete with populations using other modes of production with higher outputs.[1] Given that Wichmann's hypothesis is centrally concerned with differences between modes of production, this suggests that the Australian data are not a 'rare' exception. Rather, it is the only surviving example of language diversification patterns as they would have been before the invention of other modes of production.

A second, and central, point of this chapter is that the evidence shows that both wide geographical spread and significant high level internal differentiation within language families were recurrent patterns in Australian prehistory. A third point is that there is no compelling evidence linking the shifts that can be established in Australia to significant increases in population. Hiscock (2008: 219–244) summarizes a number of proposals of this nature in Australia, but shows that there is no compelling evidence for any of them. The currently available information on prehistoric demography is compatible with complex, non-directional change in population levels, not evidencing any significant increase in the overall continental population in the last 10,000 years.

This chapter first examines shifts in land-language affiliations at a supra-regional level (Section 15.2). The term 'supra-regional' is intended to describe shifts which extend well beyond anything that is generally recognized as a coherent region of the Australian continent. The chapter then examines shifts within a reasonably coherent region – those in the mid-central Northern Territory (Section 15.3). This region shows the most extensive and complex set of shifts currently proposed for Australia. Among these is the only well-established example of successive shifts in Australia. As we will see (Section 15.4), there is evidence for successive shifts into a particular sub-region – the Victoria River basin. The chapter examines in some detail how place names may be used to provide a linguistic stratigraphy or comparative dating for successive shifts of this nature.

15.2   Shifts in Land: Language Affiliations at the Supra-regional Level

At a continental level, attention has focused on the Pama-Nyungan (PN) family, which occupies 90% of the continent (Map 15.1). The remaining 10% is occupied by the Non-Pama-Nyungan (NPN) languages, which in diachronic

Map 15.1 Map of the area occupied by the Pama-Nyungan family of
languages in Australia.

terms are a disparate collection of a number of families and a number of isolates
(Map 15.2).

Despite the prominence of the PN versus NPN opposition, it is important to
note that most analysts propose the PN and NPN languages are ultimately
related as members of a single family, which derives from a single proto-
language, Proto-Australian (PA). Evans (2005: 275–277) provides a summary
of the hypotheses on PA. Some examples of PA reconstructions are set out in
Table 15.2.

There are only a very limited number of lexical reconstructions, such
as 'thigh' and 'liver', that can be proposed for PA. The critical evidence for
PA comes from reconstructions involving grammatical morphemes, such as
those for *pu-m 'hit-past perf' and *-ku 'dative'. Even among grammatical

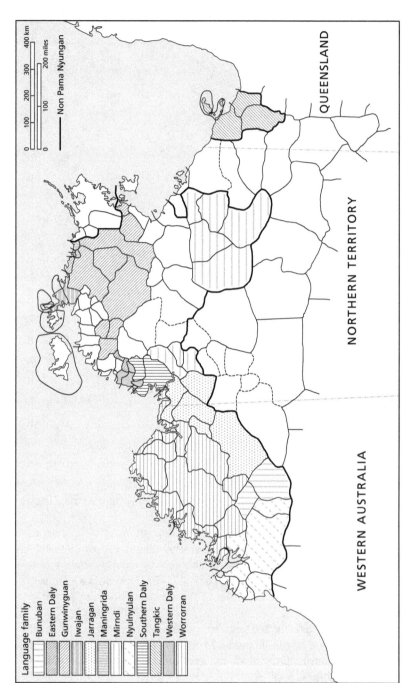

Map 15.2 Map of the area occupied by the Non-Pama-Nyungan languages in Australia.

Table 15.2 *Proto-Australian vocabulary*

	PN	NPN
*pu-m 'hit-past perf'	Dixon (2002: 120) Harvey (2008)	Alpher, Evans and Harvey (2003: 313–318); Harvey (2008)
*-ku 'dative'	Dixon (2002: 167)	Dixon (2002: 167)
*THarr(a) 'thigh'	Dixon (2002: 107)	Dixon (2002: 107); Harvey (2003a: 260)
*Thib(a) 'liver'	Dixon (2002: 112)	Harvey (2003a: 261)

morphemes, the number of reconstructions is very small. As such, the reconstruction of PA lies at the limits of the comparative method.

Though the evidence for the reconstruction of PA is limited, it is of central significance not just for general historical purposes, but also for modeling continent-level shifts in land-language affiliations. It is not possible to estimate the original spread of PA, given the subsequent spread of the PN family. It is possible that PA spread across the continent, and that the later spread of the PN family displaced other descendants of PA. It is possible that the contemporary NPN distribution was approximately the limit of the spread of PA, and that PPN was associated with an area somewhere on the borders of the PA spread, and that PPN subsequently spread to displace languages not related to PA. It is possible that some intermediate version of these two hypotheses is correct.

Whichever of these hypotheses might be true, the minimum geographical spread of PA was across the area now occupied by the NPN languages and some part of the area now occupied by the PN languages. The geographical extent of this area is well beyond anything that constitutes a coherent region of the Australian continent. As such, the spread of PA must be analysed as a supra-regional shift, belonging to the same analytical class as the spread of PPN.

Given that there have been two supra-regional shifts in Australia, the question arises as to whether these two shifts were of the same or different kinds, and whether they can be dated. One shift might have been fast and the other slow, or both might have been fast, or both might have been slow. To determine the answers to these questions, it is necessary first to examine the evidence on the internal diachrony of the NPN languages and the internal diachrony of the PN languages.

15.2.1 Internal Diachrony of the NPN Languages

As stated in the introduction, the NPN languages are a disparate collection of small families and isolates. Apart from the case of the Mirndi family discussed in Section 15.3.1, there is little evidence for significant shifts in land-language affiliations in the area where contemporary affiliations are to NPN languages. The language families which have been proposed because of evident high levels of cognacy in lexical and grammatical morphemes between the putative members are set out in Table 15.3.

There are two proposed families which do not show high levels of cognacy in lexical and grammatical morphemes, but where there is a partial reconstruction providing persuasive evidence that the putative member languages constitute a distinct genetic grouping. These two families are listed in Table 15.4.

It may be noted that none of these families involves more than five languages. I take it as the default hypothesis that contemporary land-language affiliations derive from more remote historical land-language affiliations. If there is evidence to the contrary, then other hypotheses may be favoured. For all of the families in Tables 15.3 and 15.4, the current evidence is that the default hypothesis on protolanguage territorial affiliations applies.

As set out in Tables 15.3 and 15.4, most of the families occupy comparatively small areas. Consequently, the shifts in affiliations following from the spread of the family have been comparatively small. Only the Jarragan, Nyulnyulan and Worrorran language families occupy more than 50,000 km^2.

With these three families, there must have been some more substantial movement. There is currently no material on the affiliations of Proto-Jarragan or Proto-Worrorran. Bowern (2007) reviewed flora and fauna terminology in the Nyulnyulan languages. She concluded that reconstruction in these domains appears most compatible with a reconstruction of Proto-Nyulnyulan as having affiliations in the northern Dampier Peninsula. This would imply a significant eastwards inland movement and some southwards movement to attain the contemporary Nyulnyulan affiliations.

The remaining proposed NPN family, Gunwinyguan, differs from the families listed in Tables 15.3 and 15.4 in a number of ways (Evans 2005: 250–251). There is no consensus on two critical points: first, whether the Gunwinyguan hypothesis has a satisfactory basis or not (Peiros, 'Is Gunwinyguan a language family?' [unpublished manuscript, 2002]; R. Green 2003) and second, what the full membership of the family is. For example, Alpher, Evans and Harvey (2003) provide evidence for including Mangarrayi in the family, but Merlan (2003) proposes that it is related rather to Alawa and Marra.

If consensus can be reached, then this family will be distinctive in having a much larger membership than any other NPN family. The minimum number of

Table 15.3 *Non-Pama-Nyungan language families with high-level cognacy*

Family	Area in km²	Languages	Named varieties	Sources on reconstruction
Bunuban	24,782	Bunuba	Bunuba	
		Gooniyandi	Gooniyandi	
Eastern Daly	1,635	Kamu	Kamu	Harvey (2003b, 2003c)
		Matngele	Matngele	
Iwajan	6,482	Amurdak	Amurdak, Gidjurra	
		Eastern Iwajan	Manangkari, Mawng	
		Iwaidja	Iwaidja	
		Northern Iwajan	Garig, Ilgar	
Jarragan	65,685	Gajirrabeng	Gajirrabeng, Wardanybeng	
		Gija	Gija, Giwajbem	
		?	Nyiwanawu[a]	
		Miriwoong	Miriwoong	
Nyulnyulan	56,317	Bardic	Bardi, Jawi	Stokes and McGregor (2003); Bowern (2004a, 2004b)
		Nimanburru	Nimanburru	
		Nyulnyulic	Jabirr-Jabirr, Nyulnyul	
		Eastern Nyulnyulan	Ngumbarl, Nyikina, Warrwa, Yawuru	
Tangkic	31,365	Kaiadilt-Yangkaal	Kaiadilt, Yangkaal	Evans (1990, 1995)
		Lardil	Lardil	
		Mainland Tangkic	Ganggalida, Nguburindi	
		Minkin	Minkin	
Western Daly	5,124	Marranj	Emmi-Yangal, Mendhe-Yangal, Warrgat	
		Marramaninjsji	Marramaninjsji	
		Marringarr	Marringarr	
		Marrithiyel	Marriammu, Marridan, Marrisjebin, Marrithiyel	
		Matige	Matige	
Worrorran	137,187	Ngarinyinic	Andajin, Ngarinyin, Wurla	McGregor and Rumsey (2009)
		Worrorric	Umiide, Unggurranggu, Worrorra, Yawijibaya	
		Unggumi	Unggumi	
		Wunambalic	Bayimbarr, Dulngarri, Gaambera, Gwini 1, Gwini 2, Gwini 3, Winambal, Wunambal	

[a] Nyiwanawu is extinct and unrecorded. It is unknown whether it was an independent language, or dialectal with either of Gajirrabeng or Miriwoong.

Table 15.4 *Non-Pama-Nyungan language families with low-level cognacy*

Family	Area in km^2	Languages	Named varieties	Sources
Maningrida	1,656	Burarra Gurr-goni Na-kara Ndjebbana		R. Green (2003)
Southern Daly	15,766	Ngan'gityemerri	Ngan'gikurrunggurr, Ngan'gimerri, Ngan'giwumirri	I. Green (2003)
		Murriny-Patha	Murriny-Kura, Murriny-Patha	

members would be eight languages – Bininj Gunwok, Dalabon, Jawoyn, Ngalakgan, Ngandi, Rembarrnga, Warray and Wubuy. Even at this minimum size, the family would have a substantial territorial affiliation of 90,019 km^2. Its contemporary geographical distribution would involve some significant shifts from the affiliations of Proto-Gunwinyguan.

15.2.2   Internal Diachrony of the PN Languages

Given that the PN languages occupy 90% of the continent, the patterns of movement from the original territorial affiliations of PPN are likely to have been complex. Research to date has focused on the central and western parts of the continent. McConvell (2001: 158–163) summarizes research proposing a major westward movement from approximately the area of the Southern Ngarna languages (Map 15.3). McConvell and Laughren (2004: 174–176) discuss linguistic evidence connecting the Ngumbin-Yapa language family to the Ngarna languages.

The geographical distribution of diversity within the PN family supports these proposals. There is less diversity among the PN languages of Western Australia than is found elsewhere in PN. O'Grady (1966: 121) provides figures for cognacy across most of the area associated with Pama-Nyungan in Western Australia. Table 15.5 contains figures for neighbouring languages from the Pilbara region.

The lowest percentage is 30%. As illustrated in Table 15.6, this same level is found with three, non-adjacent, representatives of the major language groups in the south-west.

In central and eastern Australia, there is a much greater range in cognacy figures between neighbouring languages. As illustrated in Table 15.7, in some cases, neighbouring languages have quite low cognacy figures (Breen 2007: 184; Eades 1979: 250).

Table 15.5 *Cognacy rates among PN languages in Western Australia*

Languages		Cognacy
Kurrama	Panyjima	65
Kurrama	Yindjibarndi	78
Ngarla	Ngarluma	41
Ngarla	Nyamal	65
Ngarla	Yindjibarndi	38
Ngarluma	Yindjibarndi	67
Nyangumarta	Ngarla	30
Nyangumarta	Nyamal	30
Nyangumarta	Palyku	33
Nyamal	Palyku	58
Nyamal	Yindjibarndi	43
Palyku	Panyjima	79
Palyku	Yindjibarndi	52
Purduna	Payungu	59
Purduna	Tharrkarri	46
Payungu	Tharrkari	35
Payungu	Yingkarta	51
Thalanyji	Purduna	79
Tharrkari	Wajarri	31

Table 15.6 *Cognacy rates among non-adjacent languages in Western Australia*

Languages		Cognacy
Mirniny	Wajuk	29
Wajarri	Mirniny	29
Wajarri	Wajuk	32

Table 15.7 *Cognacy rates among PN languages in central and eastern Australia*

Languages		Cognacy
Antekerrepenh	Wangka-Yutjurru	16
Gumbaynggirr	Bandjalang	22
Gumbaynggirr	Djangadi	20
Pitta-Pitta	Kungkari	21

The smaller range of lexical cognacy figures in the west is matched by a smaller range of diversity in the geographical extent of associations among Pama-Nyungan languages in Western Australia. The south-western portion of Western Australia includes a large coastal and subcoastal area which is as well watered as most of the eastern coast. Yet this entire area was associated with dialects of a single language – Nyungar – which extended along the coast for about 900 km. There is nowhere on the eastern coast where the affiliations of a single language extend for anything remotely approximating 900 km.

The standard interpretation of this kind of difference in diversity is that territorial associations in the less diverse area are more recent than those in the more diverse area (Sapir 1949: 223). Therefore, in terms of current evidence, the best hypothesis is that summarized in McConvell (2001), that there has been a major continental level westwards and to some degree southwards shift in PN affiliations.

15.2.3   *The Nature and Dating of Continental-Level Shifts in Land-Language Affiliations*

For both the Australian language family and the Pama-Nyungan language family, the available evidence suggests that the spread was relatively rapid. With regard to the Australian family, the evidence necessarily comes from the NPN languages, as these were not displaced in the subsequent spread of the PN family.

As we have seen (Section 15.2.1), none of the NPN families, apart from the putative Gunwinyguan family involve more than five languages. Most of the NPN families occupy comparatively small geographical areas. There is currently no evidence that any of these families, or the NPN isolates, are genetically related at any level lower than that of PA.

There are reconstructions to varying extents of a number of NPN families. Some of these are at the limits of the comparative method. For example, the reconstruction of Proto-Mirndi is close to the limits of the comparative method and only a very limited quantity of morphemes can be reconstructed (Harvey 2008). The reconstruction of Proto-Southern-Daly is involves a slightly greater quantity of morphemes, but is still very limited (I. Green 2003). The reconstruction of Proto-Gunwinyguan, whatever the ultimate resolution of the potential relations among the languages in this putative family (Section 15.2.1), involves a somewhat greater quantity again, but still limited (Alpher, Evans and Harvey 2003; Harvey 2003a).

These reconstructions are therefore in essentially the same class as the reconstruction of PA itself, which as discussed in Section 15.2, is at the limits of the comparative method. The overall situation is therefore that PA and a number of its daughter NPN proto-languages show much the same quantity of reconstructible materials. Further, most of its NPN daughters occupy small geographical areas.

The hypothesis, which currently provides the most plausible analysis of these facts, is that PA spread rapidly across the NPN area, and then the various NPN families and isolates diverged in situ, with some subsequent shifts, nearly all of them minor.

With regard to the PN family, much research remains to be undertaken on its internal genetic structure. However, it is clear that there are a large number of first order subgroups of PPN (Bowern and Koch 2004). Many of these involve only a few languages, and there are a number which are isolates within the overall PN context. As with PA, the most plausible explanation of this situation is that PPN spread rapidly across the PN area, and then the various PN families and isolates diverged in situ, with some subsequent shifts, nearly all of them minor.

Dating these shifts, as with any potential dating in historical linguistics is a problematic exercise. There are two types of evidence which can be used to propose timelines for the spread of language families. The best known and most reliable is written records, preferably detailed written records. Written evidence is obviously absent from Australia.

The other type of evidence is the reconstruction of a reasonable sized lexical domain which can be associated with datable archaeological materials. To construct an example, there might be an area where there were a number of language families, and the innovation of agriculture in this area could be dated with reasonable reliability. If agricultural terminology could be reconstructed only for one of the language families, then this would be evidence that the proto-language for that family was at least as old as the innovation of agriculture. There are no well-established examples of the second kind of evidence in Australia.

However, this is not to say that there are no general criteria for determining the comparative plausibility of one particular hypothesis as against other hypotheses. There is one basic fact about spoken language which provides an ultimate limit on the reach of the comparative method. All spoken languages necessarily undergo some quantity of continuous change. It is a fact that no utterance is ever physically the same as a preceding or following utterance, even if a speaker repeats exactly the same words. While this variation does not affect speakers' modeling of spoken input in most cases, it necessarily does do so in a proportion of cases.

Over time, the cumulation of this process of differentiation means that it becomes impossible to establish that languages are related, and the comparative method can no longer be satisfactorily applied. Consequently, in this respect, change is unidirectional – evidence of genetic relatedness will necessarily decrease over time. There is currently no way of determining a minimum for this rate of decrease. However, materials from the two reasonably reliable dating sources previously discussed – written records and correlations between archaeology and language families – do converge to suggest a probable maximum for the application of the comparative method of 10,000 years (Diamond and Bellwood 2003; Rankin 2003: 207–208).

This probable maximum argues that one obvious dating hypothesis about language spread in Australia is implausible. In terms of the Australian language family, this obvious hypothesis is that its spread follows from the colonization of Australia. The hypothesis would be that the original colonists spoke Proto-Australian, and that as they spread across the continent, they took the Australian language family with them.

The archaeological evidence supports occupation of Australia for at least 40,000 years (Hiscock 2008: 20–44). This is radically incommensurate with the probable maximum of 10,000 years for the time depth of the comparative method. It should not be possible to relate all the languages of Australia by any generally accepted application of the comparative method, even a reconstruction at the limits of the method such as PA is. Rather, the situation in Australia should be similar to that in New Guinea or western North America. There should be a number of language families which could not be related to one another by any generally accepted application of the comparative method.

Therefore, colonization of previously unoccupied territory is not a plausible explanation for the geographical spread of the Australian language family. It is evidently not an explanation for why one subgroup of this family, the PN family, has such an extensive geographical spread. Consequently, explanations for the spread of these two families must be sought elsewhere.

Sutton and Koch (2008: 497–500) discuss some of the possibilities in relation to PN. They note a correlation with Hiscock's (2008: 154–161) proposals that changes in the frequency distribution of particular stone tools are best modelled in terms of adaptation to levels of economic risk. Hiscock notes that there was an El Niño intensification, and that 2,000 to 4,000 years ago, Australia's climate was at its driest, and therefore most economically marginal.

It remains to be established if there is a connection between periods of greater economic marginality and language spread at a supra-regional level. Particularly, the more specific social factors that might underlie such a connection remain unclear. It also remains to be established what the directions of spread were. This chapter does not address the first question (see Chapter 16 by McConvell, this volume, on PN spread). It does address the second in Section 15.3, though only partially.

15.3   Regional Shift, Genetic Discontinuities, and the Mid-central NT

In terms of historical linguistics, the mid-central NT[2] is distinguished from the rest of Australia by the concentration of discontinuities (Map 15.3). There are four major discontinuities in Australian historical linguistics.

1. The Mirndi language family. There are two geographical groupings in Mirndi. The associations of the Eastern Mirndi varieties – Binbinka, Gudanji, Jingulu, Ngarnka, Wambaya – extend south and west from the south-western Gulf. The associations of the Western Mirndi varieties – Jaminjung, Ngaliwurru, Nungali – are in the Victoria River area. The distance between the two groups is approximately 220 km.
2. The Ngarna language family. There are two geographical groupings in Ngarna. The associations of the northern Ngarna varieties – Wilangarra,[3] Yanyuwa – are with the south-western Gulf coast. The associations of the southern Ngarna varieties – Bularnu, Wakaya, Warluwarra, Yinjilanji – are with the watersheds and associated rivers of the eastern Barkly Tableland. The distance between the two groups is approximately 280 km.
3. The separation of Tangkic from other NPN languages, by the intervening Garrwan language family, which is Pama-Nyungan (Harvey 2009).
4. The separation of Yolngu from other PN languages.

Only the fourth discontinuity, the Yolngu discontinuity, does not involve the mid-central NT. This chapter is concerned with the other three discontinuities. I do not examine the Yolngu discontinuity.

15.3.1   Proto-Mirndi and Proto-Ngarna

As we will see, the available linguistic evidence argues that the territorial affiliations of Proto-Mirndi and Proto-Ngarna were to areas on or adjacent to the south-western Gulf of Carpentaria. Consequently, the current overall affiliations of the Mirndi and Ngarna languages involve significant southwards and westwards movements.

The linguistic evidence on the territorial affiliations of Proto-Mirndi is discussed in Harvey (2008: 127–129). The evidence is limited, but the various pieces concur in favouring an affiliation in the north-eastern portion of the area to which the Mirndi languages are synchronically affiliated, that is, to the area affiliated with Binbinka and Gudanji. The relevant kinds of evidence are summarized following:

(a) Contemporary geographical distribution of subgroups within the Mirndi family
(b) Lexical and grammatical cognates with other non-Mirndi languages

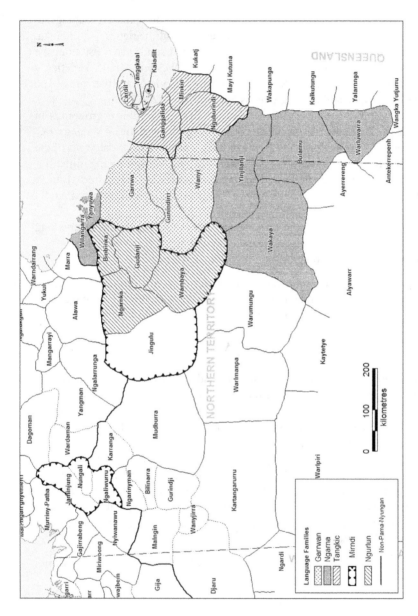

Map 15.3 The mid-central NT, distinguished from the rest of Australia by the concentration of discontinuities.

Table 15.8 *Mirndi language family*

A. Eastern Mirndi geographical group		
(i) Jingulu subgroup:	1 language	Jingulu
(ii) Ngurlun subgroup:	2 languages	Ngarnka, Wambayan (Binbinka, Gudanji, Wambaya)
B. Western Mirndi geographical group		
(i) Yirram subgroup:	1 language	Jaminjungan (Jaminjung, Ngaliwurru, Nungali)

(c) Areal typological associations of morphological systems which can be reconstructed for Proto-Mirndi

There are three subgroups in the Mirndi family. Their geographical distribution is set out in Table 15.8.

There are two subgroups in the east and one in the west. This favours an eastern affiliation for Proto-Mirndi (Sapir 1949: 223).

The overall quantity of lexical and grammatical reconstructions for Proto-Mirndi is quite limited. Therefore the possibility of finding cognates in non-Mirndi languages is even more limited. Nonetheless, there are two patterns of interest. Firstly, there are two Proto-Mirndi reconstructions which have cognates in Proto-Ngarna. They are the prefixed noun *ma-ngarra 'III-food' (Harvey 2008: 10–12) and the noun class prefix *ji- 'Class I' (Harvey 2008: 116–119). These reconstructions cannot, with any certainty, be assigned to PA, the only common ancestor of Proto-Mirndi and Proto-Ngarna.

Therefore, the common presence of these two items establishes borrowing between Proto-Mirndi and Proto-Ngarna, which in turn supports neighbouring territorial affiliations for these two proto-languages. Given that the Ngarna languages are all synchronically to the east of the Eastern Mirndi geographical bloc, this supports Proto-Mirndi having had an affiliation to the easternmost territories now associated with the Mirndi varieties.

The other pattern of lexical cognacy involves languages to the north of the Mirndi languages, principally the Gunwinyguan languages (Map 15.2). There are four Proto-Mirndi reconstructions which have cognates in Proto-Gunwinyguan – *thanga 'foot', *wany 'armpit', *ruma-ny 'come-PP' and *wonga-ny 'leave-PP' (Harvey 2008: 15–16). The Gunwinyguan languages are to the north of the Mirndi languages. This supports a north-eastern affiliation for Proto-Mirndi as opposed to a south-eastern affiliation.

Proto-Mirndi shares not only lexical cognates with Proto-Gunwinyguan but also a significant morphological structure. In the languages of north-central and north-Western Australia, verbal predicate meanings are expressed in two distinct part-of-speech classes. One class is a closed class of directly inflecting

Table 15.9 *Coverb structure*

(a) $_{wd}$[Coverb]$_{wd}$ $_{wd}$[Prefix complex-Verb root-Tense/Aspect suffixes]$_{wd}$
(b) $_{wd}$[Prefix complex-Coverb-Verb root-Tense/Aspect suffixes]$_{wd}$

verbs. The other class is an open class of non-finite forms, known as coverbs. These two classes combine in two different ways.

The structure in Table 15.9(a) is the structure reconstructed for Proto-Mirndi (Harvey 2008: 23–31), and is the structure found in nearly all neighbouring languages. However, there is evidence that the structure in Table 15.9(b) was the structure earlier in Proto-Mirndi (Harvey 2008: 31–33). The structure in Table 15.9(b) can be reconstructed for Proto-Gunwinyguan, and the closest languages which synchronically have the structure in Table 15.9(b) as their principal verbal structure are the Gunwinyguan languages. This shared structural pattern is further evidence for a northern affiliation for Proto-Mirndi.

There is another reconstructed pattern which supports a northern affiliation. A prefixal noun class system may be reconstructed for Proto-Mirndi (Harvey, Green and Nordlinger 2006; Harvey 2008: 63–79). Within this reconstruction, demonstratives show a portmanteau class/case opposition. There is one prefix form in Absolutive functions, and another in non-Absolutive functions. This kind of opposition is rare in Australian languages, being only otherwise found in a block of languages to the north of Eastern Mirndi – Alawa, Mangarrayi, Marra and Yanyuwa.

The reconstruction of Proto-Mirndi geographical affiliations as north-eastern has implications for the reconstruction of Proto-Ngarna geographical affiliations. The modern Ngarna languages appear in a northern and a southern block. As discussed, there is evidence that Proto-Ngarna and Proto-Mirndi had adjacent territorial affiliations. Therefore, this favours a northern territorial affiliation for Proto-Ngarna over a southern affiliation.

There is internal evidence from the reconstruction of Proto-Ngarna which provides some support for a northern affiliation. Like Proto-Mirndi, a prefixal noun class system may be reconstructed for Proto-Ngarna (Harvey 2008: 113–116). Areally, prefixal noun class systems are a northern feature.

As discussed, the default hypothesis is that contemporary land-language affiliations derive from more remote historical land-language affiliations. For the Mirndi and Ngarna languages, there is no evidence against the default hypothesis. The contemporary affiliations of the Northern Ngarna languages, Wilangarra and Yanyuwa, are saltwater affiliations. They are to the coastal area which includes the mouth of the MacArthur River and to the adjacent Vanderlin Islands. I reconstruct Proto-Ngarna as having had this territorial association. The contemporary affiliations of Binbinka and Gudanji are essentially freshwater affiliations. They are to the lower half half of the MacArthur drainage basin, other than the immediate coastal portion of this drainage basin. I reconstruct Proto-Mirndi as having had this territorial affiliation.

Given these historical affiliations, the current overall affiliations of the Mirndi languages involve a significant westward movement and also some degree of southward movement. The current overall affiliations of the Ngarna languages involve a significant southward movement.

15.3.2   Proto-Garrwan and Proto-Tangkic

The southward movement of Ngarna land-language affiliations necessarily requires consideration of the Garrwan family. The Garrwan family is the only family whose classification with respect to the PN versus NPN opposition has been analysed as uncertain (Blake 1988: 40, 1990: 62; Evans 2003: 10). Harvey (2009) argues that a review of the overall evidence shows Garrwan to be a PN language.

A substantial quantity of Garrwan grammatical morphemes, both free and bound, have no correspondents beyond Garrwan. This establishes that Proto-Garrwan was a protolanguage characterized by a high degree of innovation. It is only with pronominals that there is any substantial quantity of forms which have correspondents elsewhere. Consequently, it is the historical classification of pronominals that determines the historical classification of Garrwan. The data on pronominals is summarized in Table 15.10 (Harvey 2009: 238–239).

Table 15.10 *Proto-Garrwan pronominal roots and suffixes*

	PPN	Proto-Garrwan	Proto-Ngurlun
ACC	*-NHa	*-nya	
OBL	*-n	*-n	
REFL/RECIP		*-ngka	*-ngka
1sgACC	*ngaNHa	*ngana	
3sgNOM	*NHulu	*nyulu	
3sgOBL		*nanga	*nanga
1dlexc	*ngali-ya	*ngaliya	
2dl	*NHumbVlV	*nimbala	
3dl	*bula	*bula	
1plexc	*ngambala	*ngambala	
where	*waNHDHa	*wanyja	

Of the 10 forms which have clear correspondents elsewhere 8 are reconstructable for PPN. The remaining two forms correspond to forms in Proto-Ngurlun. Simple weight of numbers favours the classification of Proto-Garrwan as a PN language. Further, no plausible account can be provided for the PN forms as loans (Harvey 2009: 232–234). If Proto-Garrwan had borrowed pronouns on such a significant scale, then it should also show signs of extensive borrowing in the lexicon and elsewhere in the grammatical morphology. It does not (Harvey 2009: 239).

The two forms which correspond to Ngurlun forms, on the other hand, can be explained as loans following standard patterns. The Ngurlun languages are the eastern neighbors of the Garrwan languages, and as such are standard candidates for source or recipient loan relations with Garrwan. The Garrwan and Ngurlun languages also show a correspondence in verbal morphology which involves borrowing (Nordlinger 1998: 159–160).

This evidence of loans between Proto-Garrwan and Proto-Ngurlun establishes that these two proto-languages must have been adjacent to one another. In this respect, it may be noted that these loan forms are all innovatory in Ngurlun. There is evidence against their reconstruction in Proto-Mirndi, the parent language of Proto-Ngurlun (Green 1995: 422–423; Harvey 2009: 227–232). Consequently, while there is evidence that Proto-Garrwan and Proto-Ngurlun were adjacent, there is no evidence that Proto-Garrwan and Proto-Mirndi were adjacent.

This fact, combined with the fact that the Garrwan languages separate the two groups of Ngarna languages, and the fact that the Garrwan languages separate the Tangkic languages from the other NPN languages argue that there has been an alteration in the territorial associations of the Garrwan languages. It seems most likely that the territorial affiliations of Proto-Garrwan were such that they did not divide the Ngarna family, nor separate Tangkic from other NPN languages, nor were they adjacent to Proto-Mirndi. There is not presently, however, evidence which might indicate a more specific set of territorial affiliations for Proto-Garrwan.

15.4   Successive Region-Level Shifts: The Victoria River Basin

At colonization, there were two principal sets of affiliations to the freshwater ecozones of the Victoria River basin. The lower freshwater areas were associated with a language consisting of three named varieties – Jaminjung, Ngaliwurru and Nungali. Within this language, Jaminjung and Ngaliwurru are very similar to one another, and Nungali is considerably more divergent. This language constitutes the Yirram subgroup within the Mirndi language family (Harvey 2008: 126–127).

The upper freshwater areas were associated with two Eastern Ngumbin languages. One language consists of two named varieties – Karranga and Mudburra. The other consists of a number of named varieties – Bilinarra, Gurindji, Malngin, Ngarinyman and Wanyjirra. This second language also includes Djaru and Kartangarurru which were not associated with the Victoria River basin.

The Mirndi affiliations in the Victoria River basin result from a shift, in this case from the east (Section 15.3.1). McConvell (2009), summarizing a number of publications, proposes that the Eastern Ngumbin affiliations to the upper freshwater ecozones result from a shift which displaced Mirndi, and possibly other NPN affilations. This involves the shifts into the Victoria River basin occurring in the order Mirndi (Yirram) and then Eastern Ngumbin. However, an alternative hypothesis must be considered, that the freshwater ecozones in the basin were originally associated with Ngumbin and the Mirndi affiliations represent a later displacement.

There are two types of evidence which argue against this alternative hypothesis. The first follows from the historical status of the Mirndi family. As stated in Section 15.3.1, only a very limited quantity of material can be reconstructed for Proto-Mirndi. By contrast, a much greater quantity of material can be reconstructed for Proto-Ngumbin (McConvell and Laughren 2004). This necessitates that Proto-Ngumbin is a more recent proto-language than Proto-Mirndi. This in turn implies that the spread of the Mirndi varieties is older than the spread of Ngumbin varieties. As such, the association of Mirndi varieties with the Victoria River basin is likely to be older than the association of Ngumbin varieties with the Victoria River basin.

The second type of evidence comes from the patterning of place names in areas associated with the Yirram varieties as opposed to those associated with the Eastern Ngumbin varieties. McConvell (2009) is a detailed discussion of place names in the Victoria River basin, and it serves as the basis for the following discussion.

Place names show a range of morphological structures in the Victoria River basin. One type is unanalysable place names. McConvell states that unanalysable place names are relatively rare among the Eastern Ngumbin varieties (around 10% McConvell p.c.). The situation is very different in areas associated with the Yirram varieties. In these areas, the great majority of place names are unanalysable. A relatively extensive and detailed data-base of approximately[4] 550 place names from areas associated with the Yirram varieties, around 70% had no evident synchronic or diachronic analysis.

There are two hypotheses which could explain a high proportion of unana-lysable place names in areas associated with the Yirram varieties. One is that the names are analysable in some other language variety, not associated with the relevant areas within the contemporary period. This would imply a recent shift in land-language associations. However, the unanalysable place names in areas associated with Yirram varieties are not analysable in any of the other known language varieties from the area. Consequently, there is no reason to adopt this hypothesis.

This leaves the other hypothesis, which is that at least some reasonable proportion of the place names were historically analysable, but this analysability has been lost with the passage of time. Therefore, given that there is a very significant disparity in the percentages of unanalysable place names between the areas associated with Yirram and the areas associated with Eastern Ngumbin, this favours a longer association of Yirram with the area than Eastern Ngumbin.

The second principal type of place name in the Victoria River basin is names which consist of a noun root, and the suffix which conveys locative meanings.

Example 15.1

Burrmari-ni
scorpion-OBL
'(The place where) the scorpion is at'

In the Yirram varieties, the productive way of conveying locative meanings is with the Oblique suffix *-ni ~ -gi* which also conveys ergative and instrumental meanings. Very commonly, among the Yirram varieties, this structure is augmented with a further suffix *-wung* 'Restricted'.

Example 15.2

Garra-ni(-wung)
spider-OBL-RESTR
'(The place where) the spider is at'

As indicated in Example 15.2, the *-wung* suffix need not be obligatory. The factors determining its appearance are not known. It is standardly present, but may be omitted with at least some place names in some tokens. The Restricted suffix has a wide range of uses in the Yirram varieties. However, its appearance on place names is lexicalised (Schultze-Berndt 2002: 239). Lexicalisation in place names is evidence of comparatively greater time depth in land-language associations.

Place names involving locative suffixation are common in three of the Eastern Ngumbin varieties, Bilinarra, Gurindji and Ngarinyman. They are virtually absent in Mudburra, and rare in Malngin, Wanyjirra and Djaru. Bilinarra, Gurindji and Ngarinyman have an equivalent structure to Example 15.2. This equivalent structure is lexicalised in these varieties, as it is in the Yirram varieties.

In the Ngumbin languages the suffixes are -*ngka*, -*la*, etc. (LOCative) and -*rni* which has a range of functions similar to Restrictive in Yirram. This type of place name suffixation has a restricted geographical distribution. Particularly, for Ngarinyman which has extensive contemporary affiliations, its distribution provides evidence of differing time depths within the overall contemporary set of affiliations (McConvell 2009). The structure in Example 15.2 is absent in the other Eastern Ngumbin varieties.

In all of the Yirram varieties, and the Eastern Ngumbin varieties which have this structure, there are names which appear to involve locative marking, but where no synchronic meaning can be provided for the putative root, as in the Ngaliwurru place name in Example 15.3.

Example 15.3

Rama-ni-wung
?-OBL-RESTR

This is another kind of lexicalization, which provides further evidence for comparatively longer time depth of association. Lexicalized place names with the structure in Example 15.3, are common in the areas associated with the Yirram varieties. The previously mentioned 550 place name database contains 87 names which appear to involve Oblique suffixation. Among these 87 names, there were 62 (71%) for which no meaning could be provided for the putative root.

By contrast, among the Eastern Ngumbin varieties with place names involving locative suffix, it is only for approximately 20% (McConvell p.c.) that no meaning can be provided for the putative root. The significantly greater percentage of place names consisting of a synchronically meaningless root and a Locative suffix among the Yirram varieties, than among the Eastern Ngumbin varieties is evidence that the Locative suffix structure has a longer association with the Yirram varieties than with the Eastern Ngumbin varieties.

This is not in itself evidence that the association of the Yirram varieties to the Victoria River basin is older than the association of the Eastern Ngumbin varieties. Place names with the structure in Example 15.3, are compatible with both hypotheses as to the comparative time depths of Yirram and Eastern Ngumbin associations.

Under the hypothesis that the Eastern Ngumbin associations are older, the structure would have originated in the Yirram varieties after they displaced Eastern Ngumbin associations, and then subsequently spread into some neighbouring Eastern Ngumbin varieties. Under the hypothesis that the Yirram affiliations are older, then the structure would have been in situ in the Yirram varieties, when Eastern Ngumbin displaced previous associations, and the structure would have spread into some Eastern Ngumbin varieties.

As we have seen, the evidence from unanalysable place names favours Yirram associations being older. Further, as we will see in the following discussion, so also does evidence from Nungali place names. Therefore, the second hypothesis that Yirram associations with the Victoria River Basin are older than Ngumbin associations accords with other evidence, whereas the first hypothesis, that Ngumbin associations with the Victoria River Basin are older than the Yirram associations does not.

A further set of evidence for the Yirram varieties having a longer affiliation that the Eastern Ngumbin varieties comes from Nungali place names. Nungali differs from the other two Yirram varieties, Jaminjung and Ngaliwurru, and from the Eastern Ngumbin varieties, in that in addition to a standard system of nominal suffixation, it also has a system of nominal prefixation. This prefixal system is a closed system, and is found only in parts of the overall nominal lexicon. Synchronically, it consists of a number of partially relatable paradigms and involves a significant quantity of irregularity. The principal paradigm for nouns is set out in Table 15.11.

This paradigm has a complex history. Proto-Mirndi had a prefixal nominal classification system which was inherited into Proto-Yirram (Harvey 2008: 73–79). The morphemes in bold in Table 15.11 were inherited from Proto-Mirndi. There is both direct and indirect evidence that this system, while productive in at least some stages of Proto-Mirndi, was a closed, lexicalized system in Proto-Yirram (Harvey 2008: 78–79).

At some stage after the breakup of Proto-Yirram, Nungali innovated a new system of nominal classification, most probably through the procliticization of prefixed demonstratives to a range of heads in nominal phrases. This produced the paradigm in Table 15.11, and the other paradigms which now constitute the Nungali prefixal system.

The timeline for the innovation of the specifically Nungali prefixal class system and its subsequent closure to a set of paradigms involving significant irregularity cannot be directly dated. However, the default hypothesis is that the quantity of irregularity in a closed morphological system correlates directly with time. The hypothesis is that irregularities gradually increase in number over time in closed system. Consequently, the more irregularities

Table 15.11 *Nungali noun class prefixation*

	Absolutive	Oblique	Dative
I	*di-*	*nyi-*	*gi-*
II	*nya-*	**nga**-*nyi-*	*g-a-nyi-*
III	**ma-**	**ma-**	*gi-***ma-**
IV	*ni-*	*nyi-*	*gi-*

Table 15.12 *Terms for centipede*

Jaminjung	*Jalarrin*
Ngaliwurru	*Lirrimi*
Nungali	*Di-yalarru*

a particular closed morphological system has, the longer it has formed part of a particular language variety. There is no evidence that the irregularities in the Nungali prefixal class system have arisen by any other means. Consequently, the prefixal class system is of some reasonable time depth within Nungali.

The important point for land-language affiliations is that place names provide evidence that Nungali had essentially its contemporary affiliations for the time-span of this process. The materials on place names from a Nungali language perspective are unfortunately somewhat limited. The available evidence suggests that Nungali was not acquired as a first language by children after the early 1920s. By the time substantive research commenced in the lower Victoria River basin in the early 1980s, there was only one fluent Nungali speaker. By contrast, there were many speakers of the related Jaminjung and Ngaliwurru dialects. Consequently, most information on place names was provided from a perspective of fluency in Jaminjung and Ngaliwurru, but not from the perspective of a fluency in Nungali.

This had a couple of effects. One of these is the translation of meaningful Nungali names into Ngaliwurru or Jaminjung. This may be illustrated with the naming of a 'centipede' site in an estate which is known to have been affiliated with Nungali at colonization. The terms for 'centipede' are one of those cases where the three Yirram dialects have distinct terms.

The name universally given for the site in the period 1980–2000 is set out in Example 15.4.

Example 15.4
Lirrimi-ni(-wung)
Centipede-OBL-RESTR
'(The place where) the centipede is at.'

However, in 1996, I asked Duncan McDonald, who was then the most knowledgeable partial speaker of Nungali, what a long dead man who was an owner of the relevant estate and a fluent Nungali speaker had called the site. He stated that this owner had called the site *Nyi-yalad*. The analysis of this name is given in Example 15.5.

Example 15.5

di-yalarru   Nyi-yalad
I-centipede   OBL-centipede
'centipede'   '(The place where) the centipede is at.'

This place name shows a standard Nungali prefixation. However, it also involves a final phonological variation which has no evident motivation.

A second effect was that Jaminjung and Ngaliwurru speakers did not treat Nungali prefixation as analysable. In Nungali, prefixal nouns may only take the prefixal Oblique *nyi-*. They cannot take the suffixal Oblique *-ni*, which is the default form generally in the lexicon.

Example 15.6

*di-yimbul   nyi-yimbul   *di-yimbul-ni   *nyi-yimbul-ni*
I-man   OBL-man   I-man-OBL   OBL-man-OBL

However, Jaminjung and Ngaliwurru speakers tend to add the Oblique suffix *-ni* to Nungali forms with the Oblique prefix *nyi-*. We may consider the place name in Example 15.7.

Example 15.7

Nyi-nalij-burru(-ni)
OBL-tree sp-COM(-OBL)
'At (the place) with the *ni-nalij* trees'

The name for the relevant tree species is *ni-nalij*, with Class IV prefixation in Nungali, and *nalij* in Jaminjung and Ngaliwurru. Consequently, the place name is comprehensible to Jaminjung and Ngaliwurru speakers. However, their realizations of the name varied between *Nyi-nalij-burru*, which is the form that fluent Nungali speakers would have used, and *Nyi-nalij-burru-ni*. This second form involves the general Oblique suffix, and it would not have been a form produced in fluent Nungali speech.

There are only four place names which are synchronically analysable as involving prefixation. In addition to the two already presented in Example 15.5 and Example 15.7, there are the two in Examples 15.8 and 15.9.

Example 15.8

Nyi-marlan-burru
OBL-river red gum-COM
'At (the place) with the river red gums'

Example 15.9

Ni-yabarlawarn
IV-grindstone
'Grindstone'

The place name in Example 15.9 shows Absolutive rather than Oblique prefixation. However, in addition to these four names, there are a disproportionate number of place names with an initial /ny/ in the area associated with Nungali. The palatal nasal is a rare segment root-initially. In a Jaminjung lexicon of approximately 2,000 monomorphemic entries, only 2% have an initial /ny/. For the reasons already discussed, there is not a substantial Nungali lexicon. In the available lexicon of approximately 500 monomorphemic entries, only 2 have an initial /ny/. Therefore, there is no reason to posit that a more extensive Nungali lexicon would differ in this respect from the Jaminjung lexicon.

However, in a reasonably extensive database of Nungali place names approximately 8% (20/250) have an initial /ny/. The most plausible explanation for the disparity in percentages between the ordinary lexicon and place names is that most of the /ny/ initial place names historically involved the Oblique prefix *nyi-*. This is clearest with the place name in Example 15.10.

Example 15.10
Nyi-ngalan-burru
OBL-?-COM

This name is structurally parallel to those in Examples 15.8 and 15.9, though no meaning can be supplied for the putative root *ngalan*. The other place names with initial /ny/ appear only to have involved the Oblique prefix and a root.

Example 15.11
Nyilalgurr Nyiyalan

As with Example 15.10, no meaning can be supplied for the putative roots – *lalgurr, yalan*. A few /ny/ initial place names may involve the Class II Absolutive prefix *nya-* in Table 15.11. There are also a few names which may involve the Class IV Absolutive *ni-*, as in Example 15.9.

As discussed, nominal prefixation in Nungali is a complex system, which was created and then subsequently became closed after the breakup of Proto-Yirram. The default hypothesis is that this whole process must have taken a considerable time. There is no evidence against the default hypothesis. Consequently, the fact that there are place names, and especially many lexicalized place names, belonging to this closed, prefixal system is evidence that the land-language affiliations of Nungali have a significant time depth. A further default hypothesis is that the land-language affiliations of Nungali's close relatives and neighbours, Jaminjung and Ngaliwurru are also of the same time depth.

Overall therefore, the evidence supports two successive shifts of land-language affiliations in the freshwater ecozones of the Victoria River basin. The first was a westwards shift involving Mirndi affiliations. The second was a northwards shift involving Eastern Ngumbin affiliations. There was significant time interval between these two shifts.

One question which arises is why the prehistory of the Victoria River basin should involve two clear shifts, whereas other apparently similar basins – the Ord, the upper Daly, the Roper – do not show clear evidence of significant shifts. In this respect, Bowern's (2007) proposal that the prehistory of the lower Fitzroy basin involves spread by Nyulnyulan languages appears to be of relevance.

15.5   Conclusion

There is evidence for successive major shifts in land-language affiliations, both at the supra-regional level and the regional level. The evidence is that the spreads of PA and PPN are events of the same nature. The best hypothesis in both cases is that there was a quick expansion across a supra-regional area – in the case of PPN, this was effectively a continental expansion. This was followed by diversification in situ, with some minor shifts.

The evidence is also that the spreads of Mirndi and Eastern Ngumbin into the Victoria River basin are events of the same nature. The spread of Mirndi was a westwards spread. The spread of Eastern Ngumbin was, in immediate geographical terms, a northwards spread. However, this local northwards movement formed part of an overall westwards spread of the Ngumbin languages and their relatives. In both cases, the origin point of the shift was in the south-west Gulf of Carpentaria region.

There is clearly a significant time gap in both cases. The occurrence of events of the same kind, separated by significant time gaps, argues that these events should not be analysed as atypical, one-off events arising from an extremely rare concurrence of conditioning factors. Rather it suggests that they arise from a concurrence of social and demographic conditioning factors with a probability greater than 'extremely rare'.

It remains to be determined what these conditioning factors are, what the range of their potential concurrences is, and the probability of particular individual concurrences. Whatever these might eventually be, they should include supra-regional language spread, and westwards shift from the south-west Gulf of Carpentaria among their outputs.

The evidence presented in this chapter suggests that rapid language spread over large areas, followed by in situ diversification, cannot be causally restricted to situations where there was a rapid increase in population based on the adoption of new modes of production with a significantly higher output. While this may be the principal causal factor in some extensive spreads, it does not appear that it is a necessary or even relevant factor in all extensive spreads.

1. This point is due to Patrick McConvell.
2. As shown on Map 15.1, the 'mid-central NT' includes part of north-west Queensland. There is no generally accepted term for the area of Map 15.3. As nearly all of it does lie within the middle third of the NT, the term 'mid-central NT' is the best approximation. I avoid the term 'central NT', as this could be confused with 'central Australia', the term for the area centred around Alice Springs which is actually the southern third of the Northern Territory.
3. There is no direct linguistic information on Wilangarra. However, John Bradley reported that, in the period 1963–2007, Yanyuwa speakers who had heard Wilangarra spoken consistently described it as close to Yanyuwa. In this period, Yanyuwa speakers consistently described Garrwa as different from Yanyuwa. Place names provide some support for a connection between Yanyuwa and Wilangarra. Of the recorded language varieties in the Borroloola area – Binbinka, Garrwa, Marra, Yanyuwa – only Yanyuwa has interdentals. A number of unanalysable place names in Wilangarra country involve interdentals, including place names on the northern border with Marra. Therefore, I include Wilangarra within Ngarna.
4. There are some uncertainties about the associations of the Yirram varieties at colonization. Consequently, there are uncertainties as to the affiliations of some place names. Therefore, any statistics necessarily involve some degree of approximation.

References

Alpher, B., Evans, N. and Harvey, M. (2003). Proto-Gunwinyguan verbal suffixes. In N. Evans (ed.), *The Non-Pama-Nyungan languages of northern Australia: Comparative studies of the continent's most linguistically complex region.* Canberra: Pacific Linguistics, 305–352.

Blake, B. (1988). Redefining Pama-Nyungan: Towards the history of Australian languages. In N. Evans and S. Johnson (eds.), *Aboriginal linguistics.* Armidale: University of New England, 1–90.

(1990). Languages of the Queensland/Northern Territory border: Updating the classification. In P. Austin, R. M. W. Dixon and T. Dutton (eds.), *Language and history: Essays in honour of Luise A. Hercus.* Canberra: Pacific Linguistics, 49–66.

Bowern, C. (2004a). Diagnostic similarities and differences between Nyulnyulan and neighbouring languages. In C. Bowern and H. Koch (eds.), *Australian languages: Classification and the comparative method.* Amsterdam: John Benjamins, 269–290.

(2004b). *Bardi verb morphology in historical perspective.* PhD thesis, Harvard University.

(2007). On eels, dolphins and echidnas: Nyulnyulan prehistory through the reconstruction of flora and fauna. In Alan Nussbaum (ed.), *Verba Docenti: Studies in historical and Indo-European linguistics, presented to Jay H. Jasanoff by students, colleagues, and friends.* Ann Arbor: Beech Stave Press, 39–53.

Bowern, C. and H. Koch. (2004b). *Australian languages: Classification and the comparative method.* Amsterdam: John Benjamins.

Breen, G. (2007). Reassessing Karnic. *Australian Journal of Linguistics* 27: 175–199.

Campbell, L. (2003). What drives linguistic diversification and language spread? In P. Bellwood and C. Renfrew (eds.), *Examining the farming/language dispersal hypothesis*. Cambridge: McDonald Institute for Archaeological Research, 49–63.

Diamond, J. and P. Bellwood. (2003). Farmers and their languages: The first expansions. *Science* 300: 597–603.

Dixon, R. M. W. (2002). *Australian languages: Their nature and development.* Cambridge: Cambridge University Press.

Eades, D. (1979). Gumbaynggirr. In R. M. W. Dixon and B. Blake (eds.), *Handbook of Australian languages*, Vol. 1. Canberra: ANU Press and Amsterdam: John Benjamins, 244–361.

Evans, N. (1990). The Minkin language of the Burketown region. In G. O'Grady and D. Tryon (eds.), *Studies in comparative Pama-Nyungan*. Canberra: Pacific Linguistics, 173–207.

(1995). *A grammar of Kayardild: With historical-comparative notes on Tangkic.* Berlin: Mouton de Gruyter.

(2003). Comparative Non-Pama-Nyungan and Australian historical linguistics. In N. Evans (ed.), *The Non-Pama-Nyungan languages of northern Australia: Comparative studies of the continent's most linguistically complex region*. Canberra: Pacific Linguistics, 3–25.

(2005). Australian language reconsidered: A review of Dixon (2002). *Oceanic Linguistics* 44: 242–286.

Green, I. (1995). The death of 'prefixing': Contact induced typological change in northern Australia. *BLS* 21: 414–425.

(2003). The genetic status of Murrinh-Patha. In N. Evans (ed.), *The Non-Pama-Nyungan languages of northern Australia: Comparative studies of the continent's most linguistically complex region*. Canberra: Pacific Linguistics, 125–158.

Green, R. (2003). Proto-Maningrida within Proto-Arnhem: Evidence from verbal inflectional suffixes. In N. Evans (ed.), *The Non-Pama-Nyungan languages of northern Australia: Comparative studies of the continent's most linguistically complex region*. Canberra: Pacific Linguistics, 369–421.

Harvey, M. (2003a). An initial reconstruction of Proto-Gunwinyguan phonology. In N. Evans (ed.), *The Non-Pama-Nyungan languages of northern Australia: Comparative studies in the continent's most linguistically complex region*. Canberra: Pacific Linguistics, 205–268.

(2003b). The evolution of verb systems in the Eastern Daly language family. In N. Evans (ed.), *The Non-Pama-Nyungan languages of northern Australia: Comparative studies of the continent's most linguistically complex region*. Canberra: Pacific Linguistics, 159–184.

(2003c). The evolution of object enclitic paradigms in the Eastern Daly language family. In N. Evans (ed.), *The Non-Pama-Nyungan languages of northern Australia: Comparative studies of the continent's most linguistically complex region*. Canberra: Pacific Linguistics, 185–201.

(2008). *Proto-Mirndi: A discontinuous language family in northern Australia.* Canberra: Pacific Linguistics.

(2009). The genetic status of Garrwan. *Australian Journal of Linguistics* 29: 195–244.

Harvey, M., Green, I. and Nordlinger, R. (2006). From prefixes to suffixes: Typological change in Northern Australia. *Diachronica* 23: 289–311.

Hiscock, P. (2008). *Archaeology of ancient Australia*. London: Routledge.

McConvell, P. (2001). Language shift and language spread among hunter-gatherers. In C. Panter-Brick, P. Rowley-Conwy and R. Layton (eds.), *Hunter-gatherers: Social and biological perspectives*. Cambridge: Cambridge University Press, 143–169.

— (2009). Where the spear sticks up: The variety of locatives in place names in the Victoria River District, Northern Territory. In H. Koch and L. Hercus (eds.), *Aboriginal place names: Naming and renaming the Australian landscape*. Canberra: ANU E-Press and Aboriginal History Inc., 359–402.

McConvell, P. and M. Laughren. (2004). The Ngumbin-Yapa subgroup. In C. Bowern and H. Koch (eds.), *Australian languages: Classification and the comparative method*. Amsterdam: John Benjamins, 151–177.

McGregor, W. & Rumsey, A. (2009). *Worrorran revisited: The case for genetic relations among the languages of the North Kimberley region, Western Australia*. Canberra: Pacific Linguistics.

Merlan, F. (2003). The genetic position of Mangarrayi: Evidence from nominal prefixation. In N. Evans (ed.), *The Non-Pama-Nyungan languages of northern Australia: Comparative studies of the continent's most linguistically complex region*. Canberra: Pacific Linguistics, 353–367.

Nettle, D. (1999a). Is the rate of linguistic change constant? *Lingua* 108: 119–136.

— (1999b). *Linguistic diversity*. Oxford: Oxford University Press.

Nordlinger, R. (1998). *A grammar of Wambaya, Northern Territory (Australia)*. Canberra: Pacific Linguistics C-140.

Peiros, I. (2002). Is Gunwinyguan a language family? Unpublished MS.

O'Grady, G. (1966). Proto-Ngayarda phonology. *Oceanic Linguistics*, 5(2): 71–130.

Rankin, R. (2003). The comparative method. In B. Joseph and R. Janed (eds.), *The handbook of historical linguistics*. Malden, MA: Blackwell, 183–212.

Sapir, E. (1949/1936) Internal linguistic evidence suggestive of the Northern origin of the Navaho. In D. Mandelbaum (ed.), *Selected writings in language, culture and personality*. Berkeley: University of California Press, 213–224. *American Anthropologist* 38(2), 224–235.

Schultze-Berndt, E. (2002). Grammaticalized restrictives on adverbials and secondary predicates: Evidence from Australian languages. *Australian Journal of Linguistics* 22: 231–264.

Stokes, B. and McGregor, W. (2003). Classification and subclassification of the Nyulnyulan languages. In N. Evans (ed.), *The Non-Pama-Nyungan languages of northern Australia: Comparative studies of the continent's most linguistically complex region*. Canberra: Pacific Linguistics, 29–74.

Sutton, P. and H. Koch. (2008). Australian languages: A singular vision. *Journal of Linguistics* 44: 471–504.

Wichmann, S. (2010). Neolithic linguistics. In: Barjamovic, G., I. Elmerot, A. Hyllested, B. Nielsen and B. Okholm Skaarup (eds.), *Language and prehistory of the Indo-European peoples: A cross-disciplinary perspective*. Budapest: Archaeolingua.

16   The Spread of Pama-Nyungan in Australia

Patrick McConvell

16.1   Introduction

16.1.1   Australia, Continent of Hunter-Gatherers

In contrast to all the other continents discussed in this volume, Australia's hunter-gatherers did not share, or contend for, the land with indigenous culti-vators or pastoralists. The foraging economy reigned exclusively throughout the history of human habitation until the catastrophic events of conquest and settlement by the British caused its collapse within the last 200 years. Certainly there were differences between the way the indigenous people of Australia gained a living from the land in different regions, from more to less mobile, which will enter the picture as we focus our discussion here. But despite use of phrases like 'firestick farming' (Jones 1969) to describe strategic manipulation of the environment, and the reports of occasional scattering of wild seeds, there is no evidence of horticulture, agriculture or animal-rearing having been practised in Australia before the arrival of the British in the late eighteenth century.[1]

For many scholars of the field, this situation has provided a unique oppor-tunity – a 'laboratory' almost – for study of hunter-gatherers in a pristine situation, a window into the world in which all humans lived until about 10,000 years ago. As more and more of the hunter-gatherer studies from elsewhere in the world emphasized the intensity and complexity of interaction between hunter-gatherers and others, the contrast with Australia became more stark. Of course by the time anthropologists, linguists and others were studying Australian Aborigines with modern methods, most of them had already given up foraging as their main way of life. However, the earlier studies, and recollections of older people in later times, give a reasonably complete picture, and studies have been carried out with people still involved with traditional foraging to a greater or lesser extent.

I particularly wish to gratefully acknowledge the inspiration and assistance of Barry Alpher, a pioneer of detailed reconstruction of Pama-Nyungan lexicon. We do not necessarily agree on everything in this chapter.

There is a temptation, which has sometimes not been resisted, to project specific practices and systems of the Australian Aborigines in recent times on to Palaeolithic hunter-gatherers of other times and other places, and the general introduction to this book sets this kind of discourse in its place in the history of anthropology. Naturally the original Australians had their own cultures, quite diverse across the continent, which differ markedly from those of peoples on other continents, and – another important facet of Australia's uniqueness – a generally low level of influences from outside Australia.[2]

If the fact of being a hunter-gatherer per se has a strong influence on cultural details, then people holding this kind of view may extend it to details of language, and one might expect some scholar to have come up with the idea that Australian Aboriginal languages retain features of ancestral hunter-gatherer languages of the past in some way. As far as we know this has not happened nor does this line of inquiry offer fruitful prospects. One of the main hypotheses which could make such a link is that which differentiates the kind of ethnobiological classification in the lexicon of hunter-gatherers from that of food-producers, discussed by Cecil Brown (Chapter 4, this volume). We return to the applicability of these ideas to Australia later in this chapter.

There are many reasons why one would not go down the road of equating Australian languages with some kind of proto-typical or primordial 'hunter-gatherer language' type, but one of them is that Australian languages are quite dissimilar to each other in structure. This dissimilarity, however, is far from random and does have an interesting pattern geographically, and we would argue, historically. This is the prime focus of our chapter here.

16.1.2   The Pama-Nyungan-non-Pama-Nyungan Divide

The major striking difference in Australian languages is that between those of the bulk of the continent, which are generally termed Pama-Nyungan (PN), and those of the central north of the continent, generally termed Non-Pama-Nyungan (NPN).[3] This division correlates quite strongly with grammatical typology as well as distribution of lexicon and morphological forms. Most Australianists believe this to be a linguo-genetic division – i.e. PN languages are descended from a single proto-language, which we shall call the Pama-Nyunganist view. For NPN languages the general opinion has been that there are a number of distinct families, although the possibility that most or all of them could have a single origin has been canvassed (see Chapter 15 by Harvey, this volume, which argues that such hypotheses are not backed up by enough evidence). Another opinion has been maintained by Dixon (1997, 2002), that there is no such thing as a PN family and resemblances between languages are the result of massive diffusion both of forms and structures in the Australian 'linguistic area', which we shall label the 'Australian-arealist' view.

Within the general Pama-Nyunganist view, there are different possible hypotheses about the relationship between PN and NPN. The one followed here is that Proto-Pama-Nyungan (PPN) was a language which branched off from NPN languages, and at some early stage developed typological and lexical peculiarities and in time spread throughout most of Australia. Hypotheses about the overall tree structure and how PN and NPN families articulate to each other are being proposed and tested and no consensus has been arrived at yet.

One possible view is that represented in publications by Evans (e.g. 2003: 10) which is represented in Figure 16.1. In this conception, the core PPN (what O'Grady called Proto-Nuclear Pama-Nyungan) split from Proto-Garrwan,[4] and before that from Proto-Tangkic, then previous to that from Proto-Gunwinyguan. Garrwan and Tangkic are two small families on the southern coast of the Gulf of Carpentaria whose languages have features of both PN and NPN languages and have proved difficult to classify, but which currently people are viewing as NPN.

On this view, PN is most likely to have spread out from the region of the coast of the Gulf of Carpentaria where the languages are most differentiated within PN and the NPN neighbours most like PN. Other evidence to be reviewed in this chapter internal to PN seems to point to an origin in the north-east of the continent with movement of languages west and south from there.[5] One of the most significant things about PN was that it spread over nearly the whole continent, except for the central north. We know that people occupied the continent for more than 50,000 years and nearly every corner of it for at least 30,000 years, but the PN family has all the appearances of a family which is much younger than that, probably mid-Holocene in age (6,000–4,000 years old). As there is evidence for human occupation of most of the continent going back as much as at least 40,000 earlier than that, it follows that the PN languages replaced earlier languages over much of the continent.

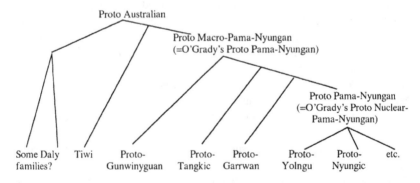

Figure 16.1 Relationship between Pama-Nyungan and Non-Pama-Nyungan.

One continental pattern in archaeology which may line up with the PN spread is the spread of backed artifacts (previously known as 'backed blades'). The distribution of these artifacts is very similar to that of PN languages. Their appearance in the archaeological record is staged from late Pleistocene-early Holocene in the north-east, with horizon dates for a more substantial proliferation going from 5–4,000 kya to 3–2,000 kya in the south-east and moving west across the continent (Hiscock 2002). This is suggestive of a parallel and linked movement and chronology with PN, and Hiscock agrees that his primary explanation, which sees development of the blades as a risk-averse strategy in a period of decreasing rainfall, is not incompatible with migration of PN speakers facing the same risks. Such correlations must, however, be treated with care. Many technological innovations are known to move quite independently of people and languages. A stronger case could be made if some of the artifact terminology could be reconstructed for PPN and other intermediate subgroups and aligned with archaeological finds. However, most of the terms which can be reconstructed are for wooden implements which are not preserved in the archaeological record and vice versa; the tools which are discovered and dated are stone and do not so far seem to have yielded any reconstructions at deep levels. One example of an 'archaeolinguistic stratigraphy' study which was at least partially successful for the mid-Holocene was McConvell and Smith's (2003) about 'mullers' (top grindstones), and more and better studies of this kind might well develop PN spread chronologies. McConvell and Smith's study does not reconstruct a term to Proto-PN or even to Proto-Ngumpin-Yapa (a northern subgroup of PN) but shows that the term for muller entered Ngumpin-Yapa as a loanword after the proto-language stage. Such loanword studies are an indispensable complement to proto-language reconstruction.

16.1.3   The Dominance of Agriculture in the Explanation of Widespread Language Families

The Holocene expansion of PN would not be an exceptional scenario – in fact it parallels the kind of picture put forward for Indo-European, Austronesian and other well-known widespread families. The apparent exceptionality arises simply because of the current dominant scholarly discourse about widespread language families which ties the phenomenon very much to the expansion of agriculture and pastoralism (e.g. Bellwood and Renfrew 2002). This discourse tends to produce an inclination to accept ultra-diffusionist 'areal' scenarios for such families as PN – to deny that they are families in the accepted sense, as Dixon (2002) does; or to allow an absence of any explanation of the phenomenon of widespread hunter-gatherer families, leaving us with an unsolved mystery. PN is not the only example of such a widespread hunter-gatherer language family as we show in the general introduction of the book. It is notable, however, that Bellwood (2013) also turns his attention to forager language expansions like PN.

16.1.4   *Pama-Nyungan: A Prime Example of a Widespread Hunter-Gatherer Language Family*

PN is a good example of a widespread hunter-gather language family because it spread across the 'continent of hunter-gatherers' and did not encounter or interact with languages of non-hunter-gatherers, except very marginally. Thus we can perhaps take the process as perhaps analogous to other hunter-gatherer language spreads before the advent of farming. Of course the process is moulded in the PN case by the specific characteristics of Australia, and in particular perhaps by the extreme aridity and variability of the climate of much of the interior. However, these characteristics are also found to a less extreme degree on other continents and there may be more general human-ecological geographical principles which help us understand both PN history and similar expansions.

The approach to this issue which denies the existence of PN (primarily pursued by Dixon) is dealt with briefly in the text that follows by referring to the mounting evidence for this family. Others concede that there may be substantial evidence for the family but regard it as an oddity in some way: for Wichman (2015) it is an exception to his generalization that hunter-gatherer language families do not have many branches (see Chapter 15 by Harvey, this volume; McConvell and Bowern 2011).

16.1.5   *Change in Meaning of Lexical Roots*

The main theme of this chapter is types of lexical semantic change referring mainly to examples in the domains of kinship and flora/fauna vocabulary. Sound change is, of course, an essential part of the reconstruction task but is not in the foreground in this chapter. Ideally one would want to have reconstructed vocabularies at the levels of all the justifiable subgroups of PN. We are not at that stage but here we discuss what general geographical distributions of forms and meanings of widespread roots can tell us in a preliminary way. The examples chosen also illustrate how the changes of meanings and borrowings can shed light on changes in culture during the PN spread. Borrowing of terms from other languages can often be complementary to meaning change and is also examined here.

The patterns in meanings of kinship terms can tell us about the types of social organization and marriage systems in a former era, and borrowing of kinship terms may indicate that groups require the new term to implement a new type of system. Changes in meanings of food terms in certain areas may indicate people encountering a new ecology in the area people are moving into, and/ or a change in the environment over time.

16.1.6   Prospectus of Sections to Come

In what follows we shall focus on the PN family, specifically the following points:

Section 16.2: PN reconstruction, especially the reconstruction of meaning of lexical roots
Section 16.3: Meaning change
Section 16.4: Meaning change in kinship terminology
Section 16.5: Meaning change in fauna vocabulary
Section 16.6: Borrowing, especially kinship and animal terminology
Section 16.7: Models of language spread in PN and meaning change/ borrowing
Section 16.8: Conclusions

16.2   Pama-Nyungan as a Family

Section 16.2 presents a brief summary of mounting evidence for the PN family. To count as evidence for the validity of the family, the reconstructions must be innovations in PN, not retentions from some earlier proto-language. However we also discuss items which are inherited from earlier proto-languages and issues about distinguishing borrowing from inheritance.

16.2.1   Innovations in Pama-Nyungan

A number of grammatical features (pronouns, noun and verb inflectional paradigms) occur exclusively in PN languages (Alpher 2004; Evans 2005), differentiating them from the other indigenous languages of Australia. These must be considered to have originated in a period of PN unity – in PPN, the language ancestral to the approximately 160 languages of the PN phylogenetic family. Those most frequently cited are a set of pronoun roots distinctively different from NPN (Blake 1988); the distinctive allomorphs of ergative and locative suffixes, some conditioned by mora-count, verb conjugations (Alpher 1990); and a sound change of initial laminalization (Evans and McConvell 1998: the latter has been questioned, however, by Alpher 2004: 112).

16.2.2   Distribution of Innovations in Lexical Roots

If, as we argue, PN is a valid language family dating back to the mid-Holocene then we will find within it a reasonably high level of roots descended from the PN proto-language which are not found outside PN except by borrowing. These are PN innovations. Contrary to a misconception Dixon seems to have about the comparative method, it is not necessary to find these roots in a high percentage of languages. To establish that the putative roots are not in fact innovations in a subgroup of PN, however, it is a reasonable heuristic to demand that reflexes of the roots be attested in a number of different geographically scattered branches of PN which are unlikely to turn out to constitute a higher-level subgroup below PN. Many roots pass this test in Alpher's PNyEtyma list, for instance (2004).

Dixon (2002) argues that there is no such bunching of a group of roots in PN languages except what may be predicted from areal convergence. His test of this proposition is flawed and the data are not presented in any case. There are of course a number of items which may be descended from a higher level grouping consisting of PN and NPN or many NPN languages (sometimes loosely referred to as proto-Australian). Further there are of course many borrowings between PN and NPN particularly around the borders of the two groups of languages. Dixon adds protection for his position by claiming that it is very hard or impossible to tell borrowings and inheritances apart. In fact there is usually evidence that allows us to distinguish them.

I have worked on languages on both sides of the PN-NPN border in the same region – the Victoria River District NT and East Kimberley WA – and it is obvious that the PN and NPN languages are very different lexically as well as grammatically. There are loanwords in both directions but these can be detected, along with the direction of borrowing in the vast majority of cases (McConvell 2009). This is the case all along the PN-NPN boundary as far as we know: despite diffusion of items and to a limited extent structures across the boundary there is a sharp divide and no sense of the smooth cline one would expect if the situation were really the result of tens of millennia of diffusion and convergence.

16.2.3   Reconstructing Proto-Pama-Nyungan Lexicon

The Indigenous languages of Australia are quite probably all related.[6] The connections between the highest-level subgroups are probably beyond the reach of the classical comparative method, however, because of the attrition of lexical cognate items. The existence of certain higher-level genetic subgroups, like PN, Tangkic, Gunwinyguan and Nyulnyulan, is, we think, beyond doubt, though many important details remain to be worked out. The relationship between PN and certain other subgroups, notably Tangkic and Gunwinyguan, seems to be right at the edge of the comparative method's power: establishment of regular sound-meaning correspondences is hindered by paucity of cognate material. There are nonetheless sets of words with strong form-meaning resemblances across these major subgroup boundaries that suggest interlanguage relationships of both the diffusional and the genetic kinds.

Lexical items reconstructed to PPN (Alpher 2004) with some degree of confidence[7] include 13 kinship terms, 32 verbs, 10 adjectives and so on, and in the flora/fauna category, 4 names of species of birds, 2 of insects, 2 of plants, 2 of molluscs and 1 of fish. While systematic phonological and lexical reconstruction of PPN has begun (see Alpher 2004), the exacting task of determining which of the reconstructed forms are exclusive to PN, and hence constitute a further argument for PN as a phylogenetic group, has not yet been systematically undertaken. Difficulties presented by this task include the large volume of NPN lexical material that must be checked, as well as the problem of determining by standard historical-comparative means just which of these forms are common inheritances and which are loans (Alpher 2004: 119–122).

In this chapter we shall touch on forms which occur in PPN which are retained from some older proto-language and show up as inherited items in some NPN languages. However, the main emphasis in this section is on form-meaning pairs which are *innovations* in PN, and are not therefore found in NPN languages except occasionally as loanwords from PN. There exists a much more extensive catalogue of such lexical innovations (Alpher 2004 and updates) but for the purposes of exposition here we shall focus on a smaller number of examples, mainly from the fields of kinship and animal and plant terms.

As noted earlier, in order to designate a term as a solid PPN reconstruction it does not have to have reflexes in a large number of languages: presence of a form with expected sound correspondences and a closely related meaning in a handful or even two languages widely separated by geographical and phylogenetic distance suffices for it to count as candidate proto-form.[8]

There are forms which occur with apparently related forms in NPN languages. Until and unless they can be definitely assigned to the category of loanwords from PN these must be suspected of going back to a pre-PPN proto-language. Such a root is *mara(ng) 'hand' of which reflexes are found spread across most PN subgroups in most parts of Australia but also in a few NPN languages such as Nunggubuyu (Wubuy). One kinship term to which we will return later because of its interesting changes in meaning is *kaala originally 'mother's brother' in PPN (see Map 16.2) but with a possible cognate in a NPN language of the west Kimberley Bardi *gaarra*.[9]

We are not dealing with arriving at regular sound correspondences in this chapter, except in passing as we discuss other matters. Sound change appears to have less impact in Australia, especially in PN than in many other language families around the world, although it is certainly present, for instance the lateralization change discussed by McConvell and Laughren (2004) and various regular lenition and other consonantal changes in many languages. In some areas sound changes produce gross distortions of proto-forms (e.g. by regular dropping of initial consonants and syllables); once understood as regular changes these are tractable and useful in the reconstruction of proto-languages. In a considerable number of cases, however, cognates are similar and may be identical in form.

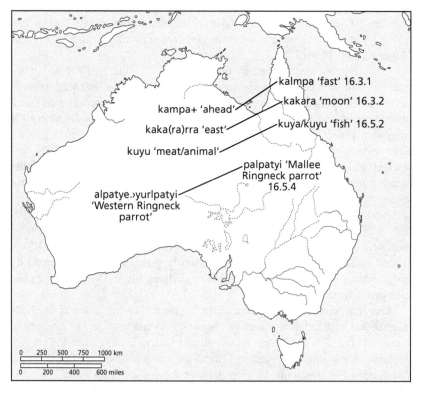

kalmpa 'fast' 16.3.1
kakara 'moon' 16.3.2
kuya/kuyu 'fish' 16.5.2
kampa+ 'ahead'
kaka(ra)rra 'east'
kuyu 'meat/animal'
palpatyi 'Mallee Ringneck parrot' 16.5.4
alpatye.›yurlpatyi 'Western Ringneck parrot'

Map 16.1 Change in meaning of some roots from east to west in Pama-Nyungan.

16.3   Meaning Change

Frequently the problem has been whether the disparate meanings of the root in different languages can be related to each other as descending from the same proto-meaning.

Lexical semantic change theory is not as well developed as sound change theory to aid in this endeavour. However, matters are improving in this regard (see Map 16.1 and examples below). Some ground-breaking work has been done by people working in the Australian languages field. Some of these lines of research are directed at discovering universal hypotheses about, for instance, the direction of extension of meaning of body-part terms (Wilkins 1996). A general principle is that change of meaning generally proceeds via a stage of polysemy. A related heuristic is that a language with the predicted polysemy between a meaning A and a meaning B, especially in the same region, can occur in a 'bridging context' for a change between A and B, that is, that sentences in discourse may be ambiguous between the two meanings, and thus increase the likelihood that the change takes place.

This Australian semantic change work has often dealt not just with semantic changes that we might expect to find in any languages but also with those which are most commonly found in Australia or regions of Australia, with relationships to general ideational and cultural patterns reflected in the languages, and trees or networks of semantic associations and change paths have been produced to map some of these connections (Evans and Wilkins 2001). An example is the very common association of words for 'ear' with the idea or knowing and understanding (Evans and Wilkins 2000). Thus for instance in PN languages across the continent (probably descended from PPN *pina) a root *pina* is found meaning 'ear' in some languages, and 'knowing' in others with a few languages having both meanings, at least in some expressions (Alpher 2004). In such a case one might want to say that the polysemy or close conceptual relatedness is ancient, and also continuing in many regions in recent times. In other cases, polysemies and meaning changes develop at certain points in more recent prehistory due to cultural or environmental changes, or language contact. The map 16.1 shows the geography of meaning changes in lexical items from east to west to be discussed in following sections.

16.3.1   *Kalmpa 'Ahead' and 'Fast'*

Forms that on phonological grounds can be reckoned cognate often carry disparate meanings in various languages, and problems arise as to whether and how these discrepancies can be accounted for. In this respect, the Indigenous languages of Australia are no different from any other. An example is PPN *kalmpa, attested in some languages as 'fast, quickly', in others as 'first', and in a few as 'hard [adverbial]'.[10] A bridging context, or sentence containing this word in which it can be understood in one or the other of two (or more) ways—in this case something like *she ran fast/first*—provides a way of formulating the conditions for the shift process (Evans and Wilkins 2000: 546–592; 2001: 493–521).

There is a non-random geographical distribution of the meanings of *kalmpa reflexes. Most Paman languages in Cape York Peninsula in the far north-east of Australia have the 'fast' meaning but among these Kok Kaper ('Koko Bera') in the south-west of Cape York Peninsula has the first/ahead meaning and Gugu Yimidhirr has the meaning 'also, more' which could be a further development from ahead/first. Throughout the rest of Australia to the west and south where reflexes of this root are attested, the meaning is 'ahead' and allied senses, and the 'fast' meaning is absent. Data that follow and in subsequent etyma lists are from an updated version of Alpher (2004).[11]

It is not possible at this stage of research to be completely sure which is the original meaning in PPN. However, it is well known that spatial terms extend to, and may shift to temporal terms and a change in the opposite direction is extremely rare. To take an example similar to the one we are looking at in Australia, in English and other European languages words for 'in front' in space like *before* shift to a temporal meaning of 'in the past' (Traugott and Dasher 2002: 57), and languages with reflexes of the root we are discussing do the same, like Gurindji where the term *kamparri* means both 'in front, ahead' and 'in the past'. This might suggest that 'fast' is a secondary development related to time, from the spatial meaning 'ahead'. There is an implication that an object X in front of an object Y has gone fast or faster in the direction object Y is going or facing so that it ends up ahead of Y. In Gurindji if someone says *kamparri yanta* 'go on ahead' that would pragmatically be understood that the addressee should go faster than the speaker, providing a hypothetical 'bridging context' for the shift from 'ahead' to 'fast'. However, so far no language has been reported with a clear case of polysemy between 'ahead' and 'fast'.

Another indication that 'ahead' is the original meaning is that other meanings for this root seem to have developed from the 'ahead' meaning: the 'also' meaning in Guugu Yimidhirr, for instance, cf. English, 'further', 'furthermore'. The development of the meanings 'up' and 'far' in some languages is also more plausibly related to 'ahead' than to 'fast'.

In this case, the, one might hypothesize that the original meaning spread widely south and west in Australia with the spread of PN but at some stage an innovation changed the meaning in a significant number of Paman languages to 'fast'.

In this case, the hypothesized proto-meaning is also the most widespread meaning in the greatest number of languages where the root is attested. This is not always the case, and this cannot be used reliably as a heuristic principle for determining proto-meanings. In discussing kinship we shall look at another kind of rule-of-thumb designed to predict proto-meanings.

Table 16.1 *Changes in meaning Proto-Pama-Nyungan *kalmpa*

\e ***kalmpa**	
\t 'fast'	
\b nAdv	
\x See also kanpa.	
\l WMungknh	\w *kamp* \g 'fast' \s (KPPW)
\l WNgathan	\w *kampvl* \g 'quickly, fast (of motion)' \q Also *kempiy* 'up, upwards, on top', with characteristic *a > *e* before *l. \s (PS)
\l Umpithamu	\w *kamparra* \g 'quick' \q Probably a loan. \s (J-CV)
\l YYoront	\w *kalpn* \g 'fast, hard'
\l YMel	\w *kalpvn* \g 'quickly'
\l KKaper	\w *kalmpá* \g 'first' \s (BA)
\l Flinders Island	\w *elmbal* \g 'quickly' \s (PS)
\l KThaypan	\w *lmbe* \g 'up, upward' \q Cognate? \s (BR)
\l GYim	\w *galmba* \g 'and, also, more' \s (JHav)
\l **pPaman**	\w ***kalmpa** \s BA
\l Biri	\w *gamba* \g 'ahead' \q Biri dialect. \s (AT)
\l Bidyara	\w *gambarri ~ gambadi* \g 'a long way away' \s (GB)
\l Margany	\w *gambarri* \g 'far' \s GB
\l Gunya	\w *gambarri* \g 'far' \s GB
\l Ngiyampaa	\w *kampirra* \g 'a day either side of the reference time, that is, yesterday or tomorrow' \q Cognate? \s (TD)
\l Yandruwandha (Innaminka)	\w *kambarri* \g 'at the front, first' \s GB
\l ECArrernte	\w *amparre* \g 'first' \q In the construction *ke+amparre*, can be reduced to *kamparre*. Per HK's analysis, the /a/ suggests that this is a loan. \s (H&D)
\l WArrernte	
\l Warlpiri	\w *kamparru* \g 'ahead, in front, first, before, at the beginning' \s (KLH)
\l Warlmanpa	\w *kampa* \g 'in front, ahead' \s (DGN)
\l Mudburra	\w *kamparra* \g 'in front, before, in the lead; old' \q Also *kambarrakambarra* 'long ago, olden days; big mob in the lead'; *kambarrambarra* 'long ago'; *kambarrajbunga* 'former (people)'. \s (DGN/PMcC, RG)
\l Payungu	\w *kamparri* \g 'before; ahead' \s (PA)
\l Thalanyji	\w *kamparri* \g 'ahead, in front, first, before' \s (PA)
\l Burduna	\w *kaparri* \g 'ahead, in front, first, before' \s (PA)
\l **PKanyara**	\w ***kamparri** \s (PA)
\l **pPNy**	\w ***kalmpa**

Some lexical semantic changes can form part of a bundle of shared innovations which define subgroups: in the kinship section we will look at an example of this. In the case of the 'fast' meaning of *kalmpa- it is possible that this is one of a set of innovations that defines Paman although in general the concept of a 'Paman' subgroup definable by shared innovation remains in doubt.

There is another change in this root which is of a more familiar kind in defining subgroups: the sound change from ***lmp to *mp*** (*kalmpa->kampa-) which is part of a more general change from a triconsonantal (liquid-nasal-oral) cluster to a nasal-oral cluster by loss of the liquid (O'Grady and Fitzgerald 1995; Alpher 2004). In this case the older conservative form is the one found in Paman (Cape York Peninsula) and the innovated form is found throughout Australia outside this area. The conservative languages retaining *lmp* are a subset of Paman not coinciding exactly with the grouping retaining the original meaning 'fast'.

16.3.2   *Kakara 'Moon' and 'East'

Of interest here are semantic shifts that are recurrent in Australian Indigenous languages. One such area is that of terms for cardinal directions. Most Australian languages attest four of them: north, south, east and west. However, in some languages, the word for one of the directions is cognate with the word for another of the directions in a nearby language.[12] One way in which meaning correspondences of this kind can arise is among adjacent languages located along a curved coastline. One pair of the cardinal terms, say east/west, is also used to designate up- or downriver – senses which can become the primary ones; down the coast, in a territory facing the ocean towards the north, 'upriver' is in fact south, and here the old 'east' term has come to mean 'south'. McConvell (1996), in relation to the Pilbara, suggests that this type of shifting of reference may have been caused by movement of people. In other areas the source of non-'cardinal' senses can be the alignment of parallel sand-ridges (Breen 1993). A further play on directional terms is pPNy *kakara, attested as 'moon' in some languages and 'east' in others. The presumed logic is that the most usual time for viewing the moon is just after nightfall, and the full moon (the presumed prototypical shape) can be seen near the eastern horizon at this time.

As noted in the text that follows, in the data from Alpher (2004, updated, cited in Table 16.2) there is an association between full moon and east because the moon rises in the east. The isoseme (semantic isogloss) lies around the central Gulf of Carpentaria, with the 'moon' meanings to the north and east and the 'east' meanings to the south and west.

The difference between the forms with *r* (retroflex glide; occasionally also retroflex stop *rt*) and those with *rr* (alveolar flap) coincides with the meaning difference 'moon' : 'east'. This does not appear to be a regular sound correspondence. The likely explanation might be found with reference to the

Watjarri forms (near the central western coast of Western Australia) where -*rra* is found suffixed to the *kakara* form as well as other spatial expressions (-*rra* is a widespread suffix in PN for 'away' direction). Reduction of -*rarra* to -*rra* in other languages of the west has probably occurred.

It is clear that 'east' is the original meaning of the cognates which have shifted compass directional meaning. There is variation: in Wakaya in the south-east Barkly Tableland on the Northern Territory-Queensland border it means 'south' for some speakers and 'east' for others. In the Pilbara, *kakarra* means 'east' in the eastern languages but in the west it means 'south' in the more southerly languages and 'west' in a more northerly language. As mentioned earlier, 'rotation' of compass point meanings is a known phenomenon in various parts of Australia (cf. Tindale 1974). For eastern examples, Breen (1993) considers that the variation correlates with the alignment of parallel sand hills.

The example of 'ahead' becoming 'fast' in Table 16.1 is unrelated to any geographical or cultural conditions in Australia and could well occur any-where. The relationship between 'moon' and 'east' (via the rise of the full moon) is similarly not obviously related to any Australian geographical or

Table 16.2 *Kakara* '*moon*' > '*east*'

\e **kakara*	
\t 'moon'	
\b n	
\c E	
\x See also *kapir, *pira.	
\l YYoront	\w *ka7ar* \g 'moon' \p Oblique case-forms in *ka7 r*(+).
\l YMel	\w *kakar* \g 'moon'
\l KKaper	\w *kakér* \g 'moon'
\l **pPaman**	**\w *kakara* \s KLH**
\l Biri	\w *gagara* \g 'moon' \q Yangga, Gangulu, Garingbal, Wiri, Biri, Baradha, and Yetimarala dialects. \s AT
\l Bidyara	\w *gagarda* \g 'moon' \s GB
\l Dharawala	\w *kakar*(*d*)*a* \g 'moon' \s GB
\l Yandjibara	\w *akarda* \g also *awara*. \s GB
\l Wadjabangayi	\w *kakara* \g 'moon' \s GB
\l Yiningara	\w *kakara* \g 'moon' \s GB
\l **pPM**	**\w *kakara***
\l Mayi-Yapi	\w *kakara* \g 'moon' \s GB
\l Wunumara	\w *kakara* \g 'moon' \s GB
\l Mayi-Kutuna	\w *kakara* \g 'moon' \s GB
\l Dyirbal	\w *gagara* \g 'moon' \q Not in RMWD 1972 (which gives *gagalum* 'moon, Masculine, for Mamu'). \s KLH
\l Duungidjawu	\w *kakare* \g 'moon' \s K&W

Table 16.2 (*cont.*)

\l Kaurna	\w *kakirra* \g 'moon' \q T&C; Gaimard gives *kaker* (with the extra sense 'shellfish') and Robinson gives *car.ca.rer* (and Wyatt *karka:ra*, per Jane Simpson [pers. com.], who regards the fluctuation in transcriptions of V2 as possible evidence that C3 is a retroflex glide and not a tapped liquid; otherwise the nature of the "rr" is uncertain). \s (T&C, RA)
\l Watjarri	\w *kakararra* \g 'east' \q Note that *-rarra* recurs in the directional *kankararra* 'up' (see *kanka). \s WD
\l pPNy	**\w *kakara** \q KLH: 'moon'. With regard to the 'moon'–'east' connection (see below, and the Watjarri attestation above), note Kayardild *balurdiinda* 'new moon' [lit. 'westward-sitter', so-called because the new moon is always in the west at dusk]' and *riyathi-ddinda* 'full moon [lit. 'far-east sitter']. The sense of this is that the prototypical form of the moon is full and that the prototypical time to view it is just after sunset. KLH gloss 'moon'. \s (KLH 82:373)
^^^	
\l Wirangu	\w *gagarrara* \g 'east' \s LH
\l Wakaya	\w *kekerril* \g 'south, east' \f "e" is a central vowel. \q Contrast *keláth* 'east'. \s GB
\l Pitjantjatjara- Yankunytjatjara	\w *kakarrara* \g 'east; on the eastern side' \q Note that /rr/ apparently does not continue *r in this position—see *yangkara. \s CG
\l Manjiljarra	\w *kakarra* \g 'east' \s PMcC
\l Warlpiri	\w *kakarrara* \g 'east' \s KLH
\l Gurindji	\w *ka:rra* \g 'east' \q Regular lenition and loss of intervocalic *k. \s PMcC
\l Djaru	\w *ga:rra* \g 'east' \ Also *ga:na*, ^ga:ni, ga:rrarra. \s TTs 26,125,259
\l Walmajarri	\w *kakarra* \g 'east' \s JHd
\l Palyku	\w *kakarra* \g 'east' \s GNOG
\l Panyjima	\w *kakarra* \g 'east' \s GNOG, AD
\l pNgayarda	**\w *kakarra** \s GNOG #604
\l Warriyangka	\w *kakarra* \g 'south' \s PA
\l Yingkarta (Northern & Southern)	\w *kakarra* \g 'south' \s PA
\l Karajarri	\w *kakarra* \g 'east' \s ASEDA 0069
\l Tharrgari (1)	\w kagarra \g 'west' \s PA

cultural conditions, although such a circumstance could not be definitively ruled out. 'Rotations' of compass points are known to have taken place elsewhere in the world, for instance Iceland (Haugen 1957), but it is possible that parallel peculiarities of migrations, social networks and local geographies could well provide further explanations of such occurrences. In the text that follows I will provide examples of kinship and flora and fauna which are more clearly related to specific cultural and environmental conditions and changes in prehistoric Australia.

16.4   Meaning Change in Kinship and Animals

16.4.1   Kinship Terminology

Kinship vocabulary is both 'basic' and 'cultural'. There is fairly high retention of kinship roots in PN which will probably permit eventual reconstruction of virtually the entire kinship terminology of PPN as well as that of many of its component subgroups. Borrowing of kinship terms occurs but this often seems to be motivated by the need to fill a gap in a system, rather than some random process like death-taboo. Affinal (in-law) terms are also commonly borrowed and McConvell (2015) discusses changes in marriage practice spreading over wide areas which motivate two of these diffusions.

Frequently the reflexes of proto-kinship roots do vary in meaning in different languages so that the problem of reconstructing the correct meaning is regularly encountered. Dyen and Aberle (1974) proposed a method for dealing with this issue in kinship reconstruction, for the Athapaskan languages, which was criticized for being over-mechanistic (Blust 1990; McConvell 2013c).

While such algorithms can play a role in assuring a higher level of objectivity in semantic reconstruction, various historical and cultural considerations need to be weighed up too. In particular reconstructions should meet two conditions:

(a) Each term (form) should be reconstructed individually, while
(b) the entire terminology made up of these terms should be assessed as a system, having regard to whether the pattern of equations (polysemies) is one which is found among the world's systems and especially if it conforms to what we know of Australian systems.

It is of course possible that ancient kinship systems in Australia were of a unique type and/or that kinship systems have radically altered their character over the millennia, but these suppositions are implausible.

Among the principles followed in all or many Australian systems (and also found in many other societies around the world) are the following:

(1) **For the purpose of reckoning kinship links,** a person is equivalent to his or her same-sex sibling.

(2) **As designated relatives,** persons in the grandparental generation tend to be called by the same term as their opposite-sex sibling (not universally true in Australia).
(3) Kinship terms tend to be repeated to designate relatives in **alternate generations**, very typically grandparent-grandchild.

Typologies of kinship systems have been constructed over many years since the pioneering work of Morgan in the mid-nineteenth century. One that brings together much of the work in the Standard Cross-Cultural Sample which in its kinship aspect is based on George P. Murdock's work (1970), and incorporates designations of systems based on names of language groups such as Iroquois, Eskimo etc. (for patterns of equation found in cousin terminology). In Australia, however, Radcliffe-Brown (1931) and Elkin (1964) invented a different scheme in which types of system took the names of language groups in Australia, and this tradition has largely been continued in more recent surveys such as Scheffler (1978).

This comparative work in anthropology on kinship systems in Australia has not involved any reconstruction of proto-terminologies or systems, until recently. However some anthropologists (e.g. Elkin 1970) have speculated that one type of system – Kariera – was the dominant system at some earlier stage and gave way to other types later. Kariera is close to a system more generally known as Dravidian in world anthropology and these earlier speculations are now echoed by others claiming a Dravidian/Kariera system to be the primordial system in world prehistory. However, no compelling evidence has been offered to back up such hypotheses for Australia.

Recent work has begun to assemble some evidence that perhaps the proto-terminology of at least PN was of the Kariera type but there is a long way to go before this is fully established. There are two primary aspects to a Kariera terminology:

(1) Dravidian cousin terminology: cross-cousins equated with each other, (and in many cases with spouse of sibling in laws), and not equated with siblings. Ex. MBS = FZS = H $\neq$ B; MBD = FZD = W $\neq$ Z.
(2) Parallel grandparents and their siblings of the same sex are equated but not equated with cross grandparents and their siblings; cross grandparents and their siblings of same sex are equated but not equated with parallel grandparents and their siblings. Ex. MMB = FF $\neq$ FM(B) or MF; MM = FFZ $\neq$ FM or MF(Z); MF = FMB $\neq$ MM(B) or FF; MFZ = FM $\neq$ MM or FF(Z).

(In some systems gender is also neutralized e.g. MM = FF, but this is not an essential criterion of Kariera systems. Grandparents and grandchildren may share the same terms and parallel grandparents may be equated to siblings but again these are not criterial for Kariera).

In what follows we examine briefly some of the issues related to how one might reconstruct PN kinship terminology and test the hypothesis that it is a Kariera system as defined in the foregoing. Each of the criteria is considered in turn: cousins and grandparents. This is not a comprehensive examination of the issue; only a few terms are discussed with emphasis on cases where the meaning of terms has changed over time between PPN and daughter subgroups.

16.4.2 Cousins, Uncles, Aunts, Nieces and Nephews

As cross-cousins are distinguished from siblings in nearly all PN languages, it is highly likely that the PPN system had this feature as well.[13] Whether there was a distinctive form for 'cross-cousin' is less clear: present indications are that none is reconstructable. On the basis of the alternate generation equivalence principle many languages equate cross-cousin with cross-grandparent (for instance, Gumbaiynggirr *ngatyi* has the meaning 'mother's father' and cross-cousin) for which terms can be reconstructed (including *ngatyi MF). Another possibility is that a PPN 'spouse' term was used for cross-cousin, assuming the cross-cousin marriage rule that usually accompanies Kariera terminologies. A term for spouse is *nyupa (with variants nhupa, ngupa) which is found over much of the PN area. It equates to cross-cousin (MBC, FZC) in language groups which have cross-cousin marriage (and Kariera kin terminology) but also to other kin where marriages rules are different (e.g. MMBDD where 'Aranda' kinship and marriage is found). However, there are indications that this is not a PPN form but an early widespread loanword.

A pair of cross-cousin spouse forms found in Yolngu Matha in North-East Arnhem Land are *galay* MBD/W and *thuway* FZS/H. These are reconstructable not to cross-cousin roots but to uncle (MB) and woman's child (fC, ZC) terms respectively in PPN: *kaala and *thuwa.

This is a case of a change in meaning which is well defined geographically. The 'uncle' and 'woman's child' meanings are confined almost entirely to the north-eastern part of Australia, mostly in Queensland, and the cross-cousin/spouse/sibling-in-law meanings in the west and south.[14]

This is also a case of a meaning change which reflects a well-known polysemy across generations: the equation of a mother with a mother's brother's daughter, and mother's brother with mother' brother's son; and reciprocally, woman's child with father's sister's child. This is known as Omaha skewing and occurs in pockets throughout the world. In Australia it was known mainly in the literature from the North Kimberleys (and labelled the 'Ngarinyin' system by Elkin [1964] but it is actually more widely distributed [Alpher 1982; McConvell and Alpher 2002; McConvell and Keen 2011; McConvell 2012]).

What has occurred with the reflexes of *kaala and *tyuwa is that the terms have altered to ego's generation going down one generation in the patriline and up one generation in the patriline respectively. This is identical to the pattern of extension of terms in Omaha skewing and we hypothesize that Omaha skewing occurred first then loss of the original mother's brother and woman's child meanings. Optional and contextual Omaha skewing appears in western Cape York Peninsula in language groups geographically between those with the original meanings in the north-east and the skewed meanings elsewhere in the west and south, as predicted by the hypothesis. For instance there is, in YirYoront, 'ad hoc' skewing of certain terms, which retain their basic sense as well. This change is depicted on Map 16.2.

Table 16.3 *Grandparental terms in proto-Pama-Nyungan*

*kami	mother's mother and FFZ
*ngaji	mother's father and FMB
*papi	father's mother and MFZ
*mayi-ri/li	father's father and MM

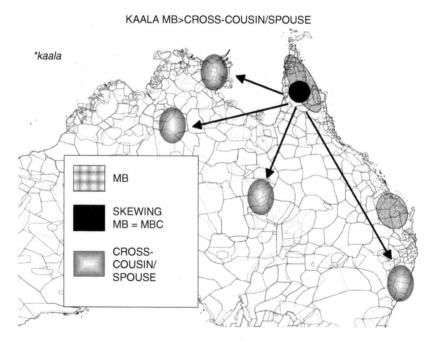

Map 16.2 *Kaala 'mother's brother'>'cross-cousin/spouse'.

16.4.3   Grandparents and Grandchildren

Kinship terminology in PN includes a quite distinctive set of widely distributed roots some of which can be confidently reconstructed back to PPN – and no further. That is, these forms do not occur in NPN languages except as demonstrable loanwords. Take the four grandparent terms (Table 16.3) proposed for PPN (McConvell 2008).

The maps in McConvell (2013) show the distribution of reflexes of the root *kami (cf. McConvell 1997b, 2008). There is variation in its meaning but it is clear that it comes back to a fundamental meaning of 'mother's mother'. For instance, *kami* means 'father's mother' in a couple of areas: around the Lake Eyre Basin and neighbouring areas another term *kany(i)*, also fairly widespread in PN takes over as the MM term. If this term is borrowed in, this could be seen as a push-chain which shifts the meaning of *kami*. However, this hypothesis would be strengthened if the borrowing in of *kanyi* itself had a motivation. Borrowing can be motivated by the absence of a term which distinguishes kin types especially in the context of a change in kinship/marriage systems to one in which the distinction is important. In this case one might speculate that region around Lake Eyre once had a system in which MM and FM were not distinguished (like 'grandmother' in English and terms in Western Desert dialects) and that the proto-term *kami had been extended from an original MM meaning to MM/FM. If subsequently it became necessary to distinguish these terms – for instance because MM was in the same matrimoiety as ego and FM in a different one – then borrowing of a new MM term *kanyi-* would be motivated and the formerly extended *kami reflex would be narrowed to part of its extended scope – FM (for further discussion of this change, see McConvell 2013b).

In fact the group of languages in which the term *kanyi-* stands for MM and *kami reflexes shift to FM coincide largely with a subgroup of PN which can be established on independent grounds: Karnic (Austin 1990; cf. Bowern 2001)

> pK *kanyini* 'mother's mother' Wn, Ar: *kadnhini* [Ad *adnyani* 'mother's mother']
>
> Proto-Karnic *kanyini* 'mother's mother' Ng, Yl, Ya, Yw, Mi, Pp: *kanyini*; Wm: *kanyidja*; Di: *kanhini*
>
> Proto-Central Karnic *kami* 'father's mother' Di, Ng, Yl, Ya, Yw: *kami*

The proto-form *ngatyi 'MF' also has widespread reflexes in the PN zone, found in Eastern Australia and in the far north-west. In many Western languages, however, the form for MF is a reflex of *tyam(p)V+.(for discussion of this see McConvell 2013b). Reflexes of the latter term turn up in Western Desert and Nyungar as the generalized grandfather (MF and FF) term, even as the neutral grandparent term. This corresponds to a change from a Kariera terminological system which rigorously distinguishes between cross and parallel terms to one which neutralizes these distinctions.

The third root *papi does seem to be geographically restricted, to the east, and unlike with *ngatyi and *kanyi there is not a pocket of occurrence in the far west. There is a term for FM which appears to have a geographically complementary distribution, *ngapa- found in the west and south.

The fourth root *ma(yi)ri 'FF' has more question marks over it than the others. *Mayili* etc occurs in the far north-west as FF and *maari* in Yolngu as MM(B) with some usage which covers FF also, but in Cape York Peninsula and it has other meanings. There is another FF root in CYP with cognates also in parts of the south-east – *puːla-: this may in fact be the PPN FF.

Some preliminary conclusions may be drawn from the grandparent terms:

(1) Four grandparent terms (set A) can be reconstructed to PPN which make up a 'Kariera' system with no distinction between paternal and maternal grandparent within parallel and cross grandparents, but with gender distinctions between grandparents and granduncles/aunts.

(2) These proto-terms are found reflected most consistently in north-eastern Australia but with some outliers in the far west and the south.

(3) There is another set of four terms which appear at first sight reconstructable to PPN but may have different non-grandparental meanings in PPN.

(4) This second set of terms (set B) has a more generally western and southern distribution than Set A, and tending to be geographically complementary.[15]

(5) All these roots undergo some changes of meanings in daughter subgroups and languages. Some of these changes are clearly associated with changes in the whole kinship systems, for instance from Kariera to an Aluridja system which combines MF with FF and MM with FM.

(6) Other changes of meanings are linked to borrowing of new terms, for instance in the Karnic case. In this case an earlier extension of MM *kami to include FM (shift to a Luritja type system) is hypothesized followed by borrowing of a new MM term from neighbours completing the fill shift of the *kami reflex to solely FM meaning.

Shifts to a Luritja type system of neutralization of cross and parallel kin are associated with moves of peoples into a harsher environment where longer distance mobility and ability to be flexible about group ties becomes an advantage: this has been observed in North America as well as Australia (Ives 1998; Dousset 2012). Oscillation between this type of system and one with strict demarcation between cross and parallel (such as Kariera) is a likely feature of spread of groups in Australia and can be one of the motivating factors in shifts of meaning of kin-terms.

The pattern of a term having a distribution in some part of the east and in the far north-west could be linked to an expansion of a subgroup which is subsequently overlain with the expansion of another subgroup.

16.5   Meaning Change: Animals

16.5.1   Reconstructing Fauna Terms in Pama-Nyungan

Some of the sets of terms assembled by Alpher (2004) permit the reconstruction of forms, by the classical comparative method, in a proto-language – PPN, Proto-Gunwinyguan, Proto-Tangkic and so on. Some show evidence of having attained their geographical distributions, over at least part of the area, by diffusion. Among the widely distributed terms in this region are names for the trees pandanus, milkwood, cocky-apple and bamboo/palm species; the distribution of these plant species suggests a linguistic origin in the tropical North. Bird terms distributed in this area include names for the bird species pygmy goose, seagull, tawny frogmouth, kite-hawk, curlew, and bustard. Of these the seagull term is an Austronesian loan and at least the hawk and curlew words are Wanderwörter – long-distance travelling loans – rather than inheritances from an old proto-language. There are also names for one or more bream species; names for at least two maritime mollusc species; 'frog'; and a number of others.

Some widespread Pama-Nyungan terms have related forms in NPN including *pangkarra 'blue tongue lizard' (some reflexes referring to other goannas and lizards) which seems related to the reconstructed Proto-Kunwinykuan *pongka (goanna or lizard of some kind, local species meanings vary) and Wakiman pongko. This is possibly a Wanderwort crossing family boundaries.

Others have a somewhat restricted distribution, e.g. *kulan 'possum' found in Cape York Peninsula and Bandjalangic; *purrka 'bandicoot' around the south-eastern Queensland-NSW border, and *wapi+ 'stingray' and *tiwa+ 'green pygmy goose' via Warndarang in Cape York Peninsula (Paman) and in Yolngu in North East Arnhem Land, but not so far detected elsewhere. These may be PPN but could be instead reconstructable only as far back as some high-level subgroup of PN not yet proposed. The latter two would not count as strong evidence for a coastal or northern origin of PN unless cognates are found elsewhere.[16]

Others, however, are found in widely scattered subgroups within PN and not outside, so they qualify both as PN reconstructions and innovations within PN. These include *kalu 'rat', *tyata 'frog', *kulu 'louse', *patawangka/parturra 'bustard' (eastern and western variants, probably related), *tyuntyun 'centipede/scorpion', *tyakurra 'fish species?'

Many of the fauna roots tend to vary in meaning between different languages. The meanings of *tyuntyun reflexes are mainly 'centipede' and/or 'scorpion' in the north-east and the resemblance of the two genera perhaps makes the variability unsurprising. However to the south-west in central Queensland, there is an apparent shift to the meaning 'crayfish': although this is a fresh-water animal there is some physical resemblance. The occurrence of the meaning 'centipede' once again in a language far to the south-west in South Australia (Diyari *thilthirri*), if a valid cognate, would tend to support reconstruction of the meaning 'centipede' in PN. In the west *tyunyturl* in Walmajarri and a related form in Mangala, with the meaning 'leech', is also a creature of no use to Indigenous people and potentially a nuisance and harmful but with little physical resemblance to centipedes, or scorpions. Other regional roots have meanings which are variations of a general sense of 'creepy-crawly' (McConvell and Spronck 2011).

There is often a shift between a generic and a subgeneric species name, for instance a reflex of *tyata is a generic 'frog' word in some languages and 'green tree frog' in some others. Polysemy between a life-form generic term and a specific hyponym is a common phenomenon, both worldwide and in Australia. It appears that meaning change can go either way on this axis. The reason for association of a specific with a generic seems generally to be that the species concerned is the most salient or dominant in the area, and specifically in the lives of local people.[17]

16.5.2   Fish and Meat/Animal

At the highest level in the faunal taxonomy in most Australian languages there is a term that can be translated as both 'meat' and 'animal' or perhaps 'game' – animal which is hunted. Usually there is another hyponym, 'fish'. A term can be reconstructed very confidently to PPN is *kuyu/kuya which means 'fish' in the east and in the south as far as South Australia, and 'meat, animal' in the west.[18] It has been argued that the original meaning in this case is 'fish'. One of the arguments is that there are other roots which also follow exactly this path of semantic shift from 'fish' in the east to 'meat' in the west notably the root *wakari (McConvell 1997a).

A possible explanation of this change is that the spread of languages with *kuyu reflexes meaning 'meat' to the south-west from the Gulf of Carpentaria crosses an inland arid area where there are and were few rivers of any capacity, and fish would have been reduced to a very small component of the diet, if eaten at all. The hypothesis is that the 'meat' meaning attained dominance in that period.

There are also areas in the east (the putative earlier zone of PN before spread) where *kuya/kuyu reflexes are polysemous between 'fish' and 'meat/animal' providing the bridging context which favours the transition from one meaning to another.

16.5.3   Generic/Specific Polysemy and Other Meaning Change: Fish

In fact both *kuya/kuyu and *wakari have reflexes which denote particular fish species in some languages as well as 'fish' and 'meat' in others. In the western Torres Strait *kuyar* is 'stingray'; in Bandjalang the term *kuyang* means 'mullet'; in Nyawaygi *kuya* is 'eel' as it is in Buwandik far to the south on the Victoria/ South Australia border. In different Dyirbal dialects in the North Queensland rain forest just north of Nyawaygi it is 'black bream' in one and 'grey jewfish' in others as well as having the generic 'fish' meaning. It may be that the generic meaning is early and some of the specific meanings emerged later through the principle mentioned earlier that a significant species can be named by the generic as the 'prototypical' fish in the area. Certainly eels became a staple part of the diet for a number of groups in the south and east of Australia where they were plentiful (an economy also evident in archaeology e.g. Bulith 2003). Otherwise the existence of the same meaning in peripheral parts of a distribution like 'eel' in Nyawaygi and Buwandik could lead to the alternative hypothesis that this was the original meaning. More research is needed to decide between these hypotheses.

Wakari, as well as meaning 'fish' in several central central Queensland languages, means 'eel' in some Biri dialects with a variant *wakal* meaning 'eel' in other dialects of this languages and other north and central Queensland languages, with *wakal* being found as 'snake' in far south-west (Nyungar). Farther north *wakal* is found meaning 'crayfish' 'prawn' etc. in PN and NPN languages. This points to the crustacean meaning (probably prawn) being first with a change to 'eel' in central Queensland, subsequently to 'fish/meat' (a polysemy also found in the Pilbara in the west with *wakari*) and 'meat'. The 'snake' meaning in the south-west may be the end of a different pathway coming from 'eel'. Other fish roots change meanings without apparently, generic 'fish' being involved in the semantic change pathways

16.5.4   Birds: Same Term Refers to Different Species in Different Zones

Some roots refer to different species which are related or of similar appearance in different zones (but sometimes overlapping). Reflexes of the PN root *kurrparu are found meaning 'magpie' in southern areas and 'butcher-bird', a similar black and white carnivorous bird, in northern areas.

Another example of where there is transition in meaning corresponding to a division of distribution of similar species is that of *palpatyi whose reflexes of the same form as the reconstruction are found in the Mayi languages and in north-central Queensland refer to the Mallee Ringneck Parrot but the related *alpatye in the Arandic languages of Central Australia refers to the Port Lincoln Ringneck Parrot. The latter form with initial consonant dropping is borrowed into some Western Desert dialects to the west as *yulpatyi* and into Warlpiri to the north as *lapaji*.

In the following we will be describing cases of borrowing of environmental and flora/fauna terms by a language which moves into a new zone and acquires terms from the local people. The foregoing case of borrowing of terms for the Port Lincoln Parrot may have arisen in a similar situation: it has been argued that the Western Desert language did in fact encroach on to Arandic territory as it moved east in the last 1,000 years as well as more recently (see later on upstream [skirting] and downstream [encroaching] spread).

16.6   Borrowing, Especially Kinship and Animal Terminology

16.6.1   Borrowing

As in other language families, inherited lexical roots are replaced by borrowing in the PN family. The rates of borrowing have been said to be exceptionally high in Australia but in fact they are rarely higher than around 20–25% (Alpher and Nash 1999) with only some languages reaching levels of 40–50% loanwords due to exceptional circumstances (e.g. Heath 1978,1981; McConvell 2009).

'Cultural items' in vocabulary (new artifacts, ceremonies, social designations etc.) are frequently loanwords. When a language group is moving into a different ecological zone which is also where another language group resides, the incoming group tends to borrow environmental vocabulary heavily from the resident group. For both these categories of 'cultural' and 'environmental' vocabulary, there may be many *Wanderwörter* – words which are widely borrowed through a region.

These are the two categories which we focus on in this chapter, but not all loanwords are in these categories. Between some languages quite high numbers of basic vocabulary items (such as body parts) are also borrowed.

16.6.2   Wanderwörter and Local Borrowing

The type of borrowing found in the case of *alpatye 'Port Lincoln Ringneck Parrot' was described in the preceding text as occurring during expansion of a language group. However, diffusion of vocabulary also takes place without necessarily involving language spread. This may be motivated by a gap in vocabulary, for instance if elements of a new environment become salient to a group even if they do not actually move into it permanently, e.g. if they hear about the sea and need words for it and for its products (e.g. if shells are traded). Regarding social vocabulary, new arrangements might become known or adopted from neighbours requiring new loan vocabulary, such as new kinship terms to differentiate roles previously subsumed by a wider term. This borrowing might be quite local between two or three groups in a network.

However, if some lexical diffusion is extensive across a larger number of different groups then the roots concerned might be called *Wanderwörter.* If this diffusion is relatively recent then it may be recognizable because of relative absence of older sound changes in the borrowed words, and probably also no, or relatively minor semantic change, as compared to inheritances from the common ancestor of the languages with the root. Such words also cross major subgroup and family boundaries. While some of these distributions can be ascribed to recent cultural diffusions, we have no reason to suppose that such diffusions did not occur in ancient times also. In such cases the diffusions may have predated the sound changes which permit us to diagnose later diffusions so it may be more difficult to separate out early wide diffusions from inheritance unless there is tell-tale crossing of boundaries.

Some of the roots which are found in both PN and NPN languages may be of this type, rather than inheritances of some proto-language like Proto-Australian or some other node between PPN and Proto-Australian. Geographical distribution of the reflexes of the root is helpful here: if they are bunched together in a restricted area of NPN (albeit a wide one) this may indicate that the original transmission was significantly by lateral transmission rather than inheritance.

16.6.3   Local Borrowing and Wanderwörter in Kinship Terminology

We have already dealt with some issues of PPN kinship. The apparent reconstructability of more than one root for terms such as the grandparental terms presents a problem (McConvell 2013b).

Local borrowings to add new terms to create a new system can be illustrated by the borrowing of terms for 'father's father' by Ngumpin-Yapa languages. This is part of a move to create an Aranda' system (in which father's fathers are terminologically distinguished from mother's mother's brothers). No FF term can be reconstructed to Proto-Ngumpin-Yapa. All the father's father terms in early Ngumpin-Yapa are loanwords, each from a different neighbouring language. In Western Ngumpin the source is the

Jarragan language family to the north (*kirlaki*); in Eastern Ngumpin it is the western branch of the Mirndi family (*kaku*); and in Yapa it is the Arandic languages to the south (Warlpiri *warringiyi* from Arrernte *arrenge-ye* 'father's father').

In contrast to this local targeted borrowing, some kinship terms are widespread *Wanderwörter*. The most prominent among roots with such a distribution are affinal (spouse and in-law) terms. The reason may be that the contracting of marriage between partners in different language groups is something that becomes a common discourse over wide areas and needs common terms, and negotiations and gossip about which often occurs in large intergroup gatherings such as ritual events.

One term which is a *Wanderwort* over a very large zone from the west Kimberleys to the Gulf Country in both PN and NPN languages is *lamparra,* meaning 'father-in-law' and reciprocally 'son-in-law' of a man (McConvell 2015). People in the Victoria River District were explicit that the popularity of this term had increased over the last 100 years or so along with a greater role for the father-in-law in marriage bestowal, as opposed to the mother-in-law, and alignment with new ceremonial roles and joking relationships.

The form in Walmajarri in the western Kimberley is *lamparr,* and the augmentation with *-a* is regular in Mudburra/Karranga. The spread of the *lamparra* form probably started from the 'Murranji Stock Route' region, on into the Tableland, Gulf and Arnhem Land. As to the *lamparr* form itself it is no doubt related to *ramparr 'wife's mother' in Worrorran with the *r:rl* correspondence expected because of the *r>rl* regular sound change which is a shared innovation in Ngumpin-Yapa (McConvell and Laughren 2004). At a certain point in the west it shifted meaning as 'wife's father' became more important in the discourse of intergroup marriage and spread east by diffusion.

Another term which is quite widespread across a similar area is *ngumparna* 'husband'. As with *lamparra* in its later elaboration it is likely that there was a need for affinal terms which were not just extensions of consanguineal terms since the equations for the latter would vary according to marriage systems. Again we have to weigh up the probability of this coming from a NPN source but again it seems more likely that it is PN in origin. A connection with a very widespread PN term for 'husband' or 'spouse' *nyupa (with reflexes *nhupa, nhuwa*) is possible: ngupa forms are also found in various places.[19]

16.6.4   *Local Borrowing and Wanderwörter in Fauna Vocabulary*

An example of an old and widespread root whose distribution may be partially by wide diffusion as well as inheritance is *karrkany along with a probably related root *karrkila for a type of hawk ('falcon; kestrel; sparrow-hawk, chicken hawk'; some minor variation in denotation of species). There are many attestations of this root in NPN as well as over quite a wide area of PN, so as with other roots with this kind of distribution we are faced with the alternatives of reconstructing back to some Pre-PN proto-language and/or diffusion.[20] Diagnosis of diffusion can rest on tell-tale similarities of the forms found in different languages, that is, absence of effect of sound-changes (although this does not work if the diffusion is itself very old). Such diagnostics are compromised by lack of full understanding of sound change across Australia, but where we do have such understanding there is some evidence of irregularity in correspondences pointing to probable diffusion.

The issue then arises of why certain items become *Wanderwörter*. It is often blandly stated that these are items of economic or cultural importance across a region, but this does not explain why all such items do not diffuse in this way. It is also the case that some such items which show this kind of distribution are not on the face of it of economic or cultural significance. One type of hypothesis would be that while such items are not significant in that way in recent history, they were significant when the diffusion occurred – for which evidence may be hard to gather in a case like Australia where independent evidence of prehistoric economic and cultural events and interactions are not available in documentary history and rarely studied by other means. Songs are potentially great importance for tracing diffusion and may often contain archaic forms.

This type of hawk designated by *karrkila/karrkany* is not of any particular economic significance and its cultural significance is not documented to any extent. However in the Victoria River District *karrkany* 'chicken hawk' is a significant animal because it is linked to the Magellanic Clouds (which have the same name) and the type of death magic associated with them. Naturally such links are somewhat covert and it is not clear how widespread this or similar beliefs are over the very wide distribution of these terms.

Similarly, other *Wanderwörter* in the area around the Kimberley, Victoria River and adjacent districts are only partially immediately explicable in terms of economic or cultural significance. One such would be *kungkala* the type of tree/stick used to make fire by the fire-drill method: a technology which no doubt diffused along with the word in relatively recent prehistory.[21]

Others, however, are puzzling, for instance, *wirntiku 'stone curlew' which appears to be a relatively insignificant bird. Once again the significance may lie in past cultural configurations which are not wholly evident today but may have left some traces in some places. For instance the stone-curlew is an important ritual figure in parts of the Kimberley and its cry is said to herald the presence of a deadly sorcerer. Such beliefs, rather than the more prosaic characteristics of the bird itself could be the vector of rapid spread of its name across areal networks.

16.7   Models of Language Spread in Pama-Nyungan and Meaning Change/Borrowing

16.7.1   The Shape of the Tree

The spread of PN has been described as 'rapid' (Chapter 15 by Harvey, this volume; McConvell and Bowern 2011) and the apparent 'rake-like' structure of the tree (with multiple first-order branches and little articulation) has been attributed to this. However, if this is a valid generalization (and more work needs to be done on PN phylogeny, which may yet yield other higher level internal subgroups) it would be the early breakup involving multiple independent splits and separations relatively closely spaced in time that would be the cause. Otherwise the entire PN spread appears to have been a staged and gradual process taking place probably over several thousand years. In this chapter it is described in terms of a general model of language spread which has 'upstream' and 'downstream' phases (McConvell 1996; Evans and McConvell 1998; McConvell 2010). More recently McConvell has switched to the terminology of 'skirting' and 'encroaching' spread for 'upstream' and 'downstream' respectively to avoid confusion with the direction of river flow which does not always match movement of people. This model is also examined in Chapter 21 by Hill on North America (this volume), and in the general introduction the issue of whether it is specific to hunter-gatherers or not. In this chapter the different phases are illustrated from specific stages in the spread of PN. An upstream or skirting spread, involving movement into and along an inland corridor, is assumed to have been the type which initially spearheaded the movement of PN itself, as well as the Western Desert language expansion example used here. The downstream or encroaching spread as illustrated here by the northern movement of the Eastern Ngumpin languages out of the desert is also probably responsible for much of the current distribution of PN languages in the more fertile southern and eastern fringes of Australia. This chapter also adds to the proposed signatures of these different types of spread in bio-genetics, archaeology and linguistics, additional effects in different types of lexical semantic change.

16.7.2   Skirting versus Encroaching Spread and Lexical Semantic Change

In upstream (skirting) spreads there is a tendency for the language to change meanings of existing environmental terms as environment changes, whereas in downstream (encroaching) spreads there is wholesale borrowing of environmental terms and semantic organization from the indigenous host language.

Theories of evolution of ethnobiological terminology like that of Berlin (1973, 1992) make a strong distinction between hunter-gatherer and farmer systems, with the strong emphasis on species and varietal distinctions found in the latter (but mainly in relation to cultivars and domesticated animals)

Type-generic systems in which a prototypical specific designation is terminologically equated with a higher taxon are common in Australia. The points at which the system changes relate to changes in the ecological zone including the ecological zone a group is entering during upstream (skirting) spread (migration). Terms do not only spread to a higher taxon, but can also spread down to a generic or species.

It is proposed that the prototypical organism promoted to generic status is selected because it is the most important of its type in the foraging economy.

Shift from one species to another as the referent of a term as their respective zones are crossed is also a characteristic of downstream spread, but may not relate specifically to foraging economies.

In a downstream (encroaching) spread, by contrast, new terms are adopted for the new area from the hosts' language, as in the large amount of environmental vocabulary borrowed from Jaminjungan (West Mirndi) in the north and Jarragan in the west by Gurindji as it moved from the desert to the riverene zone.

16.7.3 Skirting (Upstream) Spread in Inland Corridors

Several of the spreads of PN including the early spread from the north-east of the continent west and south and later reoccupations of arid country like the Western Desert would have been of the skirting (upstream) type. These are primarily by migration rather than language shift/language replacement since the area being occupied is sparsely populated, and/or intensive contact with resident groups is minimal. In such a scenario there is much less contact than in the encroaching (downstream) case described in the text that follows. The hypothesis would be then that there would be less borrowing from other languages than in the encroaching (downstream) case. A second hypothesis following from this is that if lexical innovation occurs it is more likely to be coining of new terms using existing vocabulary and/or change in meaning of existing terms.

As people begin to engage in high-mobility lifestyles in less well resourced environments (usually inland corridors in Australia) there seems to be a tendency observed both in Australia and elsewhere, for kinship systems to lose strong distinctions between cross and parallel relations, at least in some contexts. This is, following the perspective being explored here, an internal development with internal causation, not caused by external links and therefore unlikely to involve any borrowing of kinship terms. In fact most such changes involve simplification of systems – reduction in number of terms, by extending the meanings of some terms to cover the meanings formerly covered by distinct terms. For instance, in the Western Desert the term *tyamu* 'grandfather' descended from *tyam(p)V 'MF' extends to cover the parallel grandparent FF as well as MF.

As far as environmental terms are concerned we similarly expect, in skirting (upstream) spread, change in meaning of existing terms to accommodate to new environmental conditions rather than borrowing. Apart from the examples of change in at least two roots from 'fish' to 'meat' already discussed, the change in *wakal* from 'eel' to 'snake' could be an example.

Of course words may be borrowed by groups before embarking on a skirting (upstream) spread and these words may subsequently change meaning. The Western Desert word for meat *kuka* (so typical of this group that a number of the dialects have their ethnonyms constructed from the word) may be of this kind. Its cognate in the south-west Nyungar *kwaka* and *kwak*, descended from *kuka by regular sound changes (and borrowed into English as *quokka*) means a specific small marsupial which was once so abundant that it was the staple and commonest meat in the diet of Aborigines in the region. This circumstance puts it in line to be extended to a generic 'meat/animal' meaning.

16.7.4   *Encroaching (Downstream) Spread*

Downstream (encroaching) spread is the typical spread of languages into more resource-rich regions with languages already occupying the region quite densely. Language contact is intense, including high levels of borrowing, and language shift from one language to another occurs, including shift from the resident languages to the incoming language. McConvell (2009) attributes high levels of loanwords in Gurindji especially from NPN languages to its north and west to the fact that both adstratal loans and substratal vocabulary uptake from resident languages form components. It is possible that the other widely discussed example of a high-borrowing regime, Ngandi (NPN) and Ritharrngu (PN) in north-east Arnhem Land is attributable to a similar combination of types of flows of vocabulary (Heath 1978, 1981).

Particularly high levels of loans in the environmental domains of vocabulary are typical of this situation, and are also found in the Gurindji and Ritharrngu cases (McConvell 2009). The new incoming PN languages in the Victoria River District are moving into riverine districts from semi-desert and encountering new flora and fauna in the new environment. Their strategy to meet this need was overwhelmingly adoption of vocabulary from the resident languages, e.g. *yawu* 'fish' and *warrij* 'crocodile' from Western Mirndi (Jaminjungan). Some of these loanwords are old as they predate sound changes, e.g. *yawu* has undergone lenition (<*yaku, currently *yak* in Jaminjung due to loss of final vowels in western Mirndi after the loan). Other vocabulary not directly related to change in environment is also borrowed from already existing resident languages, e.g. *ngarin* 'meat' from the NPN language Miriwung or a closely related Jarragan language – this item replaces the 'meat' item reconstructable for Proto-Ngumpin-Yapa, the previously discussed *kuyu* found as *kuyi* in this subgroup.

It should be noted that the use of the terms 'upstream' and 'downstream' in this approach is metaphorical and does not always match with literal upstream and downstream spreads, and this is one reason why a change of terminology to 'skirting' and 'encroaching' respectively is recommended here. An interesting hypothesis bearing on language spread not far to the west of the Victoria River District examples is that of Bowern (2007), who proposes that the Nyulnyulan languages spread south-east from a coastal marine environment in the Dampier Peninsula to the lower basin of the Fitzroy River. This is in the opposite direction from the spread highlighted in the Victoria River District and in literal terms this is mainly upstream. Some of the crucial examples in arguing for this spread involve change of meaning of Nyulnyulan roots from a marine animal to a land animal. This type of change has been argued in the skirting versus encroaching approach to be typical of a skirting (upstream) change – migration without heavy interaction with the resident languages. However, one might suppose that the Fitzroy Valley would have been already heavily occupied at the time that the Nyulnyulan languages moved in, unless some event like a cataclysmic flooding of the river (such events are known to have taken place every several hundred years) had taken place and movement into abandoned country was the situation. Modelling of this change with further consideration of loanword data is necessary before it is certain how, or if, it fits with a skirting versus encroaching model as currently formulated.

Regarding kinship in an encroaching (downstream) spread, there is likely to be significant borrowing in the kinship domain during a period of intense social interaction and (often mutual) accommodation of social systems which would often have been different. To take the north-east Arnhem Land case (Heath 1978, 1981) we do find borrowing of kin terms in both directions. Following Shapiro (1977), Heath models this as Yolngu with a Kariera-type system accommodating to an Aranda type system among NPN neighbors, yielding a 'compromise' system of asymmetrical marriage and kinship, with borrowing patterns reflecting this. McConvell and Keen (2011), building on McConvell and Alpher (2002), instead show that the asymmetrical features of Yolngu are also found in western Cape York Peninsula along with many cognate terms and the Omaha skewing, which is a crucial part of the transition. They thus interpret many features of the Yolngu systems as internally driven and starting prior to interaction with immediate neighbours in northeast Arnhem Land. However clearly kinship loanwords have been drawn from local neighbours, and more surprisingly from groups farther to the south-east, and these each have filled strategic gaps in the Yolngu system which still remains populated mostly with PN inherited items.

This is a system of increasing complexity with high levels of loans, which fits better with an encroaching (downstream) spread. This is one of the few areas in Australia where population-genetic data are available to assist us in determinations of whether language shift has taken place and to what extent (White 1997). Here there is clear evidence of a genetic connection between Yolngu and Western Cape York Peninsula, which fits with the ancestry of the core kinship terminology being also closely related to the Paman languages of that area. There is also evidence of gene transfer between Yolngu and NPN neighbours in Arnhem Land but not enough to obscure the clear signal of the Cape York Peninsula connection.

16.8   Conclusions

The history of hunter-gatherers includes expansions of proto-languages into widespread language families, and Pama-Nyungan is a prime example. This is not something which occurs only after the 'neolithic revolution'.

The PN language family is now on a solid footing based on reconstructions at the highest level including several hundred proto-forms. Substantial work is ongoing on reconstructions of PN subgroups which will build up a picture of the shape of the family and assist in the task of tracing its prehistory. How PN links to NPN is also the subject of detailed investigation and constructive debate.

One of the main issues in reconstruction is determining which meaning or meanings a proto-form had, when the cognates might vary considerably in the glosses they have been given. This issue may be so severe that the reconstruction itself becomes doubtful. We need a method which is rigorous rather than speculative, but not overly mechanistic, so that our insights into possible semantic systems and semantic changes both universally and in the particular cultures and environments of Australia can be taken into account.

There is a two-way process between our understandings of ancient Australian cultures and environments and our linguistic reconstructions. Clearly we must operate relatively independently on reconstructions of meanings of proto-roots so that we do not compromise them by circular thinking using preconceived notions of the proto-cultures and proto-environments. On the other hand such knowledge from outside linguistics is very important in testing our results.

One of the particularly useful lexical domains for reconstruction is kinship. Anthropology has provided us with typologies of existing systems or patterns of polysemy (equations) and other social correlates of the types, both universally and in Australia. Once we have reconstructed individual terms, this anthropological knowledge provides a way of checking the plausibility of the entire system we have reconstructed. Changes in kinship term meanings often result from polysemies which are well known and understood from these system studies.

Changes in meanings of faunal terms also show regularities, for instance, as we have emphasized in this chapter, changes between generic and specific meanings which result from generic-specific polysemy. This type of polysemy seems to occur primarily with species which are most dominant, abundant or economically significant so investigation of such relationships in terms of (prehistoric) ecology and economy becomes important.

Both these domains, and others, may vary in their patterns of meaning change and borrowing of terms depending on the type of language spread which has gone on.

Hunter-gatherer language spreads. like those of other groups, often include two phases – *skirting* ('upstream') where people migrate through a sparsely populated corridor and little language shift takes place on the part of others contacted; and *encroaching* ('downstream') spread where the peripheral upstream spreaders move in on hosts and the hosts shift to the newcomers' language.

In the PN language family of Australia, the spread of the Western Desert dialects is a skirting spread, whereas the move of Eastern Ngumpin languages into the Victoria River District is an encroaching spread. Other spreads, of Nyulnyulan and Yolngu in Australia, and other language groups in North America, have also been mentioned as potentially amenable to the skirting/ encroaching (upstream/downstream) approach.

Another important question for this book is the extent to which the approaches to language spread, semantic change and borrowing outlined in this chapter are specifically applicable to hunter-gatherers or are in fact more generally applicable to language dynamics in other types of economy.

NOTES

1. It has been suggested (Denham, Donohue and Booth 2009) that there may have been agriculture/horticulture in parts of Australia in earlier times and that there was subsequent 'regression' to foraging. The evidence so far is the presence of plant species in northern Australia which are cultivars in New Guinea, combined with some claims of linguistic typological similarity between Papuan and Cape York Peninsula languages. The evidence is not at all persuasive. 'Firestick farming' has also been challenged, Mooney et al. (2011) asserting this use of fire is less significant and more recent than claimed.

2. Two areas in particular have been subject to influence from outside: the northern coast of Australia, especially Arnhem Land, visited by seafarers from Indonesia ('Macassans') in the last few hundred years, which resulted in substantial loan vocabulary, and the Torres Strait and parts of Cape York Peninsula affected by contact with Papua. While it is possible that some cultivation was practised by the Indonesians on their visits, this was not taken up by Indigenous Australians. The northern Torres Strait Islanders had gardens alongside fishing and hunting: the western Island language is Australian and Pama-Nyungan (Alpher and Bowern 2008) while the eastern island language is affiliated to Papuan languages. Biogenetically both groups are predominantly Papuan, indicating perhaps language shift on the part of the western islanders at some point in prehistory. Why farming never spread further through the Torres Strait and into the Australian mainland is the subject of much debate and conjecture. There are some as yet unsubstantiated indications that speakers of Oceanic Austronesian languages visited Northern Queensland at a much earlier period than the 'Macassans' visited the Northern Territory, around 2,500 years ago (Australia and Pacific Science Foundation 2012).

3. See also Chapter 14 by Sutton and Chapter 15 by Harvey (this volume). Tasmanian languages, from the scanty documentation recorded before their demise, are fairly definitely not related to PN languages, nor probably to the northern NPN languages either (Plomley 1976; Crowley and Dixon 1981). Greenberg's Indo-Pacific hypothesis (Greenberg 1971; Pawley 2009) which attempts to link them to Papuan, Andamanese etc. has no plausible evidence to support it.

4. Harvey (2009, this volume) argues that Garrwan is a PN subgroup, but this does not necessarily entail a change to Evans's tree, just a shifting of the label 'Pama-Nyungan' up one node, unless Harvey is proposing that Garrwan is a sister of previously proposed first-order PN branches. However, some of the evidence linking Garrwan to PN is not particularly strong, and some could be interpreted as borrowing.

5. Clendon (2006) proposed a different scenario in which the origin point of PN was around the Great Dividing Range far east of the Gulf of Carpentaria. Evidence provided in the article was not strong, but such alternatives are worth considering. Other proposals in the article are less plausible: see critical comments following it, including by McConvell.

6. O'Grady estimated its age at 4–5,000 years ago, McConvell earlier, around 6–7,000 years ago (1996). Alpher prefers a yet earlier date perhaps 10,000 years ago or more to fit in with a hypothesis that the Yolngu subgroup of PN languages was in the Gulf of Carpentaria before it was inundated with the Holocene sea-level rise about

9,000 years ago. Methods of estimating proto-language dates are not yet reliable or agreed on.

7. With the exception of Meriam, the language of the Eastern Torres Strait Islands, and Tasmanian.

8. The list of some 160 etyma in Alpher (2004) had as a central point is the validity of PN as a genetic group. Alpher tried to limit himself to as uncontroversial as possible a set of forms, but not all of these, of course, will be acceptable to all students of the subject.

9. This is a statement of a widely accepted principle in comparative linguistics, and is contrary to the unorthodox method of Dixon (e.g. 2002) which seems to require, for PN at least, reflexes of a reconstructed root in all daughter languages or close to that. On that criterion every proposed proto-language in the world of more than minimal size and complexity fails the test. A near-universal distribution with few gaps is also suspicious. The real gold standard etyma are attested in four or five widely scattered languages.

10. As we shall see later, the PN reflexes of *kaala- outside eastern Australia do not mean 'mother's brother' so the presence of this original meaning in Kimberley NPN in the far west tends to support the idea that is is a cognate by inheritance, not a loanword, as does the difference between *l* and *rr* in the root (yet to be established as a regular sound correspondence, however). Another kinship root which has a wide distribution within PN and outside is *tyam(p)V- 'mother's father'. This was explained as an early loan into some high-level PN subgroup from NPN in McConvell (1997b) but on reconsideration the presence of this root in a number of NPN languages is probably due to pulse of diffusion from PN (McConvell 2013b).

11. Reconstructed forms without giving the attestations, discussing which of the senses 'came first', or discussing problems with correspondences. They are listed in the appendix to Alpher (2004) and can be checked there.

12. Similar 'rotations' are attested in Iceland (see Haugen 1957). See Tindale (1974) for an extensive compilation of such examples for Australia. In the Pilbara, similar processes have been at work for the term *yapurru – 'west' in the east but 'north' in western languages such as proto-Mantharda (Austin 1992): here the reference seems to be 'the direction towards the Hamersley Range' in both cases. Since this is a watershed, this may be explicable in terms of association of these directions with 'downstream'.

13. The Wati subgroup (Western Desert) is an apparent exception, with neutralization of cross/parallel in cousins. Dousset (2012) argues that this is not a fundamental feature of the system but a contextual overlay. In any case, it is likely that this is relatively recent innovation related perhaps to the particular kind of expansion which occurred in Western Desert.

14. There are probable reflexes of *kaala in the far western Pilbara/Gascoyne with the 'mother's brother' meaning, e.g. Yinggarda *kawa* (Austin 1992). This together with other evidence of similar geographical patterning may indicate that the far western languages are part of an earlier spread from the east and the other languages which have the meaning shifted to ego's generation part of a later spread, but this would require more justification. In the west there is also an anomalous meaning of *tyuwa* a reflex of the *tyuwa root in Ngarluma, 'father's sister, son's son's daughter'.

15. See McConvell (2009, 2013) on the roots *tyampV- and *ngatyV-.

16. The roots *kuntya 'Pandanus spiralis' and *ngarka 'pandanus nut' are among plant etyma which have a similar distribution in Yolngu and Paman and would count as evidence for a tropical northern homeland of PN if these two subgroups are not connected in any other subgroup nor shared because of diffusion.

17. This is frequently a matter of economic importance but can also be other types of cultural importance, e.g. significance in ritual life. The circumstances which determined the association relate of course to the period at which the polysemy came into being, which may be long ago, so current significance may have changed with ecological, economic or cultural shifts without affecting the polysemy. An example in the plant domain is the term *warr(a)pa, which is found as a generic term for 'grass' in some Ngayardic languages of the Pilbara but with an additional meaning 'spinifex' in some. This polysemy is no doubt related to the dominance of Spinifex in the Pilbara. Cognates in the PN subgroup to the east Ngumpin-Yapa (*warrpa*, and *warrwa* in Eastern Ngumpin by regular lenition of *p*) mean generic 'spinifex' or 'spinifex seed heads' (Warlpiri *warrpa*). In these areas Spinifex is less dominant as a grass, and the Ngumpin-Yapa proto-form for 'grass (generic)'; is *yuka. In this case the probable proto-form *warr(a)pa is most likely to have been 'spinifex' of some kind in at least some western higher-level subgroup of PN with extension to a generic 'grass' where the ecology favours spinifex as the dominant species.

18. See McConvell (1997a) for details including some discussion of the difference in the final vowels in the proto-form which has an interesting geographical distribution but which has not yet been fully explained. The changed meaning 'meat, animal' is found only with the *kuyu variant. In McConvell (1996) it is suggested that this innovation may define a western PN high-level subgroup including a number of Nyungic groups but not equivalent to Nyungic.

19. Correspondences between initial *ng* and *ny* are found (and between *k* and *ty*) although these are generally in the environment of a following *i*. It is possible that nyupa/ngupa term had wide diffusion as part of its history.

20. Many bird-names are onomatapoeic so a third possibility in some cases is independent invention based on a common perception of the bird's call. This seems unlikely in this case.

21. See McConvell and Smith (2003) for references to the two technologies of fire-saw and fire-drill and their relationships to other cultural patterns in different zones and language groupings.

References

Alpher, Barry. (1982). Dalabon dual-subject prefixes, kinship categories and generation skewing. In J. Heath, F. Merlan and A. Rumsey (eds.), *Languages of kinship in Aboriginal Australia*. Sydney: Oceania Linguistic Monographs 24, 19–30.

(1990). Some Proto-Pama-Nyungan paradigms: A verb in the hand is worth two in the phylum. In G. N. O'Grady and D. Tryon (eds.), *Studies in comparative Pama-Nyungan*. Canberra: Pacific Linguistics C-111, 155–171.

(2004). Pama-Nyungan: Phonological reconstruction and status as a phylogenetic group. In C. Bowern and H. Koch (eds.), *Australian languages: Classification and the comparative method*. Amsterdam: John Benjamins.

Alpher, Barry and David Nash (1999). Lexical replacement and cognate equilibrium in Australia. *Australian Journal of Linguistics (AJL)* 19(1): 5–56.

Alpher, Barry, Geoffrey O'Grady and Claire Bowern. (2008). Western Torres Strait language classification and development. In Claire Bowern, Bethwyn Evans and Luisa Miceli (eds.), *Morphology and language history: In honour of Harold Koch*. Amsterdam; John Benjamins, 15–30.

Austin, Peter. (1990). Classification of Lake Eyre languages. *La Trobe University Working Papers in Linguistics* 3: 171–201.

(1992). *A Dictionary of Yinggarda*. Bundoora: La Trobe University Department of Linguistics.

Australia and Pacific Science Foundation. (2012). The distribution, abundance and diversity of the Lapita Cultural Complex along the Great Barrier Reef coastline in the third millennium BP. www.apscience.org.au/projects/APSF_09_9/apsf_09_9.html

Bellwood, Peter. (2013). *First migrants: Ancient migration in global perspective*. Chichester: Wiley/Blackwell.

Bellwood, Peter and Colin Renfrew. (2002). Examining the farming/language dispersal hypothesis. McDonald Institute for Archaeological Research, University of Cambridge.

Berlin, Brent. (1973). General principles of classification and nomenclature in folk biology. *American Anthropologist* 75(1): 214–242.

(1992). *Ethnobiological classification: Principles of categorization of plants and animals in traditional societies*. Princeton, NJ: Princeton University Press.

Blake, B. J. (1988). Redefining Pama-Nyungan: Towards the prehistory of Australian languages. In N. Evans and S. Johnson (eds.), *Aboriginal linguistics*. Armidale: Department of Linguistics, University of New England, 1–90.

Blust, Robert. (1990). Language and culture history. *Asian Perspectives* 27(2): 205–227.

Bowern, Claire. (2001). Karnic classification revisited. In Jane Simpson, David Nash, Mary Laughren, Peter Austin and Barry Alpher (eds.), *Forty years on: Ken Hale and Australian languages*. Canberra: Pacific Linguistics, 245–261.

(2007). On eels, dolphins, and echidnas: Nyulnyulan prehistory through the reconstruction of flora and fauna. In Alan Nussbaum (ed.), *Verba Docenti: Studies in historical and Indo-European linguistics, presented to Jay H. Jasanoff by students, colleagues, and friends*. Ann Arbor, MI: Beech Stave Press, 39–53.

Breen, Gavan. (1993). East is south and west is north. *Australian Aboriginal Studies* no. 2: 20–33.

Bulith, Heather C. (2003). The archaeology and socioeconomy of the Gunditjmara: A landscape analysis from southwest Victoria, Australia. *Australian Archaeology* 56: 57.

Clendon, Mark. (2006). Reassessing Australia's linguistic prehistory. *Current Anthropology* 47(1): 39–61.

Crowley, Terry and R. M. W. Dixon. (1981). Tasmanian. In R. M. W. Dixon and Barr Blake (eds.), *Handbook of Australian languages*, Vol. 2. Oxford: Oxford University Press, 392–421.

Denham, Tim, Mark Donohue and Sara Booth. (2009). Horticultural experimentation in Northern Australia reconsidered. *Antiquity* 83(321): 634–648.

Dixon, Robert M. W. (1997). *The rise and fall of languages*. Cambridge: Cambridge University Press.

(2002). *Australian languages: Their nature and development*. Cambridge: Cambridge University Press.

Dousset, Laurent. (2012). "Horizontal" and "vertical" skewing: Similar objectives, two solutions? In Thomas R. Trautmann and Peter M. Whiteley (eds.), *Crow-Omaha: New light on a classic problem of kinship analysis*. Tucson: Arizona University Press, 261–277.

Dyen, Isidore and David Aberle. (1974). *Lexical reconstruction: The case of the proto-Athapaskan kinship system*. Cambridge: Cambridge University Press.

Elkin, A. P. (1964). *The Australian Aborigines: How to understand them*. Sydney: Angus and Robertson.

(1970). The Aborigines of Australia: 'One in thought, word and deed'. In S. Wurm and D. Laycock (eds.), *Pacific linguistic studies in honour of Arthur Capell*. Canberra: Pacific Linguistics C-13, 697–716.

Evans, N., ed. (2003). *The Non-Pama-Nyungan languages of Northern Australia: Comparative studies of the continent's most linguistically complex region*. Canberra: Pacific Linguistics.

Evans, Nicholas and Patrick McConvell. (1998). The enigma of Pama–Nyungan expansion in Australia. In Roger Blench and Matthew Spriggs (eds.), *Archaeology and language*, Vol. 2. London: Routledge, 174–191.

Evans, Nicholas and David Wilkins. (2000). In the mind's ear: The semantic extensions of perception verbs in Australian languages. *Language* 76(3): 546–592.

(2001). The complete person: Networking the physical and the social. In Jane Simpson, David Nash, Mary Laughren, et al. (eds.), *Forty years on: Ken Hale and Australian languages*. Canberra: Pacific Linguistics 512, 493–521.

Greenberg, Joseph H. (1971). The Indo-Pacific hypothesis. In Thomas A. Sebeok (ed.), *Current trends in linguistics,* Vol. 8: *Linguistics in Oceania*. The Hague: Mouton, 808–71. (Reprinted in Greenberg, *Genetic Linguistics*, 2005, 193–275.)

Harvey, Mark. (2009). The genetic status of Garrwan. *Australian Journal of Linguistics* 29(2): 195–244.

Haugen, Einar. (1957). The semantics of Icelandic orientation. *Word* 13(3): 447–459.

Heath, Jeffrey. (1978). *Linguistic diffusion in Arnhem Land*. Canberra: AIAS.

(1981). A case of intensive lexical diffusion: Arnhem Land, Australia. *Language* 57: 335–367.

Hiscock, Peter. (2002). Pattern and context in the Holocene proliferation of backed artifacts in Australia. *Archeological Papers of the American Anthropological Association* 12(1): 163–177.

Ives, John W. (1998). Developmental processes in the pre-contact history of Athapaskan, Algonquian, and Numic Kin systems. In Maurice Godelier, Thomas R. Trautmann and Franklin Tjon Sie Fat (eds.), *Transformations of Kinship*, Washington, DC: Smithsonian Institution Press, 94–139.

Jones, Rhys. (1969). Fire-stick farming. *Australian Natural History* 16: 224.

McConvell, Patrick. (1996). Backtracking to Babel: The chronology of Pama-Nyungan expansion in Australia. *Archaeology in Oceania* 31: 125–144.

(1997a). The semantic shift between "fish" and "meat" and the prehistory of Pama-Nyungan. In M. Walsh and D. Tryon (eds.), *Boundary rider: Essays in honour of G. N. O'Grady*. Canberra: Pacific Linguistics, 303–325.

(1997b). Long lost relations: Pama-Nyungan and Northern kinship. In Patrick McConvell and Nicholas Evans (eds.), *Archaeology and linguistics: Aboriginal Australia in global perspective*. Melbourne: Oxford University Press, 207–236.

(2008). Grandaddy morphs: The importance of suffixes in reconstructing Pama-Nyungan kinship. In B. Evans and C. Bowern (eds.), *Morphology and language history: In honour of Harold Koch*. Amsterdam: John Benjamins.

(2009). Loanwords in Gurindji, a Pama-Nyungan language of Australia. Chapter and database in M. Haspelmath and U. Tadmor (eds.), *Loanwords in the world's languages: A comparative handbook*. Berlin: Mouton de Gruyter, 790–822.

(2010). The archaeolinguistics of migration. In L. Lucassen, J. Lucassen and P. Manning (eds.), *Migration history in world history: Multidisciplinary approaches*. Leiden: Brill, 155–190.

(2012). Omaha skewing in Australia: Overlays, dynamism and change. In T. Trautmann and P. Whiteley (eds.), *Crow-Omaha: New light on a classic problem of kinship analysis*. Tucson: University of Arizona Press, 243–260.

(2013a). Introduction: Kinship change in anthropology and linguistics. In P. McConvell, I. Keen and R. Hendery (eds.), *Kinship systems: Change and reconstruction*. Salt Lake City: University of Utah Press, 1–18.

(2013b). Proto-Pama-Nyungan kinship and the AustKin Project: Reconstructing proto-terms for "mother's father" and their transformations. In P. McConvell, I. Keen and R. Hendery (eds.), *Kinship systems: Change and reconstruction*. Salt Lake City: University of Utah Press, 190–214.

(2013c). Granny got cross: Semantic change of *kami* in Pama-Nyungan from 'mother's mother' to 'father's mother'. In R. Mailhammer (ed.), *Beyond word histories: Lexical and structural etymology*. Berlin: De Gruyter, 147–184.

(2015). Long-distance diffusion of affinal kinship terms as evidence of late Holocene change in marriage systems in Aboriginal Australia. In P. Toner (ed.), *Strings of connectedness*. Canberra: ANU Press, 287–316.

McConvell, Patrick and Barry Alpher. (2002). The Omaha Trail in Australia: Tracking skewing from east to west. In P. McConvell, L. Dousset and F. Powell (eds.), special number of *Anthropological Forum* (2002) on 'Kinship Change'. 12(2): 159–176.

McConvell, Patrick and Claire Bowern. (2011). The prehistory and internal relationships of Australian languages. *Languages and Linguistics Compass* 5(1): 19–32.

McConvell, Patrick and Nicholas Evans (eds.). (1997). *Archaeology and linguistics: Aboriginal Australia in global perspective*. Melbourne: Oxford University Press.

McConvell, Patrick and Ian Keen. (2011). The transition from Kariera to an asymmetrical system: Cape York Peninsula to North-east Arnhem Land. In Doug Jones and Bojka Milicic (eds.), *Kinship, language and prehistory: Per Hage and the Renaissance in kinship studies*. Salt Lake City: University of Utah Press, 99–132.

McConvell, Patrick and Mary Laughren. (2004). Ngumpin-Yapa languages. In H. Koch and C. Bowern (eds.), *Australian languages: Classification and the comparative method.* Amsterdam: John Benjamins, 151–178.

McConvell, Patrick and Mike Smith. (2003). Millers and mullers: The archaeolinguistic stratigraphy of seed-grinding in Central Australia. In H. Andersen (ed.), *Language contacts in prehistory: Studies in stratigraphy.* Amsterdam: John Benjamins, 177–200.

McConvell, Patrick and Stef Spronck. (2011). Meaning change in the flora, fauna, artefact and social domains in the prehistory of the Kimberley region, Western Australia. Paper presented to Australian Linguistic Society conference, Canberra.

Mooney, S. D., S. P. Harrison, P. Bartlein, et al. (2011). Late Quaternary fire regimes of Australasia. *Quaternary Science Reviews* 30: 28–46.

Murdock, George P. (1970). Kin term patterns and their distribution. *Ethnology* 9(2): 165–207.

O'Grady, G. N. and S. Fitzgerald. (1995). Triconsonantla sequences in proto-Pama-Nyungan. *Oceanic Linguistics* 34: 454–471.

Pawley, A. (2009). Greenberg's Indo-Pacific hypothesis: An assessment. In Bethwyn Evans (ed.), *Discovering history through language: Papers in honour of Malcolm Ross.* Canberra: Pacific Linguistics, 153–180.

Plomley, N. J. B. (1976). *A word-list of the Tasmanian Aboriginal languages.* Launceston, Tas: N. J. B. Plomley in association with the Government of Tasmania.

Radcliffe-Brown, A. R. (1931). *The social organisation of Australian tribes.* Sydney: Oceania Monograph 1.

Scheffler, Harold. (1978). *Australian kin classification.* Cambridge: Cambridge University Press.

Shapiro, Warren. (1977). *Structure, variation and change in "Balamumu" social classification.* Albuquerque: University of New Mexico.

Tindale, Norman. (1974). *Aboriginal tribes of Australia: Their terrain, environmental controls, distribution, limits, and proper names.* Berkeley: University of California Press.

Traugott, Elizabeth Closs and Richard Dasher. (2002). *Regularity in semantic change.* New York: Cambridge University Press.

White, Neville. (1997). Genes, languages and landscapes Australia. In Patrick McConvell and Nicholas Evans (eds.), (1997). *Archaeology and linguistics: Aboriginal Australia in global perspective.* Melbourne: Oxford University Press, 45–82.

Wichmann, Søren. (2015). Neolithic linguistics. In Gojko Barjamovic, Irene Elmerot, Adam Hyllested, Benedicte Nielsen and Bjørn Okholm Skaarup (eds.), *Language and prehistory of the Indo-European peoples: A cross-disciplinary perspective.* Budapest: Archaeolingua.

Wilkins, David P. (1996). Natural tendencies of semantic change and the search for cognates. In Mark Durie, and Malcolm Ross (eds.), *The comparative method reviewed.* Oxford: Oxford University Press, 264–304.

Part V

Northeastern Eurasia

17 Typological Accommodation in Central Siberia

Edward J. Vajda

17.1 Introduction

When Russians penetrated Siberia in the late sixteenth century they found most of the area inhabited by reindeer herders or nomadic pastoralists speaking Uralic, Turkic, Mongolic, and Tungusic languages. Western Siberia contained Khanty (Ostyak) and Mansi (Vogul) dialects belonging to the Ugrian subgroup of Uralic. Across the northeast were Nenets, Enets, and Nganasan tribes speaking Uralic languages of the Samoyedic branch. Southern Samoyedic peoples included the Selkup (Ostyak-Samoyed), as well as the now vanished Mator, Karagas, and Koibal north of the Altai-Sayan Mountains. Turkic speakers, whose modern descendants are the Khakas, Altai, Chulym, Tuvan, and Tofalar, occupied the lion's share of south Siberia's forest-steppe zone. Mongolic speakers (Halh and Buryad) lived to the south and east. Tungusic tribes speaking western dialects of Evenki had recently begun moving into central Siberia from the east. The predominant ethnolinguistic presence across North Asia was pastoral nomad groups speaking suffixal-agglutinating languages. The distribution of languages in central Siberia c. 1600 is known from tsarist *yasak* (fur tax collection) records (Dolgikh 1960).

Amid the more familiar linguistic groups, the middle Yenisei and its tributaries was home to scattered bands of hunter-gatherer-fishers whose only domesticate was the dog. These groups, known as Yeniseians, spoke languages genetically unrelated to the surrounding families. Yeniseian (Yeniseic) languages also differ typologically in having a prefixing verb morphology, pronominal possessive prefixes, phonemic distinctions in prosody, and a basic vocabulary stock without analog elsewhere in Northern Eurasia except for loanwords (Vajda 2009). The languages of Siberia's animal breeders, by contrast, conform to a well-known typological profile. All of them are non-tonal and display vowel harmony with strongly suffixal-agglutinating nominal and verbal inflectional morphology.

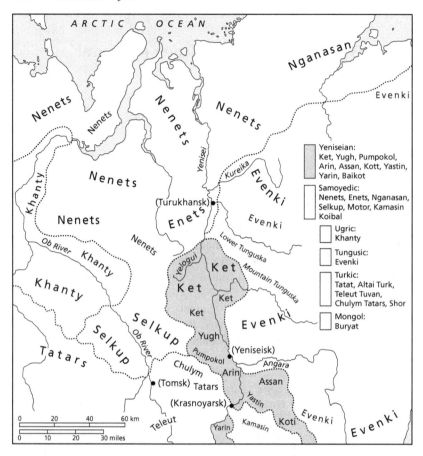

Map 17.1 Language map of central Siberia in the 1600s.

This chapter surveys the sociolinguistic interaction between Yeniseian hunter-gatherers and the pastoralists who eventually supplanted them across most of central Siberia. Although a scattering of Yeniseian substrate elements appears across a vast area of Inner Eurasia, none of the characteristic Yeniseian typological traits were borrowed. Language contact affected Yeniseian grammatical structure much more profoundly, though it likewise left the vocabulary basically untouched. Modern Ket contains few loan words yet has evolved a unique partial mimicry of originally alien morphological traits from neighboring families. The present chapter argues that long-term bilingualism by Yeniseian speakers led to this interesting typological hybridization. The Uralic, Turkic, and Tungusic speakers of the region, on the other hand, were less often conversant in a Yeniseian language. Even where their ancestors shifted from Yeniseian, the shift occurred in a way that yielded only sporadic substrate influence. Samoyedic and South Siberian Turkic acquired virtually no Yeniseian structural features, and speakers of these languages borrowed only a modest number of lexical items from their hunter-gatherer neighbors. This chapter explains how and why interethnic contact in central Siberia yielded this particular set of linguistic outcomes. It also examines in detail the issue of typological accommodation arising in Yeniseian – a family genetically related to the strongly prefixing Na-Dene (Athabaskan-Eyak-Tlingit) family of North America – to patterns of suffixal agglutination common to all of the other languages of central Siberia.

17.2   Yeniseian: Prehistoric Distribution and Internal Subgrouping

Substrate river names reveal that groups speaking Yeniseian languages once occupied a much larger portion of Inner Eurasia than where the Russian found them in the seventeenth century. Distinct pronunciations of cognate elements in Siberian hydronyms suggest that some Yeniseian languages vanished unrecorded, and that the family originally had considerable internal depth and variation. Map 17.2, following Maloletko (2002) and Werner (2005), shows the approximate distribution of Siberian river names containing cognates of Common Yeniseian words for 'river' or 'water'. The chart on the left identifies, where possible, the language from which each element appears to have originated.

The lone survivor of this erstwhile diversity is Ket, the family's northernmost member, now spoken on the fringe of the original Yeniseian range. The ethnonym Ket derives from *kɛˀt* 'man, person, human being'. Before the 1930s Ket was known as 'Yenisei Ostyak', from Russian *ostʲak*, a word of uncertain origin (see Georg 2007: 11–12). The Ket refer to themselves as *ɔstɨ́ɣan* 'Ostyaks' when speaking Ket. Most of the 1,200 ethnic Ket live today in small villages on the Yenisei and its tributaries in the Turukhansk District of Krasnoyarsk Province or in the Evenki District's Baikit Region. At present, fewer than 50 people probably speak the language fluently. Few if any children of the past two generations have acquired genuine fluency. Given this pace of replacement by Russian, Ket must be regarded as highly endangered (Krivonogov 1998, 2003). Several local elementary schools have taught it as a second language since the late 1980s using materials developed by linguist Heinrich Werner in collaboration with native pedagogues. Based on fairly minor phonetic and lexical differences, Ket is divided into Southern (SK), Central (CK), and Northern (NK) dialects. The largest concentration of Ket people lives in Kellog on the Yelogui River in the Southern Ket zone.

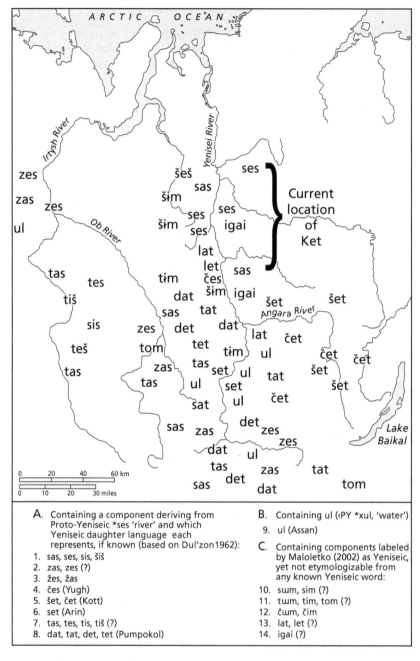

A. Containing a component deriving from Proto-Yeniseic *ses 'river' and which Yeniseic daughter language each represents, if known (based on Dul'zon1962):

1. sas, ses, sis, šiš
2. zas, zes (?)
3. žes, žas
4. čes (Yugh)
5. šet, čet (Kott)
6. set (Arin)
7. tas, tes, tis, tiš (?)
8. dat, tat, det, tet (Pumpokol)

B. Containing ul (‹PY *xul, 'water')

9. ul (Assan)

C. Containing components labeled by Maloletko (2002) as Yeniseic, yet not etymologizable from any known Yeniseic word:

10. sum, sim (?)
11. tum, tim, tom (?)
12. čum, čim
13. lat, let (?)
14. igai (?)

Map 17.2 Yeniseian substrate hydronyms and their probable language of origin.

As the last true hunter-gatherer-fishers of landlocked northern Eurasia (the sole domesticated animal was a type of Samoyed dog), the Ket and their extinct relatives should interest historians and anthropologists as much as their languages have intrigued linguists. Before Soviet collectivization efforts in the mid-1930s, most Ket lived in isolated family groups who traveled great distances on foot between forest hunting trails in winter and fishing encampments near the Yenisei or its tributaries in spring and summer (Alekseenko 1967, 2005; Vajda 2011). Of the extinct Yeniseian tongues, grammatical descriptions exist only of Yugh, which survived into the 1970s (Werner 1997b) and Kott, which disappeared by the mid-1800s (Castrén 1858; Verner 1990a; Werner 1997a). The remaining documented languages – Assan (extinct by 1800), Pumpokol (extinct by 1800), and Arin (extinct by 1750) – are known only from word lists compiled by eighteenth-century travelers (see Werner [2005] for a complete inventory). Other groups – Buklin, Baikot, Yarin, Yastin – are identifiable as Yeniseian-speaking from seventeenth-century tsarist *yasak* records, though little remains of their languages except a few proper names (Dolgikh 1960). Yugh is similar enough to Ket that Soviet-era linguists often regarded the two as dialects, referring to Yugh as Sym Ket and the three downriver Ket dialects as Imbat Ket. Ket and Yugh comprise the family's northern branch. Kott and Assan, the family's southeastern branch, are even more closely related (Verner 1990b; Werner 2005). Recordings of Kott by early explorers and linguists suggest the existence of at least two distinct Kott dialects (Verner 1990a: 45–51). Arin and Pumpokol may be two additional primary branches, though Arin verb morphology shares innovations with Ket and Yugh suggestive of an early connection with that branch (Vajda 2012).

The documented Yeniseian languages appear related at a time depth of at least 2,000 years, though the initial breakup of Common Yeniseian may have occurred earlier. It is conceivable that the first dispersals of Yeniseian speakers occurred in the Scythian Era (700–200 BC), with some groups entering western Siberia from the Altai-Sayan region. The diversity of Yeniseian substrate river names across western, southern, and central Siberia strongly suggests that some primary branches vanished unrecorded. Hydronyms containing *tis, tyš, tas, taš* – the geographically most prominent of which is the Irtysh River itself – indicates the existence of an additional primary node of Yeniseian. River names containing *zis, zaš, zes* indicate yet another.

Dispersal northward into the Yenisei watershed of speakers ancestral to the Ket/Yugh branch probably began as a response to pastoral expansions during the Hunnic (Xiong-nu) Era (300 BC–AD 200). This migration must have been underway before the rise of the First Turkic Kaganate in AD 552. A Ket legend tells of being pushed farther north up the Yenisei River by *kilikidze* (almost certainly the Yenisei Kirghiz Turks). The same legend relates that much earlier the Ket were driven north over the Altai-Sayan into the Yenisei basin by a people called the *tusta* (Anuchin 1914: 1), whose ethnic affiliation remains unidentified.

Just as it is impossible to provide a firm date for the breakup of Common Yeniseian, it is likewise not possible to place Yeniseian-speaking groups in the historic record before tsarist rule. It is conceivable that the Dingling hunter-gatherer tribes along China's northern border in the second millennium BC represent the first historically mentioned linguistic forbearers of the Ket (cf. Ket *dɛʔŋ* 'people'). Suggestions that at least some ethnic elements among the Xiong-nu (Hsiung-nu) spoke a Yeniseian tongue are difficult to substantiate due to the paucity of data. Fewer than twenty Xiong-nu words are known to have been recorded in Chinese texts, with creative guesswork required to deduce their original pronunciation; see Vovin (2000, 2002), however, for a well-reasoned identification of several of these as Yeniseian. The general absence of Yeniseian grammatical or phonological influence on known Eurasian languages, a point elaborated in Section 17.3, would seem to argue against the enormously influential Xiong-nu or later Huns being primarily speakers of Yeniseian. It is more likely that the first Asian pastoralists spoke some sort of suffixal-agglutinating language.

Table 17.1 gives rough estimates of time depth for the family and its sub-branches.

Phonological comparisons of Yeniseian core vocabulary support the division of the family's documented languages into the four primary nodes shown in Table 17.2.

The extant documentation of Kott, Assan, Arin, and Pumpokol dates from the eighteenth and nineteenth centuries and likely omits key phonetic details, notably back unrounded vowels. Any tonal distinctions in these languages were also not recorded. The first accurate recordings of phonemic tone in Ket and Yugh were made only in the late 1960s, beginning with the pioneering work of Heinrich Werner – more than a century after the first published grammar appeared (cf. Vajda 2002).

Table 17.1 *Family-internal branching and estimated time depth*

Today	AD 1700	AD 1200	AD 700	AD 500	AD 1	BC 500
Ket (>200 speakers)			Proto-Ket-Yugh		Common Yeniseian	
Yugh (extinct 1970s)						
Kott (extinct 1850)		Proto-Kott-Assan				
Assan (extinct 1800)						
Arin (extinct 1730s)						
Pumpokol (extinct early 1800s)						

Table 17.2 *Yeniseian cognate sets*

	Ket/Yugh				Kott/Assan		Arin	Pumpokol
	SK	NK	CK	Yugh	Kott	Assan		
larch	sɛʔs	sɛʔs	šɛʔš	sɛʔs	šet	čet	čit	tag
river	sēˑs	sēˑs	šēˑš	sēs	šet	šet	sat	tat
stone	tʌʔs	tʌʔs	tʌʔš	čʌʔs	šiš	šiš	kes	kit
finger	tʌʔq	tʌʔq	tʌʔq	tʌʔχ	thoχ	?	intoto	tok
resin	dīˑk	dīˑk	dīˑk	dʲīk	čik	?	?	?
wolf	qū̃ˑt	qū̃ˑti	qū̃ˑtə	χū̃ˑt	(boru <	Turkic)	qut	xotu
winter	kɨ̃ˑt	kɨ̃ˑti	kɨ̃ˑte	kɨ̃ˑt	keːtʰi	?	lot	lete
light	kʌʔn	kʌʔn	kʌʔn	kʌʔn	kin	?	lum	?
person	kɛʔd	kɛʔd	kɛʔd	kɛʔdʲ	hit	het	kit	kit
two	ūˑn	ūˑn	ūˑn	ūn	in	in	kin	hin
birch	ùs	ùːse	ùːsə	ùːʰs	uča	uuča	kus	uta
snowsled	súùl	súùl	šúùl	sɔ̀ùl	čogar	čegar	šal	tsɛl

Modern Ket and Yugh contain four phonemic tonal contours: high, laryn-gealized, rising/falling, and falling. Following Vajda (2002, 2004), a glottal stop transcribes laryngealized tone, and a macron transcribes high tone, with a raised triangular dot added to indicate the half-length that accompanies this tone in all Ket words as well as Yugh words of this type that correlate with second-syllable echo vowels in Proto-Yeniseian.

High tone occurs in 'river', 'resin', 'wolf', 'winter', 'two'. Laryngealized tone appears in 'larch', 'stone', 'finger', 'light', and 'person'. Werner (Verner 1990b) makes a plausible case that systematic peculiarities in the premodern transcription of Kott, Assan, Arin, and Pumpokol indicate the presence of high and laryngealized tones in these languages, as well. The high versus laryngea-lized contrast appears to date back to Proto-Yeniseian.

Falling tone (Ket/Yugh words for 'birch') is connected with the loss of a fricative segment in the second part of the word. In Yugh this element remains as pharyngealization of the second mora of the nucleus: *ùːʰs* 'birch'. It is unclear whether Pumpokol, Kott, and Assan had falling tone; if they did, then it too existed already in Common Yeniseian. Rising-falling tone mono-syllables are a Ket/Yugh innovation that derive from the elision of certain intervocalic consonants (cf. cognates for 'snowsled').

The divergence of Ket and Yugh dates after the Kirghiz (Turkic) intrusion into the Yenisei region (c. AD 700). The divergence of Kott and Assan is probably linked to population shifts triggered by Mongol expansion after AD 1206. The spread of Arin and Pumpokol was possibly connected with the rise of the historic Turks after AD 552. These languages show some notable similarities, such as velars instead of palatals (cf. cognates for 'stone'), the odd liquid reflex /l/ from PY *g ('winter', 'light'), and the reduction of certain original disyllables to short-vowel monosyllables ('snowsled'). Similarities between Arin and Pumpokol also include what are apparently shared retentions, such as the preservation of non-labialized velars before *i ('two') and in Arin before *u as well ('birch'); non-labialized velars dropped before high vowels in the remaining languages. Innovations in the other two branches include the Kott/Assan change of unaspirated, unlabialized *k to /h/, with Kott /k/ representing the reflex of an original labialized velar (cf. cognates for 'winter', bright). Another is Ket/Yugh back unrounded vowels /ɯ/ from /i/ and /ɤ, ʌ/ from /e, ɛ/[1] after an original aspirate ('two', 'stone') or to compensate the loss of labialization in the preceding velar or uvular ('wolf', 'winter').

The genetic and typological contrast in grammar and lexicon between Ket and other Siberian families is a recurrent topic of comment in the linguistics literature, even by scholars who do not realize that Yeniseian, unlike all other north Asian languages, contains phonemic tones. In truth, Yeniseian also shares significant contact-induced traits with the South Siberian Turkic, Samoyedic, and Evenki. These include long-distance nasal harmony, a tendency toward deaffrication, and bound relational morphemes attaching to finite verb forms to express a wide range of clausal subordination types (Anderson 2003). Yeniseian nominal enclitics mimic in many ways the suffixal case systems of geographically contiguous families. Such commonalities probably accrued over the centuries as small populations of Yeniseian speakers interacted with neighboring groups. At the same time, Ket appears to have remained fairly impervious to deliberate borrowing. Most fully assimilated loanwords derive from Russian, and even these are surprisingly few. In contrast to its phonology and morphological typology, the Ket lexicon displays little historical influence from other North Asian languages. Yeniseian influence on the neighboring languages appears limited to loanwords, with the characteristic Yeniseian phonological and morphological patterns having little or no impact.

17.3   Yeniseian Substrate Elements in Modern Siberian Languages

This section provides a sampling of Yeniseian elements – mostly loan vocabulary – known to have been acquired by other languages of central Siberia. These include northern Samoyedic and western Evenki, which borrowed a few words through adstrate influence during centuries of contact with Yeniseian speakers. In most cases, contact occurred between separate and often hostile groups. Also discussed are Yeniseian substrate influences on Southern Samoyedic and South Siberian Turkic that accrued when these peoples shifted from an original Yeniseian language.

The clearest attestation of Yeniseian substrate influence can be found in Ös (Chulym Turkic), the most northerly Turkic language of the Yenisei watershed and still spoken on the Chulym River in former Pumpokol territory. Dul'zon (1952) noted the calqued 13-month calendar and the name of the Big Dipper constellation, imitating Yeniseian *qàj* 'elk'. This influence reflects a continuity of elements of hunter-gatherer lifestyle long after this group adopted Turkic speech. An obvious Yeniseian substrate also appears in northern dialects of South Siberian Turkic, where the names of certain ethnic subdivisions among the Northern Altai, Shor, and Khakas, and presumably the actual clans themselves, originate from Yeniseian. Maloletko (2002: 255) identified as Yeniseian the Khakas clan (*seok*) names *tiin, kobïj, kïj*, the first of which is clearly cognate with Ket *dɛʔŋ* 'people'. The Todji division of Tuvan also shows Yeniseian influence on its vocabulary. The extinct Southern Samoyedic languages Koibal and Karagas, peoples known to have originally been speakers of some Yeniseian language, apparently contained numerous loanwords. This is attested by the presence of obvious Yeniseian words in the nineteenth- century word lists gathered from these languages (Dul'zon 1962; Verner 1990b). Eastern Khanty dialects also contain Yeniseian loanwords. This is not surprising, given the presence of Yeniseian toponyms in many areas of the Ob-Irtysh watershed.

Butanaev (2004: 227–228) has made the most detailed study of Yeniseian lexical influence in South Siberian Turkic, particularly Khakas. He identified a few dozen loans and calques. These can be placed in four semantic groups that reflect an original hunting-gathering forest culture:

1. Landscape and other natural features: 'snow on tree branches' – Khakas *tikper*, Ket *tokpul*; 'swampy ground': Khakas *ïlban*, Ket *lumba*; 'summit, top': Khakas *tigej*, Altai *tegej*, Tuvan *tej*, Ket/Kott *tiɣïj, tagaj* (from an older Yeniseian word meaning 'head'). Modern Ket 'head', *kʌjgá*, was borrowed as Khakas *xïjga* 'smart, clever'. Khakas also contains calques based on Yeniseian models, such as *kugurt čolï* 'rainbow'; cf. Modern Ket *ɛkkaŋna qɔʔt* 'rainbow', both literally meaning 'lightning road'.

2. Flora: Kott *šet* 'larch (*Larix*)' > Khakas *čet*, Altai/Tuvan *šet* 'young larch'; 'mountain ash (*Sorbus*)': Khakas dialectal *sojbe*, Arin *šulbe*; 'alder (*Alnus*)': Khakas *sug agazï*, Ket *sojga*; Khakas dialectal *emin* 'pine nut, kernel' versus Ket *èm*; 'sweet substance beneath the bark of pine trees': Khakas dialectal *malïn*, Yugh *falan*; 'dead tree, snag': Khakas *xoolgan*, Altai/Tuvan *kuulgï*, Ket *kɔlɛn*; 'moss growing on trees': Khakas dialectal *tabïj*, Kott *topaːk*.

3. Fauna: 'squirrel': Khakas *saxïl*, Ket *saʔq*, Yugh *saʔχ*; 'seagull': Khakas *xajlax*, Ket *qalɛŋ*; 'curlew': Khakas *tondolbus*, Ket *tógdùlt*.

4. Hunting and fishing: 'wood-tipped arrow': Khakas *sogan*, Yugh *soham*; Khakas *tolanat* 'weir' vs. Ket *tɔltɛn* 'dam, weir'; Chulym Khakas *ajbun* 'drop net' vs. Yugh *ajfen* 'drop net'; Khakas *ulban* 'lake bank where a freshwater steam is flowing' versus Ket *ulbaŋ* 'bank'; Khakas *kürüp* 'pit trap' versus Kott *kurup* 'burrow'; 'pouch, bag': Khakas *meleček*, Kott *falančak*; snow sled – Khakas *soor*, Siberian Tatar *tsuir*, Arin *čel*, Kott *čogar*. The South Siberian Turkic ethnonym 'Shor' may also derive from Yeniseian 'snow sled', reflecting the fact that the Shor, after shifting to Turkic, continued to live as forest hunters, with the snow sled their essential means of winter travel.

Yeniseian loanwords in the languages of more northerly peoples with whom the Ket interacted in historic times are less numerous. Of all their neighbors in the Yenisei River watershed, the Selkup maintained the closest and most friendly relations with the Ket, often interchanging marriage partners. Not surprisingly, a number of words for family relations and spiritual culture were borrowed between the two peoples. The Ket word for Selkup, *laʔk* derives from the Selkup word for 'friend'. Kim-Maloney (2004) identifies several possible Ket loans in the southern Selkup dialects, including *aqlalta* (< Ket *allɛl*), a term for the wooden figures with beaded eyes that housed the family's guardian spirit.

Adjacent groups with whom the Ket maintained a more adversarial relationship borrowed fewer terms. The Evenki, who were pushing into the Yenisei basin at the time of the Russian's arrival in the early seventeenth century, were hostile to the Ket. Only a few words for local material culture have been identified in the western dialects of Evenki. The Enets to the north, whom the Ket called *dudɛŋ* (possibly from Ket *duʔ* 'hat' + *dɛʔŋ* 'people'), likewise had adversarial relations with the Ket. They are generally referred to as 'Yurak', in other words 'Nenets', in Russian accounts of Ket-Samoyedic relations (Alekseenko 1957, 2005), but the historic *dudɛŋ* were more likely the Enets. The modern Forest Enets language contains a few Ket loans, including possibly the third-person singular pronoun *bu*. This pronoun is nearly identical to Ket *bū·* 'he, she', though a Turkic origin for both is also conceivable.

Beyond this rather modest lexical influence, borrowed Yeniseian grammatical and phonological features are difficult to substantiate. Badgaev (1988) suggests that the affricates *dz, ts* in Buryat Mongol diffused from Kott, which, however, did not have these sounds as phonemes. Rassadin (1971) traces the origin of pharyngealized Tuvan vowels to a Yeniseian substrate, a position rejected by Werner (Verner 1973). The feature in question appears in native Turkic vocabulary and does not seem to correlate with the pharyngealization found in Yeniseian falling tone monosyllables. Janhunen (1986: 167–8) suggests that the glottal stop in Nenets diffused from Ket. Once again, without evidence for more extensive Yeniseian influence on Nenets phonology and language structure, it is likely that the shared feature in question is a coincidence. Greg Anderson (personal communication) noted that the high back unrounded [ɯ] could have been borrowed into South Siberian Turkic from Yeniseian. But even if such isolated features represent Yeniseian substrate or adstrate influence, they are certainly not part of any larger, more significant contact-induced change.

While the lexical items noted earlier are by no means intended as an exhaustive inventory of Yeniseian loan vocabulary in the languages of western and central Siberia, they do provide a sense of how limited was the impact of the once extremely widespread Yeniseian family on the region's subsequent language families. Also noteworthy is the general absence of phonological influence from Yeniseian on neighboring families. The probably reason for this absence is that in instances of language shift to Turkic or Samoyedic occurred over a few generations. This left a scattering of substrate loanwords, mostly having to do with the natural landscape or forest life, but did not produce any creolizating effect on the grammar or phonology of the group's newly acquired non-Yeniseian mother tongue. In cases of adstrate contact between Ket and neighboring Siberian peoples, whether amicable or hostile, it was the Ket who typically learned to communicate in the outside language – a bilingualism largely unreciprocated. With such limited exposure to Ket linguistic structures, speakers of Nenets, Enets, Selkup, and Evenki typically acquired only a few isolated Yeniseian loanwords but none of the typically Yeniseian grammatical and phonological characteristics, such as phonemic tones, possessive prefixes, or prefixing verb morphology.

17.4   Grammatical Features Shared by Ket with Other Inner Eurasian Languages

While Yeniseian influence on other Siberian language families appears limited almost exclusively to the lexical realm, it is interesting to note that Yeniseian languages themselves generally show an even stronger resistance to adopting foreign vocabulary. This continues to be true even of the last generations of fluent Ket speakers today. The informants I have worked with reject most Russian words in Ket, preferring instead to coin their own neologisms, such as *ēˑɣ suul* 'iron sled' for 'car', and *hilaŋ naˀn* 'sweet bread' for 'cake', and *qʌliŋ ūˑl* 'bitter water' for 'coffee'. A survey of Modern Ket loan vocabulary (Vajda 2009) reveals that over the past two millennia only a few foreign words have taken firm root. All of these name important acquired items of material culture, such as *talún* 'flour' from Turkic, *saˀj* 'tea' from Russian *čaj, kančá* 'pipe (for smoking)' from Chinese, and possibly *naˀn* 'bread' from some

Indo-Iranic source. None of the core Ket vocabulary is borrowed, and most of it is clearly inherited from Proto-Yeniseian, judging from cognates in the other Yeniseian daughter languages. While it is more difficult to gauge the degree of borrowing in the extinct Yeniseian languages, owing to the fragmentary documentation of their lexicons, Yeniseian appears to resemble Athabaskan in its resistance to lexical borrowing. Turkic and Russian loanwords in Kott and Assan appear to have been more numerous. But this may reflect the fact that these languages were recorded only during the final stages of obsolescence, when all of the remaining speakers had already switched to one of the Siberian Turkic dialects or in Russian for most of their communication needs.

The morphological influence of the surrounding languages on Yeniseian was much farther reaching, and appears to have been well under way even during the time of Common Yeniseian. In this sense, Yeniseian languages belong firmly to the broader Inner Eurasian spread zone with its penchant for suffixal agglutination, despite their stark underlying genetic and typological dissimilarity with the other language families of Eurasia. Shared features include an extensive system of postposed bound relational morphemes. Yeniseian cases and postpositions are functionally and structurally analogous to the case suffixes and clausal subordinating enclitics found in neighboring Turkic and Samoyedic languages (Anderson 2004). In Yeniseian, however, the morphemes in question show signs of having arisen by coalescence. What are usually described as cases in Yeniseian still pattern phonologically as enclitics rather than true suffixes (Vajda 2008a). The system of grammatical enclitics in Yeniseian also shows morphological heterogeneity in their origins. One set of these bound relational morphemes derives from postpositions that cliticize directly to the preceding nominal stem. These include the instrumental, caritive (meaning 'without'), locative (used only with inanimate-class nouns), and the prosecutive (meaning 'past' or through'). In particular, the prosecutive (meaning 'through' or 'past'), is typical of North Asian case systems (Anderson 2004). Table 17.3 provides an example of these relational suffixes added to Ket nouns:

Table 17.3 *Case-like enclitics in Ket that attach directly to the noun stem*

	Masculine animate class		Feminine animate class		Inanimate class	
	'god'	'gods'	'daughter'	'daughters'	'tent'	'tents'
locative	—	—	—	—	qus-ka	quŋ-ka
prosecutive	ɛs-bɛs	ɛsaŋ-bɛs	hun-bɛs	hɔnaŋ-bɛs	qus-bɛs	quŋ-bɛs
instrumental	ɛs-as	ɛsaŋ-as	hun-as	hɔnaŋ-as	qus-as	quŋ-as
caritive	ɛs-an	ɛsaŋ-an	hun-an	hɔnaŋ-an	qus-an	quŋ-an

Table 17.4 *Case-like enclitics in Ket that require a possessive connector*

	Masculine animate class		Feminine animate class		Inanimate class	
	'god'	'gods'	'daughter'	'daughters'	'tent'	'tents'
ablative	*ɛs-da-ŋal*	*ɛsaŋ-na-ŋal*	*hun-di-ŋal*	*hɔnaŋ-na-ŋal*	*qus-di-ŋal*	*quŋ-di-ŋal*
dative	*ɛs-da-ŋa*	*ɛsaŋ-na-ŋa*	*hun-di-ŋa*	*hɔnaŋ-na-ŋa*	*qus-di-ŋa*	*quŋ-di-ŋa*
benefactive	*ɛs-da-ta*	*ɛsaŋ-na-ta*	*hun-di-ta*	*hɔnaŋ-na-ta*	*qus-di-ta*	*quŋ-di-ta*
adessive	*ɛs-da-ŋta*	*ɛsaŋ-na-ŋta*	*hun-di-ŋta*	*hɔnaŋ-na-ŋta*	*qus-di-ŋta*	*quŋ-di-ŋta*

The other set requires an augment in the form of a possessive morpheme as connector, analogous to the way possessive noun phrases are constructed (Example 17.1).

Example 17.1 Possessive Noun Phrases

hun=d quʔs   *huɯp=da quʔs*   *duɯlgat=na quʔs*
daughter=POSS.FEM tent son=POSS.FEM tent children=POSS.ANIM.PL tent
'daughter's tent'   'son's tent'   'children's tent

As they do in true possessive phrases, these augments reflect class and number distinctions of the preceding (possessor) noun: *da* (masculine class singular), *na* (animate class plural), *di* (feminine class singular or inanimate class singular and plural) (Table 17.4).

There are also numerous postpositions and relational nouns in Modern Ket, most of which can concatenate with the case-like enclitics shown above, forming long agglutinative strings (Example 17.2).

Example 17.2 Suffix-Like Concatenations of Relational Enclitics in Ket

déŋ-na-huɯt-ka   *húɯp-da-ʌʌt-di-ŋa*   *qúŋ-d-inbal-di-ŋal*
people-PL-under-LOC   son-PL-M-on-N-DAT   tents-N-between-N-ABL
'located under the people' 'onto the son'   'from between the tents'

Etymologically, many Ket postpositions are obvious adaptations of body part nouns or other noun roots: *-huɯt* 'under' < *hūɯj* 'belly'; *-ʌʌt* 'on the surface' < *ʌʁat* 'back'; *-inbal* 'between' < *inbal* 'gap, space between objects'. The resulting concatenations superficially resemble the strings of suffixes in Turkic and Samoyedic languages.

Also in imitation of other North Asian suffixal agglutinating languages, many of the bound relational morphemes used in the Ket nominal system can also be added to finite verb forms to express various kinds of clausal subordination:

Example 17.3 Ket Temporal Subordination with Kupka 'Before' (Literally, 'on the Beak') (Werner 1997c: 351)

āt qáre éŋŋuŋ   bɔyɔ́tn-kupka āt qaséŋ kiʔ   quʔs   tháptɔ
I   that village I.walk-before I   there new house I.stand.it
'Before I move to that village, I'll build a new house there.'

Example 17.4 Ket Non-temporal Subordination with the Non-augmented Postposition dɔy·t 'Because, Since' (Werner 1997c: 350)

āt émilta-ŋ Dáŋatɛt-dɔyɔt   ɔ́kŋ   āt qáriya ī·m   kátnibɛtn
I cone-PL   I.hit.them-since you.PL I   later   pine.nuts you.give.them
'Since I'm knocking down the cones, you give me the pine nuts later.'

All of this closely parallels the use of postposed bound relational morphemes in other North Asian languages (Anderson 2004).

Vajda (2008a) argues that Ket nominal relational enclitics are not a true case system, but function as transpositional suffixes to negate the head status of the nouns and verbs by converting them to adjuncts. The stem-like nature of the resulting concatenations is clearly evident when such forms are reconverted to nouns by adding the nominalizing suffix *-s* (Examples 17.5 and 17.6).

Example 17.5 Nominalizations Made from Nouns with Case-like Enclitics

qus-di-ŋal-s   qay-an-s
tent-N-ABL-NMLR   speech-CARITIVE-NMLR
'the thing (or person) from the tent' 'speechless one, mute person'

Example 17.6 Nominalizations Made from Postpositional Constructions in Ket

qus-t-huut-di-ŋal-s   aq-na-inbal-ka-s
tent-N-under-N-ABL-NMLR   trees-ANIM.PL-between-LOC-NMLR
'the one from under the tent'   'the one between the trees'

The fact that bound-relational morphemes in Ket do not build a discrete inflectional paradigm parallels their etymological heterogeneity. As seen earlier, some case-like morphemes are added to the bare stem (*-as* 'with', *-an* 'without', *-ka* 'in, at', *-bes* 'past, through'), while others require a possessive augment (*-di-ŋal* 'from', *-di-ŋa* 'to', *-di-ta* 'for', *-di-ŋta* 'at'). Possessive augments are likewise obligatory, with many morphemes conventionally described as 'postpositions' due to their more specific relational semantics or their transparent denominal etymologies (*-d-huut-* 'beneath', *-d-ʌʌt-* 'on', *-d-huj* 'inside', *-d-kup-* 'in front of', *-d-tan* 'toward', *-d-qɔn* 'up to', etc.). Other postpositions are added to stems directly, exactly like the set of non-augmented case suffixes: *-dɔyɔt* 'for the sake of', *-asqa* 'resembling'. And morphemes belonging to all four of these semantic and etymological subgroups may attach to finite verbs as clausal subordinators: augmented and case-like (-*di-ŋal* 'since'), non-augmented and case-like (-*ka* 'while'), augmented and postposition-like (-*d-kup-ka* 'before'), and non-augmented and non-postposition-like (-*dugde* 'during', *dɔyɔt* 'because').

Although a system of case-like enclitics was clearly present in Common Yeniseian, having been documented for Kott (Castrén 1858; Werner 1997a) as well as for Ket and Yugh, the actual morphological material used to create it varies tellingly across the Yeniseian daughter languages. This further suggests typological adaptation to the neighboring suffixal agglutinating languages rather than inheritance from Proto-Yeniseian. Kott uses different shapes of pronominal augments: masculine singular *a* rather than *da*, feminine singular or inanimate-class *i* rather than *di*. Note also Kott -*čaŋ* vs. Kett -*ŋal* for ablative meaning. Kott -*čaŋ* derives from a root meaning 'drag, path', while Ket -*ŋal* may be connected with morphemes meaning 'extend' (cf. Ket -*la* 'more, rather', *bìl* 'distance'). Such etymological heterogeneity further suggests that the case-like system of enclitics in later Yeniseian languages arose in imitation of suffixal agglutination. Although the enclitic shapes themselves do not appear to have been borrowed, their overall formal and functional similarity to the nominal case and postpositional systems of Turkic, Samoyedic, and other Inner Eurasian families further supports the probability that they developed in Yeniseian on the basis of long-term language contact. The use of bound relational morphemes in Yeniseian as well as Turkic and Samoyedic to subordinate finite verb forms to a main clause (Anderson 2004) further demonstrates the degree to which key typological features of Inner Eurasian languages have influenced Yeniseian linguistic structure.

The vehicle for grammatical adstrate influence on Yeniseian appears to have been the tendency for Yeniseian speakers to maintain communicative skills in the languages of surrounding peoples. This bilingualism was not reciprocated. Even among the Selkup, traditional friends and marriage partners of the Ket, the Ket language had the reputation of being difficult to learn, so that interethnic communication normally occurred in Selkup. This situation changed only during the mid-twentieth century with the adoption of Russian as a lingua franca by all Siberian peoples. Women from other ethnic groups taken into exogamous Ket society as wives may also have affected Yeniseian grammar and phonology over the centuries. The resultant situation of few loanwords but significant grammatical and phonological influence would parallel that observed by Aikhenvald (2003) for Tariana – an Amazonian language that likewise resists lexical borrowing but whose grammatical structure was strongly influenced by the neighboring languages. Unlike the situation with Tariana, there is no record of linguistic exogamy in Inner

Eurasia; however, the exogamous moieties (*hɔʁɔtpuul*) observed among the Ket in the seventeenth century may be a vestige of interethnic social accommodation between Yeniseian tribes and their neighbors dating back to Common Yeniseian, the era that witnessed the beginning of significant adaptation to the suffixal agglutinating morphology of neighboring languages. In historic times, the rarity of outsiders learning Ket appears due to the language's phonemic prosody and especially to its highly complex prefixing verb morphology – core Yeniseian features with no analog in the surrounding families. But over the centuries even these most typical Yeniseian typological traits were strongly influenced by the predominant Inner Eurasian language type. Because these traits were not replaced, but rather uniquely adapted to create intermediate patterns, the result of contact produced a hybrid morphological patterning that could be called typological accommodation.

17.5   Accommodation of Core Yeniseian Typological Features to the Inner Eurasian Linguistic Area

Beneath the underlay of Inner Eurasian areal features, Yeniseian languages display a core of features that radically distinguish them from all of the surrounding families. These features are the basic vocabulary, phonemic tones, pronominal possessive prefixes, and complex prefixing verb morphology. Family-internal comparisons demonstrate that these traits are autochthonous to the family, predating the influence of Samoyedic, Turkic, Mongolic, and Tungusic – families that spread at the expense of Yeniseian via the economic dominance of reindeer and stock breeding over forest hunting and gathering. A further, more striking demonstration that these features have no historical connection with other known language families of Eurasia comes from examining linguistic parallels with Na-Dene (Athabaskan-Eyak-Tlingit), a family with which Yeniseian appears to share a demonstrable genetic link (Vajda 2006a, b, 2010). Cognate lexical items and morphological structures in both families provide an additional vantage for estimating the typological state of Proto-Yeniseian before the spread of animal husbandry in Inner Eurasia.

This section examines how core Yeniseian morphological traits were gradually modified to become more like the radically different language type of the surrounding peoples – a process I have called typological accommodation. Malcolm Ross's (2001) term metatypy, or grammatical calquing, is too strong, since the results of accommodation do not represent a complete shift in typology but rather the achievement of a new, unique hybrid between two originally radically different morphological types.

The areally unique Yeniseian features that underwent typological accommodation to Uralic and Turkic languages – particularly the phonemic prosody that came to be eroded in longer, agglutinative word forms and the prefixing verb structure, which came to be restructured as suffixing – all display unmistakable genetic parallels to Na-Dene, the language family of the last group of American Indians to become established in North America. This link further attests to the originally alien typology of Proto-Yeniseian vis-à-vis the suffixing, non-tonal families of Inner and North Asia. Modern Ket, the best documented Yeniseian language, provides the most complete illustration of how these traits came to mimic, without actually being replaced by, the prevailing morphological and phonological patterns of the surrounding languages. The resulting uniqueness of Modern Ket morphology is largely a product of this process of structural hybridization.

17.5.1   Phonemic Tone in Proto-Yeniseian and Its Link with Na-Dene Glottalized Codas

The first known speculation that the Ket, among other Siberian peoples, share a special connection with Native Americans dates back to Adriaan Reeland in 1708 (Vajda 2001: 2). The first scholar to suggest a specific linguistic connection with Na-Dene was the Italian Alfredo Trombetti in 1923, on the basis of random lexical similarities between Ket, Kott, Tlingit, and Athabaskan (Vajda 2001: 280). Evidence precise and extensive enough to prove a genetic connection across Bering Strait would shed invaluable light on the typological structure of Proto-Yeniseian before areal influence from the suffixal-agglutinating languages of contemporary northern Eurasia. Vajda (2006b) provided interlocking sound correspondences in several dozen basic vocabulary words to argue that Yeniseian and Athabaskan-Eyak-Tlingit (Na-Dene minus Haida) are indeed genetically related in a family that could be called Dene-Yeniseian. One striking piece of phonological evidence is how the distribution of Yeniseian high and glottalized tones parallels that of high versus low tone in Athabaskan. In both families, the phonemic contrast in prosody arose based on an original contrast between glottalized and non-glottalized codas consonants. As is known (cf. Krauss 2005), modern Athabaskan languages are of three prosodic types. In non-tonal languages such as Koyukon and Ahtna, coda glottalization disappeared without any effect on vowel prosody. The Athabaskan languages that did develop a phonemic contrast in tone are of two types. In high-marked languages such as Dene (Chipewyan), coda glottalization yielded high tone, while syllables without an original glottalized coda became low tone. In low-marked languages such as Navajo, the opposite situation prevailed: syllables with original glottalized codas became low tone, while other kinds of syllables became high-tone by contrast.

Yeniseian cognates to Athabaskan show a pattern of high tone in syllables originally ending in a glottalized coda, and lower, laryngealized tone in other syllables. Compared to Athabaskan, Yeniseian resembles a high-marked language, with the added feature of laryngealization in the contrasting low tone. Table 17.5 shows this precise correlation, which applied only in the case of Yeniseian cognates that have not undergone further tonogenetic processes, such as the loss of a fricative in the second part of the word, which yielded falling tone. The Dene and Navajo consonants in Table 17.5 largely follow their modern orthographies. The proto forms are rendered in IPA, with voiceless unaspirated obstruents written /č, t, k, q/ rather than /dž, d, g, ɢ/, as is more customary in the writings of historical Athabaskanists. The symbol /v/ represents any vowel nucleus, short or long. Except for these transcriptional adjustments, the Proto-Athabaskan-Eyak forms provided below follow the

Table 17.5 *Systematic correspondences in tone between Yeniseian and Athabaskan*

Modern Yeniseian		Modern Athabaskan			*Proto-Athabaskan-Eyak	
High marked		High-marked	Low-marked		Non-tonal proto-forms with phonemic coda glottalization	
Ket	Yugh	Dene	Navajo			
CṽC	CṽC	Cv́(C)	Cv̀(C)	< *CvC$^?$	(original glottalized coda)	
dīˑk	dʼīk	dzé	džèèh		*čeˑq$^?$	*conifer resin*
sēˑŋ	sēŋ	thə́r	sèd		*sənt$^?$	*liver*
hūˑn	fũun	sí^{n}th	sèè^{n}s		*xeˑn$^?$ts$^?$	*wart*
Cv$^?$C	Cv$^?$C	Cv̀(C)	Cv́(C)	< *CvC	(original non-glottalized coda)	
qu$^{?a}$	χu$^?$	gòr	geed		*q^{w}eˑd	*poke/skewer*
sʌ$^?$n	sʌ$^?$n	zèn	(žìn)^b		*x^{w}en^j	*dark color*

^{a} Yeniseian-internal morphology reveals a closer match to the Proto-Athabaskan-Eyak forms than this chart would suggest. For example, in Ket *qu$^?$* 'skewer, ray', the original coda /d/ reappears in the plural *qʌdeŋ* 'skewers, rays' and in the CK infinitive *qʌːdə* 'to poke', which developed falling tone through erosion of the infinitive suffix. Falling tone is a Yeniseian innovation from fricative deletion and has no analog in the tonal systems of Na-Dene, where the fricative is retained instead: cf. CK *kùːnə* 'wolverine' versus Proto-Athabaskan-Eyak *k^{h}una$^?$s* 'wolverine'; Yugh *čìːʰx*, Ket *tìx* 'snake' versus Proto-Athabaskan *tɬ$^?$əɣəš*. Irregular plural forms of Ket nouns can often be explained by comparison with Athabaskan-Eyak. In *seŋn-in* 'livers, innards' (cf. *sēˑŋ* 'liver'), and *hutn-an* warts' (cf. *huˑt* 'wart'), the plural stem augments echo the original presence of coda clusters. The velar coda in Yeniseian words for 'resin' derives from an earlier uvular: cf. the Ket verb root *-daqŋ* 'glue down with resin'. Sequences of /iq/ are entirely lacking in Yeniseian, since uvular /q/ became /k/ everywhere before /i/.

^{b} In Modern Navajo all short-vowel closed syllables (cf *žin* 'black') have lost high tone through analogical leveling obscuring the original tonal correspondence.

well-reasoned system of Pre-Proto-Athabaskan reconstructions developed by Jeff Leer (cf. Leer 1999).

Ket/Yugh high-tone words ('resin, liver, wart') correlate with Athabaskan high tone in a high-marked language (Dene) but with low tone in a low-marked language (Navajo). This pattern exists because each of these sets of tonal contrasts reflects the same original opposition, presumably in an earlier Proto-Dene-Yeniseian language, between the presence versus absence of coda glottalization.

While the origin of high versus low tone in Athabaskan can be deduced from a comparison with non-tonal Eyak, which preserved the original glottalized codas, the Ket/Yugh contrast between high versus laryngealized tone requires external comparison with Na-Dene to reveal its ultimate origin, since the tonal opposition was apparently present already in Proto-Yeniseian.

17.5.2   Typological Accommodation of Ket Prosody

Under the influence of the root-initial agglutinating languages of Inner Eurasia, the tonal prosody in Yeniseian developed so that phonemic differences in pitch are largely the domain of monosyllabic words (Vajda 2004).

Ket monosyllabic phonological words contain four phonemic prosodemes. These can be called 'tones', though they actually consist of an amalgam of melody, vowel length, vowel height, and tenseness (in the case of mid vowels), and the presence or absence of laryngealization (creaky voice).

In polysyllables, many of which were created by attachment of relational morphemes after a root, distinctions in monosyllabic prosody generally erode, being replaced by a rise and fall of pitch on the first two syllables that resembles word-initial stress. The degree of prosodic erosion – in other words the degree of clitic-like versus suffix-like behavior of the relational morpheme – is free to vary to express distinctions in focus (Example 17.7).

Table 17.6 *Phonemic prosodemes in Southern Ket monosyllables*

	Tonal melody	Vowel length (syllable type)	Phonation type	Mid-vowel quality
sūˑl 'blood'	high-even	half-long (closed or open)	neutral	tense [e, ɤ, o]
suˀl 'salmon'	abrupt rising	short (closed or open)	laryngealized (creaky)	lax [ɛ, ʌ, ɔ]
súùl 'snowsled'	rising-falling	long (closed or open)	neutral	lax [ɛ, ʌ, ɔ]
sùl 'holding hook'	falling	short (closed only)	neutral	lax [ɛ, ʌ, ɔ]

Example 17.7 Degrees of Prosodic Erosion in *ōˑp* 'Father' + *da-ŋal* 'from'

under focus   neutral focus   backgrounded   nominalized as a stem
ōˑp=da-ŋal   *ōp=da-ŋal*   *ɔb-da-ŋal*   *ɔbdaŋals 'the one from father'*

Disyllabic stems have rising/falling pitch under focus or when pronounced in isolation. In a few, the pitch peak falls on the second syllable, giving the impression of stress on the second syllable. These are marked with an acute accent on the second syllable. The much more common syllable-initial prosodic prominence is left unmarked. This low-yield distinction in disyllables is likewise eroded by the attachment of relational morphemes (Example 17.8).

Example 17.8 Phonemic Contrast in Disyllabic Stem Prosody and Its Erosion before Relational Morphemes

rising-falling pitch: *qɔpqun* 'cuckoos' > *qɔpqun-di-ŋal* 'from the cuckoo'
rising-high falling   *qɔpqún* 'cuckoos' > *qɔpqun-na-ŋal* 'from the cuckoos'
pitch:

The discourse-related replacement phonemic prosody with a generally non-contrastive word-initial emphasis in polysyllables renders Modern Ket phonology closer to that of the surrounding languages. Yeniseian failed to develop vowel harmony, but combinations of stem plus strings of grammatical suffixes or clitics – with only the first vowel capable of reflecting the language's full range of phonemic distinctions – organizes the phonological word in an analogous fashion.

17.5.3   Typological Accommodation of Relational Morphemes in the Yeniseian Nominal System

It has already been show in Section 17.4 how Yeniseian encliticized relational nouns to nominal forms to build a system resembling the case suffixes of Turkic and Samoyedic. The addition of enclitics to Yeniseian nouns – sometimes with the help of possessive augments, sometimes without – closely mimics the system of nominal inflectional suffixes of the surrounding languages. Table 17.7 provides examples of postposted relational morphemes in the nominal morphology of several Inner Asian languages:

Vajda (2008a) showed that the Yeniseian case suffixes are actually enclitics with variable prosodic behavior. They only sometimes fuse with the preceding noun to form a single phonological word. When the preceding noun or pronoun is focused, these morphemes are enclitics, and the monosyllabic tonal prosody of their host is partly or fully retained.

Table 17.7 *Ablative, dative, instrumental, and locative forms of 'rock' in some Inner Eurasian languages*

	'from the rock'	'to the rock'	'with the rock'	'on the rock'
Ket	*tʌs-di-ŋal*	*tʌs-di-ŋa*	*tʌs-as*	*tʌs-ka*
Yugh	*čʌs-di-ŋə:r*	*čʌs-di-ŋ*	*čʌs-faj*	*tʌs-kɛj*
Khakas	*tas-taŋ*	*tas-xa*	*tas-naŋ*	*tas-ta*
Tuvan	*daš-tan*	*daš-ka*	*daš-bile*	*daš-ta*
Selkup	*pʊ-kɔlɪk*	*pʊ-nɪk*	*pʊ-sa*	*pʊ-qɪn*
Evenki	*xi:sɛ-duk*	*xi:sɛ-du:*	*xi:sɛ-t*	*xi:sɛ-lə*
Mongolian	*čʊlʊn-as*	*čʊlʊn-ru*	*čʊlʊn-ał*	*čʊlʊn-d*

Retention of select prosodic features as a means of expressing contextual focus

Example 17.9 Focus on the Addressee: Host Remains Prosodically Separate from the Clitic

ā·m   ō·p=da-ŋa   da=qaiŋna
mother father-M-ADESS FEM.SBJ=told
'Mother told *father*.'

Example 17.10 Unfocussed Addressee: Relational Morpheme Fuses with Its Host, Forming a Polysyllabic Phonological Word

ā·m   ɔb-da-ŋa   da=qaiŋna
mother father=M-ADESS FEM.SBJ=told
'Mother told father.'

Conversely, if the referent in question is entirely backgrounded in discourse, as in Example 17.12, the pronoun can drop altogether, leaving the relational morpheme to stand entirely on its own, something no true case suffix can do.

Example 17.11 Presence or Absence of the Pronoun Host of the Dative Morpheme Used as a Discourse-Tracking Device

ō·p   búŋ-na-ŋa   t=qáiŋna
father 3P-ANIM.PL-ADESS MASC.SBJ-told
'Father told them (neutral focus, not backgrounded).'

Example 17.12

ō·p   ná-ŋa   t=qáiŋna
father ANIM.PL-ADESS MASC.SBJ-told
'Father told 'em (backgrounded).'

Bound relational morphemes after non-focused nouns or pronouns in Ket mimic the suffixal case systems of Turkic and Samoyedic. But these morphemes are not true inflections, since their phonological and morphological behavior varies between the prosodic status of suffix, clitic, and independent word depending on discourse factors. The part-suffix, part-clitic status of the so-called case affixes in Ket represents another example of typological hybridization between an originally prefixing, somewhat isolating language and the suffixal agglutination typical of the nominal systems of the surrounding languages.

Possessive prefixes – an original feature of both Yeniseian and Na-Dene – have likewise undergone an interesting evolution in Yeniseian. In Ket and Yugh, these prefixes are capable of attaching to either the previous or following word – an unusual type of clitic called 'ditropic'. In Modern Ket, whenever a preceding word is available, even a word outside the possessive phrase itself, the possessive morpheme normally encliticizes to that word. Only when no such word is available, such as in sentence initial position or after a pause, do these morphemes procliticize to the possessum. This development, while preserved the possessive morphemes as proclitics in some environments but adapted them as suffixes or enclitics in others, caused Ket morphology, once again, to move partly in the direction of suffixal agglutination. The resulting morphological change created a hybrid between a proclitic and an enclitic/suffix rather than a complete shift to suffixation. Example 17.13 shows the variable phonological behavior of possessive morphemes in Modern Ket.

Example 17.13 Possessive Pronominal Clitics

enclitic on possessor	enclitic on unrelated word	proclitic on possessum
qàl-da ki$^?$s	*en-da ki$^?$s*	(pause) *da=ki$^?$s*
grandson=MASC.POSS foot	now=MASC.POSS foot	MASC.POSS=foot
'the grandson's foot'	'now his foot ...'	'his foot'

Interestingly, no reduction of root prosody is ever triggered across the proclitic boundary, regardless of distinctions in pragmatic focus. This contrasts with the variable ability of relational enclitics to fuse with the root into a single phonological word, like suffixes normally would. Presumably, all enclitics in Ket developed such fusional properties in mimicry of suffixation, whereas possessive proclitics display no prefix-like fusion with their host, since none of the languages surrounding Yeniseian possessive prefixes. When the possessive morphemes attach to a preceding word, however, they usually trigger prosodic erosion in their host.

Compare the prosodic leveling in the roots *ē·s* 'son' and *ē·s* 'God' caused by possessive enclisis (Example 17.14) with the absence of leveling with possessive proclisis (Example 17.15).

Example 17.14

hub-da ē·s	*es-da hu$^?$p*
son-MASC.POSS foot	God-MASC.POSS son
'the son's God'	'God's son'

Example 17.15

da=ēˑs   *da=huⁿp*
MASC.POSS=God   MASC.POSS=son
'his God'   'his son'

Though recorded as proclitics in all documented Yeniseian languages, the possessive morphemes of Modern Ket now take the form of suffix-like enclitics in all instances except word-initial position or when preceded by a significant pause. Typological accommodation to the possessive and genitive suffixes of the surrounding languages has influenced their evolution into a rare morphological object called a ditropic clitic.

The prosodic behavior of bound relational morphemes appears to have evolved under the typological influence of suffixing languages, as enclitics often fuse with their host in mimicry of suffixes, while grammatical proclitics never do.

17.5.4   Typological Accommodation of Ket Verb Prefixation

The most striking morphological feature of Modern Ket is its rigid series of verb prefixes, which stand out starkly against the exclusively suffixing inflectional morphology of other verb systems in western and southern Siberia. Modern Ket finite verbs conform to a morphological model consisting of eight prefix positions, an original root or base position (P0), and a single suffix position (Table 17.8).

Several features of Modern Ket verb morphology are extremely unusual typologically. First, the configuration of subject/object markers is not determined by an overall grammatical rule, so that agreement morphemes may appear in various positional combinations depending on the verb in question. There are two productive transitive subject/object configurations, and five productive intransitive subject configurations (Vajda 2003, 2004). Which configuration a given verb belongs to is determined by idiosyncratic etymological

Table 17.8 *Position classes in the Ket finite verb*

P8	P7	P6	P5	P4	P3	P2	P1	P0	P-1
subject	left base (lexical stem)	subject or object	thematic consonant (originally shape or animacy classifier)	tense/ mood or 3p animate subj or obj.	3p in- animate subj. or obj.	tense/ mood	subject or object	right base (original root position)	anim. subj. plural

factors rather than semantics and must be listed in the verb's lexical entry. Second, the position of the primary lexical root – the verb's semantic head – can be located either in position 7 near the beginning of the verb, or in position 0, near the end, depending on the stem in question. All of the intervening affixes therefore appear as prefixes in some verbs but as suffixes in others. A third feature of note is that tense and mood are expressed by lexically chose combinations of morphemes in two positions (P4 and P2). These morphemes interact to build six productive tense-mood classes, with nearly all verbs belonging to one of these classes as part of its lexical entry. Finally, the Yeniseian verb-internal themantic consonant prefixes, which seem to historically have played a role in shape and animacy classification, are typologically unique in northern Eurasia.

The variable position of the verb's basic root morpheme and the lexical subject/object configurations, evolved when the original Yeniseian prefixing structure partly realigned itself toward suffixal agglutination by incorporating a new root verb initially. This process, along with the breakdown in the system of animacy classifiers, some of which became agreement markers, also led to the rise of what could be called lexical inflection[2] – the idiosyncratic choice of agreement marker configuration. The discussion below concentrates on the shift of the root position from end to beginning, the central typological change that was triggered by accommodation to the suffixing verb paradigms of other Inner Eurasian languages.

A comparison of verb structure across Yeniseian demonstrates that the Proto-Yeniseian verb was exclusively prefixing, with the root, or base, always in final position, as shown in Table 17.9 (see also Vajda 2008b:143).

In contrast to this prefixing structure, every one of the more than two dozen productive patterns of finite verb creation in Modern Ket place a lexical stem at the beginning of the phonological verb. In most of these models, an infinitive form occupies position 7, while the original root position (position 0) has come to be filled with a morpheme that marks transitivity or aspect, derived from a

Table 17.9 *Proto-Yeniseian finite verb morphology*

Morphemes outside the phonological verb		P4	P3	P2	P1	
Subject NP	Verbal complement (adverb, object NP)	Thematic consonant (*d, n,* *hʷ*, etc.)	Animacy classifier *d* - anim. *b* - inan.	Tense, mood, aspect (conjugation prefix *s, ɣa,* *o* + suffix *l, n*)	Undergoer subject agreement (1 or 2p)	Verb base (bare root or verb-deriving prefix *d,* *l* + root)

semantically eroded verb root. Still, the original root position continues to be obligatorily filled in all verbs, so that it cannot simply be called a suffix. A few examples are shown in Example 17.16.

Example 17.16 Root-Initial verb forms in Modern Ket containing the infinitive ū·s 'thaw, warm up'

da=usqibit	'she thaws it (once)'	$[da^8=us^7-q^5-b^3-t^0$ 3F.SBJ^8-thaw^7-CAUS^5-3 N.OBJ^3-MOM.TRANS$^0]$
da=usqabda	'she thaws it (often)'	$[da^8=us^7-q^5-a^4-b^3-da^0$ 3F.SBJ^8-thaw^7-CAUS^5-PRES^4-3 N.OBJ^3-ITER.TRANS$^0]$
da=usqisatn	'she thaws out (once)'	$[da^8=us^7-q^5-s^4-a^1-tn^0$ 3F.SBJ^8-thaw^7-CAUS^5-PRES^4-3SG.SBJ^1-MOM.INTR$^0]$
da=usqajaɾij	'she thaws out (often)'	$[da^8=us^7-q^5-aj^4-a^1-dij^0$ 3F.SBJ^8-thaw^7-CAUS^5-PRES^4-3SG.SBJ^1-ITER.INTR$^0]$
úsíɣaʁan	'it begins to thaw'	$[ū·s^7-i^6-k^5-a^4-qan^0$ thaw^7-3 N.SBJ^6-TH^5-PRES^4-INCEPT$^0]$

In productive patterns of verb formation, only word forms can occupy P7, though these words may contain suffixes marking event or participant number (Example 17.17).

Example 17.17 Examples Showing Punctual and Iterative Suffixes on P7

da=táʁajɔksa	'she (a wasp) stings him (once)'	$[da^8=taʁaj^7-o^6-k^5-s^4-a^0$ 3f.sbj^{8}sting.MOM^7-3 M.SBJ^6-PRES^4-action.occurs$^0]$
da=táqtijiŋɔksa	'she stings him (often)'	$[da^8=taqtijiŋ^7-o^6-k^5-s^4-a^0$ IC^8-sting.ITER^7-3 M.SBJ^6-TH^5-PRES^4-action.occurs$^0]$

In all productive verb patterns in Modern Ket, a lexical root occupies phonological verb initial position. The position 8 subject markers located in front of this root are actually ditropic clitics (just like the possessive morphemes in nominal morphology) and normally encliticize to any available preceding word (Example 17.18).

Example 17.18 The Phrase 'She Makes an axe', Showing Encliticization of the Subject Marker

búra tóksivɛt
$bū·=da^8 tō·k^7-s^4-bet^0$
she=3F.SBJ^8 axe^7-PRES^4-make^0
'she makes an axe'

Most Modern Ket verbs contain a phonological word-initial root and thus mimic the root-initial suffixal agglutination typical of verbs in other Inner Asian languages.

The only productive patterns that retain a functional verb root in position 0 are verbs that incorporate their patient or instrument nouns. Incorporation is an innovation in Yeniseian and such patterns fewer than a dozen verb roots allow it. Most incorporate the patient or theme: *-aq* 'become', *-bet* 'have, make', *-ej* 'kill', *-dop* 'drink', *-a* 'eat, feed on'. Two incorporate only only instrument-role nouns: *-kit* 'rub with object' and *-tet* 'hit endwise with a long object'.

Example 17.19 Noun Incorporation in Modern Ket

kerataq	'he becomes a man'	$[ke^2d^7\text{-}a^6\text{-}t^5\text{-}a^4\text{-}aq^0$ man^7-3 M.SBJ^6-TH^5-PRES^4-INCEPT$^0]$
inijbet	'she has a needle'	$[i^2n^7\text{-}ij^4\text{-}bet^0$ needle^7-3F.SBJ^4-have$^0]$
da=insivet	'she makes a needle'	$[da^8\text{=}i^2n^7\text{-}s^4\text{-}bet^0$ 3F.SBJ^8-needle^7-PRES^4-make$^0]$
da=selsej	'she kills a reindeer'	$[da^8\text{=}sel^7\text{-}s^4\text{-}ej^0$ 3F.SBJ^8-reindeer^7-PRES^4-kill$^0]$
da=ularɔp	'she drinks water'	$[da^8\text{=}\bar{u}\cdot l^7\text{-}a^4\text{-}dop^0$ 3F.SBJ^8-water^7-PRES^4-drink$^0]$
da=imsa	'she eats pine nuts'	$[da^8\text{-}\bar{i}\cdot m^7\text{-}s^4\text{-}a^0$ 3F.SBJ^8-pine.nuts^7-PRES^4-eat$^0]$
da=donbayatet	'she knifes me'	$[da^8\text{-}do^2n^7\text{-}ba^6\text{-}h^5\text{-}a^4\text{-}tet^0$ 3F.SBJ^8-knife^7-1SG.OBJ^6-TH^5-PRES^4-hit$^0]$
da=tʌɣaŋtayit	'she salts them (fish)'	$[da^8\text{-}tʌ^{?7}\text{-}aŋ^6\text{-}t^5\text{-}a^4\text{-}kit^0$ 3F.SBJ^8-salt^7-3PL.ANIM.OBJ^6-TH^5-PRES^4-rub$^0]$

These incorporation patterns are connected with the rise of root-initial verb forms. Incorporated nouns cannot be preceded by free modifiers. Plural noun forms can be incorporated, however (Example 17.20).

Example 17.20 Singular and Plural Noun Forms in P7

t=qussivet	'he makes a tent'	$[du^8\text{-}qu^2s^7\text{-}s^4\text{-}bet^0$ 3 M.SBJ^8-tent^7-PRES^4-make$^0]$
t=quŋsivet	'he makes tents'	$[du^8\text{-}qu^2ŋ^7\text{-}s^4\text{-}bet^0$ 3 M.SBJ^8-tents^7-PRES^4-make$^0]$
qusdivet	'I have a tent'	$[qu^2s^7\text{-}di^1\text{-}bet^0$ tent^7-1SG.SBJ^1-have$^0]$
quŋdivet	'I have tents'	$[qu^2ŋ^7\text{-}di^1\text{-}bet^0$ tents^7-1SG.SBJ^1-have$^0]$
keratɔnɔq	'he became a man'	$[ke^2t^7\text{-}a^6\text{-}t^5\text{-}o^4\text{-}n^2\text{-}oq^0$ man^7-3 M.SBJ^6-TH^5-PAST$^{4/2}$-INCEPT$^0]$
deŋaŋtɔnɔq	'they became men'	$[de^2ŋ^7\text{-}aŋ^6\text{-}t^5\text{-}o^4\text{-}n^2\text{-}oq^0$ men^7-3AN.PL.SBJ^6-TH^5-PAST$^{4/2}$-INCEPT$^0]$

Once again, the placement of an easily recognizable root or stem in phonological verb-initial position approximates a suffixing structure.

An examination of the oldest verbs in Ket reveals that most of the language's basic word stock are exclusively prefixing and root final. This suggests that root-initial verb formations, which now represent the only productive patterns

in Modern Ket, arose only later, on the basis of an original prefixing configuration of morpheme position classes.

Example 17.21 Root-Final Verbs in the Oldest Layer of Ket Vocabulary

duɣaraq	'he lives'	[du^8-ya^4-daq^0 3 M.SBJ^8-PRES^4-live^0]
dɔldaq	'he lived'	[du^8-o^4-l^2-daq^0 3 M.SBJ^8-PAST$^{4/2}$-live^0]
duptaŋ	'he drags it'	[du^8-b^3-$taŋ^0$ 3 M.SBJ^8-3 N.OBJ^3-drag^0]
dɔbiltaŋ	'he dragged it'	[du^8-o^4-b^3-l^2-$taŋ^0$ 3 M.SBJ^8-PAST$^{4/2}$-3 N.OBJ^3-drag^0]
duptɛt	'he hits it'	[du^8-b^3-tet^0 3 M.SBJ^8-3 N.OBJ^3-hit^0]
dibbɛt	'he makes it'	[du^8-b^3-bet^0 3 M.SBJ^8-3 N.OBJ^3-make^0]

Note also that the position 8 subject markers in root-final verbs are regular
prefixes, forming part of the phonological verb. This contrasts with their
behavior in stems with initial roots, before which these subject markers encliticize to the previous word whenever possible, insuring root-initial pronunciation of the verb in most cases.

The verbs in all documented Yeniseian languages show the same tendency
for the semantic peak to migrate from final to initial position, with only the
oldest layer of vocabulary consistently retaining the original root-final, prefixing structure. Root-final verbs play a core lexical role in Yeniseian similar to
strong verbs in Germanic.

External comparison with Na-Dene languages provides additional evidence
that Yeniseian was originally prefixing. Much of the prefixing structure of
Proto-Yeniseian appears cognate with the oldest layers of Tlingit, Eyak, and
Athabaskan verb morphology. Although no one has yet reconstructed the
Proto-Athabaskan verb, let alone that of Proto-Na-Dene, there are many
obvious parallels with Yeniseian. These possibly include the use of shape
classifying consonants in both Yeniseian and Athabaskan: *d* for long shape, *n*
for round shape, and h^w (*qʊ* in Athabaskan) for a flat surface (Vajda 2010:
53–55).

Example 17.22 Ket and Kott Verb Stems with Shape and Animacy Classifying Prefixes

Ket: -*d-a-b-do* 'subject cuts, hews a long rigid object, such as a log'
       -LONG-PRES-3 N.OBJ-cut -*a-b-do* 'cut (object shape unspecified)'

Kott: -*dʲ-a-tʰex* 'subject hits with long object, such as a whip'
       -LONG-PRES-hit (cf: Kott -*a-tʰex* 'hit [object shape unspecified]')

Kott: -*dʲ-a-gič* 'subject rows (< turns long rigid object')
       -LONG-PRES-twist (cf: Ket *hùs* 'twisted')

Ket: -*n-a-b-gil* 'subject cuts it around the edges' (e.g., uneven edges off
       birchbark or rawhide)
       -AROUND-PRES-3 N.OBJ-cut

Ket: -*n-a-b-i* 'subject brushes away snow from around an object'
       -AROUND-PRES-3 N.OBJ-brush

Ket: *-h-a-b-daq* 'subject propels an object at a target'
        1SG.SBJ-FLAT.AREA-PRES-3 N.OBJ-propel
Ket: *-h-a-b-daqŋ* 'subject glues, sticks object onto a surface'
        1SG.SBJ-FLAT.AREA-PRES-3 N.OBJ-stick
Ket: *-h-ul-tes* 'subject stood up', Yugh *f-ul-tes* 'subject stood up'
        1SG.SBJ-FLAT.AREA-PAST-occupy.from.above
        (/u/ after /h/ or /f/ is a vestige of original labialization *h^w*)
Kott: *dʲ-a-fel,* 'he/she grows'   Vs.   *b-a-fel,* 'it grows'
        ANIM-PRES-grow   INAN-PRES-grow

The morpheme positions of shape-classifying consonants, animacy classi-fiers, conjugation markers, and first- and second-person subject agreement prefixes are generally identical in Yeniseian and Athabaskan.

Two striking differences in verb morphology likewise have explanations. Na-Dene languages are famous for their system of pre-root classifier pre-fixes. In Modern Athabaskan these include *d* used for transitivity lowering and *ł* for transitivity raising of various sorts. Proto-Yeniseian apparently possessed a *d*-prefix that converted body part nouns into verb. Vestiges of this in Modern Ket include many verb roots with initial *d: dàχ* 'laugh', *dàm* 'bark', *dìs* 'scold', *-dop* 'drink', etc. In some instances, Ket contains doublet stems, such as *in* 'light' versus *dīˑn* 'emit light'; *īˑt* 'a smell' versus *dīˑt* 'to smell', and possibly *ūˑp* 'opening, burrow' vs. Ket *-dop* 'drink', that suggest the initial *d-* was a prefix. Proto-Yeniseian also possessed a second verbaliz-ing prefix, preserved as verb-base initial *bʲ* in Arin, *χ* in Yugh, *q* in Ket – used to derive action verbs from stative verbs: Arin *-bʲon* 'look, watch'; Yugh *-oŋ* 'see', *-χoŋ* 'watch, look'. Vajda (2006b) proposed that these consonants are cognate with the Athabaskan classifiers and that the system of Na-Dene transitivity marking classifiers developed out of verb-deriving prefixes that originally did not interact to mark lexical differences in transitivity. In Yeniseian these morphemes did not evolve into a productive grammatical system. On the Na-Dene side, their origin from verb deriving prefixes might explain anomalous instances where these morphemes are not associated with transitivity raising or lowering. The most striking example is the *d*-classifier found in transitive verbs meaning 'to drink' – an ancient feature represented across Na-Dene. The original use of the *d-* prefix to create verbs denoting actions performed without the aid of an external instrument – including actions performed by the subject's own body part – might explain why it evolved into a valence-lowering device in Na-Dene, since it already signaled that agent and instrument were naturally one.

The other classic feature of the Na-Dene verb that at first glance seems entirely missing from Yeniseian is the ancient system of verb-final tense-aspect-mood suffixes, which includes *ł* for imperfective and a nasal component for perfective. In Modern Athabaskan these elements fused with

Table 17.10 *Morpheme position classes in the Modern Navajo verb*

10–7	6	5	4	3	2	1	0
Disjunct prefix slots	Direct object	Thirdperson subject	Consonantal lexical prefixes	Conjugation marker (interacts lexically with verb stem allomorphs to express grammatical tense, mood distinctions)	First, secondsubject	Classifier (valence prefix: Ø, d, l, l̥)	Verb stem (fusion of root + TAM suffix: l, n̥, etc.)
		Conjunct prefixes		**Conjugation/subject portmanteau**		**Classifier + stem**	

the original verb root to form allomorphic stem sets (Leer 1979). These interact with the conjugation prefixes located directly before the first- and second-person subject markers. Modern Navajo provides an illustration (Table 17.10).

There is no evidence for verb-final suffixes in Proto-Yeniseian, and the Ket verb base lacks suffix-induced allomorphs conveying tense-mood-aspect distinctions. However, the same elements that appear as verb-final suffixes in Athabaskan were suffixed in Yeniseian to the auxiliary verb (homologous with the Athabaskan conjugation prefix), so that they show up as prefixes rather than suffixes in the Yeniseian verb form as a whole. As mentioned earlier, Modern Ket contains six lexical tense-mood-aspect combinations of the position-4 auxiliary verb ($\gamma a, o, s$) and the original aspectual suffix (l, n) still found in prefix position 2. These morphemes are adjacent in Yugh and Kott, but were separated in Ket verb forms with an inanimate-class marker b, which migrated from the thematic consonant slot (P5) to Modern Ket position 3. The aspect-related distinctions expressed in Modern Ket by l and n are highly lexicalized and appear only in past tense and imperative forms (Example 17.23).

Example 17.23 Example of Aspectual Distinctions in the Past Tense and Imperative Forms of Modern Ket Verb Stems Meaning 'Hit Endwise Using a Long Object'[3]

-aptet	'hits it'	$[a^4\text{-}b^3\text{-}tet^0$ -PRES^4-3 N.OBJ^3-hit$^0]$
-bintet	'hit it (once)'	$[b^3\text{-}n^2\text{-}tet^0$ -3 N.OBJ^3-PAST^2-hit$^0]$
-obiltet	'hit it (iterative)'	$[o^4\text{-}b^3\text{-}l^2\text{-}tet^0$ -PAST$^{4/2}$-3 N.OBJ^3-hit$^0]$
-ntet	'Hit it! (once)'	$[n^2\text{-}tet^0$ -IMP^2-hit$^0]$
-ltet	'Hit it! (iterative)'	$[a^4\text{-}l^2\text{-}tet^0$ -IMP$^{4/2}$-hit$^0]$

Example 17.24 Example of Aspectual Distinctions in Past-Tense Forms of Modern Ket Verbs Meaning 'Break a Long Rigid Object'

t=hastet	'he breaks it'	$[du^8=ha^7\text{-}s^4\text{-}tet^0$ 3 M.SBJ^8-perpendicular^7-PRES^4-hit$^0]$
t=hantet	'he broke it (once)'	$[du^8=ha^7\text{-}n^2\text{-}tet^0$ 3 M.SBJ^8-perpendicular^7-PAST^2-hit$^0]$
t=haltet	'he broke them (iterative)'	$[du^8=ha^7\text{-}l^2\text{-}tet^0$ 3 M.SBJ^8-perpendicular^7-PAST^2-hit$^0]$
hantet	'Break it (once)'	$[ha^7\text{-}n^2\text{-}tet^0$ perpendicular^7-IMP^2-hit$^0]$
haltet	'Break them (iterative)'	$[ha^7\text{-}l^2\text{-}tet^0$ perpendicular^7-IMP^2-hit$^0]$

Morphological parallels with Na-Dene, along with Yeniseian-internal evidence, thus provide confirmation that Yeniseian was originally prefixing and later underwent a partial readaptation to resemble the suffixing verb morphology of other Inner Eurasian languages. Cross-Yeniseian comparisons, as well as an examination of productive and unproductive verb creation patterns in Modern Ket likewise point unmistakably to a partial shift from prefixation to suffixation. This process left mostly intact the relative order of the oldest position classes. But it also added new subject/object marker positions, creating one of the most bizarre morphological entities to be found anywhere on earth – the Ket finite verb.

17.6   Conclusions

Developments in the verb morphologies of Ket and other Yeniseian languages could be summed up as attempts to accommodate a prefixing morphology toward a suffixing model by innovating a new root position at the phonological verb's rightmost edge. The creation of ditropic clitics from possessive prefixes and verb-initial subject prefixes is also connected with the tendency to imitate a general root + suffix pattern. The resulting hybrid morphological typology of Yeniseian strongly imitates the suffixal agglutination common to Inner Eurasia. I have applied the term typological accommodation, to instances where original phonological, morphological, or grammatical traits come to partially mimics a radically different language type. Yeniseian provides a rare and fascinating example of what can happen when a strongly prefixing morphology with syllabic tones similar in many ways to modern Athabaskan or Tlingit is subjected to prolonged areal influence from exclusively suffixing, toneless languages. This influence is all the more interesting in light of the conservative sociolinguistic attitudes toward borrowing maintained by Yeniseian peoples, who as small and isolated bands of hunter-gatherers spoke languages not shared by the surrounding peoples.

Much less unusual from a cross-linguistic perspective is how Yeniseian languages ultimately came to be supplanted by the languages of Inner Eurasia's food producers – stockbreeding Turk and Mongols; the reindeer-herding Ugrians, Evenki, and Samoyedic peoples; and finally the Russians. The elimination of hunter-gatherer languages due to the inexorable and rarely reversed spread of farmers and pastoralists has its beginnings in the earliest Neolithic at least ten thousand years ago. In the case of Yeniseian, as in most similar scenarios, the incoming languages borrowed only a limited number of vocabulary items, with toponyms being the most widespread and enduring feature of substrate influence. The unique phonological and grammatical patterns inherent to the hunter-gatherer languages, on the other hand, were in most cases almost entirely submerged. This is definitely true across western and central Siberia in the case of the once widespread Yeniseian family.

It is interesting to speculate about the social mechanisms whereby the surviving Yeniseian languages gradually accommodated themselves to the phonology and grammar of their food-producing neighbors during millennia of contact. This process, which produced a unique hybrid morphological typology rather than more complete typological replacement (metatypy), probably began during the earliest spread of animal husbandry into south Siberia. The acquisition of a case-like system of nominal relational morphemes and a root-initial phonological verb word is most likely to have begun during the late Scythian or Hunnic periods, more than 2,000 years ago. This is the probable time for the dispersal of Yeniseian daughter languages. Evidence of incipient typological accommodation is already evident in Common Yeniseian.

A final interesting aspect of Ket sociolinguistic history is the perennial resistance of its speakers to borrowing words and morphemes outright. This tendency can still be seen among the last speakers of Modern Ket today. Linguistic conservatism may yet provide another reason why Yeniseian speakers only partly assimilated outside typological patterns during centuries of one-sided Ket-Turkic and Ket-Samoyedic bilingualism.

Abbreviations

ABL	ablative enclitic
AC	animacy classifier
ADESS	adessive enclitic
ANIM, or AN	animate class
BEN	benefactive enclitic
CAR	caritive enclitic (denotes lack or absence)
CAUS	causative affix
FEM, or F	feminine class (a subset of animate class)

CAR	caritive enclitic (denotes lack or absence)
IC	involuntary causative (fossilized agreement marker used to reduce transitivity)
IMP	imperative mood
INSTR	instrumental enclitic (also conveys comitative meaning)
INTR	intransitive
ITER	iterative
LOC	locative enclitic
MASC, or M	masculine class (a subset of animate class)
MOM	punctual, momentaneous, or single-event verb
N	neuter (= inanimate) class; either singular or plural
NMLR	nominalizing suffix (converts other word forms into nouns)
OBJ	verb-internal direct object agreement affix
PL	plural
POSS	possessive clitic
PRED	predicate concord suffix (converts most words except uninflected nouns into predicate nominals)
PAST	past tense
PRES	present (or future) tense
PROS	prosecutive enclitic
RES	resultative marker in verbs (denoting a state caused by a previous action)
SG	singular
SMLF	semelfactive (instantaneous action)
SBJ	verb-internal subject agreement affix
TH	thematic consonant (rarely, two consonants) appearing in P5 in more than half of all Ket verbs
TRAN	transitive
VOC	vocative suffix

NOTES

1. The distinction between /ɤ, ʌ/ and /e, ɛ/ in Ket and Yugh is allophonic; the raised variants [ɤ, e] occur only in high-tone syllables.
2. This term was first introduced by Ruth Singer (2007), who found lexical uses of agreement morphemes in the Australian language Mwang, a feature she compares typologically to Yeniseian.
3. The inanimate-class object marker *b*, which now separates the auxiliary verb (position 4) and its aspectual suffix (position 2), was originally part of the animacy classifying system located to the left of the auxiliary. This object marker does not show up in stems that use the contrasting animacy classifier *d*, where absence of the animacy classifier is sufficient to signal inanimate-class agreement; hence the lack of object marker in verbs meaning 'break a long object'. Animacy classifier *d* is found

only in a few stems (Vajda 2003), where it appears to the left of both tense-mood markers in the original classifier position: *thadontet* 'he broke it (animate-class tree)'. The inanimate-class object marker *b* also regularly deletes as part of the rule of imperative formation (hence its absence in forms meaning 'Hit it!').

References

Aikhenvald, Alexandra Y. (2003). *Language contact in Amazonia*. Oxford: Oxford University Press.

Alekseenko, E. A. (1967). *Kety: étnograficheskie ocherki*. Leningrad: Nauka.

(2005). "Kety." *Narody Zapadnoj Sibiri*. Moskva: Nauka, 629–740.

Anderson, Gregory. (2003). Yeniseic languages in Siberian areal perspective. *Sprachtypologie und Universalienforschung* 56.1(2): 12–39.

(2004). The languages of Central Siberia. In Edward J. Vajda (ed.), *Languages and prehistory of Central Siberia*. Amsterdam: John Benjamins, 1–119.

Anuchin, V. I. (1914). *Ocherk shamanstva u enisejskikh ostjakov*. Sankt-Peterburg: Imperatorskaja Akademija nauk.

Badgaev, N. B. (1988). Altajskie affrikaty *ts* i *dz* v svete altajskoj lingvistiki. In *Fonetika i grammatika jazykov Sibiri*. Novosibirsk: Nauka, 154–158.

Butanaev, Viktor. (2004). Linguistic reflections of Khakas ethnohistory. In Edward J. Vajda (ed.), *Languages and prehistory of Central Siberia*. Amsterdam: John Benjamins, 215–233.

Castrén, M. A. (1858). *Versuch einer jenissej-ostjakischen und kottischen Sprachlehre*. Sankt-Peterburg.

Dolgikh, B. O. (1960). *Rodovoj i plemennoj sostav narodov Sibiri v XVII veke*. Moscow: Akademija nauk.

Dul'zon, A. P. (1952). Chulymskie tatary i ikh jazyk. *Uchenye zapiski TGPI* 9: 76–211.

(1962). Byloe rasselenie ketov po dannym toponimiki. *Voprosy geografii* 58: 50–84.

Georg, Stefan. (2007). *A descriptive grammar of Ket. Part 1: Introduction, phonology and morphology*. Kent: Global Oriental.

Janhunen, Juha. (1986). *The glottal stop in Nenets*. Helsinki: MSFO.

Kim-Maloney, Alexandra. (2004). Shared Selkup-Ket spiritual terminology. In Edward J. Vajda (ed.), *Languages and prehistory of Central Siberia*. Amsterdam: John Benjamins, 169–178.

Krauss, Michael. (2005). Athabaskan tone. In Sharon Hargus and Keren Rice (eds.), *Athabaskan prosody*. Amsterdam:: John Benjamins, 55–136.

Krivonogov, V. P. (1998). *Kety na poroge III tysjaheletija*. Krasnoyarsk.

(2003). *Kety desjat' let spustja (1991–2001g)*. Krasnoyarsk.

Leer, Jeff. (1979). *Proto-Athabaskan verb theme categories: I. Phonology*. Fairbanks: Alaska Native Language Center, University of Alaska, Fairbanks.

(1999). Tonogenesis in Athabaskan. In Shigeki Kaji (ed.), *Proceedings of the symposium: Cross-linguistic studies of tonal phenomena, tonogenesis, typology, and related topics*. Tokyo University of Foreign Studies: Institute for the Study of Languages and Cultures of Asia and Africa, 37–66.

Maloletko, A. M. (2002). *Drevnie narody Sibiri. Tom II: Kety*. Tomsk: TGU.

Rassadin, V. I. (1971). *Fonetika i leksika tofalarskogo jazyka*. Ulan-Ude: Burjatskoe kn. izd.

Ross, Malcom. (2001). Contact-induced change in Oceanic languages in North-West Melanesia. In A. Y. Aikhenvald and R. M. W. Dixon (eds.), *Areal diffusion and genetic inheritance*. Oxford: Oxford University Press, 134–166.

Singer, Ruth. (2007). *A grammar of Mwang*. Unpublished doctoral dissertation, University of Melbourne.

Vajda, Edward J. (2001). *Yeniseian peoples and languages: A history of their study, with an annotated bibliography and a source guide*. London: Curzon Press.

(2002). The origin of phonemic tone in Yeniseic. *Chicago Linguistics Society* 37(2): 305–320.

(2003). Ket verb structure in typological perspective. *Sprachtypologie und Universalienforschung* 56.1(2): 55–92.

(2004). *Ket (Languages of the world/materials 204)*. Munich: Lincom.

(2006a). Origin of the Na-Dene d- and l- classifier components. Talk presented at the Na-Dene Workshop, Max Planck Institute for Evolutionary Anthropology, Leipzig, August 7, 2006.

(2006b). Yeniseic linguistic and human prehistory: A Siberian link to Native North America. Seminar talk presented at Max Planck Institute for Evolutionary Anthropology, Leipzig, September 15, 2006.

(2008a). Head-negating enclitics in Ket. In Edward J. Vajda (ed.), *Subordination and coordination in the languages of Eurasia,*. Amsterdam: John Benjamins, 179–201.

(2008b). Losing semantic alignment: From Proto-Yeniseic to Modern Ket. In Mark Donohue and Soren Wichman (eds.), *Semantic alignment*. Oxford: Oxford University Press, 140–161.

(2009). Loanwords in Ket. Martin Haspelmath and Uri Tadmor (eds.), *Loanwords in the world's languages: A comparative handbook*. Berlin: Mouton, 471–95.

(2010). A Siberian link to the Na-Dene. In Jim Kari and Ben Potter (eds.), *The Dene-Yeniseian connection*. Archeological Papers of the University of Alaska 5: 33–99.

(2011). Siberian landscapes in Ket traditional culture. In Peter Jordan (ed.), *Landscapes and culture in Northern Eurasia*. Cambridge: Cambridge University Press, 297–304.

(2012). The persistence of complex templatic verb morphology in Yeniseian. Talk presented at the 85th Annual Meeting of the Linguistics Society of America, Portland, Oregon, January 6, 2012.

Verner, G. K. (= Heinrich Werner) (1973). Review of Rassadin 1971. *Narody Azii i Afriki* 3: 209–210.

(1990a). *Kottskij jazyk*. Rostov-na-Donu.

(1990b). *Sravnitel'naja fonetika enisejskikh jazykov*. Taganrog.

Vovin, Alexander (2000). Did the Xiong-nu speak a Yeniseian language? *Central Asiatic Journal* 44(1): 87–104.

(2002). Did the Xiongnu speak a Yeniseian language? Part 2: Vocabulary. In *Altaica Budapestinensia MMII, Proceedings of the 45th Permanent International Altaistic Conference, Budapest, June 23–28*, 389–394.

Werner, Heinrich (1997a). *Abriss der kottischen Grammatik*, Wiesbaden: Harrassowitz.

(1997b). *Das Jugische (Sym-Ketische)*. Wiesbaden: Harrassowitz.

(1997c). *Die ketische Sprache*. Wiesbaden: Harrassowitz.

(2005). *Die Jenissej-Sprachen des 18. Jahrhunderts*. Wiesbaden: Harrassowitz.

18 Hunter-Gatherers in South Siberia

Gregory D. S. Anderson and K. David Harrison

18.1 Introduction

In this chapter we examine linguistic and language-encoded cultural data from two indigenous groups of South Siberia. Both groups practice a traditional lifeway of hunting and gathering accompanied by herding of domesticated reindeer. Both speak languages that arose through in situ language shift and belong to the Siberian areal group of the Turkic family. The languages show significant substrate effects, unique areal and typological features, results of long-term contacts with neighboring peoples, and considerable adaptation to the ecological niche of the South Siberia *taiga*. In the spirit of this volume, we will examine how the hunter-gatherer lifeway may be reflected in the development and current state of these languages. Areas investigated include (1) historical evidence for language shift with cultural retention, (2) archaisms in the substrate lexicon, phonology, and morphology; (3) adaptations to the superstrate languages and loanwords; and (4) linguistically encoded environmental knowledge (e.g., taxonomy, topography, mimesis, etc.).

The Tofa (population ca. 700) and Todzhu (also called Tuvan-Todzhan, population ca. 1,500) peoples are hunter-gatherers with reindeer. They inhabit the Sayan Mountains of South Siberia at the extreme southern fringe of the boreal forest ecoregion and still within the permafrost zone (see Map 18.1). Their cultures have been shaped by long-term contact with the culturally very different *steppe* zone inhabited by pastoral nomads (e.g., present-day Tuvans and their Turkic predecessors; Buriats, Mongolians, and their Mongol predecessors) to their south. The Tofa and Todzhu are presumably of Samoyed origin, and possibly prior to that Yeniseic, but underwent a linguistic shift to Turkic at an undetermined time in the past.

This chapter was invited for presentation in August 2006 at the workshop *Historical Linguistics and Hunter-Gatherer Populations in Global Perspective*, held at MPI-EVA, Leipzig. We thank the participants for their helpful feedback. Our field research, carried out in 1998–2005, was generously funded by the Volkswagen-Stiftung and institutionally supported by the MPI-EVA, Leipzig. Sven Grawunder, Brian Donahoe and Afanasij Myldyk joined us in field expeditions. We gratefully acknowledge the help of Tofa and Todzhu native speaker consultants.

The Tofa population was counted as 669 in 1998, and according to calculations that take into account all historical sources, their population appears to have been historically stable, averaging ca. 400 persons from 1675 through 1930 (Mel'nikova 1994: 35–36). They inhabit an area of more than 21,000 square kilometers, entirely composed of *taiga* (mountain forest) on the northern slopes of the Sayan mountain range. The Todzhu, now considered a sub-ethnos of Tuvans (Vainshtein 1961), reside in the Republic of Tyva on the southern slopes of the aforementioned Sayan Mountains, and number approximately 1,500. Contemporary Tofa and Todzhu continue to live off the land, using domesticated reindeer for transport, and relying on hunting and subsistence gathering of boreal forest products. Now sedentarized either partly (Todzhu) or fully (Tofa), they have adopted some food production, and also rely on some imports of food, but also still actively hunt, fish, and gather many forest products.

The date these groups acquired domesticated reindeer (likely from the Evenki, their neighbours to the north) is undetermined, as is the date of their linguistic shift to Turkic. A substantial substrate influence of an unknown (presumably Samoyed, though some have argued for Yeniseic, and some for both) language renders Tofa (now moribund) and Todzhu (now rapidly being replaced by Tuvan) quite divergent from South Siberian Turkic, and from Turkic as a family, at multiple levels of grammatical structure.[1] Some such structures, for example, the prolative case, are common to other Siberian languages spoken by hunter-gatherers.

At the same time, and somewhat surprisingly, these highly peripheral (to the Turkic family) languages each preserve some archaic Turkic structures that were subsequently lost to the rest of the family (Rassadin 1971: 71–87). Tofa, for example, has lexical archaicisms traceable to Old Turkic and subsequently lost in nearby Turkic languages (page numbers in Example 18.1 are from Rassadin 1995).

Example 18.1

qaluup   'prehistoric time'(217) < Old Turkic *kalp* < Sanskrit *kalpa* 'mythical time'
quusuul   'ravine, narrow place' (224) < Old Turkic *quusuul*
turuq-   'to remain' (said of thick liquid) (235); cf. Old Turkic *turuq-* (said of blood)

Also traceable to Old Turkic is an archaic form of the conditional mood that is preserved in Tofa and lost in all other extant Turkic varieties. Todzhu, similarly, retains an archaic Turkic limitative suffix *-kuja* ~ *-kuja* < Old Turkic diminutive *-kuja*, and collective numbers (Chadamba 1974: 90).

Further evidence of deep substrate and/or shared innovation are the fact that both languages have complex consonant clusters (Tofa in particular has consonant clusters atypical for [Siberian] Turkic, *rh, rɲ, lh, pq, pf, ŋh, gʒ*), contrastive vowel nasality, and robust pitch accent systems (noted by researchers but as yet undocumented), all features that make them radically different from both neighboring non-Turkic and related Turkic languages.

Evidence of the importance, scope, and character of hunting and gathering activities – key to survival in a mountain forest milieu – is encoded at multiple levels of the languages. We find, for example, in Tofa and Todzhu phonology, highly productive sound mimesis reflecting a keen perception of, and physical interaction with, the ambient sound environment. In Tofa morphology, we find a unique olfactory morpheme, and a prolative case suffix that is most frequently attested in our corpus in the use of rivers for wayfinding. Todzhu has a directional postposition, also frequently attested with reference to bodies of water.

In the substrate lexica of both we find numerous specialized terms relating to hunting and gathering activities. In the superstrate lexicon, we find words that in the donor language (e.g., Mongolian) expressed notions relevant to pastoral nomads, that underwent semantic shift to encode notions more relevant to a hunter-gatherer ecology. Beyond the lexicon proper, we find highly structured semantic systems that encode hunter-gatherer technologies (Section 18.4). These include ecological calendars linked to animal and plant cycles; animal and plant taxonomies; river-based topographic/orientation systems; an extensive taboo/euphemism lexicon for hunted animals (e.g., bear, wolf); and a large clan/kinship lexicon reflecting patterns of relatedness, reciprocity, and food sharing. In the course of our documentary fieldwork on these two languages, undertaken in 1998–2005, we amassed a rich corpus of narratives, as well as songs, stories, myths, and lexica relating to traditional hunting and foraging lifeways. These provide a still limited yet intriguing glimpse into the perseverance and transfer of hunting-gathering knowledge, along with the lexical and grammatical structures that encode it, across a language shift and wide cultural gap.

Placing this in a broader context, Tofa and Todzhu may reveal certain types of change or lack thereof, whether grammatical, phonological, or lexical-semantic, characteristic of a linguistic shift that is largely unaccompanied by cultural shift. Pending future research, our conclusions are preliminary and are based on our own field data and published sources cited herein. Much remains to be discovered in this arena, and we feel a sense of urgency. Both Tofa and Todzhu are now endangered and rapidly undergoing language shift. Tofa retains just 20 to 30 elderly speakers and a comparable number of semi-speakers in an ethnic population of ca. 700. Nearly the entire Tofa community has shifted to exclusive use of Russian. Todzhu has an undetermined but small percentage of elderly speakers in an ethnic population of about 1,500. It is

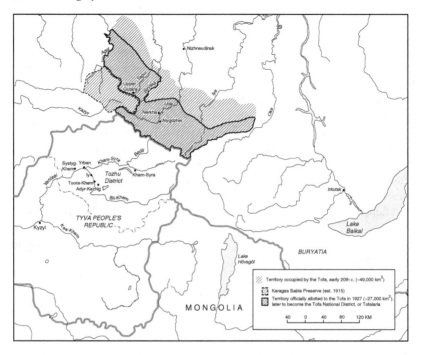

Map 18.1 Map showing the traditional Tofa territory (shaded), located in the administrative district of Irkutsk, and just to the south of that, the Todzhu (Tozhu) District, in the Republic of Tuva. (Map by Brian Donahoe, for the Altai-Sayan Language and Ethnography Project.)

rapidly being absorbed into Tuvan, a much larger language with which it forms a dialect continuum. The issues raised in this chapter are therefore deserving of urgent research.

18.2   Reindeer Herders as 'Foragers'

In attempting to establish a working definition to help frame the discussion of hunter-gatherer societies, Lee and Daly (1999: 3) explain that "Foraging refers to subsistence based on hunting of wild animals, gathering of wild plant foods, and fishing, with no domestication of plants, and no domesticated animals except the dog. In contemporary theory this minimal definition is only the starting point in defining hunter-gatherers." But as Panter-Brick et al. (2001: 2) note: "There will always be problematic cases with such a working definition. Thus contemporary foragers often practise a mixed subsistence – for example, gardening in tropical South America, reindeer herding in northern Asia . . . " In arguing for the inclusion of the Tofa and Todzhu as hunter-gatherers, we note that other Siberian reindeer herding peoples (e.g., Khanty, Evenki) are included both in the expanded foregoing definition and in the *Cambridge Encyclopedia of Hunters and Gatherers* (Lee and Daly 1999).

The Tofa and Todzhu are hunter-gatherers with reindeer, and among the circumpolar reindeer herding peoples these two groups, along with the Dukha (also called Tsaatan) of Mongolia, are singled out as belonging to a particular subtype, dubbed "South Siberian" (D. Anderson 2004). They historically lacked domesticated cultivars. On acquiring domesticated reindeer, they used them primarily as a means of transport for hunting (Vainshtein 1961; Mel'nikova 1994). Reindeer milk was typically reserved for very young children, as it is produced in small quantities.[2] Reindeer did not provide a significant source of calories; their meat was and still is eaten only in extremity, or if an animal dies of natural causes. The Tofa and Todzhu collect edible flora such as cedar nuts, berries, edible lily root, various grasses (some medicinal), and bark. They hunt and trap fauna including sable, moose, bear, wild pig, squirrels, birds, and fish.

Both Tofa and Todzhu, at least well into the first half of the twentieth century, and within living memory of our elderly consultants, would have met Hunn and William's (1982) proposed threshold criteria of deriving less than 5% of their diet from 'cultivated products' (e.g., tea, potatoes, reindeer). They clearly no longer meet this threshold, as they now rely on imported flour and cultivated vegetable plots for perhaps 50% or more of their diet. Nonetheless, many important aspects of the hunting-gathering lifeways have remained vibrant or left clear traces in these languages and cultures.

The Tofa are now completely sedentary, though elders over the age of 65 can recall clearly at least a part-time annual migration pattern and the forced transition to village life. Among the Todzhu, who have never been fully sedentarized, the number of currently nomadizing families does not exceed 50 (Donahoe 2004). Historically, Tofa lived in birchbark teepees (summer) or fur-covered huts (winter), moving to new campgrounds seasonally and, during the summer as often as every three days (Mel'nikova 1994). The Todzhu also lived in birchbark teepees, and those that still nomadize live in canvas tents for up to nine months a year while migrating with reindeer herds. Hunting and gathering are still widely practiced by both sedentary and nomadic people, supplemented by vegetable gardens and imported flour and other goods. Sedentary Tofa and Todzhu live in remote villages, some accessible only by helicopter, boat, on horseback, or by reindeer.

Both groups espouse an animistic belief system, venerating spirits believed to reside in topographic features and in animals. Both once had an elaborate cosmology of the invisible world, largely vanished without adequate documentation, and mediated by male and female shamans (Diószegy 1963). After the Tofa were nominally and forcibly converted to Orthodox Christianity in 1940s, the practice of shamanism was banned and practitioners persecuted. The Todzhu were never converted to Christianity, and like their Tuvan compatriots, practice a form of animism syncretic with later-adopted elements of Lamaist Buddhism.

Both women and men traditionally hunted, trapped, and fished. Ancestral hunting grounds were strictly delineated and inherited with clan membership. Technologies important to survival included (1) riverine topographic orientation systems; (2) reindeer domestication with use of by-products (e.g., leather, hair, antlers, milk); and (3) production of leather and fur clothing, bows and arrows, fur-covered wooden skis, wooden artifacts (e.g., birchbark buckets, wooden knives, mallets), braided hair rope, and many types of devices used to lure, snare, trap, and kill game and fish (e.g., nets, basket traps, line-triggered bow traps, pit traps, birchbark whistles, and birchbark horns) (Vainshtein 1961; Mel'nikova 1994). They adopted new technologies (guns, kettles, axes) as these became available due to contact with outsiders.

18.3   Language Shift and Contact

Tofa and Todzhu both show a Samoyedic language substrate and evidence of an in situ shift. Whether this shift was rapid or gradual is still a matter of debate. The eighteenth-century imperial explorer R. S. Pallas (1788: 524–526) noted that the Tofa spoke a purely Samoyedic language. Having traveled extensively among Siberian peoples and collected comparative lexica, he would have been well qualified to make such a judgment, and as evidence he collected contemporary Tofa lexemes: e.g., *sira* 'snow', *kale* 'fish', *merge* 'wind', *gide* 'two', *negur* 'three', *muktut* 'six'. These bear no resemblance to modern-day (and fully Turkicized) Tofa words: *xar* 'snow', *baluq* 'fish', *qat* 'wind', *ìhi* 'two', *yƒ* 'three', *àltu* 'six' (Rassadin 2005: 5). The ethnographer I. Georgi (1799) also visited the Tofa at the close of the eighteenth century and concluded that they spoke a purely Samoyedic language.

This poses a conundrum, because just 50 years later, when the ethnographers Shtubendorf (1854) and Castrén (1856) visited the Tofa, they found them to be completely Turkicized in their language. Rassadin (2005: 22–23) argues it unlikely that such a shift could have been completed in just 50 years, and Old Turkic archaisms attested in Tofa also argue against a late shift to Turkic. As an alternative, Rassadin proposes that the Tofa had already Turkicized, perhaps as early as the sixth to eighth centuries, within the period contemporary to old Turkic. They subsequently assimilated some small Samoyedic groups at a much later date. At the time of the late eighteenth-century visits by Pallas and Georgy, these Samoyedic groups, Rassadin suggests, had not yet undergone linguistic Turkicization though they were already integrated into the Tofa clan structures (as evidenced by their clan names, which are the same as present-day ones). It may have been, though somewhat improbably given the small overall size of the Tofa community, precisely these not-yet-Turkicized groups that outsiders encountered.

This scenario is not inconsistent with the view that Tofa may have arisen from a deeper Yeniseic substrate (Vainshtein 1961), perhaps including a process by which some of the constituent groups shifted first from Yeniseic to Samoyedic, then to Turkic, while others shifted directly from Yeniseic to Turkic. Evidence for any particular scenario will probably prove inconclusive, as both prior to and after the language shift, there were constant areal contacts between Tofa and languages belonging to the Mongolic (Mongolian, Okinski Buriat, Soyot – the latter still retaining a Turkic language related to Tofa in some individuals), attested Sayan Samoyedic (Taigi, etc.), Tungusic (Evenki), and Yeniseic (Ket) families. The Tofa superstrate lexicon is discussed in Rassadin (1995), we provide here just a few examples to illustrate the type of cultural contact that may be discerned, in this case with Buriat and (Old) Mongolian (page numbers refer to Rassadin 1995).

Example 18.2 Tofa Loanwords

amur mendɪ	'farewell' (wishing health & well-being to those departing). (154) < Old Mongolian *amur* 'peace', < Old Mongolian *mendy* 'health'
ap	'magic, wizardry' (154) < Buriat *ab* 'charm(s), magic power'
helbe	'oar' (187) < Buriat *helbe*
tabun saqaan	'a five-petalled white flower used for medicinal purposes' (232) < Buriat *taban sagaan* 'five white'.
toraj	'bear cub up to one year old' (235) < Mongolian *toroj* 'piglet'[3]
tuqul	'cow calf up to one year old' (235) < Mongolian *tuɣul*
yleger	'tale' (238) < Mongolian *yliger*

Todzhu had a similar range of contact influences. But it was not documented at all prior to Turkicization, and thus only substrate evidence – most of it yet unanalyzed – remains to support scenarios for language shift.

18.4   Cultural Evidence

In this section we survey briefly a range of linguistically encoded cultural phenomena and knowledge systems that provide evidence for the importance of hunting-gathering lifeways in Todzhu and Tofa. These include performative speech genres, personal narratives, ecological calendars, ethnotopographic knowledge, sound mimesis, and specialized semantic subfields within the lexicon.

18.4.1   Hunting-Gathering in the Verbal Arts

Tofa songs and stories are filled with references to hunting and gathering, and to a lesser extent, to reindeer. Some examples may be found in the rather obscure published literature (e.g., Sherkhunayev 1977; Stoyanov 1980, Rassadin 1996,). We reproduce a few examples here from our own fieldwork (Examples 18.3–18.6).

Example 18.3 Traditional Tofa Song (Marta Kangarayeva [b. 1930]. K. David Harrison Field Notes 2001)
"I'll take a shortcut and pick some cedar   *[doora bar mæn quzuqtaar mæn]*
nuts,
take a shortcut and catch a wood grouse,   *[doora bar mæn bariiqalaar mæn]*
take a shortcut and catch a quail."   *[doora bar mæn yſpyllæær mæn]*

Todzhu verbal arts, though considerably less well documented, are similarly saturated with themes of nature's abundance, hunting, and gathering.

Example 18.4 Traditional Todzhu Song (Elizaveta Kenden [b. 1945?]. Recorded by Brian Donahoe 2001. Translated by K. David Harrison.)
"In the shade of my fresh little pine,
I grew up cool, a Todzhu am I.
With my pelts and squirrels abundant,
I grew up sated, a Todzhu I am."

"In the shade of my young little pine
I grew up cool, a Todzhu am I.
With my pine-nuts and berries abundant,
I grew up sated, a Todzhu I am."

Personal narratives elicited from Tofa and Todzhu reveal an animistic belief system premised on belief in local spirits residing, for example, in bodies of water, in fire, and in animals. We found evidence in these narratives for a rapidly fading system of ritualized hunting practices, including offerings to spirits to ensure success in hunting.

Example 18.5 Tofa Hunter Sergei Kangarayev (b. 1959). (David Harrison unpublished field notes 2001, p. 98.)
"Of course I still keep the old customs. When I am out in the forest I offer tea and food to the fire for success in hunting. How could I not do it? And how could I forget my native language?"

Figure 18.1 Viktor Sambuu, Todzhu herder departing Xam-Syra village, 2001. (Photo by Brian Donahoe for the Altai-Sayan language and ethnography project.)

Example 18.6 Tofa Hunter Pavel Ungushtayev (b. 1916).
Recorded in Alygdzher village, Nov. 2000. Unpublished field notes 2000, translated from the Russian and Tofa by K. David Harrison.
" ... [After killing a bear] you had to take care skinning it ... then you had to remove the excrement, wrap it up in cedar and find a thick tree to bury it under, then do the same with the stomach. That's the way we used to do it, religiously, so that there would be more success in hunting ...

Nowadays youngsters won't do it, they've abandoned it all. Earlier when the old folks would kill a sable, they would skin it, wrap the stomach specially in cedar, and in a thicket lay it down, bury it. They treated it carefully, buried it.

Nowadays everybody, **tʃaraʃ aŋ ølyrer** [when a sable dies], they throw it all away. But we don't discard it, we eat it all winter, cooking it for three hours, and there's still plenty left. We eat it all in its entirety. Russians don't eat it, they discard it."

18.4.2   Ecological Calendars

Beyond performative genres, we find structured knowledge systems within the lexicon. Such systems, by efficiently packaging information, helped to ensure

Figure 18.2 (Upper) Sergei Kangarayev (b. 1962), Tofa hunter, and (lower)
Marta Kangarayeva (b. 1930), expert Tofa hunter. (Photos by Thomas
Hegenbart for the Altai-Sayan language and ethnography project.)

Table 18.1 *Tofa calendars*

	Tofa 'Hunting'* calendar	Tofa 'Gathering'† calendar
January	great white month	empty month
February	small white month	big log month
March	hunting with dogs month*	tree bud month
April	tree bud month	good birch bark collecting month†
May	hunting in the taiga month*	digging edible lily (*saranki*) root month†
June	(unattested)	bad birch bark collecting month†
July	hay cutting month	hay cutting month†
August	(unattested)	collecting edible lily (*saranki*) root month†
September	preparing skins month*	preparing skins month
October	round up male deer month*	move to Autumn campsite month
November	sable hunting month*	hunting month
December	cold month	braiding (rope-making) month†

Sources: Tofa calendars elicited by K. David Harrison from Sergei and Marta Kangarayeva. Hunting terms are marked with *, and gathering terms with †.

the effective transmission of foraging and survival technologies. The Tofa and Todzhu, like most indigenous peoples, would have used 13-month ecological calendars that linked lunations to predictably occurring plant and animal cycles (Harrison 2007). These calendars survive in remnant form across Siberia, now no longer widely known and rapidly being replaced by world calendars. By the time of their earliest attestation, the Tofa calendar had already been revised to fit a modern 12-month format. Two Tofa versions are attested in our corpus: the first, from the village of Alygdzher, has a preponderance of month names associated with hunting (but also some gathering activities); the second, from the village of Verkhnyaya Gutara, has notably more gathering terms.

A comparable Todzhu calendar, now largely forgotten, marks similar activities, e.g., birchbark harvesting, hunting with dogs, collecting edible lily root, and meteorological events such as wet snowfall.

The Tofa "Gathering" and Todzhu calendars notably lack any mention of reindeer. This may provide evidence for the relatively late adoption of reindeer herding, as ecological calendars of reindeer herding peoples tend to include at least a few months named for reindeer life-stages.[4] In northern Siberia, for example, the calendar of the Dolgan, a Turkic speaking people who adopted reindeer only in the nineteenth century omits any mention of reindeer, while the calendar of the neighboring Nganasan people, who had reindeer much earlier, names several months after them (Ziker 2002: 29–30).

The fate of ecological calendars provides additional information about linguistic and cultural shift and its progressive stages. They can be predicted to be found among any active practitioners of hunting-gathering. They are

Gregory D. S. Anderson and K. David Harrison

Table 18.2 *Todzhu calendar*

January	'last cold month'	*soŋgu sook aj*
February	'white month'	*ak aj*
March	'wet snow month'	*öl xarluɡ aj*
April	'hunting with dogs month' *	*ùdalaar aj*
May	'young grass month'	*ʃomur aj*
June	'birch bark peels badly month' †	*bàk tozaar aj*
July	'birch bark peels well month' †	*eki tozaar aj*
August	'edible lily collecting month' ᵃ †	*ajnaar aj*
September	'wild elk (hunting) month' *	*xylbys aj*
October	'sable hunting month' *	*aldulaar aj*
November	'snow falls day and night month'	*ørgyleer aj*
December	'first cold month'	*bàʃku sook aj*

From Chadamba (1974).
ᵃ *Fritillaria camschatcensis.*

diagnostic in that they seem to be one of the more fragile knowledge systems and one of the earliest to be abandoned under pressure from global time-reckoning norms. Their demise often precedes and presages language endangerment or shift.

18.4.3   Ethnotopographic Knowledge

Like all Siberian peoples, both Tofa and Todzhu historically relied on rivers as a primary means of transport, wayfinding, and orientation. They possessed highly detailed topographic, and especially hydrographic, knowledge systems attuned to river geography (Map 18.1). These are now undergoing rapid attrition as fewer Tofa and Todzhu spend less time hunting in the *taiga*.

The most basic element, a riverine orientation system, is morphologically encoded in verbs for 'go' (go upstream, go downstream, go cross-stream), wherein a topographically (hydrographically) content-full term is always preferred to a generic word for 'go'. The system requires speakers to constantly attend to features such as ground slope and river current direction in order to choose the appropriate verb for 'go' in any given situation. This system is not unique to foragers, however, and is shared with others, including Tuvan steppe pastoralists to the south and west (Harrison 2007).

Beyond morphological encoding of river current, and more specific to a densely forested *taiga* environment where river knowledge crucially enables wayfinding and long-range views of the landscape are quite rare, both groups reportedly possessed highly detailed hydrographic nomenclature. These are now largely forgotten, and were never adequately documented. A lifelong Russian inhabitant of the Tofa village of Alygdzher reported to the authors in

Table 18.3 *Tofa cardinal directions*

qaraŋɢaaru	'North(ward)' < qaraŋɢu 'dark'
hyngeerı	'South(ward)' < hyn keerı 'day come-P/F-3'
buruŋɢaaru	'East(ward)' < murnun '(in) front', 'before'
hyn yner tʃaruq	'East(ward)' < 'sun rises direction'
soŋgaaru	'West(ward)' < soŋ 'after(wards)', 'behind'

Table 18.4 *Tuvan cardinal directions*

soŋgu	'North' cf. soŋ, soonda 'after(wards)'
murnuu	'South' < Turkic 'in front' 'before'
tʃøøn	'East' < Mongolian
baruuun	'West', 'right(ward)' < Mongolian

2001 that he had personally collected a list of more than 600 Tofa hydronyms over a period of 10 years, primarily by hiking the river systems and eliciting the data on site from Tofa elders. He had entrusted this collection some years previously to a regional museum, where it met an unknown fate. We are certain that the bulk of this knowledge has now vanished from memory as hunting practices decline, the elders rarely venture out into the forests, and the language that would have rendered many hydronyms transparent is itself nearly extinct.

Absolute orientation also shows unique cultural (and likely substrate) traits. Cardinal Tofa orientation is toward the east, the direction they call 'in front', or 'before'. Neighboring peoples, by contrast, including the Soyots, Tuvans, and Todzhu, consider south to be the direction located out in front of them.

18.4.4   Taboo Lexicon

Perhaps the most dramatic evidence for the Tofa hunter-gatherer lifeway, and an area which unlike ecological calendars shows some perseverance, is the lexicon for bear and other sacred animals. The importance of hunting rituals in Tofa culture is amply illustrated by Pavel Ungushtayev's narrative (Section 18.2) about preparation of bear and sable carcasses, and by his poignant lament that this knowledge is eroding. Euphemistic Tofa animal names still in use include: fox = 'mountain dog', dog = 'smelly', snake = 'ground fish', wolf = 'tailed thing'. The Tofa bear lexicon is remarkable in its precision, profusion, and expansion via metaphorical extension. The bear lexicon shows the strongest substrate effects we have noticed thus far in any lexical field. Many lexemes are complex, opaque, and completely non-Turkic in their morphophonology. In Tables 18.5–18.7 we present 39 Tofa bear euphemisms,

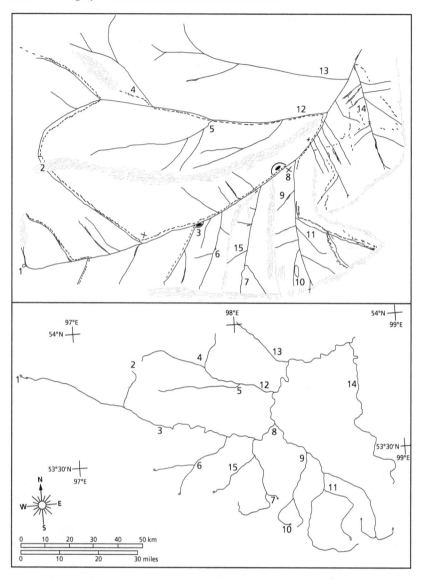

Map 18.2 Two riverine views of Tofa territory, encompassing the Uda river watershed. Above, a 'naive' Tofa map above (c. 1908, published in Adler 1910) shows the Uda river system, mountains (in gray), and trails (dashed lines). Below it is an accurate (modern-day) topographic map. Names have been removed here for clarity. Shared features are numbered for comparative purposes. Note the straightening out of river bends and meanders, greater detail of tributaries, enlargement of significant features (e.g., lakes), conflation of some distances in the first map, indicating clear cultural attenuation of spatial-topographic knowledge. (Adapted from Harrison 2007.)

Table 18.5 *Tofa bear euphemisms*

Names for bear	Compositional meaning	Gloss/translation
ene aŋ	'mother animal'	female bear
qara tɨktɨɣ tʃɣme	'black furred thing'	bear
qara tʃɣme	'black thing'	bear
qulaqtuɣ	'having ears'	bear
irezaŋ ~ erezaŋ	'grandfather animal'	bear
ire	'grandfather'	male bear
eeʃ	*	female bear (or female sable)
ene aŋ	'mother animal'	female bear
dàhɨrqan	*	female bear
aʃnʲaq aŋ	'man animal'	bear
qara aŋ	'black animal'	bear
qara tɨktɨɣ aŋ	'black furred animal'	bear
qàħʲaraarluɣ aŋ	* 'bear's fat animal'	bear
tʃoorhannuɣ	'has a blanket / hide'	bear
tʃoorhannuɣ aŋ	'has a blanket / hide animal'	bear
ʃujduŋɣalaa aŋ	* 'makes bear tracks animal'	bear
ìrhek	'male'	large male bear
toraj	'piglet' (Mongolian loan)	bear cub
irezaŋ oglu	'grandfather animal's son'	bear cub

Table 18.6 *Tofa bear part names*

Names for bear parts	Compositional meaning	Gloss / translation
quɪzar	'turn red'-P/F	bear's meat
tʃoorhan	'blanket'	bear's hide
qàħʲaraar	*	bear's fat
don dʒaa	'coat's fat'	bear's fat (from back/spine)
mɨdɨrgɣʃ	*	bear's entrails
salbar	*	bear's bones
dɪsɪleeʃ	*	bear's heart
ʃojutqu ~ ʃøjtqu	*	bear's teeth
tʃedʒaq	*	bear's rib(s)
bùtuk tøzɣ	'branch's root'	bear's ear(s)
ʃumuraaʃ	'rustle' (sound symbolic)	bear's ear(s)
tʃuttaa	'it smells'	bear's nose
eleŋneeʃ	'twinkling'	a bear's eye(s)
tʃùtuk udʒu	*	bear's head
ʃujduŋɣa	*	bear tracks
arbaq	*	claws/paws of predator or bear

Table 18.7 *Tofa bear verbs*

Names for bear actions	Compositional meaning	Gloss / translation
eleŋneer	'to twinkle'	'to look' (said only of a bear)
ʃojudaar	* 'bite'-P/F	to bite (said only of a bear)
ʃumuraar	'rustle'-P/F (sound symbolic)	to hear (said only of a bear)
uʃtaar	*	to shoot a bear (in the head)

Table 18.8 *Tofa sibilants + liquid*

ʃuɯ	'a rain sound'
ʃuɯla(ʃ)-	'to make rain sounds'
ʃyyr	'a noise'
ʃaala-	'to make water or river sounds'
ʃajula-	1.'to make a whistling wind sound', 2.'(to have) a strong voice'
ʃay	'(a) noise'
ʃuɯlura- ~ ʃalura-	'to rustle'
ʃart	'blacksmith sounds'
sartula-	'to squeak, as snow underfoot'

including 23 of Tofa origin, and 16 (denoted by asterisks) that contain unidentified substrate elements, and one Mongolian loanword.[5]

While no equivalent system has yet been documented for Todzhu, it may be seen in remnant form. Euphemistic naming of sacred, hunted, and significant animals was and still is widely practiced across Siberia.

18.4.5 Sound Mimesis

Heightened attention to ambient sounds may reflect at least in some cultures a long-term adaptation to living and foraging in a densely forested environment, where sounds are crucial indicators of the presence of game, and of meteorological and hydrological conditions.[6] This perceptual emphasis may also come to be reflected in the expressive or sound symbolic lexicon. Tofa seems to have once employed a rich and highly productive sound symbolic lexicon, though it is now undergoing rapid attrition and is not as well attested as the comparable system employed by Tuvans (Harrison 2004).

The system operates on a bi-consonantal template, in which the consonants indicate a certain family of sounds (e.g., friction, impact, etc.), while vowels, which are filled in according to principles of vowel harmony, may indicate relative pitch of a given acoustic phenomenon. Data in Tables 18.8 and 18.9 are from Rassadin (1995) and our fieldwork with Tofa consultants.

Table 18.9 *Tofa velars + nasals*

qoŋgura-	'to croak, cluck, chirp'
qugura-	'to creak, as a tree in the wind'
qujurtula-	'to creak'
qogʒura-	'to crunch on the teeth'
qoŋgura-	'to quack'
qaŋgura-	'to cackle, to call (as a bird)'

Table 18.10 *Tofa substrate lexemes with no discernible cognate or known etymology*[a]

ajamdut	'reindeer saddle pad / underblanket made of wild boar hide' (152)
boq	'now' (164)
boriiqa	'wood-grouse' (164)
byj	'skin from upper leg of animal' (167) (= Rus. *pax*)
enegææhee	'small fish' (181)
haŋgan	'very tall, thick cedar tree' (*Pinus sibirica*) (186)
haan	'white partridge' (187)
kyltys	'place in the taiga where a small stream flows underneath moss' (204)
kyskehe	'medicinal tea from a shrub' (205)
h̆ĕĕrij	'four-strand hair belt' (188)
kùmsar	'special bag for collecting roots'
hèbuq	'year old partridge' (187)
murɲæœʃqa	'mouse' (208)
ɲeeɲæœ	'fat of large wild elk or moose' (209)
øsken	'rain' (214)
qoruʃ	'birchbark back-pack' (221)
ʃuŋ	'rocky ground' (232)
ʃujduŋga	'bear track' (232)
tarhuʃ	'one year old reindeer (pejorative)' (233)
tʃoraanda	'bad' (197)
tʃurut	'small pine tree' (*Abies sibirica*) (200)
uta	'solid top layer of snow' (238)
ykese	'three year old taimen' (*Salmo taimen*) (238)

[a] Page numbers in these data refer to Rassadin (1971).

18.4.6 Substrate Lexicon of Hunting-Gathering in Tofa

We now turn to an admittedly very preliminary analysis of the lexicon of Tofa, hoping to gain some insight into the contact processes that shaped it. The transition to Turkic is likely to have been gradual, not sudden, given the prominence of substrate words in the language, especially in key areas: bear cult, hunting, reindeer taxonomy, and hydronyms (Table 18.10).

Table 18.11 *Shared Tofa and substrate lexemes*

Tofa	Todzhu	Gloss
hajduŋ	*xajduŋ*	'moss' (185)
hamzɯl	*xamzel*	'wintering small birds' (185)
iniɣ		'female moose' (201)
onoʃ	*onyʃ*	'standing water in forest', 'puddle' (212)
qadurgɯ	*kadurgɯ*	'grayling' (*Thymallus thymallus*) (216)
qùya	*kùga*	'(under)surface made of flexible twigs' (221)
qumsar	*kùmzar*	'basket for collecting *sarana* edible lily root' (222)
salhuq	*sàlgut*	'cry of an elk' (225)
sɯstɯ	*sɯstɯɣ xem*	'perpetually green grass that grows in the upper reaches of streams'. (230), Todzhu hydronym ('Grassy river')
ʃeeʃkis	*ʃeeʃkiiʃ*	'white-winged kite' (*Falco milvus*), (231)
ʃomuq	*ʃomuq*	'birch forest' (231)
ʃuruʃ	*ʃuruʃ*	'luce, northern pike' (*Esox lucius*) (232)
tʃàpal	*tʃùval*	'fern' (*Asplenium*) (194)
tʃàjhjan	*tʃàjan*	'supporting pole in teepee' (p. 195)
tʃeŋge	*tʃeŋgii*	'copper cooking pot' (p. 195)
ujgut	*ùjgut*	'poplar' (236)

Though we regard the data set as far too small to make any firm conclusions, it does suggest that among substrate words, there is a preponderance of highly specific terms related to subsistence and foraging.

A number of similarly themed substrate words are shared apparently only between Tofa and Todzhu, to the exclusion of related Turkic languages. Nearly all of these are environmental entities. Tofa terms are given in the left-hand column, Todzhu equivalents at the right.

18.4.7   Contact Lexicon

The loanword lexicon of Tofa is quite large, and has been only minimally analyzed with respect to etymology (e.g., Rassadin 1971). Much more research is needed in this domain. We wish here to simply point out the usefulness of comparative etymology in identifying linguistic adaptation to a specific ecological niche. In Tables 18.12 and 18.13, we see Tofa and Todzhu borrowing words from the lexicon of plains-dwelling pastoralists and adapting them to a mountain *taiga* context. We restrict our attention here to examples of words that have undergone semantic narrowing (Chadamba 1974; Tatarintsev 2000, 2002).

Processes of semantic specialization such as these show adaptation to a specific ecological/economic niche. They may also be useful in determining the relative chronology of language shift and/or contact events.

Table 18.12 *Weather terms*

Todzhu	*boraan*	'first snowfall'
Tofa	*boraan*	'freshly fallen snow'
Tuvan	*boraan*	'inclement weather'
Old Mongolian	*boruyan*	'rain'
Old Turkic	*bora*	'storm'

Table 18.13 *Wayfinding terms*

Todzhu	*belgi*	'a sapling placed by hunters to mark a campsite'
Tofa	*belbɪ*	'a marker (typically an arrow) placed on a hunting trail to mark clan hunting territory'
Tuvan	*belgi*	'foretelling, augury'
Turkic (various)	*belgi*	'sign', 'characteristic', 'brand', 'gravestone', 'landmark'
Old Mongolian	*belge*	'sign', 'mark'

18.4.8   Substrate Morphology

We turn lastly to substrate elements (or possibly isolated innovations) in Todzhu and Tofa morphology, restricting our attention to just those elements that strike us as having some relevance to or resonance with a foraging lifeway. These include a unique (to our knowledge) and fully productive Tofa olfactory suffix (Example 18.7); a Tofa prolative suffix (most frequently attested in our corpus with hydronyms) (Table 18.8), a Todzhu allative suffix (also typically attested with hydronyms), and a Tofa/Todzhu unproductive diminutive of unknown origin (attested in toponyms).

Example 18.7 Tofa Olfactory Suffix (fully productive)

uʃ-suɯ	'smoke'-OLF	'smelling of smoke'
ʃej-sɪɣ	'tea'-OLF	'smelling of tea'
ivi-sɪɣ	'reindeer'-OLF	'smelling of reindeer'

Example 18.8 Tofa Prolative Suffix ('upstream', 'upward along stream')

xem-ʃaru	'river'-PROL	'upstream along the river', or possibly 'uphill'

Example 18.9 Todzhu Allative Suffix

xem-gidi	'river'-ALL	'towards the river' (cf. Tuvan *kudu* 'down[ward]')
azas-kɯdu	'Azas lake'-ALL	'towards Azas lake'

Example 18.10 Diminutive /-VI/ (attested only in place names, Tatarintsev 2000:165)
Tofa
ba-al < /bag-uul/   'little linking stream'
Todzhu
art-ul   'little mountain pass'

In presenting this final data set, we make no claims about causal relations between lifeway and language. But we take seriously the notion of language and culture as adaptive mechanisms. We consider the foraging lifeway to be a stern test of adaptability, one likely to leave clear traces in a language, especially one whose speakers still practice the lifeway to the extent the Tofa and Todzhu do. Any potential correlations must be noted, both in the languages we are studying and in other hunter-gatherer languages, as a prelude to forming or (dis)proving useful hypotheses.

18.5   Tentative Conclusions and Further Research

Tofa and Todzhu represent a special type of Siberian forager culture, namely hunter-gatherers with reindeer. Though both groups are currently in advanced states of language shift and transition to sedentary living, they still practice a significant amount of hunting and gathering activities year round.

An unidentified substrate language, now lost and presumably Sayan Samoyed, though possibly Yeniseic, is most clearly discernible in Tofa and Todzhu in the taboo/euphemistic lexica, and in semantic fields linked to a foraging lifeway. We also find evidence of the traditional lifeway in conceptual systems and domains of knowledge (expressed in clusters of related semantic terms), e.g., sound mimesis, topographic, and directional systems. We find evidence to a lesser extent, in (often unproductive) morphological structures that bear at least some plausible utility for forest-dwelling foragers.

Do these domains of linguistically encoded knowledge, taken individually or collectively, serve as indicators of adaptations to a forager lifeway? Can the rates of attrition in such systems provide insights into the historical course (or even chronology) of language shift vis-à-vis cultural retention or shift? Our aim here has been to address just those systems in Tofa and Todzhu that to us, as specialists in Siberian Turkic, stand out as unusual or atypical. How these systems might eventually be used as evidence for a broader dynamic, perhaps one that would link specific types of linguistic retention or innovation to change or persistence in foraging lifeways, is left to future comparative research of the type that we hope will be fostered by this volume.

NOTES

1. For an account of historical and ongoing efforts to clarify the ethnic and linguistic origins of the Tofa, see Rassadin (2005).
2. Lactating reindeer in captivity can produce an average of 983 grams per day of milk for up to 26 weeks (Gjostein et al. 2004). We were unable to find figures for migratory domesticated reindeer, but surmise these to be significantly less productive.
3. The Tofa expanded their already very large bear lexicon (see data 10–13) with this loanword.
4. There is of course one exception in the Tofa 'hunting' calendar and that is October, which likely references their reindeer, but it is otherwise lacking entirely. For more on Siberian and other indigenous calendrics, and the attrition of these systems, see Harrison (2007, chapter 3). Non-base-10 number systems are similarly diagnostic in that their demise often precedes and presages language shift (Harrison 2007, chapter 5).
5. These data are from Rassadin (1995) and from our Tofa consultants. For more on the bear cult among the Tofa, see Rassadin (2013).
6. See Gell (1995) and Feld (1990) for discussions of this phenomenon in Papua New Gunea, and Levin (2005) for an analysis of the perception and aestheticization of the ambient soundscape by Tuvans.

References

Adler, Bruno F. (1910). Karty pervobytnykh narodov. [Maps of primitive peoples]. *Izvestiya Imperatorskago Obshestva Lyubiteley Yestestvoznaniya, Antropologii i Etnografii: Trudy Geograficheskago Otdeleniya* [Proceedings of the Imperial Society of the Devotees of Natural Sciences, Anthropology and Ethnography: Transactions of the Division of Geography] 119(2).

Anderson, Gregory D. S. (2003). Towards a phonological typology of native Siberia. In D. A. Holisky and K. Tuite (eds.), *Current trends in Caucasian, East European and Inner Asian linguistics*. Amsterdam: John Benjamins, 1–22.

(2004). The languages of central Siberia: Introduction and overview. In Edward J. Vajda (ed.), *Languages and prehistory of central Siberia*. Amsterdam: John Benjamins, 1–119.

Anderson, Gregory D. S. and K. David Harrison. In preparation. *A Grammar of Tofa, a Turkic language of Siberia*.

Chadamba, Z. B. (1974). *Todzhinskij dialekt tuvinskogo iazyka*. Kyzyl, Republic of Tuva: TKI.

Diószegi, Vilmos. (1963). *Zum Problem der ethnischen Homogenität des tofischen karagassischen Schamanismus*. Budapest: Akadémiai Nyomda.

Donahoe, Brian. (2004). Hey, you get offa my taiga: Hunting and land use among the Tozhu Tuvans. PhD thesis, Indiana University, Bloomington.

Feld, Steven. (1990). *Sound and sentiment: Birds, weeping, poetics, and song in Kaluli expression*. Philadelphia: University of Pennsylvania Press.

Gell, Alfred. (1995). The language of the forest: Landscape and phonological iconism in Umeda. In E. Hirsch and M. O'Hanlon (eds.), *The anthropology of landscape: Perspectives on place and space*. Oxford: Oxford University Press. 232–254.

Georgi, I. (1799). *Opisanie vsekh obitayushchikh v Rossijskom gosudarstve narodov.* Sankt-Peterburg.

Gjostein, H., O. Holand and R. Weladji. (2004). Milk production and composition in reindeer (*Rangifer tarandus*): Effect of lactational stage. *Comparative Biochemistry and Physiology A: Molecular & Integrative Physiology.* 137(4): 649–656.

Harrison, K. David. (2004). South Siberian sound symbolism. In E. Vajda (ed.), *Languages and prehistory of Central Siberia.* Amsterdam: John Benjamins, 199–214.

    (2007). *When languages die: The extinction of the world's languages and erosion of human knowledge.* New York: Oxford University Press.

Hunn, E. S. and N. M. Williams. (1982). Introduction. In N. M. Williams and E. S. Hunn (eds.), *Resource managers: North American and Australian hunter-gatherers.* Canberra: Australian Institute of Aboriginal Studies, 1–16.

Lee, Richard B. and Richard Daly (eds.). (1999). *Cambridge encyclopedia of hunters and gatherers.* Cambridge: Cambridge University Press.

Mel'nikova, L. V. (1994). *Tofy.* Irkutsk: Vostochnoe sibirskoe knizhnoe izdatel'stvo.

Pallas, P. S. (1788). *Puteshestviye po raznym provintsiyam rosijskogo gosudarstva, t. III.* Sankt-Petersburg.

Panter-Brick, C., R. Layton and P. Rowley-Conwy. (2001). Lines of enquiry. In Layton Panter-Brick and P. Rowley-Conwy (eds.), *Hunter-gatherers: An interdisciplinary perspective.* Cambridge: Cambridge University Press, 1–11.

Rassadin, V. I. (1971). *Fonetika i leksika tofalarskogo iazyka.* Moscow: AN SSSR.

    (1995). *Tofalarsko-russkij rossko-tofalarskij slovar'.* Irkutsk: Vostochnoe sibirskoe knizhnoe izdatel'stvo.

    (1996). *Legendy, skazki I pyesni sedogo Sayana.* Irkutsk.

    (2005). *Khozaistvo, byt i kul'tury tofalarov.* Ulan Ude: BNTs SO RAN.

    (2013). O kul'te medvedja u tofalarov [Elektronnyj resurs]. *Novye issledovanija Tuvy. Elektron. zhurnal* 2013(3). www.tuva.asia/journal/issue_19/6481-rassadin.html.

Sherkhunayev, R. A. (1977). *Skazki i skazochniki Tofalarii.* Kyzyl.

Stoyanov, A. (1980). *Tofalarskie narodnie pyesni.* Irkutsk.

Tatarintsev, B. I. (2000). *Etymologicheskij slovar' tuvinskogo iazyka. Tom I, A-B.* Novosibirsk: Nauka.

    (2002). *Etymologicheskij slovar' tuvinskogo iazyka. Tom II, D-I.* Novosibirsk: Nauka.

Vainshtein, S. I. (1961). *Tuvintsy-todzhintsy: istoriko-etnograficheskie ocherki.* Moscow: Izdatel'stvo Vostochnoi Literatury.

Ziker, John P. (2002). *Peoples of the Tundra: Northern Siberians in the post-communist transition.* Prospect Heights, IL: Waveland Press.

Part VI

North America

19 Primitivism in Hunter and Gatherer Languages

The Case of Eskimo Words for Snow

Willem J. de Reuse

19.1 Introduction

The Eskimo[1] branch of the Eskimo-Aleut language family can be divided into three subgroups: Inuit-Inupiaq, Yupik, and Sirenikski. Inuit-Inupiaq is a group of closely related varieties that form a dialect chain, extending from eastern Greenland over the Canadian Arctic to northern Alaska, and southward to the northern and eastern shores of Norton Sound. Four mutually unintelligible languages can be distinguished within the Yupik subgroup of Eskimo: Naukanski, spoken exclusively on the Russian mainland; Central Siberian Yupik (henceforth CSY), the language I will take my examples from, spoken on some points of the Chukotka peninsula and on St. Lawrence Island, Alaska; Central Alaskan Yupik in southwestern Alaska; and Pacific Yupik or Alutiiq, on the southern coast of Alaska, including Alaska Peninsula and Kodiak Island (Woodbury 1984). Sirenikski, which became extinct when the last speaker died in 1997, has long been considered a member of the Yupik subgroup, but it is better to consider it the unique member of a third subgroup (Vakhtin 2000). All these languages belong to what were originally hunter-gatherer peoples (with different emphases on animals hunted, mostly marine mammals in coastal areas, caribou in more inland areas, and fishing everywhere).

The debate about the validity of "Eskimo words for snow" as an anthropological example was initiated by Martin (1986). This seminal article made the main points about the question, which are still valid: misinterpretations of what Boas' (1911a) point was; misuse of the example by Benjamin Whorf as part of his exposition of the "Sapir-Whorf" hypothesis; and further unscholarly quotation and inaccurate statements by various influential books and textbooks. Martin also adds that the question of how many "words for snow" there are depends on the correct definition of the word in a polysynthetic language like Eskimo, and she concludes that there are really but two distinct roots (or stems) meaning "snow" in any Eskimo language (Martin 1986: 422).

The two most recent accounts of "Eskimo words for snow" are Krupnik and Müller-Wille (2010), which emphasize the importance of Franz Boas' studies of Eskimo peoples in the history of the issue, and the relationship of the issue to technical terms for "ice," and Cichocki and Kilarski (2010), a historically oriented article that builds on the points in Krupnik and Müller-Wille (2010), emphasizes that Franz Boas was not entirely clear and consistent in his usage of the example, and summarizes much of the recent literature, including that from Marxist, relativist, and ecological points of view.

In this contribution, I will not attempt to summarize all the valid points made by Krupnik and Müller-Wille (2010) and Cichocki and Kilarski (2010), and I certainly agree with these authors and with Halpern (2010) that the discussions of "Eskimo words for snow" are becoming tiresome, and have been used as "strawmen" to make various points.

Rather, I want to focus on one issue, which has not been sufficiently discussed in the literature on the debate, although it is certainly present in it. What I would like to address is the so-called "primitivism" of hunter and gatherer cultures, i.e., their being so close to nature that they fail to see the forest for the trees, i.e., in this case, that there exists a unitary phenomenon that more "evolved" peoples call "snow." What the layman[2] often believes, and which is reinforced by a defective understanding of the "Sapir-Whorf hypothesis" (Martin 1986: 418) is not only: "Wow, they have so many words for snow," but also that they do not have a general term for "snow."[3] This is not only a layman's perception of hunter and gatherer languages, but, as we will see in Section 19.4, implied in some early anthropological work as well.

19.2   What Exactly Is an "Eskimo Word"?

Before discussing the issue of primitivism, it is useful to discuss in detail what the layman means by "word," what a linguist means by "word," and especially what the linguist specializing in Eskimo considers a "word" in Eskimo.

For the layman speaker of an western Indo-European language, the issue of what a word is, regarding the discussion of "Eskimo words for snow," is a rather straightforward one: a word is a stem (or root), and by that definition the only "word" we have in English that unambiguously refers to "snow" is *snow* (German *Schnee*, Dutch *sneeuw*, French *neige*, Spanish *nieve*, Russian *sneg*, and so on). For the layman, words such as *snowfall, snowflake, snow corniche*, and so on, are not going to count, since these are compounds of stems, not stems. Also the layman will have some idea that the words for snow have to be dedicated terms (using Johns [2010: 403–404] apt terminology). That is, the words have to refer to "snow" only, and not to "snow" and other things. So for the layman, *sleet, flake*, or *slush* will not count. Finally, the layman also has the idea that words for snow-related phenomena, but that do not refer to the substance itself, such as *blizzard* or *avalanche*, should not count. One hopes of course, that the layman, should she or he become an Eskimologist linguist, apply the same criteria to an examination of the Eskimo languages. But, as we will see, there are many morphological characteristics of the Eskimo word that make deciding what counts as a "word" a particularly hazardous task, even for linguists. So for the layman, the question is really, how many stems for "snow" does an Eskimo language have?

The linguist has intuitions similar to the layman's regarding the terms "stem" or "root," but in addition she or he is acutely aware of the eternal problems with a definition of the "word," which for linguists cannot of course be equated with the term "stem" or "root."[4] What the linguist will mean by "word" in the discussion will be the "lexeme," i.e., a basic unit of the lexicon with a unitary meaning, or, in Halpern's (2010) terminology, a "fixed locution" or a "fixed construct," such as what one finds as an entry in a dictionary. For examples of lexemes in English and in Eskimo, see Woodbury (1994). So for the linguist, the question is really, how many lexemes for "snow" does an Eskimo language have?

Finally, we get to the issue of what the "word" is for Eskimologist linguists, and hopefully, for native speakers of the languages themselves. Eskimo, as already pointed out in Woodbury (2003), is typologically quite remarkable in that it is the most polysynthetic language family on earth.

In this section, I will describe the structure of the word in one Eskimo language, Central Siberian Eskimo, in an amount of detail not reached in the typical discussions by Eskimologists of the issue of "Eskimo words for snow." It should be pointed out that the discussion and illustrations are valid for all Eskimo languages. Although there is a fair amount of lexical variation from one Eskimo language to another, all Eskimo languages share essentially the same morphological structure, sometimes down to minute detail.

The structure of the CSY word (and actually for the word in all Eskimo languages), is described by the formula in Example 19.1, taken from Woodbury (1981: 104).

Example 19.1

$$\text{base} + \text{postbases}_0^n + \text{ending} + \text{Enclitics}_0^m$$

The *base* is the lexical core of the word. Some bases must take at least one postbase before they can be inflected; such bases are called *roots*. *Postbases* are derivational suffixes; the *ending* is a morphologically simple or complex unit, and functions as an inflectional suffix.[5] An *expanded base* is a base followed by one or more postbases. Expanded bases are called bases when the difference between the two is not relevant to the point under discussion. *Enclitics* are suffixes because they are bound, but syntactically they are particles; they are discussed in de Reuse (1994a: 231–294).

An example of a CSY word is Example 19.2. The first line is the word in the standard spelling, the second line the morphological analysis with morphopho-nemics undone, the third line a morpheme-by-morpheme gloss, and the fourth line a free translation. The first morpheme, *angyagh-* 'boat', is the base, the following morphemes: *-ghllag-*[6] 'big N', *-nge-* 'to acquire N', and *-yug-* 'to want to v' are postbases; finally *-tuq* is the third person subject Indicative mood ending, and *=llu* 'also', is an enclitic.

Example 19.2

angyaghllangyugtuqlu
angyagh-ghllag-nge-yug-tuq=llu
boat-big.N-acquire.N-want.to.V-IND(3s)=also[7]
'also, he wants to acquire a big boat'

The description of the CSY word so far might not sound too bizarre, but it is the derivation by postbases which shows that Eskimo is truly unique in degree of polysynthesis. Postbases are most often productive and semantically trans-parent and can be added one after another in sequences of most often two or three, the maximum encountered being more than a dozen.

Following the seminal work of Kleinschmidt (1851:108–109), but using the modern terminology of Woodbury (1981: 342–343), postbases can be classified into four basic categories: those deriving nouns from verbs (VN), for example *-(s)te-* (Example 19.12)[8], *-vig-* (Example 19.14), *-yaghqagh-* (Example 19.12), *-(u)sigh-* (Example 19.13); those deriving verbs from nouns (NV), for example *-ke-* (Example 19.9), *-lgu-* (Example 19.10), *-nge-* (Example 19.2), *-ngllagh-* (Example 19.11), *-(ng)ughte-* (Example 19.12), *-(ng)ite-* (Example 19.13), *-(ng)u-* (Example 19.13, Example 19.14); those elaborating nouns into more complex nouns (NN), for example *-rukutaagh-* (Example 19.3), *-ghllag-* (Examples 19.2, 19.3, 19.10, 19.14), *-yag-* (Example 19.4), *-ghrugllag-* (Example 19.11), *-ghhagh-* (Example 19.13); and those elaborating verbs into more complex verbs (VV), for example *-(u)te-, -laatagh-* (Example 19.5), *-lleqe-* (Example 19.6), *-pigllag-, -kayugu-, -fte-* (Example 19.7), *-yaghtugh-* (Example 19.8), *-nghite-* (Examples 19.8, 19.11), *-yagh-* (Example 19.8), *-yug-* (Examples 19.2, 19.11), and *-niigh-* (Example 19.12).

From a semantic and grammatical point of view, Eskimo postbases can indicate a wide variety of phenomena, including, for nouns, quantification (*-yag-* [Example 19.4], *-ghllag-* [Example 19.14]), adjectival modification (*-rukutaagh-* [Example 19.3], *-ghllag-* [Examples 19.2, 19.3, 19.10], *-ghrugllag-* [Example 19.11], *-ghhagh-* [Example 19.13]), being and becoming, (*-(ng)ughte-* [Example 19.12], *-(ng)u-* [Example 19.14]), a type of verbal noun-incorporation (*-lgu-* [Example 19.10], *-nge-* [Example 19.2], *-ngllagh-* [Example 19.11]), and for verbs, changes in transitivity (*-(u)te-* [Example 19.5]), adverbial modification (*-pigllag-* [Example 19.7], *-yagh-* [Example 19.8]), aspect

(-*laatagh*- [Example 19.5], -*niigh*- [Example 19.12]), evidentiality (-*fte*-[Example 19.7]), modality (-*kayugu*- [Example 19.7], -*yug*- [Example 19.2, Example 19.11]), negation (-*nghite*- [Examples 19.8, 19.11]), tense (-*lleqe*-[Example 19.6]), agent noun formation (-*(s)te*- [Example 19.12]), relative clause formation (-*yaghqagh*- [Example 19.12]), and various types of verbal complementation (Examples 19.20, 19.21).

Example 19.3

qawaagpagrukutaaghllak
qawaagpag-rukutaagh-ghllag-ø
legendary.large.bird-huge.N-big.N-AB.S
'huge big (legendary large) bird'

Example 19.4

meteghllugyaget
meteghllug-yag-t
raven-multitude.of.N-RL.P
'a lot of ravens'

Example 19.5

itemullaataamii
iteme-(u)te-laatagh-(i/u)ma-ii
come.undone-TR-V.again-PST-IND(3S-3P)
'he has freed them again'

Example 19.6

Esghaghlleqamken unaami.
esghagh-lleqe-amken unaagh-mi
see-FUT-IND(1s-2s) morning-LC.S
'I will see you tomorrow.'

Example 19.7

iflapigllakayuguftuq
ifla-pigllag-kayugu-fte-uq
get.lost-really.V-able.to.V-appear.to.V-IND(3s)
'he appears to be able to get really lost'

Example 19.8

aqelqaghniighyaghtunghisaghamken
aqelqaghniigh-yaghtugh-nghite-yagh-amken
challenge.guests-go.and.V-NEG-V.in.vain-IND(1s-2s)
'I did not come to challenge you, but ... '

Example 19.9

Miinglum ighneqaanga.
Miinglu-m ighnegh-ke-aanga
(name)-RL.S son-have.as.one's.N-IND(3s-1s)
'I am Miinglu's son.' (lit. 'Miinglu has me as a son.')

Example 19.10

mangteghaghllalguuq
mangteghagh-ghllag-lgu-uq
house-big.N-have.N-IND(3s)
'he has a big house'

Example 19.11

mangteghaghrugllangllaghyunghitunga
mangteghagh-ghrugllag-ngllagh-yug-nghite-unga
house-big.N-make.N-want.to.V-NEG-IND(1s)
'I did not want to make a big house'

As shown in Examples 19.12–14, there can be switches back and forth between verb and noun bases by successive derivations with VN and NV or VN and NV sequences.

Example 19.12

unangniightengughsaghqaq
unange-niigh-(s)te-(ng)ughte-yaghqagh-ø
catch.a.seal-habitually.V-one.who.V.s-become.N-someone.who.will.V-AB.S
'one who ought to become a hunter'

Example 19.13

Sangusighhiisin?
sa-(ng)u-(u)sigh-ghhagh-(ng)ite-zin
something-be.N-instrument.for.V-ing-little.N-not.have.N-INT(2s)
'Don't you have a little device for being something (i.e. a weapon)?'

Example 19.14

angliviglllaguuq
angli-vig-ghllag-(ng)u-uq
make.a hole-place.to.V-lots.of.N-be.N-IND(3s)
'there are lots of places to make a (fishing) hole'

Such postbases are quite numerous. CSY, like all Eskimo languages, has about 400 of them. Clearly, many of such postbases behave differently from the derivational suffixes linguists are accustomed to. First, regardless of their semantics, they are completely productive. Second, the way they are ordered is determined by semantic scope much more often than by morphological constraints, so their ordering constraints are more typical of syntax than of morphology; in some cases the order of two postbases appears to be free without affecting meaning, again more typically a characteristic of syntax than of morphology. An example of free ordering involving the postbases *-nanigh-* 'to cease to v', and *-(u)tke-* 'to v on account of' is given in Examples 19.15 and 19.16. Dialectal or idiolectal variation is not involved here, as these forms were found within three lines from each other in the same story.

Example 19.15

aananiitkumakanga
aane-nanigh-(u)tke-(i/u)ma-kanga
go.out-cease.to.v-v.on.account.of-PST-TRP(3s-3s)
'he ceased going out on account of it (watching his child)'

Example 19.16

aanutkennanighaa
aane-(u)tke-nanigh-aa
go.out-v.on.account.of-cease.to.v-IND(3s-3s)
'he ceased going out on account of it (watching his child)'

Third, as seen in the examples above, the meaning of these postbases is often lexical (even though some have grammatical meanings more typical of inflectional morphology). Finally, postbases interact with syntax in complex ways, which I will not go into here. These complex ways show that postbase morphology and syntax are tightly intertwined. For all these reasons, the postbase morphology is reminiscent of syntax, and has been called an "internal syntax," a term first applied to Nootka by Swadesh (1939), and then to Greenlandic Eskimo (Swadesh 1946: 50). Internal syntax thus contrasts with the "external syntax," which deals with the relationships between and arrangements of independent words. Regarding our discussion of "Eskimo words for snow," this means that Eskimo "words" will often correspond to, and translate as, syntactic phrases or even sentences.

There is, however, more to CSY postbase grammar than "internal syntax," and this makes the issue even more complex. Actually, not all postbases are elements of the "internal syntax"; many of them turn out to be "real" derivational morphology, reminiscent of the derivational morphology of more analytic languages, which is not fully productive. So, the fully productive elements of an "internal syntax" have to be carefully distinguished from elements of the "real" derivational morphology. Further discussion of the difference between "internal syntax" and "real" derivational morphology is in de Reuse (2006) and in de Reuse (2009). In both these articles, the catchy but rather vague term "internal syntax" is replaced by the much less catchy but more accurate term "productive noninflectional concatenation" (PNC).

I should point out that the distinction I am making between inflection, "internal syntax" (or PNC) and "real" derivational morphology is not accepted by other Eskimologist linguists, as far as I know. This is understandable, as many linguists are not happy with the difference between inflectional morphology and derivational morphology in the first place, and many consider the distinction between inflectional and derivational morphology to be a matter of degrees on a continuum. So having a tripartite distinction between inflection, "internal syntax" (or PNC) and "real" derivational morphology does not seem to be a theoretically popular way to go. I am suggesting, however, that this tripartite distinction will turn out to correspond to the unconscious linguistic competence of Eskimo speakers themselves. In my fieldwork experience, the conscious linguistic competence of native speakers of CSY can distinguish phonological "words," corresponding to the formula in Example 19.1, but cannot (yet) distinguish elements inside that "word," be they inflectional, derivational, or other.[9]

It is certainly the case that making the distinction between "internal syntax" (or PNC) and "real" derivational morphology in an Eskimo language is not a simple feat. This is due to the fact that the postbases that are part of the "internal syntax" (or PNC) and the postbases that are "real" derivational morphology are quite often homonymous. Their meaning and productivity, but usually not their phonological shape, allows one to make the distinction. Position within the word often, but not always, helps in distinguishing the two. Whereas it is true that "real" derivational postbases will occur closest to the stem, and postbases of the "internal syntax" (or PNC) farther to the right, it is also the case that many postbases of the "internal syntax" (or PNC) are built of the nonproductive combinations of two or more "internal syntax" (or PNC) postbases, which are in effect functioning as "real" derivational postbases. As a result any apparent sequence of postbases within an Eskimo word could be either one postbase of the "internal syntax" (or PNC) or a nonproductive combination of such postbases. Only semantic and productivity considerations allow one to make the difference.

Let me illustrate the distinction between "internal syntax" (or PNC) and "real" derivational morphology with a discussion of two homonymous postbases, one belonging to the "real" morphology and occurring immediately after the base and one belonging to the "internal syntax."[10] The "real" morphological postbase is -*yug*- 'to feel v', which is common in lexicalized combinations with roots of emotion. So, from the root *efqugh*- 'pleased, satisfied', one can derive the verb *efqughyug*- 'to be pleased, satisfied'. Also, from the root *igamsiqa*- 'thankful', one can derive the verb *igamsiqayug*- 'to feel thankful'. This postbase is not to be confused with the "internal syntax" postbase -*yug*- 'to want to v', which can be added to any verb (provided the result makes sense, of course). While it is true that these two postbases are etymologically and semantically related, they are quite different in terms of productivity and precise semantics. Both postbases (in boldface) can occur in the same verb word, as in Example 19.17.

Example 19.17

igamsiqayugviksugapung
igamsiqa-**yug**-vike-**yug**-apung
thankful-**feel**.v-have.an.object.of.one's.v-**want.to**.v-IND(1D-3P)
'we wish to thank them'

In this case, evidence that these two postbases have to be kept distinct is provided not only by their position with respect to another, but also by their position with respect to another postbase. It appears that when -*yug*- is followed by the "internal syntax" causative postbase -*(te)ste*- 'to cause to v', it is an element of "real" derivation, as in Examples 19.18 and 19.19.

Example 19.18

kaynguyugtestekaqii
kayngu-yug-(te)ste-kaqe-ii
embarrassed-feel.V-CAUS-PST-IND(3S-3P)
'(s)he caused them to feel embarrassed'

Example 19.19

qinuyugtestaqaa
qinu-yug-(te)ste-aqe-aa
sick-feel.V-CAUS-PROG-IND(3S-3S)
'it is making him/her sick'

On the other hand, when the order is -*(te)ste-yug*-, one has to do with a fully productive sequence 'to want to cause to v', i.e. 'to want someone to v', as in Example 19.20.

Example 19.20

Yugem aghnamun neghesugaa kayu.
yug-m aghnagh-mun negh-(te)ste-yug-aa kayu-ø
man-RL.S woman-TM.S eat-CAUS-want.to.V-IND(3S-3S) fish-AB.S
'The man wants the woman to eat the fish.'

From the foregoing discussion one should not conclude that if one sees two homophonous postbases in a word, the one farthest to the left will be "real" derivational and the one farthest to the right will be "internal syntax." As in external syntax, postbases of the "internal syntax" can be used recursively, as in Example 19.21, a sentence from an *ungipaghaan* or traditional tale with a word containing "internal syntax" -*sqe*- 'to ask to V' twice.

Example 19.21

Nanevgam	*aghnaghaat*	*kayagtii*
Nanevgagh-m	aghnaghagh-t	kayagte-ii
old.man-RL.S	girl-AB.P	send-IND(3S-3P)

iitghesqesaghtiisqelluku	*Qawaak*
itegh-sqe-yaghtugh-sqe-luku	qawaag-ø
come.in-ask.to.V-go.V-ask.to.V-APO(3S-3S)	bird-AB;S

Qatelghii.
qategh-lghii-ø
be.white-INP-AB;S

'The elderly eagle sent the girls out to have them tell the White Eagle to come in', or more literally: 'The old man sent the girls$_i$, asking them$_i$ to go and ask him$_j$, the White Eagle$_j$, to come in.'

As mentioned earlier, the "real" derivational morphology is also used in forming lexicalized combinations of postbases which are themselves part of "internal syntax." Once recognized as such, these lexicalized combinations are formally easy to analyze, but are semantically idiosyncratic, and often contain postbases in orders not occurring productively. Examples of lexicalized combinations of postbases are given now. These examples are built with the productive VV postbases *-(ng)inagh-* 'to only V', *-kayugu-* 'to be able to V', *-(i/u)ma-* 'Past Tense', *-naqe-* 'to try to V', and *-yug-* 'to want to V'.

The productive VV postbase *-kayugunaqe-* 'to learn to V', is a lexicalized combination of the productive postbase *-kayugu-* 'to be able to V', and the productive postbase *-naqe-* 'to try to V'. See Example 19.22.

Example 19.22

qimugsiqayugunaqnaqaquq
qimugsigh-kayugunaqe-naqe-aqe-uq
drive.a.dogteam-learn.to.V-PROSP-PROG-IND(3s)
'he intends to learn to drive a dogteam'

The postbase *-(i/u)manginagh-* is not a productive sequence of *-(i/u)ma-* 'Past Tense' and *-(ng)inagh-* 'to only V' since it means 'to V continuously, all the time' and not necessarily the predictable 'to only V in the past'. In Example 19.23 the inherent tense is Past, but in Example 19.24 the tense is Future, and Future Tense is incompatible with Past Tense *-(i/u)ma-*.

Example 19.23

kumlaaghqumanginaghaa
kumlaaghqe-(i/u)manginagh-aa
freeze-V.continously-IND(3s-3s)
'it kept freezing'

Example 19.24

iknaqughsaamanginaghnaaghii
iknaqugh-sagh-(i/u)manginagh-naagh-ii
become.stronger-CAUS-V.continously-FUT-IND(3s-3P)
'he will keep them stronger continuously'

The reverse sequence *-(ng)inagh-(i/u)ma-* is semantically transparent and not lexicalized, as seen in Example 19.25.

Example 19.25

igleghtengnginaamaluteng
igleghte-(ng)inagh-(i/u)ma-luteng
travel-only.V-PST-APO(3P)
'they were only travelling'

The lexicalized combination *-yuguma-* 'to be easy to V', from *-yug-* and *-(i/u)ma-*, occurs in Example 19.26, and can be used with a productive Past Tense *-(i/u)ma-*, as seen in Example 19.27.

Example 19.26

pelimyugumaaqut
pelime-yuguma-aqe-ut
shatter-be.easy.to.V-PROG-IND(3P)
'they are easily shattered'

Example 19.27

sugagyugumamaaq
sugag-yuguma-(i/u)ma-uq
be.offended-be.easy.to.V-PST-IND(3S)
'he was easily offended'

The postbase *-yuguma-* also contrasts semantically with the sequences of "real derivational" *-yug-* 'to feel v' (Example 19.28), or *-yug-* 'to want to v' (Example 19.29) and Past Tense *-(i/u)ma-*.

Example 19.28

alingyugumalghii
alinge-yug-(i/u)ma-lghii
be.afraid-feel.V-PST-INP(3S)
'he was apprehensive'

Example 19.29

neghyugumaaq
negh-yug-(i/u)ma-uq
eat-want.to.V-PST-IND(3S)
'he wanted to eat'

The point of this long discussion was to demonstrate with verbal postbases what is true of any postbase in all Eskimo languages: the postbases of an Eskimo word can be "real" derivational or part of the "internal syntax," and often the average Eskimo word contains both "real" derivational and "internal syntax" postbases. Sometimes of course, an Eskimo word is just a base (or stem), i.e., without any postbases at all.

Comparing the English "word" with the Eskimo "word" will clarify why more definitions of the "word" are possible for Eskimo than for English (Table 19.1).

As one can observe in Table 19.1, every CSY example under columns (1), (2), (3), and (4) looks like one "word" to an English speaking reader. Of course, because Eskimo also has external syntax, it *also* has under column (3), the possibility of "idiomatic syntactic phrases," and under column (4), the possibility of "non-idiomatic syntactic phrases."

Table 19.1 *The English and Eskimo "word" compared*

	1	2	3	4
English grammatical terminology:	"stem"	"derived word" (by affixation or compounding)	"idiomatic syntactic phrase"	"non-idiomatic syntactic phrase"
English examples:	snow	snowdrift	powdery snow	snow that is good for snowballs
Eskimo grammatical terminology:	"base"	"derived word" (by "real" derivational postbase)	"idiomatic internal syntax" (by postbase)	"non-idiomatic internal syntax" (by postbase)
CSY examples:	*qanik*	*qanigraak*	*qanivleghaq*	*qanigllak*
Glosses of CSY examples:	'snowflake; falling snow'	'intermittent or light but continuous snowfall'	'light snow'	cf. discussion on the next page

Looking at the CSY examples first, the "words" under columns (1), (2), and (3) are lexemes, and will be further referenced in Appendix 19.1. The CSY "word" *qanigllak* in column (4) was constructed by myself from *qanig-* 'snowflake, falling snow' and the "internal syntax" postbase *-ghllag-* 'big N, large N, lots of N'(Badten et al. 2008: 612).[11] This "word" was checked with two native speakers of CSY during the Inuit Studies Conference in Washington, DC on October 26, 2012. One of the speakers, Vera Metcalf, from Savoonga, St. Lawrence Island, suggested the gloss 'big snowflake', and added that she had never heard this word and prefers *qaniglluk* (which is a lexeme, referenced in Appendix 19.1). The second speaker, George Noongwook, also from Savoonga, suggested the glosses 'big snow coming down; huge snowflakes' and commented: "similar to *qaniglluk*." The point is that both speakers accepted this item as a possible "word", and understood it, although they both appeared to prefer the lexeme *qaniglluk*.[12] I conclude from these native speaker reactions that the apparent "word" *qanigllak* is equivalent to a non-idiomatic phrase and is thus not a lexeme. Another potential example of a "word" that is not a lexeme is *qaniggaq,* glossed as 'snowflake' by Vakhtin and Emelyanova (1988: 27). This is *qanig-* followed by the "internal syntax" postbase *-ghhagh-* 'little N, small N, bit of N' (Badten et al. 2008: 610). So I suggest that a more precise gloss for *qaniggaq* would be a non-idiomatic phrase such as 'little snowflake', or 'bit of snow falling down'.

Concerning English, if we define a "word" as a stem (or root), i.e., a free morpheme that is not further analyzable, then only column (1) is relevant, which would contain *snow* only.

If we define a "word" as a morpheme or phonologically tightknit sequence of morphemes with a clear lexical meaning, then columns (1) and (2) are relevant, and many more "words" such as *slushsnow, snow bank, snowdrift*, and *snowflake* become candidates, as mentioned at the beginning of this section.

If we define a "word" as a lexeme, then idioms composed of more than one "word" have to be included. Then columns (1), (2), and (3) become relevant, and a technical term such as *powdery snow* also becomes a candidate.

Expressions in column (4) are purely syntactic and are not lexemes, so there is never any reason for considering them "words" by any definition.

So, depending on what definition of the English "word" we use, we can thus have between one and several dozen English "words for snow." As we have seen at the beginning of this section, the layman counting "English words for snow" only counts stems, i.e. column (1).

To be consistent, people counting "Eskimo words for snow" should count them in the same way. So, they could only count forms in column (1), i.e. bases (the Eskimologist term exactly corresponding to stems).

Or they could count forms in columns (2) and (3) as well. The problem is that unless one has an extensive knowledge of Eskimo morphology, one is not going to be able to distinguish between columns (1), (2), (3), and (4), as all of them can correspond to phonologically tightknit elements, superficially looking like columns (1) or (2) in English (and written as sequences of letters without breaks). If one defines the Eskimo word as corresponding to columns (1) *and* (2), one will have to distinguish between "real derivational" postbases and "internal syntax" postbases, and as we have seen above, this is not an easy thing to do.

If one defines an Eskimo word as a lexeme, i.e. as corresponding to columns (1), (2), *and* (3.), then one will have to distinguish between "internal syntax" postbases idiomatically used, and such postbases not idiomatically used, which also presupposes an advanced knowledge of the language. Again, to be consistent, one would have to revise one's definition of the "word" in English to match columns (1), (2), and (3) also.

If one wants to include the Eskimo column (4) in one's definition of the "Eskimo word," on the grounds that the elements in that column look like phonological words similar to the English columns (1) through (3) (and they really do look that way), one is in trouble because the elements in that column correspond to non-idiomatic syntactic phrases in English. To be consistent, one should then include the English column (4) in the possible definition of a "word," and we would have to accept phrases such as *the snow that my granddaughter put in my wife's neck yesterday* as an English "word for snow." Indeed, if one wants to include column (4) in the count, one should not even try to count. Because of the high number and full productivity of Eskimo postbases, one can say without batting an eye, that there are millions and millions of Eskimo words for "snow" (and actually millions and millions of words for anything else in this language), as already pointed out by Martin (1986: 419).

It would be unfair to blame the situation described in the preceding paragraphs only on the lack of linguistic sophistication on the part of people counting "Eskimo words for snow." Many of the specialized dictionaries, such as Schneider (1970a, 1970b, 1985) used by people counting "Eskimo words for snow" do not distinguish clearly between columns (1), (2), and (3), and sometimes even include constructions of column (4), which certainly should not count as dictionary entries, since they are not lexemes. The list of snow-related terms for Central Alaskan Yupik in Fienup-Riordan and Rearden (2012: 211–214), otherwise a superb work on Arctic weather, similarly does not make such distinctions. Jacobson's (1984) dictionary of Central Alaskan Yupik and the Badten et al. (2008) dictionary of CSY are two dictionaries that carefully avoid entries corresponding to column (4).

So from the point of view of this Eskimologist linguist, how many "words for snow" one can distinguish in Eskimo will depend on whether to count bases or lexemes, and if one counts lexemes, which is the sensible thing to do, one should be careful to include forms from columns (1), (2), and (3) in the count, but not a "word" from column (4) because these are not lexemes. Nevertheless, let me reemphasize that the forms from column (4) are phonologically, and in the perception of the linguistically unsophisticated native speaker of CSY, just as much "words" as the forms in columns (1) through (3).

To summarize this section, the exact number of "Eskimo words for snow" depends entirely on who counts, and on what one counts. If one counts bases (i.e. stems) (column 1) like the layman, one will find a few "words," and this is of course what Martin (1986) and following her, Pullum (1989), have done when stating that there are not "many words for snow."[13] The only and seemingly minor difference from English is then that English has one stem for "snow," whereas Eskimo languages appear to have at least two. The potential importance of this difference will be discussed in Section 19.4.

If one counts lexemes (i.e. bases, derived words, and idioms in columns 1, 2, and 3) one will find quite a few words, representing probably more technical terms than in English. At this level, Eskimo languages do indeed have an interesting terminology for "snow," but it should be remembered that the English technical terminology used by meteorologists and skiers is fairly rich too.[14]

If one consistently counted Eskimo phonological words (i.e. all four columns), the number of "words" becomes nearly infinite, and the exercise becomes absurd.

19.2   An Example: Central Siberian Yupik "Words for Snow"

I now turn to a detailed discussion of a CSY list of Eskimo terms relating to snow. Reliable lists of lexemes for other Eskimo languages can be found in Woodbury (1994) (Central Alaskan Yupik), in Kaplan (2003) and Sturm (2009) (both North Alaskan Iñupiaq), and especially the lists from six Eskimo varieties in Krupnik and Müller-Wille (2010: 392–393).[15] There are references to other lists in Krupnik and Müller-Wille (2010: 388–389).[16]

The list, given in Appendix 19.1, was culled by myself from Badten et al. (2008), using their definitions, and from Walunga (1987: 20–21), with occasional remarks from Silook et al. (1983), and references to Vakhtin and Emelyanova (1988), abbreviated as VE, followed by their page number.[17] Krupnik and Müller-Wille (2010: 389) in their table 6.2, count 56 terms for snow in the CSY of St. Lawrence Island. They only give the numbers, not the terms themselves; they distinguish 15 terms for snow on the ground, 3 terms for falling snow and snowfall, 13 terms for snow on ice and water, 4 terms for snow forms, and 21 others, including derivatives.[18] For comparison with their counts, I adopt the same classification in Appendix 19.1.[19]

Rather than giving a synchronic morphological analysis, I have attempted to give a morphological analysis which is at the same time an etymology, and traced all elements of the word back to their proto-forms as given in the *Comparative Eskimo Dictionary*, (Fortescue, Jacobson, and Kaplan [2010], henceforth CED). This procedure is harder to follow than a synchronic analysis, but it has the benefit of facilitating comparison with other Eskimo languages. All forms preceded by the abbreviations PE, PI, and PY are from the CED[20], and are in a transliteration provided in Table 19.2.[21] Note, however, that the abbreviations D, DIS, IS are valid for the postbase discussed in the particular language, not for its PE, PI, or PY ancestors, because we are not always sure of what the status of a particular postbase was in the proto-languages.

The original spelling, the same as in the foregoing CSY examples, is retained, but the nouns are spelled in their underlying forms, because this facilitates comparison with the proto-forms.[22]

We have in Appendix 19.1 a list of 38 terms related to "snow," organized in five sections. By my count, which is different from that in Krupnik and Müller-Wille (2010: 389), there are 9 terms for snow on the ground (Section A), 5 for falling snow (Section B), 3 for snow on ice and water (Section C), 5 for snow forms (Section D), and 16 for others and derivatives (Section E).

Depending on what we want to count, there will be different terms that count as "words for snow." If we count bases (or stems) that basically mean "snow," in column (1) of Table 19.1, there are two general terms meaning "snow" in CSY: *anigu-* (A.1.)[23] and *qanig-* (B.2.).[24] We also have to put in column (1) four more specialized terms that mean "snow": *kagerghu-* (A.3) (Siberian)[25], *pightugh-* (B.1)[26], *qaalghwaag-* (A.7), and *qangaari-* (A.8). Using the criteria under column (1), one could just say that there are then six words for 'snow' in CSY, i.e. two general terms and four specialized ones.

Thirteen terms referring to "snow" proper are derived by D postbases, and thus belong under column (2) of Table 19.1. These are: *apenghaate-* (A.2), *kalevnagh-, kalefkag-, kalefkagnagh-* (A.4), *kiivnite-* (C.1), *mughayanegh-* (A.5), *nekginagh-* (A.6), *nutaqiigh-* (C.2), *pightughpag-* (E.8), *pightughrug-* (E.9), *qanigpag-* (E.11), *qanigraag-* (E.12), *ughuges-nagh-* (A.9), *umegreghagh-* (B.3), and *ungavisqwaagh-* (B.5). Note that only five of these: *pightughpag-* (E8), *pightughrug-* (E.9), *qanigpag-* (E.11), and *qanigraag-* (E.12) are derived from unanalyzable bases that refer to "snow," and not from nondedicated bases.

There are also six terms that refer to "snow" most of the time, but not all of the time; these are then nondedicated terms and would not count for many people. These are also belonging in column (2) of Table 19.1, and are all in Section E of Appendix 19.1. They are: *aghpumla-* (E.1), *aghqetghagh-* (E.2.), *anurga-* (E.4), *apumeg-* (E.6), *patugnagh-* (E.7), and *qetumla-* (E.15).

Also belonging in column (2) of Table 19.1, there are nine forms that do not refer to the substance snow, but to snow formations or snow storms, and would not be counted as "snow terms" by some people either. The snow formations can be found in Section D of Appendix 19.1: *alqimiite-* (D.1), *alukanegh-* (D.2), *alungutellegh-* (D.3), *peghyi-* (D.4) and *qengaghugh-* (D.5). Forms referring to types of storms are *kaftekrag-* (E.5), *qateghnagh-* (E.14), *sighyag-* (E.16), and *umegnegh-* (B.4).

Finally, four words are derived from snow bases (stems) by idiomatic use of an "internal syntax" postbase, and thus belong under column (3) of Table 19.1: *aniguvzeghagh-* (E.3), *qanigllug-* (E.10), *qanigvig-* (C.3), and *qanivleghagh-* (E.13).

As should be the case, none of the terms in Appendix 19.1 belong to column (4) of Table 19.1.

19.4   Snow and Ice: A Comparison Regarding the Alleged "Primitivism" of Hunter and Gatherer Languages

As seen in the preceding section, the number of common unanalyzable bases that CSY (and most Eskimo languages) has to refer to the general concept "snow" is thus an unimpressive two (or three), and of course there is a lot of additional technical terminology, some derived from these bases, and much of it not. Note that the dichotomy *qanig-* 'snow in the air', versus *anigu-* 'snow on the ground', is not even a characteristic of Eskimo languages. Indeed, many languages in the world, such as Lakota (Siouan family) have a similar dichotomy: *ičámna* 'to snow (heavily), snowstorm', and *wá* 'snow (usually on the ground)' (Ullrich 2011).

Nevertheless, ever since Boas (1911a), the fact that there is not one "word for snow" in Eskimo has intrigued the layman. Boas himself did not intend to place a value judgement on "primitive people," but as Cichocki and Kilarski (2010: 351–352) point out, some quotes from Boas' later publications are relevant to the issue:

the first impression gained from a study of the beliefs of primitive man is, that while the perception of his senses are excellent, his power of logical interpretation seems to be deficient. (Boas 1938 [1911b]: 220, quoted in Cichocki and Kilarski 2010: 351).

... large numbers of ancient elements are found that have very specific meanings. This is true of objects that are of cultural importance in many ways and for many purposes. In the life of the Eskimo snow means something entirely different as falling snow, soft snow on the ground, drifting snow or snowdrift. ... In many cases in which the specific functions of the object in the life of the people are quite distinct, a general term is missing. (Boas 1938: 130, quoted in Cichocki and Kilarski 2010: 351)

Cichocki and Kilarski (2010: 351) point out that such quotes "seem to suggest the lack of a general term for "snow" in Eskimo. Read together and out of their context, such quotes will easily be picked up on by both anthropologists and sociologists, and ultimately by the general public. Let me provide two example quotes, the first from an anthropology book, by the respected Danish anthropologist Kaj Birket-Smith, originally published in 1936:

... the Eskimo language may with full justification be described as *primitive*; but poverty and primitiveness are not the same in language – in certain respects they are rather opposites. ... It is another primitive trait that despite the crowd of proper names, the universal and more abstract words are lacking. For instance there is no term for snow in general in Eskimo; but only specific terms for the various forms of snow." (Birket-Smith 1963:63–64)[27]

The second one is from a sociology textbook, Federico and Schwartz (1983:56), quoted in Cichocki and Kilarski (2010:365):

"Eskimos (...) have no general word for snow. Instead, they know between twenty and thirty different kinds of snow, each expressed by a different word."

The "Sapir-Whorf hypothesis" also, more implicitly, might lead the layman to believe that since Eskimos "see" snow differently, they cannot be expected to need a general term, even though, as seen as in the preceding section, they do have several general terms. Further discussion of the myth that Eskimo languages do not have a general term for "snow" is in Steckley (2008: 58, 71–72).

Such statements and Whorfian assumptions can easily, even in this century, be read as "primitivist" statements and assumptions. While it is obvious that no present-day anthropologist or linguist would call the Eskimo language "primitive", (and actually would call no hunter-gatherer group "primitive"), we cannot be assured that the general public will no longer draw conclusions about the primitiveness of the Eskimos on the basis of what they hear regarding the "Eskimo words for snow" issue. Therefore, it will not hurt to remain vigilant regarding such opinions. It is, of course, encouraging to see that the modern lay literature on the subject, such as the delightful and informative children's book by Sturm (2009) does not even mention the supposed lack of general terms for "snow" in Eskimo and even glosses the Alaskan North Slope Iñupiaq term *apun* as "the snow cover, a general term for snow on the ground."

It is also good to remember that in the older anthropological literature, "words for snow" was not the most popular example to illustrate the lack of abstracting abilities of so-called "primitive" hunter-gatherer people. In the nineteenth-century literature, that distinction went to "Eskimo words for fishing." Eskimos, as "primitive" people, had lots of specific terms for "fishing," but no general term, as discussed in Cichocki and Kilarski (2010: 366). But it is the example of "Eskimo words for snow" which caught on in popular imagination.

In this regard, it is instructive to compare the discussion about "Eskimo words for snow," with the accounts of Eskimo words for "ice," of which the first have been by Boas (1894) as pointed out by Krupnik and Müller-Wille (2010: 382–383). A later but pioneering account by Nelson (1969) has also been influential. The most recent and most accurate accounts of "ice" are surveyed in Krupnik and Müller-Wille (2010) and in Krupnik (2011), and useful lists of ice terms are in Johns (2010: 410–412) (Canadian Utkuhiksalingmiutut), Krupnik and Weyapuk (2010: 347–352), Weyapuk and Krupnik (2012) (both Iñupiaq of Wales, Alaska), and Tersis and Tavernier (2010: 415–412) (Western and Eastern Greenlandic).[28]

One particularly impressive collection of "ice" terms, by the St. Lawrence Island Yupik scholar Conrad Oozeva is a Yupik Sea Ice Dictionary, which was first published in Walunga (1987: 22–30), and was expanded and elaborated on in Oozeva et al. (2004: 29–53). This last publication has detailed CSY descriptions of 99 terms, their translations, and even carefully crafted illustrative drawings for every word. And this terminology is not surprising, as for a marine mammal hunting group such as the CSY Eskimo, "ice" is much more important for survival, and more dangerous than snow. In much of the Arctic, it does not snow all that much; whatever does come down stays, of course, and blows around quite a bit. Only in some areas with more deep snow like the central Canadian Arctic was there ever enough snow to build igloos.[29] But ice varies in thickness, quality, shape, and moves around, and melts and refreezes in ways much more interesting than snow. Hence the very elaborate terminology.

One wonders then, as Krupnik and Müller-Wille (2010) do, why there has been all this focus on "Eskimo words for snow," when there is a very impressive and elaborate technical terminology for "ice" and ice conditions, and why is there no comparable debate about "Eskimo words for ice"?[30] My guess is that there is one general Eskimo term for "ice" (CSY *siku*), which has cognates in every known Eskimo language (except Sirenikski), whereas there is never, in any Eskimo language, just one term for "snow," there are at least, as we have seen, two bases (or stems), and sometimes three. And in the CSY technical definitions of "ice" (Walunga 1987: 22–30, Oozeva et al. 2004: 29–53), the term *siku* is almost always mentioned in the definitions. So nothing could be said about Eskimo being a "primitive" language, because the cover term functions pretty much like English "ice."

So from the layman's point of view, the "snow" and "ice" situations are not quite parallel, pace Kaplan (2003), Harrison (2010: 71–76), Krupnik and Müller-Wille (2010: 378), and Cichocki and Kilarski (2010: 343). And the fact that there is one "Eskimo word for ice," but several for "snow," might well remain prevalent in the popular imagination, as much as it can be considered a "red herring" in the scholarly literature.

Conclusions

How many "words for snow" there are in Eskimo depends entirely on who counts, on how one defines the word, and as I have argued at length, the difficulties in counting accurately are exacerbated by the fact that the structure of the Eskimo "word" is more complex than generally assumed in the Eskimologist literature, let alone in laymen's accounts.

It is also certain that Eskimo has a technical vocabulary for talking about "snow," as for any weather, sea, and ice conditions that affect Eskimo life, particularly regarding hunting and gathering activities, and that such a vocabulary is indicative of precious indigenous knowledge.

Finally, it is also certain that there is no evidence that Eskimos "see" snow differently from other people, and that they do not, or cannot, visualize snow as a unitary phenomenon. So the example provides no evidence whatsoever for the assumption that hunters and gatherers do not have normal powers of generalization and abstraction.

Even though no scholar any longer believes that the Eskimo "words for snow" issue tells us anything of interest about the psychology of hunting and gathering peoples, it is a good idea to make two points concurrently when "Eskimo words for snow" come under discussion, as they are, in my view, equally important.

First, as non-Eskimologist linguists such as Martin (1986) and Pullum (1989), an Eskimologist anthropologist such as Steckley (2008: 67), and

Eskimologist linguists such as Woodbury (1994) and Kaplan (2003) have shown, it is not trivial to emphasize that there are but a few general bases (or stems) for "snow" in Eskimo languages.

Second, as noted by Krupnik and Müller-Wille (2010), and Krupnik (2011), publicized by Harrison's (2010: 71–73) popular account, and in Sturm's (2009) teaching guide for children, the interesting features of the rich Eskimo technical terminology of lexemes for natural phenomena should be pointed out.

It is therefore important to read the latest article on this topic (Robson 2012) in the *New Scientist* with caution. The title of this article: '*Sno myth*, and its subtitle: *Eskimos really do have at least 50 words for snow, says David Robson*, are potentially misleading. The article lamentably ignores the first point above, while eloquently emphasizing the second point in the foregoing, and seems to imply that something (but we are not sure what) considered a myth is now established as a scientific truth. But certainly, if Robson had pointed out that it is no myth that computer scientists have a rich terminology for computer technologies, his article would not have been considered science nor newsworthy! The myth of there being something quite unusual about the powers of abstraction of hunting and gathering peoples such as the Eskimos, is not addressed, and the layman, (through no direct fault of Robson's, to be sure), might well draw "primitivist" conclusions long discarded by professional anthropologists and linguists.

APPENDIX 19.1 CSY ESKIMO TERMS RELATING TO SNOW

A.   Snow on the Ground

1. *anigu-* 'snow on ground' (Badten 61, Walunga 21, VE 26). PE N B *anigu-* 'snow (fallen)'.
2. *apenghaate-* 'hard snow (on the ground)' (Walunga 21); 'fresh fluffy snow' (Badten 67, VE 26). PE V B *ape-* 'become covered in snow', PE VV D *-n(e)rar(ar)-* 'recently or for first time', PE VN DIS *-ute-* 'means for doing'.
3. *kagerghu-* 'hard crust on snow' (Chukotkan) (Badten 179, VE 27). From Chukchi *kewir'əl*, plural *kewir'əlti* 'dry snow that is frozen through' (Badten et al. 2008:179).
4. *kalevnagh-, kalefkagnagh-* 'snow into which sled runners can sink while travel-ing' (Badten 182), *kalefkag-* (Walunga 21). PE V B *kaleve(t)-* 'sink into mud (or water or snow), CSY VN D *-nar-* 'something that causes V-ing', related to PE VV D *-nar-* 'be such as to or -able', etymology and meaning of CSY VV D *-kag-* is not clear.

5. *mughayanegh-* 'deep soft snow' (Badten 266). PE V B *maru-*, PY V B *muru-* 'sink into soft ground or snow', PE VV D *-ya-* 'be apt or be liable to' (?), PE VN D *-ner-* 'nominalizer'.

6. *nekginagh-* 'powdery snow' (Walunga 21, Badten 298). CSY R *nekeg-* 'matured, quietened down, put in place' (?), PE DIS *-nginnar-* 'only'.

7. *qaalghwaag-* 'fine snow on the ground' (Walunga 21); 'fine snow' (Badten 377). Analysis and etymology are unclear.

8. *qangaari-* 'soft snow in spring that makes traveling difficult' (Chukotkan) (Badten 385, VE 27). Etymology unknown, possibly from Chukchi.

9. *ughugesnagh-* 'sleet; wet snow' (Badten 546, Walunga 21). PY V B *urug-* 'melt', possibly PY VV DIS *-(arar)te-* 'suddenly', PE VN DIS *-nginnar-* 'only'.

B.   Falling Snow, Snowfall

1. *pightugh-* 'drifting blowing snow' (Badten 351, Walunga 20, 21). PE N B *pirtur-* 'snowstorm'.

2. *qanig-* 'snowflake; falling snow' (Badten 386, Walunga 20, 21); 'falling snow'(VE 24). PE N B *qanig-* 'falling snow'.

3. *umegreghagh-* 'snow flurries' (Badten 558, VE 24). PE V B *umeg-* 'close off or cover', PY VN DIS *-vzherar-* 'a little (more)'.

4. *umegnegh-* 'blizzard' (Badten 558, Walunga 20, 21, VE 24). PE V B *umeg-* 'close off or cover', PE VN D *-ner-* 'nominalizer'.

5. *ungavisqwaagh-* 'falling flakes' (Walunga 21, Badten 562). PY N B *ungag-* 'beard or mustache', PE VN DIS *-vig-* 'place or time of' (?), CSY NN D *-sqwaagh-* 'old, aged, decrepit'.

C.   Snow on Ice and Water

1. *kiivnite-* 'snow in sea water' (Walunga 21); 'slush snow in sea water impeding boat travel and sometimes sinking below the surface or even to the shallow bottom near the shore' (Badten 215). PE V B *kive-* 'sink or settle', PE VN D *-ner-* 'nominalizer', CSY NV D *-i-* 'to make N', PE VN DIS *-ute-* 'means for doing'.

2. *nutaqiigh-* 'frost snow on sea ice' (Walunga 21, Badten 320); also: 'new ice with frost crystals on surface' (Badten 320). PE R *nutar-* 'renew', etymology and meaning of CSY D *-qiigh-* are not clear.

3. *qanigvig-* 'water covered with snow' (Walunga 21); 'snow covering narrow open lead in sea ice, looking deceptively like solid sea ice covered with snow (Badten 386); 'thin ice covered with snow; time when the snow falls' (VE 27). PE N B *qanig-* 'falling snow', PE NN DIS *-vig-* 'place or time of'

D.   Snow Forms

1. *alqimiite-* 'snow overhang' (Walunga 21); 'overhang of ice or hard snow, cornice' (Badten 40). PY V B *alqimar-* 'to lick food from fingers', PE VN DIS *-ute-* 'means for doing'.
2. *alukanegh-* 'low ridge on surface of snow (caused by wind); sastrugi[31]; low obstructions in waves on surface of snow (or sand) caused by wind; wavy surface caused by drifting snow' (Silook 103, Badten 40, Walunga 21). PE V B *alug-* 'to lick', and an unidentified VN D element (see below).
3. *alungutellegh-* 'area in lee of building without much snow, so called because it seems as if a hollow has been licked out there'; 'snow bank' (Walunga 21, Badten 40). PY V B *alunge-* 'to lick', somehow derived from PE V B *alug-* 'to lick', PE VV D *-ute-* 'to do with or for', PE VN DIS *-ller-* 'nominalizer'.
4. *peghyi-* 'snowdrift on the way after a storm' (Chukotkan) (Badten 430, VE 27). Etymology unknown, possibly from Chukchi.
5. *qengaghugh-* 'snowdrift' (Badten 406, Walunga 21, VE 27). PE N B *qengar-* 'nose', PE NN D *-zhug-* 'big (?)'.

E.   Others, Including Derivatives

1. *aghpumla-* 'any substance that is soft and bumpy like snow' (Silook 14); 'deep, soft, powdery snow' (Badten 9, Walunga 21). PE N B *qapug-* 'foam', only existing as the CSY R *aghpu-*, CSY D *-mla-* meaning unclear, also found in *qetumla-* (see 5.15).
2. *aghqetghagh-* 'springtime snow frozen by cold wind and night cold, after its moisture had drained and has become porous; can be hard to walk on as parts of it easily crush underfoot, but sleds slide on it much easier than on moist, soft, warm weather snow' (Silook 15); 'frozen ground in spring; frozen crust on snow' (Badten 10); 'frozen crust on snow' (Walunga 21); snow crust; frozen upper crust of soft snow built in the evening (VE 26). PY V B *qiretrar-* or *qiqetrar-* 'form hard crust (snow)', from the PE V B *qire-* or *qiqe-* 'freeze', PE VV D *-ter-* 'repeatedly', PE VN D *-ar-* thing resembling sth.'
3. *aniguvzeghagh-* 'first snow on ground in fall' (Badten 62, VE 26). PE N B *anigu-* 'snow (fallen)', PY NN DIS *-vzherar-* 'a little (more)'.
4. *anurga-* 'eternal or permanent ice or snow' (Badten 64). Etymology unknown, possibly from Chukchi.
5. *kaftekrag-* 'small hailstorm, frozen raindrops, hailstone (Silook 71); 'hail' (Badten 178); 'hard falling snow' (Walunga 21). Probably a CSY N B *kafte-* and the CSY NN D *-krag-* 'small; thing like'.
6. *apumeg-* 'soft snow or dirt' (Badten 68). PE V B *ape-* 'become covered in snow', PE VN DIS *-ute-* 'means for doing' (?), etymology and meaning of CSY D *-meg-* is not clear.

7. *patugnagh-* 'frosty weather; freezing rain' (Badten 336), 'freezing falling snow' (Walunga 21). PE V B *patug-* 'frost or ice forming a crust', CSY VN D *-nar-* 'something that causes V-ing', related to PE VV D *-nar-* 'be such as to or -able'.

8. *pightughpag-* 'heavy drifting snow' (Badten 350).[32] PE N B *pirtur-* 'snowstorm', PE NN D *-pag-/-vag-* 'big or much'.

9. *pightughrug-* 'light drifting snow' (Badten 350, VE 24). PE N B *pirtur-* 'snowstorm'. PE NN D *-dhug-* 'big (?)'.

10. *qanigllug-* 'heavy snow' (Silook 137, Walunga 20, Badten 386). PE N B *qanig-* 'falling snow', PE NN DIS *-llug-* 'bad'.

11. *qanigpag-* 'snow falling hard in large flakes' (Badten 386, VE 27). PE N B *qanig-* 'falling snow', PE NN D *-pag-/-vag-* 'big or much'.

12. *qanigraag-* 'intermittent or light but continuous snowfall' (Badten 386, VE 27). PE N B *qanig-* 'falling snow', CSY NN D *-raag-* probably related to the CSY VV IS *-raag-* 'to do some V-ing'.

13. *qanivleghagh-* 'light snow' (Walunga 20, Badten 387). PE N B *qanig-* 'falling snow', PE NN IS *-vlar-* 'a little', with entanglement with PY NN DIS *-vzherar-* 'a little (more)'

14. *qateghnagh-* 'white out' (Walunga 20); white out weather conditions (Badten 392). PE V B *qater-* 'be white or pale', CSY VN D *-nar-* 'something that causes V-ing', related to PE VV D *-nar-* 'be such as to or -able'.

15. *qetumla-* 'soft dirt or snow that one sinks into as he walks' (Badten 412), PE V B *qetut-* 'be soft and pliable', CSY VN D *-mla-* meaning unclear, also found in *aghpumla-* (see 5.1.).

16. *sighyag-* 'ice fog' (Walunga 20, 21, Badten 472); also fog-like condition from tiny snow or ice particles suspended in the air' (Badten 472). CSY V B *siigh-* 'for weather to clear up; for fog or blizzard to dissipate', CSY VN D *-yag-* of unclear meaning and analysis.

NOTES

1. I am aware of the fact that the term "Eskimo" is considered derogatory in Canada, although it is not necessarily considered objectionable in Alaska or Siberia. I will use "Eskimo" as a convenient cover term for all branches of the 'Eskimo language family', as the only truly inclusive alternative 'Inuit-Yupik-Sirenikski language family' is too unwieldy.

2. By "layman" I mean any person without any training in linguistics or anthropology.

3. Other indigenous peoples who are not primarily hunting and gathering, such as the Saami, who are traditionally reindeer herders, are also described as having interesting and elaborate technical vocabularies (Ryd 2001), but, as far as I can tell, the claim that the Saami do not have a general word for, say, "snow" or "ice" has not been made in the literature.

4. The latest survey of the well-known problems with a cross-linguistic definition of the term "word" is in Haspelmath (2010).

5. Not shown in the formula in (1) is the fact that a few postbases can occur after certain noun endings. This need not further concern us, and is discussed in de Reuse (1994a: 170–230).

6. The forms of the suffixes on the second line, and when quoted in isolation, are slightly simplified underlying forms.

7. Abbreviations used in the synchronic morphological analyses of CSY examples are the following:

AB	Absolutive case
APO	Appositional mood
CAUS	Causative
FUT	Future tense
IND	Indicative mood
INP	Intransitive participial mood
INT	Interrogative mood
LC	Locative case
N	Insert gloss of preceding noun base here
NEG	Negative
P	Plural
PROG	Progressive aspect
PROSP	Prospective aspect
PST	Past tense
RL	Relative (i.e., ergative or genitive) case
S	Singular
TM	Terminalis case
TR	Transitivizer
TRP	Transitive participial mood
V	Insert gloss of preceding verb base here
3S	Third-person singular subject
3P	Third-person plural subject
3S-3P	Third-person singular subject, and third-person plural object
1D-3P	First-person dual subject, and third-person plural object and so on with all persons and numbers.

8. (n) means: see number (n) among the CSY examples.

9. My take is that it is better to postulate a three-way distinction, until I am proved wrong by linguistically sophisticated native speakers, rather than refusing to make this (possibly spurious) distinction, because nonnative speaker linguists dislike it for theoretical reasons.

10. At this point I will continue using just the "internal syntax" term, even though the term PNC is more accurate.

11. This postbase also occurs in Examples 19.2, 19.10, and 19.14.

12. Nikolai Vakhtin, a linguist from St. Petersburg, and expert in CSY, suggested at the same Conference that *qanigpak* (also a lexeme, cf. Appendix 19.1) "would be the correct form."

13. Both Krupnik and Müller-Wille (2010: 391) and Cichocki and Kilarski (2010: 342–341) criticize Martin (1986) and Pullum (1989) for this position. Balanced linguistic criticism of Martin (1986) is in Kaplan (2003). Nevertheless, one should remain grateful to Martin (1986) for initiating a serious scholarly discussion of the issue. And while Pullum can maybe be criticized for his entertaining way of dealing with the issue, which trivialized it somewhat, the criticism in Cichocki and Kilarski (2010: 368–369) of his tone seems needlessly harsh.

14. I do not agree, however, with Sturm, p.c. quoted in Cichocki and Kilarski (2010: 343) who "maintains that English allows a comparable degree of characterization of snow textures and features as found in Iñupiaq." Following Krupnik and Müller-Wille (2010: 391), I agree that the Eskimo technical terminologies for weather phenomena tend to be somewhat more elaborate than the terms used by English speaking meteorologists and snow experts.

15. A subset of these lists, from four Eskimo varieties is reproduced in Cichocki and Kilarski (2010: 344–345).

16. It would be quite unrealistic to list all the unreliable lists of "Eskimo words for snow" available in the popular literature and on the internet.

17. The analysis is partly from Badten et al. (2008), partly from CED, but mostly my own. Translations of Russian glosses from Vakhtin and Emelyanova (1998) are by Igor Krupnik, p.c. Igor Krupnik, p.c., also points out that the Badten et al. (2008) dictionary was not compiled with the help of experts in snow phenomena. This is certainly correct, but the fact that Badten et al. (2008) incorporates information from texts, and from knowledgeable sources such as Walunga (1987) and Silook et al. (1983) should alleviate this problem.

18. Krupnik and Müller-Wille (2010:389) in the same Table 6.2., also count 59 terms for snow in the CSY of Chukotka, Russian Far East, taken from Vakhtin and Emelyanova (1998). Here they distinguish 12 terms for snow on the ground, 24 terms for falling snow, snowfall, no terms for snow on ice and water, 8 terms for snow forms, and 15 others, including derivatives. My own study of Vakhtin and Emelyanova (1998) reveals quite a few derived verbs as well as other non-lexemes, and words not referring uniquely to "snow." I refer to their terms in Appendix 19.1, if other authors provide them as well, but I have not added to Appendix 19.1 the few items in Vakhtin and Emelyanova (1998) which might be otherwise unattested lexemes.

19. Why our numbers are different must have to do with the fact that I count forms from Badten et al. (2008), which is supposed to include the forms from Walunga (1987).

20. Abbreviations used in this section are the following: B, Base; CED, Comparative Eskimo Dictionary, (Fortescue, Jacobson, and Kaplan [2010]); CSY, Central Siberian Yupik; D, "real" Derivational postbase; DIS, Postbase of the "internal syntax" used derivationally; IS, Postbase of the "internal syntax" (or PNC); N, Noun; NN, Noun to noun postbase; NV, Noun to verb postbase; PE, Proto-Eskimo; PI, Proto-Inuit; PY, Proto-Yupik; R, Root; V, Verb; VN, Verb to noun postbase; VV, Verb to verb postbase.

21. The table below indicates the correspondences between CSY graphemes (not historical correspondences), our transliteration of CED, and the original CED symbols, where they differ. A dash indicates a sound which does not exist in CSY.

Table 19.2 *Transliterations of the Comparative Eskimo Dictionary (CED)*

CSY	CED (transliterated)	CED (original)
—	*dh*	eth
e	*e*	schwa
g	*g*	gamma
gh	*r*	small capital R
ll	*ll*	slash-l
ng	*ng*	engma
r	*zh*	z-hachek

22. In order to derive the forms in the Absolutive singular, the form used in dictionary entries, first delete dashes; if you encounter a vowel *i, a,* or *u,* you have the dictionary form; if you do not encounter these vowels, perform one of the following three operations on what precedes the dash: change *-te* to *-n*, change *-g* to *k*, and change *-gh* to *q*.

23. The letter and number combinations in parentheses mean the following. The letters A, B, C, D, E refer to the Sections in Appendix 19.1, and the numbers refer to the numbered words under each Section of Appendix 19.1.

24. As Igor Krupnik, p.c. pointed out to me, most Eskimo languages also have a third general term, Proto-Eskimo **apute-* 'snow on the ground' (Fortescue, Jacobson, and Kaplan 2010: 40). This form, however, seems to be more prevalent in the Inuit branch, and does not occur as a separate stem in CSY, although it is certainly etymologically connected to the words *apenghaate-* and *apumeg-* (cf. Appendix 19.1).

25. In Badten et al. (2008), (Siberian) means that the word is attested only in Chukotka, Russian Far East.

26. The term *pightugh-* might well have the basic meaning 'snowstorm,' which it has in most Eskimo languages.

27. Thanks to Geoffrey Pullum, p.c., for pointing out this reference.

28. It should be noted that even in such lists, compiled by experienced Eskimologist linguists and anthropologists, one should be cautious about nonlexeme items (i.e. belonging to column (4) of Table 19.1) having crept in. In particular, some of the forms in the list by Tersis and Tavernier (2010: 415–425) should be rechecked as to their actual lexeme status.

29. The Eskimo word *iglu* (from Canadian Inuktitut) originally means '(semi-subterranean) house', not 'snow house' (Fortescue, Jacobson and Kaplan 2010: 123).

30. The first to point out the importance of words for "ice" in discussions of Eskimo words for "snow," seems to have been de Reuse (1994b). Then the issue was also taken up by Halpern (2010) and Kaplan (2003).

31. Sastrugi (a loanword from Russian) are irregular dips and ridges in snow formed by wind or other types of erosion.

32. Vakhtin and Emelyanova (1988: 24) have *pightughllag-* 'very strong snowstorm', which is most likely not a lexeme.

References

Badten, Linda W., Vera O. Kaneshiro, Marie Oovi, Christopher Koonooka, and Steven A. Jacobson. (2008). *St. Lawrence Island/Siberian Yupik Eskimo dictionary*. 2 vols. Fairbanks: Alaska Native Language Center, University of Alaska.

Birket-Smith, Kaj. (1936). *The Eskimos*. London: Methuen. [Original Danish edition Copenhagen 1927].

Boas, Franz. (1894). Der Eskimo-Dialekt des Cumberland-Sundes. *Mittheilungen der Anthropologischen Gesellschaft in Wien*, Band XXIV (Neue Folge, Vol. XIV). Vienna: Alfred Hölder, 97–114.

— (1911a). Introduction. In Franz Boas (ed.), *Handbook of American Indian languages*. Vol. 1. Washington, DC: Smithsonian Institution, 1–83.

— (1911b). *The mind of primitive man: A course of lectures delivered before the Lowell Institute, Boston, Mass., and the National University of Mexico, 1910–1911*. New York: Macmillan. [2nd revised edition, 1938].

— (1938). Language. *General anthropology*, edited by Franz Boas. Boston: D. C. Heath & Co., 124–145.

Cichocki, Piotr, and Marcin Kilarski. (2010). On 'Eskimo words for snow': The life cycle of linguistic misconception. *Historiographia Linguistica* XXXVII(3): 341–377.

Federico, Ronald C., and Janet S. Schwartz. (1983). *Sociology*, 3rd edn. Reading, MA: Addison-Wesley.

Fienup-Riordan, Ann, and Alice Rearden. (2012). *Ellavut. Our Yup'ik World & Weather: Continuity and change on the Bering Sea coast*. Seattle: University of Washington Press.

Fortescue, Michael, Steven A. Jacobson, and Lawrence Kaplan. (2010). *Comparative Eskimo dictionary, with Aleut cognates*, 2nd edn. Fairbanks: Alaska Native Language Center, University of Alaska.

Halpern, Mark. (2010). *The Eskimo snow vocabulary debate: Fallacies and confusions*. www.rules-of-the-game.com/lin003-snow-words.htm

Harrison, K. David. (2010). *The last speakers: The quest to save the world's most endangered languages*. Washington, DC: National Geographic.

Haspelmath, Martin. (2010). *The indeterminacy of word segmentation and the nature of morphology and syntax*. www.eva.mpg.de/lingua/staff/haspelmath/pdf/WordSeg mentation.pdf

Jacobson, Steven A. (1984). *Yup'ik Eskimo dictionary*. Fairbanks: Alaska Native Language Center, University of Alaska.

Johns, Alana. (2010). Inuit sea ice terminology in Nunavut and Nunatsiavut. In Igor Krupnik, Claudio Aporta, Shari Gearhead, Gita Laidler, and Lene Kielsen Holm (eds.), *SIKU: Knowing our ice: Documenting Inuit sea ice knowledge and use*. Dordrecht: Springer, 401–412.

Kaplan, Lawrence. (2003). Inuit snow terms: How many and what does it mean? In François Trudel (ed.), *Building capacity in Arctic societies: Dynamics and shifting perspectives*. Proceedings from the 2nd IPSSAS Seminar, Iqaluit, Nunavut, Canada: May 26–June 6, 2003. Montréal: Ciéra, Faculté des Sciences Sociales, Université Laval.

Kleinschmidt, Samuel. (1851). *Grammatik der grönländische sprache, mit theilweisem einschluss des Labradordialects*. Berlin: G. Reimer.

Krupnik, Igor. (2011). 'How many Eskimo words for ice?' Collecting Inuit sea ice terminologies in the International Polar Year 2007–2008. *The Canadian Geographer/Le Géographe Canadien* 55(1): 56–68.

Krupnik, Igor, and Ludger Müller-Wille. (2010). Franz Boas and Inuktitut terminology for ice and snow: From the emergence of the field to the "great Eskimo vocabulary hoax." In Igor Krupnik, Claudio Aporta, Shari Gearhead, Gita Laidler, and Lene Kielsen Holm (eds.), *SIKU: Knowing our ice: Documenting Inuit sea ice knowledge and use.*Dordrecht: Springer, 377–400.

Krupnik, Igor, and Winton (Utuktaaq) Weyapuk Junior. (2010). Qanuq Ilitaavut: 'How we learned what we know' Wales Inupiaq sea ice dictionary.In Igor Krupnik, Claudio Aporta, Shari Gearhead, Gita Laidler, and Lene Kielsen Holm (eds.), *SIKU: Knowing our ice: Documenting Inuit sea ice knowledge and use.* Dordrecht: Springer, 323–354.

Martin, Laura. (1986). 'Eskimo words for snow': A case study in the genesis and decay of an anthropological example. *American Anthropologist* 88(2): 418–423.

Nelson, Richard K. (1969). *Hunters of the northern ice.* Chicago: University of Chicago Press.

Oozeva, Conrad, Chester Noongwook, George Noongwook, Christina [sic] Alowa, and Igor Krupnik. (2004). *Watching ice and weather our way/Akulki, Tapghaghmii, Mangtaaquli, Sunqaanga, Igor Krupnik. Sikumengllu Eslamengllu Esghapalleghput.* Edited by Igor Krupnik, Henry Huntington, Christopher Koonooka, and George Noongwook. Washington, DC: Arctic Studies Center, Smithsonian Institution.

Pullum, Geoffrey K. (1989). The great Eskimo vocabulary hoax. *Natural Language and Linguistic Theory* 7: 275–281. [Reprinted in Pullum, Geoffrey K. 1991. *The great Eskimo vocabulary hoax and other irreverent essays on the study of language.* Chicago: University of Chicago Press, 159–171.]

de Reuse, Willem J. (1994a). *Siberian Yupik Eskimo: The language and its contacts with Chukchi.* Salt Lake City: University of Utah Press.

(1994b). Eskimo words for "snow", "ice", etc. *The Linguist List* 5/5. http://linguist list.org/issues/5/5–1293.html#1

(2006). Polysynthetic language: Central Siberian Yupik. In Keith Brown (ed.), *Encyclopedia of language & linguistics,* 2nd edn, Vol. 9. Oxford: Elsevier, 745–748.

(2009). Polysynthesis as a typological feature: An attempt at a categorization from Eskimo and Athabaskan perspectives. In Marc-Antoine Mahieu and Nicole Tersis (eds.), *Variations on polysynthesis: The Eskaleut languages.* Typological Studies in Language, 86. Amsterdam: John Benjamins, 19–34.

Robson, David. (2012–2013). 'Sno myth. *New Scientist* Vol. 216, Iss. 2896/2897 December: 72–73.

Ryd, Yngve. (2001). *Snö – En renskötare berättar.* (Snow: A reindeer herder tells.) Stockholm: Ordfront.

Schneider, Lucien. (1970a). *Dictionnaire esquimau-français du parler de l'Ungava.* Quebec: Les Presses de l'Université Laval.

(1970b). *Dictionnaire français-esquimau du parler de l'Ungava.* Quebec: Les Presses de l'Université Laval.

(1985). *Ulirnaisigutiit. An Inuktitut-English dictionary of Northern Quebec, Labrador and Eastern Arctic Dialects* (with an English-Inuktitut Index). Quebec: Les Presses de l'Université Laval.

Silook, Roger S., Elinor Oozeva, Grace Slwooko, Vera Kaneshiro, David Shinen, and Linda Badten. (1983). *St. Lawrence Island junior dictionary.* Anchorage: Materials Development Center, Rural Education, University of Alaska.

Steckley, John L. (2008). *White lies about the Inuit.* Peterborough, Ontario: Broadview Press.

Sturm, Matthew. (2009). *APUN: The Arctic snow.* Teacher's Guide. Fairbanks: University of Alaska Press.

Swadesh, Morris. (1939). Nootka internal syntax. *International Journal of American Linguistics* 9: 77–102.

(1946). South Greenlandic (Eskimo). In Harry Hoijer and Cornelius Osgood (eds.), *Linguistic structures of Native America.* Viking Fund Publications in Anthropology 6. New York: Viking Fund, 30–54.

Tersis, Nicole, and Pierre Taverniers. (2010). Two Greenlandic sea ice lists and some considerations regarding Inuit sea ice terms. In Igor Krupnik, Claudio Aporta, Shari Gearhead, Gita Laidler, and Lene Kielsen Holm (eds.), *SIKU: Knowing our ice: Documenting Inuit sea ice knowledge and use.* Dordrecht: Springer, 413–426.

Ullrich, Jan. (2011). *New Lakota dictionary: Lakhótiyapi-English/English-Lakhótiyapi.* Bloomington, IN: Lakota Language Consortium.

Vakhtin, Nikolai B. (2000). *Jazyk Sirenikskix Eskimosov (The old Sirenik language).* Munich: Lincom Europa.

Vakhtin, Nikolai B., and N. M. Emelyanova. (1988). *Praktikum po leksike eskimosskogo iazyka (Practical Aid to the Eskimo Lexicon).* Leningrad: Prosveshchenie Publishers.

Wales Inupiaq Sea Ice Dictionary/Kiŋikmi Sigum Qanuq Ilitaavut. (2012). Winton Weyapuk, Jr. and Igor Krupnik, compilers. Igor Krupnik, Herbert Anungazuk, and Matthew Druckenmiller, editors. Washington, DC: Arctic Studies Center: Smithsonian Institution.

Walunga, Willis. (1987). *St. Lawrence Island curriculum resource manual.* Gambell, AK: St. Lawrence Island Bilingual Education Center, Bering Strait School District.

Woodbury, Anthony C. (1981). *Study of the Chevak dialect of Central Yup'ik Eskimo.* PhD dissertation, University of California, Berkeley.

(1984). Eskimo and Aleut languages. In David Damas (ed.), *Handbook of North American Indians*, Vol. 5: *Arctic.* Washington, DC: Smithsonian Institution, 49–63.

(1994). Counting Eskimo words for snow: A citizen's guide; lexemes referring to snow and snow related notions in Steven A. Jacobson's (1984) Yup'ik Eskimo Dictionary. *LINGUIST List* 5.1239. http://linguistlist.org/issues/5/5–1239.html

(2003). The word in Cup'ik. In R. M. W. Dixon and Alexandra Y. Aikhenvald (eds.), *Word: A cross-linguistic typology.* Cambridge: Cambridge University Press, 79–99.

20   Language Shift in the Subarctic and Central Plains

Richard A. Rhodes

In much of the study of the phenomenon of language spread the focus has been on attempting to explain the distribution of languages at a particular attested time in history based on events in the remote and largely historically unattested past based on inferences from archeological data alone.[1] In recent work the present author and Johanna Nichols have been developing a broad-based approach to explaining language distribution by focusing first on language spreads attested within the historical period to inform our theorizing about spreads that took place in prehistory. One of our examples focuses on the various indigenous Algonquian speaking hunter-gatherer groups living in the general region of the Great Lakes of North America. In this chapter I will review how some of these groups have moved, expanded, and contracted into their present distribution over the last 500 years. I will show that every logically possible type of language spread is attested in this area, all but one involving only hunter-gatherers. In this area we find (1) migration into unoccupied territory, (2) migration with one population replacing another, and a number of spreads with intermingling populations both with (3a) migrators switching to the local language and (3b) with migrators language supplanting the local language, and finally there are instances of (4) languages moving without migration, i.e., classical language shift.

This chapter is organized into three general sections. In the first I will review the language spread history of the study area. In the second I will run through examples of each of the logically possible types of language spread out of the history. Because there are so many instances of language spread represented in the history, not all of them equally well documented, I will simply draw on the best understood examples of each type. Finally, in the third section, I will focus on the interaction of Cree and Ojibwe and suggest a way of looking at language spread between languages that are closely related.

The Great Lakes region of North America is unusually good for the study of language spread among hunter-gatherer populations because many of the details regarding which groups were speaking which languages in which places are available as part of an unusually rich and well-worked over historical record that covers a 350-year-long period thanks in no small part to the fur trade. Furthermore, the archaeology of the proto-historical period links specific prehistorical archaeological traditions in this general area directly to attested historical groups, making it possible to set a reliable baseline in spite of the complexities and disruptions associated with early contact. This level of historical attestation makes it possible to talk about the conditions associated with various language spreads and shifts in this general area with comparatively little speculation. Because the area is large and complex and was home to as many as 25 languages from 4 distinct families, we cannot cover all languages throughout the whole area, even in outline; therefore the discussion in this chapter will focus on the varieties of Cree and Ojibwe-Potawatomi in the area immediately around the Great Lakes and to the north and west. There are also varieties of Cree and Ojibwe spoken to the northeast of this area, but they have a somewhat separate history. I will mention them only as necessary. The linguistic neighbors of the Ojibwe-Potawatomi and Cree in the study area include the Algonquian languages Blackfoot, Gros Ventre, Menomini, Miami-Illinois, and Sauk-Fox-Kickapoo-Mascouten; the Siouan languages, Assiniboine-Dakota-Santee, and Winnebago; the Athabaskan languages, Chippewyan and Beaver; and the Iroquoian languages, Huron, Neutral, and the Five Nations languages. No attempt will be made to discuss any of these other languages beyond their interactions with the Cree and Ojibwe-Potawatomi. Figure 20.1 gives a family tree of the whole Algic family.

Let me digress briefly to point out that the languages called Cree and Ojibwe in the literature should more properly be called subfamilies within the Algonquian language family. Each is a complex of very closely related, but not all mutually intelligible varieties (*Ethnologue* 2006), with language splits that are fairly old. The deepest division in Ojibwe dates from AD 1200, when Potawatomi (Dumaw Creek culture) divided from the rest of Ojibwe (Denny, p.c.). The deepest Cree division is probably older, ca. AD 600 when the bearers of the Laurel culture (prehistoric Cree) arrive at Lake Nipissing, but there is no easy archaeological horizon there to say for certain. Some of these dialect/languages are separately named. For the Cree, these names include Montagnais, Naskapi, and Attikamek, none of which are in the study area. For the Ojibwe the named varieties are Algonquin, Nipissing Ottawa (also now often spelled Odawa), Chippewa, Saulteaux, and Potawatomi. Of these named varieties only the two dialects that call themselves Algonquin (Algonquin and Nipissing) are not in the study area. As implicit in the previous assertion, such names do not necessarily correlate with dialect/language boundaries, and most dialects/languages are not separately named. I will clarify the names as necessary. The Ojibwe subfamiliy is given in Figure 20.2.[2]

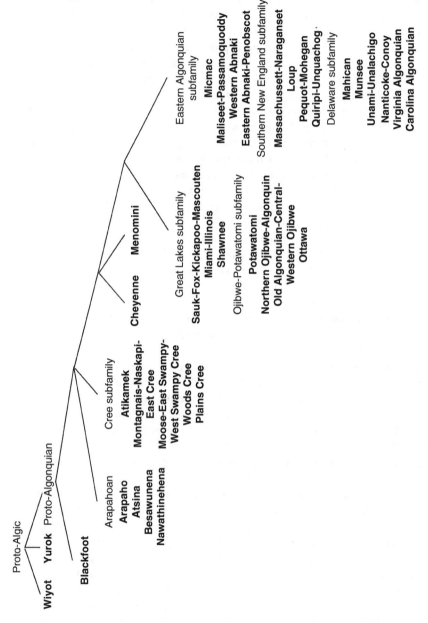

Figure 20.1 A family tree of the whole Algic family.

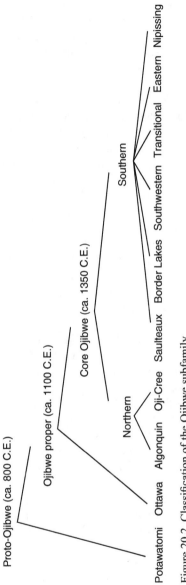

Figure 20.2 Classification of the Ojibwe subfamily.

Returning to the topic, history attests that during the first 250 years of the historical period (AD 1600–present) the speakers of all varieties of Cree and Ojibwe supported themselves primarily by subsistence hunting. Many followed a seasonal cycle of living on a lakeshore in the summer and heading into the bush in the winter to establish a winter camp. In the summer they exploited small game and fish and supplemented their diet by gathering. In the winter they hunted large game and returned to the summer residence only after the break up of the ice in spring. Many of the groups of Cree and Ojibwe participated in the fur trade, and speakers of the two southernmost varieties of Ojibwe, Ottawa, and Potawatomi also practiced some agriculture in the proto-historical period (squash, beans, potatoes, and maize). (Most groups of Ojibwes practiced a type of preagriculture, cultivating food and tobacco plants found growing wild and tapped maple trees to make sugar.) It was only after settlement on reserves (in Canada) and reservations starting in the mid-1800s, that subsistence agriculture became more widely practiced by those groups that found themselves settled in climates sufficiently warm for meaningful agriculture. But they did so only because they were under pressure from the respective white governments and because the loss of land base made it necessary. To this day all but the most urbanized Cree and Ojibwe men hunt.

The distribution of languages in the study area in the time frame of first contact has never been adequately worked out. Just as the first explorers were coming into the Great Lakes region in the early 1600s, the ripple effects of extensive contact between indigenous groups and Europeans to the east and south reached the Great Lakes in full force. The historical record is confusing to interpret because these ripple effects – massive epidemics and the pressures of new trade economies which made metal items readily available – resulted in extensive warfare and population movements. The largest recorded upheaval in the study region during that period was the Iroquois War between the Five Nations and the Huron and Neutral in what is now southern Ontario. The war raged between 1650 and 1700 and was sufficiently violent to cause the various Algonquian populations of the lower peninsula of Michigan allied to or friendly with the Hurons and Neutrals to abandon Michigan altogether and move north and/or west around the lakes. All of the reference materials prior to the 1980s reflect the post-Iroquois War locations for these languages. Volume 17 of the *Handbook of North American Indians (Languages)* has a reconstruction of the language map of the study area that is mostly correct. The relevant section is included here as Map 20.1.

Nonetheless, two general corrections need to be made. First, the eastern half of the region labeled Potawatomi was Ottawa speaking. The archaeology of the coast of Lake Huron north of Saginaw Bay connects it to the area north and east of Sault Ste. Marie (the Juntunen complex) into the 1500s, but not to the Dumaw Creek culture to its west on the northern shores of Lake Michigan.

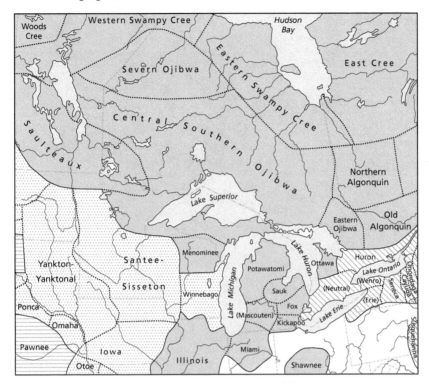

Map 20.1 Detail of language distribution in the Great Lakes area according to *Handbook of North American Indians* (*Languages*), Vol. 17 (Goddard [1996]).

Since Juntunen culture has been connected directly to historical Ottawa speakers (Fox 1990), this places the center of the Ottawa at Sault Ste. Marie, not down on the Bruce Peninsula, as the Handbook map suggests (Denny 1992).

Second, the map errs in having varieties of Ojibwe spread too far north and west for first contact. A more accurate picture of the area immediately north and west of the Great Lakes is one constructed directly from the historical record by Hamilton (1985), given in Map 20.2.

This map, too, suffers inaccuracies to the south (Hamilton was focused on the interactions to the west). The Menomini were between the Sioux (i.e., the Assiniboine-Dakota-Santee) and the Ojibwe in what is now eastern Wisconsin. The Ojibwe speaking groups, here labeled Chippewa, extended into the northern end of the lower peninsula of Michigan. These Ojibwe groups included both Ottawa and Potawatomi. The best guess at this point is that by 1650 there were at least five dialects/dialect groups of Ojibwe-Potawatomi: Potawatomi,

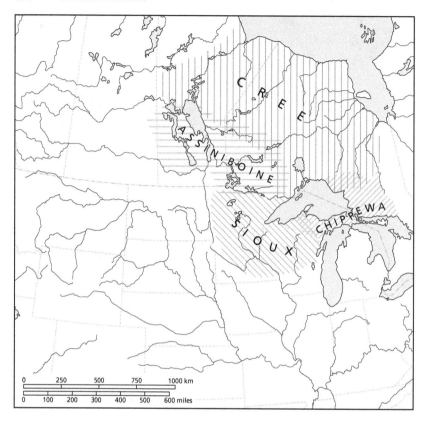

Map 20.2 Approximate distribution of the western Great Lakes tribes ca. 1650 (Hamilton [1985]).

Ottawa, Algonquin, a group that I'm calling Southern Ojibwe, and a group that I'm calling northern Ojibwe. The southern group gave rise to the dialect chain that stretches across the Subarctic Shield out Saskatchewan and down in to Minnesota and Wisconsin. It includes, most notably, Saulteax, Southwestern Ojibwe, and Eastern Ojibwe, as well as all the transitional varieties north and west of Lake Superior. The northern group gave rise to Oji-Cree, Saulteaux, and Southwestern Ojibwe. The baseline should look something like Map 20.3. All boundaries are approximate, particularly that between Northern and Southern Ojibwe. Also please note that the distinction between Eastern and Western Cree on this map is one that reflects the deepest division in the Cree subfamily, the eastern branch being Montagnais-Naskapi, and the variety known as East Cree being the easternmost edge of the western branch.

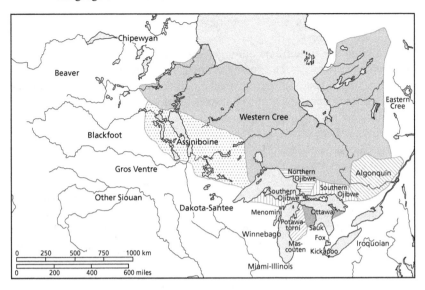

Map 20.3   Approximate distribution of languages around the Great Lakes ca. 1650 (following Hamilton [1985]).

As just mentioned, the incursions of the Iroquois War waged by the Five Nations against the Huron and Neutral to their west spilled over into the lower peninsula of Michigan, and the various groups there abandoned Michigan and moved south, west, and north. The exact details of the transition period are unknown. But after 1700 the Potawatomi, Ottawa, and some groups of Ojibwes returned to Michigan.

During this same period and continuing to ca. 1750, the Cree and Assiniboine pressed westward, pushing the Algonquian-speaking groups to their west, Blackfoot and Gros Ventre, westward. During this period Cree reached approximately its present northern extent (Ray 1974), displacing the Athabaskans to their north and northwest, Chipewyan and Beaver, respectively. In this case access to trade goods through the fur trade gave the Cree, in particular, the desire to control more beaver-rich territory to the northwest and the means to do it. Denny (1994) proposed that Blackfoot speakers shifted to Cree, but I think this is unlikely. The Cree-Blackfoot border is, and has long been, a short one. Where they have come in contact the Cree have moved north above the Blackfoot. The Assiniboine and the Gros Ventre have been between the Cree and the Blackfoot for most of the period of westward movement. My best guess is that these are all cases of population movement displacing the groups to the west in a chain reaction. Incidentally, the Assiniboines' choice 50 or so years earlier to ally themselves with the increasing wealthy and threatening Cree at the cost of enmity with their Dakota cousins to the south paid off handsomely.

Finally, in this time frame other groups of Ojibwes began pushing to the west and southwest, at the expense of the Dakota groups. The fur trade also played a crucial role in these expansions, in that differential access to trade goods gave the various groups both reasons to want to expand territory and weaponry to be more effective in warfare (Hamilton 1985). The likely distribution of languages by 1750 was as in Map 20.4, in which the position of languages around Lake Michigan is as reference maps prior to 1980 had it for precontact times.

The next hundred years in this area are again turbulent. People of European descent, both American born and immigrants from Europe, start showing up in this area in the late 1700s. By the early 1800s they begin pouring into the southern half of the study area. Starting with the Treaty of Greenville in 1795, the United States government brings increasing pressure on the various tribes in this area first to move west and, when that fails, to settle on reservations. The Canadians are about 50 years behind, but their solution is likewise to settle First Nations living on desirable land onto reserves. Both governments meet with mixed success. Because the Indians organize themselves in small bands, the white governments have to deal with many small polities. Some bands move west; a few were actually marched off at gunpoint. Many bands were moved onto reservations. In the first half of the 1800s some families moved from the US portions of Great Lakes territory to adjacent areas in Canada because Canada hadn't yet developed a hard-nosed policy. A surprising number found ways not to move at all, buying back small parcels of the land they were forced to sell to the government with their settlement monies.

The end result is that bands speaking various languages and/or dialects ended up on the same reserves/reservations, and the social networks linking bands on reserves/reservations with relatives settled on non-reservation land remain. In some real sense the languages still cover much of the same territory even though whites now fill most of the area. It wasn't until after World War II that language loss became a real matter of concern.

By the end of the nineteenth century, the languages had settled into the places where we see them in the surveys that fieldworkers started to make beginning in the 1950s. The extent of Cree and Ojibwe in the 1980s is as in Map 20.5.

What is immediately obvious is that Cree and Ojibwe have moved very far west, and Ojibwe has moved north, both in the Algonquin area to the east, and in the Oji-Cree area north of Lake Superior. As for Potawatomi, by 1980 it was so severely endangered that it makes no sense trying to map it. It was spoken only by individuals on most of the reserves and reservations around the

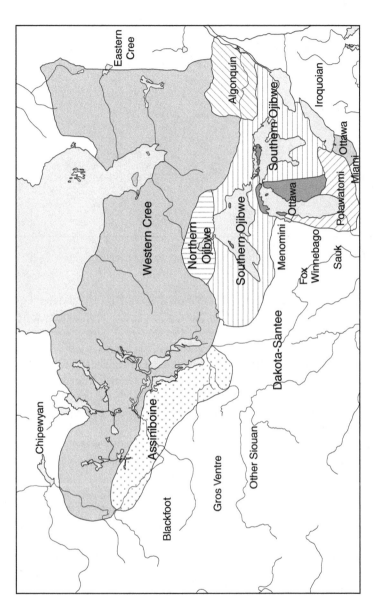

Map 20.4 Approximate distribution of languages around the Great Lakes ca. 1750 (after Tanner [1987] and Ray [1974]).

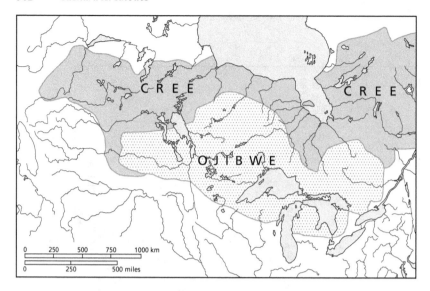

Map 20.5 Approximate distribution of Ojibwe and Cree ca. 1980.

southern Great Lakes mostly along side of Ottawa, as well as on the Menomini reservation. All Potawatomi speakers on those reserves and reservations were bilingual in the other Algonquian language (Rhodes 1992). There were also a few settlements with concentrations of Potawatomi speakers, one in Mayetta, Kansas, two in northern Wisconsin, and one on Grand Traverse Bay, in western Michigan. The distribution of the rest of the Ojibwe dialects is as in Map 20.6. (This is a major revision from Rhodes and Todd [1981], largely due to Valentine [1994], but not fully in agreement with his dialect groupings.) We will talk more about them later.

Now that we have seen the languages mapped at various stages, and seen how they changed territory, we are ready to talk about the mechanisms by which the various changes represented here take place.

In the period from 1650 to 1750, we see two types of language spread for which we can identify the mechanisms, one that accompanies migration into unoccupied territory, and one that accompanies the displacement of one group by another.

The spread of Potawatomi, Ottawa, and Southern Ojibwe into Michigan from 1700 to 1750 constitutes the first kind, movement into unoccupied territory, emptied by the Iroquois War as discussed earlier. The causes of such spreads are always the same. Whenever a barrier to the occupation of the land is removed, then the groups who are in the best position to occupy the territory move in, bringing their language with them. The barriers to occupation

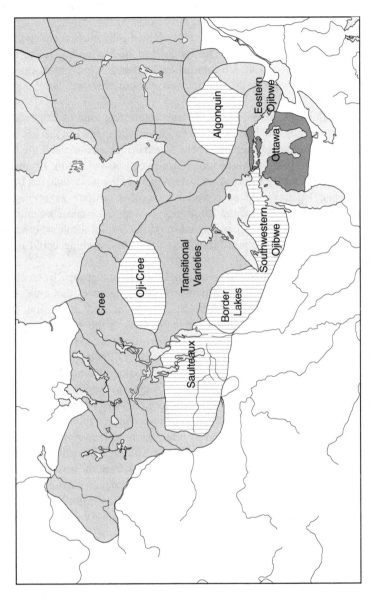

Map 20.6 Approximate distribution of Ojibwe dialects ca. 1980 (after Denny [1992] based on work ultimately published in Valentine [1994]).

can be of various sorts and removed in various ways. In this case the barriers were politics and safety. More commonly worldwide a group develops a technology that allows for the exploitation of previously uninhabitable or unreachable land, as, for example, in the case of the Polynesian spread. Yet another way a barrier to occupation is removed is by climate change, as in the case of Yokuts movement from the foothills of the Sierra into the central valley of California, ca. 1400, after the end of a 100-year drought. In any case, hunter-gatherers can spread by this mechanism without changing their approach to subsistence.

In any linguistic sense, this is the least interesting kind of language spread. People move into land bringing their language with them. But there is a point of significance for the archaeologist here. The particular example of the desertion and repopulation of Michigan took place over a 50-year span. At any serious time remove, looking solely at artifacts, a gap of 50 years would not be visible. An archaeologist would be tempted to look at artifact assemblages with distributions like those of the languages in Maps 20.3 and 20.4 and say that the Ottawas and Ojibwes had moved in on the Potawatomis who had driven out the Sauk-Fox-Kickapoo-Mascouten. In reality, nothing could be further from the truth.

The second kind of language spread, in which one group displaces another in a given territory, is exemplified in several places in this area. As mentioned earlier, the Cree/Assiniboine movement and expansion probably involves population replacement. But the facts of the expansion of Ojibwe into Dakota territory are a matter of historical record. The Ojibwe historian Warren (1984 [1885]) makes it clear that the Ojibwes pushed the Dakotas out. Subsequent historical work attempts to explain the mechanisms in detail (Hamilton [1985]), but we can afford to take a simple view. A militarily superior group with a reason to want more territory or to want to move can displace an inferior group, with the linguistic consequence that the languages follow their speakers. This kind of population replacement seems to be the assumed default case for the archaeologist, although it is not clear to me why that is. There are examples of all sorts of results from these initial conditions. The Romans, for example, conquered Gaul, but never moved in large numbers into the territory. Their language didn't take over until later, when they used Gauls (and other conquered people) extensively as military recruits. Alternatively, consider the Visigoths' conquest of northern Spain. They came in numbers, but they quickly became Ibero-Romance speakers. The Basques provide yet another possibility. They were conquered first by the Romans and later by the Visigoths, but never succumbed linguistically to either. It must be stressed that other conditions must be understood to interpret the relation between military or political success, migration, and language spread.

The third general class of language spread comes about where there are populations in contact. The contact can arise when migrations or population growth give rise to intermingled populations, or it can be with populations that are essentially stable geographically. In the study area there are instances of migrating groups resulting in intermingled populations. This happened particularly in the early reservation period in the mid- to late 1800s, mostly involving Ojibwe- and Potawatomi-speaking groups. On the reservations in Michigan and the adjacent areas of Ontario, the result was uniformly the same. Potawatomi speakers took up speaking Ottawa, which had become the "standard" Ojibwe language in that area. All but the most conservative families stopped speaking Potawatomi within a generation or two of arrival on these reservations.

What was the mechanism that determined which of the languages spread? In Rhodes (1982) I reported that all around the Great Lakes area there was a hierarchy of ethnic prestige that placed Cree over Ojibwe over Menomini over Potawatomi. In places where these populations mingle the more ethnically prestigious speak their own language. The ethnically less prestigious speak the language(s) of whichever groups above them they are in extensive contact with in addition to their ethnic language. At some point the languages of the lower prestige groups die. This is what happened to Potawatomis settled on reservations next to other Algonquian-speaking groups. The Potawatomi language seems to have been preserved only in those few places where its speakers were not mingled with speakers of other Algonquian languages. One can speculate about why Potawatomis were of low prestige. They were moved by the US government very early, and were probably in the weakest position when they were moved onto reservations with speakers of other languages. But they were already low prestige when Baraga put together his dictionary in the 1830s (published 1853) and wrote on the title page that Potawatomis used Ojibwe. (See Figure 20.3.)

Ascertaining exactly why any particular group falls where it does is beyond the scope of the present study. The fact remains that language spreads from high-prestige groups to low-prestige groups, independent of the means of subsistence. The facts of relative prestige in a mixed population, not to mention the mere fact of the existence of mixed populations, would almost certainly be invisible in any archaeological record. *Caveat fossor.*[3]

The next logical type of language spread is one in which the migrators mingle with local populations and language shifts to the migrators' language. In the study area this is happening with English, but I argue that this is just a special case of spread based on prestige. Because it does not involve groups consisting of only hunter-gatherers, let me pass over this example for the time being, except to report one mechanism by which the language shift happens.

A

DICTIONARY

OF THE

OTCHIPWE LANGUAGE,

EXPLAINED IN ENGLISH.

THIS LANGUAGE IS SPOKEN BY

THE CHIPPEWA INDIANS,

AS ALSO BY

THE OTAWAS, POTAWATAMIS and ALGONQUINS,

WITH LITTLE DIFFERENCE.

FOR THE USE OF

MISSIONARIES,

AND OTHER PERSONS LIVING AMONG THE ABOVE MENTIONED
INDIANS.

By the Rev. Frederic Baraga,

ROMAN CATHOLIC MISSIONARY AMONG THE OTCHIPWE INDIANS.

CINCINNATI, 1853.

PRINTED FOR Jos. A. HEMANN.

PUBLISHER OF THE „WAHRHEITSFREUND".

Figure 20.3 Title page from Baraga's Dictionary of the Otchipwe language
(1853).

Barbara Burnaby (p.c.) reports that in northern communities the shift to English can be quite sudden. These communities start with an increasing proportion of the population learning English in school – white teachers are sent onto the reserves – and by the ubiquity of television and radio. In time the communities reach a stable state of widespread bilingualism that can last for years. But at some point a cohort of teenagers decides to express its rebellion by refusing to speak the Indian language. The result is that their younger siblings no longer have full access to the Indian language and the language of the reserve shifts to speaking English in many social contexts, including in the home, and within a matter of only a few years the maturing of the half-generation of non-Indian-speaking younger siblings forces English in almost all contexts.

A variation on this type of language shift occurs when two populations in contact grow at differential rates and the language of the faster growing group grows with the group. It is reported that the recent northwestward spread of Plains Cree at the expense of Athabascans is happening in this way, but that is, at this point, only speculation based on Canadian census data.

The final logical type of language spread is that which takes place with populations in contact not significantly intermingled. An example of this type took place in the study area between Ottawa and Southern Ojibwe. We have good historical attestation that in the early 1800s the variety of Northern Ojibwe that would become Southwestern Ojibwe was the prestige dialect across the Ojibwe-speaking region which included the lower peninsula of Michigan. This documentation comes from three sources: Schoolcraft, the Indian agent in the 1830s; Baraga, who wrote most of his dictionary of Southwestern Ojibwe while living in an Ottawa-speaking area; and, most tellingly, a letter recently uncovered in the Notre Dame archives from Saenderl, the Austrian priest (who replaced Baraga when he was moved to the northern peninsula) to his bishop in Detroit. The relevant line from that letter is

Ich bemühe mich *Chippeway* zu erlernen, weil diese Sprache die Hof- und Diplomatische Sprache aller Indianer ist und das *medium communicationis* der verschiedenen Stämme. Ein gebildeter Indianer muß *Chippeway* sprechen, so wie in Deutschland ein Mann von Erziehung das Französische.

I am endeavoring to learn *Chippewa*, because this language is the official and diplomatic language of all the Indians and the *medium communicationis* of the different tribes. An educated Indian must speak Chippewa, just as in Germany, a man of good breeding must speak French.

At some point in the late 1800s Ottawa replaced Southwestern Ojibwe as the prestige dialect (Rhodes 1982), and by the time fieldwork began in that region in 1939 (Bloomfield [1958]), all the descendants of the Southern Ojibwe speakers were speaking Ottawa, with only a few remembered shibboleths from Southern Ojibwe. The one further notable thing about this language shift is that people from reserves that were settled primarily by Southern

Ojibwe speakers call their language Chippewa, not Ottawa. This is the source of the confusion in the title of Bloomfield (1958), *Eastern Ojibwe*, when the dialect reported is, in fact, Ottawa (Rhodes 1976).

I want to close this chapter with a series of observations on language contact phenomena between Algonquian groups. I will start by showing that the spread represented in Map 20.6 is a maturing spread. (Nichols and I have been proposing the spreads age in predictable ways. As they mature there is a diffusion of traits and then secondary spreads.) In the case of Ojibwe, the diffusion of traits has already begun. Contiguous communities of Ojibwe speakers have been spreading traits across dialects after the dialects are well differentiated.

Map 20.6 is based on the breakdown of the Ojibwe subfamily that was given in Figure 20.2. This follows Valentine (1994) in having three main divisions in Ojibwe proper, but differs in details. Some of those details have to do with language contact effects. Innovations have been spreading between adjacent dialects even where the divisions between dialects are deep. For example, Potawatomi developed a vowel reduction/deletion process in the early 1800s. In the late 1800s to early 1900s, the Ottawa on some reservations started reducing unstressed vowels as a substrate effect of Potawatomis switching to Ottawa. By the 1940s these vowels were all deleted on the southernmost reservations.[4] By the 1960s these vowels were all deleted on all Great Lakes area Ottawa reservations.[5] Early in this process, this innovation spread to Eastern Ojibwe, which in turn had only recently split from Nipissing. Valentine (2001: 3–5) makes the mistake of grouping Eastern Ojibwe with Ottawa on the basis of this vowel change, when it is lexically and morphologically much closer to Nipissing. Nipissing speakers, in turn, identify themselves as Algonquins and have borrowed traits from the "real" Algonquins to their north, since they were moved from their settlement at Oka on Georgian Bay to Maniwaki, Quebec just south of the Algonquin dialect area, in the late 1800s.

There are other phonological innovations, most of which have been spreading north (and west), the voicing of simplex obstruents being the most prominent. This precipitates a chain shift in which older hC becomes geminate CC. This is summarized in Example 20.1.

Example 20.1

(a) old obstruent system

    p t $\check{c}$ k vs. hp ht $h\check{c}$ hk

      s $\check{s}$ hs $h\check{s}$

(b) new obstruent system (effectively lenis-fortis)

    b d $\check{j}$ g vs. pp tt $\check{c}\check{c}$ kk

      z $\check{z}$ ss $\check{s}\check{s}$

The details of how this sound change plays out differs slightly from dialect to dialect, particularly in the treatment of simplex obstruents on word edges. Potawatomi does not voice word final simplexes and generally shortens geminates, especially word finally, so there is a loss of contrast in word final position making Potawatomi look like German or Russian in this regard. Algonquin (but not Nipissing) does not voice word initial simplexes, but as there are no word initial clusters, there is no merger. There are more traits being passed around, but these are the main examples and should suffice to make the point that even though the spread of Ojibwe is only a few hundred years old, it is already a maturing spread.

Now let us turn to the last point. Traits of the general sort just mentioned have been traded back and forth between Cree and Ojibwe for a very long time. This is not an accident. Almost any two Algonquian languages are close enough that people bilingual in two of them could legitimately be considered to be diglossic. Once there is a diglossia, then the possibility arises that borrowings (both lexical and structural) between the two languages could be seen as analogous to the so-called creole continuum. That is to say that the two languages involved in diglossia could be seen as analogous to basilect and acrolect, with speakers shifting between the two, or even just between traits of the two, as the communicative situation demands, and language shift can be almost unnoticeable in the short term in the shifting community. Thus, this situation is more like language creep than language shift. Cree and Ojibwe are a case in point. See Wolfart's (1973) study of a Cree-Ojibwe community on the edge of Ojibwe northward expansion. The area of his study is on the border between Oji-Cree (known as Severn Ojibwe in those days) and West Swampy Cree. As early as the 1960s fieldworkers were reporting the gradual morphing of Ojibwe into Cree as one moved north through this region (Rogers 1963).

The Cree-Ojibwe interface has always been interesting. Crees and Ojibwes have been influencing one another's way of speaking for a very long time. Various mentions have been made of some examples of this contact effect have been made for years (Rhodes 1985, 1988, 1989; Goddard 1994; Rhodes 2001; Pentland 2003). Three morphological innovations have passed from Cree to Ojibwe. One is the development of a classifier system; the second is the development of a past tense; and the third is the development of a predictive future as distinct from volitional future (Rhodes 1989). See Example 20.2.

Example 20.2

	Cree	Ojibwa	Miami	Fox	Shawnee	
(a)	classifiers	classifiers	—	—	—	
(b)	*kî(h)*- past	*kii(h)*- past	—	—	—	'past tense'
(c)	*ka-* ~ *ta-* ~	*ka-* ~ *ta-* ~	*kati* only	*wiih-* only	*weh-* only	'future'
	(ka)ci-/wî(h)-	*(ka)ci-/wii(h)*-				

The direction of influence can be seen from the fact that the closest relatives to Ojibwe lack the traits Ojibwe shares with Cree. In fact, these traits are unique to Cree in the family as a whole, and there is, therefore, reason to believe that these are ultimately substrate effects (contra Denny 1994) from the language of the Boreal Forest culture in contact with Cree during the early north- and eastward spread of Cree language and culture (following Denny's [1992] analysis).

The second set of influences is phonological (Rhodes 1989). They are given in Example 20.3. Again the influences are from Cree to Ojibwe, as shown by the closest relatives of Ojibwe. In the case of Example 20.3c the influence happened after Potawatomi split from the rest of Ojibwe.

Example 20.3

	Cree	Ojibwa	Miami	Fox	Shawnee
(a)	PA *$e > i$	PA *$e > i$	PA *$e > e/i$	PA *$e > e$	PA *$e > e$
(b)	PA *$V\# > \emptyset$	PA *$V\# > \emptyset$	PA *$V\# > V\#$	PA *$V\# > V\#$	PA *$V\# > V\#$
(c)	PA *$Cy > C$	PA *$Cy > C$	PA *$Cy > Cy$	PA *$Cy > Cy$	PA *$Cy > Cy$
(d)	PA *$nC > hC$	PA *$nC > hC/nC$	PA *$nC > nC$	PA *$nC > C$	PA *$nC > C$
		Oji-Cree hC			
		Ojibwe nC			

Finally, there has been considerable vocabulary swapped between Cree and Ojibwe as well. In the case of lexical items the trade has been in both directions. Pentland (2003) recently presented a list of words more sophisticated than the list of 40 some odd words in Rhodes (1989), which includes the time frames in which the borrowings occurred. A number of Pentland's forms can be found in Rhodes (1989, 2001) and Goddard (1994), which he does not credit, but Pentland's list is better organized, so we cite it here.

While Rhodes (1989) argued for borrowing based on differences in cognates with Miami, Fox, and Shawnee, the arguments for the borrowed status in Pentland's presentation are all of the form: language X has the reflex of some proto-segment, proto-cluster, or proto-morpheme appropriate to language Y, but not to language X. His list is given in Examples 20.4–20.11.

Example 20.4

Very early Ojibwa loans in Cree-Montagnais (Mt = Montagnais, East Cree in the maps above)

(a) PC *mi·cim*, Mt *mi·čim* (not **mi·cihp*) 'food': O *mi·čim* < PA **mi·tye?mi*

(b) PC *e·yikohk*, MC *e·likohk*, etc. (not **e·tikisk*) 'so big': O *e·nikokk* < PA **e·θekexkwi*

(c) PC *niya·nan*, SwC *niya·nan*, MC *niya·lan*, wMt *niya·yan* (not **na·tan*) 'five': O *na·nan* < **nya·lan* < PA **nya·θanwi,* cf. Ar *yo·θón*

(d) PC *oto·nipiy*, dim. *oco·nipi·s* 'tullibee (fish)' (not **oto·yipiy*): O *oto·nipi·* < PA **weto·lepye·wa*

(e) PC *kistika·n*, Mt *čistika·n* (not **kistokan*) 'field': O *kittika·n* < PA **ke?twika·ni*

Most of the forms in Example 20.4 are straightforward. The most difficult form is PC *niyānan*. It was first explained in Goddard (1994: 196–197). Two sound changes are crucial. First, after Cree split off, the remaining languages merged *θ and *l as l. Since the medial consonant in all Cree dialects (with one exception to be explained in the text that follows) show the reflex of Proto-Cree *l, the forms must have been borrowed from Ojibwe early. This is consistent with the second pattern of reflexes. Proto-Cree dropped post-consonantal *y. Proto-Ojibwe retained post-cononantal *y, as shown by Potawatomi, e.g., *ginya* 'it is sharp'. But Ojibwe proper lost post-consonantal y under influence of Cree, after undifferentiaed Cree had borrowed the word for 'five' from Ojibwe. That explains all the Cree forms except Plains Cree, which has a medial n instead of y, showing that the Plains from must have been borrowed through Swampy Cree.

Example 20.5

Early Cree loans in Ojibwa
(a) O *kaškipita·kan* 'tobacco pouch': C *kaskipita·kan* 'fire-bag' < PA *$kaškipi\theta a·kana$ (?)
(b) O *ka·skattay* 'parchment hide': C *ka·hkahtay* (Woods *ka·skahtay*) < PA *$ka·skah\theta aya$
(c) O *(ta)ta·ttapi·* 'he goes fast': C *(ta)ta·stapi·w* < PA *$\theta api·wa$ (reduplicated, as if **$ta·\mathit{?}tap$-;
        cf. Western Abenaki *nanapi* 'fast', Unami Delaware *láhpi*)

Example 20.6

Late prehistoric period (1000–1600 A.D.), Ojibwa loans in Cree
(a) C (east) *ni·swa·s* 'seven': O *ni·šwa·sswi* < PA *$nyi·šwa·(ši)$ 'seven' + *$(ta)h\theta wi$ 'so many'
        Old Woods C *ni·swa·sik*, Mt *ni·šwa·šč* < PA *$nyi·šwa·ši$ + *-ka*
        PC *te·pakohp* (etym. unknown, perhaps "enough (skins) for a blanket")
(b) C (east) *ota·mihkan*, Mt *uta·mihkan* 'jaw': O *ota·mikkan* < PA *$weta·\mathit{?}mexkani$

The forms in Example 20.6a were discussed in Rhodes and Costa (2003). Number word borrowing is quite extensive in Algonquian.

Example 20.7

Late prehistoric period, Cree loans in Ojibwa
(a) O *oštikwa·n* (most dialects) 'head': C *ostikwa·n*, Mt *uštikwa·n* < PA *$we\mathit{?}tekwa·ni$
(b) O *oskattik* (Nip., Alg.), *okkattik* 'forehead': C *oskahtik*, Mt *uskahtikw* < PA *$we\theta kantekwi$
(c) C (west) *kahkiyaw*, Atik. *kaskina*, Mt *kasčinuw* 'all': O *kakkina*

The form in Example 20.7c requires some discussion. Reflexes of this word are found only in Ojibwe and Cree. It is more likely that the direction was Cree to Ojibwe, although Pentland (2003) has it the other way around. Pentland also reconstructs PA *kaxkinawi*, although this author thinks that it is highly unlikely to go back to PA. Potawatomi has *jayék* 'all' which is a reflex of the morpheme used by the rest of the Great Lakes subfamily (see Figure 20.1). There are a large number of morpheme reflexes shared only by Cree and Ojibwe. The sheer number of them suggests that innovations (including substrate borrowings) in one or the other language might be shared between them. The mere fact that Ojibwe shares so much with Cree lexically in comparison to the other Great Lakes subfamily only supports that view.

Example 20.8

Early contact period (AD 1600–1750), Ojibwa loans in Cree
- (a) C *pa·skisikan* (all dialects), Mt *pa·sčikan* 'gun': O *pa·škisikan* < pseudo-PA *pa·škesikani*
- (b) C *iskote·wa·pow, -poy,* Mt *iškutua·puy* [!] 'fire-water, liquor': O *iškote·wa·po* < pseduo-PA *eškwete·wa·powi*
- (c) C *ko·hko·s,* Mt *ku·hku·š* 'pig': O *ko·kko·šš* < French *cocoche*
- (d) C *asapa·p* 'string, twine': O *assapa·p* < PA *aʔlapa·pyi*
- (e) C (east) *mahkate·w* 'gunpowder': O *makkate·* < PA *maxkate·wi* 'ember, charcoal'
- (f) C (east) *pi·wa·nak* 'gunflint': O *pi·wa·nak* < PA *pi·wa·(n)θakwa*

These forms are understood to have been borrowed or coined very early when contact was limited and then moved west and north through trade networks.

Example 20.9

Early contact period, Cree loans in Ojibwa
- (a) O *ma·višta·nišš,* wMt *ma·višča·niš* 'sheep': C *ma·nista·n, ma·nisca·nis* < PA *mya·leʔθa·na*

Logically, Example 20.9a should be like the forms in 20.8, where the first contact was further east and south but the *št* cluster is found only in Cree borrowings into Ojibwe.

Late loans spread dialect by dialect, so they tend to be found in just one or two dialects.

Example 20.10

Fur-trade period (AD 1750–1870), Ojibwa loans into Cree dialects
- (a) PC *kihci-mo·hkoma·n* 'American': O *kičči-mo·kkoma·n* < PA *keʔti* 'big', *mo·hkwema·ni* 'knife'
- (b) PC *taso·ye·w,* Mt *taso·le·w, tiso·le·w* 'he catches him in a (steel?) trap': O *tasso·na·t* < PA *taʔθo·le·wa,* cf. Men *taʔnone·w*
- (c) PC *pihkihkoma·n,* Mt *pihčihkuma·n,* but also PC *piskihkoma·n* 'jack-knife': O *piskikkoma·n* < pseudo-PA *peskehkwema·ni*
- (d) SwC *ase·ma·w* 'tobacco': O *asse·ma·* irr. from PA *θeʔθe·ma·wa,* cf. PC *ciste·ma·w,* cf. Men *nɛʔnema·w,* Meskwaki *nese·ma·wa.*
- (e) archaic PC *mihtimo·ye·w* 'old woman' (Lacombe 1874): O *mintimo·ye·nʔ* < PA *metemwa* + Oj. dimin.
- (f) Moose *onikam* 'portage': O *onikam* < PA *wenikaʔmi,* cf. PC *onikahp*

The Ojibwe-ism (*gichi-*)*mookomaan* (Example 20.10a) is also found in Meskwaki. In Example 20.10b and 20.10d the Menominee forms guarantee the PA reconstruction of the cluster *$?\theta$, which should show up in Cree as *st*. Possibly the most interesting form is the archaic Plains form in (Example 20.10e), which is Ojibwe in formation, but pronounced as if it were Cree. This phenomenon is also found in the mixed language Métchif as reported in Rhodes (2009).

Example 20.11

Fur-trade period, Cree loans in various Ojibwa dialects

(a) O (Nip., Oji-Cree) *mitone·ntam* 'he contemplates': C *mitone·yihtam* < PA *meθwene·lentamwa*

(b) O (Nip., Oji-Cree) *pikkoči·ssi* 'blackfly': C *pihkoce·siw, -e·si·s* < PA *penkwetye·hsiwa*

(c) O (Sault.) *mištatim* 'horse': C *mistatim* < PA *me?θaθemwa* 'big dog'

(d) O (Sault.) *mittanask* 'badger': C *mistanask* < PA *me?θakaxkwa* (cf. 'woodchuck', see (f) below)

(e) O (Oji-Cree) *pi·ssim* 'sun': C *pi·sim* (not PA – C loan from a pre-Algonquian language)

(f) O (Oji-Cree) *wi·našk* 'woodchuck': C *wi·nask* < PA *wi·naθkwa*

Two dialects of Ojibwe, Saulteaux and Oji-Cree, moved into areas where Cree was formerly spoken (and Blackfoot and then Assiniboine before that). Notice that these are where there are the most recent loans from Cree into Ojibwe, as in Example 20.11.

Although the exact details of population movement in the areas where Ojibwe is encroaching on Cree are not well known, we do know that Saulteaux, at least, involves some population movement. Looking at the linguistic innovations that differentiate each of these dialects from the neighboring Ojibwe dialect, we can perceive that Oji-Cree bears more Cree traits than Saulteaux, suggesting that Oji-Cree is showing more substrate effects reflecting more recruitment of Cree speakers than Saulteaux. This would accord with the fact that Oji-Cree speakers refer to themselves as Cree, even though the language they speak is clearly a variety of Ojibwe, parallel to the ethnic identification of Southern Ojibwe speakers as Chippewa when the language they speak is Ottawa.

Recent work on the mixed language, Métchif (Rhodes 2009), sheds some light on the relationship between Plains Cree and Saulteaux, which is more complex than we have the time to fully explore here. In short Métchif is a mixture of Plains Cree and French, clearly a product of language contact, but the Cree of Métchif differs from Plains Cree in that it shows considerably more substrate influence from Ojibwe, and this reflects points made in Métchif oral history about who the native ancestors of the Métis actually were.

In conclusion, to say why a particular shift took place, requires a more sophisticated and detailed account than is generally available based on a simple comparison of the archaeological record with a language map, no less for hunter-gatherers than for agriculturalists. In particular, mechanisms of shift in the study area of this chapter include ones that are invisible to current archaeological methods. They involve bilingualism limited to related languages, i.e., de facto diglossia, and long-term stable bilingualism. When a diglossic or bilingual system is stressed, how can we predict which language will survive? If we fail to be able to answer that question, we fall into the trap captured in the famous quote generally attributed to the influential stage designer Lee Simonson: "Any event, once it has occurred, can be made to appear inevitable by a competent historian." Our theories of language shift must take into account factors less tangible than simple access to resources.

NOTES

1. This chapter was written for presentation and is based on material intended for a chapter in a larger written work on language spread being developed by the present author and Johanna Nichols. In its current form this paper should be considered preliminary. Some of the ideas appearing here have been jointly developed between Prof. Nichols and myself. She is in no way responsible for the detailed content of this chapter, but has contributed significantly to the general thinking behind it. She deserves some of the credit but none of the blame.

2. This classification largely follows Valentine (1994). Valentine, however, distinguishes the separate dialects within the Transitional group (formerly called Central Ojibwe in Rhodes and Todd [1981]). Because the whole region encompassing Saulteaux, Border Lakes, Southwestern, and the Transitional group is a dialect continuum, little is gained for the purposes of this study by factoring out North of Superior, Berens River, and Northwest. All, like Nippising in the east, show contact phenomena with the adjacent Northern branch varieties.

3. Let the digger beware.

4. There is internal evidence in Bloomfield (1958) that at least some of the reduced vowels which are in every form in the book were resupplied by Bloomfield. The evidence comes from forms with morphological restructurings that only make sense if the vowels were actually deleted. The resupplying of the vowels probably happened as early in the process as at the initial transcription phase. Trager was a student taking the field methods class from which Bloomfield (1958) was written, and we have Trager's notebook covering about half of the material in the ultimate publication. Trager's book has the reduced vowels neatly transcribed throughout, just as they appear in Bloomfield (1958). This only makes sense if, knowing where the vowels should be, Bloomfield resupplied them for the class while writing transcriptions on the board for students to copy.

5. There is a small group of Ottawas in Oklahoma who moved there early in the reservation period losing contact with the rest of the Ottawa speech community and their Ottawa did not participate in this sound change.

References

Baraga, Fredrick. (1853). *A dictionary of the Otchipwe language.* Cincinnati: Jos. A. Hermann.

Bloomfield, Leonard. (1958). *Eastern Ojibwa: Grammar, texts, and word list.* C. Hockett, ed. Ann Arbor: University of Michigan Press.

Denny, J. Peter. (1992). The entry of the Algonquian language into the boreal forest. Paper read to the Canadian Archeological Association, London, Ontario, May 1992.

(1994). Why is there so little substrate beneath Cree-Montagnais? *Algonquian and Iroquoian Linguistics* 19(2): 17.

Fox, William A. (1990). The Odawa. In Chris J. Ellis and Neal Ferris (eds.), *The archeology of southern Ontario to AD 1650.* Occasional Publication of the London Chapter, Ontario Archeological Society, 457–473.

Goddard, R. H. Ives. (1994). The west-to-east cline in Algonquian dialectology. In William Cowan (ed.), *Actes du 25e Congrès des Algonquinistes.* Ottawa: Carleton University, 187–211.

(ed.) (1996). *Languages,* Vol. 17. *Handbook of North American Indians.* Washington, DC: Smithsonian Institution.

Hamilton, Scott. (1985). Competition and warfare: Functional versus historical explanations. *The Canadian Journal of Native Studies* 5(1): 93–113.

Pentland, David. (2003). Interaction between Cree and Ojibwa: A historical perspective. Paper presented to WSCLA, March 8.

Ray, A. J. (1974). *Indians in the fur trade: Their role as hunters, trappers and middlemen in the lands southwest of Hudson Bay 1660–1870.* Toronto: University of Toronto Press.

Rhodes, Richard A. (1976). A preliminary report on the dialects of Eastern Ojibwa-Odawa. In Wm. Cowan (ed.), *Papers of the Seventh Algonquian Conference.* Ottawa: Carleton University, 129–156.

(1982). Algonquian trade languages. In Wm. Cowan (ed.), *Papers of the Thirteenth Algonquian Conference.* Ottawa: Carleton University, 1–10.

(1985). The consequential future in Cree and Ojibwa. *International Journal of American Linguistics* 51: 547–548.

(1988). On the classification of Central Algonquian. Paper read at the 27th Algonquian Conference. Hull, Quebec, October 1988.

(1989). The Cree connection. Paper read at the 28th Algonquian Conference. Washington, DC, October 1989.

(1992). Language shift in Algonquian. *International Journal of the Sociology of Language* 93: 87–92.

(2001). Some implications of Algonquian number word borrowings. Paper read at the 33rd Algonquian Conference. Berkeley, CA, October 2001.

(2009). Ojibwe in the Cree of Métchif. In K. Hele and R. Darnell (eds.), *Papers of the Thirty-ninth Algonquian Conference.* London, Ont.: University of Western Ontario, 569–580.

Rhodes, Richard A., and David Costa. (2003). The history of Algonquian number words. In Blair A. Rudes and David J. Costa (eds.), *Essays in Algonquian, Catawban and Siouan linguistics in memory of Frank T. Siebert, Jr.* Memoir 16 Algonquian and Iroquoian Linguistics. Winnipeg: Algonquian and Iroquian Linguistics, 181–215.

Rhodes, Richard A., and Evelyn M. Todd. (1981). Subarctic Algonquian languages. In June Helm (ed.), *Handbook of North American Indians*, Vol. 6: *Subarctic*. Washington, DC: Smithsonian Institution, 52–66.

Rogers, Jean H. (1963). Survey of Round Lake Ojibwe phonology and morphology. Ottawa. *National Museum of Canada Bulletin* 194: 92–154.

Tanner, H. H. (1987). *Atlas of Great Lakes Indian history*. Norman: University of Oklahoma Press.

Valentine, J. Randall. (1994). *Ojibwe dialect relationships*. PhD thesis, University of Texas, Austin.

Valentine, J. R. (2001). *Nishnaabemwin reference grammar*. Toronto: University of Toronto Press.

Warren, William W. (1984). *History of the Ojibway people*. St. Paul: Minnesota Historical Society.

Wolfart, H. Cristoph. (1973). Boundary maintenance in Algonquian: A linguistic study of Island Lake, Manitoba. *American Anthropologist* 75: 1305–1323.

21   Uto-Aztecan Hunter-Gatherers

Jane H. Hill

21.1   Introduction

Evans and McConvell (1998) and McConvell (2001) proposed that long-term hunter-gatherer adaptations in Australia required the capacity for both "upstream" movements toward the center of the continent, into relatively empty territory, drawn by improving climatic conditions in the interior, and "downstream" movements back toward the edges of the continent, into populated territory, when conditions in the interior deteriorated. They argued that these phases of adaptation should be reflected in hunter-gatherer languages, especially by an increase in substratum phenomena in languages in a "downstream" phase. In Hill (2002, 2004) I suggested that similar dynamics can be identified in western North America. The Takic and Numic subgroups of Northern Uto-Aztecan (NUA) have often been thought to illustrate these contrasting processes, with Takic speakers spreading downstream into populated areas of Southern California between 3,000 and 1,500 years ago, while Numic speakers spread upstream across the relatively unpopulated Great Basin between 2,000 and 1,000–700 years ago. If this simplified prehistory is roughly correct, we would expect the Takic languages to show more evidence of substratum influence than the Numic languages.

To explore this hypothesis, I look at lexical and typological evidence, revisiting Miller's (1984) suggestion that Takic was a more lexically diverse group than Numic, consistent with the hypothesis of greater substratum influence in that subgroup. I explore the lexical diversity in more detail, extending Bright and Bright's (1976 [1969]) study of substratum influence in Takic. The results suggest that Takic and Numic languages exhibit roughly equal percentages of non-Uto-Aztecan lexicon, a finding that is not consistent with the hypothesis of greater substratum influence in Takic. Finally, I examine typological diversity in Takic and Numic, using the the WALS inventory of typological features (Haspelmath et al. 2005). The two subgroups exhibit very similar levels of typological variability, and are similar in the proportion of rare versus common realizations of typological variables. Again, the hypothesis that Takic should show more evidence of substratum influence is not supported.

These results suggest several possible conclusions: (1) the Evans-McConvell hypothesis about the linguistic effects of the two phases of hunter-gatherer movements may be over-simplified; (2) different language-ideological and other factors in North American versus Australian populations may mean that their model does not work for North America, at least in this case; or (3) the simplified version of Takic versus Numic prehistory is wrong.

First, I review the language groups and their prehistory. Second, I summarize the Evans-McConvell proposal, along with other theories about the relationship between types of language change and diversity and the social/geographical environments of language spread. Third, I present the methods used in the present chapter. Finally, I give results and discussion.

21.2   The Takic and Numic Languages and Their Prehistory

21.2.1   *Languages and Sources*

Takic and Numic are branches of Northern Uto-Aztecan (NUA). The Takic languages discussed here include three members from one sub-branch, Cupan (Bright and Hill 1967), consisting of Cahuilla, Cupeño, and Luiseño. Three other Takic languages, Gabrielino, Serrano, and Kitanemuk, share some innovations but have not been demonstrated to constitute a single branch of Takic.[1]

The three branches of the Numic subfamily are each composed of a language spoken in California and a language of the Great Basin (and, in the case of Southern Numic, the Colorado Plateau). Western Numic includes Mono in California and Northern Paiute in the Basin. For the Central Numic languages, Tümpisa Shoshone (Panamint) is spoken in California; the Great Basin language is the immense dialect continuum of Shoshone, extending east to Comanche, spoken by Shoshone who became horse nomads in the mid-eighteenth century. Southern Numic includes Kawaiisu in California, and a dialect continuum comprising, from west to east, Chemehuevi on both sides of the Colorado River in California and Arizona, Southern Paiute, and Ute. Like the Comanche, the Ute were horse nomads in the historic period.[2]

Takic and Numic languages both occupy linguistically homogeneous regions surrounded by linguistically complex peripheries. Hinton (1991) found several areal features linking Takic and Yuman languages, which border Takic on the south and east. In the northwest the boundary language is Chumashan, in the northeast, Yokuts. Also to the east are the Southern Numic languages Kawaiisu and Chemehuevi. Bright and Bright (1976 [1969]) found minimal evidence of loans from any of the existing languages of the Takic periphery, and suggested that the Takic lexical substratum attested to languages that have long been extinct.

The languages of the Numic periphery in California include (from south to north) Yokuts, Sierra Miwok, Maidu (probably all distantly related in Yokutian [Callaghan 1997]) and Achomawi-Atsugewi. To the north, the Numic frontier borders on Chinookan, Sahaptian, and Interior Salishan. On the Plains to the east, contacts included Blackfoot, Arapaho, and Cheyenne in the Algonquian family, Siouan languages such as Lakota, and Kiowa. To the south are the various Puebloan languages, including Hopi, Zuni, Keresan, and Tanoan. In the late prehistoric period Apache and Navajo were also in this region. Studies of loans into Numic are few; Loether (1997) has examined loans between Western Mono and Yokuts and Sierra Miwok (deeply related to one another in Yokutian [Callaghan 1997]). I have identified loans from Yokuts into Western Mono, but also into Proto-Southern Numic.[3]

Several languages believed to be Takic were extinct by the early twentieth century, and it is likely that the same is true for Numic. Both Takic and Numic languages were internally diverse, although the sources attest only a very limited range of the known dialectal variation. In Takic, Serrano-Kitanemuk is believed to have had four dialects, Cahuilla had three, and even tiny Cupeño had two varieties (Jacobs 1975). Numic diversity included four major dialect divisions in Mono (Lamb 1958b). Tümpisa Shoshone and neighboring varieties of Western Shoshone (Miller et al. 1971) also had substantial dialect diversity, although Kawaiisu is said to have been homogeneous (Miller 1986). Diversity in the Great Basin varieties of Numic is reported to be low. However, the published sources hint that at least phonological and lexical diversity are confounding efforts to develop revitalization materials for these languages.

21.2.2   What Kind of 'Hunter-Gatherers' Are the Numic and Takic Peoples?

Bellwood (2005) distinguishes three types of hunter-gatherers. The first group includes the "niche" hunter-gatherers of Africa, Asia, and perhaps Siberia: populations such as the Hadza of Tanzania and the Agta of the Philippines who are surrounded by cultivators (or, in the Siberian case, pastoralists) and trade regularly with them. The second group includes the "unenclosed" hunter-gatherers of Australia, the Andaman Islands, and the Americas. Until very recently, most scholars would have placed speakers of Numic and Takic in this second group. However, I believe that they should be classified in Bellwood's Group 3: hunter-gatherers who descend from former cultivators.

Bellwood (1997) suggested that the geography of the Uto-Aztecan languages is largely the result of a Neolithic spread originating in a population of primary cultivators located within Mesoamerica. I have identified three types of linguistic evidence in support of Bellwood's proposal: a lexicon for maize cultivation and processing reconstructed to Proto-Uto-Aztecan (PUA) (Hill 2001), a small set of loans within this maize vocabulary that I believe originate in Proto-Western Otomanguean and were adopted by PUA communities in central Mexico about 4,500 years ago (Hill 2012), and a larger set of loans between PNUA and Proto-Kiowa-Tanoan (PKT), exchanged between about 3,500 and 3,000 years ago (Hill 2008). These include loans in PKT of maize vocabulary of PNUA origin, and PNUA words of PKT origin for several of the major economic plants of the Colorado Plateau (Hill 2003, 2008). I believe the PNUA were probably the group known archaeologically as the Western Basketmaker II, the earliest cultivators on the Colorado Plateau, appearing there by about 3,500 years ago (Matson 1991, 2003; LeBlanc 2003). If this is the case, then the NUA hunter-gatherers, including Takic, Tübatulabal, and Numic-speaking peoples, represent examples of "agricultural regression" (Balée 1994).

Bellwood (2005: 38) observes of the Numic peoples that they "still have give-away characteristics of their remote agricultural ancestry, such as pottery-making, irrigation of stands of wild plants, and farmer-like attitudes to resource ownership." I have reviewed the linguistic, archaeological, and ethnohistoric evidence for cultivation among Numic peoples (Hill 2003). UA cultivation vocabulary is preserved, albeit spottily, in both Takic and Numic languages (Hill 2007, 2012), and these languages also preserve traces of PUA words for pottery (Hill 2012).

Throughout the history of NUA, demographic pressure at the northern and western edges of the regime of summer rainfall that permitted maize cultivation would have forced lower-ranking groups into a lifestyle dependent on hunting and gathering in all but the best years, a process ethnographically attested in several UA groups (Hill 2003). A catastrophic series of 20-year-long droughts during the twelfth and thirteenth centuries drove regional abandonment and refugee movements among cultivator populations in NUA territories. NUA groups identified historically as hunter-gatherers are probably the descendants of communities that had included cultivation in a diverse set of subsistence strategies, and who committed to a permanent hunter-gatherer way of life rather than join communities of cultivators as refugees.[4]

Among speakers of languages discussed here, the Agua Caliente band of the Cahuilla, the Chemehuevi, the Kaibab band of the Southern Paiutes, and at least two Southern Ute bands were cultivating in the earliest historic period (Hill 2003). Although the continuity of this cultivation through prehistory cannot be securely established, their identification as hunter-gatherers, even of Bellwood's third type, is dubious. However, they are included here because they have been considered to be hunter-gatherers in much of the anthropological literature.

21.3   The Archaeology of the Takic and Numic Spreads

21.3.1   The Takic in Southern California

That the spread of Takic-speaking communities across Southern California must have replaced substratum languages across a heavily populated area is uncontroversial. However, the chronology is in dispute; dates for arrival of Takic speakers in California of 3,500 years ago (Moratto 1984) or 3,000–2,500 years ago (Sutton 1994) may be too early. I have argued that the PNUA community appears archaeologically as the Western Basketmaker II of the Four Corners region by about 3,500 years ago, but the earliest evidence for these archaic cultivators as far west as the Mojave Desert (along the Colorado River) dates only to about 2,500 years ago (Lyneis 1995: 208). Hale's (1958) glottochronological estimate for the breakup of NUA is less than 3,000 years ago; his date for the separation of Cahuilla and Tübatulabal, 2,229 (glottochronological) years ago, is reasonably consistent with the archaeological dates for the Western Basketmaker II in the extreme western end of their range. Sutton (2000: 298) suggests that the Takic diversification and spread from the eastern Mojave Desert began around AD 1.

Some scholars continue to support a very early, mid-Holocene, date for the arrival of the Takic peoples on the Pacific Coast.[5] However, while McCawley (1996: 2) notes that a date as late as AD 700 for Takic arrival on the Pacific coast has been proposed, it is likely that they had reached there by AD 500, a period when Grenda (1997: 20) notes "clear changes" in the archaeological record in southern California west of the Coast Ranges.

Takic groups were probably just one of several involved in significant changes in Southern California archaeological cultures, which include the arrival of the bow and arrow between AD 500 and 800 (Kennett and Kennett 2004) and the intensification of acorn use by AD 500–1000 (Basgall 2004). Southern Californians suffered severe climate instability, similar to the situation further east in the US Southwest, with several episodes of 20-year-long droughts, causing famine, violence and social disruption, between AD 800 and 1350. The middle of the twelfth century, between 1120 and 1150 was especially catastrophic in Southern California, and some depopulation has been identified for this period (Jones et al. 2004). However, the Takic spread took place hundreds of years before this episode.

21.3.2   The Numic Expansion into the Great Basin

Lamb (1958) proposed that the three California Numic languages, Mono, Tümpisha Shoshone, and Kawaiisu, represent an initial stage of Numic differentiation that took place about 2,000 years ago, with a second stage beginning around 1,000 years ago when descendant groups split off from their California neighbors and moved across the Great Basin and the Colorado Plateau: Northern Paiute to the north, Shoshone to the northeast, and the Chemehuevi-Southern Paiute-Ute continuum to the east. Linguistic evidence in support of Lamb's model includes the directionality of isoglosses in each of the subgroups, which form a series of concentric bands, the greater dialectal differentiation the closer to the California languages, and the suggestion of greater antiquity in place names in the California languages and in the daughter dialects nearest to these (Miller 1986).

The archaeological evidence does not unequivocally support Lamb's model of a "Numic spread" (Rhode and Madsen 1994). Some of the authors in Rhode and Madsen's (1994) volume argue that the Numic presence in the Great Basin is very ancient, dating back at least to mid-Holocene times.[6] Rhode and Madsen (1994) report optimistically that there is general concurrence about what happened at the peripheries of the Numic Spread, with debate centering mainly on characterizing the processes that drove the initial expansion out of the core area. In asserting this, Rhode and Madsen dismiss without discussion the possibility that components of the Numic population include former cultivators. This idea was suggested by Gunnerson (1962) and, most recently, by Roberts and Ahlstrom (2006), in a refined version that takes into account fine-grained details of the archae-ological record for the Virgin Anasazi-Southern Paiute transition in south-western Utah and southeastern Nevada.

Rhode and Madsen (1994) review the debate which is especially crucial to the present discussion: whether the Numic spread into the Great Basin was into relatively unpopulated territories. Many prehistorians believe that the eastward expansion of the Shoshone and the Southern Numa entered "a void left by the disintegration of traditional Fremont and Anasazi subsistence/ settlement systems ... there may be some evidence that Numic groups and some of these other peoples intermingled, at least for a while, but nowhere is the evidence for protracted interaction between Numic popula-tions and other groups very strong ... " (Rhode and Madsen 1994: 215). Bettinger (1994), however, argues that the Basin was not empty at the time of the Numic expansion, but that the autochthonous inhabitants were simply outcompeted by the Numic, who had developed a set of "processor" subsistence strategies focussing on resources "that are time-costly but more reliable and abundant" (Bettinger 1994: 46; see also Bettinger and Baumhoff 1982). For the Southern Numic, Lyneis (2000) has pointed out a long period of interaction between the westernmost Puebloans along the Muddy River in southern Nevada near Las Vegas and hunter-gatherers to their west. Ahlstrom (personal communication July 30, 2006) reports that in the Las Vegas area the frontier between cultivators and hunter-gatherers probably shifted several times between about 100 BC and AD 700. Ambler and Sutton (1989) argued that Numic aggression played a major role in pushing out Puebloans in the Virgin River region and further east in the San Juan drainage. Populations of Fremont cultivators persisted into the middle of the fourteenth century in what in the historic period was Shoshone territory, making an episode of contact likely.

In summary, while the idea that Takic-speaking people spread into populated areas in Southern California has not been controversial, the demographic circumstances of the Numic spread are by no means settled. While some archaeologists have suggested a classic "upstream" spread into depopulated areas, others have proposed that expanding Numic peoples encountered other populations under diverse circumstances. The data reported here are more consistent with the second position.

21.4   Sociogeographical Factors in Hunter-Gatherer Language Variation

The immediate inspiration for this paper is the work of Evans and McConvell (1998) and McConvell (2001) on the linguistic results of hunter-gatherer expansions in Australia. They argue that we can identify there two types of spreads, which occur in pulses driven by climatic variation induced by the El Niño-Southern Oscillation (ENSO) climatic periodicity. Their "inward" (Evans and McConvell 1998) or "upstream" (McConvell 2001) type involves expansion into relatively depopulated areas as climatic amelioration opens these for human occupation. Their "outward" or "downstream" type involves retreats from the interior into populated areas during periods of ENSO-induced drought.

Evans and McConvell suggest that upstream expansions into depopulated territories resemble initial colonizations. In this phase the problems faced by the spreading groups can be addressed by innovations in material technology. Language change will take place in relative isolation from other groups, so we will not expect substratum effects. However, in downstream spreads migrants confront established populations. Evans and McConvell argue that success in this phase requires social technologies that will draw target groups into the socioeconomic and ritual systems of the downstream-moving groups. They predict that in this phase we will see important episodes of language shift, as migrants will use a strategy of claiming special ritual potency for their language and customs in order to win over those they encounter. Such episodes of shift on the part of autochthonous populations to the language of the expanding group should produce significant substratum impact in the expanding languages.

Linguistic geographers have pointed out a number of factors that need to be taken into account as we refine the Evans and McConvell model. For instance, spreads into "accretion zones" (Nichols 1992) such as California should have rather different effects from expansions into "spread zones" such as the Great Basin. Accretion zones exhibit high genetic and structural diversity, mediated by multilingualism. Spread zones exhibit low genetic and structural diversity, mediated by the formation of *lingue franche*. Multilingualism within accretion zones should favor the spread of substratum and superstratum effects among languages, while *lingue franche* are less likely to have such an effect.[7]

Both Takic and Numic first spread into the California accretion zone. All of the Takic peoples, as well as the Southern Numic Kawaiisu and the Western Numic Mono, had acorn-based economies; these favor the formation of "tribelets" focused in small territories (Basgall 2004; Jackson 2004). Miller et al. (1971) report considerable dialect differentiation within Tümpisa Shoshone, on the edge of the California system in the Death Valley area. Of the three California Numic languages, only Kawaiisu was reported (by Maurice Zigmond, in a personal communication to Wick Miller [1986]) to be relatively homogeneous, although the Kawaiisu economy was also largely based on acorns. Mono was divided into Western and Eastern groups, and the Western variety alone had four subdialects (Lamb 1958a). Thurston (1987) proposed that small languages of the type favored by acorn-based subsistence will exhibit tendencies toward 'esoterogeny', which can be defined broadly as a tendency for very small languages to drift in the direction of rare and highly marked feature realizations. We would predict such a drift in Takic and in the three California Numic languages. If, however, these languages are incorporating substratum speakers, the effects of esoterogeny might be mitigated by shift-based interference, which may favor change to relatively unmarked typological realizations (Thomason 2001).

Speakers' ideological relationships with their environment, both natural and social, and the way that these are expressed sociolinguistically, may vary somewhat independently of other factors. People who believe that they possess primary claims on the major resources necessary for subsistence are likely to adopt "localist" stances, which yield relatively homogeneous linguistic communities and resistance to innovation and shift. Part of a localist stance may be to see certain linguistic features as important emblems of rights to resources, with resulting marginalization of speakers who cannot display these emblems (J. Hill 2000). Acorn-based economies might be associated with this pattern, especially during favorable climatic episodes. People who believe that their claims on basic subsistence resources are only secondary are likely to adopt "distributed" stances, which yield heterogeneous linguistic communities that are very open to innovation and shift if this will strengthen some secondary claim. Hunter-gatherer populations expanding into arid regions, like the Numic popula-tions, are very likely to exhibit a "distributed" stance toward language variation, favoring contact-induced change and language shift. Miller (1970) pointed out for the Western Shoshone an active inattention to dialect differences, which are thereby detached from any role as emblems of claims on resources. This stance facilitates constant reassortment of populations across a landscape where resources are highly unreliable in any one local area. In such a situation we might expect a great deal of language mixing and the rapid spread of innovation; Nichols (1974) believes that in Numic languages such mixing took place not only within each dialect continuum, but across the boundaries between Western, Central, and Southern Numic.

21.5   Approaches to Language Variation in Takic and Numic

In the discussions that follow, I look at three types of diversity in the Takic and Numic languages: internal lexical diversity, frequency of apparent substratum vocabulary, and internal typological diversity. Only on the measure of internal lexical diversity, determined by Miller (1984), do we find the results predicted by the Evans and McConvell model if Takic is a spread into a populated area and Numic is a spread into an unpopulated area.

21.5.1   Miller's Lexical Survey

A survey of lexical diversity in a 100-word list of basic vocabulary in UA published by Miller (1984) yielded results consistent with the predictions made by simplified models of a Numic spread into relatively unpopulated territory and a Takic spread into populated territory. Miller found more internal lexical diversity in Takic than in Numic. On chronological grounds we would not expect much difference between the two branches, as the dates of the Takic and Numic spread are probably only a few hundred years apart. Sutton's (2000) estimated date of AD 1 for the beginning of the Takic spread, and Lamb's identical date for the initial breakup of Numic suggest that the initial diversification of the two sub-branches may be almost contemporaneous.[8]

Miller's results for Numic are shown in Table 21.1, those for Takic appear in Table 21.2. The numbers represent percentage of cognacy. The tables show that average cognate density among Numic languages are much higher than the average density among Takic languages. This measure of diversity is consistent with the hypothesis of a Takic spread into populated areas, versus a Numic spread into unpopulated areas.[9]

Table 21.1 *Cognate density in Numic languages*

Mno	Mno								
Pno	77	Pno							
TSh	59	58	TSh						
Sho	58	58	87	Sho					
Cmn	57	58	79	88	Cmn				
Kws	52	56	54	55	49	Kws			
Cmh	50	55	61	58	54	75	Cmh		
Put	53	58	62	62	59	79	86	Put	
Ute	52	57	59	61	59	76	78	87	Ute

From Miller (1984: 14).

Table 21.2 *Cognate density in Takic languages*

Gbo	Gbo				
Srr	45	Srr			
Cah	42	50	Cah		
Cup	34	38	65	Cup	
Lui	38	35	50	48	Lui

From Miller (1984: 14).

21.5.2   Bright and Bright's Lexical Survey, Amended

Bright and Bright's (1976 [1969]) lexical survey was undertaken to explore the sources of substratum vocabulary in the Takic languages. Their sample included 116 Uto-Aztecan etyma, taken from Voegelin, Voegelin and Hale (1962).[10] They compared Gabrielino and Luiseño to their non-UA neighbors, Chumash and Diegueño, and concluded that very few items of non-UA vocabulary could be traced to these sources. Instead, they suggested, substratum vocabulary in Gabrielino and Luiseño came from extinct and undocumented languages. I added to their lists data from Kitanemuk in Takic, from the three California Numic languages, Western Mono, Tümpisa Shoshone, and Kawaiisu, and three Great Basin/Colorado Plateau languages, Northern Paiute, Comanche, and Ute. As I consider NUA to be a securely established sub-branch of UA (cf. Manaster Ramer 1992; Hill 2001), to count as "UA" for my purposes, an item must have a resemblant form attested in a southern UA language. Table 21.3 shows the results of this comparison. While Northern Paiute in Numic has the lowest frequency of non-UA words, and Gabrielino in Takic has the highest frequency, in general the Numic and Takic languages are not very different. This result is not consistent with sociolinguistic effects predicted by the Evans and

Table 21.3 *UA Etyma versus Non-UA Etyma in Takic and Numic Languages*

Language	Number of words	Non-UA Words	% Non-UA Words
Takic			
Gabrielino	85	32	38%
Luiseño	114	34	30%
Kitanemuk	113	41	36%
Average Takic			35%
Numic			
W. Mono	106	37	35%
Tümpisa Sh.	114	41	36%
Kawaiisu	113	39	35%
N. Paiute	105	26	25%
Comanche	112	40	36%
Ute	113	35	31%
Average Numic			33%

McConvell model from a simplified picture of the Takic versus the Numic expansion.

21.5.3   *Measuring Typological Variability*

To examine typological diversity, I coded six Takic and nine Numic languages for 131 different typological features from the World Atlas of Linguistic Structures (WALS) survey (Haspelmath et al. 2005). The calculation of diversity in each subfamily is based on 91 of these. Twenty-one WALS features were excluded from the diversity measure because all the languages are identical.[11] Thirteen features were excluded because data were missing for more than one Takic, or more than one Numic, language.[12] Three WALS features were dropped because I found it too difficult to reliably interpret the discussions by the WALS authors in relation to the available data.[13] I rechecked all feature assignments for the languages in articles in Haspelmath et al. (2005), and in a few cases decided to code features differently from the way they are coded in the published WALS materials.[14]

Three lexical features, (129) "Hand and Arm", (130) "Finger and Hand", and (131) "Numeral Bases" were coded but are not counted in the diversity measures. For feature (129), Numic generally distinguishes 'hand' and "arm", but Takic lacks the distinction. Nearly all languages in both subgroups make the distinction between 'finger' and 'hand'. This is consistent with the hypothesis that these languages are spoken by descendants of cultivators;

Brown (2005: 526) claims that groups that are "not fully agrarian tend substantially more strongly to show identity than those of full agriculturalists." For feature (131), all the languages have decimal numeral bases.

Diversity was calculated as a ratio of minority and majority features. For example, for Feature (1), Consonant Inventory, four of the Takic languages have an inventory of average size, and are coded as "3" (Maddieson 2005). Serrano has a "moderately large" inventory and is coded "4", while Gabrielino has a "moderately small" inventory and is coded "2." Thus, on this feature, two of six Takic languages exhibit minority realizations, yielding variability of 2/6, or 0.33. For the same feature, seven of the Numic languages are "average" and coded "3." Ute and Comanche have "moderately small" inventories and are coded as "2." Thus Numic has two languages out of nine with "minority" realizations of this feature, yielding variability of 2/9, or 0.22. Therefore, for this feature, Numic is less variable than Takic.

A second measure counts how many "minority" features each language exhibits. For instance, Cahuilla is in the minority in Takic for 22 features, while Luiseño is in the minority for only 8. Where the languages in a sub-branch split evenly, the split is counted as part of the measure of sub-branch variability, but the individual languages are not credited with a minority feature realization. For instance, for Feature (29), "Syncretism in verbal person/number marking", Takic has a 3–3 split, because Luiseño, Serrano, and Gabrielino have no person-number marking on the verb and are coded as "1", while Cahuilla, Cupeño, and Kitanemuk have person-number marking but no syncretism, and are coded as "3." Takic is credited with 1.00 variability on this feature, but no language is credited with a "minority" realization. Similarly, with 3/3/3 splits in Numic, Numic is credited with 1.00 variability, but the languages involved are not credited with a "minority" feature realization.[15]

21.5.4   *Results and Discussion*

The survey of typological diversity between Numic and Takic failed to identify the kind of diversity that the simplified model of the Takic versus the Numic spreads would predict. While there are differences between the two groups, these are complex and subtle.

Table 21.4 summarizes the results of the survey by WALS feature groups (A) through (H) (Haspelmath et al. 2005: v–vii). Variabilities are summed for each group. Where a data point is missing, the number of languages in the denominator is reduced by one for that feature. For instance, for "Phonology", 13 features are included in the sample. For Takic, there are 21 minority realizations on these 16F features, while for Numic there are 29. For these 13 features, no language is missing data. So the total of languages times

Table 21.4 *Variability in Takic and Numic for WALS feature groups*

		Takic		Numic	
A.	Phonology (13 features)	21/78	0.27	29/117	0.25
B.	Morphology (6 features)	12/36	0.33	20/54	0.37
C.	Nominal categories (16 features)	15/96	0.16*	47/144	0.33*
D.	Nominal syntax (8 features)	2/48	0.04*	27/70	0.39*
E.	Verbal categories (9 features)	10/52	0.19	19/81	0.23
F.	Word order (16 features)	23/94	0.24	42/144	0.29
G.	Simple clauses (18 features)	30/105	0.29*	28/162	0.17
H.	Complex sentences (4 features)	15/52	0.71*	5/36	0.14*
Total		130/536	0.26	217/808	0.27

features for Takic is 6 × 13 = 78. For Numic it is 9 × 13=117. Thus the total measure of variability for "Phonology" for Takic is 21/78, or .27. For Numic, it is 29/117, or 0.25. That is, the two subfamilies are almost exactly equally variable for "Phonology."

The starred numbers in Table 21.4 show where the sub-branches are significantly different. Numic is the more variable group in Nominal Categories and Nominal Syntax. Takic exhibits greater variability in Simple Clauses and Complex Sentences (the latter measure, with only four features, should probably not be taken very seriously)[16]. If typological diversity is an index of substratum effects, we would expect greater diversity in Takic than in Numic, given the well-established linguistic complexity of aboriginal California, the site of the Takic spread, and the likelihood of very low populations in the Great Basin, the site of the Numic spread. However, this prediction is not supported by these data; the average variability for the two sub-branches is nearly identical.

Are all the languages contributing equally to the variability, or are there differences among them? Table 21.5 shows the number of minority feature realizations exhibited by each of the languages, sorted into Takic and Numic (remember that where the languages split evenly, languages are not credited with minority feature realizations).

Table 21.5 reveals some striking differences in how much individual languages are deviating from the typological majority. However, the most deviant

Table 21.5 *Numbers of minority feature
realizations by language and subgroup*

Takic		Numic	
Cahuilla	22	Kawaiisu	37
Cupeño	21	Tümpisa Shoshone	25
Serrano	13	Chemehuevi	25
Gabrielino	13	Northern Paiute	20
Kitanemuk	10	Southern Paiute	22
Luiseño	8	Mono	21
		Comanche	19
		Ute	18
		Shoshone	18

languages are not in Takic, where Luiseño of all the languages is the most ordinary within its subbranch; instead, they are in Numic: Kawaiisu, Tümpisa Shoshone, and Chemehuevi. These are all part of the California accretion-zone system (Chemehuevi is technically a part of the Southern Numic spread, anchoring the western end of a dialect chain that extends east to Ute, but consists of a community of cultivators along the Colorado River in close contact with Yuman languages). However, Mono is also a California language, but does not show exceptionally high levels of minority typological realizations.

California Numic may be skewing Numic typological diversity to the high side. A better match to the simplified model of the Takic and Numic spreads might be found if we compare the six Takic languages with only the six Numic languages involved in the second stage of Numic spread, into the Great Basin and across the Colorado Plateau: Northern Paiute, Shoshone, Comanche, Chemehuevi, Southern Paiute, and Ute (I will refer to these henceforth as the "spreading" languages). This comparison is shown in Table 21.6. This comparison still does not reveal the kind of typological diversity difference that we might expect based on the simplified model, of a Numic second-stage spread into a depopulated area. The total variability is nearly identical for the two groups.

Another manipulation of these data that we can undertake is to look at the nature of minority feature realizations. Here we confront the two issues. The first is that "minority realization" is not necessarily "innovation"; a minority feature realization might, of course, represent the proto-language type. However, as accomplishing the complete syntactic reconstruction of NUA is a task that lies beyond the scope of this chapter, "minority realization" serves here as a rough stand-in for "innovation" except where the evidence is clear

Table 21.6 *Variability in spreading Numic languages compared to Takic*

		Takic		Numic	
A.	Phonology (13 features)	19/78	0.24	21/78	0.27
B.	Morphology (6 features)	5/36	0.14*	12/36	0.33*
C.	Nominal Categories (16 features)	29/96	0.30*	15/96	0.16*
D.	Nominal Syntax (8 features)	17/47	0.36*	2/48	0.04*
E.	Verbal Categories (9 features)	15/54	0.28	12/58	0.21
F.	Word Order (16 features)	22/96	0.23	23/94	0.24
G.	Simple Clauses (18 features)	15/108	0.14*	30/105	0.29*
H.	Complex Sentences (4 features)	4/24	0.17*	15/21	0.71*
Total		126/539	0.26	130/536	0.24

against this conclusion. The second is the complex issue of exactly how language contact affects typological profiles. Thomason (2001) points out that the literature includes two precisely opposite claims: that language contact yields a less marked typology in the receiving system, and that language contact yields a more marked typology in the receiving system. I will explore both possibilities in the text that follows.

Thomason distinguishes "borrowing", where imperfect learning plays no role in the interference between languages in contact, from shift-induced interference, where members of a shifting group produce a new version of the target language. She observes that markedness seems to be most important in cases of shift-induced interference, where marked features in the target language are less likely to be acquired by members of the shifting group, and, similarly, target language speakers are unlikely to acquire marked features from the language of the shifting group. While language ideologies and attitudes can confound this pattern, Thomason's generalization does provide a hypothesis, that the Takic spread into heavily populated Southern California, which must have incorporated substratum features, will show up in the presence of shift to unmarked feature realizations.

For this exercise, I use those features where there is a clear difference between rare and common realizations as reported in the WALS survey and where there is variation within each of Numic and Takic. "Common" and "unmarked" realizations are probably not exactly the same thing, but I will use "common" here as a rough-and-ready stand-in for Thomason's "unmarked." Table 21.7 shows those cases in which a language exhibits a minority feature realization that is of a significantly more common type than is the majority realization for the subfamily. Examples of this type are few, so I show complete information for each realization. Keeping in mind the caveat noted above, I will refer to the development of these feature realizations as "innovations."

Some developments of minority realizations clearly occurred in common ancestral languages, and so are shown at that level. Sometimes changes in two or more WALS features involve only a single grammatical innovation. The

Table 21.7 *Minority feature realizations that are more common in type than the majority realizations*

Takic = 10		
Proto-Cupeño-Cahuilla = 2		
	(92) > 6	Loss of question particle
	(116) > 6	Question intonation only
	(102) > 5	Both A and P marked on verb
Cahuilla = 1		
	(126) > 1	Balanced "when" clause
Cupeño = 3		
	(37) > 1	Definite article distinct from demonstrative
	(43) > 1	P3 pronoun unrelated to demonstrative
	(103) > 2	Zero P3 not permitted
	(127) > 1	Balanced "reason" clause
Luiseño = 0		No examples
Gabrielino = 1		
	(6) > 1	Loss of uvular stop
Serrano = 1		
	(127) > 1	Balanced "reason" clause
Kitanemuk = 2		
	(103) > 2	Zero P3 not permitted
	(127) > 1	Balanced "reason" clause
Numic Core = 7 Numic Great Basin = 12		
Proto-Central Numic = 1		
	(48) > 2	No person marking on adpositions
	(58) > 2	No obligatorily possessed nouns
Tümpisa Shoshone = 2		
	(25) > 2	Dependent marking instead of double
	(37) > 5	No definite or indefinite articles
	(38) > 5	No definite or indefinite articles
Shoshone = 1		
	(34) > 6	All nouns have obligatory plural
Comanche = 1		
	(124) > 1	Implicit subject in "want" complements

Table 21.7 (*cont.*)

Kawaiisu = 1		
	(92) > 6	No question particle
	(116) > 6	Question intonation only
Chemehuevi = 4		
	(77) > 1	No grammatical evidentials
	(113) > 1	Symmetric negation only
	(126) > 1	Balanced "when" clause
	(127) > 1	Balanced "reason" clause
Southern Paiute = 0		No examples
Ute = 2		
	(106) > 2	Reflexives formally distinct from reciprocals
	(124) > 1	Implicit subject in "want" complements
Mono = 3		
	(58) > 2	No obligatorily possessed nouns
	(113) > 1	Symmetric negation only
	(127) > 1	Balanced "reason" clause
Northern Paiute = 4		
	(37)>1	Definite article distinct from demonstrative
	(58)>2	No obligatorily possessed nouns
	(113)>1	Symmetric negation only
	(127)>1	Balanced "reason" clause

numbers following the equals sign and language name represent the number of such innovations, not the count of feature changes. For instance, two changes in feature realizations in Proto-Cupeño-Cahuilla, the loss of the question particle and the shift to intonation-marked questions, should be considered as a single grammatical innovation. In Cupeño, the changes in realizations of features (37) and (43) both involve a single innovation, the emergence of a new third person pronoun, distinct from the demonstratives, that functions also as a definite article. Similarly, the changes in Proto-Central Numic in realizations of (48) and (58), are due to a single grammatical innovation, the loss of possessive prefixes. Changes in features (37) and (38) in Tümpisa Shoshone are due to a single change involving the absence of articles.

The data in Table 21.7 do not support the hypothesis that Takic, having moved into a populated area, should show more evidence of shift-induced interference in the form of innovations of common feature realizations. The six spreading Numic languages, which supposedly moved into depopulated territories, actually have more minority features of a more common type (12) than do either the California Numic (7) or the Takic languages (10).

While minority feature realizations of the "common" type, suggesting shift-induced interference, are relatively rare in these languages, minority feature

Table 21.8 *Minority feature realizations that are rarer than the majority type*

Takic	N	%	Numic	N	%
Proto-Cupeño-Cahuilla = 3			Proto-Southern Numic = 3 (7 feature changes)		
Serrano	6	0.46	Chemehuevi	6	0.29
Gabrielino	5	0.38	Southern Paiute	7	0.37
Cupeño	3	0.17	Kawaiisu	10	0.32
Luiseño	2	0.25	Comanche	7	0.37
Cahuilla	1	0.05	Ute	2	0.17
Kitanemuk	1	0.10	Northern Paiute	8	0.40
			Tümpisa Shoshone	6	0.24
			Shoshone	5	0.28
			Mono	6	0.29
Average		0.24			0.30

realizations that are rarer than the majority realizations appear widely in both Takic and Numic. These suggest that esoterogeny is overriding shift-induced interference in these languages. They are shown in Table 21.8. In this table, the numbers refer to changes in realizations of individual WALS features, except in the case of Southern Numic where I have indicated that six WALS feature realizations represent only two innovations.

Table 21.8 shows that Numic exhibits more rare minority features than does Takic. While Northern Paiute has the highest frequency of rare minority features, Southern Numic also stands out. Six of the rare feature realizations shared by the Southern Numic languages appear in at least three of the languages and thus probably date to the proto-language. These are due to two innovations: the development of an animate/inanimate gender distinction in the pronouns and demonstratives, picked up in four WALS features (30, 31, 32, 44), and the emergence of relatively free word order for OV (83) and AdjN (87). Also, these languages exhibit rare negative types with variation between a negative word and an affix (a rare realization of (112)). Double negation (another relatively infrequent realization of (112)) appears in Chemehuevi and Ute, and I have considered it to be a proto-language innovation. Comanche, which often deviates from the rest of Numic as well as from Central Numic, also stands out in Table 21.8. It is possible that the tendency to move toward rarer feature realizations in Comanche is due to language contact influences resulting from its move into the multilingual environment of the Great Plains.

In Takic, Proto-Cupeño-Cahuilla innovated a system of possessive classifiers (a rare realization of (59), most elaborated in Cahuilla), and developed person marking on the verb of both A and P arguments (102), with the marked

PA order (104); at least in Cupeño, the prefix for P may be best analyzed as a proclitic. Serrano and Kitanemuk have often been considered to be dialects of the same language. However, although they are lexically quite similar, they diverge from one another on several phonological, morphological, and syntactic typological markers, with Serrano clearly tending to move in the direction of more "esoterogenic" realizations.

21.6   Summary and Conclusions

Based on the Evans and McConvell model and a simplified understanding of the difference between the Takic spread and the Numic secondary spread that has been dominant among prehistorians of Western North America, we hypothesize that Takic languages, established as strikingly more diverse lexically than Numic (Miller 1984). should show also more significant substratum effects, which should be attested by such symptoms as a high level of non-UA lexicon in basic vocabulary, and high diversity in realization of typological features. The data summarized here do not support this hypothesis. Even when Takic is compared only with the six spreading Numic languages, the overall level of variability on both lexical and typological measures is nearly identical between the two groups. Indeed, some Southern Numic languages, especially Kawaiisu, are even more deviant within Numic than are the most differentiated Takic languages within their subgroup. This is consistent with conclusions advanced by Shaul ("The Numic unspread: Bad linguistics, convenient archaeology," manuscript, 1999), who suggested that Southern Numic is much more variable internally, with less mutual intelligibility among the dialects in the spread zone, than in the other two Numic branches.

There are no doubt many reasons why the hypothesis is not clearly supported by these data. One is that the data constitute a palimpsest representing the effects of at least 3,000 years of history, in which the complexity of intersecting demographic, ecological, and ideological processes have yielded a sort of reduction to the mean that blurs over effects that may have been striking in particular historical periods. Second is that the methods used here are blunt instruments. We have very few cases of identifiable substratum vocabulary that can be traced to a known language, so unidentifiable items that lack Uto-Aztecan etymologies stand in for substratum vocabulary in the lexical survey. In the typological survey, minority feature realizations stand in for innovations, even though we sometimes cannot be sure that they do not represent the conservative state. However, the data also suggest that the understanding of the contrast between the Takic and Numic spreads that has been shared by many historical linguists and archaeologists is greatly oversimplified. For instance, the Numic spread perhaps involved a spread into populated territories, at least at some periods, as has been suggested by several scholars. The data for Southern Numic are compatible with this idea.

It is interesting to note that both acorn-based economies (Jackson 2004) of the type adopted by Takic speakers and by speakers of two California Numic languages, Kawaiisu and Mono, and intensive "processor" procurement strategies of the type that Bettinger and Baumhoff (1982) suggested as the basis for the success of the Numic spread, place a premium on female labor. Thus all of these groups were under similar pressure to continually recruit outsider women. The similarities in diversity suggested by this survey are consistent with this idea, that second-language speakers were being continually incorporated into these communities. The role of foreign women in NUA adaptations is hinted at by the lexical data. NUA may have incorporated very early a number of Kiowa-Tanoan words for important economic plants such as pinyon pine and acorn-bearing oak, where processing was the province of women (Hill 2008). Non-UA vocabulary in Numic includes the words for "mother", three terms for grandparents (FaFa, MoFa, MoMo), and several basic body parts including "fat", "foot", "head", "heart", "leg", "stomach/belly", and "tongue", suggesting a possible foreign female "nursery" vocabulary. Although "feces", "urine", and "breast" are all UA in Numic, "feces" is a non-UA word in Takic. The word for "to grind", nearly universal throughout UA as a reflex of *tusu, has been replaced with non-UA words in Takic, and a number of other Takic items in individual languages also hint at this picture. This kind of sociolinguistic situation, where a community is recruiting foreign women for female-intensive subsistence strategies, is deserving of study as a general case, and such study might produce some refined hypotheses for examining the sociolinguistics of language spreads.

NOTES

1. Data sources for Takic are as follows: Cahuilla: Seiler (1977); Cupeño: J. Hill (2005); Luiseño: Kroeber and Grace (1960) and Hyde (1971); Serrano: K. Hill (2000) and field notes; Kitanemuk: Anderton (1988); Gabrielino: J. P. Harrington field notes and Munro (2000).
2. Data sources for Numic are as follows: Western Mono: Lamb (1958a) and Bethel et al. (1993), dictionary example search cued by Gould and Loether (2002) on Owens Valley Paiute or Eastern Mono; Northern Paiute: Snapp et al. (1982), Thornes (2003); Tümpisa Shoshon: Dayley (1989); Western Shoshone: Crum and Dayley (1993), Miller (1996); Comanche: Charney (1993); Kawaiisu: Zigmond et al. (1990); Chemehuevi: Press (1979); Southern Paiute: Sapir (1930); Ute: Givón (1980).

Numic phonological inventories are normalized to reflect a "phonemic" approach. Except for Kawaiisu, Chemehuevi, and Tümpisa Shoshone, I use the arrays proposed by Davis (1966). Davis's Shoshone array is for Wind River Shoshone, an eastern variety, while the remainder of my data for Shoshone come mainly from the western dialect of Duck Valley.

3. I propose that Western Mono *tsede* 'anus' reflects Yokuts *teda* (Kroeber 1907: 241). Yokuts *to:t: 'head, hair, skull'* may be the source for Kawaiisu *toci-* in 'head' and 'hair', and Ute *tiči-* 'head'. However, these Southern Numic forms may also be reflexes of a PUA word for 'head, hair' (Stubbs 2011: 206 [1107a]) with a chance resemblance to the Yokuts form (or a loan into Yokuts – or an ancient inherited resemblance?).

4. This theory of the archaic cultivator origins of NUA hunter-gatherers is by no means universally accepted (cf. Campbell 2003, Justeson and Kaufman 2009). However, as the history of maize cultivation in the US Southwest is being rewritten, pushing back the dates of the earliest cultivation to 4,000 years ago, many archaeologists now entertain the idea that expansions by communities of Mesoamerican cultivators, including the Uto-Aztecans, may have played a role in the spread of maize (Matson 1991, 2003; LeBlanc 2003; Coltrain et al. 2007; Staller et al. 2006). An opposing point of view is found in Merrill et al. (2009).

5. I dismiss suggestions that Takic peoples have been in California since the middle Holocene 8,000–5,000 years ago as incompatible with the linguistic evidence.

6. As with the similar suggestion for Takic in California, a mid-Holocene date for Numic differentiation is incompatible with the linguistic evidence. Miller (Miller et al. 1971) and Shaul (1986) suggested that adaptation to the Great Basin favored widespread dialect borrowing that might have constantly erased incipient differentiation and made the various Numic dialect continua look younger than they really are. However, it is most unlikely that such processes would skew Numic differentiation to such a degree that we could justify a Middle Holocene date for the proto-language.

7. Consistent with both the Nichols and the Evans and McConvell models, Golla (2002) notes the presence of widespread substratal effects in California Athabascan languages that have moved into the California accretion zone.

8. Miller concluded based on his data for lexical diversity that Takic was much older than Numic. The review of the archaeological data given here suggests that this is wrong.

9. Abbreviations are as follows: Cah, Cahuilla; Cmh, Chemehuevi; Cmn, Comanche; Cup, Cupeño; Gbo, Gabrielino; Kws, Kawaisu; Lui, Luiseño; Mno, Mono; Pno, Northern Paiute; Put, Southern Paiute; Sho, Shoshone; Srr, Serrano; Tsh, Tümpisa Shoshone. "Ute" is not abbreviated.

10. Two of these items, 'hill' and 'owl', are not valid Uto-Aztecan etyma and have been removed from the restudy. New knowledge has permitted some revisions of Bright and Bright's (1969) etymological conclusions. For instance, Gabrielino *wosi* 'dog' is not from Chumash; it is cognate with Southern UA words like Tepiman *gogosi* 'dog'. Other items can also be related today to UA origins. Thus, instead of Bright and Bright's 52% non-UA vocabulary for Gabrielino, I recognize only 38%. They find that 47% of Luiseño items are not U-A; I identify only 30%. They required that an item be a reflex of the corresponding Voegelin, Voegelin, and Hale reconstruction. I have counted as UA all items that appear to have widespread cognates or resemblants in Miller's (1989) provisional list of UA resemblant sets, as amended and edited by Kenneth C. Hill.

11. Since the relative stability of these features may be of interest to typologists, they are shown in the following list according to WALS feature numbers.

7) Glottalized consonants (None in these languages)

10) Vowel nasalization (Never contrastive in these languages)

13) Tone (None in these languages)

18) Common consonants missing (None in these languages)

19) Uncommon consonants present (None in these languages)

20) Fusion (All languages are concatenative)

21) Exponence (All languages are monoexponential)

27) Reduplication (All languages have productive partial reduplication. Only some have productive full reduplication but Rubino [2005] does not admit a distinction.)

42) Pronominal vs. adnominal demonstratives (Identical in all languages)

45) Politeness (None of the languages have politeness encoded in pronominals)

46) Indefinites (All languages have interrogative-based indefinite pronouns)

48) Intensive/reflexive (These are different in all the languages)

52) Comitative/instrumental (These are different in all the languages)

55) Numeral classifiers (None in these languages)

56) Conjunction and universal quantifier (These are different in all the languages)

69) T/A suffixes (All the languages have these)

72) Imperative/Hortative (No such distinction in these languages)

73) Optative (None in these languages)

98) Alignment (All languages are nominative-accusative)

110) Periphrastic causative (These are not attested for any of these languages)

119) Noun vs. locative predicates (These are different in all the languages)

12. WALS features excluded because data are missing in more than one language in a sub-family are listed below by feature number

17) Rhythm type

36) Associative plural

53) Ordinal numbers

54) Distributive numbers

74) Situational possibility

75) Epistemic possibility

76) Overlap of situational and epistemic possibility

91) Degree word-adjective order

115) Negatives with indefinites

121) Comparatives

123) Oblique relative clauses

125) Purpose clauses

128) Utterance complement clauses

13. Features excluded because of difficulty in interpreting data in relation to WALS statements include (22) Verb Synthesis, (49) Number of cases, and (78) Coding of Evidentiality.

14. Complete spreadsheets for coding for the 15 languages and 131 features are available from the author. Also, I have submitted coding corrections to the WALS website.

15. Some sites of variability are over-represented in the WALS sample. For instance, person-number marking on the verb figures in seven WALS features, including (29) "Syncretism in Verbal Person/Number Marking," (40) "Inclusive/Exclusive Distinction in verbal inflection," (100) "Alignment of verbal person marking,"

(101) "Expression of pronominal subjects," (102) "Verbal person marking," (103) "Third-person zero of verbal person marking," and (104) "Order of person markers on the verb." These features pick up kinds of variability among the languages that do have person marking. However, the languages that do not have person marking count either as majority or minority realizations in the same way for all seven features. I have not been able to develop a principled way to solve this problem, and have decided to ignore it, but it does cause a slight distortion.

The WALS feature system often fails to pick up kinds of local variability that are of interest to students of these languages. However, I do not consider this a serious problem. WALS provides a replicable set of features and realizations that permits the same kinds of measurements of diversity in any group of languages. This makes it difficult for the scholar with a theoretical bias to use only the most favorable anecdotal evidence.

A third problem involves the incomparability of grammars written from different theoretical perspectives. Different treatments of Numic-language phonologies required normalization, as noted in note (2). Another difficulty comes with the word order features. All of these languages are "head-final" in general type. In the case of the language that I know best, Cupeño, deviations from SOV order always involve marked pragmatics, such as topicalization or afterthought. Some grammarians count such deviations as demonstrating that the language has "no dominant order." Others specify a basic order. I have coded the word-order properties as specified in the grammars. Where word order is not specified, I have looked for constructions in text or in the example sentences and made a judgment on my own. This problem is not solvable without consultation on each feature with experts on each of the languages. Almost certainly some of my interpretations are wrong, not only for word order features, but for others. However, I have identified several cases where the feature codings for these languages published in the WALS survey are also wrong, suggesting that this kind of noise in the data is probably inevitable. This is one reason for using as large a sample of features as possible.

16. We have almost no data on complex sentences for the Takic language Gabrielino.

References

Ambler, J. Richard and Mark Q. Sutton. (1989). The Anasazi abandonment of the San Juan drainage and the Numic expansion. *North American Archaeologist* 10: 39–55.

Anderton, Alice Jeanne. (1988). *The language of the Kitanemuks of California*. Ph.D. dissertation, University of California at Los Angeles.

Balée, William. (1994). *Footprints of the forest*. New York: Columbia University Press.

Basgall, Mark E. (2004). Resource intensification among hunter-gatherers: Acorn economies in prehistoric California. In L. Mark Raab and Terry L. Jones (eds.), *Prehistoric California: Archaeology and the myth of paradise*. Salt Lake City: University of Utah Press, 86–98.

Bellwood, Peter. (1997). Prehistoric cultural explanations for widespread language families. In P. McConvell and N. Evans (eds.), *Archaeology and linguistics*. Melbourne: Oxford University Press, 123–134.

Bellwood, Peter. (2005). *First farmers*. Oxford: Blackwell Publishing.

Bethel, Rosalie, Paul V. Kroskrity, Christopher Loether and Gregory A. Reinhardt. (1993). *A dictionary of Western Mono*, 2nd edn. Completely corrected, updated and revised by Christopher Loether and Rosalie Bethel.

Bettinger, Robert L. (1994). How, when, and why Numic spread. In David B. Madsen and David Rhode, *Across the West: Human population movement and the expansion of the Numa*. Salt Lake City: University of Utah Press, 44–55.

Bettinger, Robert L. and Martin A. Baumhoff. (1982). The Numic spread: Great Basin cultures in competition. *American Antiquity* 47(3): 485–503.

Bright, William and Marcia Bright. (1969 [1976]). Archaeology and linguistics in prehistoric Southern California. Reprinted in Anwar S. Dil (ed.), *Variation and change in language: Essays by William Bright*. Stanford, CA: Stanford University Press, 189–205.

Bright, William and Jane H. Hill. (1967). Linguistic history of the Cupeño. In D. H. Hymes and W. Biddle (eds.), *Studies in Southwestern ethnolinguistics*. The Hague: Mouton and Company, 352–391.

Brown, Cecil. (2005). Finger and hand. In Martin Haspelmath, Matthew S. Dryer, David Gil and Bernard Comrie (eds.), *The World atlas of linguistic structures*. Oxford: Oxford University Press, 526–529.

Callaghan, Catherine A. (1997). Evidence for Yok-Utian. *International Journal of American Linguistics* 18–64.

Campbell, Lyle. (2003). What drives linguistic diversification and language spread? In Peter Bellwood and Colin Renfrew (eds.), *Examining the farming/language dispersal hypothesis*. Cambridge: McDonald Institute for Archaeological Research, 49–64.

Charney, Jean Ormsbee. (1993). *A grammar of Comanche*. Lincoln: University of Nebraska Press.

Coltrain, Joan Brenner, Joel C. Janetski and Shawn W. Carlyle. (2007). The stable- and radio-isotope chemistry of Western Basketmaker burials: Implications for early Puebloan diets and origins. *American Antiquity* 72: 301–321.

Crum, Beverly and Jon Dayley. (1993). *Western Shoshoni grammar*. Occasional Papers and Monographs on Cultural Anthropology and Linguistics Volume No. 1. Boise, ID: Department of Anthropology, Boise State University.

Davis, Irvine. (1966). Numic consonantal correspondences. *International Journal of American Linguistics* 32: 124–140.

Dayley, Jon P. (1989). *Tümpisa (Panamint) Shoshone grammar*. University of California Publications in Linguistics Volume 115. Berkeley: University of California Press.

Evans, Nicholas and Patrick McConvell. (1998). The enigma of Pama-Nyungan expansion in Australia. In Roger Blench and Matthew Spriggs (eds.), *Archaeology and Language II*. London: Routledge, 174–192.

Givón, Talmy (Southern Ute Tribe). (1980). *Ute reference grammar*, 1st edn. Ignacio, CO: Ute Press.

Golla, Victor. (2002). Language history and communicative strategies in aboriginal California and Oregon. In O. Miyaoka and M. Oshima (eds.), *Languages of the North Pacific Rim*, Vol. 5. Suita, Japan: Faculty of Informatics, Osaka Gakuin University, 43–64.

Gould, Drusilla and Christopher Loether. (2002). *An introduction to the Shoshoni language: Dammen daigwape*. Salt Lake City: University of Utah Press.

Grenda, Donn R. (1997). *Continuity and change: 8,500 years of Lacustrine adaptation on the shores of Lake Elsinore*. Statistical Research Technical Series 59. Tucson, AZ: Statistical Research, Inc.

Gunnerson, James H. (1962). Plateau Shoshonean prehistory: A suggested reconstruction. *American Antiquity* 28: 41–45.

Hale, Kenneth L. (1958). Internal diversity in Uto-Aztecan: I. *International Journal of American Linguistics* 29: 101–107.

Haspelmath, Martin, Matthew S. Dryer, David Gil and Bernard Comrie (eds.) (2005). *The World atlas of linguistic structures*. Oxford: Oxford University Press.

Hill, Jane H. (2000). Languages on the land. In J. Terrell (ed.), *Language, archaeology, and history*. Westport, CT: Bergin and Garvey, 257–282.

Hill, Jane H. (2001). Proto-Uto-Aztecan: A community of cultivators in central Mexico? *American Anthropologist* 103: 913–934.

Hill, Jane H. (2002). Language spread among hunter-gatherers. Paper presented to Arcling II, Canberra, ACT, October 2–5, 2002.

Hill, Jane H. (2003). Proto-Uto-Aztecan and the northern devolution. In Peter Bellwood and Colin Renfrew (eds.), *Examining the farming/language dispersal hypothesis*. Cambridge: McDonald Institute for Archaeological Research, 331–340.

Hill, Jane H. (2004). Language spread among hunter-gatherers: The North American evidence. Paper presented to The Ecology of Language: A Symposium in Honor of Murray B. Emeneau on his 100th Birthday. Department of Linguistics, University of California-Berkeley, February 20, 2004.

Hill, Jane H. (2005). *A Grammar of Cupeño*. University of California Publications in Linguistics Volume 136. Berkeley: University of California Press.

Hill, Jane H. (2007). 'External evidence' in historical linguistic argumentation: Subgrouping in Uto-Aztecan. Workshop on Alternative Approaches to Language Classification at LSA Linguistic Institute at Stanford University.

Hill, Jane H. (2008). Northern Uto-Aztecan and Kiowa-Tanoan: Evidence for contact between the proto-languages? *International Journal of American Linguistics* 74(2): 155–188.

Hill, Jane H. (2012). Proto-Uto-Aztecan as a Mesoamerican language. *Ancient Mesoamerica* 23: 57–68.

Hill, Kenneth C. (2000). A typological sketch of Serrano. Paper presented to the Seminar in Typology at the Research Centre for Language Typology, La Trobe University, Bundoora, VIC, December 2000 (Manuscript, 21 August 2003 in possession of author).

Hinton, Leanne. (1991). Takic and Yuman: A study in phonological convergence. *International Journal of American Linguistics* 57: 133–157.

Hyde, Villiana. (1971). *An Introduction to the Luiseño Language*. Banning, CA: Malki Museum Press.

Jackson, Thomas L. (2004). Pounding acorn: Women's production as social and economic focus. In L. Mark Raab, and Terry L. Jones (eds.), *Prehistoric California: Archaeology and the myth of paradise*. Salt Lake City: University of Utah Press, 172–182.

Jacobs, Roderick. (1975). *Syntactic change: A Cupan case study*. University of California Publications in Linguistics 79. Berkeley: University of California Press.

Jones, Terry L., Gary M. Brown, L. Mark Raab, et al. (2004). Environmental imperatives reconsidered: Demographic crises in western North America during the

Medieval Climatic Anomaly. In L. Mark Raab and Terry L. Jones (eds.), *Prehistoric California: Archaeology and the myth of paradise*. Salt Lake City: University of Utah Press, 12–32.

Kaufman, Terrence and John Justeson. (2009). Historical linguistics and pre-Columbian Mesoamerica. *Ancient Mesoamerica* 20: 221–231.

Kennett, Douglas J. and Jampes P. Kennett. (2004). Competitive and cooperative responses to climate instability in coastal southern California. In L. Mark Raab and Terry L. Jones (eds.), *Prehistoric California: Archaeology and the myth of paradise*. Salt Lake City: University of Utah Press, 138–148.

Kroeber, A. L. (1907). *The Yokuts language of South Central California*. University of California Publications in American Archaeology and Ethnology 2(5). Berkeley: University of California Press.

Kroeber, A. L. and George William Grace. (1960). *The Sparkman grammar of Luiseño*. University of California Publications in Linguistics Volume 16. Berkeley: University of California Press.

Lamb, Sydney M. (1958a). *Mono grammar*. PhD dissertation, University of California at Berkeley.

Lamb, Sydney M. (1958b). Linguistic prehistory in the Great Basin. *International Journal of American Linguistics* 24: 95–100.

LeBlanc, Steven A. (2003). Conflict and language dispersal: Issues and a New World example. In Peter Bellwood and Colin Renfrew (eds.), *Examining the farming/ language dispersal hypothesis*. Cambridge: McDonald Institute for Archaeological Research, 357–368.

Loether, Christopher. (1997). Yokuts and Miwok loanwords in Western Mono. In Jane H. Hill, P. J. Mistry and Lyle Campbell (eds.), *The life of language: Essays in honor of William Bright*. Berlin: Mouton de Gruyter, 101–121.

Lyneis, Margaret. (1995). The Virgin Anasazi, far western Puebloans. *Journal of World Prehistory* 9: 199–241.

Lyneis, Margaret. (2000). Life at the edge: Pueblo settlements in southern Nevada. In Michele Hegmon (ed.), *The archaeology of regional interaction: Religion, war- fare, and exchange across the American Southwest*. Boulder: University of Colorado Press, 257–274.

Madsen, David B. and David Rhode. (1994). *Across the West: Human population move- ment and the expansion of the Numa*. Salt Lake City: University of Utah Press.

Manaster Ramer, Alexis. (1992). A Northern Uto-Aztecan sound law: *-c-* → *-y-*. *International Journal of American Linguistics* 58: 251–268.

Matson, R. G. (1991). *The origins of southwestern agriculture*. Tucson: University of Arizona Press.

Matson, R. G. (2003). The spread of maize agriculture in the U.S. Southwest. In Colin Renfrew and Peter Bellwood (eds.), *Examining the farming/language dispersal hypothesis*. Cambridge: McDonald Institute for Archaeological Research, 341–356.

McCawley, William. (1996). *The first Angelinos: The Gabrielino Indians of Los Angeles*. Banning, CA: Malki Museum Press and Novato, CA: Ballena Press.

McConvell, Patrick. (2001). Language shift and language spread among hunter-gatherers. In C. Panter-Brick, P. Rowley-Conwy and R. Layton (eds.), *Hunter-gatherers: Cultural and biological perspectives*. Cambridge: Cambridge University Press, 143–169.

Merrill, William L., Robert J. Hard, Jonathan B. Mabry, et al. (2009). The diffusion of maize to the southwestern United States and its impact. *PNAS* 106(50): 21019–21026.

Miller, Wick R. (1970). Western Shoshoni dialects. In Early H. Swanson Jr. (ed.), *Languages and cultures of Western North America: Essays in Honor of Sven S. Liljeblad*. Pocatello: Idaho State University Press, 17–36.

Miller, Wick R. (1984). The classification of the Uto-Aztecan languages based on lexical evidence. *International Journal of American Linguistics* 50: 1–24.

Miller, Wick R. (1986). Numic languages. In Warren D'Azevedo (ed.), *Handbook of North American Indians*, Vol. 11: *Great Basin*. Washington, DC: Smithsonian Institution Press, 98–106.

Miller, Wick R. (1996). Sketch of Shoshone, a Uto-Aztecan language. In Ives Goddard (ed.), *Handbook of North American Indians,* Vol. 17: *Languages.* Washington, DC: Smithsonian Institution, 693–720.

Miller, Wick R., James L. Tanner and Lawrence P. Foley. (1971). A lexicostatistic study of Shoshoni dialects. *Anthropological Linguistics* 13(4): 142–164.

Moratto, Michael J. (1984). *California archaeology.* Orlando, FL: Academic Press.

Munro, Pamela. (2000). The Gabrielino enclitic system. In Eugene H. Casad and Thomas L. Willet (eds.), *Uto-Aztecan: Structural, temporal and geographic perspectives.* Hermosillo, Sonora: Editorial UniSon, 183–201.

Nichols, Johanna. (1992). *Linguistic diversity in space and time.* Chicago: University of Chicago Press.

Nichols, Michael. (1974). *Northern Paiute historical grammar.* PhD dissertation, University of California-Berkeley.

Press, Margaret L. (1979). *Chemehuevi: A grammar and lexicon.* University of California Publications in Linguistics, Vol. 92. Berkeley: University of California Press.

Raab, L. Mark and Terry L. Jones (eds.) (2004). *Prehistoric California: Archaeology and the myth of paradise.* Salt Lake City: University of Utah Press.

Rhode, David and David B. Madsen. (1994). Where are we? In David B. Madsen and David Rhode, *Across the West: Human population movement and the expansion of the Numa.* Salt Lake City: University of Utah Press, 213–222.

Roberts, Heidi, and Richard VN Ahlstrom. (2006) "Numic spread sure goes good with white bread: a test of the Numic spread model in Washington County, Utah." Manuscript on file at HRA, Inc., Conservation Archaeology, Las Vegas.

Sapir, Edward. (1930). *Southern Paiute: A Shoshonean language.* Proceedings of the American Academy of Arts and Sciences Volume 65, No. 1. Boston, MA: American Academy of Arts and Sciences.

Seiler, Hansjakob. (1970). *Cahuilla texts.* Indiana University Publications Language Science Monographs Vol. 6. Bloomington: University of Indiana and The Hague: Mouton and Company.

Seiler, Hansjakob. (1977). *Cahuilla frammar.* Banning, CA: Malki Museum Press.

Seiler, Hansjakob and Kojiro Hiroki. (1979). *Cahuilla dictionary.* Banning, CA: Malki Museum Press.

Shaul, David L. (1986). Linguistic adaptation and the Great Basin. *American Antiquity* 51: 415–416.

Snapp, Allen, John Anderson and Joy Anderson. (1982). Northern Paiute. In Ronald W. Langacker (ed.), *Studies in Uto-Aztecan frammar,* Vol. 3: *Uto-Aztecan grammatical sketches.* Dallas, TX: Summer Institute of Linguistics and Arlington, TX: University of Texas at Arlington, 1–92.

Staller, John, Robert Tykot and Bruce Benz (eds.). (2006). *Histories of Maize: Multidisciplinary approaches to the prehistory, linguistics, biogeography, domestication and evolution of maize.* Burlington, MA: Academic Press.

Stubbs, Brian. (2011). *Uto-Aztecan: A comparative vocabulary.* Blanding, UT: Rocky Mountain Books and Productions.

Sutton, Mark. (1994). The Numic expansion as seen from the Mojave Desert. In David B. Madsen and David Rhode, *Across the West: Human population movement and the expansion of the Numa.* Salt Lake City: University of Utah Press, 133–140.

Sutton, Mark. (2000). Prehistoric movements of Northern Uto-Aztecan peoples along the northwestern edge of the Southwest: Impact on Southwestern populations. In Michele Hegmon (ed.), *The archaeology of regional interaction: Religion, warfare, and exchange across the American Southwest.* Boulder: University of Colorado Press, 295–316.

Thomason, Sarah G. (2001). *Language contact: An introduction.* Washington, DC: Georgetown University Press.

Thornes, Timothy J. (2003). *A Northern Paiute grammar with texts.* PhD dissertation, University of Oregon.

Thurston, William R. (1987). *Processes of change in the languages of North-Western New Britain.* Pacific Linguistics Series b, No. 99. Canberra: Department of Linguistics, Research School of Pacific Studies, ANU.

Voegelin, Carl F., Florence M. Voegelin and Kenneth L. Hale. (1962). Typological and Comparative Grammar of Uto-Aztecan: I (Phonology). *International Journal of American Linguistics* Memoir 17.

Zigmond, Maurice L., Curtis G. Booth and Pamela Munro. (1990). *Kawaiisu: A grammar and dictionary with texts.* University of California Publications in Linguistics Vol. 119. Berkeley: University of California Press.

Part VII

South America

22   Language and Subsistence Patterns in the Amazonian Vaupés

Patience Epps

22.1   Introduction: Foragers and Farmers

The majority of contemporary hunter-gatherer populations do not subsist in isolation, but maintain regular relations with neighboring sedentary cultivators. Such interactions have been documented in many parts of the world. In Africa, for example, we find the relatively well-known cases of Pygmy groups such as the Mbuti and Efe, who interact with Bantu and other neighbors (Turnbull 1965; Bahuchet and Guillaume 1982; Grinker 1994), as well as relationships between the foraging !Kung and the Bantu/Tswana (Lee 1979), the Okiek of Kenya and the Maasai (Woodburn 1988), and the Hadza of Tanzania and their various agriculturalist neighbors (Woodburn 1988). In Southeast Asia and the Philippines, similar relations exist between the foraging Agta and the farming Palanan (Peterson 1978; Headland and Reid 1989), the Batek Semang and the Senoi (Endicott 1984), and other groups. In South India, likewise, foraging Paliyans interact with neighboring agriculturalists (the Tamils; Gardner 1972), as do the Malapantaram (Morris 1982) and the Naiken (Bird 1983).

Despite the profound geographic and cultural differences that exist among these various groups, the relationships themselves are often strikingly similar. A common pattern has been described as a 'symbiosis' (e.g., Maceda 1964; Ramos 1980; see Peterson 1978: 337) in which the hunter-gatherer groups provide hunted meat, forest products such as honey and fruit, and labor in exchange for the carbohydrates and trade goods possessed by the agriculturalists (Garvan 1963: 51; Peterson 1978: 334–337). Individuals or families often enter into long-term contracts (as is the case between the Agta and Palanan; see Peterson 1978: 342). However, the farmers almost invariably treat the foragers as inferior, savage, and even 'animal-like' (e.g., Woodburn 1988: 38), such that the latter typically get the worst of the relationship (leading some scholars to suggest that 'symbiosis' may not be an entirely appropriate characterization; see Spielmann and Eder 1994: 309). Accordingly, intermarriage tends to be limited; where it does occur, it is usually the hunter-gatherer woman who marries into the agricultural community, rather than the reverse.

The social imbalance resulting from this interaction tends to have profound linguistic consequences for the foraging populations. One-sided bilingualism is the norm, and in many cases this has resulted in language shift at some point in the past (cf. Spielmann and Eder 1994: 307). For example, the Philippine Agta apparently switched to Austronesian between 1,000 and 3,000 years ago (the variants have since become fully distinct; see Blust 1976; Reid 1987); various Aslian groups of Malaysia today speak Mon-Khmer languages (also probably adopted more than 2,000 years ago; Junker 2002: 151); and contemporary Pygmy groups speak Bantu and other languages (e.g., Bahuchet 1993). Many of these hunter-gatherers have nonetheless retained a specialized vocabulary relating to forest products and activities, kin relations, etc. (Peterson 1978: 338; Bahuchet 1993). Linguistic influence in the opposite direction is extremely rare, although cases do exist (most notably the adoption of clicks into Bantu languages; see Woodburn 1988; Chapter 6 by Güldemann, this volume).

The Amazon basin is likewise home to peoples whose mode of subsistence prioritizes hunting/gathering or horticulture, although most actually depend to some degree on both.[1] The interactions among many of these groups have much in common with those described for Africa, Southeast Asia, and elsewhere. This chapter focuses on one such example of forager-farmer relations, that existing between the Naduhup (Makú)[2] peoples, who maintain a foraging focus, and the more horticulturalist Tukanoan peoples of the northwest Amazon. While this relationship bears many of the hallmarks of forager-farmer interaction as encountered elsewhere in the world, it is particularly noteworthy in that, unlike the languages of many other foragers, the Naduhup languages have been maintained despite widespread bilingualism and profound language contact. The Naduhup languages thus provide us with a rare glimpse into the past, and allow us to address questions that have been raised regarding Amazonian foragers more generally, as well as foragers in other parts of the world: In particular, how old is the association of the Naduhup hunter-gatherers with their more horticulturalist neighbors, and indeed with horticulture generally? How well does the Amazonian case fit the profile of forager-farmer relations elsewhere in the world? An evaluation of lexical data, numeral systems, and language contact phenomena suggests that the current dynamics between these groups are a relatively consistent reflection of those that have existed for many generations, but that we can nevertheless determine an approximate point at which the interaction began.

Map 22.1 Location of Naduhup and neighboring indigenous languages.

22.2   Contemporary Foragers and Farmers in the Amazonian Vaupés

22.2.1   The Vaupés Region

The interaction between Naduhup hunter-gatherers and Tukanoan farmers is concentrated in the Vaupés region of the northwest Amazon (see Map 22.1). This strikingly multilingual region is home to some four different language families: East Tukanoan (which includes Tukano, also used as a regional lingua franca, and Desano, Tuyuka, Kotiria/Wanano, and perhaps a dozen other languages); Arawakan (of which Tariana is the sole representative in the Vaupés, Baniwa is spoken just to the northeast, and other languages were once spoken along the middle and lower Rio Negro); Naduhup (composed of Hup and Yuhup within the Vaupés, and Dâw and Nadëb outside it); and the sister languages Kakua and Nukak (formerly thought to be relatives of the Naduhup family; see Epps and Bolaños 2017 and Section 22.2.4). Also represented in the general area are the more recent imports Nheengatú (also known as Lingua Geral, a Tupi language spread in colonial times), Spanish, and Portuguese.

22.2.2   "People of the River" and "People of the Forest"

The Tukanoan and Arawakan peoples of the region are all settled agricultural-ists. Most live along major rivers and cultivate large gardens in which bitter manioc is the principal crop, and bananas, chili peppers, potatoes, and other items are also grown. Fish provide the major source of protein. The Vaupés river peoples are best known for their institutionalized practice of linguistic exogamy, or obligatory marriage across language groups (see, e.g., Sorensen 1967; Jackson 1983; Chernela 1993; Stenzel 2005). Speakers identify with their father's language, but tend to be highly multilingual because they grow up surrounded by the multiple languages spoken by their mothers, aunts, and other married women in the village.[3] This practice has fostered a regional conception that language and identity are essentially inseparable, and that mixing of languages is inappropriate. Code-switching and lexical borrowing are limited (even in the current circumstances of language shift); however, profound grammatical convergence has been shown to have taken place between Tariana and Tukano (Aikhenvald 2002.).

In contrast to the river dwellers, the Naduhup peoples of the region – and likewise the Kakua and Nukak peoples (see Silverwood-Cope 1972; Politis 1996, 2007; Cabrera et al. 1999) – are traditionally seminomadic forest dwellers. They rely heavily (or did until very recently) on hunting and gathering for subsistence, together with small-scale manioc farming. These foraging-focused peoples do not participate in the regional system of linguistic exogamy, preferring to marry among their own people, across clans. The discussion in this chapter, while comparative, focuses in particular on the Hup people (or Hupd'əh), who have a particularly close relationship with Tukanoans, and with whom I have had the most interaction.[4]

The Hupd'əh – like most of the other forest peoples of the region – have experienced relatively profound changes in lifestyle over the past three to four decades; these were initiated by missionaries who encouraged them (and in some cases coerced them; see Reid 1979) to move closer to the rivers and to settle in larger, more settled communities of as many as 200 people or more. While this has led to a more sedentary pattern and a greater reliance on horticulture than existed previously (see Reid 1979), the Hupd'əh have continued to spend extended periods of time away from their villages, often deep in the forest on hunting and gathering trips. Most Hupd'əh readily voice a strong preference for foraging, which they typically refer to as 'knocking about' in the forest (*g'etg'oʔ-*) (see also Reid 1979; Pozzobon 1991); agricultural activities, in contrast, are referred to as 'work' (*biʔ-*). A few families do not have their own gardens, and those that do almost invariably plant small patches and harvest the manioc long before it has grown to full size – in clear contrast to River Indian (Tukanoan and Arawakan) practices.

The forest orientation of the Hupd'əh is clearly an important part of their culture and their sense of identity, consistent with Rival's (1999: 81) observation that for foraging peoples generally, "hunting and gathering is as much a social and cultural phenomenon as a form of ecological-economic adaptation" (see also Rival [2002] for the Waorani; Pozzobon [1994] for the Nadëb; Politis [1999, 2007] for the Nukak). For the Hupd'əh, this is illustrated by their self-reference as *j'ugan ʔuyd'əh* 'people of the forest' (in contrast to the Tukanoans, whom they call *dehmian ʔuyd'əh* 'people of the river'), and by the words of one Hup patriarch, Henrique Monteiro, as he recounted a mythical tale: "So Bone-Son [the creator] sent us up from the river, in order to live here in this land ... We are to live here; here in the forest world it is good."

22.2.3   Dynamics of the Relationship

Within the Vaupés, the hunter-gatherer Naduhup peoples and the horticultur-alist Tukanoans maintain a close relationship (see, e.g., Reid 1979; Ramos 1980; Jackson 1983; Milton 1984; Fisser 1988; Pozzobon 1991). Often described as 'symbiotic,' this interaction has much in common with that described for other foraging and farming peoples elsewhere in the world. The Hupd'əh – and similarly the Yuhup – provide their horticulturalist neighbors with meat, forest products, and labor, and receive agricultural products (espe-cially manioc) and manufactured trade goods in exchange. Long-term 'patron-client' contracts exist between individuals and families, and an enormous amount of cultural material – rituals, religious beliefs, stories, and songs – is common to both groups (and widespread within the Vaupés generally). Little intermarriage takes place, and when this does occur it virtually always involves a Naduhup woman and a Tukanoan man; the children are thus considered Tukanoan, in keeping with the regional convention of patrilineal descent. The social imbalance is profound; Tukanoans consider Naduhup peoples inferior, incestuous (because they do not practice linguistic exogamy), and animal-like (see Reid 1979; Jackson 1983).

Bilingualism in Hup and Tukano (the East Tukanoan language that is used as a regional lingua franca) is almost 100% among Hup adults,[5] and a similar situation appears to hold for most Yuhup in Brazil. However, unlike foragers in many other parts of the world, the Naduhup peoples have not experienced language shift, despite this long-term bilingualism and social imbalance. This fact can probably be attributed to the widespread cultural attitude in the Vaupés that essentializes the link between language and identity.

The social dynamic between hunter-gatherers and horticulturalists described here – and its linguistic consequences – is most profound within the Vaupés region, but also exists beyond it. On the western side of the Vaupés, the Kakua people are reported to have had until quite recently a relationship with the Tukanoans of the region comparable to that maintained by the Hupd'əh (Silverwood-Cope 1972; Bolaños 2016). The Dâw (the Naduhup group on the eastern periphery of the Vaupés) and the River Indians in the vicinity appear to have once had a similar relationship; however, possibilities for interaction with Tukanoans are more limited, because Dâw territory is outside the principal area occupied by Tukanoans (and is currently adjacent to the Brazilian town of São Gabriel da Cachoeira, where opportunities for interaction with non-Indians are also available). The Naduhup Nadëb people, on the other hand, are far removed from the Vaupés and have virtually no contact with Tukanoans; although they apparently had some interaction with Arawakan peoples in the past, this is limited today (see Pozzobon 1991: 40; Epps 2017).

22.2.4   Who Are the 'Makú'?

In the linguistic literature, the name 'Makú' refers to a proposed language family that includes the four here termed 'Naduhup' (Hup, Yuhup, Dâw, and Nadëb). However, within the northwest Amazon region itself, the meaning of the term 'Makú' is quite different. The word is used exclusively by River Indians (and by some non-Indians) to refer to any of the various groups of foragers in the area – i.e. those who are considered 'wild' or 'animal-like' forest-dwellers by the region's more settled inhabitants. The most likely origin of the term is Arawakan (Koch-Grünberg 1906b: 877; cf. Baniwa-Kurripako *ma-aku* [NEG-speak] 'without speech'); it is considered highly offensive by the forest peoples themselves.

The name 'Makú' is thus used in reference to a range of peoples, including Naduhup, Yanomami, and others, who have no necessary relationship among themselves other than a subsistence pattern that is, in the eyes of the river dwellers, diametrically opposed to their own settled lifestyle. Early European visitors to the region were hosted by the River Indians, and what they learned of the region's more nomadic peoples (with whom they had little contact themselves) was necessarily colored by the River Indian perspective – as well as their own, perhaps not dissimilar cultural biases. This general use of the term 'Makú' was observed by one of these early visitors, Theodore Koch-Grünberg, who wrote that "under this name are grouped a whole quantity of groups with languages that are very different from each other and very primitive" … "[all are] hunting nomads, who have no agriculture" (1906a: 180–181, my translation).

Koch-Grünberg himself compiled word lists of many of the region's languages, and suggested a relationship among the Naduhup languages Dâw and Yuhup, and Kakua, spoken in Colombia and clearly related to the nearby language Nukak (see Map 22.1; Koch-Grünberg 1906a, 1906b). His suggestion was widely accepted, largely because data on these languages have always been scarce, and the inclusion of Kakua and Nukak in the 'Makú' language family became the convention (see, e.g., Rodrigues 1986; Campbell 1997; Martins and Martins 1999).

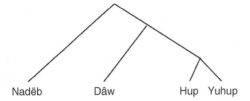

Figure 22.1 Relationships among Naduhup languages.

Yet, as Epps and Bolaños (2017) have argued, a closer evaluation of the available data (including Kakua documentation by Katherine Bolaños; see Bolaños 2016) indicates that there is at this point no conclusive evidence for a relationship between Kakua/Nukak and the four Naduhup languages (see also Martins 2005). As for the handful of close similarities that can be identified among Hup/Yuhup and Kakua/Nukak words, language contact is a likely explanation; indeed, contact between Hup and Kakua speakers – whose territories are adjacent – has been documented by Silverwood-Cope (1972; see also Reid 1979: 23). It is likely that the common identity of these 'Makú' peoples as forest-dwelling foragers, particularly when viewed in contrast to the settled Tukanoan agriculturalists, is part of what led outside observers to assume deeper similarities where none may actually exist.

On the other hand, the relationship between the four Naduhup languages – Hup, Yuhup, Dâw, and Nadëb – is well established on the basis of lexical and grammatical evidence, including many cognates and regular sound correspondences (Martins 2005; Epps and Bolaños 2017). The available data suggest the family tree in Figure 22.1, which is taken as a working assumption in this chapter. However, further historical work awaits more documentation, especially of Nadëb.

22.2.5 Tracing the First Inhabitants of the Vaupés

Of the three groups present in the Upper Rio Negro region today, there has been considerable speculation that the Naduhup peoples were the original inhabitants (Stradelli 1890; Koch-Grünberg 1906b: 878; Nimuendajú 1927/1950: 164; Aikhenvald 1999: 390). Within the Vaupés itself, ethnohistorical accounts of the Arawakan Tariana indicate that they arrived late to the area (possibly around 600 years ago) from the direction of the Rio Aiari to the north, moving into lands already occupied by Tukanoans (Cabalzar and Ricardo 1998: 57; Aikhenvald 2002: 24). According to Neves (2001: 281–283), the region of the Papuri and middle Vaupés Rivers had already been home to Tukanoan-speaking groups for hundreds of years by the beginning of the fifteenth century. Whether the Naduhup actually preceded them in the Vaupés or the Rio Negro region more generally has yet to be determined; at least some of the claims to this effect may be no more than assumptions based on their foraging subsistence pattern, commonly associated with a more 'primitive' status (see the discussion in Aikhenvald [2002: 24]; also Headland and Reid [1989] concerning the Philippines). However, the distribution of languages today does support this scenario; only the Naduhup languages are spoken uniquely within the Rio Negro region (although more distant relations may yet turn up elsewhere). In contrast, Tukanoan languages are found as far away as Peru and Ecuador to the west, and the Arawakan family is widespread, with a likely homeland in northern Amazonia between the Rio Orinoco and Rio Negro (Aikhenvald 1999; Heckenberger 2002; Chacon 2014).

22.3   Past Subsistence Patterns in the Vaupés: Foraging or Horticulture?

22.3.1   *Characterizing the Naduhup Association with Horticulture*

Horticulture today clearly plays an important role in the lives of the Hupd'əh and other Naduhup peoples, despite the cultural preference for hunting and gathering. Even for those families who do not consistently maintain small manioc plantings, cultivated foods – especially manioc and chili peppers – are nevertheless a dietary staple. No meal is considered complete in the Vaupés region without manioc, whether this appears as flatbread (*beiju* in the local Portuguese), coarse meal sprinkled on food or eaten in handfuls (*farinha*), or as a drink (usually *chibe*, manioc meal in water, or *mingau*, water thickened with tapioca). Those Hupd'əh who have no manioc of their own, or who wish to supplement the yield from their own small plantings, have a number of strategies for procuring it: they provide labor (e.g., in planting or clearing fields, building houses, etc.) to neighboring Tukanoans, to be paid in manioc; they help other Hupd'əh with chores of planting or manioc processing in exchange for a small share; or, occasionally, they simply help themselves from others' gardens. Tukanoans who live near Hupd'əh are particularly familiar with this latter strategy and typically take pains to locate their gardens well out of harm's way – often as much as a half-hour's paddle downriver.

While the contemporary Naduhup association with horticulture is relatively well established, it is less clear what the picture has been in the past. Are the Naduhup peoples' own horticultural practices and reliance on cultivated foods recent? Ancient? Representative of a stable semi-horticultural situation or a relatively abrupt transition toward cultivation? Is their association with horticulture historically independent of their relationship with River Indian agriculturalists, or have these always been linked? There appear to be at least four possible characterizations of Naduhup horticultural history. These four hypotheses are presented in the text that follows, and then evaluated on the basis of lexical evidence from the Naduhup languages in the subsequent discussion.

In the first scenario, Naduhup horticulture as practiced today may be indicative of a recent, relatively abrupt shift from a foraging to an agricultural lifestyle, which is not yet completed. This would presumably imply that the Naduhup had little or no contact with either an agriculturalist lifestyle or those who practiced it – i.e., the River Indians – until a few generations ago, but were quickly impressed by the benefits of the new technology upon encountering it. The Naduhup peoples' current lackadaisical attitude toward agriculture would thus constitute a temporary and short-lived stage, and they could be expected to settle down and become more like the River Indians in the near future.[6] Ethnographic and archaeological accounts of shifts from foraging to farming elsewhere in the world offer little or no evidence for such an abrupt transition, but it is nonetheless considered here as a possibility.

In the second hypothetical picture, Naduhup horticulture as it appears today may represent a long-term, limited assimilation of a secondary subsistence strategy. Horticulture would thus have been a peripheral part of the foragers' lives for many generations, but its adoption would be incomplete and potentially never fully realized. This scenario appears to have precedent among a variety of present-day foragers; comparable cases have been reported in southern Africa (Solway and Lee 1990; Wilmsen and Denbow 1990), Southeast Asia (Headland and Reid 1989), and other parts of the world. As Bellwood observes:

Agriculturalists and foragers can interact quite successfully for long periods, even millennia, under certain ecological situations where agriculture may be slightly marginal or where niches can be kept geographically separate ... I know of no ethnographic cases where the erstwhile foragers have come to adopt agriculture to the same degree of intensity and success as their agriculturalist neighbors. In all cases the interaction or symbiosis seems merely to be slowing down of a process which elsewhere occurred much more quickly, that is, the ultimate assimilation of the foragers into the agricultural population. (Bellwood 1997:130)

While this second scenario assumes that the foragers' association with horticulture is old, it does not require it to be ancient – that is, it may be possible to establish a point in time before which the foragers truly were foragers, with no reliance on actively cultivated foods. In contrast, the third scenario calls even this into question, proposing that the foragers' secondary reliance on horticulture has necessarily been in place for millennia, and must in fact be as old as human habitation in the rain forest ecosystem itself (as we know it today). This possibility is based on the proposal that contemporary tropical rain forests are lacking in resources required for long-term human survival, and that access to cultivated foods – whether direct or indirect – is essential (see Bailey et al. 1989; Headland and Bailey 1991). This proposal has been convincingly contested on the basis of contemporary ethnographic and archaeological evidence (see Brosius 1991; Endicott and Bellwood 1991 for Southeast Asia; also Bahuchet et al. 1991; Colinvaux and Bush 1991; Piperno and Pearsall 1998), but the possibility that some version of horticulture is ancient in the case of the Naduhup calls for consideration.

Finally, in a fourth possible scenario, the Naduhup may have been a primarily horticulturalist people at some time in the past, but later gave up their horticultural emphasis in favor of foraging. Such a reversion to hunting and gathering has been shown to have taken place among ethnographic foragers in various parts of the world, such as the Penan and Tasaday peoples of Southeast Asia (Bellwood 1985: 133–135), the prehistoric southern Maoris of New Zealand (Bellwood 1997: 130), and certain Bantu groups in southern Africa (Nurse et al. 1985: 149–153). In Amazonia, similar shifts affected a number of Tupi-Guaraní peoples, in particular, such as the Guajá (Balée 1999), the Yuqui, and the Sirionó of Bolivia (Roosevelt 1998, 1999; Neves and Petersen 2006: 284). In fact, the extreme pressures of conquest and the debated adequacy of food resources in the rain forest have led some scholars to suggest that perhaps such a shift affected *all* Amazonian hunter-gatherers, such that "the contemporary foraging societies of the humid tropics of South America ... may have generally regressed from a past horticultural mode of production" (Balée 1999: 26; see also Lathrap 1968; Levi-Strauss 1968; Bailey et al. 1989).

22.3.2   *Testing the Hypotheses: Lexical Evidence*

The tools available for piecing together Naduhup history are limited. The archaeological record is not extensive in the region, as material remains are mostly biodegradable and rarely preserved, and the relative remoteness of the areas where Naduhup languages are spoken makes investigation difficult. Historical and ethnohistorical evidence is also inconclusive, in part because stories of origins and other historical events are highly prone to diffusion within the Vaupés. The traditional stories and myths I encountered among the Hupd'əh do not appear to indicate a shift in subsistence pattern. Early explorers in the region, Koch-Grünberg and Nimuendajú, reported a forager-farmer relationship much like that seen today (Koch-Grünberg 1906b: 880–881; Nimuendajú 1927/1950: 159, 164–165).[7]

Linguistic evidence appears to provide a promising route to reconstructing the history of the Naduhup peoples and their association with horticulture. A comparative-historical assessment of lexical data, in particular, allows a relatively fine-grained approach. The following discussion relies on the basic assumptions of the 'Wörter und Sachen' methodology of cultural reconstruction (e.g., Sapir 1949: 439–444; Campbell 1997: 413–415; Epps 2014). According to these assumptions, if the word can be reconstructed to the proto-language, the concept it represents was probably present in the culture of its speakers. The concept also was likely to have been relatively important; studies of Tupi-Guaranian languages (Balée and Moore 1994; Balée 2000) and Mayan languages (Leonti et al. 2003), for example, suggest that plant names relating to culturally useful plants (as opposed to nonexploited plants) tend to be relatively time stable. Second, morphologically complex words (such as compounds and derivations) are more likely to be recent innovations than are monomorphemic words. Finally, calques and loanwords are more likely to represent new concepts than old, familiar ones, and the borrowed word and the concept are likely to have the same source; this is based on the recognition that lexical borrowing motivated by need appears to be more common cross-linguistically than lexical replacement for prestige or other reasons.

Clearly, these assumptions do not always apply, and conclusions based on individual words are suspect – especially in the case of the Naduhup languages, where only preliminary efforts at reconstruction have been made. Nevertheless, the Wörter und Sachen assumptions can be applied to an entire semantic *domain* (as opposed to an individual word) with some reliability. The following discussion presents a cross section of semantic domains relating to useful wild-occurring plants, domesticated plants (both those requiring little active cultivation and those that are more intensively cultivated), and other horticultural vocabulary, in order to test the following predictions: First, if horticulture is ancient among the Naduhup (whether as a primary or secondary subsistence strategy), the horticultural lexicon should not be significantly more innovative (i.e., newer) than the useful noncultivated plant lexicon, and (conversely) comparable numbers of cultivated and noncultivated plant terms should reconstruct to Proto-Naduhup. Second, if horticulture is very recent among the Naduhup, the horticultural vocabulary should be highly variable across all four languages, and should not reconstruct to any branch of the family.

In considering the following tables, it should be kept in mind that (as indicated in the introduction with respect to horticulture and hunting/gathering in Amazonia generally) the distinction between cultivated and noncultivated plants is not necessarily clear-cut. Several of the plants species listed here as noncultivated are nevertheless managed and/or semidomesticated (e.g., barbasco, *Lonchocarpus* spp.; ayahuasca, *Banisteriopsis caapi*) by Vaupés peoples, including the Naduhup. Other plants are domesticated species or varieties, but are like nondomesticates in that they do not require intensive or regular care, and may be susceptible to unintentional 'planting' and to harvesting by others than those who planted them. For example, plants such as achiote (*Bixa orellana*) and peach-palm (*Bactris gasipaes*) were widely dispersed throughout Amazonia by indigenous peoples in ancient times, such that current stands are presumably anthropogenic (at least by descent), but are not necessarily actively managed; their exploitation is thus more consistent with a hunting-gathering lifestyle than is the exploitation of more intensively managed crops (see, e.g., Clement et al. [2009] on the foraging Waorani people's use of the peach-palm). For some plants, a domesticated variant may have wild counterparts (i.e., different species, varieties, or even some other plant with a common resemblance or use), and these may share a name (e.g., cacao, *Theobroma* spp.; cashew, *Anacardium* spp.). The precise origin of a given plant and the degree to which it has been spread by human hand is not always clear, so particular distinctions made here may require some revision in future work.

The following tables contrast the semantic domains of useful wild-occurring plants (Table 22.1), relatively low-maintenance domesticates (Table 22.2), more intensively cultivated domesticates (Table 22.3), and other terms relating to cultivars (Table 22.4) across the four Naduhup languages. Tukano (Eastern Tukanoan) and Baniwa (Arawakan) counterparts are also provided for comparison.[8] Conventions for interpreting the tables are as follows: bolded items are presumed to be cognate[9] across all four languages of the Naduhup family; underlined items are cognate *either* across Hup and/or Yuhup and Dâw *or* across Dâw and Nadëb (and not identified as loans into their common ancestor; see the discussion that follows). Words identified as likely candidates for borrowings and calques are shaded and discussed in footnotes, and morphologically complex forms are glossed in parentheses (but note that information on morphological complexity is particularly scarce for Nadëb, and the identification of loans is made more difficult by a lack of data from other regional languages, which in many cases are underdocumented or extinct).

A comparison of the tables suggests that horticultural and nonhorticultural vocabulary is not of an equivalent age in the Naduhup languages. In Table 22.1, which presents a representative sample of terms for useful wild-occurring plants across the Naduhup languages and in two of their River Indian neighbors (Tukano and Baniwa), at least half the terms are likely candidates for cognates across all four Naduhup languages. The picture is roughly comparable to that which emerges when we compare other semantic domains of core vocabulary, such as body parts, native animals, etc. Among the terms for domesticated plants (Tables 22.2 and 22.3) and other vocabulary associated with horticultural activities (Table 22.4), in contrast, we find very few cognates across the four languages, but many compounds and morphologically complex forms, and a number of likely lexical borrowings and calques. Even if we rule out terms for

Table 22.1 *Useful wild-occurring plants (may be semidomesticated or managed)*

		NADUHUP				E. TUKANOAN	ARAWAKAN
Gloss		Hup	Yuhup	Dâw	Nadëb	Tukano	Baniwa
açai palm[a]	*Euterpe precatoria*	*g'ædʔæg* ['ʔ-fruit']	*k'ædʔæg* ['ʔ-fruit']	*nǎk*	*manǎg*	*mipí*	*manákhe*
black palm	*Oenocarpus bacaba*	*ciwíb*	*wíb*	*wǐm*	*fiwí:m*	*yumú*	*póoperi*
buriti palm	*Mauritia flexuosa*	*jʼǎk*	*cʼǎk*	*cǎk*	*ʌ́:k*	*ne ê*	*íitewi*
ayahuasca/caapi[b]	*Banisteriopsis caapi*	*kapiʔ*	*kapiʔ*			*kapí*	*kaápi*
caraná (thatch palm)	*Mauritiella armata*	*tɔ́p-gʼet* ['shelter-leaf']		*pɔ̌j*	*tapɔ:ɲ*	*muhí*	*ttiiña*
cashew[c]	*Anacardium* spp. (wild and domesticated types)	*jǎhǎm*	*jǎhǎm*	*waʃap*	*akaɟ*	*sõrã*	*akáyo*
cipó vine	*Heteropsis* spp.	*jǔb*	*jǔb*	*jum*	*ju:m*	*misí*	*dápi*
kapok cotton	*Ceiba pentandra*	*cuwǔk*	*wúk*	*wǔk*	*fíwik*	*buʃá*	*pirimítsi*
tree-grape	*Pourouma cecropiifolia*	*buhúh, píɲ*		*huh*	*farapu:ʔ*	*i'sê*	*kamhéro*
cunuri	*Cunuria spruceana*	*pěd*	*pěd*	*pǎ:d*	*pɔɔd*	*wapí*	*kóonoli*
genipap	*Genipapa americana*	*dʼǎd, bobo-ʔag*	*deh dʼǎd*	*jenipapu*	*karawiñ*	*weʔé*	*dúana*
inga[d]	*Inga* spp.	*mín*	*mín*	*mǐn*	*kamɛʔpiʔ*	*mene*	
japurá	*Erisma japura*	*jawák*	*wǎk*	*wak*	*jawak*	*baʔti*	*dzáapora*
mushroom	(edible generic)	*pɔ́b'*	*pɔ́b'*	*pɔb, pɔm'*	*pʌm*	*eheka'* [no generic]	*iralída, keerípa*
seje palm[e]	*Jessenia bataua*[e]	*wǎh*	*wǎh*	*wax*	*wak*	*yumú*	*ponáma*
paxiuba palm[f]	*Iriartea exorrhiza*	*púp-teg*	*pǔp teg*	*pup bax*	*baʔbui, kako:r*	*watá*	*éeña, póopa*

Table 22.1 (cont.)

Gloss		NADUHUP				E. TUKANOAN	ARAWAKAN
		Hup	Yuhup	Dâw	Nadëb	Tukano	Baniwa
barbasco/timbó	*Lonchocarpus* spp.	*d'ǔç*	*d'úç*	*dǔʃ*	*dṳ:j*	*ehú*	[no generic]
tucumã palm	*Astrocaryum aculeatum*	*g'öb*	*j'ɨ̈p*	*tukma*[g]	kajero	*yaí-beta*	
ucuqui	*Pouteria ucuqui*	*mǐh*	*mǐh*	*mi*	*mʌʔ*	*pupiã*	*hiíniri*
umari	*Poraqueiba serica*	*pɛ̌ɟ*	*pɛ́ɟ*	*peɟ*	*pɑːt'*	*wami*	*dòomali*

[a] The Nadëb and Dâw forms are borrowed from Arawakan.

[b] This word is shared across Hup, Tukanoan, and Arawakan languages in the region; see discussion that follows. *Banisteriopsis caapi* (a vine used to produce a hallucinogenic drink) is semidomesticated, but wild varieties are native to the northwest Amazon.

[c] The Nadëb and Baniwa forms are loans from Nheengatú (Tupi).

[d] It is possible that the Hup, Yuhup, and Dâw forms are borrowed from Tukanoan.

[e] Also known as *Oenecarpus bataua*.

[f] It is possible that the Hup, Yuhup, and Dâw forms are Arawakan loans.

[g] Borrowed from Nheengatú (Tupi) *tucumã*.

Table 22.2 *Relatively low-maintenance domesticates*

	Gloss	NADUHUP				E. TUKANOAN	ARAWAKAN
		Hup	Yuhup	Dâw	Nadëb	Tukano	Baniwa
achiote (annato)	*Bixa Orellana*	**hə̂w**	**hə̂w**	**hə̂w**	**ha:w**	*mosã*	*phirimáapa*
avocado	*Persea americana*	juhúm	juhǔm	hûm	baraja:ʔ	ũyú	piirídza
calabash tree[a]	*Crescentia cujete*	bʼɔ́ʔ	bʼɔ́ʔ	bɔ́ʔ	ʔǝk	wahá	kóoya
cocoa[b]	*Theobroma* spp.	kakáwa, baʔuk (wild sp.)	kakawa	húlʔ (ahoro wild sp.)	kʼa:w, koro, ahoro		kákawa
peach-palm	*Bactris gasipaes*	ɨ́w	cʼɨ́w	cɨ́w	ji:h, ji:hʔ	ĩrẽ	piipiri

[a] The same indigenous names may also apply to the domesticated bottle-gourd, *Lagenaria siceraria*.

[b] In Hup, the borrowed variant of Portuguese *cacao* (ultimately from Nahuatl) apparently refers to the cultivar *Theobroma cacao*, while other names refer to the wild species. Balée (2003) attributes the prevalence of borrowed variants of *cacao* in Amazonian languages to the greatly heightened importance of the plant after European contact, when it became an export crop. Dâw and Nadëb *ahoro* is probably also a loan; source is unknown.

Table 22.3 *More intensively cultivated domesticates*

Gloss	NADUHUP				E. TUKANOAN	ARAWAKAN
	Hup	Yuhup	Dâw	Nadëb	Tukano	Baniwa
banana, plantain[a] *Musa* spp.	*pihit*	*wihit, panah*	*ʃel,' nál'*	*maseːr, pãnãːr*	*ohó*	*palána*
cane (sugar)[b] *Saccharum officinarum*	*mũh teg* ['arrow stick']	*nɘ̃ɲ-teg* ['honey stick']	*xãr'*	*kaːn*	*ãrɨ*	*máapa*
carár[c] *Dioscorea* spp.	*j 'áh*	*c 'áh*	*ʔĩn*	*ʔĩːn*	*yaʔmũ*	*áaxi*
coca[c] *Erythroxylum coca*	*pïʔãk* [*ʔuk-* 'pick up loose material']	*cohó*	*tuʔ*	*batoʔ*	*paáĩu*	*hiípato*
maize[d] *Zea mays*	*pihit jĩm* ['banana-sow' (v.)]	*hóka*	*w'at*	*janatĩ*	*ohóka*	*káana*
manioc[e] *Manihot esculenta*	*kajak tɔʔ; kijak tɔʔ* [*tɔʔ* 'tuber']	*jãk tɔʔ*	*jãk*	*boːg*	*kii*	*káini*
sweet manioc *Manihot esculenta*	*kajak wɜ̃d* ['manioc-eat']; *wɜ̃d kijak* ['eat-manioc']	*jak wɜ̃d* ['manioc-eat']	*jãk jaʔ* ['manioc-grill']	*mahɔur*		*kapíwali*
papaya[f] *Carica papaya*	*mamáw*	*mamáw*	*mãw*	*mapah*	*mamu*	
peanut *Arachis hypogaea*	*j 'æʔ tutú* ['feces into.ground']	*j 'æʔ tutú* ['feces into.ground']				
hot pepper *Capsicum* spp.	*kɔ̃w*	*kɔ̃w*	*xɔw*	*pɔːh*	*biá*	*áati, mítsa*

pineapple[g] *Ananas comosus*	canā, jɔ̃j	jɔ̃j	wãn	mawã:d	sẽrã	mãawiro
sweet potato[h] *Ipomoea batatas*	piʔ	jɔʔhãh	jɔʔ / limã	karahí:r	yãpí	kaliri
squash[i] *Cucurbita* spp.	bɔʔ-wĩd ['gourd-eat']	bɔʔ-wĩd ['gourd-eat']	hũt	hĩ:t	mirô	
tobacco *Nicotiana* spp.	**hũt**	**hũt**	**hũt**	**hũt**	džeema	

[a] The cultivated banana was probably brought to Brazil in the 1500s. The Hup and Yuhup terms are identical to those used for a wild plant resembling a banana plant (*Heliconia* sp., with similarly large useful leaves), and may have been derived via semantic shift. The Baniwa term *palána* may be borrowed from Portuguese/Spanish; the Yuhup, Dâw, and Nadëb variants were probably borrowed via Arawakan.

[b] Sugar cane is not native to South America. The Hup name is the same as that used for the native arrow cane; the Dâw and Nadëb forms are borrowed from Portuguese *cana* 'cane.'

[c] Words for 'coca' appear to be lexical borrowings shared across Arawakan, Tukanoan, Dâw, and Nadëb. The most likely source is Arawakan.

[d] 'Maize' in Yuhup is a Tukanoan borrowing; the Dâw and Nadëb terms are probably loans from Nheengatú (*awací*). Maize is of Mesoamerican origin, and was probably a relatively late pre-Colombian arrival to Amazonia (Piperno and Pearsall 1998).

[e] It is possible that the syllable *ki/ka* in the Hup terms for manioc is borrowed from Tukanoan.

[f] Words for 'papaya' appear generally to be borrowed variants of Portuguese *mamão*; the Nadëb term is borrowed from Arawakan (e.g., Piapoco *mapaya*; Arawakan languages are the most likely source of the Spanish/English term *papaya*).

[g] Hup *canā* is borrowed from Tukano; the Nadëb and Dâw forms from Arawakan.

[h] The Hup term may be related via borrowing to Tukano *yãpi*; the Nadëb form is an Arawakan loan.

[i] The Dâw form is probably a loan from Nheengatú.

Table 22.4 *Other terms relating to cultivars*

Gloss	NADUHUP				E. TUKANOAN	ARAWAKAN
	Hup	Yuhup	Dâw	Nadêb	Tukano	Baniwa
caxiri[a] (manioc beer)	húptok ['person-belly']	ʔə̀g [nominalized form of verb 'drink']	ʔə̀g [nominalized form of verb 'drink']	jaraka	peéru	pádzawaro
comatá (strainer)	kojój		tun	juh, jaraʔta:	tõhõpaha	ttiiroli, báats
manioc meal[b]	kə̃n [toast(v.)]; cíh [also means 'grass']	cak pój ['mash toasted']	fɨ̃k	maʃu:k	poká	matsóka
manioc mash	cə̆k	cə̆k	jə̆k-dəp ['manioc mash']	maru:h	kii kurá, kii siʔti	hipoanhi, phóakhe
grater	**híp**	**híp**	**hi:p**	**híp**	sõkõro (v. oé)	áada
griddle	bɔ̆k káb ['pot ?']	b ɔ̆kʔã́h	bɔ̆d	afi:ra	ata	póali
manicuera/tucupi (boiled manioc juice)	kajak dě̃h ['manioc liquid']	ki-dě̃h ['sour-liquid']	jək-nəx ['manioc liquid']	karahi:	yõka (manicuera) kii-boo koo (tucupi)	kainia
manioc bread[c]	b ã̀ʔ, pə̆n' [any flat cake]	k'ŏj	baʔ?	madáo, kanapĩh	ãhú [cf. baʔá 'eat']	peéthe
mingau	wɔ̃n'	wɔ̃n'	lã̀j	kajahar	yumúka (non-manioc: koo)	koriakaa kamókaa
plant/sow/sprout (v.)	**jum-** (seeds) **cíj'-** ['poke in'; 'plant manioc cuttings']	**jum-**	**júm**	**jɔ:m, i-pih, fiing** 'plant manioc cuttings'	oé	-pana
garden field	b ɔ̆t [from 'chop down trees' (v)]	b ɔ̆t	kaw	gə:w ['chop down trees' (v)]	wesé	kenike
sifting basket	cim'	cim'	bɔj lig	jerata, napid	siʔapahá (v. siʔa)	dopitsi, oropéma
tapioca[d]	**nǔh**	**nǔh**	**nǔh**	**nú:h, ʃɛ:j**	wetá	mhéetti
tipití[e] (manioc press)	jɔ̃h	lume?	lume?	harum	wáti-kẽʔewa	ttirolipi
tripod	mɔhɔj (='deer')	có (='deer')	có (='deer')	hetfɨd doo	yamá (='deer')	mháitsi

[a] The Nadêb term for caxiri (beer) is probably an Arawakan loan, e.g., from Mandawaka *jaláki*; the Tukano word may be derived from 'bubble, ferment.'

[b] The Dâw and Nadêb terms for 'manioc meal' are probably borrowed from Arawakan.

[c] The Hup and Dâw words for 'manioc bread' may be related by borrowing to Tukano *baʔa* 'eat.'

[d] Refers to any solid matter that settles out of liquid.

[e] The Yuhup, Dâw, and Nadêb terms are almost certainly loans of Arawakan or Cariban origin (Konrad Rybka p.c. 2019).

plants that are post-European-contact imports from outside the region (such as banana and sugar cane), the horticultural vocabulary in the Naduhup languages appears much more innovative, and thus probably newer, than the nonculti-vated plant terminology. Consider the words for 'maize,' for example: the Hup term is a lexical innovation ('planting banana'), the Yuhup and Dâw terms are loans (from Tukanoan and Nheengatú, respectively), and the Nadëb term is of uncertain origin.

There are nevertheless a few words in the horticultural vocabulary that do appear to be cognate across all four Naduhup languages. The most noteworthy are the terms for tobacco (*Nicotiana* spp.) and achiote (*Bixa orellana*). Both of these plants are early domesticates that probably originated elsewhere in South America. Tobacco has two main cultivated variants in South America (*N. tabacum* and *N. rusticum*), which are thought to have originated via hybridization in far southern Amazonia and on the western slopes of the Andes, respectively (Brücher 1989: 181); achiote, used widely as a dye and body paint, was probably domesticated in southwestern Amazonia and spread widely by people at an early date (Clement et al. 2009). That the names of these plants apparently reconstruct to proto-Naduhup, and are not identifiable as loans from outside this language family, suggests that Naduhup involvement with these domesticates is very old. However, whether or not the speakers of proto-Naduhup actually cultivated these plants themselves remains a mystery; alternative explanations include trade, early borrowing among daughter languages, and/or early semantic shift of terms that originally designated some wild counterpart.

Among the other terms relating to cultivars or to their processing, we find three cognates across the Naduhup languages: 'grater,' 'plant/sow/ sprout,' and 'tapioca'. However, most of these terms are not limited to horticultural meanings. The term 'grater' is a nominalized form of the verb 'grate,' a means of processing a variety of wild foods (such as seeds, fruits, and even leaves) in addition to manioc. In Hup, the term used for 'plant, sow' also means 'sprout, germinate' (regardless of human inter-vention), and the word for 'tapioca' is a generic term applied to any solid matter that settles out of a liquid, such as arrow poison (information on whether these variations in meaning are found in Hup's sister languages is not available).

The relative newness of most of the Naduhup horticultural vocabulary, in contrast to the domain of useful wild plants, suggests strongly that active cultivation is not ancient among the Naduhup peoples. It is undoubtedly the case that Naduhup foragers have managed their forest resources to some degree, and the presence of cognates for tobacco and achiote may indicate some early knowledge of domesticated plants (though not necessarily their active cultivation). However – and especially given that neither tobacco nor achiote are raised as food – the linguistic data suggest that even a secondary dependence on domesticated plants is not ancient for the Naduhup, and postdates the breakup of the proto-language. Active horticulture does not therefore appear to have been necessary for their long-term survival; nor is there any evidence that the Naduhup experienced a reversion from horticulture to foraging at any time in their history, in contrast to the Amazonian Guajá (Balée 1999).

Just as the lexical evidence does not support an ancient dependence on horticulture, it also is not consistent with a scenario in which the Naduhup are undergoing an abrupt, recently initiated shift to horticulture. The data in Tables 22.2–22.4 suggest that many horticultural terms predate the later splits in the family; similarly, several of the candidates for lexical borrowing from neighboring languages appear quite old (in contrast to many other, less well integrated Tukanoan borrowings that appear in Hup).

Yet for those horticultural terms that do appear to reconstruct to lower-level groupings within the Naduhup family, their distribution presents a fuzzy historical picture. Several terms in the tables are common to Hup-Yuhup-Dâw but are not shared by Nadëb (e.g., 'calabash tree,' 'manioc,' 'peach-palm,' and 'hot pepper') – as we would expect given the family tree suggested in Figure 22.1. However, other terms are common to Dâw-Nadëb but not to Hup-Yuhup ('banana,' 'pineapple,' 'garden field' ['chop down trees (v.)'], as well as the Arawakan borrowings 'manioc meal,' 'coca,' and 'açaí,' among others). If these words are indeed shared innovations (i.e., words that entered the lexicon since the breakup of Proto-Naduhup), this distribution would suggest two competing possibilities for subgrouping the Naduhup languages. A likely explanation is that contact among Naduhup groups continued for some time after the initial breakup of the Naduhup family, with the geographically intermediate Dâw speakers continuing to interact with the other groups. This is a plausible scenario given Naduhup mobility (for example, Hup speakers undertake frequent treks to other Hup villages to visit relatives, look for spouses, etc.), and there are historical accounts of Dâw contact with the Nadëb (e.g., Assis 2001). It is also possible that one or more groups of River Indians had contact with Dâw, Nadëb, and/or with Hup-Yuhup speakers in these early days and were a source of loanwords into more than one Naduhup group. This picture will become clearer as historical work progresses.

The various loans and calques from Tukanoan and Arawakan languages that appear in the Naduhup horticultural vocabulary suggest that the source of the Naduhup peoples' horticultural knowledge was indeed their River Indian neighbors. Probable borrowings from Tukanoan include 'maize' in Yuhup, 'pineapple' in Hup, and possibly 'manioc bread' in Hup and Dâw (which bears a close resemblance to 'eat' in Tukano). 'Coca,' 'manioc meal,' and other terms in Dâw and Nadëb are Arawakan borrowings, and a few loans from Nheengatú (Tupi) are also encountered (probably borrowed since European contact). A few other, more recent horticultural terms ('cocoa,' 'sugar cane,' and 'papaya') in several Naduhup languages are of Portuguese origin (but in many cases probably entered via Tukano or Arawakan). That the languages of the neighboring cultivators were the sources of these loans in Naduhup, rather than vice versa, is established by the fact that many of these horticultural terms appear to have cognates across the Arawakan and Tukanoan families (or large branches thereof; see Huber and Reed 1992), but this is clearly not the case for the Naduhup languages.

In summary, the lexical evidence suggests that Naduhup horticulture is a secondary subsistence strategy that has been in place for many generations, but is not ancient. The Naduhup peoples' association with horticulture probably intensified between the initial and subsequent splits of the family, through contact with the river-dwelling farmers in region.

22.4   Further Linguistic Clues to Forager-Farmer Interaction in the Vaupés

22.4.1   Additional Lexical Evidence

Horticultural vocabulary is not the only source of evidence for reconstructing the history of the Upper Rio Negro region. Perhaps the most intriguing additional lexical clue is the word meaning 'River Indian,' which is common to Hup (wɔ̃h), Yuhup (wɔh), and Dâw (wɔ̃h) (see Martins 2005: 270), but is apparently absent from Nadëb. This fact suggests a forager-farmer interaction that is later than the initial family split, but older than the subsequent splits – consistent with the horticultural evidence discussed earlier. However, we cannot at this point definitively rule out the possibility that the word is older, and was subsequently lost in Nadëb, or that it is younger, and was borrowed among the Naduhup languages – although contact between Dâw and Hup/Yuhup speakers would itself have to be quite old, since a considerable distance separates their contemporary territories.

Other vocabulary provides clues to what Naduhup life may have been like before there was intensive contact with agriculturalists. Cognate terms pertaining to material culture (listed in Table 22.5) suggest that the Naduhup peoples were familiar with these concepts early on, before the breakup of the proto-language.[10]

Particularly striking in this list is the presence of words for 'hammock' and 'canoe.' Koch-Grünberg, one of the earliest European visitors to the region, described the Naduhup peoples as "crude nomadic hunters,

Table 22.5 *Cognate Naduhup terms relating to material culture*

Gloss	Hup	Yuhup	Dâw	Nadëb
hammock	*jág*	*jăg*	*jæg*	*jag*
canoe	*hɔh-tĕg*	*hɔ́h*	*xɔ*	*h'ɔːh*
axe	*mɔ̃m*	*mɔ̃m*	*mãm*	*miːm*
shoot with blowgun	*cɔw*	*cɔw*	*ʃɔw*	*ʔeʃoːw*
shaman	*cɔ́w*	*cɔ̆w*	*ʃəw*	*ʃəːw*
fishhook	—	*dáj'*	*lăj'*	*(ko)rãːj*

who ... know neither hammock nor canoe, but who have an excellent knowledge of the woods" (1906b: 877; my translation). However, the lexical data suggest that the Naduhup peoples not only knew the hammock and canoe in Koch-Grünberg's time, but had known them for many generations. That 'canoe' appears to reconstruct is perhaps particularly noteworthy, since Naduhup peoples occupy the forest zones between the larger rivers, and associate canoe travel with the River Indians.[11] Koch-Grünberg's description is probably once again a reflection of the unequal relationship between the horticulturalists and the foragers of the region – he and other European visitors attained much of their knowledge of the Naduhup peoples through the River Indians.

Conversely, a number of terms relating to ritual life are widely shared among the languages of the Upper Rio Negro region.[12] The common 'dabu-curi' ritual (so called in the local Portuguese, borrowed from Nheengatú), in which one group makes a ceremonial presentation of fruit or some other commodity to another group (and all celebrate with large quantities of manioc beer), is a calqued form of the verb 'pour out' in both Tukano and Hup (but not in Dâw or Nadëb, which have different terms of uncertain origin). The name of the hallucinogenic plant *Banisteriopsis caapi* is a loanword shared across Tukano, Baniwa (Arawakan), and Hup within the Vaupés (and likely by other languages as well), and the name of the principal deity or culture hero is likewise a widespread calque ('Bone-Son' in Hup, Dâw, and Tukano, 'One on the Bone' in Baniwa). The fact that Baniwa, an Arawakan language spoken outside the Vaupés, has more limited contact with Tukanoan, and does not seem to be a major source of other loans in Tukanoan languages or vice versa (as far as the available information suggests), suggests that Arawakan languages were the source of these shared lexical items, and possibly of other elements of ritual culture common to the peoples of the Upper Rio Negro generally.[13]

22.4.2   Numeral Systems

Additional clues to the history of the Vaupés peoples come from their numeral systems. It has been widely observed that a correlation exists between numeral systems of minimal complexity and hunter-gathering societies, or societies generally having little in the way of social stratification, division of labor, or complex trading patterns – in other words, little socioeconomic need to manipulate exact quantities of items (see, e.g., Greenberg 1978:291, Stampe 1976:596, Winter 1999:43).

In the Vaupés, the River Indian languages (East Tukanoan and Arawakan) all have numeral systems of comparable complexity and very similar structure. These include etymologically opaque lexical 'atoms' (i.e. forms not based on any smaller number) for 'one,' 'two,' and 'three'; a term for 'four' which translates as 'has sibling/is accompanied,' a term for 'five' which translates as 'one hand';[14] and a base-five system for 5–20 using fingers and toes. This level of complexity is typical of the Tukanoan and Arawakan families in general (see Huber and Reed 1992).

In contrast, the Naduhup numeral systems vary considerably. Nadëb may have established terms for 1–3 only, and even these are not 'basic' numerals in that they are reported to have alternative and approximate meanings. Dâw has lexical atoms for 1–3, but then reportedly employed the calqued expression 'has a sibling' for all even numbers up to 10, and 'has no sibling' for the corresponding odd numbers. The numeral systems in Hup and Yuhup closely resemble those in the Vaupés River Indian languages: lexical atoms 1–3, calqued terms for 'four' meaning 'has sibling/is accompanied' and for 'five' meaning 'one hand,' and a base-five strategy using fingers and toes for 5–20.[15]

There is little doubt that the Naduhup numeral systems are relatively young in comparison to those of the River Indians (see Epps [2006] for a detailed discussion). Not only does the variation within the family suggest some amount of independent innovation since the days of Proto-Naduhup, but the terms for 1–3 in Hup, Yuhup, and Dâw are for the most part etymologically transparent (and not cognate in Nadëb, with the exception of 'three'): 'one' appears to be related to a demonstrative in all three cases, 'two' is derived from 'eye-quantity' in Hup and Dâw, and 'three' is derived from 'rubber-tree-seed quantity' (the rubber tree (*Hevea* sp.) has a distinctive three-lobed seed). Moreover, the terms for 'four' in these Naduhup languages, and for 'five' and up for Hup and Yuhup, are Tukanoan calques, suggesting that the Naduhup development of higher numerals was motivated by language contact and by an increased need for numerals in trade. The Vaupés numeral systems thus support the picture presented earlier, in which the Naduhup peoples developed more complex patterns of subsistence and trade through their contact with the River Indians, since the breakup of the proto-language.

22.4.3   Grammatical Convergence

Although the contact between the Naduhup and the River Indians has not led to language shift, the Naduhup languages within the Vaupés region have nonetheless been profoundly affected. Within the Vaupés linguistic area, the cultural association between language and personal identity has led to a conscious avoidance of language mixing, such that lexical borrowing, code-switching, and ultimately language shift have been actively resisted; however, areal diffusion has resulted in profound grammatical convergence. This has affected the language of the horticulturalist Tariana, whose participation in the linguistic exogamy system has put them in close contact with Tukano (Aikhenvald 2002), but has had a similar effect on the languages of the Hup and Yuhup foragers, who today experience nearly complete unilateral bilingualism in Tukano (Epps 2007). Outside the Vaupés, contact with Tukanoan speakers today is very limited for the Dâw, and essentially completely absent for the Nadëb; this is reflected in their languages, which have undergone much less convergence toward Tukano than that undergone by Hup and Yuhup.

Examples of the effects of Tukanoan contact on the Naduhup languages of the Vaupés are many and pervasive (see Epps 2007, 2008a, 2008b for detailed discussion). Contact has probably been responsible for the spread of phonological features such as tone (which today is found in Hup, Yuhup, and Dâw) and nasalization as a morpheme-level prosody (in Hup and Yuhup only). The development of a complex system of evidentiality distinctions in Hup and Yuhup has clearly been carried out on a Tukanoan model (though the markers themselves have been grammaticalized from native material); only a single reported marker reconstructs to Proto-Naduhup, while Hup now has four distinct evidential markers and a five-way contrast (Epps 2005, 2008b). Similarly, Hup and Yuhup have developed a recent versus distant past tense distinction that closely parallels the Tukanoan pattern, and Hup's recently grammaticalized future suffix probably had the same catalyst. Other features in Hup and Yuhup that are probably due (at least in part) to Tukanoan contact include the many lexical calques (such as those discussed earlier), extensive verb compounding, nominal number marking patterns, noun classification, and many more.

The effects of contact with Tukanoan on the Naduhup languages are closely correlated with their proximity to the Vaupés region, where foragers and farmers interact most closely today. This suggests a period of intense contact between Hup/Yuhup and Tukanoan speakers, less intense contact for Dâw speakers, and no contact between Tukanoans and Nadëb. This fact (and that

Nadëb speakers were in contact with Arawakan groups in the past) may explain some of the striking differences between Nadëb's typological profile and those of Hup, Yuhup, and Dâw – such as ergative-absolutive versus nominative-accusative alignment, a strong preference for prefixing versus suffixing, head-marking versus dependent-marking, etc.

Finally, although it is not clear how much time is required for extensive grammatical convergence like that exemplified by Hup/Yuhup to take place, it is probably a relatively long-term process. (Compare, for example, the Xingu region of Brazil, where 150–200 years of cultural and linguistic exchange has not yet led to extensive areal diffusion of linguistic features, although multilingualism in this region is more limited; see Seki 1999.) Because linguistic categories are borrowed in the Vaupés, but the borrowing of words and morphemes themselves is generally avoided, extensive reanalysis and grammaticalization are required to generate new native morphemes to fill the slots in the developing paradigms. This process probably requires several generations, at a minimum (see also Aikhenvald 2002: 24), and thus supports the picture of long-term forager-farmer interaction that is emerging here.

22.5   Conclusion

A variety of features of the Naduhup languages – a relatively innovative horticultural lexicon; cognate terms for 'River Indian' in Hup, Yuhup, and Dâw; recent, Tukanoan-inspired numeral complexity; and grammatical convergence of Naduhup languages toward Tukanoan within the Vaupés – all support a consistent historical picture. The Naduhup peoples probably relied almost exclusively on hunting and gathering in the days when they spoke Proto-Naduhup, but this began to change soon after the initial break-up of the family, when they came into contact with horticulturalist Tukanoan and Arawakan peoples (Figure 22.2; see also Neves 2001). Around this time, the Naduhup presumably established a trade relationship with their farming neighbors that gave them consistent access to horticultural products, and then began to engage in small-scale cultivation themselves. While it is impossible at this point to date this interaction chronologically, the degree of separation among the Naduhup languages suggests that – in a cautious estimate – perhaps 1,500 to 3,000 years have passed since the breakup of Proto-Naduhup; the initiation of contact with horticulturalists would be somewhat more recent.

The available evidence thus suggests a long history of forager-farmer interaction with maintenance of separate lifeways. This scenario is consistent with other cases of contemporary and historically documented forager-farmer interaction elsewhere in the world, as observed by Bellwood:

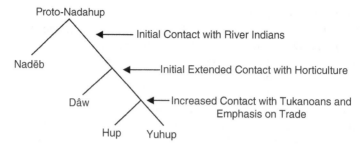

Figure 22.2 Naduhup languages and contact with horticulturalists.

Ethnographic foragers have never [fully] adopted agriculture. Even when they occasionally include a small amount of cultivation in their subsistence round . . . they never do this to the extent that they are able to compete both demographically and technologically with surrounding long-term agriculturalists. (Bellwood 1997: 131–132)

It is also consistent with what archaeological data has revealed about such cases of interaction in the past (Price and Gebauer 1995: 7–8). In Mesoamerica, for example, "agriculture was adopted only slowly, and the hunter-gatherer communities show a marked reluctance to give up their foraging life and to make a commitment to farming" (Bray 1977: 294).

While in contemporary cases the typical linguistic outcome of this interaction is language shift on the part of the foragers, the Vaupés case – like that of the !Kung and other hunter-gathering peoples in southern Africa – shows that the long-term separation of lifeways can also foster language maintenance where cultural conditions are right. But the Vaupés situation shows that such maintenance is nevertheless likely to come at a cost: the Naduhup languages have undergone significant grammatical convergence toward the horticulturalists' language.

The linguistic dynamics of forager-farmer interaction may have profound implications for our understanding of the contemporary distribution of the world's languages. While we must exercise caution in extrapolating from contemporary relationships to those in prehistory (see, e.g., Spielmann and Eder 1994: 316, Roosevelt 1998: 200), it is nevertheless likely that past relationships had much in common with those we witness today. As interaction between hunter-gatherers and agriculturalists has probably existed on all continents where agriculture has taken hold, and has probably been present since agriculture's inception, we can suppose that for some 12,000 years at least part of the earth's population has been involved in "highly significant intercultural exchange" (Peterson 1978: 347). Linguistic exchange has clearly been an inseparable part of this interaction. The spread of many language families (such as Bantu, Austronesian, and Indo-European) over wide geographic areas has been attributed to the spread of agriculture, via the complete assimilation or out-competition of hunting and gathering peoples (Renfrew 1987; Bellwood 1997, 2001, inter alia). Similarly, where cultural factors favor language maintenance rather than complete assimilation – as in the Vaupés case – a likely outcome is grammatical convergence, resulting in multiple unrelated languages with very similar typological profiles. It is possible that such scenarios of maintenance and convergence were even more common in the distant past, before agriculture gained a firm foothold. Thus, just as the spread of agriculture may have been responsible for the widespread distribution of many large language families, the interaction between hunter-gatherers and farmers on the fringes of these spreads could have played a role in establishing the large-scale areal patterns (Dahl 2001; Haspelmath et al. 2005) observed among the languages of the world today.

Acknowledgments

Information on Hup (aka Hupda, Jupde) was obtained via original fieldwork on the Rio Tiquié, Amazonas, Brazil, conducted in 2000–2004. Support for this research from Fulbright-Hays, the National Science Foundation (BCS0111550), and the Max Planck Institute for Evolutionary Anthropology, Leipzig is gratefully acknowledged. My thanks go to my Hup hosts and language teachers, as well as to the Museu Parense Emílio Goeldi and the Instituto Socioambiental in Brazil for practical assistance with fieldwork. Additional work on the material discussed in this chapter was supported by NSF ('Dynamics of Hunter-Gatherer Language Change' HSD0902114). I am also grateful to participants in the Workshop on Historical Linguistics and Hunter-Gatherer Populations in Global Perspective (MPI EvA, Leipzig, 2006) for comments on the material in this chapter.

NOTES

1. Defining hunter-gatherers and agriculturalists, and distinguishing the one from the other, is not as clear-cut a task in Amazonia as it is in some other parts of the world. Nearly all contemporary Amazonian foragers also practice limited cultivation, and have been shown to manage forest resources and to depend on foodstuffs sprung from past habitation sites and garden fallows (e.g., Posey 1984; Balée 1992, 1993; Politis 1996, 1999, 2007; Zent and Zent 2004). Similarly, Amazonian horticulturalists commonly rely on fishing and some hunting and gathering for their protein and other needs (as is the case for the Tukanoan and Arawakan peoples discussed in this chapter). Thus the distinction between the two subsistence patterns is best considered a continuum (Piperno and Pearsall 1998: 7; Rival 2006: S82–83; see also Smith 2001). Nevertheless, as work by Rival (2002, 2006 inter alia), Politis (1999 inter alia), and others has demonstrated, different groups can be characterized *relatively* as foragers or farmers on the basis of their primary subsistence strateg(ies) and corresponding cultural emphasis.

2. The name 'Naduhup' is preferred because (a) the name 'Makú' occurs in the literature in reference to several unrelated language groups in Amazonia and is thus prone to confusion, and (b) the name 'Makú' is widely recognized in the Vaupés region as an ethnic slur, directed against the members of this ethnic/linguistic group (see Section 22.2.4). 'Naduhup' combines elements of the names of the four established languages that make up the family (Nadëb, Dâw, Yuhup, Hup); see Epps and Bolaños (2017).

3. This practice has begun to break down in recent years as speakers of local languages experience a shift to Tukano and/or Portuguese; however, marriages are still determined by ethnic affiliation (Tukano, Desano, etc.), which retains a close ideological association with the heritage language (Stenzel 2005).

4. See Epps (2008b) for a comprehensive grammar of Hup. The Hup language is also known as Hupda, from the ethnonym Hup-d'əh (people-PL) 'the people.'

5. This figure is based on my experience among the Hup people living between the Tiquié and Vaupés Rivers.

6. Of course, the current interaction with non-Indian society represents an additional force encouraging a more sedentary lifestyle.

7. Koch-Grünberg also wrote that the Naduhup peoples he encountered "ha[d] no agriculture" (1906b: 877) and were "very primitive" (but see Section 22.4.1).

8. Gaps in the tables are due to unavailability of data. Sources for data are: Hup: my fieldnotes; Yuhup: Ospina (2002), Martins (2005), and my fieldnotes; Dâw: Martins (2004), Martins (2005), and my fieldnotes; Nadëb: Schultz (1959), Weir (1984), and Martins (1999, 2005); Tukano: Ramirez (1997b); Baniwa: Ramirez (2001). The data for Naduhup are given in a slightly adjusted version of the regularized phonemic transcription given in Martins (2005) (because transcriptions vary across sources); the Tukano and Baniwa data are given in the orthographies used in their sources.

9. Judgments of likely cognates are based on my analysis and on the correspondences identified in Martins (2005); they are still somewhat tentative.

10. While we cannot at this point absolutely rule out borrowing in the past among the daughter languages or parallel semantic shift, the probable status of these words as cognates – like the word for 'River Indian' discussed earlier – is supported by the presence of regular sound correspondences (see Martins 2005: 225–228).

11. Contemporary Naduhup peoples do use canoes, primarily for fishing. At least within the Vaupés region, the Naduhup do not make the canoes themselves, but trade for them with the River Indians. This is in keeping with the general economic system in the region, in which the various groups maintain a system of divided labor, such that each contributes a different aspect of material culture to the trading circuit: along the Tiquié River, for example, the Tukanos make painted benches, the Hupd'əh make baskets, and the canoe-making falls to the Tuyuka (an East Tukanoan group).

12. Unfortunately, however, documentation of these terms is particularly scant.

13. The peoples of the region (despite their linguistic differences) share a wide range of rituals (*dabucuri*, initiation, etc.), and most notably the *yuruparí* complex, which involves sacred trumpets that only men may see; a comparable tradition of sacred trumpets is widely represented among Arawakan peoples throughout Amazonia (see Wright 2011). A range of song styles, myths, and other cultural practices is also shared throughout the Upper Rio Negro region.

14. Aikhenvald (2002: 107–108) has shown that the terms for 'four' and 'five' in Tariana are calqued from Tukanoan and have replaced earlier terms.
15. Sources of data for the discussion in Section 22.4.2–3 are: Yuhup (Ospina 2002), Dâw (Martins 2004), Nadëb (Weir 1984), Tukano (Ramirez 1997a), and Tariana (Aikhenvald 2002, 2003).

References

Aikhenvald, Alexandra. (1999). Areal diffusion and language contact in the Içana-Vaupés basin, north-west Amazonia. In R. M. W. Dixon and Alexandra Aikhenvald (eds.), *The Amazonian languages*. Cambridge: Cambridge University Press, 385–416.

(2002). *Language contact in Amazonia*. Oxford: Oxford University Press.

(2003). *A grammar of Tariana*. Cambridge: Cambridge University Press.

Assis, Elias. (2001). *Patrões e fregueses no Alto Rio Negro: As relações de dominação no discurso do povo Dâw*. BA thesis, Universidade do Amazonas, Brazil.

Bahuchet, Serge. (1993). History of the inhabitants of the central African rain forest: Perspectives from comparative linguistics. In C. M. Hladik, H. Pagezy, A. O. Hladick, and F. Linares (eds.), *Tropical forests, people, and food: Biocultural interactions and applications to development*. Paris: UNESCO and Parthenon, 37–54.

Bahuchet, Serge and Henri Guillaume. (1982). Aka-farmer relations in the northwest Congo basin. In Eleanor Leacock and Richard Lee (eds.), *Politics and history in band societies*. Cambridge: Cambridge University Press, 189–211.

Bahuchet, Serge, Doyle McKey, and Igore de Garine. (1991). Wild yams revisited: Is independence from agriculture possible for rainforest hunter-gatherers? *Human Ecology* 19: 213–243.

Bailey, Robert, Genevieve Head, Mark Jenike, Bruce Owen, Robert Rechtman, and Elzbieta Zechenter. (1989). Hunting and gathering in tropical rain forest: Is it possible? *American Anthropologist* 91(1): 59–82.

Balée, William. (1992). People of the fallow: A historical ecology of foraging in lowland South America. In Kent H. Redford and Christine Padoch (eds.), *Conservation of Neotropical forests: Working from traditional resource use*. New York: Columbia University Press, 35–57.

(1993). Indigenous transformation of Amazonian forests: An example from Maranhão, Brazil. In Philippe Descola and Anne C. Taylor (eds.), *La remontée de l'Amazone: Anthropologie et histoire des sociétés amazoniennes*, 231–254. Special ed. L'Homme 126–128, 33(2–4).

(1999). Modes of production and ethnobotanical vocabulary: A controlled comparison of Guajá and Ka'apor. In Ted L. Gragson and Ben Blount (eds.), *Ethnoecology: Knowledge, resources, and rights*. Athens, GA: University of Georgia Press, 24–40.

(2000). Antiquity of traditional ethnobiological knowledge in Amazonia: The Tupi-Guarani family and time. *Ethnohistory* 47: 399–422.

(2003). Historical-ecological influences on the word for cacao in Ka'apor. *Anthropological Linguistics* 45: 259–280.

Balée, William and Denny Moore. (1994). Language, culture, and environment: Tupí-Guaraní plant names over time. In Anna Roosevelt (ed.), *Amazonian Indians from prehistory to the present: Anthropological perspectives*. Tucson: University of Arizona Press, 363–380.

Bellwood, Peter. (1985). *Prehistory of the Indo-Malaysian archipelago*. Sydney: Academic Press.

(1997). Prehistoric cultural explanations for widespread language families. In Patrick McConvell and Nicholas Evans (eds.), *Archaeology and linguistics: Aboriginal Australia in global perspective*. Melbourne: Oxford University Press, 123–134.

(2001). Early agriculturalist population diasporas? *Farming, languages, and genes. Annual Review of Anthropology* 30: 181–207.

Bird, Nurit. (1983). Wage-gathering: Socioeconomic change and the case of the Naiken of South India. In Peter Robb (ed.), *Rural South Asia: Linkages, changes, and development*. London: Curzon Press, 57–90.

Blust, Robert. (1976). A third palatal reflex in Polynesian languages. *Journal of the Polynesian Society* 85: 339–358.

Bolaños, Katherine. (2016). *A descriptive grammar of Kakua, a language of Northwest Amazonia*. PhD dissertation, University of Amsterdam.

Bray, Warwick. (1977). From foraging to farming in early Mexico. In J. V. S. Megaw (ed.), *Hunters, gatherers and first farmers beyond Europe*. Leicester: Leicester University Press, 225–250.

Brosius, J. Peter. (1991). Foraging in tropical rain forests: The case of the Penan of Sarawak, East Malaysia (Borneo). *Human Ecology* 19(2): 123–150.

Brücher, Heinz. (1989). *Useful plants of Neotropical origin and their wild relatives*. Berlin: Springer-Verlag.

Cabalzar, Aloisio and Carlos Alberto Ricardo. (1998). *Povos indígenas do Alto e Medio Rio Negro*. São Paulo: Instituto Socioambiental; São Gabriel da Cachoeira, AM: FOIRN – Federação das Organizações Indígenas do Rio Negro.

Cabrera, Gabriel, Carlos Franky, and Dany Mahecha. (1999). *Los Nïkak: Nómadas de la Amazonía Colombiana*. Santafé de Bogotá: Universidad Nacional de Colombia, Fundación Gaia – Amazonas.

Campbell, Lyle. (1997). *American Indian languages*. New York: Oxford University Press.

Chacon, Thiago. (2014). A revised proposal of Proto-Tukanoan consonants and Tukanoan family classification. *International Journal of American Linguistics*. 80(3): 275–322.

Chernela, Janet. (1993). *The Wanano Indians of the Brazilian Amazon: A sense of space*. Austin: University of Texas Press.

Clement, Charles R., Laura Rival, and David M. Cole. (2009). Domestication of peach-palm (*Bactris gasipaes*): The roles of human mobility and migration. In Miguel N. Alexiades (ed.), *Mobility and migration in indigenous Amazonia*. New York: Berghahn Books, 117–140.

Colinvaux, Paul and Mark Bush. (1991). The rain-forest ecosystem as a resource for hunting and gathering. *American Anthropologist* 93(1): 153–160.

Dahl, Östen. (2001). Principles of areal typology. In Martin Haspelmath, Ekkehard König, Wulf Oesterreicher, and Wolfgang Raible (eds.), *Language typology and language universals: An international handbook*. Berlin: Mouton de Gruyter, 1456–1470.

Endicott, Kirk M. (1984). The economy of the Batek of Malaysia: Annual and historical perspectives. *Research in Economic Anthropology* 6: 26–52.

Endicott, Kirk M. and Peter Bellwood. (1991). The possibility of independent foraging in the rain forest of peninsular Malaysia. *Human Ecology* 19: 151–185.

Epps, Patience. (2005). Areal diffusion and the development of evidentiality: Evidence from Hup. *Studies in Language* 29(3): 617–650.

(2006). Growing a numeral system: The historical development of numerals in an Amazonian language family. *Diachronica* 23(2): 259–288.

(2007). The Vaupés melting pot: Tukanoan influence on Hup. In Alexandra Aikhenvald and R. M. W. Dixon (eds.), *Grammars in contact: A cross-linguistic typology*. Explorations in Linguistic Typology 4. Oxford: Oxford University Press, 267–289.

(2008a). Grammatical borrowing in Hup. In Yaron Matras and Jeanette Sakel (eds.), *Grammatical borrowing: A cross-linguistic survey*. Berlin: Mouton de Gruyter.

(2008b). *A Grammar of Hup*. Mouton Grammar Library 43. Berlin: Mouton de Gruyter.

(2014). Historical linguistics and socio-cultural reconstruction. In Claire Bowern and Bethwyn Evans (eds.), *The Routledge handbook of historical linguistics*. London: Routledge, 579–597.

(2017). Subsistence pattern and contact-driven language change: A view from the Amazon basin. *Language Dynamics and Change* 7: 47–101.

Epps, Patience and Katherine Bolaños. (2017). Reconsidering the 'Makú' family of northwest Amazonia. *International Journal of American Linguistics* 83(3): 467–507.

Fisser, Anne. (1988). *Wirtschaftliche und soziale Beziehungen zwischen den Tukano und Maku Nordwest-Amazoniens*. Hohenschäftlarn: Klaus Renner Verlag.

Gardner, Peter. (1972). Paliyan social structure. In David Damas (ed.), *Contributions to anthropology: Band societies*. Ottawa: National Museums of Canada, 153–171.

Garvan, John M. (1963). *The Negritos of the Philippines*. Horn-Wien: Verlag Ferdinand Berger.

Greenberg, Joseph. (1978). Generalizations about numeral systems. In Joseph Greenberg, Charles A. Ferguson, and Edith A. Moravcsik (eds.), *Universals of human language*, Vol. 3. Stanford: Stanford University Press, 249–295.

Grinker, Roy. (1994). *Houses in the rainforest: Ethnicity and inequality among farmers and foragers in Central Africa*. Berkeley: University of California Press.

Haspelmath, Martin, Matthew Dryer, David Gil, and Bernard Comrie (eds.). (2005). *The world atlas of language structures*. Oxford: Oxford University Press.

Headland, Thomas and Robert Bailey. (1991). Introduction: Have hunter-gatherers ever lived in the tropical rainforest independently of agriculture? In Thomas Headland and Robert Bailey (eds.), *Human foragers in tropical rain forests*. New York: Plenum. Special issue of Human Ecology, 19(2): 115–122.

Headland, Thomas, Robert Bailey, and Lawrence Reid. (1989). Hunter-gatherers and their neighbors from prehistory to present. *Current Anthropology* 30(1): 43–66.

Heckenberger, Michael. (2002). Rethinking the Arawakan diaspora. In Jonathan Hill and Fernando Santos-Granero (eds.), *Comparative Arawakan histories*. Urbana: University of Illinois Press, 99–122.

Huber, Randall and Robert Reed. (1992). *Vocabulário comparativo: Palabras selectas de lenguas indígenas de Colombia*. Bogotá: SIL.

Jackson, Jean. (1983). *The fish people: Linguistic exogamy and Tukanoan identity in northwest Amazonia*. Cambridge: Cambridge University Press.

Junker, Laura. (2002). Introduction: Southeast Asia. In Kathleen Morrison and Laura Junker (eds.), *Forager-traders in South and Southeast Asia: Long-term histories*. Cambridge: Cambridge University Press, 131–166.

Koch-Grünberg, Theodore. (1906a). Die Indianner-Stämme am oberen Rio Negro und Yapurá und ihre sprachliche Zuhörigkeit. *Zeitschrift für Ethnologie* 38: 167–205. (1906b). Die Makú. *Anthropos* 1: 877–906.

Lathrap, Donald. (1968). The 'hunting' economies of the tropical forest zone of South America: An attempt at historical perspective. In Richard Lee and Irven Devore (eds.), *Man the hunter*. Chicago: Aldine, 23–29.

Lee, Richard. (1979). *The !Kung San: Men, women, and work in a foraging society*. Cambridge: Cambridge University Press.

Leonti, Marco, Otto Sticher, and Michael Heinrich. (2003). Antiquity of medicinal plant usage in two Macro-Mayan ethnic groups (México). *Journal of Ethnopharmacology* 88: 119–124.

Levi-Strauss, Claude. (1968). The concept of 'primitiveness'. In Richard Lee and Irven Devore (eds.), *Man the hunter*. Chicago: Aldine, 349–352.

Maceda, Marcelino. (1964). *The culture of the Mamanua*. Manila: Catholic Trade School.

Martins, Silvana A. (2004). Fonologia e gramática Dâw. PhD dissertation, University of Amsterdam.

Martins, Silvana A. and Valteir Martins. (1999). Makú. In R. M. W. Dixon and Alexandra Aikhenvald (eds.), *The Amazonian languages*. Cambridge: Cambridge University Press, 251–268.

Martins, Valtier. (2005). Reconstrução fonológica do Protomaku Oriental. PhD dissertation, Vrije Universiteit, Amsterdam.

Milton, Katherine. (1984). Protein and carbohydrate resources of the Maku Indians of northwestern Amazonia. *American Anthropologist*, 86: 7–27.

Morris, Brian. (1982). *Forest-traders: A socio-economic study of the Hill Pandaram*. London: Athlone Press.

Neves, Eduardo G. (2001). Indigenous historical trajectories in the upper Rio Negro basin. In Colin McEwan, Cristiane Barreto, and Eduardo Neves (eds.), *Unknown Amazon: Culture and nature in Ancient Brazil*. London: British Museum Press, 266–285.

Neves, Eduardo G. and James Petersen. (2006). Political economy and Pre-Colombian landscape transformations. In William Balée and Clark L. Erickson, *Time and Complexity in Historical Ecology: Studies in the Neotropical Lowlands*. New York: Columbia University Press, 279–309.

Nimuendajú, Curt. (1927/1950). Reconhecimento dos rios Içana, Ayarí, e Uaupés: Relatório apresentado ao Serviço de Proteção aos Indios do Amazonas e Acre, 1927. *Journal de la Société des Américanistes* 39: 125–183 and 44: 149–178.

Nurse, George T., J. S. Weiner, and Trefor Jenkins. (1985). *The peoples of southern Africa and their affinities*. Oxford: Clarendon Press.

Ospina Bozzi, Ana Maria. (2002). Les structures élémentaires du Yuhup Makú, langue de l'Amazonie Colombienne: Morphologie et syntaxe. PhD dissertation, Université Paris 7 – Denis Diderot.

Peterson, Jean Treloggen. (1978). Hunter-gatherer/farmer exchange. *American Anthropologist* 80: 335–351.

Piperno, Dolores and Deborah Pearsall. (1998). *The origins of agriculture in the lowland Neotropics*. San Diego: Academic Press.

Politis, Gustavo. (1996). *Nukak*. Colombia: Instituto Amazonico de Investigaciones Cientificas.

(1999). Plant exploitation among the Nukak hunter-gatherers of Amazonia: Between ecology and ideology. In Chris Gosden and John Hather (eds.), *The prehistory of food: Appetites for change*. London: Routledge, 97–124.

(2007). *Nukak: Ethnoarchaeology of an Amazonian people*, trans. Benjamin Alberto. Walnut Creek, CA: Left Coast Press.

Posey, Darrell. (1984). A preliminary report on diversified management of tropical rainforest by the Kayapó Indians of the Brazilian Amazon. *Advances in Economic Botany* 1: 112–126.

Pozzobon, Jorge. (1991). Parenté et demographie chez les Indiens Maku. PhD dissertation, Université de Paris VII.

(1994). Indios Por Opção. *Porto e Virgula* 17: 34–39. Porto Alegre, RS.

Price, T. Douglas and Anne B. Gebauer. (1995). New perspectives on the transition to agriculture. In T. Douglas Price and Anne B. Gebauer (eds.), *Last hunters – first farmers: New perspectives on the prehistoric transition to agriculture*. Santa Fe: School of American Research Press, 3–20.f

Ramirez, Henri. (1997a). *A fala Tukano dos Ye'pa-Masa*, Vol. 1: *Gramática*. Manaus: Inspetoria Salesiana Missionária da Amazônia, CEDEM.

(1997b). *A Fala Tukano dos Ye'pa-Masa*, Vol. 2: *Dicionário*. Inspetoria Salesiana Manaus: Missionária da Amazônia, CEDEM.

(2001). *Dicionário Baniwa-Português*. Manaus: Editora da Universidade do Amazonas.

Ramos, Alcida Rita. (1980). *Hierarquia e simbiose: Relações intertribais no Brasil*. São Paulo: Editora Hucitei.

Reid, Howard. (1979). Some aspects of movement, growth and change among the Hupdu Maku Indians of Brazil. PhD dissertation. University of Cambridge.

Reid, Lawrence. (1987). The early switch hypothesis: Linguistic evidence for contact between Negritos and Austronesians. *Man and Culture in Oceania* 3 (Special Issue): 41–60.

Renfrew, Colin. (1987). *Archaeology and language*. London: Jonathan Cape.

Rival, Laura. (1999). Introductory essay on South American hunters-and-gatherers. In Richard Lee and Richard Daly (eds.), *The Cambridge encyclopedia of hunters and gatherers*. Cambridge: Cambridge University Press, 77–85.

Rival, Laura (2002). *Trekking through history: The Huaorani of Amazonian Ecuador*. New York: Columbia University Press.

Rival, Laura (2006). Amazonian historical ecologies. In Roy Ellen (ed.), *Ethnobiology and the science of humankind: A retrospective and a prospective*. Special issue of *JRAI*, S79–S94.

Rodrigues, Aryon Dall'Igna. (1986). *Línguas Brasileiras: Para o conhecimento das línguas indígenas*. São Paulo: Ed. Loyola.

Roosevelt, Anna C. (1998). Ancient and modern hunter-gatherers of lowland South America: An evolutionary problem. In William Balée (ed.), *Advances in historical ecology*. New York: Columbia University Press, 190–212.

(1999). Archaeology of South American hunters and gatherers. In Richard Lee and Richard Daly (eds.), *The Cambridge encyclopedia of hunters and gatherers*. Cambridge: Cambridge University Press, 86–91.

Sapir, Edward. (1949). Time perspective in aboriginal culture: A study in method. In David G. Mandelbaum (ed.), *Selected writings of Edward Sapir in language, culture, and personality*. Berkeley: University of California Press, 389–467.

Schultz, Harald. (1959). Ligeiras notas sobre os Maku do Paraná Boá-Boá. *Revista do Museu Paulista*, n.s., v. XI: 129–131.

Seki, Lucy. (1999). The Upper Xingu as an incipient linguistic area. In R. M. W. Dixon and Alexandra Aikhenvald (eds.), *The Amazonian languages*. Cambridge: Cambridge University Press, 417–430.

Silverwood-Cope, Peter. (1972). A contribution to the ethnography of the Columbian Maku. PhD dissertation, University of Cambridge.

Smith, Bruce D. (2001). Low-level food production. *Journal of Archaeological Research* 9: 1–43.

Solway, Jackie S., and Richard B. Lee. (1990). Foragers, genuine or spurious? *Current Anthropology* 31: 109–146.

Sorensen, Arthur P. (1967). Multilingualism in the Northwest Amazon. *American Anthropologist* 69: 670–684.

Spielmann, Katherine and James Eder. (1994). Hunters and farmers: Then and now. *Annual Review of Anthropology* 23: 303–323.

Stampe, David. (1976). Cardinal number systems. *Chicago Linguistic Society* 12: 594–609.

Stenzel, Kristine. (2005). Multilingualism in the northwest Amazon, revisited. In *Memorias del Congreso de Idiomas Indígenas de Latinoamérica-II*. University of Texas at Austin. Available at www.ailla.utexas.org/site/cilla2_toc_sp.html.

Stradelli, Ermanno. (1890). L'Uaupés e gli Uaupés. *Leggenda del Jurupary. Boll. Soc. Geogr., Series III* 3, 659–689 and 798–835.

Turnbull, Colin. (1965). The Mbuti Pygmies of the Congo. In James L. Gibbs, Jr. (ed.), *Peoples of Africa*. New York: Holt, Rinehart and Winston, 281–317.

Weir, E. M. Helen. (1984). A negação e outros tópicos da gramática Nadëb. Master's thesis, UNICAMP, Campinas.

Weir, Helen, Rodolfo Senn, and Beatrice Senn Martins. (1999). *Dicionario Nadëb-Português, Português-Nadëb*.

Wilmsen, Edwin N. and James R. Denbow. (1990). Paradigmatic history of San-speaking peoples and current attempts at revisionism. *Current Anthropology*, 31: 489–524.

Winter, Werner. (1999). When numeral systems are expanded. In Jadranka Gvozdanovic, ed. *Numeral types and changes worldwide*. Trends in Linguistics 118. Berlin: Mouton de Gruyter, 43–54.

Woodburn, James. (1988). African hunter-gatherer social organization: Is it best understood as a product of encapsulation? In Tim Ingold, David Riches, and James Woodburn (eds.), *Hunters and gatherers: History, evolution, and social change*. New York: Berg Press, 31–64.

Wright, Robin. (2011). Arawakan flute cults of lowland South America: The domestication of predation and the production of agentivity. In Jonathan H. Hill and Jean-Pierre Chaumeil (eds.), *Burst of breath: New research on indigenous ritual wind instruments in lowland South America*. Lincoln: University of Nebraska, 325–353.

Zent, Eglée and Stanford Zent. (2004). Amazonian Indians as ecological disturbance agents: The Hoti of the Sierra de Maigualida, Venezuelan Guyana. In T. J. S. Carlson and Luisa Maffi (eds.), *Ethnobotany and conservation of biological diversity*. Bronx, NY: New York Botanical Garden, 79–112.

23   The Southern Plains and the Continental Tip

Alejandra Vidal and José Braunstein

"Todo esto nos prueba que las lenguas del Chaco han sufrido las más violentas mezclas, de suerte que voces, partículas y raíces de un tipo se han connaturalizado en otro ... (...) ... **Cuanto más conozco la historia de nuestras lenguas más me convenzo que todo es mezcla** ...." Lafone Quevedo (1894: 186) in his Introduction to *Los Lules*.[1]

23.1   Introduction

The main obstacle to understanding the history of the Gran Chaco peoples and their languages lies in some particular facts: linguistic descriptions are relatively recent or are in progress; the available archeological data are scarce; and some historical written sources have given rise to confusion. Basically, we have a chronology of dates *post quem*: the geomorphology of the region suggests that the peopling process may have begun 6,000 years ago. However, archaeological findings provisionally pose that it began 2,000 years ago (according to the few available radiocarbon tests). Finally, none of the documents date back to more than 500 years. But, leaving aside the few significant seventeenth-century sources, the historical documentation appears to be concentrated in the second half of the eighteenth century, especially in the Jesuits' chronicles that were mostly published after their expulsion. In addition, the congruence of the information in the Jesuits' documents compared to later sources is doubtful. This scenario suggests that to a certain degree, the description of the processes occurring during these distinct periods will necessarily be, at least in part, speculative.

The aim of this chapter is to describe the hunter-gatherer peoples of Gran Chaco from a historical perspective.[2] To that end, we first present the characteristics of the Chaco region and its languages. We then focus on the dynamics of the population and the communication between the peoples. Finally, we examine some linguistic characteristics of the area, concluding that a brief comparative examination of various Chaco languages shows evidence of linguistic contact among all the hunter-gatherer peoples of the area that could have occurred several centuries ago.

23.2   Characteristics of Gran Chaco

The Chaco region in the South American lowlands includes the great woody plain bounded on the west and southwest by the Andes and the Salado River basin, on the east by the Paraguay and Parana Rivers and on the north by the Moxos and Chiquitos Plains. This vast region spans 1,000,000 square kilometers across western Paraguay, eastern Bolivia, northeastern Argentina, and a small portion of Brazil. It is characterized by a patchwork of savannah grasslands and semiarid vegetation with forests along the riverbanks. In its central part, two rivers run NW to SE: the Bermejo and the Pilcomayo Rivers. Gran Chaco's current landscape was shaped by alluvial sediments and by the slow drying out of a large water system formed during the Andean genesis.[3] Owing to these ecological characteristics, it was practically impossible to carry out traditional agricultural activities in the area. Several thousand years ago, huge areas surrounding this large inundated territory became inhabitable and it is possible that various peoples began to settle. For historical and geographical reasons, Gran Chaco became a refuge for diverse indigenous groups whose subsistence was based on hunting wild animals, gathering wild plant foods, and fishing. Over the centuries, this region served as a kind of sanctuary for the local populations when Europeans landed in America, as well as for others that settled there as a consequence of colonial pressure. It was only at the beginning of the twentieth century that the countries that claimed to have right to the region gained territorial control and a massive presence that forced the natives into sedentarization. According to Braunstein (1992), some 50 social units exist that speak 18 different languages.

23.3   Linguistic Stocks, Languages, and Their Speakers

Historical linguistics in the Chaco is still quite rudimentary compared with studies on other languages and families around the world. The reasons are several. First, Chaco languages belong to several families and it is uncertain whether any of these have a genetic relationship with languages outside Gran Chaco. Second, few historical studies on the Chaco languages have rigorously applied the comparative method because of the lack of evidence on all of the linguistic varieties involved. Finally, some languages have yet to be documented thoroughly, in extensive dictionaries or comprehensive reference grammars, and most of what we currently know about others is incipient

Chaco peoples speak a number of languages that have been traditionally cast in six stocks. The historical relationship among the languages comprised within the Mataguayan, Guaycuruan, Enlhet-Enenlhet, Zamucoan, Lule-Vilela and Ava Guarani stocks is widely recognized by linguists. At present, we estimate[4]

Table 23.1 *Linguistic classification of the indigenous peoples in Gran Chaco*

Genus/stock		Languages			
Mataguayan	Wichi	Chorote	Nivacle	Maka	
Guaycuruan	Toba	Pilagá	Mocoví	Caduveo	
Enlhet-Enenlhet	Enxet	Sanapaná	Angaité	Guaná	Enlhet-Enenlhet
Zamucoan	Chamacoco	Ayoreo			
Lule-Vilela	Vilela				
Tupi-Guaraní	Ava-Guaraní	Tapiete			

Based on Braunstein and Miller (1999); Fabre (2007); Unruh and Kalish (2003).[5]

that between 150,000 and 250,000 people speak the 18 surviving indigenous languages listed in Table 23.1. Table 23.2 shows the population size and approximate locations.

Map 23.1 presents all of the languages in Tables 23.1 and 23.2 as they are distributed in Gran Chaco.

23.4 Population Dynamics of Gran Chaco: Historical Peopling Processes and the Later Dynamics of the Conquest

Chaco peoples share the fact that they are indigenous to this South American area, that all of them are and have inhabited the area for the last three centuries as hunter-gatherer societies and that a great deal of exchange has occurred owing to contact (Braunstein 1992; Golluscio and Hirsch 2006).

In the next section we review the archaeological and geomorphological information as a first approach to understanding the ancient peopling processes during the past centuries. In this regard, and based on the available records and sources, it is useful to distinguish between several periods: prehistory, the Conquest, and the colonial period. To date, these periods cover a span of almost 4,000 years.

23.4.1 Prehistory: Early Peopling and Spreads (6000 BP)

Even if the cultural history of the region can be traced to a much earlier period, the only incipient archeological studies (Calandra and Salceda 2008:39)[7] consider the first years of AD to be the period when a precursory human group moved from north to south across the sub-Andean hills.[8] New ceramic characteristics began to appear after AD 500, frequently found in the Paraná and

Table 23.2 *Population size and locations*[6]

Laguage	Population size	Locations
Wichi	45.000/ =	Arg.: Formosa, Chaco, Salta
		Bol.: Tarija
Chorote	2.000/ =	Arg.: Salta.
		Par.: Boquerón
Nivacle	13.200/ =	Par.: Boquerón, Presidente Hayes
		Arg.: Salta, Formosa
Maka	1.200/ =	Par.: Central, Presidente. Hayes
Toba	60.000/+25%	Arg.: Chaco, Formosa, Salta
Pilagá	4.000–6000	Arg.: Formosa
Mocoví	3.000–5.000/+50%	Arg.:Santa Fe, Chaco
Caduveo	1.600	Br.: Mato Grosso do Sul
Enxet	3.788/5.844	Par.: Presidente Hayes
Sanapaná	914/2.2.71	Par.: Presidente. Hayes, Alto Paraguay
Angaité	780/3.694	Par.: Presidente Hayes, Boquerón, Alto Paraguay
Guana	242	
Enlhet	7.221/ =	Par.: Boquerón, Presidente Hayes
Enenlhet	1.275/1.474	Par.: Presidente Hayes, Alto Paraguay
Chamacoco	1.571 (Par.)	Par.: Alto Paraguay
	40 (Br.)	Br.: Mato Grosso do Sul, Municipio Puerto Murtinho
Ayoreo	2000/ = (Par.)	Par.: Boquerón, Alto Paraguay
	?/2.500 (Bol.)	Bol.: Pcia. Santa Cruz
Vilela	moribunb (2 sp.)	Arg.: Chaco and Buenos Aires
Tapiete	524/ =	Arg.: Salta (Tartagal)
		Bol.: Tarija
		Par.: Boquerón
Ava-Guaraní	58,000	Arg.: Salta y Juluy
		Bol.: Santa Cruz y Tarija
		Par.: Boquerón

Paraguay basin,[9] a factor that could suggest a second peopling process by those who had moved in the opposite direction (from south to north). That is, despite the little archeological evidence, the data are congruent with the distribution of the two groups with the highest number of speakers: the groups speaking Mataguayan languages that settled in Gran Chaco from the northwest following the central river basins toward the southeast, while the groups speaking Guaycuruan languages took the opposite direction from southeast and penetrated the northwest following the same basins (Map 23.2).[10] Undoubtedly, these early peoples bore cultural elements that would include them in the category of hunter-gatherers.

Finally, a third group partially overlapped the Chaco region. These are the ancestors of those speaking today's Zamucoan languages, corresponding to cultural forms on the periphery of Brazil's Planalto area.

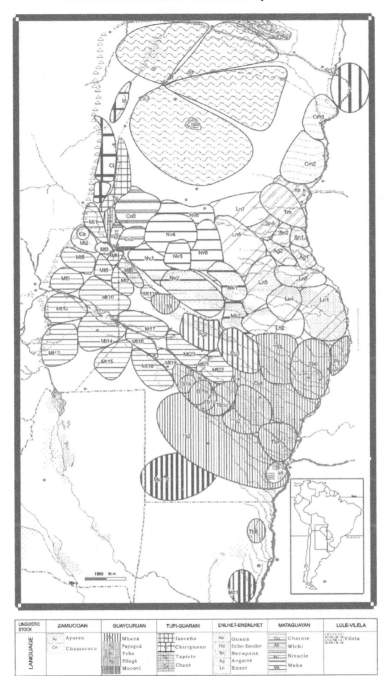

LINGUISTIC STOCK	ZAMUCOAN	GUAYCURUAN	TUPI-GUARANI	ENLHET-ENENLHET	MATAGUAYAN	LULE-VILELA
LANGUAGE	Ay Ayoreo Cm Chamacoco	Mbayá Payaguá Toba Pilagá Mocoví	Izoceño Chiriguano Tapiete Chané	Ka Guaná TM Enlhet-Enenlhet Sn Sanapaná Ag Angaité Ln Enxet	Co Chorote Mi Wichí Nv Nivaclé Mk Maka	Vilela

Map 23.1 Ancient socio-political units (Braunstein 1992).

The full lines in Map 23.2 represent the population speaking Mataguayan languages. Sušnik (1972: 24) says that the Mataguayan-speaking population may have moved toward the southeast due to the pressure of Amazonian groups, speakers of Arawak languages. If this effectively happened, it could have developed quite slowly. The occupation of the area was likely rooted in a fission and displacement mechanism that was akin to these societies. Before reaching the area, some kind of interchange with local Arawak-speaking agriculturalists living at the foot of the mountains must have taken place because ancient archaeological levels of Gran Chaco reveal similar but more rudimentary-decorated pottery. The dotted lines in Map 23.2 represent the probable direction that speakers of the Guaycuruan languages took. As in the previous case and following the same kinds of social mechanisms described earlier (fission and fusion), they must have "borne" cultural features (farming, pottery, and navigation, among others) that were typical of the peoples living on the periphery of the area. The opposite, although overlapping, direction that the movement paths took and the dynamics of the Chaco hunter-gatherers must have generated recurring situations for genetic and linguistic mixtures. For example, it is likely that the Payaguá boatmen, who presumably spoke a language related to the current Guaycuruan and Mataguayan languages, were early representatives of these dynamics in which boating practices were introduced by the Guaycuruans who were in close contact with the river-sailing peoples of the coastal region, as archeologists can clearly identify.[11] Those multiple and varied loan phenomena can blur the historical picture to such a degree that scholars that privilege genetic explanations have posed kinship relationships between Guaycuruan and Mataguayan (Greenberg [1959:22], and more recently Viegas Barros [1993]). No distant genetic relationships with languages outside Gran Chaco have been proposed.

23.4.2   The Conquest (500 BP)

We have a clearer idea of the movements of the Gran Chaco peoples after the Spanish conquest (see Map 23.3). By the time the conquest had begun, a considerable number of agriculturalists and horticulturalists had already settled in Gran Chaco. In brief, the main forces that generated these peoples' dispersal were: first, the arrival of Guaraní Amazonian agriculturalists in Chaco from the fifteenth century, who for supposedly religious reasons crossed the region and settled along the eastern mountain range of what is today southern Bolivia (see long-dash arrows); and second, the pressure of the Spanish from colonial Tucumán, which compelled various sub-Andean agriculturalists to settle in Chaco (see short-dash arrows).

It may be a coincidence that both forces acted somewhat concomitantly. It is probable that the Guaraní movements and the displacement of populations

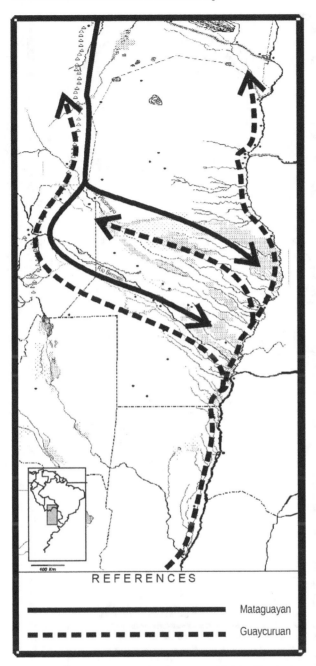

Map 23.2 Early peopling.

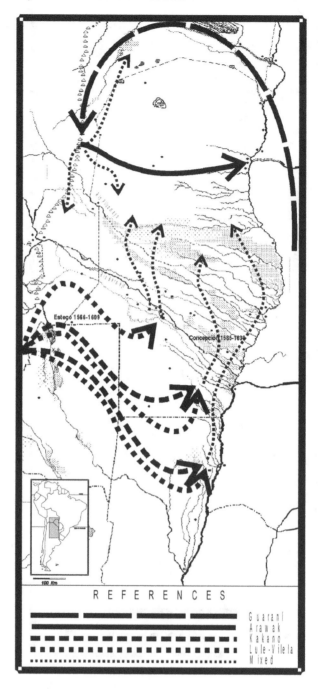

Map 23.3   Gran Chaco after the Spanish conquest.

that these movements produced may have begun before the conquest. However, when the Guaranís occupied the Andes area, a cultural and linguistic mixture commenced with some of the earlier inhabitants of the region that led to the formation of what we now call "the Chiriguano-Chané complex." The rest of the Arawak-speaking peoples settled in the Chaco region. The language of the Guaraní immigrants prevailed in the Chané-Chiriguano complex, although more marked substrata Arawak groups exist that were concentrated in isolated enclaves, for instance, around the Isozog and the Parapetí Rivers).

Similarly, the numerous Lule-Vilela-speaking peoples (short-dash arrows), who had expanded southward of the Bermejo River due to the conquest and remained there until the mid-1700s, were partially able to continue their agricultural customs. One hundred years later they had become practically integrated with the hunter-gatherer groups, undoubtedly experiencing distinct processes of mixing and ethnogenesis.[12] It is also very likely that the Diaguitas (identified in the sources as Kakanos, see the long-dash arrows on Map 23.2) and who were defeated in the so-called Calchaquí wars were then expelled and divided up.

In northern Chaco, signs of the Enlhet-Enenlhet linguistic group only begin to appear from the 1800s, although some references claim that indications of their presence already existed in the late 1700s. These indigenous populations from eastern Chaco show evidence of an agricultural substratum marked by cultigens of Andean origin. This seems to result from a particular ethnogenesis in the historical process of the Spanish colonization of Gran Chaco. This process first began with the foundation of two cities during the 1500s—Esteco and Concepción del Bermejo—which were abandoned after indigenous groups revolted in the early 1600s. As in other parts of South America, the process was characterized by the legal regime of *encomiendas*.[13]

In short, the first indigenous reaction that destroyed the Spanish cities in this region is likely to be directly related to the process of intermixing and homogenization of cultural patterns that must have been generated in the indigenous populations living in the *encomiendas*. Many sub-Andean agriculturalists are likely to have come into direct contact with each other, including Diaguitas that had been exiled after the military defeat, as well as various Lule-Vilela peoples that made contact with native hunter-gatherers. The spreading adoption of the horse and equestrian life among these groups gave them the means to block the advance of European colonization in the following centuries. Also, cultural patterns that conditioned the social organization and reproductive capacities of these societies must have occurred in the *pueblos de indios*. In this case, the arrows on the map do not indicate sudden migration. Rather, the symbols try to represent the processes that the indigenous peoples experienced under the *encomienda* system, forcing them to live in mostly ethnically heterogeneous *pueblos de indios*. More than 100 *encomiendas* existed under the jurisdiction of the first two and short-lived Chaco cities, Esteco and Concepción. Thousands of indigenous peoples worked to maintain the irrigation system of Esteco and the chronicles indicate that hundreds of Matarás[14] were forcibly taken to the city to work in domestic service. Many of these indigenous peoples are certain to have experienced Spain's withdrawal from Chaco in the early 1600s as a true liberation and the beginning of a new cultural and, eventually, linguistic life.

23.4.3   The Colonial Period (250 BP)

Once the European enclaves had been eliminated in the area, a frontier was established that constituted a strip of land where mixture and assimilation took place together with the formation of the *criollo* cultures outward, and a combination of cultural elements inwards that may have fostered accelerated ethnogenesis processes. Key military campaigns following the early eighteenth century produced important demographic changes and substantially contributed to giving Gran Chaco the physiognomy it has today.

Map 23.4 synthesizes the ethnic dynamics of the mid- and late-colonial periods after the indigenous groups adopted the use of the horse. The solid arrows represent "entries," that is, large-scale military expeditions, in particular those carried out from the city of Santa Fe against the Calchaquís and from Tucumán (Argentina) in the early eighteenth century against the Guaycuruans at the foot of the Andes. The thick black arrows represent the ensuing migrations. The three arrows that take the direction of the river represent the breaking-up of the "horsemen" and "warring" "Pilagá," "Toba," "Aguilote," and "Mocoví," among others, who had concentrated at the foot of the mountains. At present, we can locate their descendants and understand the processes that triggered their sudden migration.

As we have said, the first peoples to populate Chaco were hunter-gatherers. This does not mean that they had no knowledge of agricultural technology. As some ancient archaeological levels on the Peruvian coast show,[15] those entering from the north employed basic horticulture methods and cultivated cucurbitaceae crops (melon and pumpkin as their main cultigens; they probably cultivated cotton and tobacco.) Those coming from the south surely cultivated at least tobacco. Nevertheless, archaeological studies have not yet uncovered the presence of populations without pottery at the ancient levels of Gran Chaco, although this may be attributed to the lack of fieldwork, the scarcity of durable utensils, and the unfavorable climatic conditions of the region that hinders conservation.

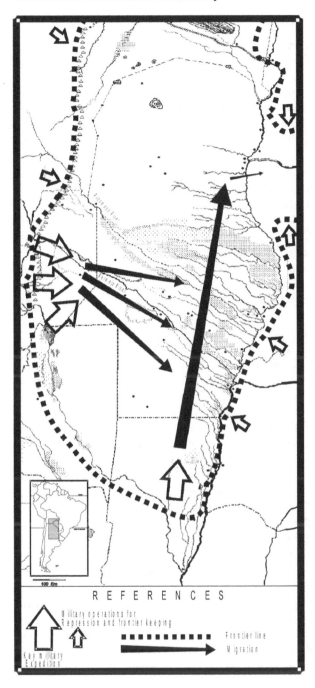

Map 23.4 The colonial period.

23.5   The Dynamics of Communication

Until the beginning of the twentieth century, the organization of traditional societies of various Chaco hunter-gatherer peoples could be categorized as a series of inclusive social units, that is, social units that included some within others. Extended families were constituted by a nucleus grouped together with other individuals that were somehow considered related.[16] Such a group shared kinship terms, although these were not always explicit or traceable to a link showing how the members of the distinct extended families were related. This set of family groups that was technically denominated a "band" lived and moved together in a regular and cyclical pattern around a territory they considered their own.[17] Each one established itself in temporary villages on the banks of water sources. In turn, a varying number of these social units maintained alliances among themselves making up larger units called "nations," "tribes," or "peoples." In the past each of these nations corresponded to a system of norms, a chiefdom and a system of independent social control. Even today the descendants of their members share the awareness of an exclusive history. The non-indigenous classification (the way in which the non-indigenous referred to indigenous peoples) considers, for example, that the "Toba," "Mocoví," and "Wichi," among others, are separate indigenous groups in Gran Chaco, although in reality they are social units formed by various tribes. Despite their internal differences, they all had an "air of family" among them, but presented considerable differences with respect to their language and customs. Thus, referring to the "Chaco indigenous peoples" implies the recently defined socio-political units in Gran Chaco with undeniably individual characteristics, that is, territorial, linguistic, and historical units that had a unique and distinct organization prior to the social disarticulation that resulted from the National States' occupation of their land.

With respect to the languages in the region, some data indicate that diverse and complex phenomena occurred in Gran Chaco involving contact, and borrowing. This is highly coherent with the aforementioned social organization and ethnohistory. In effect, the communication phenomena between the traditional populations undoubtedly depended on the foregoing social model that is characterized by the somewhat stable alliances of bands, which traditionally moved within a specific territory and that constituted the most extensive political groups. In addition, by concentrating the social and cultural interchange among them, these units could delimit the sphere of solidarity and their shared historical awareness.

On examining this model on a synchronic level, we can find two different degrees in the intensity of their communication. On the one hand, the alliances of bands or "tribes," with a population of about 2,000 individuals, concentrated the majority of the circuits regarding matrimony, goods, and linguistic interchange. On the other hand, a lower degree of quantitative and different qualitative communication existed between the neighboring tribes, consisting of circumstantial alliances with extratribal bands, reciprocal thefts, or the kidnapping of women and children. The situation becomes even more complicated if we think diachronically. The stability of these units often depended on short-term situations, like the prestige of the charismatic chiefs or the accessibility of the resources, producing the breakdown of bands and tribal transformation with allies that differed linguistically and culturally with varying frequency.[18]

Overall, we could mention a corollary of this social model. Periods of unrest and tension surely favored a tendency to unify cultural patterns in Gran Chaco – including language – owing to the frequency of rupture and tribal transformation, while periods of stability probably led to differentiation and diversification. The second scenario explains the intense dialectal differentiation (understood as "linguistic complexes" or even true "dialectical chains") that can be observed in the languages with the highest number of speakers.

However, it would be a mistake to overlook the fact that these contradictory tensions operate simultaneously in Chaco societies since the progressive differentiation and specialization at the heart of the tribes is countered by the eventual cultural mix within the confines of these units. This leads to the conclusion that peripheral areas of the tribal groups that speak varieties or similar linguistic dialects – larger groups that can be denominated "ethnic complexes" – must have formed new cultural varieties, including the generation of languages with elements coming from different linguistic sources. With respect to the communication of cultural patrimonies, we consider two kinds of movements: some centripetal of a cultural and linguistic derivation in periods of stability and at the center of great ethnic complexes; and, other centrifugal ones, of a mix and interference in periods of unrest and on the periphery of areas of greater homogeneity. The recurring image of regional unity must have developed from the combination of these forces, together with the surprising dynamic of differentiation that presents the current vivid kaleidoscope of more than 50 discrete ethnic units that speak 18 languages.

Population geneticists Neel and Salzano (1967: 554–574) proposed a model for American hunter-gatherers known as "fission and fusion," which well adapts to the social dynamics of the Chaco indigenous populations. Briefly, the groups exchange genetic, social, cultural, and linguistic information quite stably over long periods. However, under extreme positive or negative conditions, that is, as the population decreases or increases, groups fuse or fission with others to maintain a demographic stability. Although the codes involved may have been initially heterogeneous, the continuous exchange led to homogenization. Inversely, the fission processes produced by an increase in the population and the formation of new associations between groups sharing an important percentage of exchangeable elements logically led to the genetic and cultural (linguistic) drift. Despite this linguistic diversification, we find that each Chaco language or dialect exhibits elements from many linguistic sources (see Sections 23.7.3 and 23.7.4), a situation that is comparable to what modern geneticists observed in the studies of mitochondrial DNA (Demarchi *et al.*, *apud* Mendoza 2004).

There are differences between this Chaco model of dynamics of genetic, cultural and linguistic communication and what Dixon (1997) proposes for the general evolution of language. As with Chaco peoples and languages, the stability and instability of the historical events condition the dynamic characteristics. However, in Dixon's model, the periods of "equilibrium" would determine the mix and homogenization of the linguistic forms, whereas the moments of "punctuation" would produce the formation of linguistic groups that can be diagrammed using the classic family tree.

We follow Dixon's belief that "stability" does not exist in languages. Interchange adopts different modes that condition the forms in which the social and linguistic modifications take place, these being normal and inevitable given the very nature of language. These modalities depend on the thread of the communication and this, in turn, depends on the social norms and institutional functioning. We ask whether or not Australian societies, whose linguistic dynamics Dixon takes as a model, present a social structure that conditions Chaco's opposite dynamic characteristics.

23.6   Gran Chaco as a Linguistic Area

As was stated before and also suggested in Citro, Golluscio and Vidal (2006), Chaco constitutes a cultural area in which the prolonged and ongoing interaction between the distinct peoples generated shared features of subsistence practices, political organization, and worldview. Following the ideas discussed earlier, a number of linguistic features suggest that a connection runs through all of the languages of this area.

23.6.1   *The Languages of Gran Chaco from the Perspective of Eighteenth-and Nineteenth-Century Ethnographers*

As followers of the tradition initiated by Hervás y Panduro (1787) on American philology, a number of travelers, ethnographers and historians have concentrated on the description and study of Chaco peoples since the eighteenth century. Sources from the 1700s until the beginning of the twentieth century used a variety of terms for the languages and ethnic groups to whom these were attributed – the ethnonyms that each group used to refer to others, together with the very transcription modes of travelers and historians, a fact that brought about some degree of confusion for the complete identification of the groups. The Nivacle (Mataguayan), also referred to as the "Chulupí," (pej.) constituted a clear example of the mixing of terms that several peoples were subject to in ethnographic literature. "Chunupí" refers to the speakers of the Lule-Vilela family (which is a hispanization of the name the Toba gave to the Vilela), and sources refer to the Chulupí or Nivacle as "Tapiete," confusing them with the Tapiya (or Tapiete) of the Tupi-Guaraní linguistic group. However, this has not discouraged the emergence of hypotheses related to the linguistic groupings among them all.[19]

In the late 1800s, the Argentine Geographic Institute (Instituto Geográfico Argentino) promoted the publication of a series of documents on the peoples of Chaco in its bulletin. Lafone Quevedo (1895) collected, organized, and wrote the prologues of the works of Franciscan monks Massei (1895), Remedi (1890), of the traveler D'Orbigny (1839), and the engineer Pelleschi (1897) about the Wichi language and their dialectic varieties, later taken up by the missionary Hunt (1913). At this time, Ducci (1904) published two papers on the Toba people and language and Boggiani (1900) on the Caduveo language and the linguistic cartography of Chaco and the classification of Brinton (1898).

All of the comments in the sources result from direct observations about the regions and the Chaco peoples. This is one reason why the work of the first European ethnographers and historians was so influential: they not only acknowledged Gran Chaco as a particular ethnolinguistic area, but also made attempts to consider their peoples and languages as a whole and from a comparative perspective. In the first half of twentieth century, these ideas were continued by Nordenskiöld (1912), Lehmann-Nitsche (1907), Furlong (1939), Karsten (1932), Métraux (1946), Sušnik (1972, 1986/87, 1988), and Tovar (1951, 1964).[20]

23.6.2   Adscription to the Genealogical Model of Languages

The linguistic groupings presented in Section 23.2 have sometimes been taken for granted and other times proved (for the Mataguayan languages, see Tovar [1951, 1964]; on Guaycuruan languages, Koch-Grünberg [1903], Ceria and Sandalo [1995]; Viegas Barros [1993] on Greenberg's hypothesis of a supposedly Macro-Mataco-Guaycuruan group; Dietrich [1986, 2006], on the place of Chiriguano within the Tupi-Guaraní family, and González [2005] on the location of Tapiete within the Tupi-Guaraní family also, inter al.). Most of these historical-comparative studies overlooked linguistic borrowing because the tradition in linguistics states that languages must have an identified genealogical origin. In effect, there is a bulk of linguistic evidence that cannot be explained from a genealogical standpoint (Fabre 1998). Moreover, the genealogical model fails to account for the transference of features which nineteenth-century sources had already suggested and has been confirmed in our field notes.

In general, there are a number of cross-linguistic patterns in the data on most Chaco languages that can be synthesized as follows: dialect-formation due to fission of larger socio-political and socio-linguistic units, with or without further contact with other dialects and/or languages, contact phenomena evidenced in the grammar of quite closely related languages or languages of seemingly different affiliation, lexical borrowings, and strong similarities in semantic organization.

23.6.3   *Language Diversification and the Fusion/Fission Model*

The demographic increase and the conflicts over leadership have been the main causes for the fission of the groups (a process that was described in Section 23.4), giving rise to the formation of new socio-political units across various generations, which constitute groups of speakers of different varieties of the same language. This would explain the dialectal continuum of Wichi (which is spoken in a territory covering three provinces in Argentina and part of the department of Tarija in southern Bolivia) and presents so many differences between the distinct varieties that speakers can sometimes find them mutually unintelligible. Based on Viñas Urquiza (1974), who worked with a linguistic variety spoken in the province of Salta, Messineo and Braunstein (1990) compare their data with the Bazanero dialect (Formosa), detecting a regular vowel change ($a > e$, $i > u$, $o > \ddot{a}$) between the two. The hypothesis of a dialectal continuum between Toba and Pilagá was proposed by Messineo (1988, 1992). The fission process proposed here might explain the existence of the current Toba ethnic partialities in the provinces of Chaco and Formosa and the correlation with linguistic differences between them (Messineo 1988: 15–21), although the extent of this linguistic variation is not yet clear. Toba data compared to the Pilagá (central Formosa) and Metraux's (1946) Toba-Pilagá (western Formosa) data suggest that the lexical differences and phonological reductions accentuate both in the east-west and north-south directions of the territory occupied by all of these dialects. Different lexical forms are used for the same concept by speakers of the eastern and southeastern varieties of Toba (Las Palmas and Saenz Peña, Chaco) compared to speakers in central and western Formosa. Moreover, syllable-reduction characterizes different varieties of Pilagá (central and western Formosa). Examples are presented in Table 23.3.

Table 23.3 *Selected lexical forms across the continuum Toba-Pilagá languages*

	Toba (Las Palmas, Chaco)	Toba (Saénz Peña, Chaco)	Pilagá (Central Formosa)	Toba-Pilagá (Western Formosa)
arm	*napike*	*napike*	*nalte*	*(na)lte*
mouth	*halap*	*alap*	*degaʕat*	*ndeɢaɢat*
hot	*dapaqa*	*dapaqa*	*p'e*	*piyi*
water	*etarat*	*netaʕat*	*noʕop*	*noɢop*

Likewise, the fact that the dialects may have arisen based on contact with other dialects or languages spoken by neighboring peoples may also have developed from the same fission and fusion processes of the groups. (See de la Cruz [1991] on Nivacle dialects based on the work by Chase Sardi [1972], Seelwische [1980], and Stell [1972].) As was mentioned, when fission occurs in the center of the areas where related languages or dialects of a same language are spoken, new dialectal varieties develop from this same language. However, if these are mixed with other nonrelated groups, the result will be different. Bilingualism or multilingualism may occur for one or more generations of speakers and they then adopt just one language, incorporating characteristics from one or the others one prevailing over the other or others, or generating an entirely new language.

The Enlhet traditional narrative corpus includes myths to explain the "change (abandonment) of languages," which is particularly revealing given the hypothesis of language contact and mixture advanced by Lafone Quevedo. Grubb (1914: 66ff), in his chapter on Chaco folklore, comments on a story by which the Maka (called Towothli by the Enlhet) migrated southwards. Facing great hunger, they eat part of the rainbow on the advice of their witch doctor. Their language suddenly becomes confused and the people end up speaking differently. Curiously, according to the Enlhet, the Aii (the name used by the Enlhet to refer to the Guaycuruan Pilagá) ate a plant that thrived in the swamps and they too lost their language. The myth on the exchange suggests that language shift could actually have taken place. Azara (1847) documented the presence of Enimagá indigenous peoples mixed with the Pilagá south of the Pilcomayo River in the late 1700s. Neither the language nor the Maka people now living near the city of Asunción in Paraguay until the early twentieth century appear to have been identified by that name at the time. According to Schmidt (1936), there is a close relationship between the modern Maka and the old Enimagá. The lack of data about the Enimagá a century later and the appearance of the Maka as a different ethnic group at the same time gave rise to the hypothesis that they might have mixed with the Enlhet and that today's

Maka are possibly the descendents of the old Enimagá, fusioned with the speakers of distinct neighboring groups north and south of the Pilcomayo River. The literature also explains that the Maka (Mataguayan) had contact with the Pilagá (Guaycuruan) people living on the southern bank of the central Pilcomayo River, an area that they shared and disputed.[21]

23.6.4   Language Contact

This natural fission-fusion process of the groups and their languages overlaps with the numerous contact situations that appear to have generated junctures fostering linguistic exchange. Interestingly, a number of commonalities have been confirmed by the grammar and lexicon of several Chaco languages, such as some nominal deictic affixes and lexical borrowings.

The two Mataguayan languages, Nivacle and Maka, have cognate deictic forms: *na-, xa-/ha-, ka- and pa-* (Tables 23.4 and 23.5). Wichi, from the same linguistic group, shares the cognate forms -na and -pa (Table 23.6) with Nivacle and Maka, but the overall system of forms that are suffixed rather than prefixed

Table 23.4 *Nivacle nominal deictic determiners*

	Visible and known	Absent and known	Nonexistent	Unknown
Unmarked	*na*	*xa*	*pa*	*ka*
Feminine	*lha*	*lhxa*	*lhpa*	*lhka*
Plural + human	*napi*	*xapi*	*papi*	*kapi*
Plural – human	*nawa*	*xawa*	*pawa*	*kawa*

Based on Stell (1989) and Vidal and Gutierrez (2010)[22].

Table 23.5 *Maka nominal deictic determiners*

	Close				Absent	
	Touching	Not touching	Far, visible	Far, invisible	Known	Unknown
Masc.	*ha'ne-*	*na'-*	*tsa'-*	*ha'-*	*ka'-*	*pa'-*
Fem.	*ene'-*	*ne'-*	*tse'-*	*ke'-*	*ke'-*	*pe'-*
Pl (reduced form)	*ne'*	*he'-*			*ke'-*	*pe'-*
Pl (full form)	*enewe'*	*nekhewe'*	*etsiwe'*	*hekhewe'*	*kekhewe'*	*pekhewe'*

From Gerzenstein (1994).

Table 23.6 *Wichi deictic determiners*

| Close Touching | Far but visible | | Orientation | | Non-visible |
	Relative distance	Nonrelative distance	Toward	Away	Unknown
-*na*	-*l'a*	-*l'e~l'i*	-*tsi*	-*tsu*	-*pa*

From Vidal (2005)[23].

Table 23.7 *Pilagá nominal deictic determiners*

	Visible, close or moving toward	Visible but far or moving away	Distal or non-visible
Masc. sg.	*na'*	*so'*	*ga'*
Masc. pl.	*naa'*	*sa'*	*ga'*
Fem sg.	*hana'*	*haso'*	*haga'*
Fem pl	*hanaa'*	*hasoo'*	*haga'*

From Vidal (1997).

to the noun or noun phrase proves to be more divergent in Wichi, suggesting that the deictic forms in this language may be an innovation compared to the other two Mataguayan languages.

Nivacle and Maka deictics are part of the noun phrase, obligatorily prefixed to nouns but used as free demonstratives as well. Wichi's deictic forms are completely optional. In other words, in Wichi these forms are not required by heads.

Despite the fact that most of them are not cognates, demonstrative forms in Guaykuruan languages are very akin in form and meaning to the Mataguayan deictic forms. They are also obligatory, procliticized to nouns, or may combine with demonstrative roots. Also, except for the case of Wichi, deitics in Mataguayan languages and Guaykuran languages bear number and gender inflection. Table 23.7 shows the three basic deictic forms in Pilagá (Guaykuruan).

With regard to their meaning, "visibility"/"non-visibility" (absence) and "proximity" are basic organizing parameters of all such systems. "Motion" is concurrent with "visibility" in Pilagá (but this holds for the rest of the Guaykuruan languages). Wichi, conversely, has separate forms to mark "visibility" or "closeness" and "orientation." All the languages have forms to refer to what is "unknown," "distal," or "non-visible": these are either alternative forms or combinations of -*ka* and -*pa*.

Table 23.8 *Pilagá and Wichi shared vocabulary*

Wichi	Pilagá	Gloss
am	*am*	you (sg.)
amilh	*amii'*	you(pl.)
ele	*ele'*	parrot
ka	*qa'*	stone
ha	*ha'a*	yes
kha	*qa*	no
kamata	*qamata*	incorrect, bad
layalh	*layat*	breath, wind
lhawu	*law'o*	flower
nawup	*nawoʕo*	summer
pele	*pelee*	raindeer
y'umet	*y'omaʕat*	go out
na	*na'*	take it / close

Lexical similarities among Chaco languages also prove to be an incipient and fruitful field of study to understand language contact in Chaco. Shared vocabulary is found between genetically unrelated languages, as in Wichi and Pilagá. A few examples in Table 23.8 illustrate this.

When examining vocabulary, we should not overlook the influence of Quechua (a neighbouring Andean language related to the extinct Calchaquí and Diaguita populations). Quechua is also identified as Kakano, which reached the Chaco 500 years BP (see Map 23.3). Quoting Machoni's (1877 [1732]) book *Arte y vocabulario de la lengua lule y tonocoté*, Golluscio (2007) states that Quechua loanwords are documented in Vilela. But interestingly enough, they are also infrequent in the Wichi lexicon.

Thus, Quechua words in the vocabulary of several Chaco languages can be traced to pre-Hispanic times or could have penetrated the Spanish vocabulary and from there to several languages in Chaco. Quechua was largely spoken in the territory comprising the current Argentine provinces of Tucumán, Salta, Santiago del Estero and Córdoba, whose population was bilingual in Quechua and Spanish. In the late 1600s, Quechua language was so pervasive in the territory that it was even spoken in trials, and for this reason communication in that language started to be banned.

23.6.5   Notes on Areal Semantics

Klein and Braunstein (2003) pointed out overwhelmingly strong conceptual resemblances in the lexical semantic domain of most Chaco languages.

Table 23.9 *Shared Wichi and Quechua vocabulary*

Wichi	Quechua	Gloss
wuk'u	*juku, tuku*	owl
kuchi	*khuchi*	pig
mati	*mathi*	mate (calabash gourd)
mitsi	*misi*	micha, micho, michino, (colloquial, RAE)[24]
pulutu	*purutu*	bean
tuk	*tukan*	toucan
upa'	*upa*	silly (Spanish, "opa")

Guaycuruan and Mataguayan languages utilize the same word to designate both the shell of a mollusk and a spoon (the relation being functional): Abipón (Guaycuruan, extinct) *enenk,* mocoví *rekona,* Toba *conec,* Wichi *lanec* and Pilagá *konek.* Likewise, a specific fish called *sabalo* (*sp. Prochilodus platensis*) in Spanish is used for the generic name for "fish" in those languages. The words are totally different, phonetically and morphologically, yet the meaning and the use is the same: Abipón *noai,* Mocoví *naií,* Toba *niyaq, ndiaq,* Pilagá *ñiyaq,* Wichi *wahat,* and Maka *sehets.* Many other examples such as the word for the "honey" and "honey bee," for "sweet" and "happiness," "to search for" and "to gather" are the same in various Chaco languages.

Similarities in the semantic organization are evidenced in the regular expressions to designate the groups. All of the languages in the area have two main forms to organize these systems: one in relation to the location of the group, classifying it according to the cardinal points generally fixed by a river and another that identifies them by their regional, topographical, or ecological characteristics. An example of the first is the name *nachelamol'ek* that means "those from where the river runs channeled" and refers to the Toba-Pilagá from western Formosa or *pigeml'ek* that addresses the name of a Toba group living upstream. Interestingly, similar forms were registered to denominate subgroups among the Pilagás from Central Chaco, the Mocoví who inhabit southern Chaco and the Ayoreos living in northern Chaco. The three use similar names: Pilagá *waqaepil'ek,* Mocoví *xonaxaic,* and Ayoreo *totobiegosode,* all meaning "those who live where the peccary pigs are found."

Toponyms are related in different ways. On the one hand, toponyms tell us about the space that is actually known and taken, how it is used, and about the events linked with it. On the other hand, they address motifs and topics on which most Chaco peoples focus In Chaco, the *topoi* were generally either campsites (living or resting places) with water, whose names evoked past stories as well as potential functions of places and beings. For example, a Pilagá toponym, *qaqadepi layo* "the caranchos' mortar," evokes a story and a

Table 23.10 *Toponyms*

Toba (Misión Taccaglé, Wright 1988: 45)	
lawaRanaki	'sound of the well'
qagesaRalogona	'a place with many ant colonies'
Pilagá (Dell'Arciprete1991: 66)	
apaqae la'et	'place where *pacú* (sp. fish) are plentiful'
camán sere	'Camán'swell (legendary man who dug a hole)'
koché lotaRanaqa	'open place where otter worms were killed'
Wichi (Palmer 2005: 299–303)	
Nakwoyo	'place where a tree with moro-moro bees was burned'
Sacham	'accumulated water accumulated water inside a tree'
fwumahnui p'itsehyei	'place where a group of Wichi people died of thirst'

summer campsite in the surroundings of the farms of the Algarrobo (sp. *Prosopis*) woods; and "burned (animal name)" is not only a reminder of its corresponding story but also shows that it was a hunting site. Toponyms can also refer directly to an action (a place where something happened) and indicate topographic features ("open places," a "round-shapedplace" such as a hole or well, etc.). Table 23.10 provides examples taken from several ethnographic and anthropological studies.

23.7   Summary and Conclusions

We have shown that alternative forms to the genealogical model exist when analyzing the history of the languages of an area, making it possible to improve the internal coherence of the linguistic descriptions while taking advantage of the information of other fields that study Chaco's cultural history.

This chapter has retaken one of the oldest enigmas in the history of this area. In particular, the conundrum of why some of the above cultural entities disappeared or were forced to settle in Gran Chaco owing to early colonial pressure. Later came the almost mysterious appearance of peoples whose traces did not exist until the late 1700s. The researchers that examined this question first tried to identify them but had little result. We now believe that a rational explanation contemplates accentuated ethnogenetic dynamics that should be examined based on what we currently know about the phenomena of cultural change and mixture. In this dynamic, the hunter-gatherer model acts as a minimum common denominator that even assimilates agrarian societies.

In effect, the behavior of intermediate social units that we sketched above must have reproduced the situation of mixed groups from the cultural and linguistic perspective countless times, a situation that has been documented since ancient times and that can now be seen in various points of Gran Chaco.

On the other hand, certain historical events must have produced sudden modifications that made it possible to identify exchange processes within a short period.

If languages behave like genes and social structures, as in the origin of most cultural areas, we should expect the Chaco languages to show the greatest variability of origin and the least variability between groups.

Finally, we have also stressed that linguistic contact and interactions may have led to borrowing and/or to shift. We have discussed some examples and provided a sketch of a fairly plausible scenario. We will only know how certain and accurate these assertions are when future linguistic and historical research continues to study this area.

NOTES

1. "All of this proves that the Chaco languages have undergone the fiercest mixtures, so that the words, particles, and roots of one type have merged with another. (...) The more I learn about the history of these languages, the more convinced I am that everything is a mixture" (our translation).

2. This chapter was drawn up between 2010 and 2011. Due to publishing difficulties, we have been unable to update the bibliography on Chaco language studies, which since that time have increased considerably. The chapter should therefore be read on the understanding it was written nine years ago. Moreover, important archaeological discoveries have also clarified our ideas about the earliest settlement in the Gran Chaco. Today we believe that the broad base of the population comprised a group of archaic people, extending west over the Andes and the Puna region to the Pacific, before the incursion of peoples speaking Arawak languages from the Subandean fold in the northwest, who promoted the regional formative.

3. Although the traditional literature on the formation of the Chaco region coincides on this interpretation of the process (Tapia 1936; Frenguelli 1943), we should not overlook the possibility of alternative proposals in modern geomorphology. Still, the above interpretation is also supported by the absence of findings to indicate that populations inhabited the area several thousand years earlier, as happened in adjacent areas.

4. Our estimations are based on different censuses and our own data.

5. Some of the Chaco languages and stocks in the literature have been referred to by other names or by compound names: Mataguayan or Mataco-Mataguayan or Mataco-Maká; Wichí or Mataco; Nivacl or Chulupí; Maká or Enimagá; Toba or Qom; Chamacoco or Ishir; Ava-Guaraní or Chiriguano; Enlhet-Enenelhet or Lengua-Maskoy; Guaná or Kaskiha; Enenlhet or Toba-Maskoy and are also spelled slightly differently in the sources.

6. See Fabre (1998) for the languages of the Mataguayan, Guaycuruan, and Enlhet-Enenlhet stocks. For the others, see the data on Tapiete from González (2005); on Ava-Guaraní, Dietrich (2006); and on Vilela, Golluscio (2007).

7. Although Gran Chaco is the second-largest natural biome in South America, it is also the last true "black hole" of American archaeology. The scarcity of the findings can be explained by the land and weather conditions (a succession of extreme

temperatures and humidity) that quickly corrupt organic substances and, overall, hinder the conservation of objects. In addition to the impediments for human inhabitance, which is uninviting for archaeologists, we can explain the historical lack of interest in the area and the reason why archaeological research has been scarce and irregular. In 1985 B. Dougherty and H. Calandra, from the La Plata Museum, began a systematic exploration that, following Dougherty's untimely death, was carried on with the help of S. Salceda (of the same institution), O. González (from Charata, Chaco), and a group of students and research assistants. Today, after several dozen campaigns, the findings of many archaeological sites and some radiocarbon dates, we have new and significant information. While it is far from complete, it promotes further historic research in the area.

8. "(...) un grupo humano precursor, en fechas cercanas al inicio de la era cristiana (...) desplazándose de norte a sur vía las serranías subandinas."

9. "(...) "con preponderancia hacia el sector ribereño."

10. This is the most common population hypothesis and does not clash directly with Sušnik's proposals based, above all, on anthropometric features. (See Sušnik 1972 and 1988).

11. A coastal area exists with an archaeological level showing characteristics that specialists call the "culture of the coastal dwellers" (Serrano 1972). Ethnohistorians identify these findings with the inhabitants whose names are chronicled as "Mepenes" or "Chanás."

12. On this point, also see Domínguez, Golluscio, and Gutierrez (2006).

13. The *encomienda* was a socio-economic institution employed by the Spanish crown during the colonization of the Americas and the Philippines. The Spanish could exact tribute from a group of individuals in the form of some kind of labor, products, or other means in exchange for goods or services.

14. The Matarás comprised a now extinct ethnic group that lived 50 kilometers from the colonial city of Concepción, which was completely destroyed in 1631 (Morresi 1971).

15. Lanning (1967) summarizes the findings of pre-pottery sites with cucurbitaceous and cotton crops at the oldest levels on the Peruvian coast.

16. A nuclear family is by and large an adult couple with dependent persons (children, parents, or elderly grandparents without spouses, sons-in-law, and generally more distant relatives).

17. We take 'band' to be a bilateral group perceived as a single family that migrated together and was represented by one principal leader.

18. Until the Criollos and Whites settled in the Chaco (from the 1800s on) and the jurisdiction of the National State was imposed across this territory, the processes of linguistic dynamics were fluid, as was mentioned earlier. Forced sedentarization must have crystallized linguistic differences. The Chaco peoples are currently struggling to perpetuate their traditional model but they are encountering serious difficulties. For example, when social fission occurs, the Pilagás seek out new locations; but because the land was assigned, they face huge constraints to separate and, hence, inhabit the periphery of the settlements.

19. The findings of linguistic research during the late nineteenth and twentieth century contributed to the description of several Chaco languages. We refer to the works of Stell (1989) on the Chulupí, Klein (1973) on the Toba and Gerzenstein on the Chorote (1978, 1979, and 1983), and Maka (1994, 1999); and the doctoral theses

dealing with the grammars of several of these languages, in particular, on e Toba, Mocoví, Tapiete, Caduveo, and Pilagá: Censabella (2002), Gualdieri (1998), González (2005), Grondona (1998), Messineo (2000 [2003]), Sandalo (1995), and Vidal (2001).

20. For example, Pelleschi (1886) documented the personal pronouns in Wichi and the value of the pronoun particles in the verbs and nouns, which he also compared to the personal forms in the Guaycuruan languages. Tovar (1951) took up this view years later in his study of the possessive prefixes in the Chaco languages.

21. Moreover, in 1974 Braunstein documented the presence of a few Maka families still living in the Pilagá settlement of Pozo Navagán.

22. Gutierrez (2015:416) argues that the primary distinction between a is instead one of evidentiality, defined as the encoding of source of information. The determiners na, ja, and ca indicate the speaker has or had firsthand sensory evidence for the existence of an entity, where the preferred evidence type is visual. Conversely, pa is used whenever the speaker lacks that type of evidence.

23. See Nercesian (2014) for a complete description of the demonstrative/deictic subsystem. In this work, she claims that that -pa 'non visible' encodes 'unknown/ out of the visual field but sensorily evident' (op.cit:185).

24. Real Academia Española (RAE).

References

Azara, Félix de. (1847). *Descripción e historia del Paraguay y del Río de la Plata.* Imprenta de Sánchez, calle de Jardines, número 36, Madrid. 2 vols.

Boggiani, Guido. (1900). Compendio de etnografía paraguaya moderna. *Asunción: Revista del Instituto Paraguayo,* Año 3, N°23/24.

Brinton, Daniel. (1898). *The linguistic cartography of the Chaco region.* Philadelphia: Kessinger Publishing.

Braunstein, José. (1992). Presentación. *Hacia una nueva carta étnica del Gran Chaco,* IV. Las Lomitas: Centro del Hombre Antiguo Chaqueño, 1–8.

Braunstein, José, and Elmer Miller. (1999). Ethnohistorical introduction. In Elmer Miller and José Braunstein (eds.), *Peoples of the Gran Chaco.* Westport, CT: Bergin and Garvei, 1–22.

Calandra, Horacio and Salceda, Susana. (2008). Cambio y continuidad en el Gran Chaco: De las historias étnicas a la prehistoria. In José Braunstein and Norma Meichtry (eds.), *Liderazgo: Representatividad y control social en el Gran Chaco.* EUDENE (Editorial Universitaria de la Universidad Nacional del Nordeste) Resistencia, 33–43.

Censabella, Marisa. (2002). *Descripción funcional de un corpus en lengua toba. Sistema fonológico, clases sintácticas y derivación. Aspectos de sincronía dinámica.* Doctoral thesis, Universidad Nacional de Córdoba, Argentina.

Ceria, Verónica, and Filomena Sandalo. (1995). A preliminary reconstruction of Proto-Waikuruan with special reference to pronominals and demonstratives. *Anthropological Linguistics* 37(2): 169–191.

Citro, Silvia, Lucía Golluscio, and Alejandra Vidal. (2006). The Chaco languages and the socio-historical dynamics of their people. Paper presented at the Conference

Hunter-Gatherers in Historical Perspective. Max Planck Institute for Evolutionary Anthropology.

Chase Sardi, Miguel. (1972). La situación actual de los indígenas en el Paraguay. In M. Morner, (ed.), *La situación del índigena en América del Sur.* Montevideo: Editorial Tierra Nueva, 237–305.

de la Cruz, Luis María. (1991). La presencia nivaklé (chulupí) en el territorio formoseño. Contribución de la etnohistoria de Formosa. In *Hacia una nueva carta étnica del Gran Chaco*, II. Las Lomitas: Centro del Hombre Antiguo Chaqueño, 87–106.

Dell'Arciprete, Ana. (1991). Lugares de los pilagá. In *Hacia una carta étnica del Gran Chaco* II. Las Lomitas: Centro del Hombre Antiguo Chaqueño, 9–19.

Dietrich, Wolfang. (1986). *El idioma chiriguano: gramática, textos, vocabulario.* Madrid: Instituto de Cooperación Iberoamericana.

  (2006). Nuevos aspectos de la posición del conjunto chiriguano (Guaraní del Chaco boliviano) dentro de las lenguas Tupi-Guaraníes bolivianas. Paper presented at the 52nd International Congress of Americanists, Sevilla.

Dixon, R. M. W. (1997). *The rise and fall of languages.* Cambridge: Cambridge University Press.

Dominguez, Marcelo, Lucía Golluscio & Analía Gutierrez 2006 Los vilelas del Chaco: desestructuración cultural, invisibilización y estrategias identitarias. *Indiana* 23, 199–226.

Ducci, Fray Zacarías. (1904). *Los Tobas y su lengua.* Boletín del Instituto Geográfico Argentino, Tomo XXII. Buenos Aires: Instituto Geográfico Argentino.

  (1905/6). *Vocabulario toba-castellano.* Boletín del Instituto Geográfico Argentino, Tomo XXIII. Buenos Aires: Instituto Geográfico Argentino.

Fabre, Alain. (1998). Manual de las lenguas indígenas sudamericanas. Lincom Europa. München-Newcastle. 2 vols.

  (2007). Morfosintaxis de los clasificadores posesivos en las lenguas del Gran Chaco. *Revista de Lenguas Indígenas y Universos Culturales* 4: 67–85.

Frenguelli, Joaquín (1943). *Las grandes unidades físicas del territorio argentino. Geografía de la República Argentina.* GAEA, V, III. Buenos Aires: Sociedad Geográfica de la República Argentina.

Furlong Cardiff, Guillermo. (1939). *Entre los vilelas de Salta.* Buenos Aires: Academia Literaria del Plata.

Gerzenstein, Ana. (1978). *Lengua chorote I.* Archivo de Lenguas Precolombinas. Buenos Aires: Instituto de Lingüística, Facultad de Filosofía y Letras, Universidad de Buenos Aires.

  (1979). *Lengua chorote II.* Vocabulario. Archivo de Lenguas Precolombinas. Buenos Aires: Instituto de Lingüística de la Universidad de Buenos Aires.

  (1983). *Lengua chorote. Variedad número 2.* Archivo de Lenguas Precolombinas. Buenos Aires: Instituto de Lingüística. Facultad de Filosofía y Letras, Universidad de Buenos Aires.

  (1994). *Lengua Maká.* Estudio descriptivo. Colección Nuestra América, Serie Archivo de Lenguas Indoamericanas. Buenos Aires: Facultad de Filosofía y Letras, Universidad de Buenos Aires.

  (1999). *Diccionario Etnolingüístico Maká-Español (DELME).* Colección Nuestra América. Serie Archivo de Lenguas Indoamericanas. Buenos Aires:

Instituto de Lingüística. Facultad de Filosofía y Letras, Universidad de Buenos Aires.

Golluscio, Lucía. (2007). Vilela (Chaco, South America): A typological overview with special emphasis on deictics. Colloquium presented at the Max Planck Institute for Evolutionary Anthropology, Leipzig.

Golluscio, Lucía, and Hirsch, Silvia. (2006). Historias fragmentadas, identidades y lenguas: Los pueblos indígenas del Chaco Argentino. *Indiana* 23: 99–102.

González, Hebe. (2005). *Tapiete grammar.* PhD dissertation. Department of Linguistics. University of Pittsburgh.

Greenberg, Joseph. (1959). Linguistic classification of South America. In J. Steward and L. Faron (eds.), *Native peoples of South America.* New York: McGraw-Hill.

Grondona, Verónica. (1998). *A grammar of Mocoví.* PhD dissertation. Department of Linguistics. University of Pittsburgh.

Grubb, W. Barbrooke. (1914). *A church in the wilds.* London: Seeley, Service & Co. Ltd.

Gualdieri, Beatriz. (1998). *Mocoví (Guaycuruan). Fonologia e morfossintaxe.* PhD dissertation. Universidade Estadual de Campinas, Campinas, São Paulo.

Gutiérrez, Analía. (2015). Evidential Determiners in Nivacle. *Anthropological Linguistics* 57 (4): 412–443.

Hervás y Panduro, L. (1787[1990]). *Vocabulario Poligloto. Saggio Pratico delle lingue Manuel With introduction and facsímile edition by Manuel Breva-Claramonte and Ramón Sarmiento.* Madrid: Socieded General Española de Librería.

Hunt, Richard J. (1913). *El Vejoz.* Buenos Aires: Coni Hermanos.

Karsten, Rafael. (1932). The Indian tribes of the Argentine and Bolivian Chaco. Ethnological Studies. *Societas Scientarum Fennica, Commentationes Humanarum Litterarum,* 4.1. Helsingfors, Finland.

Klein, Harriet M. (1973). *A grammar of Argentine Toba.* PhD dissertation, Columbia University. Klein Harriet M., and José Braunstein. (2003). Contacts and language intermixing among Chaco indigenous populations. Paper presented at *LSA Annual Meeting.*

Koch-Grünberg, Theodor. (1903). Die Guaycuruan gruppe. *Mitt. Anthrop. Gesell.,* Vol. 33; Vienna.

Lehmann-Nitsche, Robert. (1907). Estudios antropológicos sobre los chiriguanos, chorotes, matacos y tobas (Chaco Occidental). *Anales del Museo de la Plata I* 2: 53–151.

Lafone-Quevedo, Samuel A. (1894). Los Lules. *Boletin del Instituto Geográfico Argentino,* 185–245, Tomo XV. Mayo, Junio, Julio y Agosto.

(1895). La lengua vilela o chulupí. Estudio de filología chaco-argentina fundado sobre los trabajos de Hervás, Adelung y Pellschi. *Boletin del Instituto Geográfico Argentino* 16: 37–124.

(1912). *Pronominal classification of certain South American Indian stocks.* Buenos Aires: Coni Hermanos.

Lanning, Edward. (1967). *Perú before the Incas.* Englewood Cliffs, NJ: Prentice Hall.

Machoni de Cerdeña, P. Antonio. (1877). *Arte de la lengua Lule y Tonocoté.* Buenos Aires: Coni Hermanos.

Massei, Inocencio Or. Seráfica. (1895). "Pater noster" and notes. Nocten dialect with an introduction and notes by S. A. Lafone Quevedo *Boletín del Instituto Geográfico Argentino*, Tomo XVI. Buenos Aires.

Mendoza, Marcela. (2004). Culture, Demic expansions, and bilateral kinship in the South American Gran Chaco: A response to Doug Jones. *American Anthropologist* 106: 212–213.

Messineo, Cristina. (1988). *Variantes dialectales del complejo lingüístico Toba. Hacia una nueva carta étnica del Gran Chaco*, II, 13–22. Las Lomitas: Centro del Hombre Antiguo Chaqueño.

(1992). Variantes diatópicas del toba. In *Hacia una nueva carta étnica del Gran Chaco*, V, 67–79. Las Lomitas: Centro del Hombre Antiguo Chaqueño.

(2003). *Lengua toba (Guaycuruan).Aspectos gramaticales y discursivos*. Lincom Europa Academia Publications.

Messineo, Cristina, and José Braunstein. (1990). Variantes lingüísticas del Mataco. *Hacia una nueva carta étnica del Gran Chaco*, I. Centro del Hombre Antiguo Chaqueño. Las Lomitas.

Métraux, Alfred. (1996[1946]). *Etnografía del Chaco*. Asunción: Centro de Estudios Antropológicos de la Universidad Católica.

Morresi, Eldo S. (1971). *Las Ruinas del km. 75 y Concepción del Bermejo – Primera etapa de una Investigación de arqueología histórica regional*. Resistencia: Departamento de Publicaciones e Impresiones de la Universidad Nacional del Nordeste.

Neel, J. V. and F. M. Salzano. (1967). Further studies on the Xavante Indians. X. Some hypotheses-generalizations resulting from these studies. *American Journal of Human Genetics* 19(4): 554–574.

Nercesian, Verónica (2014). *Wichi Lhomtes. Estudio de la gramática y la interacción fonología-morfología-sintaxis-semántica*. Muenchen: Lincom Studies in Native American Linguistics 74.

Nordenskiöld, Erland. (1912). *Indianerleben. El Gran Chaco (Südamerika)*, Leipzig.

Orbigny, Alcide D'. (1839). *L'Homme Américain*, Paris.

Palmer, John. (2005). *Wichi toponimy Hacia una nueva carta étnica del Gran Chaco*, VI, 3–63. Las Lomitas: Centro del Hombre Antiguo Chaqueño.

Pelleschi, Giovanni. (1886). *Eight months on the Gran Chaco of the Argentine Republic*. London: Gilbert and Rivington.

(1897). Los indios mataguayos y su lengua Introduction by Samuel. A. Lafone Quevedo. *Boletín del Instituto Geográfico Argentino*, XVII/XVIII. Buenos Aires.

Remedi, Joaquín Ord. Seráf. (1890). *Los indios matacos y su lengua. With vocabulary organized by S.A. Lafone Quevedo Boletín del Instituto Geográfico Argentino, Separate edition*. Buenos Aires.

Sandalo, Filomena. (1995). *A grammar of Kadiwéu*. PhD dissertation. University of Pittsburgh.

Schmidt, Max. (1936). Los Maká en comparación con los Enimagá antiguos. *Revista de la Sociedad Científica del Paraguay* III(6): 152–157.

Seeelwische, José. (1980). *Diccionario nivaclé-castellano*. Mariscal Estigarribia: Biblioteca Paraguaya de Antropología.

Serrano, Antonio. (1972). Líneas fundamentales de la arqueología del litoral. *Instituto de Antropología*. Vol. XXXII. Universidad Nacional de Córdoba.

Stell, Nélida. (1972). *Fonología de la lengua axluxlai*. Cuadernos de Lingüística Indígena 8. Buenos Aires: Facultad de Filosofía y Letras. Universidad de Buenos Aires.

(1989). *Gramática descriptiva de la lengua niwaclé (chulupí)*. *Tesis doctoral*. Buenos Aires. Facultad de Filosofía y Letras. Universidad de Buenos Aires.

Sušnik, Branislava. (1986/87). *Los Aborígenes del Paraguay*, VII/1, Lenguas Chaqueñas. Asunción, Paraguay: Museo Etnográfico Andrés Barbero.

(1972). *Dimensiones migratorias y pautas culturales de los pueblos del Gran Chaco y de su periferia. Enfoque etnológico. Instituto de Historia. Facultad de Humanidades*. Universidad Nacional del Nordeste.

(1988). Etnohistoria del Paraguay. Etnohistoria de los chaqueños y de los guaraníes. Bosquejo sintético. *Suplemento Antropológico* 23(2).

Tapia, Augusto. (1936). *"Pilcomayo. Contribución al conocimiento de las llanuras argentinas."* Buenos Aires: Ministerio de Agricultura de la Nación, Dirección de Minas y Geología.

Tovar, Antonio. (1951). Un capítulo de lingüística general. Los prefijos posesivos en lenguas del Chaco y la lucha entre préstamo morfológicos en un espacio dado. *Boletín de la Academia Argentina de Letras* 20: 360–403.

(1964). El grupo mataco y su relación con otras lenguas de América del Sur. *Actas del 35°Congreso Internacional de Americanistas*, tomo II, 439–452. México.

Unruh, Ernesto; Kalisch, Hannes. (2003). Enlhet-Enenlhet. *Una familia lingüística chaqueña. Thule, Rivista italiana di studi americanistici* 14/15: 207–231.

Vidal, Alejandra. (1997). Noun classification in Pilagá. *The Journal of Amazonian Languages* 1(1): 58–111.

(2001). *Pilagá grammar*. PhD dissertation. Department of Linguistics. University of Oregon.

Vidal, Alejandra. (2005). *Fieldnotes on Wichí (southern and central Bermejo, Formosa). DoBeS Project. "Endangered Languages, endangered peoples of Argentina."* Universidad de Buenos Aires-Max Planck Institute for Evolutionary Anthropology.

Vidal, Alejandra, and Gutierrez, Analia. (2010). La categoría de tiempo nominal en las lenguas chaqueñas. In Victor Castel and Liliana C. de Severino (eds.), *La renovación de la palabra en el bicentenario de la Argentina. Los colores de la mirada linguistica*. Mendoza: Universidad Nacional de Cuyo, 1347–1355.

Viegas Barros, Pedro. (1993). ¿Existe una relación genética entre las lenguas mataguayas y guaycurúes? In *Hacia una nueva carta étnica del Gran Chaco*, V. Las Lomitas: Centro del Hombre Antiguo Chaqueño, 193–213.

Viñas Urquiza, María Teresa. (1974). *Lengua Mataca. Archivo de Lenguas Precolombinas. Centro de Estudios lingüísticos, Facultad de Filosofía y Letras*. Universidad de Buenos Aires, 2 vols.

Wright, Pablo. (1988). Topónimos Tacaaglé. In *Hacia una nueva carta étnica del Gran Chaco*, V. Las Lomitas: Centro del Hombre Antiguo Chaqueño, 193–213.

Appendix A Preliminary Worldwide Survey of Forager Languages

Tom Güldemann, Patrick McConvell, and Richard A. Rhodes

To produce an exhaustive worldwide survey of ethnolinguistic communities with a foraging subsistence and analyze it regarding various linguistic and historical questions is a research project in its own right. This persisting gap is planned to be filled by Güldemann and Hammarström (in prep.), which the reader is referred to for a more extensive discussion regarding the current conditions and problems of such an undertaking. The following list of forager languages is a first step in that direction by the present editors in the form of a preliminary global inventory that combines judgments found in a variety of published and unpublished sources that deal with this issue, based on different types of data and having each their strengths and drawbacks.

The major written sources are given under (1).

(1)   Sources for Language-Forager Assignment

a. Hammarström (ms.)
b. Human relations area file (HRAF, see: http://www.yale.edu/hraf/)
c. Lee and Daly (1999)
d. Lewis (2009) = "Ethnologue, 16th edition"
e. Murdock (1967) = "Ethnographic atlas"
f. Dedicated Specialist publications, notably:
  • Bahuchet (2012) for Central Africa
  • Bulletin of the International Committee on Urgent Anthropological and Ethnological Research no. 1, 2, 3, 9, 11
  • Martin (1969) for South America
  • Roscoe (2002) for Papua New Guinea
  • Rottland (1983) for East Africa

We also relied on our own expertise as well as that of areal specialists who are listed under (2); we herewith would like to express our deep gratitude for their important help.

(2)   Personal Communication by Specialists

J. Blevins	– Andaman islands (see also Chapter 9)
N. Burenhult	– Mainland Southeast Asia (see also Chapter 8)
M. Crevels and H. van der Voort	– Guaporé-Mamoré (unpublished ms.)
P. Epps	– Vaupés (see also Chapter 22)
L. Reid	– Philippines (see also Chapter 10)
J. Rischel	– Southeast Asia (see also Chapter 7)
F. Rottland	– Eastern Africa
G. Savá and M. Tosco	– (North)eastern Africa (see also Chapter 5)
A. Soriente	– Borneo (see also Chapter 11)
U. Tadmor	– Insular Southeast Asia
E. Vajda	– Central Siberia (see also Chapter 17)

As the foregoing sources do not have the same scope and/or agree on the identification of a speech community as forager there are a number of uncertain cases (marked in the list by a question mark after the language name). This characterization applies in particular in two geographical macro-regions, namely South America and even more so Central Pacific+New Guinea, which is an interesting phenomenon in its own right and will be discussed in more detail by Güldemann and Hammarström (in prep.).

(3)   Geographical Macro-regions of the Globe

    I. Africa + Arabian Peninsula
   II. Tropical Asia + Western Pacific
 III. Central Pacific + New Guinea
 IV. Australia
  V. Northern Eurasia
 VI. North America + Mesoamerica
VII. South America

In our survey, the globe is divided into seven continent-sized macro-regions, for which see (3). The relevant languages are then organized according to language families. Our approach to genealogical linguistic relationships is oriented towards commonly accepted standards of historical-comparative methodology that are outlined, for example, by Nichols (1996) and Campbell (2003). That is, our classificatory layout does not consider genealogical language groups proposed in such works as Greenberg (1963, 1971, 1987, 2002), Ruhlen (1987, 1994a, b) etc., which are not (yet) supported by robust historical-comparative evidence, even if some may be accepted by many linguists. We are fully aware that some of our decisions will turn out to be inappropriate, because classification in many areas is still in flux. The major reference work for the language inventory was Lewis (2009); some new ISO codes from later editions are given in square brackets. Some additional languages recognized by area specialists (often without an ISO code) are included, but not systematically. Finally, the survey focuses on independent languages and thus largely disregards speech forms that are (thought to be) varieties embedded in speech communities with a predominant food-producing subsistence, as, for example, Hassaniyya Arabic spoken by the Imeraguen and Nemadi, Malagasy spoken by the Mikea, Telugu spoken by the Yanadi, and Maori spoken by the Chatham Moriori.

Family	Language	ISO code	Country
Africa + Arabian Peninsula: 45			
Afroasiatic, Cushitic	Aasáx	aas	Tanzania
	Boni	bob	Kenya
	Boon	bnl	Somalia
	Dahalo	dal	Kenya
	Elmolo	elo	Kenya
	Sanye ~ Waata	ssn	Kenya
	Yaaku	muu	Kenya
Central Sudanic, Moru-Mangbetu	Asoa	asv	DRC
	Efe	efe	DRC
Hadza	Hadza	hts	Tanzania
Kujarge	Kujarge	vkj	Chad
Khoe-Kwadi	Gǀui	gwj	Botswana
	Gǁana	gnk	Botswana
	Haiǀom	hgm	Namibia
	Khwe	xuu	Botswana, Namibia
	Kua	tyu	Botswana
	Naro	nhr	Botswana
	Shua	shg	Botswana
	Tyua	hio	Botswana
	ǀAni	hnh	Botswana
Kx'a	Juǀ'hoan	ktz	Namibia, Botswana
	Kung-Ekoka	knw	Namibia
	Maligo	mwj	Angola
	Vasekela Bushman	vaj	Angola
	!O!ung	oun	Namibia, Angola
	ǂHoan ~ ǂ'Amkoe	huc	Botswana
	ǂKx'auǀ'ein	aue	Namibia, Botswana
Niger-Congo, Benue-Kwa	Yaka ~ Aka	axk	CAR, Congo
Niger-Congo, Ubangi	Baka	bkc	Cameroon
	Ganzi	gnz	CAR
	Ngombe	nmj	Congo

(*cont.*)

Family	Language	ISO code	Country
Africa + Arabian Peninsula: 45			
Nilotic-Surmic, Nilotic	Akie	mwy	Tanzania
	Okiek ~ Sogoo	oki	Kenya
	Omotik	omt	Kenya
Nilotic-Surmic, Surmic	Koegu	xwg	Ethiopia
Ongota	Ongota ~ Birale	bxe	Ethiopia
Sandawe	Sandawe	sad	Tanzania
Shabo	Shabo ~ Mikeyir	sbf	Ethiopia
Tuu	Nǀuu ~ Nǁng	ngh	South Africa
	Seroa	kqu	South Africa
	ǀHaasi	No code	South Africa, Botswana
	ǀXam	xam	South Africa
	ǀ'Auni	No code	South Africa, Botswana
	!Xóõ ~ Taa	nmn	Botswana, Namibia
	ǂUngkwe	No code	South Africa
	ǀXegwi	xeg	South Africa
Tropical Asia + Western Pacific: 98 + 17 uncertain			
Austroasiatic, Mon-Khmer, Aslian	Batek	btq	Malaysia
	Jehai	jhi	Malaysia
	Kensiu	kns	Malaysia
	Kintaq	knq	Malaysia
	Lanoh	lnh	Malaysia
	Minriq	mnq	Malaysia
	Mintil	mzt	Malaysia
	Sabüm	sbo	Malaysia
	Semaq Beri	szc	Malaysia
	Semnam	ssm	Malaysia
	Tea-de	No code	Malaysia
	Tonga (Ten'en)	tnz	Thailand
Austroasiatic, Mon-Khmer, Other	Chut ~ Ruc/May ?	scb	Vietnam, Laos
	Mlabri	mra	Thailand
Austroasiatic, Munda	Birhor	biy	India
	Juang ?	jun	India
Austronesian, Malayic	Moken	mwt	Myanmar, Thailand
	Urak Lawoi'	urk	Thailand
Austronesian, Meso Philippine	Agta, Isarog	agk	Philippines
	Agta, Mt. Iraya	atl	Philippines
	Agta, Mt. Iriga	agz	Philippines
	Ata	atm	Philippines
	Ati	atk	Philippines
	Ayta, Sorsogon	ays	Philippines

(cont.)

Family	Language	ISO code	Country
Tropical Asia + Western Pacific: 98 + 17 uncertain			
	Ayta, Tayabas	ayy	Philippines
	Batak	bya	Philippines
	Mamanwa	mmn	Philippines
Austronesian, North Borneo	Aoheng	pni	Indonesia
	Basap	bdb	Indonesia
	Bukat	bvk	Indonesia
	Bukitan	bkn	Indonesia
	Hovongan	hov	Indonesia
	Kereho	xke	Indonesia
	Penan, Eastern	pez	Malaysia, Brunei
	Penan, Western	pne	Malaysia, Brunei
	Punan Aput	pud	Indonesia
	Punan Bah-Biau	pna	Malaysia
	Punan Batu 1	pnm	Malaysia
	Punan Merah	puf	Indonesia
	Punan Merap	puc	Indonesia
	Punan Tubu	puj	Indonesia
	Sajau Basap	sjb	Indonesia
	Sihan	spg	Malaysia
	Ukit	umi	Malaysia, Indonesia
Austronesian, Northern Philippine	Agta, Alabat Island	dul	Philippines
	Agta, Camarines Norte	abd	Philippines
	Agta, Casiguran Dumagat	dgc	Philippines
	Agta, Central Cagayan	agt	Philippines
	Agta, Dicamay	duy	Philippines
	Agta, Dupaninan	duo	Philippines
	Agta, Remontado	agv	Philippines
	Agta, Umiray Dumaget	due	Philippines
	Agta, Villa Viciosa	dyg	Philippines
	Alta, Northern	aqn	Philippines
	Alta, Southern	agy	Philippines
	Arta	atz	Philippines
	Atta, Faire	azt	Philippines
	Atta, Pamplona	att	Philippines
	Atta, Pudtol	atp	Philippines
	Ayta, Abenlen	abp	Philippines
	Ayta, Ambala	abc	Philippines
	Ayta, Bataan	ayt	Philippines
	Ayta, Mag-Anchi	sgb	Philippines
	Ayta, Mag-Indi	blx	Philippines
	Paranan	agp	Philippines
	Sambal, Botolan	sbl	Philippines

(cont.)

Family	Language	ISO code	Country
Tropical Asia + Western Pacific: 98 + 17 uncertain			
Austronesian, Southern Philippine	Manobo, Ata	atd	Philippines
Dravidian	Allar	all	India
	Aranadan	aaf	India
	Chenchu	cde	India
	Eravallan ?	era	India
	Irula ?	iru	India
	Kadar	kej	India
	Kaikadi	kep	India
	Kurumba, Alu	xua	India
	Kurumba, Jennu Nayaka	xuj	India
	Mala Malasar	ima	India
	Malankuravan ?	mjo	India
	Malapandaram	mjp	India
	Malasar ?	ymr	India
	Malavedan	mjr	India
	Muthuvan ?	muv	India
	Paliyan	pcf	India
	Sholaga ?	sle	India
	Thachanadan ?	thn	India
	Ullatan	ull	India
	Urali ?	url	India
Great Andamanese	Aka-Bea	abj	India
	Aka-Bo	akm	India
	Aka-Cari	aci	India
	Aka-Jeru	akj	India
	Aka-Kede	akx	India
	Aka-Kol	aky	India
	Aka-Kora	ack	India
	Akar-Bale	acl	India
	A-Pucikwar	apq	India
	Oko-Juwoi	okj	India
Indo-European, Indo-Aryan	Kharia Thar	ksy	India
	Veddah (Wanniyala-aetto)	ved	Sri Lanka
Kusunda	Kusunda	kgg	Nepal
Little Andamanese (Ongan)	Jarawa	anq	India
	Onge	oon	India
Sentinel	Sentinel	std	India
Shom Peng	Shom Peng	sii	India
Sino-Tibetan	Darang Deng ?	dat	China
	Drung ~ Dulong	duu	China

(cont.)

Family	Language	ISO code	Country
Tropical Asia + Western Pacific: 98 + 17 uncertain			
	Geman Deng ?	gen	China
	Jinuo, Buyuan	jiy	China
	Jinuo, Youle	jiu	China
	Kaike ?	kzq	Nepal
	Kucong ?	lkc	China, Laos
	Raji	rji	Nepal
	Raute	rau	Nepal
	Rawat	jnl	Nepal
	Sulung	suv	India
Central Pacific + New Guinea: 102 + 202 uncertain			
Abinomn	Abinomn	bsa	Indonesia (Papua)
Amto-Musan	Amto	amt	Papua New Guinea
	Siawi ~ Musan	mmp	Papua New Guinea
Arafundi	Andai	[afd]	Papua New Guinea
	Meakambut	No code	Papua New Guinea
	Nanubae	[afk]	Papua New Guinea
	Tapei	[afp]	Papua New Guinea
Austronesian	Bajau, Indonesian (Orang Laut)	bdl	Indonesia (Sulawesi)
	Biak	bhw	Indonesia (Papua)
	Huaulu	hud	Indonesia (Maluku)
	Lauje, Sinalutan	law	Indonesia (Sulawesi)
	Loncong (Orang Laut)	lce	Indonesia (Sumatra)
	Manusela ~ Maneo	wha	Indonesia (Maluku)
	Taliabu	tlv	Indonesia (Maluku)
	Titan ?	ttv	Papua New Guinea
	Toala'	tlz	Indonesia (Sulawesi)
	Tugutil	tuj	Indonesia (Maluku)
	Warembori ?	wsa	Indonesia (Papua)
	Waropen	wrp	Indonesia (Papua)
	Yoke ?	yki	Indonesia (Papua)
Awin-Pare	Aekyom ?	awi	Papua New Guinea
	Kamula	xla	Papua New Guinea
	Pare ?	ppt	Papua New Guinea
Baibai	Baibai ?	bbf	Papua New Guinea
	Nai ?	bio	Papua New Guinea
Bayono-Awbono	Awbono ?	awh	Indonesia (Papua)
	Bayono ?	byl	Indonesia (Papua)
Biksi	Kimki ?	sbt	Indonesia (Papua)
	Yetfa ?	yet	Indonesia (Papua)
Bosavi	Aimele ?	ail	Papua New Guinea
	Beami ?	beo	Papua New Guinea

(cont.)

Family	Language	ISO code	Country
Central Pacific + New Guinea: 102 + 202 uncertain			
	Dibiyaso	dby	Papua New Guinea
	Edolo ?	etr	Papua New Guinea
	Kaluli ?	bco	Papua New Guinea
	Kasua ?	khs	Papua New Guinea
	Onobasulu ?	onn	Papua New Guinea
	Sonia ?	sig	Papua New Guinea
Bulaka River	Maklew ?	mgf	Indonesia (Papua)
	Yelmek ?	jel	Indonesia (Papua)
Burmeso	Burmeso ~ Taurap ?	bzu	Indonesia (Papua)
Damal	Damal ~ Uhunduni ?	uhn	Indonesia (Papua)
Doso	Doso ?	dol	Papua New Guinea
Eastern Trans-Fly	Bine	bon	Papua New Guinea
	Gizrra	tof	Papua New Guinea
	Meriam	ulk	Australia
	Wipi	gdr	Papua New Guinea
East Geelvink Bay = East	Anasi	bpo	Indonesia (Papua)
Cenderawasih Bay	Barapasi	brp	Indonesia (Papua)
	Bauzi	bvz	Indonesia (Papua)
	Burate	bti	Indonesia (Papua)
	Demisa ?	dei	Indonesia (Papua)
	Kofei	kpi	Indonesia (Papua)
	Nisa ?	njs	Indonesia (Papua)
	Sauri ?	srt	Indonesia (Papua)
	Tefaro ?	tfo	Indonesia (Papua)
	Tunggare	trt	Indonesia (Papua)
	Woria ?	wor	Indonesia (Papua)
Elseng	Elseng ~ Morwap ?	mrf	Indonesia (Papua)
Gogodala-Suki	Ari ?	aac	Papua New Guinea
	Gogodala ?	ggw	Papua New Guinea
	Suki ?	sui	Papua New Guinea
	Waruna ?	wrv	Papua New Guinea
Inanwatan	Duriankere ?	dbn	Indonesia (Papua)
	Suabo ?	szp	Indonesia (Papua)
Kaure	Kapori ?	khp	Indonesia (Papua)
	Kaure ~ Narau ?	bpp	Indonesia (Papua)
	Kosadle ?	kiq	Indonesia (Papua)
Kayagar	Atohwaim	aqm	Indonesia (Papua)
	Kayagar ?	kyt	Indonesia (Papua)
	Tamagario	tcg	Indonesia (Papua)
Kehu	Kehu ?	khh	Indonesia (Papua)
Kembra	Kembra ?	xkw	Indonesia (Papua)
Kibiri	Kibiri ~ Porome ?	prm	Papua New Guinea
Kiwaian	Bamu	bcf	Papua New Guinea

(cont.)

Family	Language	ISO code	Country
Central Pacific + New Guinea: 102 + 202 uncertain			
	Kerewo ?	kxz	Papua New Guinea
	Kiwai, Northeast	kiw	Papua New Guinea
	Kiwai, Southern	kjd	Papua New Guinea
	Morigi	mdb	Papua New Guinea
	Waboda ?	kmx	Papua New Guinea
Koiarian	Ömie ?	aom	Papua New Guinea
Konda-Yahadian	Konda ?	knd	Indonesia (Papua)
	Yahadian ?	ner	Indonesia (Papua)
Kwerba	Airoran ?	air	Indonesia (Papua)
	Bagusa	bqb	Indonesia (Papua)
	Isirawa	srl	Indonesia (Papua)
	Kauwera ?	xau	Indonesia (Papua)
	Kwerba	kwe	Indonesia (Papua)
	Kwerba Mamberamo	xwr	Indonesia (Papua)
	Samarokena ?	tmj	Indonesia (Papua)
	Trimuris	tip	Indonesia (Papua)
Kwomtari	Fas ?	fqs	Papua New Guinea
	Guriaso ?	grx	Papua New Guinea
	Kwomtari	kwo	Papua New Guinea
Lakes Plain	Awera ?	awr	Indonesia (Papua)
	Biritai ?	bqq	Indonesia (Papua)
	Doutai	tds	Indonesia (Papua)
	Duvle ?	duv	Indonesia (Papua)
	Edopi	dbf	Indonesia (Papua)
	Eritai	ert	Indonesia (Papua)
	Fayu	fau	Indonesia (Papua)
	Foau ?	flh	Indonesia (Papua)
	Iau	tmu	Indonesia (Papua)
	Kaiy	tcq	Indonesia (Papua)
	Kirikiri	kiy	Indonesia (Papua)
	Kwerisa	kkb	Indonesia (Papua)
	Obokuitai ?	afz	Indonesia (Papua)
	Papasena ?	pas	Indonesia (Papua)
	Rasawa	rac	Indonesia (Papua)
	Saponi ?	spi	Indonesia (Papua)
	Sikaritai	tty	Indonesia (Papua)
	Tause	tad	Indonesia (Papua)
	Taworta ?	tbp	Indonesia (Papua)
	Waritai ?	wbe	Indonesia (Papua)
Left May	Ama ~ Sawiyano	amm	Papua New Guinea
	Bo	bpw	Papua New Guinea
	Iteri ?	itr	Papua New Guinea
	Nakwi ?	nax	Papua New Guinea
	Nimo ?	niw	Papua New Guinea
	Owiniga ?	owi	Papua New Guinea

(cont.)

Family	Language	ISO code	Country
Central Pacific + New Guinea: 102 + 202 uncertain			
Lepki	Lepki ?	lpe	Indonesia (Papua)
Lower Sepik-Ramu, Lower Sepik	Angoram ?	aog	Papua New Guinea
	Chambri ?	can	Papua New Guinea
	Kopar ?	xop	Papua New Guinea
	Murik	mtf	Papua New Guinea
	Tabriak ?	tzx	Papua New Guinea
	Yimas	yee	Papua New Guinea
Lower Sepik-Ramu, Ramu	Abu ?	ado	Papua New Guinea
	Aiome ?	aki	Papua New Guinea
	Akrukay ?	afi	Papua New Guinea
	Ambakich ?	aew	Papua New Guinea
	Andarum ?	aod	Papua New Guinea
	Anor ?	anj	Papua New Guinea
	Ap Ma ~ Kambot	kbx	Papua New Guinea
	Awar ?	aya	Papua New Guinea
	Aruamu ~ Mikarew ?	msy	Papua New Guinea
	Banaro ?	byz	Papua New Guinea
	Bosngun ?	bgs	Papua New Guinea
	Borei ~ Gamay ?	gai	Papua New Guinea
	Breri ?	brq	Papua New Guinea
	Gorovu ?	grq	Papua New Guinea
	Igana ?	igg	Papua New Guinea
	Inapang ?	mzu	Papua New Guinea
	Itutang ?	itu	Papua New Guinea
	Kaian ?	kct	Papua New Guinea
	Kanggape ~ Igom ?	igm	Papua New Guinea
	Kire ?	geb	Papua New Guinea
	Kominimung ?	xoi	Papua New Guinea
	Rao ?	rao	Papua New Guinea
	Romkun ?	rmk	Papua New Guinea
	Sepen ?	spm	Papua New Guinea
	Tanguat ?	tbs	Papua New Guinea
	Tanggu ?	tgu	Papua New Guinea
	Watam ?	wax	Papua New Guinea
Massep	Massep ?	mvs	Indonesia (Papua)
Molof	Molof ?	msl	Indonesia (Papua)
Mongol-Langam	Langam	lnm	Papua New Guinea
	Mongol	mgt	Papua New Guinea
	Yaul	yla	Papua New Guinea
Mor	Mor ?	moq	Indonesia (Papua)
Moraori	Morori	mok	Indonesia (Papua)
Murkim	Murkim ?	rmh	Indonesia (Papua)
Nimboranic	Gresi ?	grs	Indonesia (Papua)
	Nimboran ?	nir	Indonesia (Papua)
Odiai	Odiai ~ Busa	bhf	Papua New Guinea

(cont.)

Family	Language	ISO code	Country
Central Pacific + New Guinea: 102 + 202 uncertain			
Ok	Mian	mpt	Papua New Guinea
	Nakai ?	nkj	Indonesia (Papua)
Pahoturi	Agob	kit	Papua New Guinea
	Idi	idi	Papua New Guinea
Papi	Papi ?	ppe	Papua New Guinea
Pauwasi	Dubu ?	dmu	Indonesia (Papua)
	Emumu ?	enr	Indonesia (Papua)
	Karkar-Yuri ?	yuj	Papua New Guinea
	Towei ?	ttn	Indonesia (Papua)
	Yafi ?	wfg	Indonesia (Papua)
Pawaian	Pawaian ?	pwa	Papua New Guinea
Piawi	Haruai ?	tmd	Papua New Guinea
	Pinai-Hagahai ?	pnn	Papua New Guinea
Pyu	Pyu ?	pby	Papua New Guinea
Sause	Sause	sao	Indonesia (Papua)
Senagi	Anggor ?	agg	Papua New Guinea
	Dera ?	kbv	Indonesia (Papua)
Sentani	Demta ?	dmy	Indonesia (Papua)
	Nafri ?	nxx	Indonesia (Papua)
	Sentani ?	set	Indonesia (Papua)
	Tabla ?	tnm	Indonesia (Papua)
Sepik, Abau	Abau	aau	Papua New Guinea
Sepik, Iwam	Amal ?	aad	Papua New Guinea
	Iwam ?	iwm	Papua New Guinea
	Iwam, Sepik	iws	Papua New Guinea
Sepik, Ndu	Ambulas ?	abt	Papua New Guinea
	Boikin ?	bzf	Papua New Guinea
	Burui ?	bry	Papua New Guinea
	Gaikundi ?	gbf	Papua New Guinea
	Hanga Hundi ?	wos	Papua New Guinea
	Iatmul ?	ian	Papua New Guinea
	Koiwat ?	kxt	Papua New Guinea
	Malinguat ~ Sawos	sic	Papua New Guinea
	Manambu ?	mle	Papua New Guinea
	Ngala ?	nud	Papua New Guinea
	Sengo ?	spk	Papua New Guinea
	Yelogu ~ Kaunga	ylg	Papua New Guinea
Sepik, Nukuma	Kwanga ?	kwj	Papua New Guinea
	Kwoma	kmo	Papua New Guinea
	Mende ?	sim	Papua New Guinea
Sepik, Ram	Awtuw ?	kmn	Papua New Guinea
	Karawa ?	xrw	Papua New Guinea
	Pouye ?	bye	Papua New Guinea
Sepik, Sepik Hill	Alamblak	amp	Papua New Guinea

(cont.)

Family	Language	ISO code	Country
Central Pacific + New Guinea: 102 + 202 uncertain			
	Bahinemo	bjh	Papua New Guinea
	Berinomo	bit	Papua New Guinea
	Bikaru ?	bic	Papua New Guinea
	Bisis	bnw	Papua New Guinea
	Hewa ?	ham	Papua New Guinea
	Kaningra	knr	Papua New Guinea
	Kapriman ~ Sare	dju	Papua New Guinea
	Mari	mbx	Papua New Guinea
	Niksek ?	gbe	Papua New Guinea
	Piame ?	pin	Papua New Guinea
	Saniyo-Hiyewe	sny	Papua New Guinea
	Sumariup	siv	Papua New Guinea
	Watakatauwi	wtk	Papua New Guinea
Sepik, Tama	Ayi ?	ayq	Papua New Guinea
	Kalou ?	ywa	Papua New Guinea
	Mehek ?	nux	Papua New Guinea
	Pahi ?	lgt	Papua New Guinea
	Pasi ?	psq	Papua New Guinea
	Yessan-Mayo ?	yss	Papua New Guinea
Sepik, Wogamusin	Chenapian ?	cjn	Papua New Guinea
	Wogamusin ?	wog	Papua New Guinea
Sepik, Yellow River	Ak ?	akq	Papua New Guinea
	Awun ?	aww	Papua New Guinea
	Namia	nnm	Papua New Guinea
	Yerakai ?	yra	Papua New Guinea
Sko	Krisa	ksi	Papua New Guinea
	Puari ?	pux	Papua New Guinea
	Rawo ?	rwa	Papua New Guinea
	Vanimo ~ Dumo	vam	Papua New Guinea
	Warapu	wra	Papua New Guinea
South Bird's Head Proper	Arandai ?	jbj	Indonesia (Papua)
	Kaburi	uka	Indonesia (Papua)
	Kais	kzm	Indonesia (Papua)
	Kemberano ?	bzp	Indonesia (Papua)
	Kokoda ?	xod	Indonesia (Papua)
	Puragi ?	pru	Indonesia (Papua)
Tabo	Tabo ~ Waya ?	knv	Papua New Guinea
Taiap	Taiap ~ Gapun ?	gpn	Papua New Guinea
Tanahmerah	Tanahmerah ?	tcm	Indonesia (Papua)
Tirio	Abom ?	aob	Papua New Guinea
	Baramu ?	bmz	Papua New Guinea
	Bitur ?	mcc	Papua New Guinea
	Makayam ?	aup	Papua New Guinea
	Were ?	wei	Papua New Guinea

(cont.)

Family	Language	ISO code	Country
Central Pacific + New Guinea: 102 + 202 uncertain			
Tofamna	Tofamna	tlg	Indonesia (Papua)
Tor-Orya	Berik (Tor)	bkl	Indonesia (Papua)
	Betaf ?	bfe	Indonesia (Papua)
	Bonerif	bnv	Indonesia (Papua)
	Dabe ?	dbe	Indonesia (Papua)
	Itik ?	itx	Indonesia (Papua)
	Keder ?	kdy	Indonesia (Papua)
	Kwesten ?	kwt	Indonesia (Papua)
	Mander	mqr	Indonesia (Papua)
	Maremgi ?	mrx	Indonesia (Papua)
	Orya ?	ury	Indonesia (Papua)
Torricelli	Au ?	avt	Papua New Guinea
	One, Inebu	oin	Papua New Guinea
	One, Kabore	onk	Papua New Guinea
	One, Kwamtim	okk	Papua New Guinea
	One, Molmo	aun	Papua New Guinea
	One, Northern	onr	Papua New Guinea
	One, Southern	osu	Papua New Guinea
Trans-New-Guinea, Asmat-Kamoro	Citak, Tamnim	tml	Indonesia (Papua)
	Asmat (Central)	cns	Indonesia (Papua)
	Asmat (Casuarina Coast)	asc	Indonesia (Papua)
	Asmat (North)	nks	Indonesia (Papua)
	Kamoro (Mimika, western)	kgq	Indonesia (Papua)
Trans-New-Guinea, Awyu-Dumut	Awyu, Central ?	awu	Indonesia (Papua)
	Awyu, Jair ?	awv	Indonesia (Papua)
	Awyu, South (Siagha-Yenimu)	aws	Indonesia (Papua)
	Kombai	tyn	Indonesia (Papua)
	Sawi	saw	Indonesia (Papua)
	Tsakwambo ?	kvz	Indonesia (Papua)
	Wanggom ?	wng	Indonesia (Papua)
Trans-New-Guinea, Eleman	Kaki Ae ?	tbd	Papua New Guinea
	Keuru ?	xeu	Papua New Guinea
	Opao ?	opo	Papua New Guinea
	Orokolo ?	oro	Papua New Guinea
	Purari ~ Koriki	iar	Papua New Guinea
	Tairuma ?	uar	Papua New Guinea
	Toaripi ?	tqo	Papua New Guinea
Trans-New-Guinea, Marind	Kuni-Boazi	kvg	Papua New Guinea
	Marind	mrz	Indonesia (Papua)
	Marind, Bian	bpv	Indonesia (Papua)
	Warkay-Bipim	bgv	Indonesia (Papua)
	Yaqay	jaq	Indonesia (Papua)
	Zimakani	zik	Papua New Guinea

(*cont.*)

Family	Language	ISO code	Country
Central Pacific + New Guinea: 102 + 202 uncertain			
Turumsa	Turumsa	tqm	Papua New Guinea
Usku	Usku ?	ulf	Indonesia (Papua)
Walio	Pei ?	ppq	Papua New Guinea
	Tuwari ?	tww	Papua New Guinea
	Walio ?	wla	Papua New Guinea
	Yawiyo	ybx	Papua New Guinea
Yale	Yale ~ Nagatman ?	nce	Papua New Guinea
Yuat	Biwat ?	bwm	Papua New Guinea
	Bun ?	buv	Papua New Guinea
	Changriwa	cga	Papua New Guinea
	Kyenele ~ Miyak	kql	Papua New Guinea
	Mekmek	mvk	Papua New Guinea
Australia: 270			
Australian, Anindilyakwa	Anindilyakwa	aoi	Australia
Australian, Anson Bay	Giyug	giy	Australia
	Wadjiginy	wdj	Australia
Australian, Bunaban	Bunaba	bck	Australia
	Gooniyandi	gni	Australia
Australian, Eastern Daly	Kamu	xmu	Australia
	Madngele	zml	Australia
Australian, Gaagudju	Gagadu	gbu	Australia
Australian, Garrwan	Garawa	gbc	Australia
Australian, Giimbiyu	Erre	err	Australia
	Mangerr	zme	Australia
	Urningangg	urc	Australia
Australian, Gunwinyguan	Djauan	djn	Australia
	Gunwinggu	gup	Australia
	Kunbarlang	wlg	Australia
	Ngalakan	nig	Australia
	Ngalkbun	ngk	Australia
	Ngandi	nid	Australia
	Nunggubuyu	nuy	Australia
	Rembarunga	rmb	Australia
	Waray	wrz	Australia
Australian, Iwaidjan Proper	Amarag	amg	Australia
	Garig-Ilgar	ilg	Australia
	Iwaidja	ibd	Australia
	Manangkari	znk	Australia
	Maung	mph	Australia
Australian, Jarrakan	Gadjerawang	gdh	Australia
	Kitja	gia	Australia
	Miriwung	mep	Australia
Australian, Kungarakany	Kungarakany	ggk	Australia
Australian, Larrakiyan	Laragia	lrg	Australia

(cont.)

Family	Language	ISO code	Country
Australia: 270			
Australian, Limilngan	Limilngan	lmc	Australia
	Wulna	wux	Australia
Australian, Maran	Alawa	alh	Australia
	Mangarayi	mpc	Australia
	Mara	mec	Australia
	Wandarang	wnd	Australia
Australian, Maningrida	Burarra	bvr	Australia
	Djeebbana	djj	Australia
	Guragone	gge	Australia
	Nakara	nck	Australia
Australian, Marrku-Wurrugu	Margu	mhg	Australia
	Wurrugu	wur	Australia
Australian, Minkin-Tangkic	Ganggalida	gcd	Australia
	Kayardild	gyd	Australia
	Minkin	No code	Australia
	Nyangga	nny	Australia
Australian, Mirndi	Djamindjung	djd	Australia
	Djingili	jig	Australia
	Gudanji	nji	Australia
	Nungali	nug	Australia
	Wambaya	wmb	Australia
Australian, Northern Daly	Mullukmulluk	mpb	Australia
	Tyaraity	woa	Australia
Australian, Nyulnyulan	Bardi	bcj	Australia
	Djawi	djw	Australia
	Dyaberdyaber	dyb	Australia
	Dyugun	dyd	Australia
	Nimanbur	nmp	Australia
	Nyigina	nyh	Australia
	Nyulnyul	nyv	Australia
	Warrwa	wwr	Australia
	Yawuru	ywr	Australia
Australian, Pama-Nyungan	Adynyamathanha	adt	Australia
	Aghu Tharnggalu	ggr	Australia
	Alngith	aid	Australia
	Alyawarr	aly	Australia
	Andegerebinha	adg	Australia
	Anmatyerre	amx	Australia
	Antakarinya	ant	Australia
	Arabana	ard	Australia
	Areba	aea	Australia
	Arrarnta, Western	are	Australia
	Arrernte, Eastern	aer	Australia
	Atampaya	amz	Australia

(cont.)

Family	Language	ISO code	Country
Australia: 270			
	Awabakal	awk	Australia
	Ayabadhu	ayd	Australia
	Badimaya	bia	Australia
	Bandjalang	bdy	Australia
	Bandjigali	bjd	Australia
	Banggarla	bjb	Australia
	Barrow Point	bpt	Australia
	Bayali	bjy	Australia
	Bayungu	bxj	Australia
	Bidyara	bym	Australia
	Biri	bzr	Australia
	Burduna	bxn	Australia
	Darling	drl	Australia
	Dayi	dax	Australia
	Dhalandji	dhl	Australia
	Dhangu	dhg	Australia
	Dhargari	dhr	Australia
	Dhurga	dhu	Australia
	Dhuwal	duj	Australia
	Dieri	dif	Australia
	Dirari	dit	Australia
	Djambarrpuyngu	djr	Australia
	Djangun	djf	Australia
	Djinang	dji	Australia
	Djinba	djb	Australia
	Djiwarli	djl	Australia
	Dyaabugay	dyy	Australia
	Dyangadi	dyn	Australia
	Dyirbal	dbl	Australia
	Flinders Island	fln	Australia
	Gamilaraay	kld	Australia
	Gangulu	gnl	Australia
	Gugadj	ggd	Australia
	Gugu Badhun	gdc	Australia
	Gugu Warra	wrw	Australia
	Gugubera	kkp	Australia
	Guguyimidjir	kky	Australia
	Gumatj	gnn	Australia
	Gungabula	gyf	Australia
	Gunya	gyy	Australia
	Gupapuyngu	guf	Australia
	Gurdjar	gdj	Australia
	Gureng Gureng	gnr	Australia
	Gurinji	gue	Australia

(cont.)

Family	Language	ISO code	Country
Australia: 270			
	Guwamu	gwu	Australia
	Guyani	gvy	Australia
	Jarnango	jay	Australia
	Jaru	ddj	Australia
	Kala Lagaw Ya	mwp	Australia
	Kalarko	kba	Australia
	Kalkutung	ktg	Australia
	Kanju	kbe	Australia
	Karadjeri	gbd	Australia
	Kariyarra	vka	Australia
	Kaytetye	gbb	Australia
	Kokata	ktd	Australia
	Kukatja	kux	Australia
	Kuku-Mangk	xmq	Australia
	Kuku-Mu'inh	xmp	Australia
	Kuku-Muminh	xmh	Australia
	Kuku-Ugbanh	ugb	Australia
	Kuku-Uwanh	uwa	Australia
	Kuku-Yalanji	gvn	Australia
	Kumbainggar	kgs	Australia
	Kunggara	kvs	Australia
	Kunggari	kgl	Australia
	Kunjen	kjn	Australia
	Kurrama	vku	Australia
	Kuthant	xut	Australia
	Kuuku-Ya'u	kuy	Australia
	Lamu-Lamu	lby	Australia
	Lardil	lbz	Australia
	Leningitij	lnj	Australia
	Malgana	vml	Australia
	Mandandanyi	zmk	Australia
	Mangala	mem	Australia
	Margany	zmc	Australia
	Martu Wangka	mpj	Australia
	Martuyhunira	vma	Australia
	Mayaguduna	xmy	Australia
	Maykulan	mnt	Australia
	Mbabaram	vmb	Australia
	Mbara	mvl	Australia
	Mbariman-Gudhinma	zmv	Australia
	Mudbura	mwd	Australia
	Muluridyi	vmu	Australia
	Muruwari	zmu	Australia
	Narrinyeri	nay	Australia
	Narungga	nnr	Australia

(cont.)

Family	Language	ISO code	Country
Australia: 270			
	Ngaanyatjarra	ntj	Australia
	Ngadjunmaya	nju	Australia
	Ngamini	nmv	Australia
	Nganyaywana	nyx	Australia
	Ngarinman	nbj	Australia
	Ngarla	nlr	Australia
	Ngarluma	nrl	Australia
	Ngawun	nxn	Australia
	Ngura	nbx	Australia
	Nhuwala	nhf	Australia
	Nijadali	nad	Australia
	Nugunu	nnv	Australia
	Nyamal	nly	Australia
	Nyangumarta	nna	Australia
	Nyawaygi	nyt	Australia
	Nyunga	nys	Australia
	Pakanha	pkn	Australia
	Panytyima	pnw	Australia
	Pini	pii	Australia
	Pinigura	pnv	Australia
	Pintiini	pti	Australia
	Pintupi-Luritja	piu	Australia
	Pirlatapa	bxi	Australia
	Pitjantjatjara	pjt	Australia
	Pitta Pitta	pit	Australia
	Ritarungo	rit	Australia
	Thayore	thd	Australia
	Thaypan	typ	Australia
	Thurawal	tbh	Australia
	Tjurruru	tju	Australia
	Umbindhamu	umd	Australia
	Umbuygamu	umg	Australia
	Umpila	ump	Australia
	Uradhi	urf	Australia
	Wadjigu	wdu	Australia
	Wagaya	wga	Australia
	Wajarri	wbv	Australia
	Wakawaka	wkw	Australia
	Walmajarri	wmt	Australia
	Wamin	wmi	Australia
	Wangaaybuwan- Ngiyambaa	wyb	Australia
	Wanggamala	wnm	Australia
	Wangganguru	wgg	Australia
	Wanman	wbt	Australia

(cont.)

Family	Language	ISO code	Country
Australia: 270			
	Wariyangga	wri	Australia
	Warlmanpa	wrl	Australia
	Warlpiri	wbp	Australia
	Warluwara	wrb	Australia
	Warrgamay	wgy	Australia
	Warumungu	wrm	Australia
	Warungu	wrg	Australia
	Wik-Epa	wie	Australia
	Wik-Iiyanh	wij	Australia
	Wik-Keyangan	wif	Australia
	Wik-Me'anha	wih	Australia
	Wik-Mungkan	wim	Australia
	Wik-Ngathana	wig	Australia
	Wikalkan	wik	Australia
	Wikngenchera	wua	Australia
	Wiradhuri	wrh	Australia
	Wirangu	wiw	Australia
	Worimi	kda	Australia
	Wuliwuli	wlu	Australia
	Yalarnnga	ylr	Australia
	Yandruwandha	ynd	Australia
	Yankunytjatjara	kdd	Australia
	Yanyuwa	jao	Australia
	Yawarawarga	yww	Australia
	Yidiny	yii	Australia
	Yindjibarndi	yij	Australia
	Yindjilandji	yil	Australia
	Yinggarda	yia	Australia
	Yir Yoront	yiy	Australia
	Yugambal	yub	Australia
Australian, Southern Daly	Murrinh-Patha	mwf	Australia
	Nangikurrunggurr	nam	Australia
Australian, Tiwi	Tiwi	tiw	Australia
Australian, Umbugarla-Ngurmbur	Ngurmbur	nrx	Australia
	Umbugarla	umr	Australia
Australian, Wagiman	Wageman	waq	Australia
Australian, Western Daly	Ami	amy	Australia
	Manda	zma	Australia
	Maranunggu	zmr	Australia
	Maridan	zmd	Australia
	Maridjabin	zmj	Australia
	Marimanindji	zmm	Australia
	Maringarr	zmt	Australia
	Marithiel	mfr	Australia

(cont.)

Family	Language	ISO code	Country
Australia: 270			
	Mariyedi	zmy	Australia
	Marti Ke	zmg	Australia
Australian, Worrorran	Gambera	gma	Australia
	Kwini	gww	Australia
	Miwa	vmi	Australia
	Ngarinyin	ung	Australia
	Wilawila	wil	Australia
	Worora	unp	Australia
	Wunambal	wub	Australia
Australian, Yangmanic	Dagoman	dgn	Australia
	Wardaman	wrr	Australia
	Yangman	jng	Australia
Tasmanian	Big River	No code	Australia
	Little Swanport	No code	Australia
	Oyster Bay	No code	Australia
	Ben Lomond	No code	Australia
	Cape Portland	No code	Australia
	Piper River	No code	Australia
Northern Eurasia: 21 + 6 uncertain			
Ainu	Ainu	ain	Japan
Chukotko-Kamchatkan	Alutor	alr	Russia
	Chukot, Coastal	ckt	Russia
	Itelmen	itl	Russia
	Kerek	krk	Russia
	Koryak	kpy	Russia
Gilyak	Gilyak ~ Nivkh	niv	Russia
Tungusic	Even ?	eve	Russia
	Evenki ?	evn	Russia
	Nanai	gld	Russia
	Negidal	neg	Russia
	Oroch	oac	Russia
	Orok ?	oaa	Russia
	Udihe	ude	Russia
	Ulcha	ulc	Russia
Turkic	Dolgan ?	dlg	Russia
	Tofa (Karagas) ?	kim	Russia
Uralic	Khanty	kca	Russia
	Mansi	mns	Russia
	Nenets (Forest) ?	No code	Russia
	Nganasan	nio	Russia
	Selkup	sel	Russia
Yeniseian	Ket	ket	Russia

690 Appendix

(cont.)

Family	Language	ISO code	Country
Northern Eurasia: 21 + 6 uncertain			
	Kott	No code	Russia
	Yugh	yuu	Russia
Yukagir	Yukaghir (Kolyma)	yux	Russia
	Yukagir (Tundra)	ykg	Russia
North America + Mesoamerica: 225			
Algic	Abnaki, Eastern	aaq	USA
	Abnaki, Western	abe	USA, Canada
	Algonquin	alq	Canada
	Arapaho	arp	USA
	Atikamekw	atj	Canada
	Blackfoot	bla	USA, Canada
	Cheyenne	chy	USA
	Chippewa (Red Lake and Pillager)	ciw	USA
	Cree (Moose)	crm	Canada
	Cree (Plains)	crk	USA, Canada
	Cree (Swampy)	csw	Canada
	Cree (Woods)	cwd	Canada
	East Cree (Northern)	crl	Canada
	East Cree (Southern)	crj	Canada
	Fox, Mesquakie	sac	USA
	Gros Ventre	ats	USA, Canada
	Illinois, Miami	mia	USA
	Kickapoo	kic	USA
	Malecite-Passamaquoddy	pqm	USA, Canada
	Menomini	mez	USA
	Miami	mia	USA
	Micmac	mic	Canada
	Montagnais	moe	Canada
	Naskapi	nsk	Canada
	Nawathinehena	nwa	USA
	Ojibwa (Central)	ojc	USA, Canada
	Ojibwa (Eastern)	ojg	Canada
	Ojibwe (Northwestern)	ojb	Canada
	Ojibwa (Severn)	ojs	Canada
	Ojibwa (Western)	ojw	USA, Canada
	Ottawa	otw	USA, Canada
	Potawatomi	pot	USA
	Shawnee	sjw	USA
	Wiyot	wiy	USA
	Yurok	yur	USA

(*cont.*)

Family	Language	ISO code	Country
North America + Mesoamerica: 225			
Alsea	Alsea	aes	USA
Beothuk	Beothuk	bue	Canada
Cayuse	Cayuse	xcy	USA
Chimakuan	Chemakum	cmk	USA
	Quileute	qui	USA
Chimariko	Chimariko	cid	USA
Chinookan	Chinook (Lower)	chh	USA
	Wasco-Wishram	wac	USA
Chumashan	Barbareño	boi	USA
	Chumash	chs	USA
	Cruzeño	crz	USA
	Ineseño	inz	USA
	Obispeño	obi	USA
	Purisimeño	puy	USA
	Ventureño	veo	USA
Coahuilteco	Coahuilteco	xcw	USA, Mexico
Comecrudo	Comecrudo	xcm	Mexico
Coosan	Hanis (Coos)	csz	USA
Cotoname	Cotoname	xcn	USA, Mexico
Eskimo-Aleut	Aleut	ale	USA, Russia
	Greenlandic	kal	Denmark
	Inuktitut (Eastern Canadian)	ike	Canada
	Inuktitut (Western Canadian)	ikt	Canada
	Iñupiaq (North Alaskan)	esi	USA
	Iñupiaq (Northwest Alaskan)	esk	USA
	Yup'ik (Central)	esu	USA
	Yup'ik (Naukan)	ynk	Russia
	Yup'ik (Pacific Gulf)	ems	USA
	Yup'ik (Siberian)	ess	USA, Russia
	Yup'ik (Sirenik)	ysr	Russia
Esselen	Esselen	esq	USA
Guaicurian	Guaicurian	No code	Mexico
Haida	Haida (Southern)	hax	Canada
	Haida (Northern)	hdn	Canada
Karankawa	Karankawa	zkk	USA
Karok	Karok	kyh	USA
Kiowa-Tanoan	Kiowa	kio	USA
Kutenai	Kutenai	kut	USA, Canada
Maratino	Maratino	No code	Mexico
Miwok-Costanoan	Karkin	krb	USA

(cont.)

Family	Language	ISO code	Country
North America + Mesoamerica: 225			
	Miwok (Bay)	mkq	USA
	Miwok (Bodega ~ Coast)	csi	USA
	Miwok (Central Sierra)	csm	USA
	Miwok (Lake)	lmw	USA
	Miwok (Northern Sierra)	nsq	USA
	Miwok (Plains)	pmw	USA
	Miwok (Southern Sierra)	skd	USA
	Ohlone (Northern) ~ Costanoan	cst	USA
	Ohlone (Southern) ~ Mutsun	css	USA
Molala	Molala	mbe	USA
Na-Dene	Ahtena	aht	USA
	Apache (Jicarilla)	apj	USA
	Apache (Kiowa)	apk	USA
	Apache (Lipan)	apl	USA
	Apache (Mescalero-Chiricahua)	apm	USA
	Apache (Western)	apw	USA
	Babine	bcr	Canada
	Beaver	bea	Canada
	Carrier	crx	Canada
	Carrier, Southern	caf	Canada
	Chetco	ctc	USA
	Chilcotin	clc	Canada
	Chipewyan	chp	Canada
	Coquille	coq	USA
	Degexit'an	ing	USA
	Dogrib	dgr	Canada
	Eyak	eya	USA
	Galice	gce	USA
	Gwich'in	gwi	USA, Canada
	Han	haa	USA, Canada
	Holikachuk	hoi	USA
	Hupa	hup	USA
	Kaska	kkz	Canada
	Kato	ktw	USA
	Koyukon	koy	USA
	Kuskokwim (Upper)	kuu	USA
	Mattole	mvb	USA
	Sarsi	srs	Canada

(*cont.*)

Family	Language	ISO code	Country
North America + Mesoamerica: 225			
	Sekani	sek	Canada
	Slavey, North	scs	Canada
	Slavey, South	xsl	Canada
	Tagish	tgx	Canada
	Tahltan	tht	Canada
	Tanacross	tcb	USA, Canada
	Tanaina	tfn	USA
	Tanana (Lower)	taa	USA
	Tanana (Upper)	tau	USA, Canada
	Tlingit	tli	USA, Canada
	Tolowa	tol	USA
	Tsetsaut	txc	USA, Canada
	Tutchone (Northern)	ttm	Canada
	Tutchone (Southern)	tce	Canada
	Tututni	tuu	USA
	Wailaki	wlk	USA
Palaihnihan	Achumawi	acv	USA
	Atsugewi	atw	USA
Plateau?	Klamath-Modoc	kla	USA
Plateau, Maiduan	Maidu, Northeast	nmu	USA
	Maidu, Northwest (Konkow)	mjd	USA
	Maidu, Valley	vmv	USA
	Nisenan	nsz	USA
Plateau, Sahaptin	Nez Perce	nez	USA
	Tenino	tqn	USA
	Umatilla	uma	USA
	Walla walla	waa	USA
	Yakima	yak	USA
Pomoan	Kashaya	kju	USA
	Pomo (Central)	poo	USA
	Pomo (Eastern)	peb	USA
	Pomo (Northeastern)	pef	USA
	Pomo (Northern)	pej	USA
	Pomo (Southeastern)	pom	USA
	Pomo (Southern)	peq	USA
Salinan	Salinan	sln	USA
Salishan	Bella Coola	blc	Canada
	Chehalis (Lower)	cea	USA
	Chehalis (Upper)	cjh	USA
	Clallam	clm	USA, Canada
	Coeur d'Alene	crd	USA
	Columbia-Wenatchi	col	USA
	Comox	coo	Canada

(cont.)

Family	Language	ISO code	Country
	Cowlitz	cow	USA
	Halkomelem	hur	USA, Canada
	Kalispel ~ Pend D'oreille	fla	USA
	Lillooet	lil	Canada
	Lushootseed	lut	USA
	Nooksack	nok	USA
	Okanagan	oka	USA, Canada
	Pentlatch	ptw	Canada
	Quinault	qun	USA
	Salish (Southern Puget Sound)	slh	USA
	Salish (Straits) ~ Lummi	str	USA
	Sechelt	sec	Canada
	Shuswap	shs	Canada
	Skagit	ska	USA
	Snohomish	sno	USA
	Spokane	spo	USA
	Squamish	squ	USA
	Thompson	thp	USA, Canada
	Tillamook	til	USA
	Twana	twa	USA
Seri	Seri	sei	Mexico
Shasta	Shasta	sht	USA
Siouan	Assiniboine	asb	USA, Canada
	Biloxi	bll	USA
	Crow	cro	USA
	Dakota	dak	USA
	Hocak (Winnebago)	win	USA
	Kansa	ksk	USA
	Lakhota	lkt	USA
	Omaha	oma	USA
	Osage	osa	USA
	Stoney	sto	Canada
Siuslawan	Siuslaw (Lower Umpqua)	sis	USA
Takelma-Kalapuyan	Kalapuya	kyl	USA
	Takelma	tkm	USA
Tonkawa	Tonkawa	tqw	USA
Tsimshianic	Gitksan	git	Canada
	Nisgha	ncg	Canada
	Tsimshian (Coast)	tsi	USA, Canada
Uto-Aztecan	Cahuilla	chl	USA
	Comanche	com	USA

(cont.)

Family	Language	ISO code	Country
North America + Mesoamerica: 225			
	Cupeño	cup	USA
	Kawaiisu	xaw	USA
	Luiseño	lui	USA
	Mono	mnr	USA
	Paiute, Northern	pao	USA
	Panamint	par	USA
	Serrano	ser	USA
	Shoshone (Wind River)	shh	USA
	Tübatulabal	tub	USA
	Ute-Southern Paiute	ute	USA
Wakashan	Haisla	has	Canada
	Heiltsuk	hei	Canada
	Kwakiutl (Kwakwala)	kwk	Canada
	Makah	myh	USA
	Nootka	noo	Canada
Washo	Washo	was	USA
Wintuan	Patwin	[pwi]	USA
	Wintu	wit	USA
Yana	Yana	ynn	USA
Yokuts-Utian	Wikchamni	yok	USA
	Yokuts	yok	USA
Yuki-Wappo	Wappo	wao	USA
	Yuki	yuk	USA
Yuman	Cochimi	coj	Mexico
	Cocopa	coc	USA, Mexico
	Kiliwa	klb	Mexico
	Kumiai ~ Diegueño	dih	USA, Mexico
	Paipai	ppi	Mexico
South America: 69 + 47 uncertain			
Alacalufan	Qawasqar	alc	Chile
Arawakan ~ Maipurean	Enawené-Nawé	unk	Brazil
	Mashco Piro	cuj	Peru
Arawan	Arua ?	aru	Brazil
	Banawá ?	bnh	Brazil
	Culina ?	cul	Brazil
	Jarawara ?	jap	Brazil
	Paumarí	pad	Brazil
Arutani	Arutani ~ Awaké ~ Uruak ?	atx	Brazil
Betoi-Jirara	Betoi ?	No code	Venezuela, Colombia
Boran	Bora ?	boa	Peru, Colombia, Brazil
Cacua-Nukak	Cacua	cbv	Colombia

(cont.)

Family	Language	ISO code	Country
South America: 69 + 47 uncertain			
	Nukak Makú	mbr	Colombia
Canichana	Canichana	caz	Bolivia
Cariban	Akurio	ako	Suriname
	Arára, Pará	aap	Brazil
	Wai Wai	waw	Brazil, Guyana
Charruan	Chaná	No code	Argentina, Uruguay
	Charrua	No code	Argentina, Uruguay
	Güenoa	No code	Argentina, Uruguay
Chon	Haush	No code	Argentina
	Ona ~ Selknam	ona	Argentina
	Tehuelche	teh	Argentina
	Teushen	No code	Argentina
Chono	Chono	No code	Chile
Guahiboan	Cuiba	cui	Colombia, Venezuela
	Guahibo ~ Sikuani	guh	Colombia
	Guayabero ?	guo	Colombia
	Macaguán ?	mbn	Colombia
	Playero ?	gob	Colombia
Guaicuruan	Kadiwéu	kbc	Brazil
	Mocoví	moc	Argentina
	Pilagá ?	plg	Argentina
	Toba	tob	Argentina
	Abipon	axb	Argentina
Guamo	Guamo ?	No code	Venezuela
Harakmbut	Amarakaeri ?	amr	Peru
	Huachipaeri ?	hug	Peru
Huitotoan	Huitoto (Nüpode) ?	hux	Peru
	Nonuya ?	noj	Colombia
Itonama	Itonama ?	ito	Bolivia
Katukinan	Katukína ?	kav	Brazil
Leco	Leco ?	lec	Bolivia
Lule	Lule	[ule]	Argentina
Macro-Ge, Bororo	Borôro	bor	Brazil
	Otuke	otu	Brazil
	Umotína	umo	Brazil
Macro-Ge, Botocudo	Krenak ~ Aimoré	kqq	Brazil
Macro-Ge, Guató	Guató	gta	Brazil
Macro-Ge, Ge-Kaingang	Kaingang	kgp	Brazil
	Kayapó	txu	Brazil
	Xavánte	xav	Brazil
Macro-Ge, Kamakan	Kamakan ?	vkm	Brazil
Macro-Ge, Ofayé	Ofayé ?	opy	Brazil
Macro-Ge, Puri	Puri	prr	Brazil
Macro-Ge, Rikbaktsa	Rikbaktsa	rkb	Brazil

(*cont.*)

Family	Language	ISO code	Country
South America: 69 + 47 uncertain			
Macro-Ge, Yabuti	Arikapú	ark	Brazil
	Jabutí ~ Djeoromitxi	jbt	Brazil
Maku	Máku	[xak]	Brazil, Venezuela
Mascoyan	Emok ?	emo	Paraguay
	Guana	gva	Paraguay
	Lengua	leg	Paraguay
	Sanapaná	sap	Paraguay
	Toba-Maskoy ?	tmf	Paraguay
Matacoan	Chorote, Iyojwa'ja	crt	Argentina
	Chorote, Iyo'wujwa	crq	Argentina
	Maca	mca	Paraguay
	Nivaclé ~ Chulupí	cag	Paraguay
	Wichí Lhamtés Güisnay	mzh	Argentina
	Wichí Lhamtés Nocten	mtp	Bolivia
	Wichí Lhamtés Vejoz	wlv	Argentina
Matanawí	Matanawí ?	No code	Brazil
Movima	Movima ?	mzp	Bolivia
Mura	Pirahã	myp	Brazil
Nadahup	Dâw	kwa	Brazil
	Hupdë	jup	Brazil
	Nadëb	mbj	Brazil
	Yuhup	yab	Brazil
Nambikwaran	Nambikwara (Northern)	mbg	Brazil
	Nambikwara (Southern)	nab	Brazil
	Sabanês	sae	Brazil
Oti	Oti ?	oti	Brazil
Pano-Tacanan	Araona	aro	Bolivia
	Cavineña ?	cav	Bolivia
	Tacana ?	tna	Bolivia
	Toromono ?	tno	Bolivia
Puelche	Puelche ~ Gününa-Küne	pue	Argentina
Pumé	Pumé ~ Yaruro	yae	Venezuela
Sapé	Sapé ~ Kaliana ?	spc	Venezuela
Taushiro	Taushiro ?	trr	Peru
Trumaí	Trumaí ?	tpy	Brazil
Tupi	Aché ~ Guayaki	guq	Paraguay
	Arawete ?	awt	Brazil
	Cinta Larga	cin	Brazil
	Guajá	gvj	Brazil
	Guaraní, Mbyá ?	gun	Brazil
	Jorá	jor	Bolivia
	Mondé ?	mnd	Brazil
	Mundurukú ?	myu	Brazil
	Puruborá	pur	Brazil

(*cont.*)

Family	Language	ISO code	Country
South America: 69 + 47 uncertain			
	Sirionó	srq	Bolivia, Brazil
	Tupi ?	tpw, tpn	Brazil
	Xetá	xet	Brazil
	Yuqui	yuq	Bolivia
Vilela	Vilela	vil	Argentina
Waorani	Waorani	auc	Ecudaor
Warao	Warao	wba	Venezuela
Xukuru	Xukurú ?	xoo	Brazil
Yámana	Yámana ~ Yahgan	yag	Chile
Yanomaman	Ninam ~ Shiriana	shb	Brazil
	Sanuma	xsu	Venezuela
	Yanomámi	wca	Brazil
	Yanomamö	guu	Venezuela
Yuwana	Yuwana ~ Waruwaru ~ Joti ?	yau	Venezuela
Zamucoan	Ayoreo ?	ayo	Paraguay
	Chamacoco	ceg	Paraguay
Zaparoan	Andoa ?	anb	Peru
	Arabela ?	arl	Peru
	Aushiri ?	avs	Peru

References

Bahuchet, Serge. (2012). Changing language, remaining Pygmy. *Human Biology* 84(1): 11–43.

Bulletin of the International Committee on Urgent Anthropological and Ethnological Research no. 1, 2, 3, 9, 11.

Campbell, Lyle. (2003). How to show languages are related: Methods for distant genetic relationship. In Brian D. Joseph and Richard D. Janda (eds.), *The handbook of historical linguistics*. Oxford: Blackwell, 262–282.

Greenberg, Joseph H. (1963). The languages of Africa. Publications 25. Bloomington: Research Center in Anthropology, Folklore, and Linguistics, Indiana University Press.

Greenberg, Joseph H. (1971). The Indo-Pacific hypothesis. In J. Donald Bowen et al. (eds.), *Linguistics in Oceania*, 2 vols. Current Trends in Linguistics 8 (ed. by T. Sebeok). The Hague/ Paris: Mouton, Vol. 1: 807–871.

Greenberg, Joseph H. (1987). *Language in the Americas*. Stanford, CA: Stanford University Press.

Greenberg, Joseph H. (2000). *Indo-European and its closest relatives: The Eurasiatic language family*. Stanford, CA: Stanford University Press.

Güldemann, Tom and Harald Hammarström. (in preparation). The late global distribution of forager languages and its implications for human pre-history.

Lee, Richard B. and Daly, Richard (eds.). (1999). *The Cambridge Encyclopedia of hunters and gatherers*. Cambridge: Cambridge University Press.

Lewis, M. Paul (ed.). 2009. *Ethnologue: Languages of the world*, 16th edn. Dallas, TX: SIL International. www.ethnologue.com/16.

Martin, M. Kay. (1969). South American foragers: A case study in cultural devolution. *American Anthropologist, New Series* 71(2): 243–260.

Murdock, George P. (1967). *Ethnographic atlas*. Pittsburgh, PA: University of Pittsburgh Press.

Nichols, Johanna. (1996). The comparative method as heuristic. In Mark Durieand Malcolm Ross (eds.), *The comparative method reviewed: Regularity and irregularity in language change*. Oxford: Oxford University Press, 39–71.

Roscoe, Paul. (2002). The hunters and gatherers of New Guinea. *Current Anthropology* 43(1): 153–162.

Rottland, Franz. (1983). Zur sprachlichen Herkunft ostafrikanischer Wildbeuter. In Rainer Voßen and Ulrike Claudi (eds.), Sprache, Geschichte und Kultur in Afrika: Vorträge, gehalten auf dem III. Afrikanistentag, Köln 14./15. Oktober 1982. Hamburg: Helmut Buske, 280–289.

Ruhlen, Merritt. (1987). *A guide to the world's languages 1: Classification*. London: Edward Arnold.

Ruhlen, Merritt. (1994a). *On the origin of languages: Studies in linguistic taxonomy*. Stanford, CA: Stanford University Press.

Ruhlen, Merritt. (1994b). *The origin of language: Tracing the evolution of the mother tongue*. New York: John Wiley & Sons.

Language Index

Subject Index

Aboriginal Australia, 422–423
  Asian contact and, 366, 367
  Austronesians and, 367
  clan/estate model of, 357–358, 361
  clans of, 359–361
  colonization of, 358, 359
  egalitarianism of, 19
  equilibrium, in linguistic geography of,
    363–364
  language groups of, 356–357
    approximate locations of, 358
    size, 357–362
    small, 368–370
  nested groupings in, 358
  Pama-Nyungan languages in, 364–367
  punctuation, in linguistics on, 364–366
  tribes in, 358–359
  Western Desert language in, 359, 366
Aboriginal Malay (people), 167–168, 191
accretion zones, 584, 589–590, 597
achiote, 625–626
acorns, 82
Africa. *See also* Eastern Africa; Ethiopia;
    South Africa
  foragers in, 607
  HG groups of, 61
  pygmy groups in, 60
AGR. *See* traditional agricultural group
agricultural expansion. *See also* Bantu
    expansion
  in genetic diversity, of HG groups, 56–57
  in spread, of languages, 392
agricultural groups
  HG groups and, 50–51, 57–59, 61
agricultural revolution, 10
agriculturalists, 350–351. *See also* traditional
    agricultural groups
  Amazonian, 646–649
  binomial oak terms of, 85–86
  Borneo hunter-gatherers and, 276–279, 280,
    296, 300
  foragers and, 607–608, 632–633

HG groups and, 54–55
  Highland, in Guinea, 322–325, 326
  in Near Oceania, 319, 323–325
  Pnan groups and, 275
  Senoi, 178
agriculture
  Aslian languages and, 174
  in Australia, 403
  binomial terms and, 77–78
  of Cree, Ojibwe, 556
  in Gran Chaco, 650
  of Kalahari Khoe, 129–130
  language spread and, 392, 632–633
  in Mesoamerica, 632
  Nadahup attitude toward, 615
  Numic and, 580
  spread of, in North America, 3–4
  widespread language families and, 425–426,
    632–633
agta, 232
Agta (people), 231, 238, 256
  Casiguran Agta (people), 246–247,
    256
  Negrito groups and, 237–239
Alaska, 523
Algic language family tree, 554
Algonquian (people), 5, 16, 552, 553, 556,
    559–560, 568
  Eastern Algonquian, 5, 29
  in Great Lakes region, 552
  Southern Great Lakes, 5
Amazonian agriculturalists, 646–649
Amazonian foragers, 8–9, 608, 633
Amazonian Vaupés. *See also* Nadahup
  cultivated foods in, 614
  Dâw in, 611–612
  first inhabitants of, 613–614
  foragers, farmers in
    contemporary, 609
    grammatical convergence, 630–631
    lexical evidence of, 627–628
    numeral systems of, 629–630

710

hunter-gatherers (cont.)
Pama-Nyungan, as widespread language
family of, 426, 454
in present-day New Guinea, 323–325
Semang as, 180
of Southeast Asia, 149, 263–264, 301
specialized vocabulary of, 608
top-down model of, 92
Yeniseian, semantic groups of, 473–474
hunting, 303, 341–342
Hup (Hupd'eh) (people), 28, 610–611,
613–614, 616, 619–620, 628, 630–631,
632–633
in Amazonian Vaupés, 610–611
cacao, 621
manioc of, 614, 623, 624
'River Indian' term in, 629
traditional stories of, 616
Huron (people), 559
hydronyms, 467, 468, 510–511
hypergyny, 58

ice, words for, 538–541, 548
iglu, 540, 548
immigration, 135
Inati (people), 248–249, 257
India, 60, 150–151
Indian subcontinent, 149
indigenist perspective, 171, 174
Indonesia, 367
intermarriage, 181–182, 607–608, 611
Iroquois War, 556, 559, 562

Jarawa (people), 54, 198–201, 217–218, 219

Kakua (people), 611, 613
Kalahari Khoe (people), 137–138
Kalimantan, 265
Kangarayev, Sergei, 508
Kayan (people), 265, 267–270
Kelly, R. I., 22
Kenyah (people), 35, 267–270, 274, 275, 276,
277, 280, 282–283, 285
Badeng Kenyah, 275, 276, 282–283, 303
Ket (people)
marriage partners and, 479
Khoekhoe (people), 26, 119, 129, 130–132,
133, 138, 139
Khoe-Kwadi (peoples), 34, 115, 118–119,
133–137, 138, 139–140
colonizing population in, 140–141
early history of, 118–119, 135–136, 140
culture, reconstruction in, 128–130
genealogical relations, 125–128
proto-Khoe culture in, 129

Khoe-Kwadi languages
Bantu expansion and, 134, 137
early history of, 118–119, 135–136, 140
food production and, 133–134, 140–141
genealogy of, 115
history of, 136
expansion, diversification of, 134–139
non-Bantu languages in, 130–132
precolonial, 132–134
speaking groups, 139
immigration in, 135
Khoisan and, 114–115, 126, 128, 131–132,
139–140
Nama-Orlami migration in, 138–139
Khoisan (people), 49, 132, 133, 134,
137–138, 139
genetics, 100, 131, 134, 137, 138, 139
mtDNA, 59–60, 61
kinship systems, 437–438
kinship terminology, 161, 451–452, 453–454
in Dayak, 274–276
in Mlabri, 161
Koch-Grünberg, Theodore, 612, 616,
627–628, 634
Kra ecotone, 179
Krupnik, Igor, 540, 542, 548
Kusunda (people), 29

Lamb, Sydney M., 581–582
land-language affiliations, in Australia. *See*
Australia
landownership, 275, 302
language. *See also* Aboriginal Australia;
farming/language dispersal hypothesis;
Great Lakes region, of North America;
language index; Malay Peninsula;
multilingualism; Negrito groups
of Amazonian foragers, 8–9
Australian, 36
Austroasiatic, 165
of Boni, 100
Chaco, 38
contact, 591, 658–660
of Dahalo, 100
distribution, nodal leadership in, 19
diversification, 656–658
Dixon on, 654
East Cushitic, 107
of farmers, 4
of food producers, 37–38
spread of, 23–24
typological variables in, 68–73
of foragers, 4–5
demic diffusion, wave of advance models
of, 23

CPSIA information can be obtained
at www.ICGtesting.com
Printed in the USA
BVHW031750151222
654346BV00005B/26